CENTRAL BANKS AT A CROSSROADS

Throughout their long history, the primary concern of central banks has oscillated between price stability in normal times and financial stability in extraordinary times. In the wake of the recent global financial crisis, central banks have been given additional responsibilities to ensure financial stability, which has sparked intense debate over the nature of their role. Bankers and policy makers face an enormous challenge finding the right balance of power between the central bank and the state.

This volume is the result of an international conference held at Norges Bank (the central bank of Norway). International experts and policy makers present research and historical analysis on the evolution of the central bank. They specifically focus on four key aspects: its role as an institution, the part it plays within the international monetary system, how to delineate and limit its functions, and how to apply the lessons of the past two centuries.

Michael D. Bordo is Professor of Economics and Director of the Center for Monetary and Financial History at Rutgers University–New Brunswick.

Øyvind Eitrheim is a director at the General Secretariat, Norges Bank.

Marc Flandreau is Professor of International History at the Graduate Institute of International Studies and Development in Geneva.

Jan F. Qvigstad is Executive Director at the General Secretariat, Norges Bank.

STUDIES IN MACROECONOMIC HISTORY

Series Editor: Michael D. Bordo, *Rutgers University*

Editors: Marc Flandreau, *Graduate Institute of International and Development Studies, Geneva*
Chris Meissner, *University of California, Davis*
François R. Velde, *Federal Reserve Bank of Chicago*
David C. Wheelock, *Federal Reserve Bank of St. Louis*

The titles in this series investigate themes of interest to economists and economic historians in the rapidly developing field of macroeconomic history. The four areas covered include the application of monetary and finance theory, international economics, and quantitative methods to historical problems; the historical application of growth and development theory and theories of business fluctuations; the history of domestic and international monetary, financial, and other macroeconomic institutions; and the history of international monetary and financial systems. The series amalgamates the former Cambridge University Press series *Studies in Monetary and Financial History* and *Studies in Quantitative Economic History.*

Other books in the series:

Michael D. Bordo and Mark A. Wynne, Editors, *The Federal Reserve's Role in the Global Economy*, 2016

Owen Humpage, *Current Federal Reserve Policy under the Lens of Economic History*, 2015

Michael D. Bordo and William Roberds, Editors, *The Origins, History, and Future of the Federal Reserve*, 2013

Michael D. Bordo and Ronald MacDonald, Editors, *Credibility and the International Monetary Regime*, 2012

Robert L. Hetzel, *The Great Recession*, 2012

Tobias Straumann, *Fixed Ideas of Money, Small States and Exchange Rate Regimes in Twentieth-Century Europe*, 2010

Forrest Capie, *The Bank of England: 1950s to 1979*, 2010

Aldo Musacchio, *Experiments in Financial Democracy: Corporate Governance and Financial Development in Brazil, 1882–1950*, 2009

Claudio Borio, Gianni Toniolo, and Piet Clement, Editors, *The Past and Future of Central Bank Cooperation*, 2008

Robert L. Hetzel, *The Monetary Policy of the Federal Reserve: A History*, 2008

Caroline Fohlin, *Finance Capitalism and Germany's Rise to Industrial Power*, 2007

John H. Wood, *A History of Central Banking in Great Britain and the United States*, 2005

Gianni Toniolo (with the assistance of Piet Clement), *Central Bank Cooperation at the Bank for International Settlements, 1930–1973*, 2005

Richard Burdekin and Pierre Siklos, Editors, *Deflation: Current and Historical Perspectives*, 2004

Pierre Siklos, *The Changing Face of Central Banking: Evolutionary Trends since World War II*, 2002

Michael D. Bordo and Roberto Cortés-Conde, Editors, *Transferring Wealth and Power from the Old to the New World*, 2001

Howard Bodenhorn, *A History of Banking in Antebellum America*, 2000

Mark Harrison (ed.), *The Economics of World War II*, 2000

Angela Redish, *Bimetallism*, 2000

Elmus Wicker, *Banking Panics of the Gilded Age*, 2000

Michael D. Bordo, *The Gold Standard and Related Regimes*, 1999

Michele Fratianni and Franco Spinelli, *A Monetary History of Italy*, 1997

Mark Toma, *Competition and Monopoly in the Federal Reserve System, 1914–1951*, 1997

Barry Eichengreen, Editor, *Europe's Postwar Recovery*, 1996

Lawrence H. Officer, *Between the Dollar-Sterling Gold Points*, 1996

Elmus Wicker, *Banking Panics of the Great Depression*, 1996

Norio Tamaki, *Japanese Banking*, 1995

Barry Eichengreen, *Elusive Stability*, 1993

Michael D. Bordo and Forrest Capie, Editors, *Monetary Regimes in Transition*, 1993

Larry Neal, *The Rise of Financial Capitalism*, 1993

S. N. Broadberry and N. F. R. Crafts, Editors, *Britain in the International Economy, 1870–1939* 1992

Continued after Index

Central Banks at a Crossroads

What Can We Learn from History?

Edited by

MICHAEL D. BORDO
Rutgers University, New Jersey

ØYVIND EITRHEIM
Norges Bank, Oslo

MARC FLANDREAU
Graduate Institute of International and Development Studies, Geneva

JAN F. QVIGSTAD
Norges Bank, Oslo

CAMBRIDGE
UNIVERSITY PRESS

University Printing House, Cambridge CB2 8BS, United Kingdom

One Liberty Plaza, 20th Floor, New York, NY 10006, USA

477 Williamstown Road, Port Melbourne, VIC 3207, Australia

314-321, 3rd Floor, Plot 3, Splendor Forum, Jasola District Centre, New Delhi - 110025, India

79 Anson Road, #06-04/06, Singapore 079906

Cambridge University Press is part of the University of Cambridge.

It furthers the University's mission by disseminating knowledge in the pursuit of education, learning and research at the highest international levels of excellence.

www.cambridge.org
Information on this title: www.cambridge.org/9781108791984

© Norges Bank 2016

This publication is in copyright. Subject to statutory exception and to the provisions of relevant collective licensing agreements, no reproduction of any part may take place without the written permission of Cambridge University Press.

First published 2016
First paperback edition 2020

A catalogue record for this publication is available from the British Library

Library of Congress Cataloging in Publication data
Names: Bordo, Michael D., editor.
Title: Central banks at a crossroads : what can we learn from history? / edited by Michael D. Bordo, Rutgers University, New Jersey, Øyvind Eitrheim, Norges Bank, Marc Flandreau, Graduate Institute of International and Development Studies, Geneva, Jan F. Qvigstad, Norges Bank.
Description: New York NY : Cambridge University Press, 2016. | Series: Studies in macroeconomic history | Includes bibliographical references and index.
Identifiers: LCCN 2016015468 | ISBN 9781107149663 (Hardback : alk. paper)
Subjects: LCSH: Banks and banking, Central–History. | Monetary policy–History.
Classification: LCC HG1811 .C45974 2016 | DDC 332.1/1–dc23 LC record available at https://lccn.loc.gov/2016015468

ISBN 978-1-107-14966-3 Hardback
ISBN 978-1-108-79198-4 Paperback

Cambridge University Press has no responsibility for the persistence or accuracy of URLs for external or third-party internet websites referred to in this publication, and does not guarantee that any content on such websites is, or will remain, accurate or appropriate.

Contents

Editors and contributors		*page* ix
Preface		xvii
	Michael D. Bordo, Øyvind Eitrheim, Marc Flandreau, and Jan F. Qvigstad	
1	Introduction *Michael D. Bordo, Øyvind Eitrheim, Marc Flandreau, and Jan F. Qvigstad*	1
2	The Descent of Central Banks (1400–1815) *William Roberds and François R. Velde*	18
3	Central Bank Credibility: An Historical and Quantitative Exploration *Michael D. Bordo and Pierre L. Siklos*	62
4	The Coevolution of Money Markets and Monetary Policy, 1815–2008 *Clemens Jobst and Stefano Ugolini*	145
5	Central Bank Independence in Small Open Economies *Forrest Capie, Geoffrey Wood, and Juan Castañeda*	195
6	Fighting the Last War: Economists on the Lender of Last Resort *Richard S. Grossman and Hugh Rockoff*	231
7	A Century and a Half of Central Banks, International Reserves, and International Currencies *Barry Eichengreen and Marc Flandreau*	280

viii *Contents*

8 Central Banks and the Stability of the International
Monetary Regime 319
Catherine Schenk and Tobias Straumann

9 The International Monetary and Financial System:
A Capital Account Historical Perspective 356
Claudio Borio, Harold James, and Hyun Song Shin

10 Central Banking: Perspectives from Emerging Economies 387
Menzie D. Chinn

11 The Evolution of the Financial Stability Mandate: From
Its Origins to the Present Day 424
Gianni Toniolo and Eugene N. White

12 Bubbles and Central Banks: Historical Perspectives 493
Markus K. Brunnermeier and Isabel Schnabel

13 Central Banks and Payment Systems: The Evolving
Trade-off between Cost and Risk 563
Charles Kahn, Stephen Quinn, and William Roberds

14 Central Bank Evolution: Lessons Learnt from
the Sub-Prime Crisis 610
C. A. E. Goodhart

15 The Evolution of Central Banks: A Practitioner's
Perspective 627
Andrew G. Haldane and Jan F. Qvigstad

Index 673

Editors and contributors

Michael D. Bordo is a Board of Governors Professor of Economics and Director of the Center for Monetary and Financial History at Rutgers University, New Brunswick, New Jersey, USA. Selected publications include: *The Defining Moment: The Great Depression and the American Economy in the Twentieth Century* (1998, with C. Goldin and E. White), *The great inflation: the Rebirth of Modern Central Banking* (2013, with A. Orphanides), *A Return to Jekyll Island* (2013, with W. Roberds) and *Strained Relations: US Foreign Exchange Operations and Monetary Policy in the Twentieth Century* (2014, with O. Humpage and A.J. Schwartz).

Claudio Borio is Head of the Monetary and Economic Department at the Bank for International Settlements, Basel, Switzerland. Selected publications include: "Anchoring Countercyclical Capital Buffers: The role of Credit Aggregates", *International Journal of Central Banking* (2011, with M. Drehmann and K. Tsatsaronis), "Stress-testing macro stress testing: Does it live up to expectations?" in *Journal of Financial Stability* (2014, with M. Drehmann and K. Tsatsaronis) and "The financial cycle and macroeconomics: What have we learnt?" in *Journal of Banking & Finance* (2014). Borio is a co-editor of *The Past and Future of Central Bank Cooperation* (2011, with G. Toniolo and P. Clement).

Markus K. Brunnermeier is Edwards S. Sanford Professor of Economics at Princeton University, New Jersey, USA and director of Princeton's Bendheim Center for Finance. Selected publications include: "Hedge Funds and the Technology Bubble", *Journal of Finance* (2004, with S. Nagel), "Predatory Trading", *Journal of Finance* (2005, with L. Pedersen), "Deciphering the Liquidity and Credit Crunch 2007–2008", *Journal of Economic Perspectives* (2009), "A Macroeconomic Model with a Financial Sector", *American*

Economic Review (2014, with Y. Sannikov) and *Risk Topography* (2014, co-edited with A. Krishnamurthy).

Forrest Capie is a Professor Emeritus of Economic History at the Cass Business School City University, UK. Selected publications include: *The future of central banking: the tercentenary symposium of the Bank of England* (1994, with C. Goodhart, S. Fischer and N. Schnadt), *The Bank of England: 1950s to 1979* (2010), "Financial crisis, contagion, and the British banking system between the world wars", *Business History* (2011, with M. Billings) and *Money over Two Centuries: Selected Topics in British Monetary History, 1870–2010* (2012, with G. Wood).

Juan Castañeda is a Lecturer in Economics at the University of Buckingham, UK. He is since 2016 the Director of the Institute of International Monetary Research, established in collaboration with this University. Selected publications include: "Business cycle, interest rate and money in the euro area: A common factor model", *Economic Modelling* (2014, with J. L. Cendejas and F-F. Muñoz) and *European Banking Union: Prospects and Challenges* (2016, co-edited with D.G. Mayes and G. Wood).

Menzie D. Chinn is a professor of public affairs and economics, University of Wisconsin, USA. He served as a senior economist for international financial issues on the White House Council of Economic Advisers from 2000 to 2001. Selected publications include: *Empirical Exchange Rate Economics: Estimation and Implications* (2004), *Lost Decades: The Making of America's Debt Crisis and the Long Recovery* (2011, with J. Frieden) and "A forensic analysis of global imbalances", *Oxford Economic Papers* (2014, with B. Eichengreen and H. Ito).

Barry Eichengreen is George C. Pardee and Helen N. Pardee Professor of Economics and Political Science at the University of California, Berkeley, USA. Selected publications include: *Golden Fetters: The Gold Standard and the Great Depression 1919–1939* (1992), *Globalizing Capital: A History of the International Monetary System* (1996), *The European Economy Since 1945: Co-ordinated Capitalism and Beyond* (2008), *Exorbitant Privilege: The Rise and Fall of the Dollar and the Future of the International Monetary System* (2011) and *Hall of Mirrors: The Great Depression, The Great Recession, and the Uses-and Misuses-of History* (2014).

Øyvind Eitrheim is a Director at General Secretariat, Norges Bank. He served as Director of the Research Department at Norges Bank 2001–2009 and is currently coordinating projects related to Norges Bank's Bicentenary

Project 1816–2016. Selected publications include: *The econometrics of macroeconomic modeling* (with G. Bårdsen, E.S. Jansen and R. Nymoen) (2004), *Twenty Years of Inflation Targeting. Lessons learned and future prospects* (2010, co-edited with D. Cobham, S. Gerlach and J.F. Qvigstad), *A Monetary History of Norway 1816–2016* (2016, with J.T. Klovland and L. F. Øksendal).

Marc Flandreau is a Professor of International Economics and International History at the Graduate Institute of International and Development Studies, Geneva, Switzerland. Selected publications include: *The Glitter of Gold. France, Bimetallism and the Emergence of the International Gold Standard, 1848–1873* (2004), *Money doctors: the experience of international financial advising 1850–2000* (2005, with F. Zumer), "The vanishing banker", *Financial History Review* (2012), "The Price of Media Capture and the Debasement of the French Newspaper Industry During the Interwar" *The Journal of Economic History* (2014, with V. Bignon).

Charles Goodhart is a Professor Emeritus at the London School of Economics, UK. Selected publications include: *The Evolution of Central Banks* (1988), *The future of central banking: the tercentenary symposium of the Bank of England* (1994, with F. Capie, S. Fischer and N. Schnadt), *The Central Bank and the Financial System* (1995) and "Lessons for monetary policy from the Euro-area crisis", *Journal of Macroeconomics* (2013).

Richard S. Grossman is a Professor of Economics at the Wesleyan University, USA. Selected publications include: "The Emergence of Central Banks and Banking Regulation in Comparative Perspective", in *State and Financial Systems in Europe and the USA: Historical Perspectives on Regulation and Supervision in the Nineteenth and Twentieth Centuries* (2010), *Unsettled Account: The Evolution of Commercial Banking in the Industrialized World since 1800* (2010) and *WRONG: Nine Economic Policy Disasters and What we Can Learn From Them* (2013).

Andrew G. Haldane is the Chief Economist at the Bank of England and Executive Director, Monetary Analysis and Statistics. He is a member of the Bank's Monetary Policy Committee. He also has responsibility for research and statistics across the Bank. Selected publications include: "Complexity, Concentration and Contagion", *Journal of Monetary Economics* (2011, with P. Gai and S. Kapadia), "Systemic risk in banking ecosystems", *Nature* (2011, with R. May), "The Dog and the Frisbee", speech at the Federal Reserve Bank of Kansas City's 36th Economic Policy Symposium, Jackson Hole, Wyoming, 31 August 2012 and "Curbing the

Credit Cycle", *The Economic Journal* (2014, with D. Aikman and B. Nelson).

Harold James is Claude and Lore Kelly Professor in European Studies and Professor of History and International Affairs at Princeton University, USA. Selected publications include: *Reichsbank and Public Finance in Germany, 1924–1933* (1985), *International Monetary Cooperation Since Bretton Woods* (1996), *The End of Globalization: Lessons from the Great Depression* (2001), *The Creation and Destruction of Value: The Globalization Cycle* (2009) and *Making the European Monetary Union* (2012).

Clemens Jobst is a researcher at the Österreichische National Bank. Selected publications include: "The Empirics of International Currencies: Network Externalities, History and Persistence" (with M. Flandreau) in *Economic Journal* (2009), "Market leader: the Austro-Hungarian Bank and the making of foreign exchange intervention, 1896–1913", *European Review of Economic History* (2009) and *The Quest for Stable Money. Central banking in Austria 1816–2016* (2016, with H. Kernbauer).

Charles Kahn, Bailey Memorial Chair Professor of finance at University of Illinois at Urbana-Champaign. Selected publications include: "Allocating Lending of Last Resort and Supervision in the Euro Area", in *Monetary Unions and Hard Pegs: Effects on Trade, Financial Development and Stability* (2004, with J. Santos), "Payments Settlement: Tiering in Private and Public Systems", *Journal of Money, Credit and Banking* (2009, with W. Roberds) and "Private payment systems, collateral, and interest rates", *Annals of Finance* (2013).

Stephen Quinn, associate professor of economics at Texas Christian University, USA. Selected publications include: "Money, Finance and Capital Markets", in *The Cambridge Economic History of Modern Britain* (2004), "The Bank of Amsterdam and the Leap to Central Bank Money", *American Economic Review Papers and Proceedings* (2007) and "How Amsterdam got fiat money", *Journal of Monetary Economics* (2014, with W. Roberds).

Jan F. Qvigstad was Deputy Governor of Norges Bank 2008–2014. He is now Executive Director, General Secretariat, responsible for Norges Bank's research in monetary history. Selected publications include: *Choosing a Monetary Policy Target* (1997, co-edited with A.B. Christiansen), *Twenty Years of Inflation Targeting. Lessons learned and future prospects* (2010, co-edited with D. Cobham, Ø. Eitrheim and S. Gerlach) and *On Central Banking* (2016, Cambridge University Press).

Editors and contributors xiii

William Roberds is a research economist and senior policy adviser with the Federal Reserve Bank of Atlanta. Selected publications include: "Optimal pricing of payment services", *Journal of Monetary Economics* (2008, with C. Monnet), "Payments Settlement: Tiering in Private and Public Systems", *Journal of Money, Credit and Banking* (2009, with C.M. Kahn) and "How Amsterdam got fiat money", *Journal of Monetary Economics* (2014, with S. Quinn).

Hugh Rockoff is a Distinguished Professor of Economics at Rutgers University. He has specialized on war economics and finance. Selected publications include: *Drastic Measures: A History of Wage and Price Controls in the United States* (1984), *History of the American Economy* (with G. Walton) (2010), "Not Just the Great Contraction: Friedman and Schwartz's A Monetary History of the United States 1867 to 1960" *American Economic Review* and *America's Economic Way of War* (2014).

Catherine Schenk is a Professor of International Economic History at the University of Glasgow, UK. Selected publications include: *Britain and the Sterling Area: from devaluation to convertibility in the 1950s* (1994), "The evolution of the Hong Kong currency board during global exchange rate instability, 1967–1973", *Financial History Review* (2009), *The Decline of Sterling: managing the retreat of an international currency* (2010) and *International Economic Relations since 1945* (2011).

Isabel Schnabel is a Professor of Financial Economics at Bonn University. Selected publications include: "The German Twin Crisis of 1931" in *The Journal of Economic History* (2004), "Liquidity and Contagion: The Crisis of 1763" in *Journal of the European Economic Association* (with H.S. Shin) (2004), "Banks without parachutes: Competitive effects of government bail-out policies", *Journal of Financial Stability* (2010, with H. Hakenes) and "Bank Bonuses and Bailouts" in *Journal of Money, Credit and Banking* (2014, with H. Hakenes).

Hyun Song Shin is Director of Research at the Monetary and Economic Department at the Bank for International Settlements, Switzerland. Selected publications include: "Unique Equilibrium in a Model of Self-Fulfilling Currency Attacks", *American Economic Review* (1998, with S. Morris), *Risk and Liquidity* (2010), *Global Shock, Risks, and Asian Financial Reform* (2014, co-edited with I.J. Azis) and "Capital flows and the risk-taking channel of monetary policy", *Journal of Monetary Economics* (2015, with V. Bruno).

xiv   *Editors and contributors*

Pierre L. Siklos is a Professor of Economics and Director of the Viessmann European Research Centre at Wilfrid Laurier University. Selected publications include: *The Changing Face of Central Banking: Evolutionary Trends Since World War II*, (2002), *Challenges in Central Banking: The Current Institutional Environment and the Forces Affecting Monetary Policy* (2010, co-edited with M. Wohar and M.T. Bohl), *Central Bank Transparency, Decision-Making, and Governance: The Issues, Challenges, and Case Studies* (2013, co-edited with J.-E. Sturm) and "The Monetary Policy Council and the Governing Council: Two Canadian Tales", *International Journal of Central Banking* (2015, with Matthias Neuenkirch).

Tobias Straumann is a Professor at the Department of Economics, University of Zürich, Switzerland. Selected publications include: "A pioneer of a new monetary policy? Sweden's price-level targeting of the 1930s revisited", *European Review of Economic History* (2009, with U. Woitek), *Fixed Ideas of Money: Small States and Exchange Rate Regimes in 20th Century Europe* (2010), "Still tied by golden fetters: the global response to the US recession of 1937–1938", *Financial History Review* (2012, with U. Scott) and *The Value of Risk: Swiss Re and the History of Reinsurance* (2013, with P. Borscheid and D. Gugerli).

Gianni Toniolo, Research Professor Emeritus at Duke University (USA) and lecturer at LUISS, Italy. Selected publications include: *Economic Growth in Europe Since 1945* (1996, co-edited with N. Crafts), *The Emergence of Modern Central Banking from 1918 to the Present* (1999, co-edited with C.L. Holtfrerich and J. Reis), *Central Bank Cooperation at the Bank for International Settlements* (2005, assisted by P. Clement), *The Global Economy in the 1990s. A Long-run Perspective* (2006, co-edited with P.W. Rhode) and *The Oxford Handbook of the Italian Economy Since Unification* (2013, ed.).

Stefano Ugolini is Assistant Professor at the University of Toulouse, France. Selected publications include: "The origins of foreign exchange policy: the National Bank of Belgium and the quest for monetary independence in the 1850s", *European Review of Economic History* (2012) and "Bagehot for beginners: the making of lender-of-last-resort operations in the mid-nineteenth century", *Economic History Review* (2012, with V. Bignon and M. Flandreau).

François R. Velde, Senior Economist and Research Advisor at the Federal Reserve Bank of Chicago and Assistant Professor of Economics at the Johns Hopkins University, USA. Selected publications include: "A Model of Bimetallism", *Journal of Political Economy* (with W.E. Weber) (2000), *The Big Problem of Small Change* (2002, with T. Sargent) , "John Law's System" , *American Economic Review* (2007), "Chronicle of a Deflation Unforetold", *Journal of Political Economy* (2009), "The case of the undying debt", *Financial History Review* (2010), "The Life And Times Of Nicolas Dutot", *Journal of the History of Economic Thought* (2012).

Eugene N. White is Professor of Economics at Rutgers University and a Research Associate of the NBER. Selected publications include: *The Defining Moment: The Great Depression and the American Economy in the Twentieth Century* (1998, with M. Bordo and C. Goldin), "How Occupied France Financed Its Own Exploitation in World War II", *American Economic Review (2007),* "Competition among the exchanges before the SEC: was the NYSE a natural hegemon?", *Financial History Review* (2013) and *Housing and Mortgage Markets in Historical Perspective* (2014, with K. Snowden and P. Fishback).

Geoffrey Wood is a Professor Emeritus at Cass Business School. Selected publications include: "Defining and achieving financial stability", *Journal of Financial Stability* (2006, with W. Allen), *Designing Central Banks* (2011, with D. Mayes), *Money over Two Centuries: Selected Topics in British Monetary History, 1870–2010* (2012, with F. Capie) and *European Banking Union: Prospects and Challenges* (2016, with J.E. Castañeda and D.G. Mayes).

Preface

In 2016, the Norwegian central bank, Norges Bank, celebrates its bicentennial. This is a timely occasion to ask what is really at the core of central banks and central banking, and what defines them as institutions? Both academic experts and central bank policymakers are curious to know more about this, and developments after the global financial crisis have further stimulated this curiosity.

Internationally a number of national histories of central banks have been published in the past decades, e.g. on the Bank of England, the Federal Reserve, the Swedish Riksbank and the Bank of Finland. Our approach is inspired by the broad coverage of the historical evolution of central banks up to 1994 when the Bank of England celebrated its tercentennial.[1] Around that time the academic literature focused specifically on inflation control and central bank independence. Twenty years later, and with recent experiences of the global financial crisis in mind, we have learnt that a stable monetary system requires more than inflation control and independence. A stable monetary system requires that the three dimensions of a trinity of price stability, financial stability and a well-functioning payment system are all jointly in place, acknowledging of course their mutual interdependence. Neither the institutional accounts nor the scholarly studies which have appeared are in anyway competitors, but must be seen as complementary to our book which highlights evolutionary aspects of central banks and central banking.

Already in 2011 we started the planning of a broad, research-based, international study of the evolution of central banks and central banking

---

[1] A great inspiration has been the book by Capie F., C.A.E. Goodhart, S. Fischer and N. Schnadt (1994), *The Future of Central Banking: The Tercentenary Symposium of the Bank of England*, Cambridge University Press.

over the past 200 years. We thank Stefano Ugolini in particular for his input and contributions in the planning process. In the summer of 2012 a broad range of research along these lines was commissioned from 14 different teams of authors, most of them merited international academic experts and policymakers. Representatives from all 14 teams first met at a pre-conference at the Graduate Institute of International and Development Studies (Centre for Finance and Development) in Geneva 25–26 April 2013. The papers were subsequently revised and presented at the Norges Bank conference *Of the Uses of Central Banks: Lessons from History,* held in Oslo on 5–6 June 2014. After a new round of author revisions, responding to comments made by the discussants and participants at the conference, all drafted chapters were finished in March 2015. We would like to extend our thanks to all the authors for devoting a share of their valuable time to prepare their contributions to this project. And Norges Bank want to express our deepest gratitude to the network of international academic experts on central banking and monetary history, with whom we have had the pleasure to interact since the Norges Bank Bicentenary Project 1816–2016 was started a decade ago. The inner core of this network has included Michael D. Bordo, Forrest Capie, Marc Flandreau, Lars Jonung, Gianni Toniolo and Eugene White.

Oslo, 4 April 2016

Michael D. Bordo

Øyvind Eitrheim

Marc Flandreau

Jan F. Qvigstad

Preface xix

NORGES BANK'S BICENTENARY PROJECT 1816-2016

Norges Bank publishes four books in conjunction with its 200th anniversary in 2016:

- M. D. Bordo, Ø. Eitrheim, M. Flandreau and J. F. Qvigstad (editors) (2016). *Central Banks at a Crossroads: What Can We Learn from History?* Cambridge University Press.
- Ø. Eitrheim, J. T. Klovland and L. F. Øksendal (2016). *A Monetary History of Norway 1816-2016.* Cambridge University Press.
- E. Lie, J. T. Kobberrød, E. Thomassen and G. F. Rongved (2016). *Norges Bank 1816–2016.* Fagbokforlaget. (In Norwegian only).
- H. Bøhn, Ø. Eitrheim and J. F. Qvigstad (editors) (2016). *Norges Bank 1816–2016. A Pictorial History.* Fagbokforlaget. (In Norwegian and English).

The work on these books started in 2007. Michael D. Bordo, Rutgers University, New Jersey; Øyvind Eitrheim, Norges Bank; Marc Flandreau, Graduate Institute of International and Development Studies, Geneva; and Jan F. Qvigstad, Norges Bank have constituted the steering group for Norges Bank's Bicentenary Project 1816–2016.

COVER IMAGES

The cover images show the proposed motifs for the new Norwegian 100-krone banknote ©2014 Norges Bank. The obverse side of the notes (top) shows the 9th century Gokstad vikingship with the Norwegian designed bow X-BOW®, a design owned by Ulstein Design & Solutions AS, in the background. The reverse of the notes (bottom) bears a pixel motif of a cargo ship on the horizon. The motifs are proposals from Metric and T. Tønnessen, and Snøhetta respectively, selected after an artistic competition arranged by Norges Bank. The design of the finished notes may deviate somewhat from the competition proposals.

1

Introduction

Michael D. Bordo
Rutgers University and NBER

Øyvind Eitrheim
Norges Bank

Marc Flandreau
Graduate Institute of International and Development Studies, Geneva

Jan F. Qvigstad
Norges Bank

1 Trust and the Central Bank

A widespread view among economic historians is that a well-functioning and stable monetary and financial system is a necessary condition for a thriving economy and rising living standards. Traditional students of European economic history have long noted the association between the expansion of the banking system and economic development. At a time when economists still grappled with the notion of the neutrality of monetary institutions, Cameron (1967) posited the existence of a link between banking and development. The US experience in the nineteenth century has for a while stood as a possible counter-example to this view, in that its banking system was crisis prone and yet the economy did thrive. However, more recent work has shown that the output losses of the recurrent crises that occurred in America during the nineteenth century were limited (Rousseau and Sylla, 2006). Modern research is moving toward a better understanding of the underpinning of this long underestimated financial success.

Both fiat money and commercial bank finance are underpinned by trust but the mechanisms whereby trust is produced are still incompletely understood. The role of the rise of the modern state as a producer of trust has been emphasized. It has been traced back to Italian city states (Fratianni and Spinelli, 2006) and the British "Glorious Revolution" of 1689 (North and Weingast, 1989), which is seen as having paved the way for Britain's Financial Revolution in the eighteenth century (Dickson,

1967). The Industrial Revolution in the second half of the nineteenth century can be seen as having completed the process.

Both history and theory suggest that the construction of trust have led to the emergence and development of systems of monitoring. It is not surprising perhaps that where the consolidation of trust took place in Western Europe in the eighteenth and nineteenth century, a form of institutional proliferation occurred whereby state and privileged banks controlled one another: This makes the early history of central banking a narrative of how rents and privileges were granted by the state to private institutions (banks of issue) and how the banks of issue reciprocated by improving the credit and liquidity of state debt (Broz and Grossman, 2004). The result was an evolutionary process whereby compromises had to be found between the needs of public finance and the conduct of monetary policy. It did not go without failures or controversies. The temptation of cash-strapped governments to extract more seigniorage from the bank led to episodes of monetary exploitation, which usually resulted in a reduction of credit for both the state and the central bank. The famous episode of the "bullion controversy" during the French wars, whereby economists and policy makers debated whether the depreciation of sterling in terms of gold ("the high price of bullion") was due to the monetization of British debt facilitated by the inconvertibility of the banknotes of the Bank of England or to other factors, provides illustration. In the instance, the depreciation was moderated by the roaring expansion of the British economy, which fuelled an increase in the demand for banknotes and enabled the Bank of England to lend support to the economy. Toward the later part of the nineteenth century, the wisdom accumulated from these experiences was encapsulated in a new theory that enshrined the independence of the bank of issue, and anticipated on the modern theory of central bank independence (Flandreau, Le Cacheux, and Zumer, 1998).

In parallel, the belief had spread that leaving the establishment of trust solely to market forces was unlikely to produce satisfying results, and in Europe it was felt that the adequate solution was to be found in the replacement of free banking by central banking. Historically, many examples were invoked to underpin this view, which led contemporaries, long before the idea was emphasized by Bank of Japan Governor Masaaki Shirakawa, to think of financial stability as a public good whose provision invited the creation of a government supervised monopoly (Goodhart, 1988). The idea of a special role for the central bank to play in the midst of financial stress coagulated in the aftermath of financial crises, with the crisis of 1866 playing a distinct role through the introduction of the so-called Bagehot doctrine. Bagehot was the editor of British weekly Liberal magazine *The Economist* and, following a series of articles that went back to 1866, he eventually published in 1873 a book called *Lombard Street: A Description of the Money Market*. There he argued, on the basis of the behavior of the Bank of England during the panic of 1866, that a central bank could, and should, intervene during crises. The three pillars of Bagehot's guidelines for central bank intervention now known as "Lending of Last Resort" or LOLR (generous liquidity, against good collateral, at high rates) have been often commented upon (Bignon, Flandreau, and Ugolini (2011) and Bordo (2014)). More important for our purpose here is the question of understanding why the Bank of England rather than another institution came to be the vehicle in charge of intervening in the aftermath of the failure of Overend Gurney and Co, a leading non-bank financial institution (in the language and categories of the time the Bank of England referred to such money market funds as "bill brokers" and "Overends" was the most aggressive of them all). The answer could be that, because of the Bank of England's vast knowledge of how the market operated in normal times, it was in a unique position to determine what constituted "good collateral". This interpretation is consistent with the evidence in Flandreau and Ugolini (2013) who show the stability of the composition of the discounting portfolio of the Bank of England before and during the crisis of 1866. Based on the British experience, a crisis was an episode that called for monetary authorities to do "more of the same."

As this happened however, the state remained in a position that enabled it to continue to play a role, either in the forefront or in the background of the formation of trust. In the case of the development of modern LOLR in Britain for instance, a surrounding arrangement that accompanied the implementation of such policies was the suspension of the Act of 1844, an arrangement that effectively freed the Bank from bending the limits of the Act. In other words, the Bank's ability to conduct LOLR policies was itself constrained by the authorization of the State, which enjoyed the right to review such policies afterward (in turn creating some resistance on the part of the Bank to seek the actual suspension of the Act of 1844). Moreover, it was prescribed that, as it performed its role as a LOLR, the Bank would lose the privilege of earning revenues from such crisis lending (Flandreau, 2008). This is important, because the removal of the profit motive and its replacement by a set of rules underscores the notion of a nascent "public good logic" just emphasized (i.e., Bagehot's "Responsibility Doctrine"). This also suggests that the operation of LOLR was only as solid as was its continued societal support materialized in state guarantees. As a result, for prolonged periods of history, in a great number of countries, right up to the dawn of the twentieth century, and even when the supreme monetary authority was on the forefront, the state remained a de facto stakeholder of the management of crises and the ultimate guarantor of monetary and financial stability.

The twentieth century accelerated trends discernible in the past in some "financially advanced" countries. Institutionally entrenched central banks, continued to play a progressively more pivotal role in safeguarding the stability of money and finance. They received this role from governments, in large part, because of the superior information and experience they had accumulated.

2 Central Banks at a Crossroads: "Where Next?"

In the opening paragraph of the *Tale of Two Cities*, Charles Dickens wrote: "in short, the period was so far like the present period, that some of its noisiest authorities insisted on its being received, for good or for evil, in the superlative degree of comparison only." The same phenomenon appears to have characterized the use of adjectives to describe modern financial times. When the global financial crisis of 2008 brought the so-called Great Moderation decisively to an end, it was not long until the outcome was described as the "Great Recession." And indeed after the crisis erupted, central banks quickly made up their minds as to the seriousness and source of the problem and identified the culprits in the shape of a number of pre-crisis blind-spots – extensive credit in the banking system, but also, and more fundamentally, having escaped from their view, the burgeoning of credit by non-banks. Just as had occurred in the crisis of 1866 with bill brokers or in 1907 and 1929 with financial trusts, an enormous credit system had proliferated in the shadow of the banking system, resulting in ballooning debts. In response, central banks have reinvented themselves and although this was certainly not the first time such reinventions occurred in the history of central banks (as the birth of the Bagehot doctrine after the crisis of 1866 reminds us) the magnitude of the modern episode is truly remarkable.

A first aspect of this reinvention relates to monetary policy; it is said that extraordinary times call for extraordinary monetary measures. Global interest rates were lowered to unprecedented levels (making comparison with Bagehot's rules, which called for *raising* interest rates, somewhat irrelevant), accompanied in some major advanced countries by purchases of government securities – the so-called quantitative easing (QE). In some countries, central banks also purchased private sector assets, such as mortgage-backed securities and corporate bonds – the so-called credit easing. Others, including the Federal Reserve and the Bank of England, began to rely on announcements known as "forward guidance" to convey their future policy intentions and thereby shape the yield curve.

A second aspect of the reinvention relates to macro-prudential regulation. Inflation targeting was necessary but, by itself, insufficient to curb the financial cycle. The response of governments has been to grant central banks new powers, focused on the needs of the financial system as a whole and the needs of the nonfinancial economy, as much as the financial sector: The approach is no longer narrowly monetary, and it enables central banks to respond to perceived trends in the macro-economy. This is the meaning of 'macro' in macro-prudential.

A third aspect of the reinvention concerns central banking operations. During the crisis, central banks expanded their balance sheets as never before. When crisis lending in the nineteenth century resulted in an expansion of the central bank's balance sheet, it was typically smaller than 30 percent (Bignon, Flandreau, and Ugolini, 2011). The subprime crisis produced a revolution in central banking in that balance-sheet increases have been of an order of magnitude larger. New facilities were introduced that extended liquidity for longer durations and against expanded sets of collateral (public and private) to new counterparties (bank and non-bank). This took last-resort lending to a new level. Some central banks went one step further, becoming effective market-makers of last resort in some assets to secure market liquidity (Mehrling, 2010). These were new and bold steps.

One consequence of this is that the meaning of "normal times" has been transformed. When (if?) we get back to "normal times," will central banks go back to normal activity or will they move further ahead? Haldane (2014) refers to A. A. Milne's (1924) poem, "Halfway Down."[1] Haldane thinks this poem is a fitting description of the position central banks find themselves in today. "During the past twenty-five years or more, central banks' mandates and instruments have moved upward in steps. They have ascended the stairs. But where this leaves central banks today is not entirely comfortable. Halfway up the stairs is neither up nor down, neither nursery nor town. That begs a natural question about where next for central banks over the next quarter-century."

---

[1] In A. A. Milne (1924), *When We Were Very Young* (illustrated by E.H. Shepard), published by Methuen & Co. Ltd.

3 I Told you So: Learning from History

A recent book by Eichengreen (2015) provides important insights on the art and pitfalls of drawing lessons from history for the purpose of policy making. He argues that one source of the dynamics of the current Great Recession can be found in what he calls the progressive narrative of the Great Depression, whereby the disasters of the 1930s were ascribed to a set of correctable flaws in collective decision-making. This reading of the interwar crisis, pioneered by Friedman and Schwartz (1963) in their classic *Monetary History of the United States*, implied that scientific central banking, advances in supervision and regulation, and deposit insurance would ensure that no comparable crisis would occur again in the future. While such beliefs were counter-productive in that they created blind-spots in which financial fragilities accumulated, they also conveyed a sense of policy responsibility that ensured that policy makers reacted in a substantially more pro-active manner in the modern recession than they had in the past.

This sweet and sour conclusion on the uses of history raises important questions about how lessons are constructed. For instance, the conventional reading of the Great Depression led to the impression that bank runs occurred principally in the retail banking sector, and were thus properly addressed by deposit insurance and the supervision of commercial banks, thus creating a loophole in investment banking and the shadow banking system as the 2008 run on Lehman brothers and the repo market revealed. However, the already mentioned crisis of 1866 and the reading that Bagehot had provided of the crisis did emphasize the role of what is known today as the shadow banking system. For what was the failure of Overend, Gurney & Co., that took deposits from the banking system and invested them in short term assets that turned out to be "toxic" if not that of a "shadow bank"? It is tempting to conclude that the whole subject hinges on the selection of a proper precedent.

But if the conclusion is that selecting the right precedent, or reading the right history, is paramount this begs the question of how historical knowledge is organized. Perhaps a heuristic parallel is with the misunderstanding that develops from the parent-children relation. To the frustration of parents who see the elements of repetition in the present, children seem to be more interested in having their own experiences than listening to parents' advice. To the frustration of the children, parents seem more interested in reading the past in the present, rather than taking into account the information that children have about the new world that surrounds them.

The situation is further complicated when the grandparents enter the picture and tell, now to the parents, now to the children, that they are actually not so different from one another and that they both forget earlier lessons.

There is no agreed upon framework whereby knowledge from past experiences in economic policy making is organized and in fact there cannot be. With the tendency of modern economics to be increasingly theoretical and often detached from mundane concerns, the study of past economic successes and failures straddles the borders of economics, economic history, history, political science not to mention anthropology and sociology (Flandreau, 2016). To this scattering of wisdoms, one must add a number of hurdles which Eichengreen recognizes as having obstructed previous inference: he mentions the continuity bias (a psychological phenomenon whereby current trends are simply extrapolated), peer pressure, and the fear of being ostracized, the dominant ideology and the pressure of big financial institutions.

Something should be said also about the fact that, by bringing economic history to the fore as a legitimate source of inspiration for policy making, the current crisis will only add to the political pressures weighing on the work of scholars. This is something to reckon with, especially since the economic history profession forms a relatively tiny group. In summary, the answer to the normative question whether we should learn from history is obviously a clear "yes." As to which lessons and how one gets to pick them, this book attempts to provide some answers and the next section provides indications as to the areas in which writing the history of central banks could become the source of valuable lessons – or perhaps practical imagination. Recent research questions, which this volume reflects, suggest that the history of central banks goes way beyond the remit of the traditional history of monetary policy or the institutional response to financial turmoil. In fact central banks are at the center of social, economic, and political processes and studying them provides rich perspectives on the development of modern capitalism.

4 Lessons Waiting to be Learned

4.1 The Central Bank as an Institution

From the point of view of modern monetary policy making, the history of central banks has been narrated as one of an institution whose predominant concern typically varied between normal times (price or exchange rate stability) and extraordinary times (financial stability). What seems to draw the most interest today, in the light of the recent financial crisis, is indeed this shifting balance between price stability and financial stability raising important questions as to what role a central bank should be playing in the future. Are we actually entering a new epoch? History can provide help in order to illuminate such top of the agenda questions. Modern central banks are the result of past debates, politics and an institutionalization of "experience" and power relations which we call learning. Historically they have been embedded in processes that were part of nation-building. By extending their network of branches across the country, or by being at a center of a system of liquidity provision ultimately tied to the national currency, becoming wholesale provider of this currency, they have defined the meaning of "domestic economy" and made modern macroeconomic policy possible.

4.2 The Central Bank as Part of the International Monetary System

A national central bank is not alone in the world. Today, there is a central bank in (almost) every country and they cannot operate in isolation. A century ago, in the wake of the crisis of 1907, Italian economist Luigi Luzzatti wrote a much-commented article calling for a conference in support of what he called (in an age fixated by the risks of a European war) "international monetary peace." He emphasized that owing to rampant spill-overs the national economy did not provide a relevant entity when it came to dealing with financial stress. International monetary cooperation was needed and urgent (Luzzatti, 1908). Central banks were to be the intermediaries – in a sense the diplomats – of this international peace. Simultaneously and partly prompted by the crisis, several advanced countries such as the United States and Switzerland indeed created their own central bank. Today, it is widely recognized that, interest-rate setting in a small open economy cannot be done without regard for the interest rate abroad. Recent mentions of the currency wars of the 1930s reflect the persistence and indeed perhaps amplification, of international interdependencies (Eichengreen, 2013). And there are limits to how much banking regulation can vary across countries in a world of free capital movements. So learning from history must also draw on the experiences of the international monetary system: The way in which central banks become part of the international monetary system – influencing it or being influenced by it – is a particularly relevant research direction.

4.3 The Central Bank and the Other National Institutions – Delineations and Limitations

As argued earlier, especially in continental Europe, the nineteenth century saw central banks taking more and more responsibility in the management of crises while the government was less visible. By contrast, after World War II, governments (i.e., the Treasury) played a considerable role in supervising the banking system etc. The division of monetary power between say, central bank, government, and parliament, not to mention the agency problem which central banking raises, is a complex subject that opens many positive and normative questions. It is important to try and understand why central banks evolved the way they did, in order to better understand the underlying issues that underpin the division of monetary power. Conversely, such a better understanding can inform prescription and transformations in legal statuses (e.g. Calomiris, Flandreau, and Laeven, 2015). In other words can we learn from history with regard to the delineation of the contours of central banks and to limitations placed on their reach?

4.4 The Central Bank from a Practitioner's Perspective

It is a conventional aphorism that central banking is an art rather than a science. This captures the essence of an important feature of the evolution of central banks, which have always found themselves at the center of a two-way flow, between economic theory on the one hand and the lessons from the practice on the other. In other words an important aspect of the "learning" of central banks hinges on the practitioners' experience and learning. This experience is kept in the memory of current policy makers. It is held in the publication, archives, and personal papers of former policy makers and their staff. Most central banks have a long history, encompassing past episodes of monetary and financial instability. Memory teaches patience, and both are two crucial virtues for effective public policy. This book's message to practitioners is that they should cultivate both.

5 The Chapters

The chapters in the book are divided into four parts: I) The central bank as an institution – the historical perspective; II) The central bank as part of the international monetary system; III) The central bank and other national institutions – delineation and limitation; IV) The central bank from a practitioner's perspective. We summarize the chapters briefly in the following.

5.1 The Central Bank as an Institution - The historical Perspective

Chapter 2: "The Descent of Central Banks (1400–1815)" by William Roberds and François R. Velde

Whereas the bulk of papers in this volume concern central banks and central banking over the past two centuries from the Napoleonic era onward, this chapter provides a review over their early history from 1400 until the Napoleonic era ends in 1815. A Darwinian model is applied and the key idea is to capture evolutionary aspects and path dependence of these early banks. From this perspective, the structure of today's highly-levered, note-issuing, government-debt-backed central banks preserves a record of the successes and failures of past institutions. The authors argue that this biological metaphor also has some implications for the future of central banks. One implication is that in central banking, as in nature, there are no true steady states. Hence, the present structure of modern banks does not necessarily represent convergence. In fact the history of early public banks confirms nearly the opposite view, i.e., that unorthodox ideas of one generation of central banks may become the orthodoxy of the next. The authors see the evolution of central banking as a sort of alchemy, a continuous search for the right formula, and conclude that the search continues.

Chapter 3: "Central Bank Credibility: An Historical and Quantitative Exploration" by Michael D. Bordo and Pierre L. Siklos

Empirical measures of credibility, based on inflation performance, are supplemented with historical narratives drawing on extensive and detailed analysis of historical evidence of ten 11 central banks over their lifetime, spanning 150 years or more. The results indicate that credibility changes are both frequent and can be of quite significant magnitude. Second, the authors find that institutional factors (i.e., the quality of governance), plays an important role in preventing a loss of credibility. Third, credibility shocks are shown to depend on the type of monetary policy regime in place, such as whether the Gold Standard applies or there is central bank independence. Finally, credibility is most affected by whether the shock can be associated with policy errors.

Chapter 4: "The Coevolution of Money Markets and Monetary Policy, 1815–2008" by Clemens Jobst and Stefano Ugolini

Money market structures shape monetary policy design, but the way central banks perform their operations also has an impact on the evolution of money markets. This chapter addresses topics at the crossroad of two independent strands of the economic and financial literature. On the one hand the literature on the workings of money markets and on the other the literature on monetary policy implementation. The coevolution of money markets and monetary policy is investigated using three newly collected datasets covering ten countries over two centuries. Periods of convergence and divergence are singled out, and it is shown that exogenous factors – by changing both money market structures and monetary policy design – may impact on coevolution from both directions.

Chapter 5: "Central Bank Independence in Small Open Economies" by Forrest Capie, Geoffrey Wood, and Juan Castañeda

Could it be that central bank independence and low inflation are in fact simultaneously produced by the structure of a country's financial system? This chapter provides evidence on central bank independence in small open economies. The authors report empirical evidence which indicates that it is more likely that central bank independence is durable in small open economies than in large economies, regardless of the degree of openness of the latter. The fact that small open economies also tend to be 'high trust' societies has a bearing on this result.

Chapter 6: "Fighting the Last War: Economists on the Lender of Last Resort" by Richard S. Grossman and Hugh Rockoff

The evolution of the lender of last resort (LOLR) doctrine – and its implementation – is traced from the nineteenth century through the panic of 2008. Economists tend to behave like generals, always fighting the last battle, formulating policy guidelines that would have dealt effectively with the latest crisis, only to be confronted by new issues, requiring new solutions, in subsequent crises. Perhaps, like the military, central banks need to make "war plans" for meeting different types of threats. In the meantime, policymakers have to rely on older plans of Thornton, Bagehot, Friedman and Schwartz, Bernanke et. al, bearing in mind, as R. G. Hawtrey suggested, that central banking in financial crises will remain an art rather than a science.

5.2 The Central bank as Part of the International Monetary System

Chapter 7: "A Century and a Half of Central Banks, International Reserves, and International Currencies" by Barry Eichengreen and Marc Flandreau

The authors provide a historical perspective on central bank foreign exchange management, spanning the 150-plus years since the middle of the nineteenth century. There was a shift in reserve management practices from the late nineteenth century away from holding the reserve entirely in bullion toward also holding foreign exchange reserves and using them to intervene actively in foreign exchange markets. Three themes are emphasized: The first theme traces the evolution of the principal reserve assets: sterling before 1914, followed by the entry of the dollar, first in the 1920s and subsequently as the dominant reserve currency after the Second World War. The second theme highlights the rise of active reserve and portfolio management; and the third theme the influence of politics.

Chapter 8: "Central Banks and the Stability of the International Monetary Regime" by Catherine Schenk and Tobias Straumann

The authors ask under what historical circumstances central banks have been successful in preserving the two public goods of an international monetary regime – international currencies and external stability – over the past 200 years. The three main determining factors are shown to be the exchange rate system, the degree of international policy convergence, and the degree of central bank independence. The authors argue that the fixed exchange rate system of the twentieth century was undermined by the lack of common goals and interests. The subsequent floating exchange rate of the 1970s system was unsustainable because most central banks were not independent. After central banks were freed from political influence, the international monetary system became much more stable and their role in preserving these two public goods has become more important than ever.

Chapter 9: "The International Monetary and Financial System: A Capital Account Historical Perspective" by Claudio Borio, Harold James, and Hyun Song Shin

The authors state rather provocatively that current accounts are largely uninformative about risks inherent in the international monetary and financial system. Instead the relevant information is contained in the capital accounts and in their relationship to the broader balance sheets of the relevant economies. They argue that in a financially integrated global

Introduction 13

economy the international monetary and financial system tends to amplify the "excess financial elasticity" of national economies. Second, there is a need to go beyond the resident/non-resident distinction that underpins the balance of payments and to consider the consolidated balance sheets of decision-making units that operate across borders, including the currencies of denomination. These points are illustrated by examining two historical phases of special interest: the interwar years and the period surrounding the recent Great Financial Crisis.

Chapter 10: "Central Banking: Perspectives from Emerging Economies" by Menzie D. Chinn

The international trilemma is used to describe the constraints faced by central bank policy makers in emerging economies. Second, focus is on the evolution of monetary policy over time, with specific reference to the recent adoption of inflation targeting, more specifically how the different types of flexible inflation targeting regimes actually implemented address some, but not all, of the special concerns facing these emerging markets. The next section addresses the motivation for the marked accumulation of reserves over the past two decades, a special attribute of emerging market economies. Finally, the author offers his conjectures regarding the future of monetary policy in emerging economies.

5.3 The Central bank and Other National Institutions – Delineation and Limitation

Chapter 11 "The Evolution of the Financial Stability Mandate: From Its Origins to the Present Day" by Gianni Toniolo and Eugene N. White

This chapter traces the origins and growth of the Financial Stability Mandate (FSM) with an eye to improving policymakers' understanding of why central banks and policy regimes in the past succeeded or failed to meet their FSM. Two issues inform this chapter (1) whether supervision should be conducted by the central bank or by independent agencies and (2) whether supervision should be rules- or discretion/principles-based? The authors focus on the history of six countries, three in Europe (England, France, and Italy), and three in the New World (United States, Canada, and Colombia) to highlight the essential developments in the FSM. While a common evolutionary path can be identified, the development of the FSM in individual countries depend on their adaptation to changes in payment technologies, their disposition toward competitive markets and their degree of openness.

Chapter 12: "Bubbles and Central Banks: Historical Perspectives" by Markus K. Brunnermeier and Isabel Schnabel

This chapter categorizes and classifies some of the most prominent asset price bubbles of the past 400 years and documents how central banks (or other institutions) reacted to those bubbles. The authors describe the types of assets involved, the holders of assets, policy environments during the emergence of bubbles, the severity of crises, and policy responses. The historical evidence suggests that the emergence of bubbles is often preceded or accompanied by an expansionary monetary policy, lending booms, capital inflows, financial innovation, or deregulation. The authors find that contrary to conventional wisdom, the financing of bubbles is much more relevant than the type of bubble asset. Second, passive "cleaning up the mess" policies tend to be costly. Policy measures are in many cases shown to help mitigate crises, but whether interest-rate tools or macro-prudential tools are most effective will depend on circumstances. The complexities of assessing the bubble in real time and timing of interventions is of the essence.

Chapter 13: "Central Banks and Payment Systems: The Evolving Trade-off between Cost and Risk" by Charles Kahn, Stephen Quinn, and William Roberds

The authors present a simple theoretical framework to illustrate the evolution of central bank payment systems and, importantly, their interactions with private systems. Central bank money contributes to the effectiveness of the wider payment system and its characteristics depend on the structure of the central bank. First, the authors examine the Early Modern system of bills of exchange prevalent on the European Continent. Next, they examine the Anglo-American experience with banknotes and checks. Finally, they consider modern wholesale payments arrangements for foreign exchange, which work through multiple central banks but do not have a unifying central bank.

4 The Central Bank from a Practitioner's Perspective

Chapter 14: "Central Bank Evolution: Lessons Learnt from the Sub-Prime Crisis" by Charles A. E. Goodhart

In the wake of the recent global financial crisis central banks have been given additional responsibilities in the field of achieving financial stability through macro-prudential measures, as well as their price stability objective. This raises the question of whether central banks have now been given an overload, and whether this overload might even imperil their independence. Another potential threat to central bank independence could be that the massive expansion of central bank balance sheets, resulting from unconventional easing measures, could lead to very large losses further out, as and when interest rates return toward normal. The global financial crisis made it abundantly clear that neither central banks nor economists fully understood the working of the economic system. We cannot be sure that we have learnt the right lessons; uncertainty remains endemic.

Chapter 15: "The Evolution of Central Banks: A Practitioners' Perspective" by Andrew G. Haldane and Jan F. Qvigstad

The chapter briefly reviews the history of central banks, focusing on the Bank of England and Norges Bank. Despite differences in their origins, these institutions have converged to having similar objectives aimed at ensuring monetary and financial stability. Economic crises have contributed greatly to this evolution, as both central banks have responded to deal with them and taken steps to prevent recurrence. The recent financial crisis in particular has shown that monetary stability is unsustainable without financial stability. Endowed with both longevity and a long memory of past crisis experience, central banks are well suited to pursue long-run objectives in the spheres of monetary and financial stability. The case for operational independence in the pursuit of monetary policy is widely acknowledged. But the case is equally strong with regard to the pursuit of financial stability. In the light of the most recent crisis, central banks face a wide array of challenges in the period ahead, including their choice of objectives and instruments, and how to communicate them.

References

Bagehot, W. (1873), *Lombard Street: A Description of the Money Market*, London: H.S. King.

Bernanke, B. S. (2000), *Essays on the Great Depression*, Princeton, N.J.: Princeton University Press.

Bignon, V., M. Flandreau, and S. Ugolini (2011), "Bagehot for Beginners: The Making of Lending of Last Resort Operations in the Mid 19th Century," *Economic History Review*, 65(2), pp. 580–608, May 2012.

Bordo, M. D. (2014), "Rules For a Lender of Last Resort: An Historical Perspective," in Frameworks for Central Banking in the Next Century: A Special Issue on the Occasion of the Centennial of the Founding of the Federal Reserve, editors: Michael D. Bordo, William Dupour and John B. Taylor, *Journal of Economic Dynamics and Control*, 49, pp. 126–134.

Broz, J. L. and R. S. Grossman (2004), "Paying for Privilege: The Political Economy of Bank of England Charters, 1694–1844," *Explorations in Economic History*, 41 (1), January, pp. 48–72.

Calomiris, C. W. and S. H. Haber (2014), *Fragile by Design: The Political Origins of Banking Crises and Scarce Credit*, Princeton, N.J.: Princeton University Press.

Calomiris, C. W., M. Flandreau, and L. Laeven (2015), "Political Foundations of the Lender of Last Resort: A Global Historical Narrative", Working Paper.

Cameron, R. (1967), *Banking in the Early Stages of Industrialization: A Study in Comparative Economic History*, with the collaboration of Olga Crisp, Hugh T. Patrick, and Richard Tilly. New York: Oxford University Press.

Dickson, P. G. M. (1967), *The Financial Revolution in England. A Study in the Development of Public Credit, 1688–1756* London: Macmillan.

Eichengreen, B. (2013), "Currency War or International Policy Coordination?," *Journal of Policy Modelling*, 35 (3), May/June, pp. 425–433.

(2015), *Hall of Mirrors: The Great Depression, The Great Recession, and the Uses-and Misuses-of History*, USA: Oxford University Press.

Flandreau, M. (2008), "Pillars of Globalization: A History of Monetary Policy Targets, 1797–1997," in A. Beyer and L. Reichlin (eds.), *The Role of Money and Monetary Policy in the 21st Century*, Proceedings from Fourth ECB Central Banking Conference November 9–10, 2006, Frankfurt: ECB, pp. 208–243.

(2016), *Anthropologists in the Stock Exchange: A Financial History of Victorian Science* Chicago: University of Chicago Press.

Flandreau, M. and S. Ugolini (2013), "Where It All Began: Lending of Last Resort and the Bank of England during the Overend, Gurney Panic of 1866," in Michael D. Bordo and William Roberds (eds.), *Return to Jekyll Island: The Origins, History, and Future of the Federal Reserve*, New York: Cambridge University Press, pp. 113–161.

Flandreau, M., J. Le Cacheux, and F. Zumer (1998), "Stability without a Pact? Lessons from the European Gold Standard, 1880–1913," *Economic Policy*, 13 (26), pp. 115–162.

Fratianni, M. and F. Spinelli (2006), "Italian City-States and Financial Evolution," *European Review of Economic History*, 10 (3), pp. 257–278.

Friedman, M. and A. Schwartz (1963), *Monetary History of the United States; 1867 to 1960*, Princeton, N.J.:Princeton University Press.

Goodhart, C. A. E. (1988), *The Evolution of Central Banks*, Cambridge, Mass: MIT Press.

Haldane, A. G. (2014), "Halfway up the stairs," speech given on 5 August 2014 at the Portadown Chamber of Commerce, Northern Ireland, published in Central Banking Journal on August 5, 2014. London: Bank of England.

Hawtrey, R. G. (1932). *The Art of Central Banking*, London, New York, etc.: Longmans, Green and Co. Kindle Ebook edition.

Luzzatti, L. (1908), *Une conférence internationale pour la paix monétaire*, Paris: Chaix.

Mehrling, P. (2010), *The New Lombard Street: How the Fed Became the Dealer of Last Resort* Princeton, N.J.:Princeton University Press.

Milne, A. A. (1924), *When We Were Very Young*, (illustrated by E.H. Shepard), London: Methuen & Co. Ltd.

North, D. C. and B. R. Weingast (1989), "Constitutions and Commitment: The Evolution of Institutional Governing Public Choice in Seventeenth-Century England," *Journal of Economic History*, 49 (4), December, pp. 803–832.

Rousseau, P. L. and R. Sylla (2006), "Financial Revolutions and Economic Growth: Introducing This EEH Symposium," *Explorations in Economic History*, 43 (1), January, pp. 1–12.

Shirakawa, M. (2012), "International Financial Stability as a Public Good," Keynote address at a High-Level Seminar co-hosted by the Bank of Japan and the International Monetary Fund in Tokyo, Japan, October 14, 2012.

Thornton, H. (1802), *An Enquiry into the Nature and Effects of the Paper Credit of Great Britain* and two speeches *(1811)*. Edited with an Introduction by F. A. v. Hayek. New York: Rinehart & Company, Inc., 1939.

2

The Descent of Central Banks (1400–1815)

William Roberds and François R. Velde
Federal Reserve Banks of Atlanta and Chicago

1. Introduction

As works of financial engineering, modern central banks are at once both audacious and unremarkable. Their audacity stems from a routine degree of leverage, which, if observed in any other type of financial institution, might be described as "eye-popping." To give a familiar example, the Federal Reserve recently announced that it earned quite substantial profits ($79.5 billion) in 2013 from its $4 trillion debt portfolio, all against a capital of only $55 billion (Board of Governors of the Federal Reserve System 2014a, b). Yet such is the popularity of the Fed's own obligations, packaged as circulating notes or deposit accounts, that the publication of these figures generated only light interest in the financial press. In the twenty-first century, the near-universal acceptance of central banks' debt as money has made such leverage a commonplace, if not always uncontroversial phenomenon (Fawley and Neely, 2013).

The history of central banking shows that this was not always so. Protocentral banks (often operating as privileged private institutions) struggled to balance leverage (then as now, necessary in order to provide income for the banks and their sponsoring governments) with acceptance by the public (necessary in order to build a revenue base). A celebrated and decisive engineering breakthrough was provided by the Bank of England (founded in 1694), which, through its winning formula of restrained note issue and adroit management of government debt, was able to thrive as no other public bank had before it. The Bank of England's success was neither

---

This paper was written for the Norges Bank 2014 conference "Of the Uses of Central Banks: Lessons from History." The views presented here do not necessarily reflect those of the {Federal Reserve {System}|||{Bank of {Atlanta}||{Chicago}}}.

We thank without implicating Joost Jonker and Tom Sargent.

The Descent of Central Banks (1400–1815) 19

immediate nor inevitable, however, and the Bank itself represented but one chapter in a long process of experimentation and "natural selection" that shaped the structure of modern central banks.

This essay will review the history of early European public banks from an evolutionary perspective. We will use the evolutionary metaphor as a narrative device to organize a dozen countries over four centuries and invoke this profusion of observations as our defense when we appear to ride the metaphor too hard.

Our essay begins with the emergence of the first of these institutions, circa 1400 and ends approximately in 1815. The latter year marks the end of the Napoleonic Era, which as will be seen, served as an "extinction event" for many of these early banks. To extend the Darwinian metaphor, our essay will collect specimens (life histories of individual institutions), propose a taxonomy, and offer some hypotheses concerning the origin of today's species of central bank.[1]

Our conclusions depend crucially on the set of institutions that we review. We have tried to be comprehensive, or at least inquisitive, and avoid survivor bias.[2] The nature of the sources makes this difficult: short-lived experiments leave less of a trace in the record (unless their failure is spectacular, like the French bank of 1716–20). In addition, while it may be clear that these institutions were forerunners of modern central banks, they often did not look like them. Under the term "public bank" we include government-owned and operated banks, but also purely private institutions with unique legal privileges, as well as a range of intermediate entities whose governance structures sometimes resist taxonomic classification. The set of specimens examined is somewhat arbitrary, but all institutions studied shared the goal of creating a legally privileged, previously unavailable type of monetary asset.

All metaphors have limits, including ours. We are aware that blind forces are not at work here, but human beings grappling for solutions to problems they perhaps do not fully understand. Nor do we necessarily think that all hillclimbing algorithms find the global optimum: where one arrives often depends on initial conditions and on the path followed. So we will also use another metaphor: central banking involves a sort of alchemy, and what we see in our history is a search for the right formula.

---

[1] This review draws on the survey of the secondary literature in Roberds and Velde (2016 a, b).
[2] In terms of our guiding metaphor, if we only look for mammal fossils we will miss the dinosaurs.

2 The Primordial Soup: Medieval and Early Modern Money

We do not conclude that it has been found; if anything, we are left with a sense that the search continues.

2 The Primordial Soup: Medieval and Early Modern Money

The magic glue that binds together modern central banks' balance sheets is a factor known as "money demand": the widespread willingness of firms and individuals to hold central bank claims, bearing little or no interest, as a medium of exchange or store of value. Money demand enables central banks to generate income and to pursue policy goals while operating with little or no conventional equity. The importance of money demand can be grasped from estimates of modern central banks' "comprehensive net worth" (Archer and Moser-Boehm, 2013), which attempt to adjust central bank equity by incorporating the off-balance sheet asset of discounted future seigniorage. Performing this adjustment for the Federal Reserve, for example, yields estimates of comprehensive net worth of $1 trillion or more.[3] Such figures reflect the value of the liquidity services rendered by central banks.

Reduced to its most elemental terms, the challenge of early public banks was to create a money demand where none existed. In one sense, this should not have been a difficult task, as medieval and early modern forms of money and near-money were beset with numerous problems.

Even transactions with coin were rarely straightforward. After economic exchanges had evolved out of barter, prices were expressed and debts were settled in coined metal – and, since Roman times at least, the right to define and produce (or have someone produce) coins was a prerogative of the State. But with debasements and the introduction of coins of different sizes and contents in medieval times, coinage could not provide an unambiguous and litigation-free means of settling debts. Different coins could and did have different values over time, a fact which increasing attempts at regulation could never satisfactorily eliminate. Debasements, undertaken for both fiscal and monetary reasons, kept the stock of circulating coins in constant flux. Fluctuations in exchange rates, competition from neighboring mints, variations in the market price of different metals plagued exchanges and made it difficult to establish a stable unit of account. A coin regarded as highly desirable tended to disappear from circulation, often to reappear as "ghost money," that is, a unit of account tied

---

[3] Archer and Moser-Boehm (2013, 11), Del Negro and Sims (2014, 42). These estimates assume that the Fed would retain all future seigniorage.

The Descent of Central Banks (1400–1815)

to the seldom-circulated coin at a historic rate. The problem of instability in units of account persisted throughout our period of interest, and was not fully resolved until the nineteenth century (Sargent and Velde, 2002).

A commodity money system was inherently wasteful. Metal stocked in the form of coinage represents resources that are not used to satisfy economic wants. Hence a pressure has always existed to find ways to economize on the stock of coined metals to execute exchanges and settle debts.

These two problems, the multiplicity of coins and the desire to avoid their use, lie at the origins of banking. Medieval banking began with the *campsores* or money-changers who dealt with the first problem. In response to the second problem, the moneychangers' *depositum regulare* (a deposit claim on a specific coin) evolved into the *depositum irregulare* (a claim on fungible coin). The latter allowed fractional reserve banking, payments occurring as book-entry transfers of deposit claims. Over time a payment by book-entry transfer became accepted as a valid discharge of debt, that had the additional advantage of providing legally admissible evidence of payment. This form of payment by transfers of deposits is variously called "in bank," "transfer," or "giro."

Such payment economized on resources and reduced transactions costs but also faced problems. As well documented for Venice by Mueller (1979, 1997), private banking was fragile, because commercial and merchant banking were integrated, properly diversifying risk was difficult and enterprises that were tied to individuals had limited life-spans in the absence of the legal form of commercial corporations.[4] The fragility manifested itself in waves of bankruptcies that seriously disrupted the industry. In response to this fragility banks were regulated heavily by local governments, either as a matter of regalian rights (as in Germany) or as a matter of public policy. To interpret the regulations in modern terms, they could take the form of capital requirements by defining the pool of assets that could be seized in case of bankruptcy (the banker's own head being an extreme form of "skin in the game"). They also placed restrictions on the assets that the banker could hold, notably on the basis of their perceived risk. The liabilities were also regulated, and making deposits demandable on very short notice appears to have emerged to discipline bankers (Diamond and Rajan, 2001). Of course, given the problem with fluctuating values of coins, governments also imposed on bankers the

---

[4] Of course, non-commercial corporations could and did enter the banking business. But the Knights Templars' success as a bank may ironically have led to their early demise.

obligation of abiding legal valuations of coins. These regulations were often ineffective, either in curtailing bank failures, or in maintaining a predictable exchange rate between *moneta in obligatione* (the money owed) and *moneta in solutione* (the money repaid). Dissatisfaction with private banks led many localities to found public banks.

Private debts (or orders to pay) were also used in transactions between merchants, but these too were subject to difficulties. Full transferability of these instruments did not become possible until the development of negotiable and later bearer instruments, and even then there remained problems of settlement. In many cities, obligations could be periodically canceled through the quasi-netting process of *rescontre* (Börner and Hatfield, 2010). Customs regarding the transfer and settlement of such instruments were eventually codified into widely understood "laws merchant," but the formality of these customs limited the use of private debt as money.

Another common problem was that overuse of endorsement could lead to uncomfortably long chains of indebtedness. Merchants who advocated the founding of a public bank complained of sometimes receiving bills with as many as ten or twenty signatures (see Lattes 1869, 172 for Venice, Van Dillen 1964b for Amsterdam). As trading expanded and endorsement became more prevalent, this problem became more resistant to solution through the traditional method of *rescontre*.

Government debt, often thought of as a near-money in the modern world, was in most cases less liquid than private obligations. The traditional form of government debt was long or perpetual annuities, often secured by specific tax revenues. In areas of Roman law annuities were considered as a form of real estate and the costs of transferring ownership could be onerous. Secondary markets could be thin or nonexistent, and the threat of default made the value of government debt uncertain, even in well-run municipal governments (as the case of Genoa will show).

3 Life Histories

3.1 The First Generation of Public Banks

Into this world were born the first public banks, from 1400 to circa 1650. Banks in this "first generation" issued obligations that were transferable only as book entries, just like those of the private banks. From 1650, a "second generation" of note issuers becomes increasingly predominant.

While the early public banks differed in many details they all were charged with the task of creating claims of a more stable and liquid character than existing monies or near-monies. There were many challenges involved. At the theoretical level, the Modigliani–Miller benchmark suggests that special factors are required in order for such repackaging of assets to be relevant. At a more practical level, a public bank needed to persuade a sufficient number of typically skeptical merchants to adopt its claims as a monetary asset.

To this end, funds held in accounts at public banks were invariably given legal privileges, for example, an elevated status in the settlement of certain debts and freedom from attachment or taxation. The historical record indicates, however, that such privileges were by themselves insufficient to attract a critical mass of users to a public bank. Success instead depended on the existence of credible mechanisms for limiting the asymmetric information and enforcement frictions that hindered the use of alternative assets (which themselves were the backing assets for the public banks). There as yet was no standard technique for doing this, which led to a degree of institutional experimentation. We briefly sketch the approaches taken by some of the first generation of public banks.

One recurrent feature in the history of this first generation is the "agio," which is simply the market exchange rate between balances in the bank and "current money," meaning the current stock of coinage as valued by legal tender laws in terms of a unit of account. Current money was unstable because legal tender laws changed, and because which coin currently circulated at its legal value changed with debasements, imports of foreign coins and wear.

Barcelona and Catalonia

To Barcelona is usually given the honor of the first public bank in Europe (Usher, 1934; Sánchez Sarto, 1934; Riu, 1979; Passola, 1999). The *Taula de Canvi* was founded in 1401 as a city agency for one main purpose: to provide the city with alternate means of funding itself. To this effect the Bank, whose solvability was guaranteed by the city, received deposits and even had a monopoly on certain types of deposits (conditioned, i.e., payable when certain stipulated conditions were met). It did not keep 100 percent reserves. It provided short-term financing to the city and served as fiscal agent, and sometimes as fiscal enforcer, for example in the 1412 reform of municipal finances that tasked the Bank with applying new budgetary rules (Ortí Gost, 2007). In principle it could not lend to private parties although it appears that overdrafts were common in the fifteenth century. Its relations with the private banking sector were tense throughout its history: private bankers were repeatedly prohibited from having accounts at the Bank. At various times special privileges were given to the Bank, such as a monopoly on settling bills of exchange from 1446 to 1499, and (briefly) all transactions above a certain size. From 1468, balances at the Taula were exempt from seizure.

The Bank, like its counterparts in Europe, had to deal with periodic debasements and disruptions in rates of exchange between coins. In 1453, following a debasement of the currency of Aragon, deposits were revalued but to a lesser extent than the currency's debasement (Usher, 1943, 376). In the early seventeenth-century, monetary disorders prompted the creation of a separate bank, the *Banch de la Ciutat*, to accept deposits in all sorts of coinage (even clipped and worn) at its discretion The Bank of the City was kept separate from the Taula although it was possible to transfer balances between the two. Usher (1943, 433–58) claims that the Banch's losses on exchange were subsidized by the city.

The Bank's initial purpose as funding vehicle for the city was severely put to the test in the 1460s when the city rebelled against the crown of Aragon. Pressed to make loans to finance the war the Bank was forced to suspend convertibility of its balances in 1463. In 1468 the Bank was reorganized; new ledgers were opened while existing depositors were given a choice between receiving annuities and waiting for full redemption out of the city's future surpluses, a process that took decades. After the reorganization the Bank was prohibited from lending to the city, and abided the rule for nearly two centuries.

The next major crisis occurred when Catalonia tried to secede from the Spanish monarchy in 1640. The two Banks were pressed into service to lend to the principality of Catalonia; payments were again suspended, from 1641 to 1653. At the same time large issues of essentially fiat copper currency brought substantial inflation. After Barcelona was retaken in 1653 a lengthy and complex process began to convert existing balances: in essence, depositors were again given a choice between annuities (in amounts indexed on the depreciation of the currency at the time deposits were made) and transferring balances to the new accounts and convert therein old balances at a small fraction of face value.

The final episode of Catalonia's struggle against the Spanish monarchy, during the War of Spanish Succession, ended in 1714 with a complete loss of autonomy. The Banks were reorganized as pure transfer banks and survived uneventfully until absorption into the Bank of Spain in 1853.

It is noteworthy that the Taula inspired a series of imitations throughout Catalonia (Passola, 1999), in cities including Valencia (1407–14, 1519–1649, 1649–1720), Saragossa (1550–1707), Mallorca (several in the fifteenth century, and 1507–1833), Perpinyà (from 1404), Girona (1443, 1567–1711), Tarragona (1585–1741), Lleida (1585–1707), Manresa (1603–late eighteenth century), Tortosa (1587–late seventeenth century), Olot, Cervera and Vic (1582– 1760s). This proliferation is remarkable for the small size of some cities: Olot, the smallest, numbered less than 2,000 inhabitants in the early sixteenth century. These banks were all more or less modeled on their counterparts in Barcelona, designed to accept deposits, make transfers, lend to their municipalities and act as fiscal agents; they also endured the same vicissitudes as their counterparts in Barcelona.

Genoa

The city of Genoa had issued debt backed by specific tax revenues since the twelfth century; in 1404 the *Casa di San Giorgio* was created to consolidate various issues, represent the creditors and ensure the collection of their claims. This remarkable corporation, whose main task was monitoring tax collection and managing payments to creditors of the City, lasted as long as the Republic itself and grew into a powerful non-governmental organization.

The Casa's involvement in banking occurred in two phases, the first from 1408 to 1444 and the second from 1530, or more clearly from 1675 on. The intentions behind the creation of the bank were stated clearly: to reduce the debt (implying that banking would be a source of profit) and to enforce the legal tender laws. The bank accepted deposits, which not demandable but payable at term (Sieveking, 1906, 87, fn2). It made loans only to the city and to the tax farmers and collectors, on collateral. It dealt in foreign exchange only in relation to the collection of revenues from Genoese territories in the Eastern Mediterranean. Business developed quickly, but the Bank was unable to fulfill the city's mandate of maintaining stable exchange rates between coins. A monetary reform in 1437 (during which the Bank's balances were made legal tender) failed to stem the rise in the market price of the gold coin, and when the city gave the Casa the choice between abiding the legal valuation of the gold coin and relinquishing its banking license, the Casa chose the latter (1444).

The Casa did not formally reopen a bank until 1530, but in the meantime its ledgers provided giro services, in the following way. Payments of tax revenues were often delayed and as a convenience accrued interest became transferable between creditors on the Casa's books. These sums were actively used for a wide range of transactions. A secondary market developed for these credits, which were bought up by tax farmers to discharge their obligations. The Casa thus gradually acquired expertise in the banking business. The archives show that a new banking ledger was opened in 1530, probably for the Casa's own business at first, but soon private deposits were accepted. The mode of operation is not well known for the early years, but loans were granted sparingly. Operations become clearer when the Casa opened several banks in succession, each dedicated to a specific coin: gold (1586), Genoese silver (1606), Spanish silver (1625). Clearly the Casa was avoiding the pitfalls of the fifteenth century and protecting itself from the risks of abiding legal valuations of coins.

By the mid-seventeenth century there was a consensus that a broader form of bank was needed, and after some debate it was decided to entrust it to the Casa rather than the city. In 1675 the Casa was allowed to open a ledger in current money, for which all sorts of coins were accepted in deposit. While the bank was to obey legal valuations, it had the right to choose which coin to repay. It was denied the right to operate a Lombard facility (offering small collateralized loans to individuals), loans to the city were restricted to short terms and subject to approval by a general assembly. The new bank copied several features from foreign counterparts: the settlement of bills of exchange was mandated through the bank as in Venice and Amsterdam. It also copied from Neapolitan banks the use of circulating deposit certificates (*fede di credito*).

The agio on the bank's money was fairly stable until the early eighteenth century. The bank faced a serious crisis during the 1740s. It had been helping the city with the cost of keeping its restive Corsican possession. In addition the city abandoned its neutrality in the ongoing War of Austrian Succession but was soon occupied by Austria in 1746 and saddled with a large war indemnity. The bank was forced to suspend payments. Existing depositors were repaid in bonds and a new bank was opened. The city eventually repaid its debt to the Casa which was able to redeem its bonds.

The end of the bank came with the end of the Casa. The French-sponsored Republican regime, established in 1797, regarded the very nature of the Casa as unacceptable: the government, not a private corporation, ought to control public revenues.[5] The Casa was eventually abolished and its creditors (including creditors of the bank) became creditors of the State.

---

[5] There is an interesting parallel with the arguments used during the French Revolution to reject the creation of a central bank (Sargent and Velde, 1995).

The Descent of Central Banks (1400–1815)

When the Republic of Genoa was briefly recreated in 1814, an attempt was made to recreate the Casa and the bank, but the attempt ended when Piedmont annexed Genoa.

Venice

The history of Venice provides two quite distinct examples of public banks.

The first, called the *Banco della Piazza di Rialto* or *Banco di Rialto*, was founded only in 1587, but had been preceded by several plans or attempts to remedy what seemed to be persistent shortcomings of the private banks. Venetian banks were few (less than a half-dozen) and as elsewhere held deposits and invested in a variety of assets, restricted in various ways over time by regulations. In 1526, when bank money stood at a 20 percent discount to cash, banking supervisors were created and bankers were required to pay deposits in cash without delay when demanded. Yet by 1584 the last private bank in Venice went bankrupt, and the Senate resolved, not without dissent, to license a strictly regulated, 100 percent-reserves, privately owned bank. The banker to be chosen to operate it was to liquidate the bank after three years (a radical form of supervision) and to be held responsible for any losses.

The bank performed reasonably well, and in 1593 it was required that all foreign bills of exchange be cleared on the books of the bank, apparently to improve their settlement. Nevertheless, as the bank was founded amidst continuing movements in exchange rates between coins an agio developed on bank money relative to current money. The bank had to make decisions continually on which coins to accept and pay out.

Quite different was Venice's second public bank, the *banco del Giro*, founded in 1619 while the Banco di Rialto was still operating. Here the motivation was to make liquid a public debt. Not long before, the Grain Office had kept a ledger of its creditors (grain merchants) and allowed them to make transfers between themselves. Although that debt was redeemed within a few years, a similar debt arose from a purchase of bullion by the mint from one merchant, who proposed a similar arrangement. As a temporary measure the Senate created an office at the mint to allow the merchant to pay his own creditors by transfers on a ledger; the credits were made legal tender for large payments, and ten years later accepted in payment of taxes. Some of the bullion, minted, was kept as a reserve, and the Senate authorized regular payments to the office at the mint to meet redemptions. By trial and error an appropriate level of reserves emerged and the City found it convenient to issue more debt by creating credits on the ledger.

This new bank was so successful that the Banco di Rialto withered and was shut down in 1638. At the same time, as the agio on bank money rose, pressure increased to have the Banco di Giro accept deposits (i.e., sell its liabilities), which it did from 1645. By 1651, bank money had become the sole tender for large payments including foreign exchange (although, as is often the case with such provisions, it is not clear that it was enforced).

Its origin, a fiscal tool, exposed the Banco di Giro more directly to the vicissitudes of Venetian public finance. Throughout the seventeenth century, Venice fought expensive wars against the Ottoman Empire; heavy issues of Giro balances led to a suspension of convertibility from 1648 to 1666. When convertibility was resumed the bank's balances were effectively devalued by 20 percent, and the bank gained full discretion in the choice of which coins to pay out. Another suspension took place from 1714 to 1739; during that time the bank offered demand depositors the option to convert their balances to interest-bearing time deposits. The bank was eventually bailed out by tax revenues and convertibility restored. The rest of the eighteenth century brought no major disruptions: proposals to have the bank issue paper liabilities were rejected several times. When the French invasion of 1797 brought down the Republic the bank closed for a while and did not resume full convertibility after reopening. The new Austrian authorities refused to assume the city's debt to the bank, but the government of Napoleon did in 1805 and depositors became bondholders.

Early German municipal banks (fifteenth–sixteenth centuries)

In the German Empire, money-changing like minting was a regalian right. Both activities were originally delegated to guild-like organizations (*Hausgenossenschaften*) in most localities, but as commerce developed, city governments began to take more direct control. Public banks (*Stadtwechsel*) arose in many cities, including Augsburg, Basel, Bremen, Cologne, Erfurt, Frankfurt, Konstanz, Lübeck, Merseburg, Strasbourg and Wismar. These were often temporary operations, in some cases structured as joint ventures with private bankers, in other cases delegated entirely to the latter. The original focus of these banks was money-changing, but over a time they expanded into other banking activities, including book-entry payments, making Lombard loans, and offering interest-bearing (time) deposits. Generally speaking, however, these were modest institutions of only local significance (Hallauer, 1904; Günther, 1932).

Similar institutions (*stadswissel*) existed in the Low Countries during this time, but banking activity there, especially giro payment, soon came to be dominated by private bankers known as cashiers. In the Dutch

Republic, the cashiers were eventually displaced to a large extent by the Bank of Amsterdam and similar institutions (see next section). By contrast, in the Southern Low Countries, giro payment activity continued to be dominated by cashiers until the end of the Napoleonic period. Interestingly, from the mid-seventeenth century onward the dominant unit of account for the Southern Low Countries' transactions was the "bank florin," that is, the units of the ledger-money of the Bank of Amsterdam (Aerts, 2011).

The Dutch Republic

In 1609 the city of Amsterdam founded the Bank of Amsterdam (*Amsterdamsche Wisselbank*). At the time, commerce in Amsterdam was hindered by a unit of account based on an obsolete silver coin, and by irregularities in the settlement of bills of exchange. The initial design of the Bank borrowed heavily from Venice's Banco di Rialto The Bank's charter granted it extensive legal privileges. Bills of exchange for large amounts were to be settled exclusively through the Bank. Private bankers (cashiers) were simultaneously outlawed, though these soon returned in a secondary role. To promote confidence in the Bank, it was to accept only recognized coins at legal value, and other coins by weight only. Lending activity was prohibited. Instead, the Bank was to be funded by fee income, principally 1.5 percent charges on deposit withdrawals, which were generally restricted to full-weight Dutch domestic coins (Van Dillen, 1934, 1964b). Over its lifetime the Bank enjoyed considerable success (see Figure 2.1) and initiated a number of significant innovations.

The first innovation was to gain control over Amsterdam's (and de facto, the Republic's) unit of account. This occurred around 1641 when the Republic assigned too high a value to a coin from the Spanish Netherlands, the patagon, in effect debasing the currency. The Bank chose to ignore this valuation and to "haircut" the patagon, a move that was applauded by Amsterdam merchants and later legally sanctioned by the Republic. This gave rise to a separate unit of account for Bank funds and a domestic exchange rate (or agio) between Bank funds and circulating coin. Bank funds became the dominant unit of account for commercial transactions (Van Dillen, 1964b; Quinn and Roberds, 2009).

A second major innovation came in 1683 when the Bank began to issue negotiable receipts for deposits of coin, which allowed the bearer of the receipt to reclaim the deposited coin within six months at a much smaller fee (usually 0.25 percent of the deposit) than the traditional fee on withdrawal. Bank deposits then became de facto inconvertible, and someone with Bank funds who wished to withdraw would then buy a receipt on a market that was operated by cashiers (Van Dillen, 1964c). This reduction in the user costs increased both Bank deposits and velocity of giro payments made through the Bank (Dehing, 2012; Quinn and Roberds, 2014).

The Bank also successfully innovated in response to two late eighteenth-century financial crises. In the first (1763) it sold balances against bullion rather than coin (Quinn and Roberds, 2012); in the second (1772–73) it funded a city-operated loan facility for distressed merchants (Breen, 1900).

This indicates that the Bank did not fully adhere to the prohibition against lending in its charter. Over its history the Bank regularly lent to privileged parties, especially the Dutch East India Company (VOC). Profits from lending were returned to the city. For much of the Bank's history, the extent of such lending was well controlled, as evidenced by the Bank's lifetime reserve ratio of 82 percent (Dehing and 't Hart, 1997). Eventually, however, extensive wartime (1781–83) loans to the VOC undermined market confidence in the Bank, and collapse followed in 1795 (Van Dillen, 1964a).

The success of Amsterdam's bank encouraged the founding of similar institutions in other cities of the Republic (Delft, Middelburg and Rotterdam). These did not achieve the success of Amsterdam. A common problem was that these banks's credit activities were less disciplined than those of Amsterdam, resulting in too many suspensions. Nor were these institutions able to establish a unit of account distinct from the "current guilder" that was applied to circulating coins. After Dutch domestic coinage stabilized in the eighteenth century, much local business was conducted in current money terms, undermining the rationale for the banks' existence. These institutions did not survive beyond the early nineteenth century with the exception of Middelburg, which persisted until 1861 (Mees, 1838; Sneller, 1938a,b,c).

Hamburg

The Bank of Hamburg (Hamburger Bank) was founded in 1619 during a period of intense coin debasement in much of Germany, known as the *Kipper- und Wipperzeit*. Following Amsterdam, the Bank of Hamburg's charter granted deposits freedom from attachment and required all bills of exchange drawn on parties in Hamburg to be payable through the Bank. Differently from Amsterdam, the Bank's charter allowed it lend to the city government of Hamburg, and to private parties against collateral. Partial balance sheets compiled by Sieveking (1933, 1934b) suggest that by the mid-seventeenth century, over half the Bank's assets consisted of loans.

The Bank was successful from its beginning, but suffered many bouts of instability over the first 150 years of its existence. The 1672 French invasion of the Netherlands caused a run and forced the Bank to suspend withdrawals and to restrict eligible collateral for its loans to metal. Lengthy suspensions occurred again in 1755–61 and 1766–68 (Levy von Halle, 1891; Sieveking, 1933, 1934b).

As in Amsterdam, Bank of Hamburg money had its own unit of account (*mark banco*) and enjoyed a premium or agio over current money. Unlike Amsterdam, instability in locally prevalent current money made the Hamburg agio fluctuate wildly. By 1726, the discount on current money reached 34 percent and the city attempted to stabilize the situation by requiring the Bank to operate a "current money bank" (a parallel set of accounts kept in current marks, at fixed exchange rates). This was a money-losing operation and had to be given up in 1737 (Sieveking, 1933, 1934b; Schneider et al., 1991).

The Bank enjoyed more lasting success from 1770, when it began to allow deposits in silver bullion rather than coin. Deposits of coin were largely abolished by 1790 in favor of the "pure silver currency" (*Reinsilberwährung*) of bullion-backed ledger-money. The popularity of the Bank increased in the wake of Amsterdam's difficulties in the 1780s, and the Bank was heavily used by Hamburg merchants until its activities were taken over by the Reichsbank in 1876 (Levy von Halle, 1891; Sieveking, 1933, 1934b).

Nuremberg

The city of Nuremberg founded its Public Bank (*Nürnberger Banco Publico*) in 1621. As in Hamburg, impetus for the Bank's founding was provided by the rampant debasement of the Kipper- und Wipperzeit (Schnabel and Shin, 2006). The Public Bank was a deposit-based, fee-funded institution modeled on the Bank of Amsterdam. Use of the Bank was encouraged by freedom of attachment for bank funds, a formal requirement to settle all debts in bank, hefty fines for non-compliance, and the death penalty for anyone caught using debased coinage (Denzel, 2012; White, 2012).

Initially these measures seem to have worked. However, the Bank's popularity was soon undermined by a 1623 coinage reform and the city's policy of borrowing virtually all the Bank's reserves of coin. Although the Bank had been repaid by 1634, confidence had been lost. A renewed wave of debasements in the 1660s was poorly handled, via a partial suspension and a restriction of withdrawals to light coins. Accounts were moved to a current-money basis in 1691, and the city's adoption of a stable coinage standard in 1765 reduced the Bank's business to frictional levels. It was liquidated in 1831 (Denzel, 2012).

Common themes

Several themes are prominent in the life-histories of the first generation of public banks. One is experimentation: there were as yet no accepted norms for the creation and operation of public banks. Accordingly, some institutions were publicly owned while others operated as privileged private entities. The capitalization and the legal status of bank obligations also varied. The banks' backing assets consisted of differing mixtures of metal, private obligations and the debt of their sponsoring governments.

A related theme is instability. The experimental nature of the first-generation banks often led to loss of public confidence and runs. Lengthy suspensions of withdrawals were common, and outright closure not unheard of (e.g., Genoa 1444, Venice 1638). Ultimately, the successful public banks tended to be characterized by a high degree of conservatism in their design and operation (e.g., Amsterdam and Hamburg).

And even when successful, first-generation public banks were seen as highly specialized institutions, more akin to today's financial market utilities than today's central banks. Their clientele was seen as limited to wealthy merchants in commercial cities. Statistics compiled by Dehing (2012) for the Bank of Amsterdam support this view: about two percent of Amsterdam's population held accounts at the Bank, and the average Bank giro payment was equal to about ten times the annual income of a typical Amsterdam resident. Moreover, because a principal mission of many first-generation public banks was to discourage the circulation of debased coin, the operation of public banks was thought to conflict with the financial interests of monarchical governments that depended heavily on seigniorage as revenue source. Summarizing the accepted wisdom of the time, Frederick the Great's counselor Calzabigi wrote in 1765 that "a ledger-money bank is not allowed under a monarchy because it makes most coin payments unnecessary, and therefore reduces the income from seigniorage" (Niebuhr, 1854, 183).

3.2 Second-Generation Banks

Common themes

Views about the political prerequisites for maintaining a public bank changed with popularization of the bearer banknote. Compared with ledger-money, payment by banknote was convenient, (usually) anonymous and free from transfer fees, so was practical for smaller sums. Seen at first an experimental product, circulating notes became more accepted following their adoption by the Bank of England; see the discussion later. Banknotes were popular with governments, too, as England's example opened many Continental monarchs' eyes to the capabilities of public banks as engines of government finance.

This generational shift in public banks' product mix (from ledger money to circulating notes), customer base (from more to less wealthy) and habitat (from merchant-dominated commercial cities to monarchical states) also increased the potential for their fiscal abuse. Fiscal demands on public banks became acute during the Napoleonic period, leading to suspension of convertibility and paper-money inflations in many of the cases we study. Some degree of postwar restructuring was necessary before public banks could return to their full prewar functionality. And, for many of the early public banks, liquidation was by that point the more practical alternative.

The counterexample of Naples

The banks of Naples do not meet our definition of public banks. We nevertheless include them in the survey, not because they have often been mistaken for public banks, but for the interesting counter-example that they offer (Demarco, 2000a,b; Balletta, 2009).

Naples, the second-largest city in Europe after Paris in the sixteenth and seventeenth centuries, was ruled in the name of the Spanish king by a viceroy. As elsewhere private sector banking was unreliable, but the solution that emerged was different. From 1584 to 1597 a total of seven charitable institutions obtained from the viceroy permission to open banks. An eighth bank was created in 1661 by the administrators of the wheat tax. Until 1815 this set of banks, unchanged except for one failure, accepted deposits and provided banking services to the general public. Their specialization was geographic, except for the eighth bank which catered to the government and the court. The banks were owned by non-profit organizations (hospitals, confraternities and charitable Lombard facilities), long-lived corporations with strict governance. Their assets combined loans to the public and private sector as well as shares in tax farms, but their high level of reserves, well above 50 percent, allowed them to survive two monetary disturbances in the seventeenth century as well as the rebellion of 1648–49 against Spain. When one bank did fail in 1702 the viceroy leaned on the other banks to take over the deposits at full value.

Conservatively managed, the Neapolitan banks were nevertheless financially innovative. Naples became well-known for the *fede di credito*, originally a certificate of the sums deposited that became negotiable: a simple endorsement was sufficient proof for the assignee to be credited with the funds at the bank.

Sweden

Sweden saw extensive experimentation with banknote issue over the seventeenth and eighteenth centuries. One factor influencing the use of banknotes, unique to Sweden over this time period, was its adherence to a copper standard for long intervals (Edvinsson, 2010b). Notes were favored since the weight of copper coins made them impractical for large-value transactions. Note issue began as early as 1657 with the founding of the *Stockholms Banco*, a privileged private institution inspired by the exchange banks of Hamburg and Amsterdam. The Stockholms Banco granted credit not through its accounts, but through the issue of pre-printed redeemable notes in round denominations. Despite or perhaps due to this innovation, Stockholms Banco soon became overextended and was closed in 1664 (Heckscher, 1934).

A second attempt to set up a public bank came in 1668 with the founding of the Bank of the Parliament (*Riksens Ständers Bank*). The Bank, formally divided into separate lending and exchange operations, was overseen by an appointed commission and initially forbidden to issue notes. The Bank's operations were dominated by the lending bank, whose main asset consisted of mortgages made at legally fixed interest rates (Tarkka, 2009; Fregert, 2012).

The Bank began to issue notes in 1701, at first in only minor amounts. Fiscal demands of the Great Nordic War (1700–18) caused the Bank to venture into government finance, eventually leading to a drain on reserves and a 25-year suspension of deposit withdrawals (1710–35). Notes issued by the Bank became increasingly popular from 1726, when they became legal tender for tax payments. Additional wars began in 1740 and forced the Bank to suspend convertibility by 1745, due to extensive credits granted to both the government and the private sector (through mortgages). Convertibility was not restored until 1777, with the introduction of a new, silver-based unit of account (Riksdaler) that effectively reduced the metallic value of Bank money by half (Heckscher, 1934; Edvinsson, 2010a; Fregert, 2012).

With the renewed outbreak of war in 1788–90, the Bank's refusal to engage in inflationary finance caused the Treasury to issue its own inconvertible paper, leading to parallel units of account. Resumption of war in 1808 led the Bank to issue its own paper which itself soon became inconvertible, leading to a confusing situation of three competing units of account (on Treasury notes, the Bank's notes, and silver; see Edvinsson 2010c). A definitive monetary reform could not occur until 1834. In 1865, the Bank received its current name, the *Sveriges Riksbank* (Fregert, 2012).

England
The Bank of England was founded in 1694 soon after a revolution. However glorious it may have become in retrospect the regime it established was far from secure. A legitimate king had been expelled by a foreign invasion and the new rulers took England into a war against France that turned out to be prolonged, costly, and dangerous for the new regime. The Bank's foundation was in fact the floatation of a government loan: in return for lending money for the war effort creditors received 8 percent annuity and a banking license. The new institution would practice on a larger, corporate scale, what goldsmiths had been doing for decades in London: receiving deposits, keeping accounts, discounting bills and circulating negotiable notes.

Since the Bank's foundation was really a securitization of government debt (Quinn, 2008) the Bank was tied to government finances from birth. It ran into difficulties very early: the government pressed it for help in delivering funds to its troops on the Continent, and a badly needed but ill-conceived general recoinage reduced the available silver currency. Both drains, one external and the other internal, led to a suspension of convertibility in 1696. But further demands from the government allowed the Bank to bargain for further privileges, in particular a commitment not to charter another bank. During the following war the Bank negotiated another important privilege, a partial monopoly on note issue in England.

Trading government debt for a risky but potentially lucrative monopoly seemed to be a successful technique and it was used again when the South Sea company was created in 1711. The South Sea Company proved less adept at exploiting its trading monopoly but nevertheless convinced the government to apply the technique more generally to most of the public debt. The Bank felt compelled to come up with a competing offer but was fortunate enough to see it turned down. It came out of the South Sea fiasco unscathed and helped to government's clean-up operation by buying more debt.

The Bank's position as a key element of British public finance was consolidated over the rest of the eighteenth century. Its role was to be the government's bank, service the long-term debt and ensure the liquidity of the short-term debt issued during wars until it was funded. Although a majority of its assets was public debt it was also a classic bank, holding deposits and discounting bills, and was a dominant player in the money market. As such it played a role in mitigating the financial crises of the late eighteenth century (1763, 1782, 1793) although the example of Amsterdam shows that it was not unique in this role.

The Revolutionary and Napoleonic Wars of 1793–1802 and 1803–15 presented for Britain as for many other countries unprecedented fiscal demands. The government, however, did not use the Bank as a main fiscal tool: the Bank never held more than 5 percent of the public debt in its portfolio. The Bank did play its now traditional role of easing the Exchequer's financing, and the accidental suspension of convertibility in 1797 (initially due to an external drain prompted by France's remonetization after the collapse of its paper money) was extended for the duration of the war as a matter of convenience. As the Bank continued both to support government issues of short-term debt and to discount private bills, but freed of any convertibility constraint, the outstanding stock of money grew considerably. As a result Britain experienced what was now familiar to other countries, namely a paper-money inflation, but a mild one compared with France's earlier experience, or with Austria's contemporaneous experience. After the war the Bank gradually contracted its balance sheet and the government raised the revenues needed to redeem its debt to the Bank, and convertibility was restored in 1819.

France

Two banks make their apparition in France in our survey. The first, short-lived but spectacular, was the *Banque générale* (renamed *Banque Royale*) from 1716 to 1720. The second was the *Caisse d'Escompte* founded in 1776; abolished during the Revolution, it was nevertheless the forerunner and in many ways the ancestor of the *Banque de France* founded in 1800.

Law's Banque (1716–20)

France's first note-issuing bank was the brainchild of an itinerant Scotsman named John Law. Law's original plan, as he advertised it, was in some ways close too traditional public banks: it was to be publicly controlled and the main purpose of its notes, initially backed by 100 percent reserves, was to serve as a payments system for the numerous receivers and paymasters of the French monarchy. The government of the time was weary: it had just seen the end of the costly War of Spanish Succession which had required large tax increases and partial defaults on the debt; it was still in the process of liquidating the unfunded debt and considered that a public bank would never gain credibility. A few months later Law was allowed to open the *Banque générale*, a private venture based on securitized debt after the model of the Bank of England: shares in the initial offering could be bought with government bonds, the bank was allowed to issue notes redeemable on demand in a specific coin, hold deposits, discount bills, but could not engage in any trade except precious metals. Over the next two years, a series of government decrees conferred on the bank distinct advantages: bearer notes other than those of the bank were outlawed, tax collectors were obliged to accept the notes in payment of taxes and to redeem them on demand, and later to use them in all their transactions with the State.

The bank's success and the popularity of its notes were enhanced when, in 1718, a compulsory reminting replaced the coin in which the notes were denominated. The seigniorage tax imposed on coin-holders was partly waived for note-holders. Within a few months the private shareholders were bought out by the State and the *Banque générale* became *Banque royale*.

Law's ambitions went beyond banking; he chartered a trading company which progressively bought out existing privileged companies to become the French Indies Company and monopolize foreign trade. It also acquired other monopolies and eventually bought out the tax farms and mint leases. By August 1719 Law's company, financed by new issues of shares at increasing nominal prices, offered to refinance the whole national debt. A new, final issue of shares financed this last deal, effectively converting bondholders into shareholders of a private company in charge of collecting nearly all the taxes in France. The ensuing market frenzy drove the price of Indies shares to new heights and Law to the position of finance minister. In February 1720 the Bank, whose notes were progressively replacing gold and silver as sole legal tender, was merged with the Company. Law's extraordinary creature began like the Bank of England but mutated into the Casa di San Giorgio, but on the scale of an absolute monarchy of twenty million rather than a city-republic of sixty thousand.

While Law's debt-to-equity conversion, unlike the South Sea scheme which derived from it, was based on a fixed-price offering, the conversion itself was to take place through a sequence of payments, each of which bondholders had to be induced to make. Law had to prop up the price of his shares and eventually used his Bank's notes to do so, pegging the price of shares in terms of notes. The resulting increase in money supply drove down the foreign exchange and Law had to backtrack and find ways to reduce it; he tried to devalue the notes, but this prompted a run on the Bank in May 1720. Law's efforts to salvage the scheme at one point drew on yet another model, that of Amsterdam, creating bank accounts and requiring all bills of exchange to clear on the bank's books. In the end the Indies Company went into receivership and Law into exile. The debt conversion was undone and the long-term debt painstakingly recreated, the old tax-farming system restored, and the Indies Company returned as a pure trading company.

From the Caisse d'Escompte (1776–93) to the Banque de France (1800–present)

At the conclusion of the Seven Years War, the French Indies Company, deprived of its Indian territories, was edging once again toward bankruptcy. Proposals to turn it into a bank that would fund overseas trade went nowhere and the company was shut down, its debt assumed by the State. The proponents succeeded a few years later in convincing the new finance minister (and distinguished economist) Turgot of the advantages of a note-issuing bank to fund trade. Turgot chartered the *Caisse d'Escompte* in 1776 as a private bank. No government debt was involved (a plan to have the company post bond in the form of a loan was soon dropped) and the government at first adopted a hands-off approach to the bank. Its business was to discount bills its management comprised experienced merchants and bankers. By the early 1780s it had turned into a bankers' bank and succeeded in bringing money market rates down in Paris. A clumsy attempt by a finance minister to secure a secret loan in 1783 prompted a near-run that was skillfully avoided, and although the relations with a government always able to rewrite the charter remained fraught with ambiguity, the Caisse did well, with rising note circulation and solid dividends.

The life of the Caisse was cut short by the Revolution; in 1788, when the monarchy was running out of sources of funds, it forced the Caisse to provide loans and made its notes legal tender. Within two years the Bastille had been torn down, a national assembly was writing a constitution, and a new currency managed directly by the government was backed by the value of confiscated church lands. The Caisse was repaid its loan and allowed to return to its business, but the course of political events changed rapidly.

The French Revolutionary Wars started in 1792 and within a year the monarchy was overthrown, France was invaded from all sides, and the new currency was in free-fall. To prop up the currency the revolutionary government eliminated all alternative forms of holding wealth (aside from land), shutting down the stock-market and all joint-stock companies. The Caisse was thus forced to close in 1793, but a few years later, many of shareholders and employees regrouped to form the *Caisse des Comptes Courants*, closely patterned on the Caisse. Within a few years an expanded coalition of major bankers, including close supporters of the new First Consul of the Republic, Bonaparte, founded the *Banque de France*, with which the Caisse was merged within weeks.

Prussia

Prussia's Royal Main Bank (*Königliche Hauptbank*) was founded by Frederick the Great in 1765. A motivation for the founding of the Main Bank was the "proof of concept" provided by the Bank of England, that a public bank could be compatible with both stable money and a monarchical appetite for revenue. The initial design of the Main Bank however more closely followed the Bank of Hamburg, combining a traditional ledger-money exchange bank with a lending bank. The Main Bank in its initial implementation was a complete failure, due to both management corruption and to the decision to tie the value of the Bank's money to a favored gold coin rather than the more widely circulating silver coinage (Niebuhr, 1854).

The Main Bank was completely reorganized in 1766, and after an unsuccessful attempt at note issue, evolved into essentially a state-run savings institution. Accounts bore interest and the majority of these were redeemable at a week's notice. Loans were primarily long-term, fixed-rate mortgages. The risks inherent in this business model became apparent after 1806, when military setbacks at the hands of Napoleon led to a loss of territory and to disruptions to mortgage payments. One-third of the Main Bank's asset had to be written off, and operations were suspended until 1817 (Niebuhr, 1854).

During the final years of the Napoleonic Era (1806–13), Prussia resorted to the emission of notes. These were not issued through the Main Bank, but through a rival state-sponsored institution, the Maritime Enterprise (*Königliche Seehandlung*), probably because the Enterprise was seen as a stronger credit than the Main Bank. Convertibility of the Enterprise's notes was nonetheless soon suspended, and by 1808, their market value had collapsed to 23 percent of par (Conrad et al., 1901; Schleutker, 1920).

40 *William Roberds and François R. Velde*

At the conclusion of the Napoleonic wars, the Enterprise's notes were made convertible at their original face value and gradually retired. The Main Bank cautiously resumed note issue, at first only with 100 percent metallic backing. Following the Bank's nationalization in 1847, this was reduced to a one-third backing requirement, with the remainder of the assets consisting of obligations of the Prussian state. In 1876, the nationalized bank was merged into the Reichsbank (Lichter, 1999).

Austria

Austria's first attempt to set up a public bank came with the founding of the *Banco del Giro* in 1703, in response to a crisis in Imperial finance. This institution failed within a year, leading to the founding of a second bank in 1705, the Viennese Municipal Bank (*Wiener Stadtbank*), nominally under control of the City of Vienna. The Municipal Bank was only lightly used for payment purposes. The Bank instead emphasized interest-bearing time deposits, which it used to fund loans to the Imperial Treasury. Income was provided by tax and other dedicated Imperial revenue streams (Bidermann, 1859). Fuchs (1998) emphasizes that the Stadtbank came into existence partly as a way of addressing creditors' fears of selective default by the Imperial treasury.

While the Municipal Bank achieved some success in reducing Austria's borrowing costs, its operations were hampered by an ever-growing portfolio of government debt and by constant infighting with the Treasury. After 1759 the Municipal Bank was increasingly dominated by the Treasury, and the bank was effectively nationalized in 1782 (Fuchs, 1998).

In 1762, the Municipal Bank experimented with its first, modest issue of banknotes, which were given special advantages in transactions with the state and were soon retired from circulation. Additional, tentative emissions followed in 1770 and 1785. Following the outbreak of the Napoleonic wars, the stock of notes expanded sharply, growing at an average 23.6 percent annual rate over 1796–1811. Redeemability of the notes was soon suspended and they were given full legal tender status. As Imperial finances continued to deteriorate, an 1811 Imperial decree reduced the metallic equivalent of the notes by 80 percent from their original value. Even with this extreme devaluation, the notes did again not become redeemable until 1817, and then only partly in government bonds and partly in the notes of the newly chartered *Österreichische Nationalbank*. The Viennese Municipal Bank was formally abolished in 1818 (Raudnitz, 1917).

4 Taxonomy

Table 2.1 is a rough attempt at comparing the institutions we surveyed along certain key dimensions. In constituting this table we have tried to be "non-parametric." The characteristics that we chose consist of features that we see appear repeatedly in our historical survey.

Some features are very broad, based on the simple fact that these are all, in a modern sense, corporations: not individuals but legal entities that can hold and issue claims and therefore can sue and be sued.[6] Some form of ownership can be ascertained, although the language of the time may not be very clear: one way to think of ownership is to search for the residual claimant to profits but also losses (who is implicitly responsible for saving the entity if it runs into trouble).

Since they are financial corporations whose main business is creating claims, we can then distinguish the asset and liability side and see if any restrictions or on the contrary certain freedoms are given on the types of claims that can appear on either side.

We consider what type of services they provide. By "fiscal agent" we mean providing banking services to the State, such as managing current accounts and servicing the debt (distributing payments on interest and principal). Finally we consider two privileges that we find repeatedly conferred on the liabilities of the public banks. One is a monopoly on foreign exchange clearing: foreign bills of exchange were required to be settled on the books of the bank. The other is exemption from seizure in judicial proceedings, perhaps intended to make bank balances more competitive with cash.

The entries are arranged in chronological order of creation.

An important dimension which we have not studied is the form of governance and oversight over the public banks. A detailed study of the statutes would be required, but it is noteworthy that they are typically replete with detailed prescriptions on these matters. We also did not collect information on legal tender status beyond the requirement to clear foreign bills of exchange because it was not commonly conferred, aside from a few cases (Genoa between 1437 and 1444, France in 1719–20, Vienna after 1797, England after 1810).

Some observations can be made.

There is no clear pattern regarding public or private ownership over time: although private ownership tends to be more common among second

---

[6] In the absence of a standard legal framework to create commercial corporations until the nineteenth century, any such creation involved some kind of derogation to current law, granted by the legislator, which might be called in the language of the time "privilege" without necessarily implying monopoly or exclusive rights.

Table 2.1: *Characteristics of early public banks*

		Owner	Objectives		Assets			Liabilities			Services		Privileges	
			Profit	Stable coin values	100% reserves	Govt. debt	Private bet	Circ. paper	Deposits		Govt. fiscal agent	Giro	FX clearing	Safe from seizure
									Demand	Saving				
Barcelona Taula	1401–1853	pub	Y	Y	N	Y*	N*	N	Y	Y	Y	Y	Y*	Y*
Genoa I	1404–1444	priv	Y	Y	N	Y	N	N	N		Y	Y		Y*
German cities	1400s–1700s	mix		Y	N	Y	Y	N	Y	Y		Y		
Naples	1580s–1815	priv	Y*	N	N	Y	Y	c1650	Y			Y		
Venice Rialto	1587–1638	priv	N	Y	Y	N	N	N	Y			Y	Y	Y
Barcelona Ciutat	1609–1853	pub		Y	Y?	N*	N	N				Y		
Amsterdam	1609–1820	pub	N	Y	Y*	Y*	Y*	N	Y	N		Y	Y	Y
Dutch cities	1616–1861	pub	N	Y	N	Y*	N	N	Y	N	N	Y	Y*	Y
Venice Giro	1619–1800	pub		Y*	N	Y	Y	N	Y*			Y	Y	Y
Hamburg	1619–1875	pub	N	Y	N*	Y	N	N	Y	N		Y	Y*	Y
Nürnberg	1621–1836	pub		Y	N	Y	Y	N	Y	N	N	Y	Y*	Y
Stockholm Banco	1657–1664	priv	Y	N	N	?	Y	Y						
Sweden Ständers	1668–	pub	Y		N	Y	N	1701	Y	Y	Y	Y	Y*	Y
Genoa II	1675–1815	priv	Y	Y	N	Y*	Y	18th c.				Y	Y*	Y

England	1694 –	priv	Y	N	N	Y	N	1694	Y		Y		N	N
Vienna Giro	1703 –1705	pub	Y	Y	N	Y	N	N	Y	Y	Y	Y	Y	Y
Vienna Stadtbank	1705 –1816	pub		Y	N	Y	Y	1762	Y	Y	Y	Y	N	Y
France B. Royale	1716 –1720	priv	Y	N	N	Y	Y	1716	Y	N	Y	Y*	Y*	N
Prussia K. HauptB.	1765 –1847	pub	Y	Y*	N	Y	Y	Y*	Y*	Y	Y	Y	Y*	Y
Prussia Seehandlung	1806 –1824	pub	Y*	N	N	Y	Y*	Y*	N		Y		N	
France C d'Escompte	1776 –1793	priv	Y	N	N	r	Y	1776	Y				N	

Y = yes, N = no, r = rare. *Notes*: Taula: Overdrafts forbidden but allowed in practice. FX clearing required from 1446 to 1499. Balances safe from seizure from 1468. Taula, Ciutat: From mid-fifteenth c., prohibition on lending to the city, observed except in severe circumstances. Genoa I: safe from seizure from 1437. Naples: the banks were expected to make money, but were owned by charitable institutions. Circulating paper from mid-17th c. Amsterdam: 80% reserves in practice. Government debt sporadically held. Private debt: that of a privileged entity (the East India Company). Dutch cities: FX clearing not enforced. Hamburg: FX clearing widely evaded after 1630. Hamburg, Stockholm banco: giro banking formally separate from lending. Venice Giro: stabilizing coin values not part of the design but became one role. Deposits accepted from the 1630s and balances became fully convertible in the 1660s. Sweden, Ständers: giro banking formally separate from lending. FX clearing never viable. Notes from 1701. Genoa II (from the opening the *banco di moneta corrente* in 1675): loans to government strictly limited. Circulating paper: certificates of deposits were circulated. Vienna, Stadtbank: government debt with pledged revenue stream. Notes: from 1762, legal tender from 1797. France, Banque royale: founded as a private bank, nationalized in 1718. Notes legal tender from 1719. FX clearing and giro: briefly in 1720. Prussia, Hauptbank: ineffective in stabilizing coin values. Demand deposits unimportant in practice. Note issue sporadic until Napoleonic wars. FX clearing never viable. Prussia, Seehandlung: profit in addition to support of trading monopolies. Private debt: loans to favored industries. Circulating notes: wartime issues in 1806–24. Savings accounts: debt and instruments resembling preferred stock. France, Caisse d'Escompte: notes briefly legal tender in 1789.

generation banks, it is not the norm. Profit-making is the norm in the second generation, but it occurs earlier. The goal of stabilizing coin values is dominant among the first generation and diminishes in importance in the eighteenth century, although it is still present in the Northern banks. Having 100 percent reserves is the exception, but an important one, since it is present in the first Venice bank and its immediate progeny in Amsterdam. Although the Amsterdam bank was a great success and an important model, that feature was not generally retained (although Northern banks sometimes operated an exchange department distinct from the lending department). The reserves that were held were normally in the form of coin, of ascertained and typically high quality (although some banks, like the Barcelona bank of 1609, were established explicitly to handle a wide variety of poor-quality coinage; we do not know much about the way in which those were handled).

Holding government debt is prevalent, although with many asterisks, as lending to government was often done in violation of the bank's statutes (as in Amsterdam). The loans might be made to the bank's owner, or to privileged entities or favored individuals; typically they were not collateralized, although there is some variance in practice. Holding private debt is much less common: the public banks were generally not designed to compete with or replace the private sector's intermediation activities. When it did take place it was typically collateralized, although again with varying practices. Note issue is the characteristic of second generation banks, but emerges first with the "counter-example" banks of Naples. Demandable deposits are common, savings deposits (offering interest) much less so. The function of fiscal agent is not prevalent early on, although we must confess a large measure of uncertainty as shown by the blank entries. Monopoly on foreign exchange clearing and freedom from seizure are recurrent privileges bestowed on the banks' liabilities.

Our distinction between first and second generation is in some ways technical, based on the way the payments system is handled, via transfers of circulating notes. At a deeper level we can tentatively identify three basic models that transcend this technical distinction: a public version of a private bank accepting deposits and making loans mostly to the State (Barcelona's Taula, Stockholm Banco), a "narrow bank" holding 100 percent reserves (Venice's Rialto and Amsterdam), a "special purpose vehicle" designed to make government debt more liquid (Venice's Giro, England).

5 Understanding the Evolution

Above we have seen that the history of early public banks offers a diverse array of institutional designs and empirical outcomes. In the usual

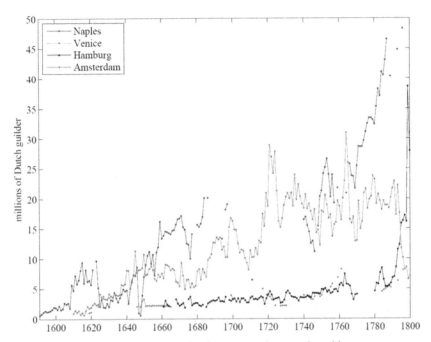

Figure 2.1: Bank balances of various banks, converted at Dutch guilder at current exchange rates (1591–1800).
Source: Roberds and Velde (2016b).

trade-off between clarity and precision we will tilt toward the former and try to discern broad patterns at the expense of institutional detail.

5.1 A quantitative overview

Figures 2.1 and 2.2 offer quantitative perspectives on the evolutionary process. In the figures, the size of the banks is measured by balance sheet for the first-generation banks and by note circulation (and/or deposits) for the second generation. The format of these comparisons was dictated by data availability. Current exchange rates were used to convert all amounts to a common currency.[7] Table 2.2 supplements the figures by comparing balance sheets at specific points in time also dictated by data availability.

---

[7] The units were chosen so as to use direct foreign exchange quotations as much as possible. To compare the two figures, note that during the eighteenth century the Dutch guilder averages 1.2 marcs banco.

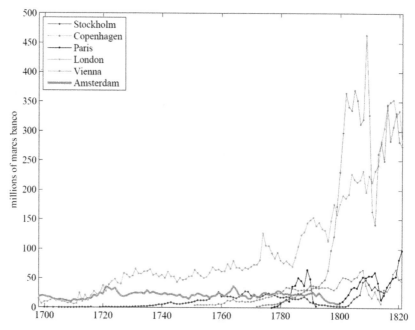

Figure 2.2: Note circulation of various banks, converted into Hamburg marcs banco at current exchange rates (1700–1821). The balance sheet of the Amsterdam Wisselbank is plotted for comparison purposes. Paris consists of the Caisse d'Escompte (1776–93) and the Banque de France (from 1800).
Source: Roberds and Velde (2016b).

The time series begin in the late sixteenth century, but Table 2.2 indicates that, even as early as 1433, Barcelona's Taula was comparable with the public banks of 1600. Figure 2.1 shows the Bank of Amsterdam's rapid rise to dominance within the first generation. After 1640 it surpasses Venice and Hamburg and continues to grow through the early eighteenth century, while Venice and Hamburg remain stagnant, and almost equal to each other. Table 2.2 suggests that Genoa probably fit in between Amsterdam and Venice, and also shows that Nuremberg was, for its brief existence, on a par with Hamburg. Also noteworthy is the combined size of the Neapolitan banks, comparable to Amsterdam for much of the sample and surpassing it by the late eighteenth century.

Figure 2.2 shows that around 1720, a mere quarter-century after its founding, the Bank of England surpassed the Bank of Amsterdam in size, and was more than double the size of its rival by the mid-eighteenth century. Moreover the Bank of England continues to grow throughout the Napoleonic era, though it is eclipsed for a short time by the aggressive

The Descent of Central Banks (1400–1815)

Table 2.2: *Total assets/liabilities of various public banks. The amounts are converted to Venetian ducats (a gold coin containing about 3.5g) at current exchange rates taken from Spufford (1986, 145) and Denzel (2010). Per capita balances are computed using the cities' populations (Bairoch et al., 1988). The figure for London excludes the exchequer bills circulated by the Bank. Sources: Balletta (2009, 286–9) (Naples); Tucci (1973, 370) (Venice); (Sieveking, 1934a, 29,33) (Genoa); Sieveking (1934b, 131–2, 139–41, 152–3, 156) (Hamburg); Van Dillen (1934, 117–23) (Amsterdam); Bank of England archives General Ledger 6, f. 665, ADM7/8 (kindly communicated by Stephen Quinn).*

	Year	Thousand ducats	Ducats/Capita
Barcelona	1433	477	13
Naples	1597	611	2
Venice	1597	950	6
Genoa, c. oro	1586	179	3
Hamburg	1621	339	8
Amsterdam	1631	1,646	30
Nuremberg	1631	462	11
Venice	1631	1,462	15
Naples	1631	1,450	5
Venice	1666	876	6
Genoa, c. moneta corrente	1675	967	15
Amsterdam	1675	2,731	13
Naples	1675	5,147	17
Venice	1721	1,722	12
Genoa, c. banco	1721	7,531	116
Amsterdam	1721	13,610	68
Naples	1721	4,298	14
London	1719	46,545	72

note issues of Vienna's Stadtbank. Figure 2.2 also captures the brief period of success of the Caisse d'Escompte before the Revolution, the fall of the Bank of Amsterdam and the emergence of the Banque de France.

5.2 Origins

Why were public banks created? To formulate this question more narrowly, what did their founders think they were doing?

To collect all our histories under a single formulation, we can say that the underlying impetus for the founding of the bank was essentially the same: a desire to introduce a new and safe (or at least reliable) type of asset. No asset is truly risk-free, but the intent was to find one that was sufficiently reliable or safe to serve as means of payment and basis for valuation.

The impetus arose from two possible directions: payments issues, stemming from failures (real or perceived) in the private sector, and fiscal issues. In the first instance, dysfunctions or failures of a private system of payments are remedied by the creation of a public bank. In the second instance, an illiquid government liability is improved by being transformed into the liability of a public bank.

Private failings

The first, payments-related, impetus is itself divisible into collapses of the banking sector or its incapacity to maintain stable units of account. The first set of concerns is exemplified by the Banco del Giro in Venice and the remarkable debates in the Senate (reported by Lattes 1869) that surrounded its creation, the payments problem arises from the persistent failing of the private banking sector. Medieval banks had risky portfolios and maturity mismatch. Public authorities, concerned about fraud and more generally wishing to make the bankers accountable to their clients, imposed demandable deposits as a general rule, setting the stage for bank runs.[8] Further regulations restricting bankers' choices of assets and increasing their equity stake were apparently insufficient to restore stability.

Why did it matter? Interestingly, in the eyes of the Venetian Senators, the key function (from their perspective) provided by banks was not maturity transformation or matching lenders and borrowers, but providing a payments system. The public policy issue was that banks provided an essential payments function: that function had to be provided somehow, by the State if need be and however reluctantly. The first sentence of the resolution founding Venice's public bank states that "It has been the most ancient and almost natural custom of this city to trade, and to complete mercantile and all other activities by means of *banchi di scritta*, whose convenience and ease of making payments is necessary in so many businesses and of such importance."

The Senators were aware that other commercial centers did well without a public bank and used multilateral netting mechanisms to facilitate payments. The mechanisms, originating in the medieval fairs of Champagne, survived in Lyon and Antwerp, but they relied on private trust that could not be depended upon in Venice. Venice created a public bank, but one that could not create credit: in fact, the possibility of

---

[8] The ultimate origin of the demand deposit, either as a prevalent form of contracting among private parties or a government regulation imposed on them, is still unclear to us.

The Descent of Central Banks (1400–1815)   49

creating credit was seen as dangerous. The main function was to provide payments services to merchants.

Venice provides the clearest example of this motivation, although the history of Catalonian public banks (in particular the disappearance of private banking in Barcelona in the early seventeenth century) may well provide another example of the potential of public banks to replace private banks in the payments arena.

The second possible failure of the private sector is a more subtle one. We analyze it in terms of the Sargent and Velde (2002) model, according to which inherent features of the multiple-coin commodity money system led to recurrent episodes of instability in the rate of exchange between various coins. Yet societies needed a predictable unit of account. The fact that the bouts of exchange rate fluctuations occurred intermittently and infrequently (a generation or more) let private parties grow accustomed to stable parities between coins of different size. Then fluctuations started again, and private parties had to decide to which coin they should peg their preferred unit of account. The result of both repeated episodes of fluctuations and lack of agreement on which coin to follow led in the first case to successive "ghost monies," units tied to coins at some long-obsolete (ghost) rate of exchange, and the second to multiple units of account tied to different coins being used at the same time.

Authorities perceived the problem but misdiagnosed its cause, and blamed specific private agents for an equilibrium phenomenon. If certain coins rose unexpectedly in value, they reasoned, it must be the fault of people who most handle these coins, bankers. And if bankers drive up the value of some coins, it must be because they have an interest in doing so. Thus, if banking were entrusted to a party that has no such interest, the problem would disappear.

This motivation for creating public banks is exemplified in Genoa's 1408 creation of the Banco di San Giorgio, as well as in the flurry of public bank creations in the early seventeenth century: not only Amsterdam and Hamburg, but also Barcelona's Bank of the City.

Public failings

Another, a priori unrelated motivation, can be discerned in the foundation of Barcelona's Taula in 1401, and much more evidently in most second-generation public banks. The concern here is to provide banking/financing services, broadly construed, to the State. In Table 2.1 we included services as fiscal agent to indicate that deficit financing was not the sole consideration: banking and accounting services were part of the package. Of course such services could and were provided by the private sector, but the history of Barcelona's Taula show that the unreliability of private banks (mentioned in the previous section) also affected the State, and also that the services provided could go farther than mere book-keeping. In fifteenth century Catalonia (as in other eras) clear accounting was not just a convenience but also a means to enforce clarity, accountability, and the respect of budgetary rules.

But our table show a number of early public banks that were allowed to hold government debt and that were profit-making institutions. In Genoa and Barcelona, the profit was intended to help extinguish the public debt. In Barcelona, as in the second-generation public banks, the motive was also to provide the State with better ways to market its debt. The transformation that a public bank could provide from an illiquid bond to a money-like instrument is transparent in the Venetian Banco del Giro, but is also at the core of the Bank of England's foundation. How exactly the alchemy works will be taken up in more detail later. For now let us note the widespread resort to legal properties of the new liability, particularly the requirement to clear foreign exchange through the bank, and the common privilege from seizure of the bank's balances. Both aspects clearly had as outcome, if not as intention, the enhancement of the liability's desirability.

One motivation that we do not see is a concern for financial stability. The foundation of the first Venetian bank was prompted by failures of private banking, but the solution was not to replace private bankers in their intermediating function, nor was it to provide a recourse or lender of last resort. That concern emerges much later, in the crises of the late eighteenth century. The crisis of 1763, in the aftermath of the Seven Years War, prompted the first use of the public bank's liquidity creation powers. If anything, bail-outs came to the public banks (from the State) rather than from them.

5.3 Evolution

General features
Our overview of early public banks provides the following insights.

Before 1820 people did not have very firm idea of what a public bank should do or how it should be structured. Generally, it was thought that a government-sponsored financial intermediary could improve on outcomes.

Whether it should be private or public was not clearly settled, and no single model emerged. The two basic impulses that we outlined above,

The Descent of Central Banks (1400–1815)   51

providing a reliable payments system and making government debt more liquid, interacted continuously throughout the banks' history.

Various countries experimented with various models. For all their stumbles and failures, public banks were an enduring genus, as governments rarely gave up on them. One can discern a process of natural selection, in which many designs failed to gain acceptance and flopped right from the start (e.g., Austria), but once a public bank was up and running, selective pressure from war-driven fiscal crises forced it to evolve in new ways. One can also see a process of mutation and propagation at work, with direct evidence and indirect suggestion for cross-border imitations.

Finally, we have one big extinction: the Napoleonic Wars left only a few public banks left intact, and even T. Rex (the Bank of Amsterdam) had succumbed by 1795.

Three eras

We observe three broad phases in the process. The first phase begins with founding of the earliest public banks around 1400 in Barcelona and Genoa. Imitations of these banks then arose in other (quasi-)independent city-states. Generally these banks were municipally owned, were often supposed to be fully backed by a metallic reserve and were geared toward a payments function. This first phase culminated with emergence of the Bank of Amsterdam (founded 1609) as a preeminent payments institution.

The second phase begins in the late seventeenth century, with beginnings of note issue (tentatively by banks in Naples and Sweden, then famously in England). The second-generation public banks differ from the first generation along multiple dimensions: they tended to operate in monarchical states, were often privately owned, held only fractional metallic reserves and were geared toward the securitization of public debt. Yet the second generation of banks was undoubtedly inspired by the success of the first generation, and by debt-management institutions such as Genoa's Casa di San Giorgio. But, although the Bank of England dominates its peers in terms of size within a few decades, just as Amsterdam had, the first generation banks coexist with it, and the model of Amsterdam and Hamburg continues to inspire new bank creations in the eighteenth century.

The third phase in the evolution comes at the end of the Napoleonic Wars, with the Bank of England's successful integration of the payment and debt management functions of earlier generations of public banks. The Bank of England's structure becomes the basis for future mutations in central bank design, but it is worth noting that this is not a spontaneous development of the early nineteenth century, but the outcome of more than 400 years of institutional evolution.

The extinction event of 1815 is a complex one. It may be tempting to see it in Darwinian terms as the triumph of a superior species over weaker ones, although the eighteenth century shows that there was no immediate or absolute advantage to the English model. It was copied, unsuccessfully at first, in France only; and it is worth noting that John Law, in his efforts to save his bank, turned belatedly to the Amsterdam model. Although note-issue became prevalent among the newly created banks, those of Northern Europe often included at their origin an exchange bank copied from Hamburg, even if that function tended to play a minor role.

Clearly the transformation of Europe's map, and the disappearance of the autonomous municipalities (earlier in Catalonia, then in Amsterdam, Venice and Genoa) deprived the oldest public banks of the political structures that had created them. Perhaps the attempt by the Genoese to recreate their bank, in the brief months of 1814 when they thought it possible to restore their ancient constitution, reflected only misguided nostalgia. But the example of Hamburg shows that the nineteenth century had not made first-generation banks obviously obsolete.

It also remains an open question, in our eyes, whether the Bank of England model was obviously superior. The nineteenth century is outside the scope of our survey, but we suspect the various countries continued to experiment while facing new political constraints.

Internal and external evolution

The difference between first-generation, ledger banks and second-generation, note-issuing banks can probably be ascribed in part to a technological innovation, the emergence of transferable bearer liabilities. At a physical level this required innovations like the replacement of parchment with cheaper paper, and the ability to produce counterfeit-proof, verifiable claims (printing). From a legal perspective, the evolution was more difficult. A claim has to be actionable in court, and people sue people, pieces of paper don't. A transferable claim requires a legal system that permits in a simple fashion the transfer of one person's claims to another. The need for such a system was felt early on in the Middle Ages but it took a long time for the law to develop the proper mechanisms. It is interesting in this respect to notice that the innovation developed fully outside of the public banks proper, in the city of Naples and among the London goldsmiths. In this, as in the provision of payments by transfer, the public banks were not adding anything to what was available in the private sector: the public bank's alchemy used existing technologies.

One can distinguish between two forms of evolution, internal and external. Internal evolution is reflected in the process of reform in response to local failures, while external evolution, perhaps more readily observed at the creation of a new institution, involves observation and imitation of best practices from other places (and at times, conscious improvement, for example in John Law's attempt to improve on the Bank of England model). The model of the Venice Banco di Rialto, via the Bank of Amsterdam, proved very influential. It is striking to see how the Hamburg Bank (1619), Stockholm Banco (1657), the Riksen Ständers Bank (1668), Vienna Giro (1703), Prussian Hauptbank (1765) all started from or included an exchange or giro function. Yet, in an instance of mutation or "genetic drift," the key ingredient of the Venice Giro, 100 percent reserves, was (formally) retained by the bank of Amsterdam, but was gradually lost in the later imitations. External evolution also involved learning from others' mistakes, for example the failure of Law's bank.

We reach here one of the many limits of our metaphor, but an interesting one: the biological model of evolution has no room for any ingredient of foresight and design.

The invention of fiat money

We have highlighted the provision of a stable unit of account as a key impetus in the creation of public banks. This goal also provided a key force in their evolution, pushing them toward the invention of fiat money, which we identify as a key moment in central banking alchemy.

A simple marker of success in this dimension can be found by perusing Denzel (2012): in this wide-ranging collection of exchange rate quotations for early and late modern Europe, one notices that quotations on certain cities (Amsterdam, Venice, Genoa, Hamburg) are expressed in terms of a "banco" unit. This was not a simple outcome of the requirement to clear foreign exchange bills through the public bank: it could be and was evaded or ignored. Merchants found it useful to use banks' liabilities to denominate and settle their obligations, because those liabilities were more reliable than current money. This outcome was by no mean pre-ordained, and it required a lot of learning on the part of the public banks.

One of the key aspects of the evolution was public banks' acquisition of the right to decide in which coin a deposit could be redeemed. Governmental insistence that a public bank maintain a non-market exchange rate could lead to failure of the bank (as occurred with Genoa's *Banco di San*

Giorgio in 1444) or its reorganization (as with Prussia's *Koenigliche Haupt-bank* in 1766). The Bank of Amsterdam was also restricted to paying out full-weight coins at fixed values, but was able to manage this issue by charging substantial withdrawal fees (1.5 percent) and then applying its own discounts to lighter-weight coins at deposit (from 1641). These policies maintained the liquidity of the bank, but their expense provided a disincentive to use bank money. Amsterdam did not gain full control of the situation until 1683, when it began issuing redeemable receipts for specific coins deposited. Since a depositor holding a receipt could now only withdraw the coins listed on the receipt, coin-to-coin arbitrages were limited, and withdrawal fees could be reduced to almost negligible levels (0.25 percent for most coins).

Perhaps the ultimate expression of public bank control of redeemability, Hamburg's *Reinsilberwährung*, appears near the end of our period (1790). Beginning in 1770, the Bank of Hamburg started accepting deposits of silver bullion in addition to coin. Coin deposits were eliminated altogether in 1790 in favor of bullion, and depositors paid only a small fee (0.45 percent) at withdrawal. But the creation of such a "virtual coin" was only possible in a city-state like Hamburg that was politically dominated by commercial interests.[9]

The history of Genoa also provides a clear case of a public bank slowly, perhaps reluctantly, venturing into the business of providing a stable unit of account. The bank at first kept separate ledgers for each type of coin, but by the mid-seventeenth century it was generally felt that Amsterdam's success needed to be emulated. The Bank formally obtained the freedom to choose the coins in which to repay, a phenomenon that also emerges in Barcelona.

Coins made of metal had failed to provide a satisfactory anchor for a monetary system based on units of account. Replacing coins while somehow retaining the anchor of intrinsic value involved substituting a new asset linked to, in a flexible way, to precious metal. Modern central banks actively manage the value of their liability: that is what we call monetary policy, and it turns out to have a much longer history than generally suspected. Open market operations go back to Amsterdam in the 1660s and were the endpoint of a long process goes back another few centuries.

---

[9] David Ricardo, who must have known the precedent, proposed a similar currency in 1816.

State and bank: finding the right distance

A second key element of the public bank alchemy was finding a "gentlemanly distance" between the institution and its sponsor.

Our survey by design has considered only institutions with a corporate charter, assets and liabilities, thus excluding the early German municipal exchange offices. We have also excluded from our survey instances of currency issued directly by the State, as in Sweden and France in the 1790s.

The early public banks were thus distinct from the State, but never far from it, because the State chartered them, gave them privileges and often owned them or eventually stepped in to bail them out when needed.

Success of a public bank required some distance from the sponsor: Law's first bank proposal was rejected by the king's advisers because it was too closely tied to the State, whose bad credit they knew would taint the bank from birth. But success led to new tensions. The higher the perceived quality of a public bank's claims, the higher the private-sector demand for these claims and the greater the potential for fiscal abuse. Managing fiscal temptation required an appropriate degree of distance between government and bank, and a flawed mechanism for maintaining such distance might cause a bank to collapse in the face of war-driven fiscal demands.

The search for the right distance went in new directions with the second generation of banks created in monarchies. Again, Law's experience is interesting in this regard: to his objectors who claimed that a public bank could never be safe in an absolute monarchy he offered the example of Naples and also pointed out the ruler's self-interest in preserving a well-functioning bank. Law's bank was created as a privately-owned company with no government control, like the Bank of England and the later Caisse d'Escompte. Vienna's Stadtbank offers another model, relying on the relative independence (and better credit) of the city relative to the crown. The Swedish bank's history reflects directly the complex tensions between crown and parliament. Prussia's experiments are also shaped by the same imperative. It is naturally tempting to see the Bank of England's dominance in the nineteenth century as partly based on it having met that imperative.

Stumbles and adaptations

From our vantage point, survival is success. In this respect most public banks we survey did well; indeed, the durability is almost astonishing. Failure, or rather stumbles, can be defined either as suspension of payments (for those banks with demand liabilities) or sharp drops in the market value of the liabilities. Nearly all banks experienced some form of stumble; indeed, the emergence of the Bank of England as model in the nineteenth century is partly due to its twenty-year suspension of convertibility.

How were stumbles handled? The outcomes differ widely. At one extreme the Bank of England's suspension ended with a return to convertibility of its notes at the original parity, without any help from the State. At the other extreme the Banque Royale's collapse in 1720 ended with a conversion of its notes into government liabilities at varying haircuts, as high as 95 percent; likewise the public banks of Catalonia had their deposits converted into government debt at severe discounts in the 1650s. In-between the extremes one finds various models, with conversion of liabilities into either new liabilities of the bank or into liabilities of the State, with varying haircuts in either case. Such are the suspensions of Genoa and Venice, during which deposits were converted more or less at par in long-term annuities and the Barcelona Taula's conversion of old deposits into new deposits and Sweden's and Vienna's conversion of notes. Amsterdam's only serious difficulties, as measured by the most violent movement in its agio, were also fatal.

Just as in the case of the Bank of England, prolonged periods of suspension were not necessarily fatal: the suspensions in Venice and Genoa lasted several decades before convertibility was resumed. Although the record is scant, it is plausible to think that, just as Amsterdam had learned to manage a fiat currency (via a pre-emptive suspension of convertibility), so Venetian and Genoese merchants learned to live with, and tolerated, a payments system based on inconvertible balances, as long as they could hold reasonable expectations that the currency would be well managed.

6 Conclusion

This essay has argued an evolutionary model can be usefully applied to the history of central banks. The key idea is one of path dependence, that is, that the structure of today's highly-levered, note-issuing, government-debt-backed central banks preserves a record of the successes and failures of past institutions. Put another way, the resemblance of today's central banks to the eighteenth-century Bank of England is due more to inheritance rather than to random coincidence.

Pushed to its logical extreme, the biological metaphor also has some implications for the future of central banks. One implication is that in central banking, as in nature, there are no true steady states. Hence, the present structure of modern banks does not represent a convergence. In fact the history of early public banks confirms nearly the opposite view, that is, that the unorthodox ideas of one generation of central banks may become the orthodoxy of the next. We have seen, for example, that banknotes began as a fringe payments instrument, and that early attempts at note issue were catastrophic failures in most implementations. Yet today circulating notes are the most widely accepted transactions medium, not to mention a profit center for the central banks that issue them.

In 2014, one does not have to look far for unorthodox ideas that could have some staying power. To give one example, many central banks implemented "unconventional" policies such as quantitative easing in the wake of the 2008 crisis. But as such policies persist, the unconventional is becoming increasingly conventional. A second example is in the area of cross-border co-operation. The debut of a global large-value payment system (CLS, in 2002) and of a major supranational currency (the Euro, in 1999) represent significant concessions of monetary responsibility by national central banks to international institutions. Such cross-border institutions may become increasingly important in the future, as commerce becomes increasingly globalized. A final and more speculative example is provided by arrangements such as Bitcoin and Ripple, which are essentially trying to offer online versions of banknotes, via online versions of ledgers; it is easy to imagine that at some point, central banks may want in on this act.

The biological metaphor also suggests, and the history confirms, that the course of central banks' evolution is unlikely to be a linear or predictable one. Both new and experimental structures will be tested by acute fiscal demands, market crises, and financial innovation. History likewise indicates that under the pressure of extreme events, even established institutions may quickly become irrelevant or extinct, as occurred with many public banks during the Napoleonic period. What can be guaranteed is continuing pressure for structural innovation, and the survival of the fittest. To anticipate otherwise is to ignore 600 years of historical experience.

References

Aerts, E. (2011). The Absence of Public Exchange Banks in Medieval and Early Modern Flanders and Brabant (1400–1800): A Historical Anomaly to be Explained. *Financial History Review*, 18 (1), 91–117.

Archer, D. and P. Moser-Boehm (2013). Central Bank Finances. Paper 71, Bank for International Settlements.

58 William Roberds and François R. Velde

Bairoch, P., J. Batou and P. Chèvre (1988). *The Population of European Cities, 800–1850: Data Bank and Short Summary of Results*. Droz, Geneva.

Balletta, F. (2009). *La circolazione della moneta fiduciaria a Napoli nel Seicento e nel Settecento (1587–1805)*. Edizioni Scientifiche Italiane.

Bidermann, H. I. (1859). *Die Wiener Stadt-Bank*. Archiv für Kunde österreichischer Geschichtsquellen, Vienna.

Board of Governors of the Federal Reserve System. (2014a). *Federal Reserve Statistical Release H.4.1*. January 2.

(2014b). *100th Annual Report*. Washington, D.C. 2014.

Börner, L. and J. W. Hatfield (2010). The Economics of Debt Clearing Mechanisms. Discussion Paper 2010/27, Freie Universität Berlin.

Breen, J. C. (1900). Eene Amsterdamsche Crediet-instelling uit het laatst der achttiende eeuw. *Tijdschrift voor Geschiedenis*, 15 (2), 137–55.

Conrad, J., L. Elster, W. Lexis and E. Loening (1901). *Handwörterbuch der Staatswissenschaften*, vol. 6. Gustav Fischer, Jena.

Dehing, P. and M. 't Hart (1997). Linking the Fortunes, Currency and Banking, 1550–1800. In 't Hart, M., J. Jonker and J. Luiten van Zanden (eds.), *A Financial History of the Netherlands*, 37–63. Cambridge University Press, Cambridge.

Dehing, P. W. (2012). *Geld in Amsterdam, Wisselbank en wisselkoersen, 1650-1725*. Verloren, Hilversum.

Del Negro, M. and C. A. Sims (2014). When Does a Central Bank's Balance Sheet Require Fiscal Support? Staff Report 701, Federal Reserve Bank of New York.

Demarco, D. (2000a). *Il banco di Napoli: Dalle Casse di Deposito alla Fioritura Settecentesca*. Edizioni Scientifiche Italiane, Napoli.

(2000b). *Il banco di Napoli: L'Archivio Storico: La Grammatica delle Scritture*. Edizioni Scientifiche Italiane, Napoli.

Denzel, M. A. (2010). *Handbook of World Exchange Rates, 1590–1914*. Ashgate Publishing Group, Farnham.

(2012). *Der Nürnberger Banco Publico, seine Kaufleute und ihr Zahlungsverkehr (1621–1827)*. Franz Steiner Verlag, Stuttgart.

Diamond, D. W. and R. G. Rajan (2001). Liquidity Risk, Liquidity Creation, and Financial Fragility: A Theory of Banking. *Journal of Political Economy*, 109 (2), 287–327.

Edvinsson, R. (2010a). Foreign Exchange Rates in Sweden 1658–1803. In Edvinsson, R., T. Jacobson and D. Waldenström (eds.), *Historical Monetary and Financial Statistics for Sweden: Exchange Rates, Prices, and Wages, 1277–2008*, 238–339. Ekerlids Förlag and Sveriges Riksbank, Stockholm.

(2010b). The Multiple Currencies of Sweden-Finland 1534–1803. In Edvinsson, R., T. Jacobson and D. Waldenström (eds.), *Historical Monetary and Financial Statistics for Sweden: Exchange Rates, Prices, and Wages, 1277–2008*, 133–237. Ekerlids Förlag and Sveriges Riksbank, Stockholm.

(2010c). Swedish Monetary Standards in a Historical Perspective. In Edvinsson, R., T. Jacobson and D. Waldenström (eds.), *Historical Monetary and Financial Statistics for Sweden: Exchange Rates, Prices, and Wages, 1277–2008*, 26–66. Ekerlids Förlag and Sveriges Riksbank, Stockholm.

Fawley, B. W. and C. J. Neely (2013). Four Stories of Quantitative Easing. *Federal Reserve Bank of St. Louis Review*, 95 (1), 51–88.

The Descent of Central Banks (1400–1815)   59

Fregert, K. (2012). The Swedish Riskbank 1668–2010: A view from its balance sheet. Working paper, Lund University.

Fuchs, R. (1998). *Die Wiener Stadtbank: ein Beitrag zur österreichischen Finanzgeschichte des 18. Jahrhunderts.* Peter Lang, Frankfurt-am-Main.

Günther, K. (1932). *Die städtischen Wechselbanken Deutschlands im Mittelalter und im 16. Jahrhundert.* Höfling, München.

Hallauer, R. (1904). *Der Basler Stadtwechsel 1504–1746.* Emil Birkhäuser, Basel.

Heckscher, E. F. (1934). The Bank of Sweden in its Connection with the Bank of Amsterdam. In van Dillen, J. G. (ed.), *History of the Principal Public Banks*, 161–99. Martinus Nijhoff, The Hague.

Lattes, E. (1869). *La Libertà delle Banche a Venezia dal Secolo XIII al XVII.* Valentiner e Mues, Milan.

Levy von Halle, E. (1891). *Die Hamburger Giro-Bank und Ihr Ausgang.* Puttkammer und Mühlbrecht, Berlin.

Lichter, J. (1999). *Preussiche Notenbankpolitik in der Formationsphase des Zentralbanksystems 1844 bis 1857.* Duncker und Humblot, Berlin.

Mees, W. C. (1838). *Proeve eener Geschiedenis van het Bankwezen in Nederland geduerende den Tijd der Republiek.* W. Messcuert, Rotterdam.

Mueller, R. C. (1979). The Role of Bank Money in Venice, 1300–1500. *Studi Veneziani, n. s.* III, 49–96.

(1997). *The Venetian Money Market: Banks, Panics, and the Public Debt, 1200–1500.* The Johns Hopkins University Press, Baltimore, MD.

Niebuhr, M. (1854). *Geschichte der Königlichen Bank in Berlin.* Verlag der Deckerschen Geheimen Ober-Hofbuchdruckerei, Berlin.

Ortí Gost, P. (2007). Les finances municipals de la Barcelona dels segles XIV i XV: Del censal a la Taula de Canvi. *Arxiu Històric de la Ciutat de Barcelona, quaderns d'història*, 13, 257–82.

Passola, J. M. (1999). *Els Orígens de la banca pública: les taules de canvi municipals.* Ed. Ausa, Sabadell.

Quinn, S. (2008). Securitization of Sovereign Debt: Corporations as a Sovereign Debt Restructuring Mechanism in Britain, 1694–1750. Tech. rep., Texas Christian University.

Quinn, S. and W. Roberds (2009). An Economic Explanation of the Early Bank of Amsterdam, Debasement, Bills of Exchange and the Emergence of the First Central Bank. In Atack, J. and L. Neal (eds.), *The Evolution of Financial Institutions from the Seventeenth to the Twentieth-First Century*, 32–70. Cambridge University Press, Cambridge.

(2012). Responding to a Shadow Banking Crisis: The Lessons of 1763. Working Paper 2012-8, Federal Reserve Bank of Atlanta.

(2014). How Amsterdam got Fiat Money. *Journal of Monetary Economics*, 66, 1–12.

Raudnitz, J. (1917). *Das Österreichische Staatspapiergeld and die Privilegierte Nationalbank: erster Theil 1762 bis 1820.* Kaiserliche und königliche Staatsdruckerei, Vienna.

Riu, M. (1979). Banking and Society in Late Medieval and Early Modern Aragon. In Chiappelli, F. (ed.), *The Dawn of Modern Banking*, 131–68. Yale University Press, New Haven.

Roberds, W. and F.R. Velde (2016a). Early Public Banks I: Ledger-Money Banks. In Wolfgang Ernst and David Fox (eds.), *Money in the Western Legal Tradition*, 321–358. Oxford University Press, Oxford.

Roberds, W. and F.R. Velde (2016b). Early Public Banks II: Banks of Issue. In Wolfgang Ernst and David Fox (eds.), *Money in the Western Legal Tradition*, 465–488. Oxford University Press, Oxford.

Sánchez Sarto, M. (1934). Les Banques publiques en Espagne jusqu'à 1815. In van Dillen, J. G. (ed.), *History of the Principal Public Banks*, 1–14. Martinus Nijhoff, The Hague.

Sargent, T. J. and F. R. Velde (1995). Macroeconomic Features of the French Revolution. *Journal of Political Economy*, 103 (3), 474–518.

(2002). *The Big Problem of Small Change*. Princeton University Press, Princeton, NJ.

Schleutker, H. (1920). *Das volkswirtschaftliche Bedeutung der Königlichen Seehandlung von 1772–1820*. Ferdinand Schöningh, Paderborn.

Schnabel, I. and H. S. Shin (2006). The 'Kipper- und Wipperzeit' and the Foundation of Public Deposit Banks.

Schneider, J., O. Schwarzer and P. Schnelzer (1991). *Historische Statistik von Deutschland. Band XII: Statistik der Geldund Wechselkurse in Deutschland und im Ostseeraum (18. Und 19. Jahrhundert)*. Scripta-MercurataeVerlag, St. Katharinen.

Sieveking, H. (1906). Studi sulle finanze genovesi nel medioevo e in particolare sulla casa di San Giorgio. In *Atti della Società Ligure di Storia Patria*. Società Ligure di Storia Patria, Genoa.

(1933). Die Hamburger Bank 1633–1875. In *Festschrift der Hamburgischen Universität ihrem Ehrenrektor Herrn Bürgermeister Werner von Melle*, 21–110. J. J. Augustin, Hamburg.

(1934a). Das Bankwesen in Genua und die Bank von S. Giorgio. In van Dillen, J. G. (ed.), *History of the Principal Public Banks*, 15–38. Martinus Nijhoff, The Hague.

(1934b). Die Hamburger Bank. In van Dillen, J. G. (ed.), *History of the Principal Public Banks*, 125–60. Martinus Nijhoff, The Hague.

Sneller, Z. W. (1938a). De Rotterdamsche Wisselbank 1635–1812. *De Economist*, 87 (1), 685–716.

(1938b). De Rotterdamsche Wisselbank 1635–1812 (Slot). *De Economist*, 87, 882–902.

(1938c). De Rotterdamsche Wisselbank 1635–1812 (Vervolg). *De Economist*, 87, 818–40.

Spufford, P. (1986). *Handbook of Medieval Exchange*. Offices of the Royal Historical Society, London.

Tarkka, J. (2009). The North European Model of Early Central Banking: Collateral Policy Before the Real Bills Doctrine. Tech. rep., Bank of Finland.

Tucci, U. (1973). Convertibilità e copertura metallica della moneta del Banco Giro veneziano. *Studi Veneziani*, XV, 349–448.

Usher, A. P. (1934). The Origins of Banking: The Primitive Bank of Deposit, 1200–1600. *The Economic History Review*, 4 (4), 399–428.

(1943). *The Early History of Deposit Banking in Mediterranean Europe*. Harvard University Press, Cambridge.

Van Dillen, J. G. (1934). The Bank of Amsterdam. In van Dillen, J. G. (ed.), *History of the Principal Public Banks*, 79–123. Martinus Nijhoff, The Hague.

The Descent of Central Banks (1400–1815)   61

(1964a). Bloeitijd der Amsterdamse Wisselbank 1687–1781. In van Dillen, J. G. (ed.), *Mensen en Achtergronden, Studies uitgegeven ter gelegenheid van de tachtigste jaardag van de schrijver*. J.B. Wolters, Groningen.

(1964b). Ondergang van de Amsterdamse Wisselbank, 1782–1820. In van Dillen, J. G. (ed.), *Mensen en Achtergronden, Studies uitgegeven ter gelegenheid van de tachtigste jaardag van de schrijver*. J. B. Wolters, Groningen.

(1964c). Oprichting en Functie der Amsterdamse Wisselbank in de zeventiende Eeuw 1609–1686. In van Dillen, J. G. (ed.), *Mensen en Achtergronden, Studies uitgegeven ter gelegenheid van de tachtigste jaardag van de schrijver*. J.B. Wolters, Groningen.

White, M. P. (2012). *The Kipper and Wipper Inflation 1619–1623: An Economic History with Contemporary German Broadsheets*. Yale University Press, New Haven.

3

Central Bank Credibility

An Historical and Quantitative Exploration

Michael D. Bordo
Rutgers University and NBER

Pierre L. Siklos
Wilfrid Laurier University and Viessmann European Research Centre

1 Introduction

Central Bank credibility is defined as a commitment to follow well-articulated and transparent rules and policy goals. More precisely, credibility refers to the "...extent to which the public believes that a shift in policy has taken place when, indeed, such a shift has actually occurred" (Cukierman 1986, p. 6). Blinder (1999, pp. 64–65) offers a more prosaic definition, namely "... that your pronouncements are believed – even though you are bound by no rule and may have an incentive to renege." He goes on to add: "...it is ... built up by a history of matching deeds to words." More generally, Brunner (1983) makes the connection between credibility and the performance of the institutions mandated to carry out policies: "Credibility depends...on the history of policy making and the behavior of the policy institution."

We recognize that central banks may have adopted several goals over time (e.g., the price of gold, exchange rate pegs, monetary targets, inflation

Presented at the 2014 Norges Bank Conference "Of the Uses of Central Banks: Lessons from History", Oslo, Norway. The second author thanks CIGI-INET for financial support. Nicolo Battestini, Samantha St. Amand, and Cesar Tamayo provided excellent research assistance. Earlier versions of this paper were presented as a keynote presentation at the 7th Conference of the South-Eastern European Monetary History Network, Bank of Albania, the Norges Bank 2016 pre-conference at the Graduate Institute in Geneva, the 7th World Congress of the Cliometrics Society, the 2014 ASSA Conference (Cliometrics Society) in Philadelphia, and the 31st SUERF Colloquium and Baffi Finlawmetrics Conference in Milan (June 2014). Comments on earlier drafts by Øyvind Eitrheim, Marc Flandreau, Peter Ireland, Lars Jonung, Josh Hausman, Athanasios Orphanides, and Eugene White, are gratefully acknowledged. We are also grateful to our discussant, Lars Svensson, for insightful comments as well as participants at the Norges Bank Conference and other conferences.

targets). Partly for practical reasons, but also because alternatives to inflation objectives are typically subservient to the goal of controlling the rate of change in the price level, we interpret credibility in terms of inflation performance. Our approach has the virtue of being quantifiable. However, we recognize that such a broad definition could also be viewed at times as being too restrictive. Put differently, model-based estimates of credibility can be sensitive to the parameterizations employed. Therefore, while numerical estimates of credibility are useful these can only tell an incomplete story. Hence, we supplement the quantitative approach with narrative evidence.

Credibility then is best thought of as a flow like variable that changes as observed inflation is seen to deviate from a time-varying inflation objective, which need not be explicit or publicly announced. Credibility is also partially determined by the relative importance the central bank attaches to real and nominal economic objectives. Regular economic shocks and the manner in which the central bank manipulates monetary policy instruments dictate how credibility evolves over time.

Credibility evolves possibly in a non-linear manner, is earned slowly and painstakingly yet susceptible to evaporate on a moment's notice. In the words of Benjamin Franklin "It takes many good deeds to build a good reputation, and only one bad one to lose it."[1] Identifying and measuring credibility is challenging. Nevertheless, as Cukierman (1986, p. 5) again points out, "...the ability of monetary policymakers to achieve their future objectives depends on the inflationary expectations of the public. These inflationary expectations depend, in turn, on the public's evaluation of the credibility of the monetary policy makers..." Paul Volcker, former Chair of the US Federal Reserve's Open Market Committee (FOMC), once underscored the point that "[T]o break the inflation cycle we must have credible and disciplined monetary policy" (Bernanke 2013, p. 35). Indeed, Volcker went on to remark that "...inflation undermines trust in government." (Silber 2012, p. 266). Therefore, autonomy, transparency, accountability, and the monetary policy strategy in place each can influence both the credibility and reputation of the monetary authority.

---

[1] Experimental evidence (e.g., List 2006) suggests that reputation and the monitoring of quality are complements. Our definition of credibility is, in effect, a quality assessment exercise, and reputation, that is, the ability of a central bank to deliver the promised monetary policy outcome over time, seems consistent with the stock-flow distinction made earlier.

Not everyone shares the view that credibility is a sought after objective of central banks. Romer (2013, p. 109), for example, claims: "There is remarkably little evidence that credibility in monetary policy making buys one much when it comes to lowering the costs of disinflation." Ball (1994), and Ball and Sheridan (2005), are similarly skeptical. Notice, however, that Romer's criticism relates to views about the costs of lowering inflation and this is also highly dependent not only on how expectations are formed but on the constraints faced by the monetary authorities. Ball and Sheridan's (2005) analysis is selective and appears to be offset by contrary evidence based on the success of regimes such as inflation targeting. Mishkin (2005), for example, reviews the arguments against a role for credibility and finds them wanting.[2]

In this paper we back up our interpretation of central bank behavior with measures of credibility. To the extent that we are able to apply reliable institutional information we can also indirectly assess their role in influencing the credibility of the monetary authority. We focus on measures of inflation expectations, the mean reversion properties of inflation, and movements in interest rates, money growth, and exchange rate movements. In addition we will place some emphasis on whether credibility is particularly vulnerable during financial crises. As Carney (2013), former Governor of the Bank of Canada (BoC), points out: "Financial imbalances ultimately breed crises, and crises threaten price stability." Crises, especially of the financial variety, play a role in influencing the ability of a central bank to maintain price stability. A monetary authority with a reputation for delivering on its promises will likely have an easier time of it, as well as the flexibility to temporarily deviate from a rule, than one with poorly established credibility. Is credibility linked to improvements in macroeconomic conditions? Is credibility in monetary policy also affected by other factors such as the growth of private credit?

Clearly, credibility will also be influenced not only by how observed inflation behaves over time but, by implication, according to how expectations of inflation are formed. As argued earlier, expectations formation lies at the core of any definition of credibility. Of course, as Eggertsson and Woodford (2003) point out that: "...the power of the expectations channel

---

[2] Part of the difficulty is that the definition of credibility is not unique. The theoretical literature also views the concept as akin to a central bank being bound by a rule and this raises the possibility of time inconsistency. The definition adopted here is, admittedly, a simpler one. More recently, Geraats (2014) has raised further doubts about the methodology used by Ball and Sheridan (2005).

of monetary policy is highly sensitive to the precise manner in which expectations are formed...". As a result, there is the possibility that our definition concerns how well central banks have achieved their target as opposed to how their actions are reflected in changing inflation expectations.[3] It is for this reason that we are careful to argue that, as imperfect as our measure may be, we strive to assess credibility on the basis of how monetary policy actions and regimes over time are reflected in some proxy for inflation expectations.[4] A study that relies on a shorter time span than the century or more of data used in this paper would be able to rely on more direct measures of inflationary expectations but at the expense of investigating the role of credibility over far fewer policy regimes.

Central banks can, at least for our purposes, be thought of as institutions responsible for price stability and economic stabilization which, for simplicity, we will refer to as monetary stability, as well as having possibly a role in ensuring financial stability. Traditionally, financial stability meant serving as a lender of last resort (LOLR) to the commercial banking system and protecting the payments mechanism. The concept has recently been extended to include the prevention of contagion from the non-bank financial sector and heading off asset price booms before they can burst.

A complication arises when one attempts to understand how these twin responsibilities are, institutionally, linked to each other. The separation can be formal, as in the case of the European Central Bank, or the Bank of England prior to the recent global financial crisis, or informal as when central banks choose to focus on one activity at the expense of the other. Reinhart and Rogoff (2013) posit that the US Federal Reserve is a case in point.

However, theirs is a revisionist view of the financial stability task assigned to the Fed. Responsibility for financial stability did not apply to non-member banks. Moreover, there was no formal mechanism which would permit the Fed to intervene in what we now call shadow banking. In other words, there was insufficient institutional flexibility to permit intervention in the financial system that might prove necessary in response to financial innovations. Legislation tended to define the circumstances under

---

[3] Indeed Lars Svensson, our discussant, drew attention to the useful distinction between inflation target achievement and credibility. For example, he argues that the Riksbank's performance in achieving its inflation target since the mid-1990s is not good (in contrast to the Canadian experience) but that the central bank's target has been credible based on market-based expectations. As stressed later our measure need not be equivalent to some publicly announced inflation target.

[4] In fact, we consider several proxies as discussed later.

which the central bank intervened and, when it did not do so, politicians reacted by placing additional limits on the Fed's room to maneuver in financial sector interventions. Finally, whereas the Fed's creation did away with seasonality in interest rate movements (e.g., see Mankiw and Miron 1991), certainly a contribution to financial stability, central banks more generally were not created to manage asset booms and busts.

Instead, the Fed was led to focus on monetary stability after World War II. Next, we have central banks where there is clear recognition that the twin responsibilities of the central bank for monetary and financial stability overlap. Arguably, most central banks were of this variety, at least until 2007 or so. Consequently, the mandate of the central bank, its autonomy with respect to the government, the governance of the institution, to name but three important determinants, also provide clues about how a central bank is able to manage its credibility over time.

Finally, the type of central bank will also dictate which instruments are at its disposal and how many are likely to be deployed at any given time. Presumably, central banks where monetary and financial stability are both integral to the conduct of policy rely on more instruments than a monetary authority where stabilization policies are effectively divorced from financial stability concerns. Ultimately, however, the scope of the LOLR function (see Table 3.1) is critical. A central bank that is statutorily prohibited from intervening under certain circumstances (e.g., the Fed and the ECB) is likely to have different consequences for financial stability than a monetary authority which is prepared to intervene on a broad scale. Therefore, the credibility and reputation of the central bank will be dictated by a more complex set of factors which, for brevity, we will refer to as institutionally driven.

In a historical study it is unclear how we should define the benchmark against which inflation deviates from some expected value. Accordingly, we consider a number of approaches. For example, we apply statistical break tests to determine breaks in the inflation rate. This permits us to evaluate one indicator of deviations of realized inflation from some expectation, namely deviations from a statistically estimated trend inflation rate.

Yet another strategy consists in comparing monetary policy performance against examples when, with the hindsight of history, policies are thought to have been delivered credibly and the reputation of the central bank was considered to be stellar. Historical examples from Germany or Switzerland, the United States during the Great Moderation from approximately 1986 to 2007, or the period since certain central banks adopted and maintained numerical inflation targets beginning in the mid-1990s, readily

Table 3.1 *The origins of ten central banks*

Year	Country	Name	Motivation
1668	Sweden	Bank of the Estates of the Realm. Forerunner of the Riksbank	Finance war
1694	United Kingdom	Bank of England	Finance war
1800	France	Banque de France	Manage public debt, generate seignorage
1816	Norway	Norges Bank	Economic crisis in Denmark-Norway prompts monetary reform
1876	Germany	Reichsbank. Forerunner of Bundesbank	Consolidation of previous note issuing authorities following unification
1882	Japan	Bank of Japan	Part of modernization of Meiji regime
1893	Italy	Banca d'Italia	Consolidation of previous note issuing authorities following unification
1907	Switzerland	Swiss National Bank	Elimination of note issuing competition
1913	United States	Federal Reserve System	Creation of lender of last resort and other banking related functions
1934	Canada	Bank of Canada	Lender of last resort

Sources: Siklos (2002) and updated from individual central bank websites accessible through the BIS's Central bank hub, www.bis.org/cbanks.htm.

come to mind. The implication then is that an evaluation of central bank credibility and reputation is enhanced by narratives of central bank actions through time.

Next, we ask how the hypothesized credibility indicator reacts to the past history of inflation, various proxies for economic growth performance, or the output gap, the stage and shape of particular business cycle events (i.e., recessions versus recoveries, their size and shape; see, for example, Bordo and Haubrich 2010) as well as other variables such as wars, financial crises and financial market conditions. We also aim to empirically establish whether credibility behaves asymmetrically over time.

A historical perspective also enables us to deal with another under-emphasized element of central bank performance, namely whether deflationary periods, or the threat of deflation, also influences central bank credibility. Burdekin and Siklos (2004b), based on a cross-section of countries covering a long span of time, have shown that macroeconomic shocks are strikingly different between inflationary and deflationary samples. We can also draw upon the rich examples of the consequences of deflation covered by several other authors (e.g., also see Burdekin and Siklos 2004a). The upshot is that there is potentially an asymmetry that could further contribute to introducing non-linearity in the behavior of central bank reputation over time.

The rest of the chapter is organized as follows. The next section provides a brief narrative exploration of the nature and evolution of credibility through time and across a select number of countries.[5] We then provide some theoretical underpinnings for the proposed empirical exercise aimed at evaluating how central bank credibility and reputation have evolved over time.[6] Next, we provide a brief description of the data and discuss some methodological considerations. Section 4 discusses our main findings. Section 5 concludes.

Briefly, we find credibility changes over time are frequent and can be sizeable. For example, there is robust evidence that the gold standard improves central bank credibility. Similarly, in the post–World War II era, central bank independence reliably improved credibility. Finally, there is some evidence that financial crises damage central bank credibility. However, the gap between observed and the central bank's inflation goal must be fairly large for this to happen. Hence, credibility is significantly affected according to whether the shock can be associated with policy errors. Bernanke (2013, p. 23), for example, has acknowledged that such errors can play an important role in explaining the severity of the most recent 'global' financial crisis. Moreover, institutional factors (i.e., the quality of governance) can play an important role in mitigating reputational loss. Lastly, credibility shocks are dependent on the type of monetary policy regime in place.

2 Credibility and Reputation Through the Ages

The history of central bank credibility is tied up with the history of policy regimes. Consider, for example, the classical gold standard as a rule based on the commitment to maintain the official peg. Central banks (independent of the fiscal authorities) in many of the advanced countries of Europe

---

[5] An Annex presents detailed Narratives on the historical evolution of eleven advanced country central banks.

[6] Some technical details are mainly relegated to an Appendix.

adhered to this rule from 1880 to 1914. According to the rule temporary suspension was allowed during a wartime emergency or a serious financial crisis. In such situations central banks issued paper money to help finance the government's fiscal deficit. Once the emergency ended the central bank was required to restore convertibility to gold at the prewar official parity. If it did this it would ensure its credibility and allow it to use its seigniorage to finance a future war (Bordo and Kydland 1995). Credible adherence to the gold standard rule allowed central banks to have some leeway to conduct stabilization policies within the gold points (Bordo and MacDonald 2012). It also insured that it could conduct LOLR actions without engendering capital flight (Eichengreen 1997). The history of the pre 1914 gold standard shows how important countries, especially Britain, France and Germany, had credible regimes (see the Annex for examples from other countries with successes; e.g., Sweden and the United States, and failures; e.g., Italy's inability to deliver credible regimes). Many other peripheral countries tried to gain it but were less successful (Bordo and Schwartz 1996).[7]

World War I ended the classical gold standard and, after the war, many countries tried to rebuild the prewar system. Restoring the prewar parity after massive wartime inflation and changes in the political economy (suffrage) delayed the restoration of the gold standard and the standard that was established – the fragile gold exchange standard – had less credibility. Britain returned to gold at the prewar parity in 1925 but at an overvalued parity which continually threatened its adherence. The United States never left gold but the newly established Federal Reserve went through a lengthy learning period to become a fully functioning member of the central banking club (Meltzer 2009). France went through a period of high inflation and its central bank lost much of its credibility in a scandal. Germany went through a hyperinflation fueled by the Reichsbank. By 1926 the gold exchange standard was up and running and its short-lived success depended upon the reputations of Benjamin Strong, Montagu Norman, Emile Moreau and Hjalmar Schacht. Despite their efforts the system collapsed during the Great Depression. In its aftermath central

---

[7] Not everyone supports the view that rules implicit in regimes of the gold standard variety can generate credibility. Ferguson and Schularik (2008) suggest that in peripheral (i.e., less developed) economies there was no credibility bonus in adhering to a policy rule of the gold standard variety. Nevertheless, this view downplays the fact that credibility and reputation are inter-connected. Hence, even if the peripheral countries intended to generate credibility, theirs is an attempt to operate under rules governed by weak central banking institutions.

70   *Michael D. Bordo and Pierre L. Siklos*

bankers were blamed for the Depression and central banks lost their independence and became virtual appendages of the fiscal authorities. Academics still debate not only if too much authority was invested in central banks but whether a series of policy mistakes by governments, and other public institutions, combined to create the perfect storm resulting in the greatest economic slump of the twentieth century (e.g., Ahamed 2009, Meltzer 2009).

While the rules versus discretion debate concerning the conduct of monetary policy has a long history, and is likely to dominate discussions of central bank credibility and reputation, the institutional approach evaluates performance through the prism of the mandate of the central bank. Indeed, evaluations of central bank performance according to how autonomous and accountable they are, continues to pre-occupy academics and policy makers. While there exists a fairly broad consensus that central bank independence and accountability are essential ingredients in maintaining credibility and reputation (e.g., see Waller 2011), it is equally clear that there are serious reservations about our ability to objectively make the link between central bank mandates and inflation performance or the success of a particular monetary policy regime (e.g., see Parkin 2012, Cargill 2013). Matters become still more complicated when attempts are made to link central bank mandates with inflation prior to the 1950s (e.g., Dehay and Levy 2000).[8]

Regardless of one's view about the importance of central bank autonomy in explaining monetary policy performance central banks have become far more talkative over time and place a premium on their ability to communicate with the public. In this regard we may trace the origins of this phase in the evolution of central banks to the late 1950s when, then Governor of the BoC, James Coyne, was the target of heavy criticism, in both the press as well as from government officials, for speaking out in public on matters beyond the usual remit of monetary policy. Not only did Coyne view speeches and other reports published by the BoC as devices to explain monetary policy to the public but as a tool to underpin the central bank's credibility and reputation (Siklos 2010, and Powell 2009). This sentiment would be echoed a little later by Karl Blessing, President of the Bundesbank (DBB) from 1958 to 1969, who argued: "A central bank which never fights,

---

[8]   Interestingly, Japan (low inflation and, until the 1990s, not an autonomous central bank) poses a problem for institutional hypotheses of central bank performance in more recent times, and also appears to be atypical of the central bank independence – low inflation nexus in the interwar era.

which at times of economic tension never raises its voice...that central bank will be viewed with mistrust." (Marsh 1992, pp. 256–257) Therefore, whereas central banks were hampered by their unwillingness or inability to express their views or influence expectations via public pronouncements, the spread of transparency especially since the late 1990s has changed rather dramatically (e.g., see Siklos 2002, Dincer and Eichengreen 2007). Central banks are no longer shy about discussing matters beyond purely monetary policy questions.

In the 1950s, the Federal Reserve gained its independence and began following gold standard orthodoxy dedicated to price stability. Few other central banks, with the exception of the DBB, the Swiss National Bank (SNB) and the BoC, followed suit. In Canada, policy makers suspended their participation in the Bretton Woods system for much of the 1950s. This allowed the BoC to regain its monetary independence although Canada's economic fortunes were increasingly linked to economic developments faced by its largest trading partner, the United States. A crisis dented the reputation of the BoC in the late 1950s but it would be restored following important institutional reforms and with the return to the Bretton Woods fold (Siklos 2010). The theme linking independence to credibility and the role of the policy regime in dictating central bank behavior is a recurring one throughout the twentieth century (Siklos 2002).

In the United States the return to monetary orthodoxy rested on the reputation of William McChesney Martin after the 1951 Fed-Treasury Accord restored the Fed's independence to conduct monetary policy. The regained central bank credibility was, however, short lived. In the 1960s central banks (with the exception of the DBB and the SNB) began following Keynesian policies to maintain full employment at the expense of higher inflation. The subsequent Great Inflation destroyed any vestiges of credibility as well as the reputations of central bankers such as Arthur Burns (Bordo and Orphanides 2013). Paul Volcker's adoption of a monetarist style tight monetary policy in 1979 broke the back of inflationary expectations at the expense of a deep recession in the United States. Previously, inflation had drifted upward in a seemingly permanent fashion (e.g., see Goodfriend and King 2013, and De Long 1997) and it appears that only a form of 'shock therapy' could restore lower long-run inflationary expectations (e.g., see Levin and Taylor 2013).

Similar strategies were followed in Canada, the United Kingdom, Japan, and other countries (see the Annex) so that by the mid-1980s the Great Moderation restored price stability in the advanced countries along with the reputations of central bankers. However, in all of these instances (with the possible exception of Switzerland), credibility did not exist in the immediate postwar. It had to be earned at an economic price over time. Indeed, the lower the credibility of policies, the more adverse the economic costs are. This relationship has been understood for some time (e.g., Fellner 1976, Haberler 1980). The commitment to rules focused on low inflation helped to restore central bank credibility (e.g., see Levin and Taylor 2013 and Goodfriend 1986). What helped these central banks to succeed was that new policies were built on the reputation of their institutions. In Germany, the DBB\gained credibility and a sterling reputation in the postwar period. The DBB was founded in 1948 with the express mandate to pursue price stability. This mandate was a reaction to the disastrous experience of its predecessor, the Reichsbank, in generating a hyperinflation in the 1920s.

Canada, like the US example under Volcker, offers another example of the trade-off between credibility and the costs of reducing inflation, occasionally referred to as the sacrifice ratio. Following years of inflation rates that were persistently higher than those in the United States, the Canadian government, in cooperation with the BoC, adopted inflation targeting. In spite of the joint declaration to aim for low and stable inflation the recession of the early 1990s was among the sharpest in Canadian history (e.g., see Cross and Bergevin 2012). It led some to suggest that Canada, as a result of the tight monetary policy that helped influence inflationary expectations delivered a "Great Canadian Slump" (Fortin 1996). The BoC replied that supply side factors played a much greater role than critics of monetary policy allowed (Freedman and Macklem 1998). The Canadian example also highlights a recurring theme, namely the difficulty of identifying the proximate source of economic downturns, particularly severe ones, and the extent to which central banks ought to have anticipated these and calibrated their policies to mitigate the costs of a transition in adopting a new policy regime.[9]

In Germany the DBB gained credibility and a sterling reputation in the postwar period. In the next fifty years the DBB had the best track record of any advanced country in maintaining low inflation (Beyer et. al. 2013). Indeed during the Great Inflation, core inflation in West Germany increased only a fraction of that of the United States and United Kingdom.

---

[9] The adoption of inflation targeting was spurred by the record of monetary policy in the 1970s and 1980s. See Crow (2002) for a first-hand account by the Bank of Canada Governor at the time.

Unlike central banks in other advanced country, the DBB did not accommodate the oil price shocks of the 1970s. This record of credible adherence to low inflation gave the DBB a very strong reputation which the ECB, founded in 1999, tried to emulate. The also followed a policy like Germany's from its origin in 1907 and had one of the best inflation fighting track records of any central bank in the twentieth century (Bordo and James 2007) (for other countries see the Annex).

The fact that central banks, mainly in Anglo-Saxon countries, appear to attach relatively more weight to the statutory relationship between central banks and governments suggests that certain cultural factors might also be in play (e.g., Eijffinger and De Haan 1996, La Porta, Lopez-de-Silanes, and Schleifer 2008). Moreover, if cultural factors also impact business cycles, at least in some parts of the world (e.g., see Altug and Canova 2013), then there exists another avenue through which the central bank's credibility and reputation can be altered.

The series of financial crises that have, since 2007, gripped the advanced economies especially led to massive discretionary intervention in financial markets by central banks around the world. Many of the actions mixed monetary with fiscal policy and appeared to violate central bank independence. The changes in the legislative and regulatory landscape that followed have expanded the role of central banks. Time will tell if their credibility to maintain low inflation will survive. However, unlike earlier episodes in the monetary history of the last century or so, it is the fear of deflation and depression that has fueled central banks' responses. It is, therefore, worth contemplating whether the ability of central banks to ease policies by historically unheard of amounts, without signs that inflation expectations are becoming unanchored, is a sign of the triumph of central bank credibility and the strength of their reputation (also see Borio and Filardo 2004).

Has the industrial world, in particular, adopted a 'culture of stability' that seemingly explains Germany's and Switzerland's success in avoiding the Great Inflation of the 1970s and 1980s? (e.g., see Beyer et. al. 2013). As Bernanke (2013, p. 63) notes: "People get used to what they see." And the industrial world has experienced low and stable inflation rates for approximately two decades. The implication of Bernanke's comment is that low and stable observed inflation rates give meaning to the concept of price stability which, as former Fed Chairman Alan Greenspan (1996, p. 1) remarks: "...obtains when economic agents no longer take account of the prospective changes in the general price level in their economic decision-making."

74   *Michael D. Bordo and Pierre L. Siklos*

Alternatively, central bank credibility may have suffered recently, based on expectations about what central banks can and cannot do, because the public does not believe the current policy is compatible with the reliance on numerical objectives for evaluating the performance of monetary policy. It may be that inflation expectations are no longer a sufficient guide of policy credibility. By the same token, changes in the responsibilities central banks are faced with also raise questions about the reputation of these institutions and whether they have become overburdened with responsibilities that are bound to conflict with each other (e.g., see Siklos 2014).

3 Quantifying Credibility

3.1 The Taylor Rule, Credibility, and Policy Regimes

Since Taylor's (1993) celebrated article many discussions about policy rules revolve around an expression of the following kind:

$$i_t = \overline{\rho} + \overline{\pi} + \alpha_2 \widetilde{\pi}_t + \alpha_3 \widetilde{y}_t + \varepsilon_{i,t} \tag{1}$$

where i_t is the central bank's policy rate, $\overline{\rho}$ is the natural real interest rate, $\widetilde{\pi}_t$ is an indicator of the inflation gap, $\widetilde{y}_t$ is the output gap. The inflation gap can either be the difference between realized and expected or forecasted inflation, or represented by some deviation from an explicit inflation objective. In Taylor's original formulation, $\overline{\rho}$ is set at 2 percent, as is the inflation objective, while α_2, α_3 were each calibrated to equal ½. Since that time many central banks have adopted a 2 percent inflation objective, generally for the medium-term (i.e., a 2 to 3 year horizon). Instead of an explicit numerical objective a model-based estimate of the central bank's implicit inflation objective can be used to generate $\widetilde{\pi}$ since central banks, generally, are not expected to meet the stated objective on an annual basis let alone at quarterly or monthly frequencies.

The output gap, $\widetilde{y}_t$, defined as deviations of observed real GDP (y_t) from potential output (y_t^*), is likely unobserved given lags in obtaining economy-wide output data (i.e., real GDP). Consequently, many empirical applications resort to $\widetilde{y}_{t-1}$ instead of relying on the contemporaneous output gap.[10] Note that (1) assumes that $\rho + \overline{\pi}$ is time-invariant. If inflation

---

[10] Alternatively, one can replace the output gap with an unemployment rate gap. There is the additional difficulty, in this connection, stemming from the fact that central banks may not make policy decisions on a monthly or quarterly basis. The US Federal Reserve, for example, renders decisions eight times a year.

An Historical and Quantitative Exploration 75

drifts over time, as was the case during the Great Inflation of the 1970s and 1980s (e.g., see Goodfriend and King 2013), then the intercept of the Taylor rule would also change over time with consequences for central bank credibility.

Arguably, a big challenge with Equation (1) is estimating potential or trend output. Several techniques are available. While the Hodrick-Prescott filter is probably the most widely used method there is no agreement on which method is best (e.g., see Dupasquier, Guay, and St-Amant 1999, van Norden and Orphanides 2002, and Mishkin 2007).[11]

If the hallmark of good policy making involves setting today's policy instrument in a forward-looking manner then it is preferable to replace $\tilde{\pi}_t$ and $\tilde{y}_{t-1}$ with their expected values (e.g., $E_t\tilde{\pi}_{t+1}, E_t\tilde{y}_{t+1}$), whether these are model generated or rely on published forecasts. Woodford (2003) demonstrates that some history dependence is required to implement policy in a stable fashion. As a result, central banks generally do not always adjust their policy instrument according to Equation (1). Instead, policy rate changes may be 'smoothed' over time. One way to introduce this feature into the reaction function is by adding a lagged dependent variable (i.e., i_{t-1}).[12] Another limitation of Taylor's original formulation, and many of its variants, stems from the role of the policy rate at or near the zero lower bound (ZLB). For example, simulations by Chung et. al. (2012) reveal that very low inflation objectives (viz., below 2 percent) frequently lead to the ZLB being reached. Consequently, either the central bank reacts more aggressively to the output gap when the policy rate is low or it reduces the policy rate to zero more quickly than any standard Taylor rule might recommend.

It is not an exaggeration to state that central banks through the decades have followed some type of 'rule', explicit or not, since most central banks have always been created, among other tasks to be carried out (e.g., an exchange rate, economic activity, or employment objective, banker for the

---

[11] Borio (2013) argues in favor of an output gap concept that incorporates financial asset prices. With few exceptions, however, such data are not available for a long span of time nor is it immediately clear whether financial assets were important prior to, say, the 1980s in influencing the output gap. Likely, a more significant influence on changes in potential output are recessions. Also, see Haltmaier (2012).

[12] Rudebusch (2006) casts doubts on the interest rate smoothing hypothesis because interest rate changes are unpredictable, among other reasons. In contrast, Goodhart (1999) posits several plausible reasons in support of the interest rate smoothing phenomenon, including the unwillingness of central banks to be seen as frequently enacting policy reversals. Also, see Sack and Wieland (2000), and Rudebusch (2002).

State, supervisory tasks, supporting the economic policies of government, to name a few), to maintain some form of price stability. Also, the instruments of policy used by a large number of central banks around the world have ranged over the decades from setting interest rates, influencing the price of gold, liquidity enhancing and credit easing measures, setting objectives for the exchange rate and money growth. The fact that one resorts to a post-1990s framework to examine central bank performance in previous decades simply means that allowances should be made for deviations from such rules. They do not, however, invalidate their use. After all, Taylor (1993, 1998) demonstrated the usefulness of his rule for the Fed using historical data for a period when few would have characterized monetary policy as acting in a rule-like manner. While it is true that focus on Taylor rules masks the fact that central banks over time have deployed different policy instruments, the formulations we develop here do not ignore other factors, such as money (or credit) aggregates in potentially influencing financial conditions.[13]

Kozicki and Tinsley (2009) explicitly demonstrate that a formulation such as (1) is consistent with a several policy strategies.[14] Hence, describing change in central bank credibility over time in these terms is possible because central banks have different views about the various natural rates in the Taylor rule (inflation, output, and the real interest rate), as well as different attitudes about how aggressively to react to inflation and output gap shocks (i.e., the size of α_1, α_2). Moreover, with some exceptions, even if central banks are clear about the primary instrument of policy used to control inflation they have also always reserved the right to resort to using other instruments at their disposal. It is only very recently that many central banks have become sufficiently transparent to allow clear identification of the instruments of policy actually used.

---

[13] Reinhart and Rogoff (2013) point out that the Fed, like a few other central banks, have seen their mandate evolve over time, from financial stability to price stability, and back again to financial stability. Consequently, they favor a greater role for credit aggregates in the conduct of monetary policy, a point repeatedly made by the BIS in recent years. Nevertheless, their analysis underestimates the connection between price stability and financial stability as well as equating financial stability with bank stability. There is no allowance made for the role of shadow banking nor does the Federal Reserve Act explicitly define what financial stability means.

[14] Their formulation is expressed in terms of an unemployment gap in part because they are interested in US monetary policy during the 1970s through the late 1990s. Data restrictions as well as comparability with most of the relevant literature, including Orphanides' (2003) historical analysis of policy rules, make it impractical, in our study, to rely on the unemployment rate. Instead, we begin with a rule expressed in terms of an output gap.

It seems reasonable then, if we are interested in evaluating central bank credibility and reputation, to focus our attention on how expected inflation evolves over time when derived from alternative formulations of Equation (1), conditioned on a chosen monetary policy instrument. Since we can allow estimates of expected inflation to evolve for both short-term economic reasons (e.g., an economic shock of some kind), as well as institutional reasons (e.g., a change in the degree of central bank independence), this serves as the starting point for our estimates of central bank credibility over time. As Kahn (2012) argues: "The Taylor rule can be seen as part of a broader movement in which commitment (and therefore credibility), transparency, and independence, replaced a culture of discretion, "mystique," and occasional political influence."

We begin with the case where interest rates are not smoothed and Equation (1) augmented by a 'speed limit' term (e.g., see Woodford 2003) that corrects for measurement type errors in specification via the addition of an output growth term. Next, strong persistence in the policy rate is accounted for by permitting dynamic adjustment of the policy rate. This yields a version of (1) which can be written as follows

$$i_t = \gamma_{1,t} + \gamma_{2,t} E_t \pi_{t+1} + \gamma_{3,t}\left(E_t y_{t+1} - y_t^*\right) + \gamma_{4,t}\Delta y_t + \gamma_{5,t}\Delta i_{t-1}$$
$$+\gamma_{6,t}\left(i_{t-1} - \bar{P}_t\right) + \bar{P}_t + \eta_t \tag{2}$$

Adapting the result from Kozicki and Tinsley (2009), the *implied inflation target* is derived as

$$\bar{\pi}_t = \frac{-\gamma_{1,t}}{\left(\gamma_{2,t} + \gamma_{6,t} - 1\right)} \tag{3}$$

When an intermediate monetary target is in place we rely on a Quantity Theory type formulation that sets money growth (Δm_t), in both realized and equilibrium terms, according to either realized or the effective inflation target, the growth rate of the economy and velocity movements (Δv_t).

Kozicki and Tinsley (2009) then demonstrate that the effective inflation target can be shown to be (also, see Orphanides 2003)[15]

---

[15] As a result, this formulation of the policy rule has the distinct advantage that it does not rely on unobservable output gap measures. See, for example, Friedman (1968) and Orphanides (2003). Nevertheless, the specification does require taking a stand on how best to measure the money supply. The formal expression is still as in Equation (3) except that, in Equation (2), $E_t\Delta x_{t+1}$ replaces $E_t\pi_{t+1}$ and $E_t y_{t+1}$ replaces Δy_t. In other words, parameters $\gamma_{3,t}$ and $\gamma_{4,t}$ are affected. Δx_t is a proxy for the nominal output growth gap obtained via Okun's Law (e.g., see Ball et. al. 2013). The difficulty is that Okun's Law requires data for the

$$\bar{\pi}_t = \Delta \overline{m}_t - \Delta \bar{y}_t + \Delta \bar{v}_t \qquad (4)$$

Finally, we consider the case of a small open economy that contemplates combining interest rate and exchange rate instruments in the manner of Ball (1999) so that the policy rule is expressed as an adapted version of Equation (1) written as follows:

$$\lambda i_t + (1 - \lambda)e_t = \bar{p}_t + \bar{\pi}_t + \tilde{\alpha}_2 \tilde{\pi}_t + \tilde{\alpha}_3 \tilde{y}_t + \tilde{\varepsilon}_{i,t} \qquad (5)$$

where e_t is the nominal exchange rate (i.e., the domestic price of foreign currency). Under a floating exchange rate regime, $\lambda = 1$, so we are left with an expression of the form of Equation (1). Next, if domestic and foreign inflation rates are related to each other via an (uncovered) interest rate parity relation the effective inflation target is reminiscent of Equation (3), but adapted to capture the trade-off between an interest rate and an exchange rate response so that we obtain the following expression for the *implied inflation target*

$$\bar{\pi}_t = \frac{-\gamma_{1,t}}{\left(\gamma_{2,t} + \gamma_{6,t} - \gamma_{7,t} - 1\right)} \qquad (6)$$

where $\gamma_{7,t}$ is obtained from a variant of Equation (2) augmented by adding a term capturing the expected depreciation of the nominal exchange rate. The upshot is that not all shocks require an immediate response of the policy instrument to maintain credibility.[16] Indeed, as long as the central bank communicates clearly (i.e., there is adequate transparency)[17], some changes in the inflation and the output gap will elicit a response such as when the economic shock is of the aggregate demand variety while other types of shocks, namely aggregate supply shocks, are responded to in a 'balanced' fashion. Both of these actions should be reflected in the ability of the central bank to 'anchor' inflation expectations.

---

unemployment rate in order to estimate the relevant gap measure and this series is likely unavailable for several countries and samples in our dataset. Instead, we proxy Δx_t by estimating $\Delta \pi_{t+1} + 0.454 \Delta y_{t+1}$. The 0.454 value is obtained for the United States from Ball et. al. (2013) and is equivalent to the value used in Kozicki and Tinsley (2009). For the other countries in the data set we also rely on estimates in Ball et. al. (2013).

[16] Indeed, as a result we do not interpret what central banks have done as if they followed an optimal control (OC) policy. Orphanides and Williams (2011) demonstrate an OC policy does not deliver better outcomes unless the information possessed by the authorities is superlative. Since this is unlikely, even in the data rich environment we live in, and almost certainly a low probability event in earlier decades, our approach is more akin to the 'robust' monetary policy type of approach in the presence of significant impairments in information.

[17] Clarity and transparency need not, of course, go hand in hand (e.g., see Siklos 2003).

An Historical and Quantitative Exploration 79

We can now define credibility. In the simplest terms a central bank is deemed credible when it delivers, subject to a random error, the implied inflation rate objective conditional on the monetary regime in place. Of course, as previously noted, there may well be economic and institutional reasons why the credibility of the central bank may be affected. Consequently, we write

$$\left(\pi_{it} - \overline{\pi}_{it}\right)^2 = \theta Z_{it} + \varphi_i\left(\pi_{i,t-1} - \overline{\pi}_{i,t-1}\right)^2 + u_{it} \tag{7}$$

Where the dependent variable is our indicator of credibility, θZ_t is the product of a vector of coefficients, θ, and Z represents economic and institutional variables that can explain departures from the effective inflation target (see the following section). Finally, as suggested earlier, credibility may be persistent because inflation tends to be persistent over time (e.g., Burdekin and Siklos 1999). The subscript i identifies the country in question. Equation (7), therefore, is estimated as a panel.[18] Since we are also interested in asymmetries that have consequences for central bank credibility we consider separately a version of Equation (7) for what we term low inflation and deflation environments. Low inflation is arbitrarily defined as CPI inflation below 1.5 percent while deflation, of course, obtains when inflation is negative.[19]

Note that credibility is independent of the level of inflation. Credibility is also independent of whether or not the central bank has other targets (e.g., money growth, exchange rate). Recall that, for reasons previously discussed, our interpretation of credibility is focused on inflation performance relative to some (implicit) inflation objective. Of course, the latter may well be indirectly influenced by performance in relation to other objectives or targets the central bank may pursue which are likely also impacted by institutional considerations. We return to this issue in the empirical section where we allow for the possibility that past inflation shocks can also impact credibility.

---

[18] Space limitations prevent the extensive reporting of the sensitivity of our results to sub-sample selection. See, however, Bordo and Siklos (2014) for additional evidence which corroborates the conclusions discussed later. We consider a variety of samples based on historical evidence dating the start and end of monetary policy regimes, the length of time the various central banks in our study have been in existence, as well as limitations due to the availability of certain institutional data (e.g., index of central bank independence or transparency).

[19] Some judgment is involved when selecting the threshold for low inflation. However, even in the modern era where 2 percent inflation targets are common, the choice of a 1.5 percent threshold seems a reasonable one.

80 Michael D. Bordo and Pierre L. Siklos

There exist, potentially, several questions that can be raised about specification (7). First, if there are any lags in obtaining and processing information then it is not clear that credibility will involve the differential between observed inflation and the contemporaneously implied inflation target. While inflation rates are observed fairly quickly it may well take some time to observe the effective inflation target.[20] Of course, to some extent, the appropriateness of Equation (7) is dependent on the sampling frequency being used. At the annual frequency, which is used in this study, the foregoing specification seems sensible.

There is no reason for the relationship between credibility and its determinants to be linear. For example, there may well be a threshold beyond which there is a loss of credibility whereas there might also exist a 'band of indifference' within which there is no appreciable loss of credibility. An alternative, commonly found in the literature on policy rules and the objective function of central banks, is to assume that the loss of credibility rises with the size of the deviation from the inflation goal. A simple specification that meets this requirement is to express credibility as the squared differential between observed and the Fed's inflation goal. Hence, the dependent variable is expressed as in Equation (7).[21] However, as will be seen later, other alternatives are also considered.

As noted previously, it is not always known a priori whether a central bank relies primarily on one instrument over another. Hence, estimates of (3) and (6) may well be implausible. As will be demonstrated later, this means that there is some value in censoring 'outliers' based on estimates of (7).

3.2 Challenges in Measuring Credibility Over a Long Time Span

Obviously, there are a number of complications when dealing with historical data especially when the span of time exceeds over a century of data.

---

[20] In principle observing the inflation target is easier in a conventional inflation targeting (IT) regime. Recall, however, that the implied inflation target, as defined here, need not to be the same as the numerically announced inflation target. All modern IT regimes are sufficiently flexible in that they are permitted to avoid missing the target from time to time as long as departures are publicly explained. Whether these departures separately influence credibility is, of course, another matter.

[21] Indeed, if credibility is only a function of whether the observed and the notional inflation objective are different from each other, so that we set $\boldsymbol{\theta}\mathbf{Z}_{it}=0$, and $\mathbf{u}_{it} \sim N(0, \sigma_{iu}^2)$, then credibility can be interpreted as observed inflation and the effective inflation objective being *attracted* to each other in the sense of being co-integrated. We do not, however, investigate this possibility here.

In no particular order of importance one might include significant changes in the quality, scope and availability of time series useful for the kind of macroeconomic analysis in place. Consequently, the evidence marshaled later is cross-checked with additional narrative evidence about the evolution of central bank credibility over time.

An additional illustration of the desirability of blending the time series econometric approach with what is known from economic history emerges when evidence that a change in the monetary policy regime is found. If such an event is associated with, say, a sudden loss of credibility then our estimates should compare favorably with historical depictions of a policy regime change. Econometrically, these could be identified from structural break tests. Of course, structural breaks come in many forms. For example, it is interesting to examine the connection between financial crises and changes in central bank reputation and credibility. The global financial crisis of 2008–2009 has been said to rest on the ineffectiveness of financial regulation and supervision by the Fed and other regulators, on the Fed keeping policy rates too low to fight the prospect of deflation, and on the inattention of central bankers to the possible link between low inflation and asset price booms leading to financial sector instability.[22]

As the foregoing discussion indicates the LOLR function of central banks is critical. Long dormant as the growth in the financial sector provided adequate liquidity until the loss of confidence in 2007–2008, the re-emergence of the LOLR role of central banks was ushered in by market failures in key financial markets. Finally, the combination of statistical testing and the narrative approach should also reduce the likelihood of identifying too many breaks.[23]

4 Data and Methodological Considerations

Our empirical investigation consists of a time series analysis of ten central banks around the world.[24] They are: Canada, France, Japan, Germany, Italy, Norway, Sweden, Switzerland, the United Kingdom, and the United

---

[22] Bernanke (2013, p. 23) admits as much. "...the Federal Reserve failed [to] ...adequately perform its function as lender of last resort..."

[23] In a sense this was the aim of Perron's (1989) seminal contribution to the literature on the time series properties of macroeconomic data. Hence, not all shifts in time series are permanent (i.e., level or intercept shifts). Indeed, some breaks simply alter the trend in a time series.

[24] Narratives were written for all of these central banks except Japan. The narratives also include the Reserve Bank of Australia and New Zealand.

States. We rely on annual data going back to when central banks were established. Table 3.1 provides information about the year when the central banks in our sample were created as well as a brief description of the proximate reason for their creation. It is interesting to note that, of the central banks surveyed, not all were created to fulfill the LOLR mandate. Indeed, other than to assist with the consequences of war finance, monetary stability is the other major proximate explanation for the creation of many central banks around the world. Since their formation central banks, and central banking more generally, have seen a broadening of their functions while shouldering ever greater responsibilities for economic stabilization.

For several countries in our sample (e.g., Japan, Norway, the United Kingdom, Sweden) we can rely on over a century of data. For other countries (e.g., the United States) annual data span almost a century of data. There is a rich historical narrative history to draw on to identify policy regimes, exchange rate regimes, the dating and identification of crises (e.g., see Bordo, Eichengreen, et. al. 2001, Reinhart and Rogoff 2009, Bordo and Orphanides 2013, Singleton 2011 James 2012, just to name a few). Moreover, thanks to efforts made by several central banks to greatly improve historical data sources (e.g., Norway) there are ample macroeconomic and financial data. In other cases (e.g., Canada and the United States) there is a long tradition of collecting historical time series and making them publicly available. To these sources must be added the sources of data the authors and their collaborators, as well as others, have compiled over the years. Finally, *Global Financial Data* (www.globalfinancialdata.com/index.html) is another source of long-term macroeconomic and financial data, especially for countries in Europe and Asia where publicly available historical time series are more difficult to obtain.

Prior to econometric estimation three preliminary steps are followed. First, either based on statistical testing or using the narrative approach, we must identify policy regimes. Since we estimate a central bank's inflation objective under the assumption that the same policy instrument is used throughout the estimated sample, it is inevitable that we end up adopting a counterfactual approach, at least for a portion of the sample in question. Consequently, one may view this approach as asking whether some monetary regimes are more credible than others over time. In a second step, Equation (2), or its variants, are estimated to obtain the key parameters of interest, namely $\gamma_{2,t}, \gamma_{6,t}$, and $\gamma_{7,t}$. Finally, we can obtain estimates of the implicit inflation target, $\overline{\pi}_t$, for each central bank. Notice that the parameters and the inflation objective are time-varying as are the estimates of the real policy rates. There exist, of course, a variety of techniques to generate such estimates. As discussed in the results section we also combine several proxies to improve the robustness of our estimates.

Credibility and, by implication, reputation might also be determined by governance structures that define the relationship between the central bank and government, including central bank independence. In this case we can resort to data originally constructed by Cukierman (1992), updated by Siklos (2002), with more recent data also available from the IMF (e.g., see Arnone and Romelli 2012, and Arnone et. al. 2009). However, these data are only available since the 1950s.

5 Empirical Evidence

5.1 Panel Estimates

Relying on the notion that the average of forecasts delivers superior performance relative to individual forecasts our estimates of expected inflation are based on mean forecasts generated from three different models.[25] First, we evaluate the three years ahead mean inflation rate, that is, $E_t \pi_{t+1} = (\pi_{t+1} + \pi_{t+2} + \pi_{t+3})/3$. Next, we estimate an AR(1) model for observed inflation and let the data select up as many breaks based on a series of econometrically determined constraints.[26]

Finally, following Stock and Watson (2007) we estimate an integrated moving average model of order 1 (i.e., an IMA (1,1)) in the change in inflation as this has been shown to be a reliable inflation forecasting model

---

[25] Obviously in a study that looks at credibility for roughly a century of data we are unable to construct a data set consisting of private sector, central bank or survey data that covers the entire span of the history of the Fed or, for that matter, any of the other central banks in our study. We also considered a fourth model, namely the difference between the yield on a long-term government bond and a ten year (moving) average of inflation (e.g., see Bordo and Dewald 2001). However, as the results were unaffected we did not include them in computing the final estimate of inflation expectations.

[26] This involves implementing the Bai-Perron (1998) test where the maximum number of breaks we restrict is set according to the rule T/25, where T is the number of available observations. In this manner we restrict the maximum number of structural breaks to, at most, 4 per century of data. The breaks are globally determined and a degrees of freedom adjustment is also applied. The samples are 'trimmed' using a 10 percent rule meaning that breaks will be located in 80 percent of the sample excluding the first and last 10 percent of the sample. It is well-known that these choices in the estimation of breaks will impact their frequency and location. This is another reason for cross-checking the choice of breaks with the historical evidence.

in a wide variety of circumstances. In a twist on the usual approach, however, the IMA (1,1) model is separately estimated for each sub-sample obtained from the analysis of breaks in the inflation process using an AR (1) model. This approach provides us with additional insights into the changing role of permanent versus transitory shocks influencing the behavior of inflation since the time the central banks in this study were founded.[27]

As with the proxy for expected inflation, the output gap measure used later is the mean of several proxies. They are: an H-P filter with the standard smoothing parameter (i.e., 100 in the case of annual data), two other versions of an H-P filter estimated with a twenty year window and changing end-points (one fixing the end-point at the beginning of the sample, the other fixing it at the end of the sample) and, finally, deviations from a linear trend applied to the logarithm of potential real GDP allowing for break-points beginning around the time of the Great Depression, one that starts at the time of the first oil price shock of the 1970s, and a final one at the end of the sample to capture the early stages of the so-called Global Financial Crisis.[28] The difficulties in estimating the output gap have been widely discussed. Admittedly, the task of estimating an indicator of economic slack is made even more difficult when a century of data is examined. However, as pointed out in Goodfriend and King (2013), if the output gap properly measures aggregate economic slack then it should be negatively correlated with future real GDP growth.[29] This seems to be the case for the proxy generated here, at least beginning around the mid-1920s (results not shown).

Next, we consider the institutional determinants of credibility. As discussed previously, our benchmark measure of credibility is evaluated as the squared deviation from a central bank's inflation objective. Other measures were considered, including distinguishing between instances when observed

---

[27] The samples are defined so that the year a structural break is found in the Bai-Perron test is the last observation of each sub-sample. Additional robustness tests were conducted when the sub-samples were short (e.g., less than fifteen years in duration). Stock and Watson (2007) also indicate that permitting some time variation in this kind of model improves the forecasting performance of this model.

[28] The break for the Depression begins in 1930 and is defined as an intercept break, the other two are slope breaks which begin in 1974 (oil price shocks) and 2006 (global financial crisis).

[29] A positive output gap signifies real GDP is above potential or trend real GDP. If the economy stabilizes around the trend over time then observed real GDP should eventually fall towards trend. Hence, a positive output gap should be associated with lower future real GDP growth.

An Historical and Quantitative Exploration 85

inflation is above as opposed to being below the central bank's inflation goal. We then consider some hypothesized institutional determinants at our disposal. Accordingly, Z_{it}, the vector of institutional determinants of credibility is specified as follows:

$$Z_{it} = \left[Gold_{it}, \dot{M}_{it}, loans_{it}, debt_{it}, OIL_{it}, CRISIS_{it}, CBI_{it}, ERR_{it} \right]$$

where *Gold* is a dummy variable that identifies when country i was on the gold standard, $\dot{M}_{it}$ is the growth rate of a broad monetary aggregate, *loans* represents the ratio of bank credit to GDP, and *debt* is the ratio of sovereign debt to GDP. Other controls include a dummy variable for the oil price shocks of the 1970s, CRISIS are dummy variables to capture various financial crises (banking, currency, stock market and/or sovereign debt of the domestic or external varieties), *CBI* is an index of central bank independence while *ERR* is a dummy indicative of the type of exchange rate regime in place.[30]

An obvious concern, among others, is that some of the determinants of credibility may be endogenous, reflecting both the impact of past credibility and, in turn, influencing future central bank credibility. This concern is considerably mitigated under the circumstances either because lags are used, the persistence properties of credibility are recognized, and the economic determinants listed are likely to influence credibility instead of the other way around. Equation (7) is estimated using GLS in a panel setting.[31] Given the wide-ranging inflation experiences of the ten countries in our sample (see later) we apply cross-section weights as well as estimate heteroskedasticity-consistent standard errors.[32]

---

[30] Data are only available since the 1950s for CBI and mid-1940s for ERR.

[31] With the limited number of instruments we also estimate the same specification using GMM. Typically, we use lagged values of the variables shown earlier although a few additional variables (e.g., lagged inflation, money growth) are also candidates. The conclusions discussed later hold when instrumental variable techniques are applied but the results, perhaps unsurprisingly, can be highly sensitive to the choice of instruments. Our metric for whether the instruments are adequate is the Stock-Yogo test (e.g., see Stock and Yogo 2005). Essentially, a linear regression of the variable suspected of being endogenous on the collection of instruments must yield an F-test statistic of at least ten, as a rule of thumb. In practice more formal tests were used to assess the weakness of the chosen instruments.

[32] It is possible that some of the determinants (e.g., the CRISIS dummies) interact with others (e.g., debt to GDP ratio). Therefore, we also consider interaction terms. However, as none of the main conclusions were affected, we omit interaction terms in the specifications presented. See, however, Bordo and Siklos (2014) who include interaction terms.

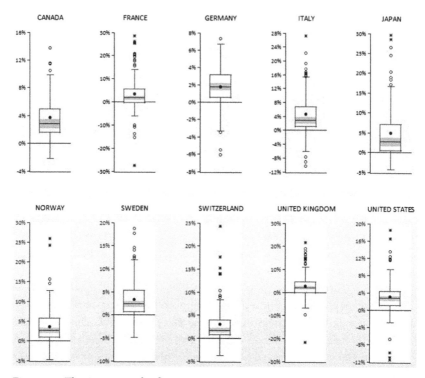

Figure 3.1 The Anatomy of Inflation in Ten Countries

Figure 3.1 provides a summary description of the inflation history of the ten countries in the sample. The boxplots allow easy visualization of the differences between mean and median inflation rates, identification of outliers, and the range of inflationary experiences in each country. One immediately notices that outliers tend to be positive not negative. That is, high inflation rates are far more likely to have been experienced than high rates of deflation. As a result, it is not surprising that median inflation rates (the bar inside the box) are always below mean inflation rates. For the most part, however, the differences between the two are small. Indeed, both mean and median inflation rates through time have tended to be less than 5 percent. The box, which provides an indication of the range of inflation rates between the first and third quartiles (i.e., 75 percent of the distribution of inflation rates), tends to be rather narrow. This suggests that while variations in inflation rates throughout history have been large the vast majority of the range of inflationary experience in the ten countries examined here has been relatively small. Nevertheless, it is notable that negative inflation rates have occurred in all countries during the course of

An Historical and Quantitative Exploration   87

their experience with central banking. We return to this issue later (see Figure 3.3). Even if one excludes outliers from the analysis (see later) double digit inflation rates are not uncommon with the exception of Germany, Switzerland, and the United States.[33] Similarly, Japan does not stand out when it comes to experience with deflation. Indeed, the deflation profile for Japan looks similar to that of Norway's and Sweden's.

Not shown are some data that pertain to the performance of the inflation expectations data compared to observed inflation. We find that the higher is observed inflation the potential for forecast errors also rises. Hence, as one would expect, it is more difficult to forecast high inflation rates than when inflation is low. Consequently, one expects that it is relatively easier to anchor low inflation rates. To the extent that these expectations errors contribute to changing credibility the data suggest considerable scope for central bank credibility to change over time.[34]

Figure 3.2 plots instances when inflation rates are low or negative. Recent events make clear that central bankers are just as concerned with low positive inflation rates as they are about the prospect of deflation. While the choice of a threshold between low and some acceptable inflation rate is admittedly *ad hoc* we have chosen to define low inflation as observed inflation rates below 1.5 percent. Deflations tend to be observed before World War II and this includes Japan. Indeed, by historical standards the recent two decades or so encounter with deflation is rather mild relative to the pre–World War II experience. Indeed, negative inflation rates, though not unheard after 1950, are dwarfed by examples from before World War II, most notably when the gold standard was operational. However, for the United States, where we have independent evidence of recessions versus expansions (i.e., the NBER business cycle chronology), the stylized facts do not appear to suggest that low inflation or deflation are strongly correlated with recessions. Canada is another country where we also have an NBER style recession indicator (Cross and Bergevin 2012). Once again, there is no obvious visual relationship between low inflation, deflation, and recessions.

Next, we move on to an analysis of the determinants of credibility based on estimates of Equation (7). The results are summarized in Table 3.2 as well as in Figures 3.3 and 3.4. To economize on space, Table 3.2 shows the

---

[33] Note that data for Germany excludes certain periods because the data are incomplete or, in the case of Germany's experience with hyperinflation, would not provide any useful insights about credibility under such extreme conditions.

[34] Recall that the expectations proxy is partially based on estimates of structural breaks in inflation performance. The Appendix provides a list of the estimated break-point dates.

88   Michael D. Bordo and Pierre L. Siklos

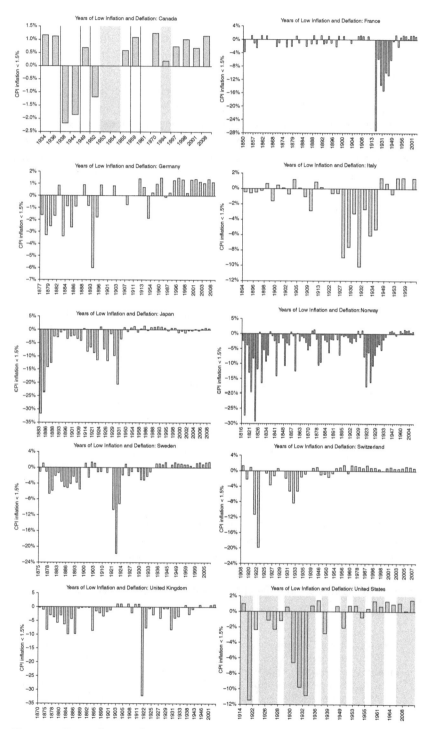

Figure 3.2 Years of Low Inflation and Deflation

Table 3.2 *Panel regression estimates of the determinants of credibility*
A. Interest Rate Instrument

	1871–2008		1950–2008		1871–2008 T		1950–2008 T		1871–2008 +ve		1871–2008 −ve		1950-2008 +ve		1950–2008 −ve	
Ind. Variables	Coeff.	s.e.	Coeff.	s.e.	Coeff.	s.e.	Coeff.	s.e.	Coeff.	s.e.	Coeff.	s.e.	Coeff.	s.e.	Coeff.	s.e.
Gold standard	−57.57†	28.04	NA	NA	−5.14‡	5.69	NA	NA	−3.67†	1.55	−2.40‡	1.49	NA	NA	NA	NA
Money growth	2.71	2.73	5.47	6.27	0.57‡	0.32	0.18	0.22	0.20*	0.06	0.18*	0.06	0.07	0.06	−0.04	0.05
Loans to GDP ratio	−1.16	1.74	−0.58	1.32	−0.19	0.27	−0.36	0.23	0.02	0.02	0.06*	0.02	0.06*	0.02	0.08*	0.02
Debt to GDP ratio	−0.52	0.71	0.56	0.79	−0.00	0.08	−0.05	0.12	−0.02	0.02	−0.02	0.01	−0.07*	0.01	−0.07*	0.02
Equity returns	0.60	0.56	0.79	0.69	−0.07	0.07	−0.09	0.08	−0.01	0.01	−0.01	0.01	−0.01	0.01	−0.00	0.01
Oil price shocks	35.27	71.30	−3.99	9.20	0.33	5.23	−0.00	0.76	2.22†	0.94	0.96	1.29	4.68*	0.97	3.58†	1.61
Financial crises	30.31†	16.69	52.13‡	32.05	0.40	1.33	1.17	1.57	0.55‡	0.31	0.29	0.32	0.44	0.46	0.10	0.34
Central bank independence	NA	NA	−18.75	14.03	NA	NA	−1.01†	0.52†	NA	NA	NA	NA	−2.71	1.98	−1.29*	1.93
Exchange rate regime	NA	NA	11.79†	5.50	NA	NA	1.47	0.69	NA	NA	NA	NA	−0.33	0.08*	−0.39	0.12
Summary statistics																
Adjusted R^2	0.10		0.11		0.11		0.48		0.43		0.44		0.49		0.46	
F-statistic	4.54		3.46		3.46		14.28		36.69		39.39		30.06		25.37	
p-value	0.00		0.00		0.00		0.00		0.00		0.00		0.00		0.00	

(a)

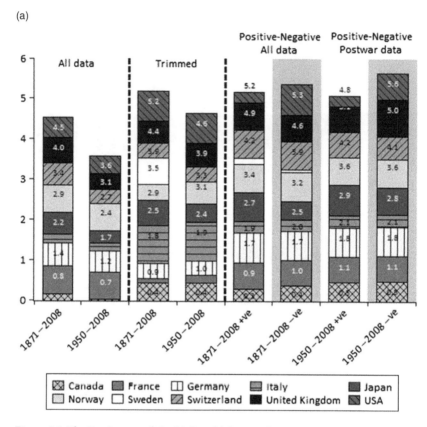

Figure 3.3 The Persistence of Credibility. (a) Interest Rate Instrument, (b) Money Growth Instrument, and (c) Exchange Rate Instrument.

estimated panel coefficients for the vector $\mathbf{Z}_{it}$ described earlier. Although fixed effects were added in virtually every case (test statistics for the redundancy of fixed effects are also provided) these are not shown. Estimates are shown for two samples and four cases. The choice of samples is partially dictated by data availability, as in the indicators of central bank independence and exchange rate regime type, as well as the earlier observation that the behavior of inflation rates before World War II appears different from the period since that conflict ended.

The three cases considered are also meant to control for the potential impact that outliers might have on the results. For example, if credibility is particularly vulnerable when inflation rates are very large, and such events are also associated with financial crises, then trimming the data set to exclude outliers should provide additional insights into the factors that

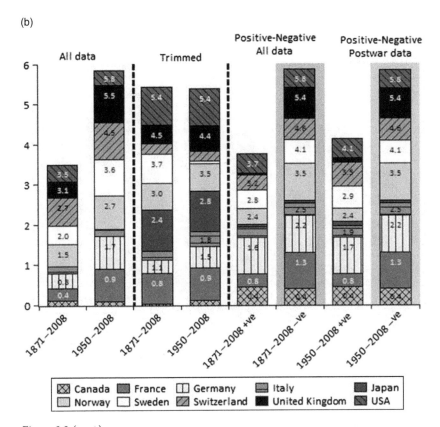

Figure 3.3 (cont.)

drive credibility. Consequently, the trimmed estimates exclude deflations that exceed -5 percent as well as inflation rates of more than 15 percent.[35] Next, we consider a variant of Equation (7) where deviations from the central bank's implicit inflation objective are not squared but, instead, we separately examine positive versus negative deviations from the model-based inflation targets used to proxy the time-varying inflation objective. Finally, since our definition of credibility is independent of the level of inflation, we also consider a version of Equation (7) augmented with a variable which asks whether credibility is affected by the interaction of inflation expectations surprises (i.e., the difference between observed and expected inflation – not the central bank's inflation objective) and a

---

[35] The Appendix provides information about the impact on sample size from the exclusion of 'outliers'.

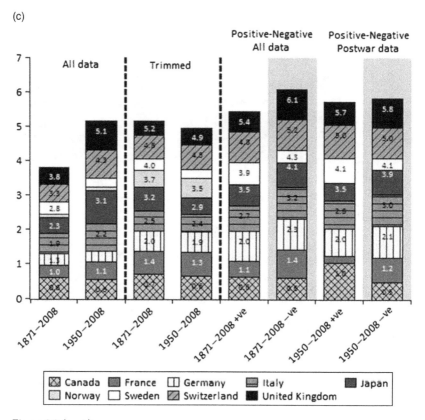

Figure 3.3 (cont.)

dummy variable that identifies positive inflation shocks (i.e., instances where the change in observed inflation is positive). A statistically significant response would indicate yet another avenue through which there are asymmetric effects on credibility. In particular, we can determine whether positive inflation shocks, combined with the size of the forecast error, contribute an additional and, presumably, negative effect on credibility.

Table 3.2 shows the coefficient estimates for the variables in $\mathbf{Z}_{it}$ as well as a few summary statistics while Figure 3.3 graphically displays the estimates of the persistence of credibility in the ten countries considered (i.e., the coefficient φ_i). We find that if an interest rate instrument is used the gold standard period reliably improves central bank credibility since the negative sign suggests that the squared gap between observed and goal inflation becomes smaller. Perhaps more interesting is the finding that when a financial crisis is present this reduces credibility with the effect significantly

An Historical and Quantitative Exploration 93

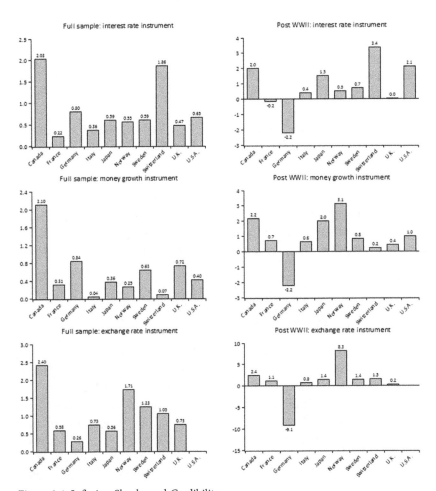

Figure 3.4 Inflation Shocks and Credibility

larger in the postwar era. Notice, however, that the effect disappears when we trim the distribution of inflation rates as defined earlier. It appears, therefore, that a financial crisis together with a bad inflation outcome contributes to significantly erode central bank credibility.[36] Otherwise, there is no separate statistically significant impact of financial crises on central bank credibility. There is also some evidence that oil price shocks

---

[36] As previously noted, we have several proxies for financial crises depending on their source. Although we experimented with each measure separately the most reliable results are obtained when financial crises are aggregated. Hence, in what follows, the financial crisis dummy refers to the sum of all types of financial crises defined earlier.

negatively impact credibility. This is not surprising since, if such events reflect a rise in observed inflation even when the central bank's inflation objective remains unchanged.[37] A reading of the international response to the oil prices shocks of the 1970s (see Bordo and Orphanides 2013) seems consistent with the view of a loss of credibility as a result of the oil shock of the 1970s.

Finally, if we examine the determinants of credibility since the 1950s, we find that central bank independence does indeed improve credibility. However, this result only obtains when we rely on the trimmed data. Consequently, central bank independence does not help when there are episodes of unusually high inflation rates. There is also a little bit of evidence that the impact of autonomy is asymmetric with the effect more pronounced when inflation is below the monetary authority's implicit inflation objective than when observed inflation is relatively higher than the goal set by the central banks.

Turning to the case of a money supply target we find more muted evidence of the credibility-inducing benefits of the gold standard. In addition, the impact of the determinants in Z_{it} appears to be relatively more asymmetric in nature when the money supply is targeted than when an interest rate instrument is assumed. For example, we find that rises in private sector credit and government debt to GDP ratios reduce credibility but only when we consider episodes where inflation is below the central bank's implicit inflation objective. Similarly, central bank independence improves credibility but, interestingly, the impact is relatively larger when inflation exceeds the central bank's goal than vice-versa. Finally, in contrast with the case where an interest rate instrument is used, financial crises appear to only weakly impact credibility and again only when inflation is above target.

Part C of Table 3.2 considers the case of the exchange rate instrument. The gold standard once again is a device that enhances central bank credibility while central bank independence is also seen to consistently raise credibility. Oil price shocks also appear to have a negative effect on credibility as do financial crises. Unlike the other two instruments considered, rising equity returns help raise central bank credibility. Somewhat counterintuitively there is solid evidence that higher government debt to GDP ratios improve credibility. Whether this reflects an expectation that central banks will not allow such a development to raise their inflation

---

[37] We also experimented with a time series of oil prices going back to the mid-nineteenth century but this did not improve the results.

objective we cannot say. Nevertheless, it is worth adding that the coefficients are economically small and are easily dwarfed, for example, by the impact of central bank independence on credibility.

Figure 3.3 stacks the coefficient estimates of the lagged dependent variable in (7) which serves as an indicator of credibility persistence. Although there is no sign or size restriction on the parameter of interest, if the maximum value in absolute terms is close to one while the minimum value is zero then the vertical axis is defined such that it ranges between zero and ten. To identify the coefficient estimate for each country one simply needs to subtract a particular value shown in the figure less its value in the bar immediately below.[38] Not surprisingly, there is less persistence when all data are considered than when we trim the inflation data to exclude large inflation and deflation rates. Nevertheless, cross-country differences are most noticeable for the full sample than when the postwar data are separately considered. Next, it appears that persistence is sensitive according to whether we proxy credibility as in Equation (7) or by separately examining positive versus negative values of the difference between inflation and the central bank's objective for inflation. Also, the total amount of persistence is roughly the same regardless whether the chosen instrument of monetary policy is an interest rate, a growth rate in the money supply or the exchange rate. To be sure, there are noticeable cross-country differences. These are seen by looking at the height of each bar in Figure 3.3. Nevertheless, the most robust estimates are ones obtained when the data are trimmed. Overall then, to obtain a clear picture of the determinants of credibility it is advisable to trim the data. The only caveat is that if one seeks confirmation that the interaction of financial crises with historically high inflation or deflation rates reduces credibility then it is necessary to use all the available data at our disposal (see Table 3.2).

Finally, Figure 3.4 uses a bar chart to display the coefficient indicating how the interaction of a positive inflation shock (i.e., a dummy equal to one when the change of inflation is positive) and forecast errors impact central bank credibility.[39] With the exception of Germany, positive shocks do indeed reduce credibility defined as in Equation (7). Note, however, that

---

[38] For example, in part A of the Figure, the top of the first bar indicates 4.5, the second 4.0. Hence, the estimate of credibility persistence for the Fed for the full sample (1914–2008 in the Fed's case) is 4.5-4.0=0.5.

[39] Complete estimates are relegated to the Appendix. Note that the addition of this variable did not alter the conclusions based on Table 3.2. We also considered other variants such as adding the level of inflation, and the change in observed inflation. Generally speaking, the conclusions are similar to the ones described later.

the credibility impact is sensitive not only to the chosen sample but to the chosen monetary policy instrument. For example, in Switzerland's case, the reduction in credibility following an inflation shock is considerably larger when an interest rate instrument is assumed. In the case of Norway, the impact on credibility is much larger when an exchange rate instrument is assumed. As far as Germany is concerned one can only assume that positive inflation shocks improve credibility if the public is convinced that the central bank will react appropriately to prevent persistent rises in inflation. Of course, we have no way of knowing whether this is the only hypothesis consistent with the data other than to rely on the historical experience of the DBB. Even if the estimates coefficients are relatively small compared to the ones found statistically significant in Table 3.2 there is some evidence that the level of inflation, particularly when it is rising, does have an independent influence on central bank credibility.

5.2 Select Individual Country Evidence

Ideally, we would have liked to discuss every country in the sample but space limitations prevent us from doing so. We note, however, that in addition to the evidence presented, the case of Japan suggests that the patterns of the gain or loss of credibility mirrors the experience of most of the other countries considered later, since the early to mid-1990s, there has been a persistent loss of credibility for the Bank of Japan. Indeed, when an interest rate instrument is assumed to be used to conduct monetary policy there is evidence of rising credibility losses until the end of the sample (2008). Rolling estimates point in the same direction though the most notable negative shock to credibility takes place in the early 1990s. Nevertheless, large credibility losses have taken place earlier in the Bank of Japan's history such as shortly after the end of World War II and during the brief but significant surge in the 1970s especially following the first oil shock of that decade.

United States

We begin with a description of some broad stylized facts. Figure 3.5(a) plots observed CPI inflation since the creation of the Fed together with our estimate of expected inflation. In this manner we identified four breaks: in 1924, 1933, 1973, and 1982. An *ex post* historical analysis suggests that the location of these breaks appear sensible. The first break occurs after the deflation of the early 1920s and when the Fed became more activist;

An Historical and Quantitative Exploration

(a)

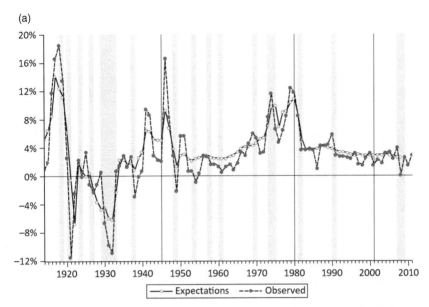

Figure 3.5(a) Inflation and Expected Inflation in the United States since the Fed's Creation

(b)

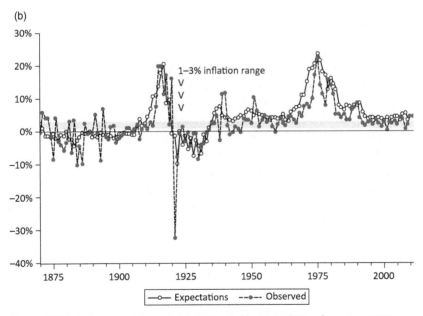

Figure 3.5(b) Inflation and Expected Inflation in the United Kingdom since 1870

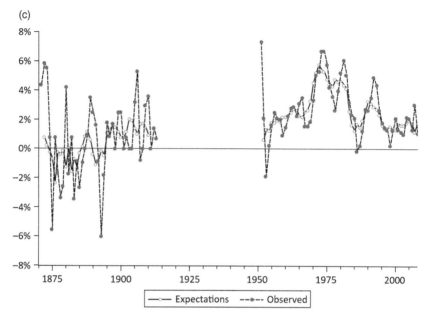

Figure 3.5(c) Inflation and Expected Inflation in Germany since 1871

the second break takes place when the monetary authorities implemented a more comprehensive response to the Great Depression. The break in 1973 is, of course, associated with the first oil price shock while the break in 1982 can be explained by the Volcker disinflation policy.

One hopes, of course, that inflation expectations track observed inflation. Nevertheless, there are gaps that occasionally persist over several years. This is particularly noticeable during the period of the Great Inflation (also see Bordo and Orphanides 2013) of the 1960s and 1970s. Another observation, also commonly encountered in the more recent literature on the behavior of inflation forecasts, is that inflation is more volatile than its expectation. As a result, expectation errors are short-lived but typically far greater, for example, before World War II than say during the period of the Great Moderation from the mid- 1980s until the end of the available sample.

Figure 3.6(a) indicates the years when the United States faced an environment of low inflation and deflation. Approximately a quarter of the Fed's existence is associated with low or negative inflation with episodes of low inflation a post–World War II phenomenon while deflation is more typical of the pre-1940s macroeconomic experience. Moreover, based on

An Historical and Quantitative Exploration

(a)

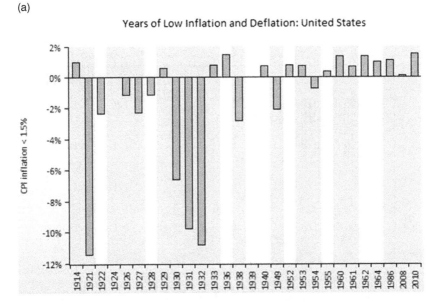

Figure 3.6(a) Low and Deflationary Periods in the United States since the Fed's Creation

(b)

Figure 3.6(b) Low and Deflationary Periods in the United Kingdom

(c)

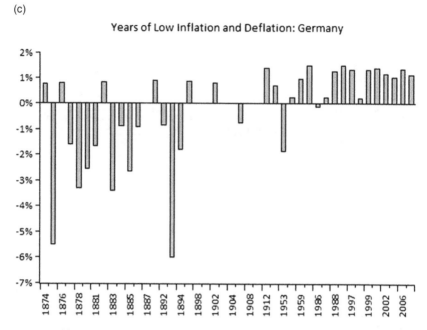

Figure 3.6(c) Low and Deflationary Periods in Germany

the NBER chronology, no one to one association between low inflation or deflation and recessions is found. This view is heavily skewed by the events of the Great Depression.

Figures 3.7(a)(i) and (ii) plot two different versions of our measure of central bank credibility (i.e., the left hand side of Equation (7)). The recursive estimates are based on Equation (3) estimates of $\pi_t - \bar{\pi}_t$. Since the weight of the last observation declines under the recursive scheme it is conceivable that our proxy for central bank credibility will too readily fluctuate with observed inflation as we approach the end of the available sample. Therefore, we also consider a measure of credibility based on rolling estimates of $\bar{\pi}_t$ using a twenty year window for the calculations. The dotted lines in Figure 3.7 plot the recursive estimates while the vertical bars represent the rolling estimates.

When the instrument of monetary policy is assumed to be an interest rate we observe that our measure of credibility, no matter how it is estimated, is fairly close to zero during much of the Fed's history. This indicates that observed inflation and the Fed's inflation goal are fairly closely matched. Nevertheless, there are notable exceptions to this rule. The first takes place during the second half of the 1930s. This is the period when the Fed was

(a)

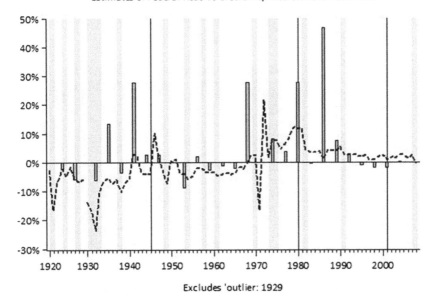

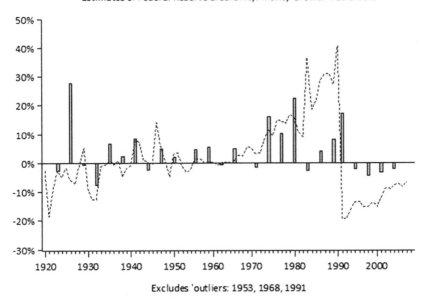

Figure 3.7(a) The Fed's Credibility Over Time: Recursive and Rolling Estimates

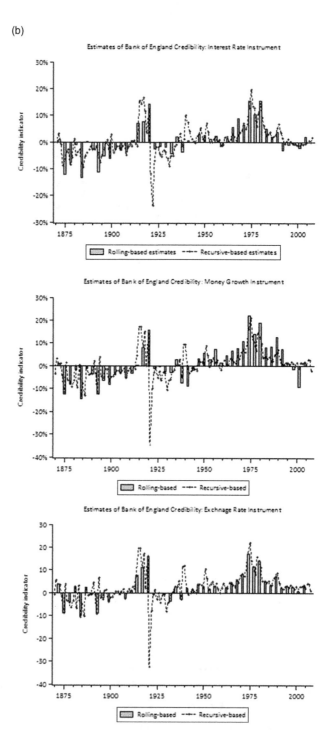

Figure 3.7(b) The Bank of England's Credibility Over Time: Recursive and Rolling Estimates

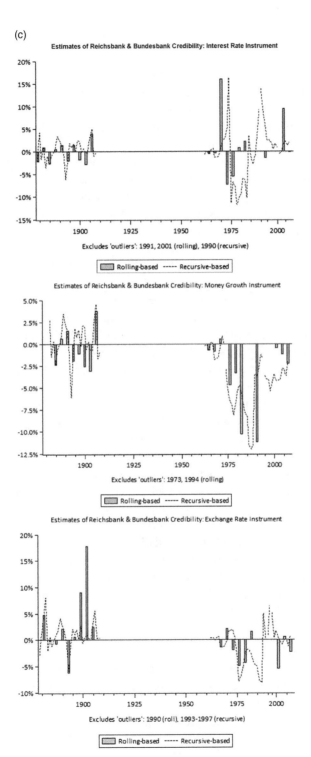

Figure 3.7(c) The Reichsbank's and the Bundesbank's Credibility Over Time: Recursive and Rolling Estimates

104   *Michael D. Bordo and Pierre L. Siklos*

attempting a return to a more 'normal' monetary policy following the Great Depression. Combined with an overly restrictive fiscal policy, in hindsight, these events combined to negatively impact the Fed's credibility. The next substantial period of reduced Fed credibility takes place during the second half of the 1960s, that is, when, again looking back, the Fed lost the battle against inflation with the consequent loss of reputation under Arthur Burns who went on to lament the high inflation in *The Anguish of Central Banking* (1979). The final episode of credibility loss takes place during the early 1980s. This period overlaps, of course, with the wrenching disinflation of the early 1980s. As Volcker himself later noted (see Silber 2012), the Fed had little credibility at the time of the temporary switch from interest rate to reserves targeting. Rising credibility would come later and benefit Volcker's successors, Alan Greenspan and Ben Bernanke. The Great Moderation is seen, therefore, as a period of high Fed credibility.

The story is much the same when we assume the Fed operates with a money growth instrument. The precise years when the Fed loses credibility in a significant way do not, of course, exactly match those of the interest rate instrument case but they come close. One interesting departure of sorts is that the money growth instrument case reveals a significant loss of credibility during the mid-1920s no doubt the culmination of the residual effects of the deflation of the early 1920s and perhaps even reflects attempts by the Congress, through the so-called Stabilization Bills, to require the Fed to target the price level rather than adhere strictly to the gold standard (e.g., see Siklos 2002). It is also difficult to argue that the loss of credibility shown in the late 1980s and early 1990s can be explained by residual effects of the Volcker era. The fed funds rate was, by then, the principal instrument of policy. What the result suggests then is that, had a money growth instrument been used, observed inflation would have been permitted to rise substantially above the Fed's inflation goal. Once again, a retrospective analysis suggests that the confluence of two events, namely the severe recession of the early 1990s may well have also contributed to reducing the Fed's credibility under the circumstances.

United Kingdom

Data limitations prevent us from examining the credibility record of the Bank of England since its inception.[40] As is the case for most of the

---

[40] We are, however, able to conduct a variety of tests on inflation for the full history of the Bank. Unless otherwise stated our conclusions for the post-1870s period are unchanged. Space limitations prevent a fuller discussion here.

advanced economies in our dataset, the United Kingdom experiences relatively volatile inflation prior to World War II. The post–World War II period is notable for a steady rise in inflation which reaches 20 percent by the early 1970s in part as a result of the first oil price shocks as well as other macroeconomic problems that were accumulating prior to the Thatcher years. Thereafter there is a steady fall in inflation with inflation relatively low and stable especially once the inflation targeting regime is in place. Our estimates of expected inflation appear to be unable to capture the volatile movements of prices prior to World War II whereas, in the postwar period, expected inflation appears to be persistently above observed inflation. These observations will impact our estimates of the Bank of England's credibility. Not shown in Figure 3.5(a) are the five estimated breaks in the inflation process. These were found in 1908, 1922, 1936, 1963, and 1977. Some of the breaks are associated with financial stresses related to currency crises, or the sharp deflation in the aftermath of World War I while the most recent breaks are associated with the impact of macroeconomic policies in the United Kingdom as well as the oil price shocks.

Figure 3.6(b) plots years of low inflation and deflation in the United Kingdom. Although most of the episodes we identify take place before World War II there are a few years of low inflation in the postwar era. It is also notable that deflationary episodes are persistent particularly during the years before 1897 when deflationary shocks to the global gold market prevailed.

Finally, Figure 3.7(b) displays our estimates of credibility for each one of the three instruments. The results across the various instruments are broadly comparable. Nevertheless, it is interesting to note that while observed inflation is often lower than the Bank of England's inflation objective, as derived from our estimated models, the reverse is true beginning in the 1940s. Moreover, whereas there is little persistence in the estimates of credibility before the 1930s credibility losses are persistent and rise throughout much of the post–World War II era, that is, until the end of the sample when the Bank of England's inflation objective and observed inflation become closely matched. It is tempting, but cannot be proven, that the adoption of inflation targets contributes to this result. Finally, rolling-based estimates support the inferences based on the recursive estimates.

Germany
Figure 3.5(c) plots inflation and our proxy for expected inflation for Germany. Note that the gap is dictated by gaps in the data due to the two

World Wars as well as the deliberate omission of the hyperinflation of the early 1920s. It is also worth bearing in mind that inflation is likely to be affected, as is the credibility of the DBB by the various phases towards the adoption of the euro in 1999.[41] Although inflation is volatile in the pre-1910 era, at least compared with inflation in the post–World War II period, the record of low German inflation is clearly visible. As a result, and paralleling the results for the other cases examined in this paper, our proxy for expected inflation does a poorer job of matching observed inflation when inflation is volatile than when volatility is low. A time series analysis of breaks in inflation dates these as follows: 1896, 1914, 1970, and 1984. One of the breaks is clearly associated with the start of World War I and is found at the end of the first sample (i.e., before the gap in the data), the 1896 break occurs at the inflexion point between gold deflation and inflation. The 1970 break can be explained by the collapse of the Bretton Woods System. The 1984 break does not appear to be directly associated with economic events. Also of interest is that the usual finding of oil price shocks influencing the behavior of inflation is not evident in the German data.

Figure 3.6(c) shows the years when inflation was low or deflation emerged. Actual periods of deflation generally take place in the late nineteenth century associated with the vagaries of the gold standard and there is considerable persistence in deflation during this period. At the other end of the sample, Germany unlike many other economies examined in this paper experiences persistently low inflation right up to and after the adoption of the euro. Indeed, Germany's record of low and stable inflation is quite noticeable in the Figure.

Finally, Figure 3.7(c) displays our estimates of credibility in Germany. In spite of the deflation that persists throughout the late nineteenth century, differences between the Reichsbank's inflation objective and observed inflation are small and do not persist. With few exceptions this result holds regardless of the instrument assumed to be used. Note, however, that there are more volatile changes in credibility when an exchange rate instrument is assumed. Indeed, as World War I approaches there are sharp differences between inflation and the central bank's objective especially when the rolling estimates are considered.

Turning to the post–World War II era, one's assumption about the instrument of monetary policy used has considerable impact on our

---

[41] The estimates presented in the Figures for Germany rely on separate pre and post gap models of German inflation. We also estimated credibility for the 'full' sample but our conclusions were largely unaffected.

interpretation of DBB credibility. Hence, when an interest rate instrument is operative, there are fairly large swings in credibility especially around the time of the two oil price shocks. In contrast, when a money growth instrument is employed, the type of instrument actually used by the central bank, observed inflation is found to be considerably lower than the Bundesbank's inflation objective particularly around the time of German reunification (i.e., 1989). It is conceivable then that while the public may have expected inflation to rise the German central bank held its inflation 'target'. This is consistent with the narrative in Beyer et. al. (2013). By the beginning of the first decade of the 2000s observed and targeted inflation closely match each other.

6 Conclusions

This paper seeks to determine how central bank credibility and reputation have changed over time in a cross-section of central banks around the world. Theory links credibility with how well the central bank is able to anchor inflation expectations relative to some implicit target over time that is allowed to change over time. In addition, there are institutional factors that also impact a central bank's credibility.

We find credibility changes over time are frequent and can be significant. Second, the frequency with which the world economy experiences economic and financial crises, institutional factors (i.e., the quality of governance) plays an important role in preventing a loss of credibility. Third, institutional factors affect credibility. For example, the gold standard improves credibility as does central bank independence. Finally, credibility is significantly affected according to whether the shock can be associated with policy errors. Bernanke (2013, p. 23), for example, has acknowledged that such errors can, for example, an important role in explaining the severity of the most recent 'global' financial crisis.

Our interest in credibility in central banking goes beyond the analysis of the experience of individual countries. Indeed, as is clear, for example, from the spread of inflation targeting as the monetary policy regime of choice in several countries beginning in the 1990s, or the linking of economies through pegged or managed exchange rate regimes, spillover effects can also play a role. Alternatively, changes in central bank credibility may contain an element of contagion. For example, a policy regime change in a core economy (e.g., the United States) may influence economic outcomes elsewhere. Consequently, there is scope for credibility effects to be imported from or exported to other economies over time. Changes in

108 *Michael D. Bordo and Pierre L. Siklos*

policy regimes may also occur via a simple demonstration effect not associated with any fundamental economic factors but simply because they appear to work elsewhere. One example often used to underscore this point is the Volcker era at the Fed (e.g., see Silber 2012). Another is the dominant position of the Bank of England in the classical gold standard (Bordo 1981). Empirically, it is certainly of interest to explore these issues. However, space constraints prevent us from directly addressing the relevant implications. This is left for future research.

References

Ahamed, L. (2009), *Lords of Finance* (New York: The Penguin Press).

Altug, S., and F. Canova (2013), "Do Institutions and Culture Matter for Business Cycles?", Working Paper, European University Institute, March.

Arnone, M., and D. Romelli (2012), "Dynamic Central Bank Independence Indices and Inflation Rates: A New Empirical Explanation", Paolo Baffi Centre Research Paper No. 2012-118.

Arnone, M., B. Laurens, S. Segolato, and J-F. Sommer (2009), "Central Bank Autonomy: Lessons from Global Trends", *IMF Staff Papers* 56 (2):263–296.

Bai, J., and P. Perron (1998), "Estimating and Testing Linear Models with Multiple Structural Changes", *Econometrica* 66 (January): 47–78.

Ball, L. (1994), "What Determines the Sacrifice Ratio?" in N.G. Mankiw (Ed.), *Monetary Policy* (Chicago: University of Chicago Press), pp. 155–182.

 (1999), "Policy Rules for Open Economies" in J. Taylor (Ed.), *Monetary Policy Rules* (Chicago: University of Chicago Press), pp. 127–144.

Ball, L. and N. Sheridan (2005), "Does Inflation Targeting Matter?" in B. Bernanke and M. Woodford (Eds.), *The Inflation Targeting Debate* (Chicago: University of Chicago Press), pp. 249–276.

Ball, L., D. Leigh, and P. Loungani (2013), "Okun's Law: Fit at Fifty?", NBER Working Paper 18688, January.

Bernanke, B. (2013), *The Federal Reserve and the Financial Crisis* (Princeton, N.J.: Princeton University Press).

Beyer, A., V. Gaspar, C. Gerbeding, and O. Issing (2013), "Opting Out of the Great Inflation: German Monetary Policy After the Break Down of Bretton Woods" in M.D. Bordo and A. Orphanides (Eds.), *The Great Inflation: The Modern Rebirth of Central Banking* (Chicago: University of Chicago Press).

Blinder, A. S. (1999), *Central Banking in Theory and Practice* (Cambridge, Mass.: The MIT Press).

Blinder, A., and J. Rudd (2013), "The Supply-Shock Explanation of the Great Stagflation Revisited" in M.D. Bordo and A. Orphanides (Eds.), *The Great Inflation: The Modern Rebirth of Central Banking* (Chicago: University of Chicago Press).

Bordo, M.D. (1981), The Classical Gold Standard: Some Lessons For Today" *Federal Reserve Bank of St. Louis Review*.

Bordo, M.D., and W. Dewald (2001), "Bond Market Inflation Expectations in Industrial Countries: Historical Comparisons, NBER Working Paper 8582, November.

Bordo, M.D., and J. Haubrich (2010), "Credit Crises, Money and Contractions: An Historical View", *Journal of Monetary Economics* 57: 1–18.

Bordo, M.D., and F. Kydland (1995), "The Gold Standard as a Rule: An Essay in Exploration", *Explorations in Economic History* 32: 422–464.

Bordo, M.D., and R. MacDonald (2012), *Credibility and the International Monetary Regime* (New York: Cambridge University Press).

Bordo, M.D., and A. Orphanides (2013), *The Great Inflation: The Modern Rebirth of Central Banking* (Chicago: University of Chicago Press).

Bordo, M.D., and A.J. Schwartz (1996), "The Operation of the Specie Standard: Evidence for Core and Peripheral Countries, 1880–1990" in B. Eichengreen and J. Braga de Macedo (Eds.), *Historical Perspectives in the Gold Standard: Portugal and the World* (London: Routledge), pp. 11–83.

Bordo, M.D., and P.L. Siklos (2014), "Central Bank Credibility, Reputation and Inflation Targeting in Historical Perspective," NBER Working Paper 20693, November.

Bordo M.D., B. Eichengreen, D. Klingebiel, and M. Soledad Martinez –Peria (2001), "Is the Crisis Problem Growing More Severe?", *Economic Policy*. April, 53–82

Borio, C. (2013), "Rethinking Potential Output: Embedding Information About the Financial Cycle", BIS Working Paper 404, February.

Borio, C., and A.J. Filardo (2004), "Looking Back at the International Deflation Record", *North American Journal of Economics and Finance* 15 (December): 287–311.

Burdekin, R.C.K., and P.L. Siklos (1999), "Exchange Rate Regimes and Shifts in Inflation Persistence: Does Nothing Else Matter?", *Journal of Money, Credit and Banking*, Vol. 31, May: 234–247.

Eds. (2004a), *Deflation: Current and Historical Perspectives* (Cambridge: Cambridge University Press).

(2004b), "Fears of Deflation and the Role of Monetary Policy: Some Lessons and an Overview" in R.C.K. Burdekin and P.L. Siklos (Eds.), *Deflation: Current and Historical Perspectives* (Cambridge: Cambridge University Press), pp. 1–27.

Brunner, K. (1983), "The Pragmatic and Intellectual Tradition of Monetary Policy-making" in Karl Brunner, (Ed.), *Lessons of Monetary Experiences from the 1970s* (Berlin: Springer), pp. 97–141.

Burns, A. (1979), The Anguish of Central Banking, Per Jacobsson Lecture, September.

Cargill, T. (2013), "A Critical Assessment of Measures of Central Bank Independence", *Economic Inquiry* 51 (January): 260–272.

Carney, M. (2013), "Monetary Policy after the Fall", Eric J. Hanson Memorial Lecture, University of Alberta, 1 May, www.bankofcanada.ca/2013/05/monetary-policy-after-the-fall/.

Chung, H., J-P. Laforte, D. Reifschneider, and J. Williams (2012), "Have We Under-estimated the Likelihood and Severity of Zero Lower Bound Events?", *Journal of Money, Credit and Banking* 44 (February): 47–82.

Cross, P., and P. Bergevin (2012), "Turning Points in Business Cycles in Canada Since 1926", C.D. Howe Commentary No. 366, October.

Crow, J. (2002), *Making Money* (Toronto: John Wiley & Sons).

Cukierman, A. (1986), "Central Bank Behavior and Credibility: Some Recent Theoretical Developments", *Review* of the Federal Reserve Bank of St. Louis (May): 5–17.

(1992), *Central Bank Strategy, Credibility and Independence: Theory and Evidence* (Cambridge, Mass.: MIT Press).

De Long, B. (1997), "America's Peacetime Inflation: the 1970s" in C.D. Romer and D.H. Romer (Eds.), *Reducing Inflation: Motivation and Strategy* (Chicago: University of Chicago Press).

Dehay, E., and N. Levy (2000), "L'independenance des banques centrales pendant l'entre-deux guerres et ses effects sur l'inflation et la croissance", Working Paper, Universite de Paris X-Nanterre.

Dincer, N. and B. Eichengreen (2007), "Central Bank Transparency: Where, Why, and With What Effects?", NBER Working Paper 13003, March, www.nber.org/papers/w13003

Dreher, A., J.E. Sturm, and J. de Haan (2008), "Does High Inflation Cause Central Bankers to Lose Their Job? Evidence Based on a New Data Set", *European Journal of Political Economy* 24 (December): 778–787.

Dupasquier, C., A. Guay, and P. St-Amant (1999), "A Survey of Alternative Methodologies for Estimating Potential Output and the Ouput Gap", *Journal of Macroeconomics* 21 (Summer): 577–595.

Eijffinger, S., and J. De Haan (1996), The Political-Economy of Central Bank Independence", Special Papers in International Economics, Princeton University, no. 19, May.

Eggertsson, G., and M. Woodford (2003), "The Zero Bound on Interest Rates and Optimal Monetary Policy", *Brookings Papers on Economic Activity* 34: 139–211.

Eichengreen, B. (1997), "The Gold Standard Since Alec Ford" in B. Eichengreen and M. Flandreau (Eds.), *The Gold Standard in Theory and Practice.* Second Edition. (London: Routledge).

Fellner, W. (1976), *Towards a Reconstruction of Macroeconomics: Problems of Theory and Policy* (Washington, D.C.: American Enterprise Institute).

Ferguson, N., and M. Schularik (2008), "The 'Thin Film of Gold': Monetary Policy Rules and Policy Credibility in Developing Countries", NBER Working Paper 13918, April.

Fortin, P. (1996), "The Great Canadian Slump", *Canadian Journal of Economics* 29 (November): 761–787.

Freedman, C. and T. Macklem (1998), "A Comment on the 'The Great Canadian Slump'", *Canadian Journal of Economics* 31 (August): 646–665.

Friedman, M. (1968), "The Role of Monetary Policy", *American Economic Review* 58 (March): 1–17.

Goodfriend, M. (1986), "Monetary Mystique: Secrecy and Central Banking", *Journal of Monetary Economics* 17 (January): 63–92.

Goodfriend, M., and R. King (2013), "The Great Inflation Drift" in M.D. Bordo and A. Orhanides (Eds), *The Great Inflation: The Modern Rebirth of Central Banking* (Chicago: University of Chicago Press).

Goodhart, C.A.E. (1999), "Central Bankers and Uncertainty", Bank of England *Quarterly Bulletin* (February): 102–121.

Greenspan, A. (1996), "Opening Remarks", in *Achieving Price Stability*, A Symposium sponsored by the Federal Reserve Bank of Kansas City, August.

Haberler, G. (1980), "Notes on Rational and Irrational Expectations", reprint 111, American Enterprise Institute (March).

Haltmaier, J. (2012), "Do Recessions Affect Potential Output?" Board of Governors of the Federal Reserve System, International Finance Discussion Papers, No. 1066, December.

James, H. (2012), *Making the European Monetary Union* (Cambridge, Mass.: The Belknap Press of Harvard University Press).

Kahn, G. (2012), "Estimated Rules for Monetary Policy", *Economic Review*, Federal Reserve Bank of Kansas City, Fall, 5–29.

Killian, L. (2009), "Oil Price Shocks, Monetary Policy and Stagflation" in R. Fry, C. Jones and C. Kent (Eds.), *Inflation in an Era of Relative Price Shocks* (Sydney: Reserve Bank of New Zealand), pp. 60–84.

Kozicki, S., and P.A. Tinsley (2009), "Perhaps the 1970s FOMC Did What It Said It Did", *Journal of Monetary Economics* 56: 842–855.

La Porta, R., F. Lopez-de-Silanes, and A. Schleifer (2008), "The Economic Consequences of Legal Origins", *Journal of Economic Literature* 46 (2): 285–332.

Levin, A., and J. Taylor (2013), "Falling Behind the Curve: A Positive Analysis of Stop-Start Monetary Policies and the Great Inflation" in M.D. Bordo and A. Orphanides (Eds.), *The Great Inflation: The Modern Rebirth of Central Banking* (Chicago: University of Chicago Press).

Mankiw, N. G., and J. Miron (1991), "Should the Fed Smooth Interest Rates? The Case of Seasonal Monetary Policy", *Carnegie-Rochester Series on Public Policy* 34 (Spring): 41–69.

Marsh, D. (1992), *The Bundesbank: The Bank That Rules Europe* (London: Heinemann).

Mauro, P., R. Romeu, A. Binder, and A. Zaman (2013), "A Modern History of Fiscal Prudence and Profligacy", IMF Working Paper 13/05, January.

Meltzer, A. (2009), *A History of the Federal Reserve, Volume 1: 1913–1951* (Chicago: University of Chicago Press).

Mishkin, F. (2005), "The Inflation Targeting Debate", John Kuszczak Memorial Lecture, Bank of Canada, May.

    (2007), "Estimating Potential Output", speech given at the Conference on Price Measurement for Monetary Policy, Federal Reserve Bank of Dallas, Dallas, Texas, available from www.c.federalreserve.gov/newsevents/speech/mishkin20070524a.htm.

Orphanides, A. (2003), "The Quest for Prosperity without Inflation", *Journal of Monetary Economics* 50(3): 633–663.

Orphanides, A. and S. van Norden (2002), "The Unreliability of Output Gap Estimates in Real-Time", *Review of Economics and Statistics* 84 (November): 569–583.

Orphanides, A. and J. Williams (2011), "Monetary Policy Mistakes and the Evolution of Inflation Expectations", Working Paper, June.

Parkin, M. (2012), "Central Bank Laws and Monetary Policy Outcomes: A Three Decade Perspective", available from http://ideas.repec.org/p/uwo/epuwoc/20131.html.

Perron, P. (1989), "The Great Crash, the Oil Price Shock, and the Unit Root Hypothesis", *Econometrica* 57 (November): 1361–1401.

Pesaran, H., T. Schurmann, and S.M. Weiner (2004), "Modelling Regional Interdependencies Using a Global Error-Correcting Macroeconometric Model", *Journal of Business and Economic Statistics* 22: 129–162.

Powell, J. (2009), *The Bank of Canada of James Elliot Coyne* (Montreal and Kingston: McGill-Queen's University Press).

Reinhart, C., and K.S. Rogoff (2009), *This Time Is Different: Eight Centuries of Financial Folly* (Princeton: Princeton University Press).

(2013), "Shifting Mandates: The Federal Reserve's First Centennial", *American Economic Review Papers and Proceedings* 103 (May): 48–54.

Romer, C. (2013), "Comments", in M.D. Bordo and A. Orphanides (Eds.), *The Great Inflation: The Modern Rebirth of Central Banking* (Chicago: University of Chicago Press).

Rudebusch, G. (2002), "Term Structure Evidence on Interest Rate Smoothing and Monetary Policy Inertia", *Journal of Monetary Economics* 49 (September): 1161–1187.

(2006), "Monetary Policy Inertia: Fact or Fiction?" *International Journal of Central Banking*, December: 85–135.

Sack, B., and V. Wieland (2000), "Interest-Rate Smoothing and Optimal Monetary Policy: A Review of Recent Empirical Evidence", *Journal of Economics and Business* 52 (January–April): 205–228.

Siklos, P.L. (2002), *The Changing Face of Central Banking* (Cambridge: Cambridge University Press).

(2003), "Assessing the Impact of Changes in Transparency and Accountability at the Bank of Canada", *Canadian Public Policy* 29 (September): 279–299.

(2008), "No Single Definition of Central Bank Independence is Right for All Countries", *European Journal of Political Economy* 24: 802–816.

(2010), "Revisiting the Coyne Affair: A Singular Event that Changed the Course of Canadian Monetary History", *Canadian Journal of Economics* 43 (3): 994–1015.

(2014), "Communications Challenges for Multi-Tasking Central Banks: Evidence and Implications", *International Finance* 17 (Spring): 77–98.

Silber, W.L. (2012), *Volcker* (New York: Bloomsbury Press).

Singleton, J. (2011), *Central Banking in the Twentieth Century* (Cambridge, Mass.: Cambridge University Press).

Stock, J.H., and M.W. Watson (2007), "Why Has US Inflation Become Harder to Forecast?", *Journal of Money, Credit and Banking* Vol 39 (February): 3–33

Stock, J., and M. Yogo (2005), "Testing for Weak Instruments in Linear IV Regressions" in D.W.K. Andrews and J.H. Stock (Eds.), *Identification and Inference for Econometric Models: Essays in Honor of Thomas Rothenberg* (Cambridge: Cambridge University Press).

Taylor, J. (1993), "Discretion versus Policy Rules in Practice", *Carnegie-Rochester Conference Series on Public Policy* 39 (December): 195–214.

(1998), "A Historical Analysis of Monetary Policy Rules" in J. Taylor (Ed.), *Monetary Policy Rules* (Chicago: University of Chicago Press), pp. 314–341.

Waller, C. (2011), "Independence and Accountability: Why the Fed Is a Well-Designed Central Bank", *Review* of the Federal Reserve Bank of St. Louis (Sept/Oct): 293–301.

Woodford, M. (2003), *Interest and Prices: Foundations of a Theory of Monetary Policy* Princeton: Princeton University Press.

NARRATIVES

1 Sweden: The Riksbank

The Sveriges Riksbank was founded in 1668 making it the world's oldest central bank. Like the Bank of England it was set up to provide government finance, then evolving over time as a banker's bank. In the nineteenth century, Sweden joined the gold standard in 1873. Sweden maintained gold convertibility and had price stability (with alternating periods of inflation and deflation) reflecting strong credibility until 1914. The Riksbank followed the rules of the game as well as most other countries (Jonung 1984). The Riksbank also acted as a LOLR in allaying financial crises in 1873 and 1907.

During World War I, although Sweden was neutral, she abandoned gold convertibility de facto until 1921. During the war, Sweden had high inflation reflecting gold inflows from the belligerents purchasing its commodities. Like the United Kingdom, Sweden followed a costly deflation to return de facto to the gold standard at the original parity in 1922, de jure 1924. The deflation contributed to a serious banking crisis in 1920 which the Riksbank handled well as a LOLR. Prices declined through the 1920s. After the United Kingdom left gold in 1931 Sweden followed suit but the Riksbank began following the unorthodox policy of stabilizing the price level(following a price level rule) and maintaining stable prices throughout the 1930s (Berg and Jonung 1999).

During World War II Sweden left the gold standard and like many countries imposed extensive exchange rate and price controls in the face of the large supply shocks it faced from the heavy demand for its resources by both the Germans and the Allies (Fregert and Jonung 2008). Sweden emerged from the war with ongoing inflation. Sweden, like many other European countries had an overvalued exchange rate in terms of dollars and it followed the United Kingdom in devaluing the krona in 1949.

Sweden joined the Bretton Woods system in 1951. Like the experience of other countries prices were relatively stable and the economy boomed. Sweden, following the war kept extensive capital and exchange controls and used the central bank to implement credit policy – the allocating of credit by non-market means. Like other countries the Riksbank was subservient to the Treasury.

After the collapse of Bretton Woods, Sweden followed an inflationary Keynesian full employment policy. It also accommodated both OPEC oil price shocks. In the face of these supply shocks and the inflationary response to them, Sweden was forced to devalue several times. According to Fregert and Jonung (2008) "the nominal anchor in the form of an ex ante fixed exchange rate for the krona quickly lost its ability to anchor long-run expectations ex post...the policy rule from the mid-1970s to the early 1990s has been characterized as a full employment policy rule accompanied by a wage price spiral caused by the use of devaluation to accommodate wage increases "page 16.

In the mid-1980s Sweden adopted a fixed exchange rate to the DM as an irrevocable nominal anchor. Adhering to this policy, once the DBB tightened monetary policy in 1991, it led to a serious currency crisis / banking crisis in the fall of 1992 accompanied by a recession with high unemployment. This led the Riksbank to abandon the peg.

In January 1993, after switching to floating exchange rates, the Riksbank adopted an explicit inflation target at 2 percent (bounded on either side by 1 percent) to be enforced after January 1995. This policy led to the greatest improvement in inflation credibility in a century measured by the length of wage contract (Fregert and Jonung 2008). The Riksbank began following a flexible inflation targeting regime – allowing supply shocks to affect inflation in the short-run and limiting fluctuations in the output gap. The Riksbank became independent in 1999. Sweden followed the Maastricht criteria of low inflation, fiscal deficits and debt ratios but stayed out of the Exchange Rate Mechanism (ERM). Sweden decided in a referendum in 1992 to not join the euro area when it would start in 1999 and has stayed out ever since. Based on the length of long-term contracts, Fregert and Jonung (2008) find that Sweden had credible inflation regimes in the Classical gold standard era, during Bretton Woods and during the inflation targeting regimes and possibly in the 1930s price stability rule period. They see the 1940s, 70s and 80s as unstable regimes.

2 United Kingdom: Bank of England

The Bank of England was founded in 1694. It was a private chartered joint stock bank with a public function. It was designed to aid the British government in placing its debt. In exchange for being the government's financier it was given the right to issue bank notes and to take on other private banking functions. Over time it evolved into a banker's bank, taking deposits from the nascent commercial banks because of its import-ant position. The Bank's charter required that it keep its notes convertible

An Historical and Quantitative Exploration 115

into gold at the official price of L 3.17s 9d per ounce of gold. By maintaining gold convertibility, the Bank gained credibility early on.

The Bank had operational independence but not goal independence, i.e., its main goal was to stay on the gold standard but it had control of its main policy tool – Bank Rate (the discount rate) – and the government could monitor its performance since its charter was subject to periodic renewal.

The gold standard rule that the Bank followed in the eighteenth and nineteenth centuries was a contingent rule, in the sense that in times of emergency, such as major wars, the Bank could request permission from the Treasury to temporarily suspend convertibility and issue inconvertible bank notes, as was indeed the case during the Napoleonic wars, during which the Bank suspended convertibility in 1797 and restored it after hostilities had ceased, in 1821. Inflation reached a peak of 10 percent per year in 1810 and then declined to its prewar level by the time of Resumption. These actions ensured the Bank's credibility (Bordo and Kydland 1995).

During the nineteenth century the Bank evolved into a LOLR in the face of banking panics. In many crises, beginning in 1825 and ending in the Overend Gurney crisis of 1866 the Bank lent too little and too late. By the Baring crisis of 1890 the Bank finally learned to follow Bagehot's (1873) Responsibility Doctrine to subsume its private interest to its public responsibility (Bordo 1990). This also enhanced its credibility.

During the heyday of the Classical gold standard 1880–1914 the Bank generally followed the "rules of the game" using its main policy tool, Bank rate, to speed up the adjustment to balance of payments disequilibria. On occasion, to make Bank Rate effective, the Bank used open market operations and gold devices (Bordo 1981). Because of its credibility the Bank had considerable flexibility to achieve goals other than convertibility, i.e., to smooth interest rates, output and prices (Bordo and MacDonald 2005).

World War I in August 1914 led to de facto suspension of the gold standard but not de jure until 1918. The Bank of England became an engine of inflation by freely discounting short-term Treasury bills at a low pegged interest rate to aid the Treasury in its war finance. For a year after hostilities ceased, prices kept rising, at close to 200 percent in total. The British monetary authorities expressed a strong interest in restoring the gold standard at the original parity as soon as possible in the Cunliffe report of 1918. Resumption would require politically unpopular deflation. The Bank engaged in tight money beginning in 1919 and the United Kingdom returned to gold at $4.866 in April 1925. Many argue that sterling was overvalued by at least 10 percent. This overvaluation in one of the key reserve currencies, along with other flaws, meant that the reestablished gold exchange standard would prove to be not as durable as the classical gold standard but it was as credible, at least until 1931 (Bordo and Macdonald 2002).

The gold exchange standard broke down in 1931 because of its major flaws of maladjustment, illiquidity and lack of confidence. Under a heavy speculative attack in summer 1931 the United Kingdom left the gold standard. The United Kingdom's experience with deflation and depression was much less than other countries like the United States that had continued to stay on gold (Eichengreen 1992). After Britain had left gold, devalued and floated sterling the Bank embarked on a reflationary policy through the 1930s.

During the Second World War the Bank again became an engine of inflation and subsumed its independence to the Treasury. This led to a period of high inflation which carried through into the 1950s. The Bank was nationalized in 1945 and officially lost whatever independence it had. The United Kingdom became part of the Bretton Woods system in 1946 but did not achieve current account convertibility until December 1958. The 1950s and 60s was a period of stop go monetary policy. Like in the interwar, sterling was overvalued and the United Kingdom ran persistent balance of payments deficits, often culminating in currency crises, ended by international rescues. Once the balance of payment constraint was relaxed the monetary and fiscal authorities would stimulate the economy leading to a run up of prices and another sterling crisis. The stop go pattern ended after the Devaluation of 1967 which also ended sterling's role as a reserve currency (Bordo 1993).

During the 1950s and 60s it was widely believed in the United Kingdom that monetary policy was impotent as described in The Radcliffe Committee Report of 1960. Radcliffe advocated the use of credit allocation policy and fiscal policy rather than monetary policy to maintain full employment (Capie 2010).

After the Bretton Woods system broke down between 1971 and 1973, sterling floated and without an external nominal anchor the United Kingdom entered the Great Inflation reaching inflation rates over 20 percent and a total loss of credibility in the later 1970s. The Treasury, which controlled monetary policy, believed inflation was caused by non-monetary, cost push forces and advocated the use of incomes policies rather than tight money to allay it (DiCecio and Nelson 2013).

The high inflation rate produced a major currency crisis necessitating an IMF rescue in 1976. The inflation spiral was finally ended in 1980 when

Margaret Thatcher came to power. Thatcher and her advisor Alan Walters adopted monetarist orthodoxy and greatly reduced money growth, liberalized the financial system, and removed capital controls. This led to a serious recession in 1980–1981 but by the mid-1980s the policy broke the back of inflation and inflation expectations as was occurring at the same time in the United States. Like the United States, this was the beginning of a period of low inflation, later called the Great Moderation. However unlike the Volcker Fed, the Bank of England did not have independence. That did not occur until 1998 when it achieved operational but not goal independence from the Treasury. The UK Treasury and the Bank in the 1980s and 1990s had the primary goal of low inflation and, following New Zealand's example, began formal inflation targeting in 1992. Since then the United Kingdom has generally had low inflation and anchored inflationary expectations.

3 France: Banque de France

The Banque de France was founded in 1803 by Napoleon Bonaparte to restore France to monetary discipline after decades of instability and high inflation. France returned to bimetallic specie convertibility and the Banque was a successful guardian of the Bimetallic system until 1878 when France switched to the gold standard. Specie convertibility was maintained until 1914 with two interruptions: in 1848–1850 following the overthrow of the July monarchy and 1870–1873 following the Franco German War. France adhered credibly to the specie standard as a contingent rule (Bordo and Kydland 1995) and like the United Kingdom and Germany maintained price stability. The Banque de France did not follow "the rules of the game" as closely as did the Bank of England and rarely varied its discount rate but its unconventional (credit rationing) policies did not threaten its credibility (Bordo and MacDonald 2005). The Banque de France also learned to be an effective LOLR in allaying financial crises in 1882 and 1889 (White 2007, Hautcoeur, Riva, and White 2014).

France left the gold standard during World War I and like the other belligerents, the BdF became an engine of inflation, freely absorbing the government's debt and maintaining a low interest peg. France had a higher inflation rate than Britain and the United States during the war (at well over 200 percent). After the war, the BdF and the Treasury favored returning to its prewar parity but the inflation and debt overhangs were so high that it would have taken a massive deflationary policy to achieve it (Bordo and Hautcoeur 2007). More importantly a struggle between the left and the right on how to reduce the debt and restore fiscal balance prevented any action. The BdF continued absorbing the government's debt and inflation mounted until 1926. In 1925 the Banque's reputation was tarnished in a scandal for falsifying its statement of its circulation leading to the fall of the incumbent government (Johnson 1997). By 1926 France had a serious currency crisis which was resolved by Poincare arranging a political deal to restore fiscal balance, aided by international loans. France returned to gold de facto with an 80 percent devaluation of the franc. Thereafter until 1936 the BdF followed a very conservative, hard franc policy to keep France on the gold standard. During the Great Depression France stayed on the gold standard after Britain and the United States had departed. It was able to do this because until 1934 the franc was undervalued. In the next two years France, like the other members of the gold bloc faced increasing competitive pressure from the devalued sterling and dollar blocs culminating in a currency crisis in 1936. To prevent a disorderly devaluation, France, the United States and Britain signed the Tripartite agreement under which the three countries coordinated intervention in their currencies to smooth the franc's descent (Bordo, Humpage, and Schwartz 2014 chapter 3). In sum, in stark contrast to the pre 1914 gold standard, the BdF's credibility was generally at a low level.

During World War II, occupied France had high inflation which continued after the war. At war's end in 1945, The Banque was nationalized losing its independence. In the early postwar period the BdF followed an inflationary policy to spur economic growth and maintain social stability. The Banque used credit rationing policies rather than the conventional tools of monetary policy. Such policies continued through much of the next three decades. According to Monnet (2013) the pursuit of such policies did not in general achieve worse countercyclical outcomes than would be the case with conventional tools.

France joined the Bretton Woods system in 1946. In the face of high inflation, parity was suspended in 1948, then restored following a devaluation in 1949. The experience was repeated in 1957 and 1958. Important fiscal reforms were instituted in 1958 which allowed France to declare current account convertibility in December 1958. In early 1960 a currency reform created the New Franc worth 100 old francs. The BdF maintained relatively low inflation in the 1960s and in 1963–1964 President DeGaulle and Jacques Rueff began campaigning to convert the Bretton Woods gold dollar exchange standard into a pure gold standard. Until 1967 France continually challenged US hegemony and undermined the Bretton Woods system (Bordo, Simard, and White 1995).

In spring 1968 political unrest led to a currency crisis which despite an international rescue, ended with another devaluation of the franc. After the collapse of the Bretton Woods system France's participation in the "Snake in the Tunnel" exchange rate arrangement was unsuccessful because of France's high inflation rate relative to Germany's. Like many other countries, France had high inflation in the 1970s. Despite the BdF's adoption of monetary targeting, it accommodated the oil price shocks. France joined the European Monetary System in 1979 as a credibility enhancing mechanism but the franc still remained weak relative to the deutschemark. In 1983 France adopted the "franc fort" policy with tight monetary policy by the BdF. Subsequent disinflation restored some credibility. However it was short lived as the European Monetary System (EMS) crisis in 1992 ended with France's exit and devaluation of the franc. France signed the Maastricht Treaty in 1992. The Banque was granted independence in 1993 and became fully committed to price stability. For the next six years until EMU and the creation of the euro in 1999, the Banque followed a credible policy of low inflation.

4 Norway: Norges Bank

The Norges Bank was founded in 1816 when Norway was made independent from Denmark. The nineteenth century, after the end of the Napoleonic Wars, was one of price stability for Norway as was the case in the other Scandinavian countries. Norway was on a silver standard until 1873 when it joined the gold standard. Norway was also part of the Scandinavian Monetary Union from 1875.

Prices tended toward long run price stability because of adherence to a specie based nominal anchor. However prices were not perfectly stable from year to year reflecting global demand and supply shocks to specie and the operation of the price specie flow mechanism. Like the other Scandinavian central banks, the Norges Bank continued to have credibility for low inflation in the years preceding World War I (Eitrheim, Qvigstad, and Skeie 2006)

Like the other Scandinavian countries, Norway left the gold standard during World War I and had high inflation reflecting the belligerents demand for its goods and services. After the war Central bank Governor Rygg vigorously pursued a deflationary policy to restore the exchange rate to its original parity in 1928. The drastic deflation in the 1920s was associated with high unemployment and falling output. Like Sweden and other countries Norway left the gold standard after Britain did in

September 1931. The Norges Bank then pursued an expansionary policy in the 1930s.

During World War II Norway was occupied by the Germans. As in the case of other occupied countries, the central bank used the inflation tax to provide revenue to be transferred to the occupiers. The inflation was accompanied by extensive controls and hence was repressed.

After the War, Norway joined the Bretton Woods System in 1946. The next two and a half decades were periods of rapid economic growth (partly fueled by Marshall Plan aid) and low inflation. Norway left Bretton Woods in 1971 and the 1970s and 80s was a period of high inflation associated with expansionary monetary and fiscal policy dedicated to maintain full employment. The Norges Bank, like other central banks in this era believed in the Phillips curve trade-off between unemployment and inflation. As a consequence of these inflationary policies and continued adherence to fixed exchange rates Norway had periodic devaluations. Like Sweden, the Norges Bank was involved in the government's credit allocation policies which were accompanied by extensive controls on financial markets (Eitrheim and Øksendal 2013)

Liberalization of the financial sector was lifted in 1984 which contributed to a real estate boom, fueled by expansionary monetary policy. The boom ended with tighter monetary policy in 1986. The legacy of the collapse of the real estate boom and the buildup in bad assets in the commercial banks was a banking crisis in 1991 when the Norges bank served as an effective LOLR (Steigum 2009).

A major policy reform occurred in 1986, The Norges Bank became dedicated to price stability as its main goal. The Norges Bank received operational independence in 1985. The reforms and new policies were successful in reducing inflation and the Norges Bank gained credibility. This was strengthened when the Bank began targeting inflation in 2001. Since the late 1980s the Norges Bank has been very successful at keeping inflation low and price expectations well anchored (Qvigstad 2013).

5 Germany: Reichsbank/Bundesbank

The Reichsbank was founded in 1876 shortly after the Franco-Prussian War, German reunification and Germany's joining the gold standard. The Reichsbank had private ownership but public management (Singleton 2008). It had operational independence within the confines of the gold standard. It was established to unify the currency, preserve gold convertibility, act as a central bank (to use its discount rate to provide liquidity for the money market based on bankers acceptances) and be a LOLR.

An Historical and Quantitative Exploration 121

The Reichsbank was successful in maintaining the gold standard until World War I and it generally followed the rules of the game (Bordo and Eschweiler 1994). It also was a successful LOLR in the financial crises of 1901 and 1907. Thus the Reichsbank had considerable credibility and the German price level was well anchored.

Germany abandoned gold convertibility at the start of World War I and the Reichsbank became part of the government. It freely discounted government paper at a low interest rate peg, becoming a major engine of inflation. After defeat in 1918 the Reichsbank under its President Havenstein continued to be an engine of inflation which became hyperinflation by 1923. The basic problem was an impossible fiscal impasse in which the Weimar government could not raise the tax revenues needed to pay for reparations and postwar reconstruction and other expenses so it resorted to the printing press. By 1923 the Reichsbank lost its credibility and the German mark became worthless. In the Currency Reform of 1923, Havenstein was succeeded by Hjalmar Schacht as President of the Reichsbank. In 1924 the Reichsmark was created, fiscal balance was restored with the aid of massive foreign loans, and the currency was pegged again to gold at a vastly devalued rate from its prewar parity. For seven years Germany had price stability and credibility was restored (Bordo and MacDonald 2002). Schacht cooperated with Montagu Norman (Governor of the Bank of England), Emile Moreau (Governor of the Banque de France, and Benjamin Strong (Governor of the Federal Reserve bank of New York) to maintain the Gold Exchange Standard (Ahamed 2009).

The Great Depression, which began in the United States, spread quickly to Germany, which had borrowed heavily in the United States and quickly lost access to the foreign capital inflows needed to service reparations. Germany had as serious a contraction and deflation as the United States. The Reichsbank, following gold standard orthodoxy maintained a tight monetary policy making things worse (Eichengreen 1992). The Creditanstalt crisis in Vienna in May 1931, which led to a bailout by the Austrian National Bank and government, provoked a run on the Austrian schilling, a freeze on foreign deposits and the imposition of exchange controls (which de facto removed Austria from the gold standard). The banking crisis then spread to Germany in July 1931. The German government bailed out most of the commercial banks, froze foreign deposits and like Austria imposed exchange controls and de facto left gold. The German financial crisis and the Depression contributed greatly to the victory of National Socialism in the elections of 1933. Under Hitler, the Reichsbank became the government's bank and greatly helped finance rearmament and then World War II. The Bank instituted a panoply of internal and external controls. World War II led to high (and suppressed) inflation which continued after defeat.

After the war, the allies established the Deutsches Lander Bank, which like the early Federal Reserve was a loose federation of regional banks coordinated by a Board. The BdL was dedicated to preserving the value of the currency (both external and internal). It was made independent from the Federal Government. The Currency Reform of 1948 ended inflation and created a new currency, the Deutschemark. The BdL based on the stability culture of postwar Germany focused primarily on price stability and led Germany into a pattern of low inflation. (Beyer et. al. 2013).

The BdL was superseded by the Bundesbank (DBB), established by the Federal Government of Germany in 1958. Like its predecessor it was dedicated overall to maintaining the value of the DMark. Under the Bretton Woods System the DBB faced a conflict between maintaining the dollar peg and internal price level stability since under a pegged exchange rate the money supply becomes endogenous. In the Bretton Woods era, West Germany, because of its rapid productivity growth and high growth rate, kept running current account surpluses which would lead to dollar inflows, which unless they were sterilized would lead to faster money growth and inflation. In response to the inflationary pressure Germany imposed controls on capital inflows and revalued the DM in 1961 and 1969 (Bordo 1993). Once the Bretton Woods system broke down between 1971 and 1973, The DBB began to focus on maintaining the internal value of the DM. Its attempts to maintain price stability were not successful with the first Oil Price shock in 1973 when inflation rose to 8 percent per year. In 1974 the DBB adopted monetary growth targeting to gradually reduce inflation. The monetary targeting framework was supposed to both control inflation and influence inflation expectations. The DBB roughly followed monetarist doctrine in targeting Central Bank Money (similar to M3) and gradually reducing its targets, but it often missed its targets. According to Beyer et. al. 2013) although the DBB missed its targets, it always explained the misses and hence followed pragmatic monetarism. The DBB's policy did succeed in making Germany's inflation rate (along with Switzerland) by far the lowest among the advanced countries during the Great Inflation. The experience of low inflation and the fact that Germany did not accommodate the second oil price shock in 1978/79 gave the DBB very high credibility before the 1980s, in sharp contrast to the United States and United Kingdom. The DBB kept following money targeting until the advent of the euro in 1999. The DBBs monetary targeting approach and

An Historical and Quantitative Exploration 123

its credibility for low inflation were incorporated into the European Central Bank as its two pillar strategy.

6 Italy: Banca d'Italia

Italy was unified in 1861 but the Banca d'Italia was not founded until 1893. Italy had competing banks of issue for its first three decades which meant that it was difficult to create a uniform national currency or to conduct national monetary policy Fratianni and Spinelli (1997). Italy initially adhered to the bimetallic standard until 1883 when it joined the gold standard. It also was a member of the Latin Monetary Union. Italy had a chequered specie adherence and inflation record until the end of the nineteenth century. Lax fiscal and monetary discipline, initially consequent upon war with Austria, led it to abandon specie from May 1861 to March 1883, float its exchange rate and issue inconvertible fiat money, and then return to the gold standard from 1883 to June 1893. It again left gold and floated from 1893 to 1902 (Bordo and Schwartz 1996). Thereafter although Italy did not join the gold standard the Bd'I began following a conservative monetary policy which kept the lira close to its de facto parity and the government greatly reduced its fiscal deficits so that Italy shadowed the gold standard (Tattara 2000).

During World War I, along with other belligerents, The Banca d'Italia served as an engine of inflation, which peaked at 44 percent in 1917. Shortly after the war ended, Mussolini came to power in 1922 and the central bank lost its autonomy to the Treasury and inflation continued. In the late 1920s the monetary authorities followed a tight monetary policy to produce a strong lira and Italy joined the gold exchange standard in 1928. Like other gold bloc countries Italy stayed on gold until 1935 which imposed deflationary pressure on the Italian economy. The lira was devalued in 1936 and Italy adopted a fiscally dominant inflationary policy which culminated in very high inflation, peaking at 90 percent per year in 1944 (Fratianni and Spinelli 1997).

After its defeat in World War II, Italy was plagued by high inflation and deep recession. The B d'I began a stabilization policy in 1947. Italy joined the Bretton Woods system in 1946 and the Bd'I was successful for a number of years in maintaining the official peg, leading to current account convertibility in 1960. However expansionary financial policy inconsistent with the peg, led to a currency crisis in 1964 which was resolved with an international rescue package (Yeager 1976). Italy adhered to Bretton Woods until it collapsed in 1971. In the 1970s, Italy returned to a fiscally

124   *Michael D. Bordo and Pierre L. Siklos*

dominant regime, with high and variable inflation, a serious currency crisis in 1976 requiring an IMF rescue and conditionality and unsuccessful adherence to the European "snake in the tunnel "arrangement.

Italy joined the EMS in 1979 as an inflation disciplining device (Giavazzi and Pagano (1991). Although its inflation rate remained one of Europe's highest, and it was forced to exit the ERM in the currency crisis of 1992. Italy signed the Maastricht Treaty in 1992, and by 1999 its inflation rate, debt to GDP ratio, and fiscal deficit were sufficiently reduced to allow it to join the euro. The Banca d'Italia became operationally independent in 1992 but never formally adopted an inflation target before it was absorbed into the ECB.

In sum, with a few exceptional episodes, the Banca d'Italia's credibility for low inflation was not stellar before joining the euro. Indeed Italy was a strong advocate for EMU because it would have an externally imposed nominal anchor to give it such credibility.

7 Switzerland: The Swiss National Bank

The SNB was founded in 1907. Unlike the earlier European National Banks of Issue established in the nineteenth century or earlier, the SNB was set up to adhere to the monetary standard and to provide financial stability. Switzerland was on gold since 1878 but was still a member of the Latin Monetary Union and in the nineteenth century had issues with depreciated Italian silver coins and with its currency being weaker than the French Franc (Bordo and James 2007). Like the Federal Reserve the SNB was to follow the real doctrine and freely discount eligible real bills from the Swiss commercial banks.

Like other European countries, Switzerland left the gold standard in 1914 and had high (internationally driven) inflation in the war although she was not a belligerent.

Following the War the SNB followed a deflationary policy to restore gold, de facto in 1924 and de jure 1929. As an important banking center, Switzerland was exposed to the crisis of the Great Depression. Several important banks faced stringency in 1931 and the SNB provided liquidity support. Switzerland stayed on the gold standard, along with France and the other gold bloc countries (Belgium, Netherlands, and Poland) and began to suffer competitive pressure after Britain and then the United States left gold and floated. Political debate between advocates of devaluation and proponents of hard money only ended when France left gold and Switzerland followed. Had Switzerland devalued earlier along with the

An Historical and Quantitative Exploration   125

United States, its real output would not have fallen nearly as much as it did (Bordo, Helbling, and James 2007).

Switzerland remained neutral during World War II. After the war, Switzerland, like Germany followed the stability culture and the SNB had an excellent track record at keeping inflation low. Switzerland did not join the Bretton Woods System but the Swiss franc was defined as a specified weight in gold so it had its own nominal anchor. Switzerland like Germany because of its low inflation ran continuous balance of payments surpluses which led to inflationary pressure. Unable to sterilize the dollar inflows, Switzerland like Germany imposed capital controls (taxes on foreign deposits). As the Great Inflation progressed and the weak dollar became more of a problem, Switzerland joined the other European countries and allowed the SF to float in 1973. Like the DBB, the SNB followed a monetary targeting strategy with the monetary base as a target (Rich 1997) and the SNB was as successful as the DBB in keeping its inflation rate lower than other advanced countries. The SNB's credible track record for low inflation combined with Switzerland's efficient banking sector (and secrecy laws) made the SF a key haven for capital flows from the rest of Europe and the less developed world. The inflows put upward pressure on the SF and made it difficult for the SNB to hit its monetary base target so that in 1978 it had to temporarily suspend its target. The SNB was generally able to hit its target until 1986, after which external shocks put upward pressure on the SF, on money supply and prices, forcing Switzerland to abandon its base control strategy and to shift to inflation targeting in 1999 while still monitoring monetary aggregates as predictors of future inflationary pressure (SNB 2007). The SNB has maintained credibility for low inflation and has anchored inflation expectations for much of its history.

8 Australia: The Commonwealth Bank of Australia/ The Reserve Bank of Australia

Although the Reserve Bank of Australia (RBA) dates from 1959 central banking actually began with the Commonwealth Bank of Australia (CBA) in 1912. The CBA was publicly owned but operated much like a conventional commercial bank (Gollan 1968). The original concept stemmed from boom and bust cycles due to Australia's position as a commodity producer and the purpose of the new bank was to act as a backstop of sorts in the event of bank failures, a common occurrence in the nineteenth century. From the outset there was considerable discussion about the independence of the

CBA. Politicians felt that the CBA ought to be independent of political interference as it sought to deepen financial markets and spur economic development not act as a tool of the politicians (e.g., Bell 2004). A common development across many of the central banks covered by our narratives is that, during major wars, the monetary authorities became, if they not already, subservient to the Treasury. The CBA was no exception (e.g., see Swan 1940). However, it is also true that war finance provided an opportunity for the institutional development of the monetary authority, especially as a 'restraining influence' (Bell 2004, p.9) on government finance.

Like its counterparts elsewhere in the Dominions, the CBA was affected by the Great Depression and, when the gold standard ended in 1931, the CBA was given authority over the exchange rate. Moreover, just as in Canada, the subject of conflict between the Governor and the central bank became an important topic of reform. While a crisis on the same level as the Coyne Affair in Canada did not take place, the government in the early 1950s eventually introduced a dispute resolution mechanism designed to defuse tension and avoid damaging the government. It is interesting that Australian politicians of the time understood that conflict would likely first damage a sitting government and not the central bank. In contrast, politicians in Canada would not understand the consequences of conflict with the central until after the Coyne Affair erupted (e.g., see Siklos 2002). Just as with Canada there has never been a conflict serious enough to appeal to the legislation to resolve any dispute.

Initially, as in the case of New Zealand and Canada, the remit of the central bank did not contradict the goal of price stability (i.e., the stability of the currency) but there was a clear requirement to support economic growth as well. By the 1970s the oil price shocks were producing higher inflation rates while the abandonment of the Bretton Woods exchange rate system, together with interest rate ceilings and heavy handed banking regulation promoted the growth of the non-bank financial sector. By the late 1970s and into the early 1980s, a financial deregulation phase was being initiated culminating with the float of the dollar in December 1983. Through the use of open market operations and the ban on funding any government budget deficit the RBA was able to influence interest rates and autonomously set the stance of monetary policy.

The 1980s would eventually bring the start of major changes in the role of the RBA. Paul Keating, who became Treasurer in 1983, was determined to fight inflation. At the RBA this led to sharp rises in the policy rate, called the cash rate, reaching a peak of over 18 percent by the end of 1985. In addition, the RBA intervened regularly in foreign exchange markets to prevent the dollar from falling too quickly since this was deemed to be unhelpful (RBA 1987). Adding to the difficulties faced by monetary policy, especially during the late 1980s, were rapidly rising housing prices and a large current account deficit. However, at the same time inflation rates began to drop quickly and, in the space of roughly six years went from near double-digit rate of change to around 2 percent by 1992.

In spite of an improved inflation record the RBA entered the 1990s with low credibility. It had been unable to counter the effects of boom and busts in the 1980s, there was no clear policy framework, supported incomes control policies, and was not seen as independent of government influence. The policy of gradualism, implicit in how monetary policy was delivered, lost favor.

By 1993, shortly after New Zealand, Canada, and the United Kingdom did the same, the RBA adopted an inflation target as an anchor of policy. However, in an important departure from the practice elsewhere of declaring an inflation target range with the aim of achieving the mid-point of the target over a specified horizon, the RBA chose to adopt a narrow range of 2–3 percent, on average, over the cycle. Part of the reason was that, as did the RBNZ and the BoC, there was sufficient uncertainty about whether the target would be reached to adopt as flexible an approach as was feasible under the circumstances. By the mid-1990s a new government ushered in some modifications in the inflation targeting policy by requiring that the Treasurer and the RBA Governor agree on the inflation targeting strategy. The resulting Statement on the Conduct of Monetary Policy has become a fixture of monetary policy making since that time (Grenville 1996).

Inflation has been low and stable since the mid-1990s in Australia and there are no indications that the monetary policy strategy will change. Unlike many other central banks Australia did not experience a recession following the GFC of 2008–2009. However, the commodity price boom, together with an asset price boom, primarily in the housing sector, made life difficult for the RBA. Policy rates were raised and lowered relatively gradually through the crisis and in response to the housing price boom but the RBA never flirted with the ZLB. Nevertheless, while the economic problems Australia has faced for decades, namely boom and bust cycles in commodity and asset prices, remain the RBA has now achieved an enviable record of low and stable inflation thanks to inflation targeting (e.g., see Stevens 2003), its independence is not in doubt, and its committee-based decision making structure is consistent with best practice in monetary policy making.

9 United States: Federal Reserve

The Federal Reserve was established in 1913 to act as a LOLR and to preserve the gold standard. The United States hadn't had a central bank since the demise of the Second Bank of the United States in 1836. The United States had been on a specie standard (bimetallism before 1873, gold thereafter) standard throughout the nineteenth century with the exception of the Greenback paper money floating exchange rate episode from 1862 to 1879. Under the gold standard, the United States had long-run price stability (alternating periods of rising and falling prices driven by the vagaries of the gold standard). The United States' inflation credibility was nearly as good (with the exception of the Free Silver threat in the early 1990s) as the advanced countries of Europe which had central banks (seen in long-term interest rate spreads on gold bonds Bordo and Rockoff 1996). The main problem in the United States was financial instability manifest in frequent banking panics (1837, 1857, 1873, 1884, 1993, and 1907) in the absence of a true LOLR.

The panic of 1907 was the event that broke the camel's back leading to the movement for monetary reform. The prototype for a US central bank was contained in the Warburg Plan of 1910 – a loose federal system of regional central banks, each modeled after the Reichsbank in Germany to be coordinated by a Board in Washington. The Reserve banks would use their discount rates to freely accommodate banker's acceptances and act as a LOLR. The Federal Reserve System founded in 1913 took on many of the aspects of the original Warburg Plan with a much stronger federal government presence in the Federal Reserve Board (Bordo and Wheelock 2013).

World War I broke out just before the Fed was to open its doors leaving the United States as one of the few countries still on the gold standard (with the exception of a gold embargo 1917–1919). Gold inflows from the belligerents' purchases of US goods fueled inflation which was aggravated after the United States joined the war in April 1917 when the Fed began financing the US Treasury's bond issues at a low pegged interest rate. By wars end the US price level had increased close to 100 percent, (the lowest rate of the belligerents).

After the war the Fed began sharply raising its discount rate in 1919 after its gold reserves were threatened by continued high inflation. This led to a serious but short-lived recession and deflation from 1920–1921. The period 1921 to 1929 was characterized by mild deflation and rapid economic growth punctuated by two mild recessions. Friedman and Schwartz

An Historical and Quantitative Exploration 129

(1963) and Meltzer (2003) gave the Fed high marks for attenuating the recessions, preventing banking panics and preserving price stability. The 1920s can be regarded as a period of high Federal Reserve credibility.

The Great Contraction, 1929–1933 can be attributed to several failures of US monetary policy. These include loose monetary policy in 1927 to aid the United Kingdom in its struggles to stay on the gold exchange standard which may have fueled asset booms in housing and later stocks (Bordo and Landon Lane 2013a); Fed tightening in early 1928 to stem the stock market boom which contributed to a downturn in August 1929 followed by the stock market crash of October; c) the failure to act as LOLR and prevent four banking panics from October 1930 to March 1933. This policy failure contributed greatly to an unprecedented collapse in money supply, real output and prices. The massive (over 30 percent) decline in prices led to a major loss of credibility.

The Great Contraction ended in March 1933 and recovery followed quickly after the incoming Roosevelt administration declared a one week banking holiday, exited the United States from the gold standard, engaged in massive gold (and silver) purchases and then devalued the dollar by 60 percent a year later. Prices and real output rebounded rapidly from 1933 to 1937, interrupted by a sharp recession 1937–1938 which Friedman and Schwartz (1963) attribute to the Fed's doubling of reserve requirements in 1936 to absorb banks excess reserves and the Treasury's policy of sterilization of gold inflows.

The Federal Reserve system was reorganized in 1933 and 1935 and the Board of Governors was given enlarged powers. However during the 1930s the Fed did not play a very active role in monetary policy which had been taken over by the Treasury. From the 1930s onward the Fed began following a low interest rate policy to accommodate the Treasury's fiscal policies (Meltzer 2003). During World War II the Fed again became an engine of inflation although prices did not rise as much as in World War I because of extensive price controls. The interest rate pegs were kept after World War II and in the 1940s inflation became a problem leading the Fed to campaign to regain its independence to raise its policy rates. This was achieved after a considerable struggle with the Treasury and the Administration in the Federal Reserve Treasury Accord of 1951. The Fed tightened policy in the early 50s and restored price stability. Under Chairman Martin the Fed followed a policy of low inflation and the economy performed well through much of the 1950s and early 60s. During this period the United States performed well in keeping inflation low as the provider of the key currency of the Bretton Woods System.

The era of credible inflation ended after 1965 when, under pressure from the Johnson administration the Fed began accommodating expansionary fiscal policies to support the Vietnam War and the Great Society. This led to the beginning of the Great Inflation (1965 to 1982). The Fed also began following Keynesian doctrine (the Phillips Curve trade-off) and made achieving full employment (at the expense of inflation) its paramount policy goal. As inflation and inflationary pressures mounted in the 1970s, several attempts by the Burn's FOMC to reduce inflation faltered when it led to recession and rising unemployment, leading to a ratcheting up in inflation and inflation expectations (Bordo and Orphanides 2013). Accommodation of two oil price shocks also contributed to the run up in inflation. By the late 1970s the Fed had lost considerable credibility for low inflation. This culminated in a run on the dollar in 1978.

In 1979 President Carter appointed Paul Volcker as Chairman of the Fed with a mandate to end inflation. Volcker followed a monetarist policy strategy, targeting non-borrowed reserves and letting interest rates be determined by market forces. Interest rates rose to close to 20 percent by 1980. Volcker's tight money policy triggered a sharp recession in 1979–1980. It was aggravated by the Carter administration imposing controls on credit card expenditures. In reaction the Fed loosened policy in late 1980. Immediately inflation and inflationary expectations rebounded. Several months later, with the support of the newly elected President Reagan, Volcker reapplied the monetary brakes triggering a second recession and this time it did not stop tightening despite the unemployment rate rising well above 10 percent until inflation and inflation expectations abated in 1982. The Fed's credibility suffered after the first recession and only was regained after the second (more severe) Fed induced downturn (Bordo, Erceg, Levin, and Michaels 2007).

The Fed reestablished its credibility for low inflation by the mid-1980s seen in declines in nominal interest rates, in the TIPs spread and in various measures of inflation expectations. The twenty-year episode of good economic performance is referred to as the Great Moderation. Alan Greenspan took over as Fed Chairman in 1987. He quickly prevented a major stock market crash from leading to a banking crisis and then followed the Volcker approach to maintaining credibility for low inflation. This policy was put to the test by the inflation scare of 1994 when rising long-term bond yields signaled a run up in inflationary expectations. The Fed tightened sharply, raising real interest rates. And then when inflation expectations eased, the Fed loosened, preventing a recession. (Goodfriend 1993).

The Great Moderation ended with the Financial Crisis of 2007–2008. Loose Federal Reserve policy of keeping the Federal Funds rate well below the Taylor rule rate from 2003 to 2005, in an attempt to head off potential deflation, added fuel to a burgeoning real estate boom which burst in 2006 triggering the crisis. (Taylor 2007, Bordo and Landon Lane 2013b). The Fed reacted to the crisis by following aggressive monetary policy of cutting the FFR in the fall of 2007, opening the discount window to many non-bank financial institutions and non-traditional markets and by a controversial bailout policy in fall 2008 (bailing out Bear Stearns, AIG and the GSEs) and letting Lehman fail in October. That action triggered a global financial crisis. The Fed reacted to the panic by cutting the FFR to zero and instituting several unorthodox discount window facilities. These policies combined with the Treasury's TARP plan, stress tests and an inter central bank swap arrangement ended the crisis. By late fall 2008 the Fed's policy rate had hit the zero lower bound and with the recession still on going, the Fed instituted its Quantitative Easing policy (QE1) – the purchase of long term Treasuries and mortgage backed securities. This unconventional policy was followed in the next four years by three other packages in the face of an unprecedented (after a financial crisis) slow recovery (Bordo and Haubrich 2012). These policies have quadrupled the Fed's balance sheet, and many argue could lead to a future inflation policy. The Fed may have lost considerable credibility with the crisis and time will tell if it regains its credibility for low inflation by how it exits from QE.

10 Canada: Bank of Canada

The Bank of Canada (BoC) was created in 1935. Two historic events during the 1930s were influential in the formation of the central bank. The first, of course, was the Great Depression. The second event was the end of the gold standard. Unlike the United States to the south Canada saw no bank failures in the 1930s. Neither did the country experience a surge in inflation when the link to gold was suspended. Indeed, part of the impetus for the creation of the BoC was the fear of deflation (e.g., Burdekin and Siklos 2004). An equally strong motive for the creation of a central bank was a political one. The MacMillan Commission, a royal commission struck in 1993 to investigate the possibility of establishing a central bank in Canada, returned a favorable, though narrow, majority report after conducting hearings nationwide. As Bordo and Redish (1987, p. 415) note: "Domestically, in an environment where traditional trust in the beneficial nature of the market system was eroding and a spirit of nationalism was rising, political pressure was mounting to halt the deflation which was frequently blamed on the concentrated banking industry."

Other political forces also contributed to the creation of the BoC. Canada had no central bank that could be used to manage monetary policy, including the exchange rate. Indeed, paralleling the creation of the BoC was the introduction of the Exchange Fund Account in 1935 to "aid in the control and protection of the external position of the Canadian monetary unit." (Statutes of Canada 1935) The Bank, which officially began operations in March 1935, was initially a private institution with stocks issued and dividends paid out to shareholders up to a stated maximum. After the 1936 election, however, the Bank was nationalized and, by 1938, the government acquired all of the shares.

Around the time of the outbreak of World War II, Canada introduced exchange controls. Price controls would also shortly thereafter be put in place. These were administered by the Foreign Exchange Control Board, chaired by the Governor of the BoC. Wage and price controls were also introduced and the war was financed by the issuance of a series of Victory bonds. These long-term loans would create some difficulties for the BoC during the second half of the 1950s (see later). More controversially, the Governor of the Bank would also preside over the Industrial Development Bank, a vehicle to spur economic growth and employment in the postwar era. The result was to effectively neutralize monetary policy as a stabilization tool to manage inflation (e.g., see Deutsch 1957).

The earliest days of the Bank in the postwar era were marked by the creation of a market for short-term government debt as well as facilitate the development of a money market. This was deemed vital given the contemporary trend toward greater government involvement in the economy. An important feature of BoC policy in the early years was the resort to moral suasion. The aim was to persuade the commercial banking system to follow lending policies that suited the macroeconomic objectives of the central bank. The highly concentrated nature of the Canadian banking system made such a policy practical.

Once World War II ended high levels of government debt, the need to re-intermediate the Canadian financial system following wartime controls, meant that the Bank needed to prepare to intervene in the financial system to ensure a smooth exit from an era of forced 'cheap money'. In addition, the postwar era would usher in the creation of the Bretton Woods system of pegged exchange rates. Canada adopted the system but, in the early 1950s, became the first country to opt out of the exchange rate system.

An Historical and Quantitative Exploration

In spite of the heavy criticism it faced, Canada adhered to a form of floating exchange rates until the early 1960s when it returned to the Bretton Woods fold (e.g., see Helleiner 2006). In spite of the flexible exchange rate regime the nominal exchange rate did not vary a great deal throughout most of the decade. Unlike other parts of the world, capital remained mobile.

The decade of the 1950s was an eventful one for at least two other reasons. First, the BoC arguably became the first central bank to adopt an interest rate instrument to signal the stance of monetary policy (e.g., see Siklos 2010). Next, and perhaps most importantly, the Bank experienced its first institutional crisis whose consequences are still being felt to this day. Following the boom and bust period in the aftermath of the Korean War the Canadian economy once again grew vary rapidly during the mid-1950s and the Bank publicly worried about rising inflation. Through its encouragement of the development of a nascent money market the Bank engineered successive increases in the interest rate even as the Canadian and US economies, the latter by far its largest trading partner, were showing signs of an imminent and sharp slowdown. The Bank also faced the soon to mature Victory bonds from the World War II era and the resulting shift in the maturity structure of the government debt complicate matters as well.

James Coyne, who became the second BoC Governor in 1955, believed strongly that the bank needed to be interventionist, especially in the control of inflation. His policy of high interest rates at a time of rising unemployment created severe tension with the government of the day led by Prime Minister John Diefenbaker. Publicly, doubts about the correctness of the Bank's monetary policy were also raised to unprecedented levels. As one notable economist of the time opined (Gordon 1961, p. 15) the Bank "...has its eye fixed on the moral wickedness of the slightest changes of inflation and is unmoved by the patent facts of growing unemployment and stagnating national income." By 1961 the controversy reached a climax when the government introduced a motion declaring the post of Governor vacant. The elected House of Commons passed the motion but the unelected Senate, where Coyne found support, did not. Coyne, feeling vindicated, resigned. Regardless of who was right or wrong during the crisis the BoC lost much of its credibility during the Coyne years.

The resignation would, however, have lasting consequences on the Bank. Louis Rasminsky, who took over as Governor, did so on the condition that a new Bank of Canada Act contain a directive such that, in the event of a disagreement over policy issues, the government was required to publicly explain its disagreement and the Governor would be directed to implement the policy. Since the so-called Rasminsky directive was included in the Bank of Canada Act, it has never been invoked. Indeed, it has proved to be the device that guarantees the autonomy of the Bank from direct political interference. Indeed, the Rasminsky era succeeded in re-establishing central bank credibility.

The period the 1960s was a time of fixed exchange rates with the Canadian dollar pegged at US 92.5 cents. Relative economic peace came to an end with the two oil price shocks of the 1970s. The resulting stagflation culminated in the Saskatoon Monetary manifesto of then Governor Gerald Bouey, who advocated the adoption of monetary targeting to buttress BoC credibility. At the time the Governor (Courchene 1976, p. 25) insisted that "Whatever else may need to be done to bring inflation under control, it is absolutely essential to keep the rate of monetary expansion within reasonable limits." Termed the strategy of gradualism the objective of the policy was to bring down the rate of money supply growth from an initial range of 10–15 percent per annum. The policy succeeded in part because, as Bouey famously stated, "we didn't abandon the monetary aggregates, the abandoned us". Once again the Bank suffered a loss of credibility when it failed to control inflation.

The failure of monetary targeting, the end of the Bretton Woods era conspired to create a void in monetary policy. There was no monetary anchor. As a result, pressure came from several quarters to stem inflation with new tools. In 1987, during the course of the Hanson Lecture, Governor John Crowe argued that "monetary policy should be geared so as to achieve a pace of monetary expansion that promotes price stability in the value of money. This means pursuing a policy aimed at achieving and maintaining stable prices." (Crowe 1988, p. 4) Shortly after New Zealand adopted inflation targeting (see later), the Bank, with the tacit encouragement of the federal government, adopted inflation reduction targets in 1991. However, the adoption of a new anchor of policy was not without considerable controversy, somewhat reminiscent of the Coyne affair three decades earlier. The issue was once again whether, in the pursuit of price stability, the Bank deliberately engineered or made worse the recession of the early 1990s.

Canada's inflation targeting regime began with goals to reduce inflation, first to 3 percent by 1992, and then to 2 percent by 1995. Inflation fell more quickly than anyone expected and a target range of between 1 to 3 percent, with a 2 percent mid-point inflation target, was adopted. Since that time the inflation target remit has been renewed every five years and inflation has remained within the target range much of the time since then. The inflation targeting regime has been in place for over two decades and is, arguably, a success story. Along with the adoption of inflation targets was a commitment to a floating exchange rate and the gradual expansion of the transparency of the BoC. Governor Gordon Thiessen was largely responsible for these and other changes (e.g., see Laidler 1991, and Laidler and Robson 1993).

The inflation targeting regime survived the global financial crisis but the regime has not been left unscathed. While Canada escaped the worst of the GFC, the events of 2008–2013 provide some fodder for the critics of the Bank. The recession of 2008–2009 was short-lived but among the sharpest of the postwar era (see Cross and Bergevin 2012). Even if the 2 percent inflation target has proved to be a durable anchor, observed inflation has been below target roughly half the time since 2005, including all of 2009 and 2013. Prior to 2005 CPI inflation also remained below 2 percent between 1998 and early 2001. Conventional central banks actions, via changes in a central bank policy rate, became less effective and appeared inoperative once the zero lower bound was reached. Consequently, much of the advanced world adopted unconventional monetary policies. The shift implies emphasis on policies that impact the balance sheet of the central bank.

Canada remained in the eye of the storm that was creating havoc across the industrialized economies. A sound banking system and little bubble-like activity in the housing sector, meant that two direct channels that propagated the financial crisis in the United States were absent in Canada. Nevertheless, the BoC could not avoid the movement of policy rates toward the ZLB. Regardless, the accommodative monetary policy stance still failed to dent the unease about negative spillovers from the deepening US recession; a phenomenon that was apparent throughout the industrial world.

Why, even if it Canada's economy was relatively resilient to the sizeable adverse shocks from abroad, could the Canadian economy not fully avoid a recession and the rapid fall in inflation? These events appeared to contradict the intent of the inflation targeting regime which relies crucially on a floating exchange rate regime believed to act as a shock absorber. Consequently, the Bank once again was thrust at the forefront of monetary policy actions when it unveiled its forward guidance policy in April 2009. The aim was convince the public that the mid-point of the inflation target would not be abandoned and, to underscore its determination to return inflation

136   *Michael D. Bordo and Pierre L. Siklos*

to its 2 percent goal, by stating that the policy rate would remain at its ZLB for up to a year. Nevertheless, worried over the possibility that inflationary expectations might become unanchored, the Bank raised the policy rate prior to the expiry date of the CC policy. By some accounts (e.g., Siklos and Spence 2010) the exit was credible. Of course, the CC strategy was modest, took place under crisis conditions, and had a limited horizon.

While the BoC has been a leader in promoting the virtues of forward guidance, to good effect, the central bank appears occasionally incapable of providing clarity about when the economy might return to a state that calls for a more 'normal' monetary policy stance. For example, in the April 2010 MPR, the BoC first sought to justify why monetary policy might remain loose even after signs of inflation and a return to capacity might otherwise have led markets to believe that the policy rate would rise. Unfortunately, the explanation was predicated on an inflation rate below target at a time when observed inflation was above target.

The BoC has the legal authority and flexibility to act as a LOLR through the provision of emergency liquidity assistance or by conducting outright asset purchases. Like other major central banks, the BoC responded to the crisis by significantly extending its lending facilities and aggressively lowering the policy rate. After hitting the zero lower bound on interest rates and worried that the expansionary macroeconomic policies were not sufficient to spark a recovery in the real economy, the BoC used calendar-based conditional commitment to maintain the policy rate at the ZLB. Other major central banks were more hesitant in making such commitments, and acted cautiously when they did.

Despite some temporary failures to control inflation or anticipate deflation risks from time to time inflation expectations remain firmly anchored at the 2 percent inflation target. Hence, there is every reason to believe that the inflation targeting regime has been a credible one.

11 New Zealand: The Reserve Bank of New Zealand

Like the BoC, the Reserve Bank of New Zealand (RBNZ) was established in 1934 following the Great Depression. The RBNZ was not created to promote monetary stability. Rather, unlike many other central banks, it was created to establish separate monetary and banking systems between New Zealand and Australia (Hawke 1973). Since commodity prices had considerable impact on the New Zealand economy it was believed that a central bank, as was the case elsewhere, could be a vehicle to soften the blows of large shifts in commodity prices. Of course, a vehicle to insulate the New Zealand economy from foreign shocks was dependent on the type of exchange rate regime. Although the New Zealand dollar's was pegged to the pound sterling the government hoped that the creation of a central bank would signal a form of independence from Australia in the financial and economic realms e.g., see RBNZ 2007).

Paralleling the Canadian experience the RBNZ was two-thirds owned by private shareholders but nationalization took place in 1936 when a labour government came into power. New legislation would soon indicate that the government intended to use the RBNZ as a tool to finance expansion of the public sector. There was no pretense of independence from the Minister of Finance. During the first two decades or so of its existence the lack of independence did not appear to matter much as the New Zealand economy grew rapidly and unemployment remained low. Nevertheless, economic imbalances were building and these are reflected in rising inflation rates and pressure on the exchange rate (e.g., see RBNZ 2007). Therefore, there is little reason to believe that the RBNZ had much credibility as it was unable to act autonomously.

The RBNZ went through World War II under an increasingly interventionist government. Surging demand for its commodities to support the war effort, combined with capital controls that would remain in place until the mid-1980s, as well as import restrictions, meant that the government took near total control of the economy. The RBNZ became a vehicle to help finance the war effort but the positive externalities of the war on New Zealand's economy also permitted the war debts to be repaid quickly following the end of hostilities. The public was willing to put up with the necessary austerity measures to assist with the effort at debt repayment. Price controls were also adopted.

When the rest of the world began to relax restrictions on the movement of capital and reduce import tariffs during the 1950s, New Zealand took a different route. It sought to protect its commodity exports, vital to national economic growth, but increasingly restricted imports and other forms of direct economic controls on its citizens. Unfortunately for New Zealand when the United Kingdom joined the European Economic Community in 1973, combined with the dying days of the Bretton Woods system, conspired to create an economic shock (e.g., See Singleton et al. 2006) that would eventually lead to major economic and financial reforms.

From the oil price shocks of the 1970s through to the loss of large export markets New Zealand's economy began to experience stagflation on a major scale. When the continued attempt to deal with the underlying pressures on New Zealand's economy by resorting to more direct controls, including wage and price controls, could no longer be sustained an economic crisis erupted. Poor economic conditions were exacerbated by the autocratic style of then Prime Minister Muldoon who was determined to avoid rising unemployment. In the event, inflation soared from below 5 percent in the early 1970s to almost 20 percent by the early 1980s. There were also other forces that would contribute to creating unsustainable tensions in the economy. Monetary policy was, during the 1970s, governed by a reserve requirement scheme. In the meantime interest rates were gradually being liberalized while the end of the Bretton Woods era brought a period where the New Zealand dollar was pegged to a changing basket of currencies. This did not prevent several large devaluations of the dollar followed by the adoption of a 'crawling peg' regime by the end of the decade of the 1970s. A currency crisis erupted in 1984 and, together with an election that year, brought in a new government. Once again it is difficult to speak of any RBNZ credibility as its ability to conduct monetary policy was severely constrained.

In the years following the elections of 1984 landmark reforms were introduced that affected all aspects of New Zealand's economy. Perhaps the most significant reforms were in the area of monetary policy. The RBNZ would eventually be made autonomous from government and accountable for meeting an inflation target. May of the reforms were introduced by the newly installed Finance Minister at the time, Roger Douglas. As part of the program of reform the New Zealand dollar would float. The determination to maintain the float is evident from the fact that the RBNZ did not intervene in foreign exchange markets until 2007.

The changes in monetary policy were enshrined in the RBNZ Act of 1989. The focus of monetary policy was the maintenance of price stability to be defined by an inflation target. Henceforth, there would be a clear indicator by which the public and markets could assess the credibility of the RBNZ. The target would be regularly revisited thanks to a Policy Targets Agreement (PTA) which would have to be signed following each election as a signal of the commitment of both the central bank and the government to maintain price stability. Although initially the inflation target range included 0 percent subsequent assessments of the conduct of monetary policy, together with the adoption of inflation targets elsewhere which explicitly excluded the 0 percent value eventually produced a 1–3 percent target range that survives to this day. Provisions were made in the legislation to bring the Governor to account in case the targets were breached. This happened on at least two occasions but, in both cases, the Governor was not removed and inflation eventually returned to target although the RBNZ's credibility was dented. Some of the difficulties lay in the manner in which inflation is measured. For example, a rise in interest rates would filter through mortgage rates and rents and these were incorporated into the CPI. Clearly, the appropriate response was not to further raise interest rates unless inflation expectations became unanchored. In large part for this reason the role of central bank communication became central to RBNZ policy and the central bank became among the most transparent in the world (e.g., see Siklos 2002, Dincer and Eichengreen 2007).

Two other events in the RBNZ's history are noteworthy. Realizing that interest rate changes and exchange rate changes are interrelated in a floating rate regime the RBNZ publicized and, later, adopted a monetary conditions index (MCI) as a primary signal in communicating the stance of monetary policy. Interestingly, the MCI has Canadian roots although the BoC never adopted the MCI as an intermediate instrument of policy. When markets became too focused on changes in the MCI this complicated the task of communicating the policy intentions of the RBNZ and it was forced to abandon its usage (e.g., see Siklos 2000). Second, in the aftermath of the Asian financial crisis of 1997–1998 followed by the Fed's reaction to the bursting of the tech bubble in 2001 and the slow tightening of monetary policy in the United States during the early 2000s, the RBNZ began to reconsider its ban on foreign exchange intervention. After some public consultations and an international conference on the monetary and fiscal policy regime in mid-2007 (RBNZ 2007), the RBNZ adopted foreign exchange intervention guidelines. In the event the RBNZ only intervened a few times since the policy was adopted and the commitment to inflation targeting and, for the floating exchange rate regime remains undiminished to this day. There is no imminent sign that the inflation targeting regime will be reconsidered. It remains a credible nominal anchor for monetary policy.

Narratives' References

Ahamed, L. (2009), *The Lords of Finance* (New York: The Penguin Press).

Bagehot, W. (1873), *Lombard Street*, rev. ed. (London: Kegan Paul, Trenh, Toubner and Co.), 1906.

Bell, S. (2004), *Australia's Money Mandarins* (Cambridge: Cambridge University Press).

Berg, C., and L. Jonung (1999), "Pioneering Price Level Targeting: The Swedish Experience 193–1937", *Journal of Monetary Economics* 43(3): 525–551.

Beyer, A., V. Gaspar, C. Gerberding, and O. Issing (2013), "Opting Out of the Great Inflation: German Monetary Policy after the Breakdown of Bretton Woods" in M.D. Bordo and A. Orphanides (Eds.), *The Great Inflation; The Rebirth of Modern Central Banking* (Chicago: University of Chicago Press for the NBER).

Bordo, M.D. (1981), "The Classical Gold Standard: Some Lessons for Today" *Federal Reserve Bank of St. Louis Review* 63(6) May.

Bordo, M.D., and B. Eschweiler (1994), "Rules, Discretion and Central Bank Independence: The German Experience 1880–1989" in P.L. Sikos (Ed.), *Varieties of Monetary Reform: Lessons and Experience on the Road to Monetary Union* (Boston: Kluwer Academic Publishers).

Bordo, M.D., and H. James (2007), "From 1907 to 1946: A Happy Childhood or a Troubled Adolescence? in SNB. *The Swiss National Bank 1907–2007*. (Zurich: Neue Zurcher Zeitung Publishing).

Bordo, M.D., and P.C. Hautcoeur (2007), "Why Didn't France Follow the British Stabilization after World War I?", *European Review of Economic History* 11(1) (April): 3–37.

Bordo, M.D., and J. Haubrich (2012), "Deep Recessions, Fast Recoveries and Financial Crises: Evidence from the American Record" NBER Working Paper 18194 June.

Bordo, M.D., and F. Kydland (1995), "The Gold Standard as a Rule: An Essay in Exploration" Explorations in Economic History. October.

Bordo, M.D., and J. Landon Lane (2013a), "Does Expansionary Monetary Policy Cause Asset Price Booms: Some Historical and Empirical Evidence" NBER Working Paper 19585 October.

Bordo, M.D., and J. Landon Lane (2013b), "What Explains House Price Booms?: History and Empirical Evidence" NBER Working Paper 19584 October.

Bordo, M.D., and R. MacDonald (2003), "The Interwar Gold Exchange Standard: Credibility and Monetary Independence", *Journal of International Money and Finance* 22 (February): 1–32.

Bordo, M.D., and R. MacDonald (2005), "Interest Rate Interactions in the Classical Gold Standard: 1880–1914; Was There Monetary Independence?", *Journal of Monetary Economics* 2 (March): 307–327.

Bordo, M.D., and A. Orphanides (2013), *The Great Inflation; The Rebirth of Modern Central Banking* (Chicago: University of Chicago Press for the NBER)

Bordo, M.D., and A. Redish (1987), "Why Did the Bank of Canada Emerge in 1935?", *Journal of Economic History* 47 (June): 405–417.

Bordo, M.D., and A. Redish 'The Lender of Last Resort: Alternative Views and Historical Experience' Federal Reserve Bank of Richmond Economic Review March.

Bordo, M.D., and A. Redish " The Bretton Woods International Monetary System: An Historical Overview" in M.D. Bordo and B. Eichengreen (Eds.), *A Retrospective on the Bretton Woods System* (Chicago: University of Chicago Press for the NBER).

Bordo, M.D., and H. Rockoff (1996b), "The Gold Standard as a Good Housekeeping Seal of Approval", *Journal of Economic History* 56 (June): 389–428.

Bordo, M.D., and A.J. Schwartz (Eds.), (1984), *A Retrospective on the Classical Gold Standard 1821–1931* (Chicago: University of Chicago Press for the NBER) pp. 361–404.

Bordo, M.D., and A.J. Schwartz (1996a), "The Operation of the Specie Standard: Evidence for Core and Peripheral Countries, 1880–1990" in B. Eichengreen and J. Braga de Macedo (Eds.), *Historical Perspectives on the Gold Standard; Portugal and the World* (London: Routledge Publishers).

Bordo, M.D., and P.L. Siklos (2014), "Central Bank Credibility, Reputation and Inflation Targeting in Historical Perspective", NBER Working Paper 20693, November.

Bordo, M.D., and D. Wheelock (2013), "The Promise and Performance of the Federal Reserve as Lender of Last Resort 1914–1933" in M.D. Bordo and W. Roberds (Eds.), *A Return to Jekyll Island* (Cambridge: Cambridge University Press).

Bordo, M.D., T. Helbling, and H. James (2007), "Swiss Exchange Rate Policy in the 1930s. Was the Delay in Devaluation Too High a Price to Pay for Conservatism?", *Open Economies Review* 18 (February): 1–25.

Bordo, M.D., C. Erceg, A. Levin, and R. Michaels (2007), "Three Great American Disinflations" NBER Working Paper No. 12982 March.

Bordo, M.D., O. Humpage, and A.J. Schwartz (2014), *Strained Relations: U.S. Monetary Policy and Foreign Exchange Operations in the Twentieth Century* (Chicago: University of Chicago Press).

Bordo, M.D., D. Simard, and E. White (1995), "France and the Bretton Woods International System" in J. Reis (Ed.), *The History of International Monetary Arrangements* (London: MacMillan).

Burdekin, R., and P.L. Siklos (2004), "Fears of Deflation and the Role of Monetary Policy: Some Lessons and An Overview" in R.C.K. Burdekin and P.L. Siklos (Eds.), *Deflation* (Cambridge: Cambridge University Press), pp. 1–30.

Capie, F. (2010), *The Bank of England 1950s to 1979* (Cambridge: Cambridge University Press).

Courchene, T. (1976), *Money, Inflation and the Bank of Canada: An Analysis of Canadian Monetary Policy from 1970 to Early 1975* (Toronto: C.D. Howe Institute).

Cross, P., and P. Bergevin (2012), "Turning Points: Business Cycles in Canada since 1926", C.D. Howe Commentary No. 366, October.

Crow, J. (1988), "The Work of Canadian Monetary Policy", Eric Hanson Memorial Lecture, January, University of Alberta.

Deutsch, J. (1957), "The Canadian Treasury and Monetary Policy", *American Economic Review* 47 (May): 220–228.

DiCecio, R., and E. Nelson (2013), "The Great Inflation in the United States and the United Kingdom: Reconciling Policy Decisions and Data Outcomes" in M.D. Bordo and A. Orphanides (Eds.), *The Great Inflation: The Rebirth of Modern Central Banking* (Chicago: University of Chicago Press for the NBER).

Dincer, N.N., and B. Eichengreen (2007), "Central Bank Transparency: Where, Why, and With What Effects?" NBER Working Paper 13003, March.

Eichengreen, B. (1992), *Golden Fetters* (Oxford: Oxford University Press).

Eitrheim, Ø., J.F. Qvigstad, and Ø.B. Skeie (2006), "Price Stability has Been the Historical Norm. What Distinguishes the Abnormal?" Norges Bank (mimeo).

Eitrheim, Ø. and L.F. Øksendal (2013), "The Cost of the Post War Economic Order in Norway: Reflections in Hindsight" Norges Bank (mimeo).

Fratianni, M., and F. Spinelli (1997), *A Monetary History of Italy* (Cambridge, Mass.: Cambridge University Press).

Fregert, K.,and L. Jonung (2008), "Inflation Targeting Is a Success So Far: 100 Years of Evidence from Swedish Contracts", *Economics Open Access E Journal* 2 :2008–2031.

Friedman, M., and A.J. Schwartz (1963), *A Monetary History of the United States 1867 to 1960* (Princeton NJ: Princeton University Press).

Geraats, P. (2014), "Monetary Policy Transparency", in J. Foessbaeck and L. Oxelheim (Eds.), *Oxford Handbook of Institutional and Economic Transparency* (Oxford: Oxford University Press), pp. 68–97.

Giavazzi, F., and M. Pagano (1991), "The Advantage of Tying One's Hands: EMS Discipline and Central Bank Credibility", *European Economic Review* 38: 303–330.

Gollan, R. (1968), *The Commonwealth Bank of Australia: Origins and Early History* (Canberra: ANU Press).

Goodfriend, M. (1993), "Interest Rate Policy and the Inflation Scare Problem 1979–1992" Federal Reserve Bank of Richmond Quarterly 79/1 (Winter).

Gordon, H.S. (1961), *The Economists versus the Bank of Canada* (Toronto: The Ryerson Press).

Grenville, S. (1996), "Recent Development in Monetary Policy: Australia and Abroad", Australian Economic Review (1st Quarter): 29–39.

Hautcoeur, P.C., A. Riva, and E. White (2014), "Can Moral Hazard Be Avoided? The Banque De France and the Crisis of 1889" Journal of Monetary Economics (forthcoming).

Hawke, G. (1973), *Between Governments and Banks* (Wellington: Reserve Bank of New Zealand).

Helleiner, E. (2006), *Towards North American Monetary Union? A Political History of Canada's Exchange Rate Regime* (Montreal: McGill-Queen's University Press).

Johnson, H.C. (1997), *Gold, France and the Great Depression, 1919–1932* (New Haven, Conn.: Yale University Press).

Jonung L. (1984), "Swedish Experience Under the Classical Gold Standard: 1873–1914" in M.D., Bordo and A.J., Schwartz (Eds.), *National Bureau of Economic Research Conference Report Series* (Chicago and London: University of Chicago Press), pp. 361–399.

Laidler, D.E.W. (1991), *How Shall We Govern the Governor?: A Critique of the Governance of the Bank of Canada* The Canada Round 1 (Toronto: C.D. Howe Institute).

An Historical and Quantitative Exploration 143

Laidler, D.E.W., and W.P. Robson (1993), *The Great Canadian Disinflation: The Economics and Politics of Canadian Monetary Policy in Canada, 1988-93* (Toronto: C.D. Howe Institute).

Meltzer, A. (2003), *A History of the Federal Reserve* Volume 1 (Chicago: University of Chicago Press).

Monnet, E. (2013), "Monetary Policy without Interest Rates. Evidence from France's Golden age (1948-1973) Using a Narrative Approach" Banque de France (mimeo).

New Zealand Treasury and Reserve Bank of New Zealand (2006), *Testing Stabilization Policy Limits in a Small Open Economy: Proceedings from a Macroeconomic Policy Forum* (Wellington: NZ Treasury).

Qvigstad, J.F. (2013), "On Institutions—Fundamentals of Confidence and Trust" Norges Bank (mimeo)

Reserve Bank of Australia (1987), *Annual Report* (Sydney: Reserve Bank of New Zealand).

Reserve Bank of New Zealand (2007), *The Reserve Bank and New Zealand's Economic History* (Wellington: Reserve Bank of New Zealand).

Rich, G. (1997), "Monetary Targets as a Policy Rule: Lessons from the Swiss Experience", *Journal of Monetary Economics* 39(1): 113-141.

Siklos, P.L. (2000), "Is the MCI a Useful Signal of Monetary Policy Conditions? An Empirical Investigation", *International Finance* 3 (November): 413-438.

(2002), *The Changing Face of Central Banking* (Cambridge: Cambridge University Press).

(2010), "Revisiting the Coyne Affair: A Singular Event That Changed the Course of Canadian Monetary History", *Canadian Journal of Economics* 43 (August): 994-1015.

Siklos, P.L., and A. Spence (2010), "Face-Off: Should the Bank of Canada Release Its Projections for the Interest Rate Path?", C.D. Howe Backgrounder 134, October, available from www.cdhowe.org/pdf/Backgrounder_134.pdf.

Siklos, P.L., and O. Karagedikli (2013), "A Bridge Too Far? RBNZ Communication, The Forward Interest Rate Track, and the Exchange Rate" (with Özer Karagedikli) in *Central Bank Transparency, Decision-Making, and Governance: The Issues, Challenges, and Case Studies* (Cambridge, Mass.: MIT Press), pp. 273-310.

Singleton, J. (2011), *Central Banking in the Twentieth Century* (Cambridge: Cambridge University Press).

Singleton, J., A. Grimes, G. Hawke, and F. Holmes (2006), *Innovation and Independence: The Reserve Bank of New Zealand* (Wellington: Auckland University Press).

Statutes of Canada (2014), laws.justice.gc.ca/eng/.

Steigum, E. (2009), "The Boom and Bust Cycle in Norway" in L. Jonung et. al. (Eds.), *The Great Financial Crisis in Finland and Sweden* (Northampton, Mass.: Edward Elgar Publishers), pp. 202-244.

Stevens, G. (2003), "Inflation Targeting: A Decade of Australian Experience", Reserve Bank of Australia Bulletin, April: 17-27.

Swan, T.W. (1940), "Australian War Finance and Banking Policy", Economic Record 16 (June): 50-67.

Swiss National Bank (2007), *The Swiss National Bank 1907-2007* (Zurich: Neue Zurcher Zeitung Publishing).

144 *Michael D. Bordo and Pierre L. Siklos*

Tattara, G. (2000), "Paper Money but a Gold Debt: Italy on the Gold Standard" *Explorations in Economic History* 40: 122–142.

Taylor, J.B. (2007), "Housing and Monetary Policy" in *Housing Finance and Monetary Policy. Federal Reserve Bank of Kansas City* (Kansas City: Kansas City Fed Symposium) pp. 463–476.

White, E.N. (2007), "The Crash of 1882, Counterparty Risk, and the Bailout of the Paris Bourse" NBER Working Paper 12933

Yeager, L. (1976), *International Monetary Relations; Theory, History and Policy* Second Edition (New York: Harper and Row).

4

The Coevolution of Money Markets and Monetary Policy, 1815–2008

Clemens Jobst

Oesterreichische Nationalbank and CEPR

Stefano Ugolini

University of Toulouse – Institute of Political Studies and LEREPS

That in their activities and operations, the Federal Reserve banks influence and are influenced by developments in the money market is but the statement of a truism. Central banks must adapt their policies to the particular credit economy in which they operate, and these policies, in turn, influence and shape money market trends (Beckhart 1932, p.3).

1 Motivation

Before 2008, central banks in developed countries not only pursued a similar macroeconomic policy – viz., slightly different versions of inflation targeting. They also implemented this policy in a broadly similar way and by relying on one main instrument: a short-term uncollateralized interbank market rate, which was kept close to the target value by liquidity-providing or liquidity-absorbing repo operations. These operations – often labelled open market operations – were done against safe assets, most often government debt, and on the central bank's own initiative. The standing facility or

---

Contact: clemens.jobst@oenb.at or stefano.ugolini@ut-capitole.fr. We thank the editors Michael Bordo, Øyvind Eitrheim, Marc Flandreau, and Jan Qvigstad for their invitation for contribution and helpful advice. We owe a great debt to Olivier Accominotti, Bill Allen, Vincent Bignon, Ulrich Bindseil, Philippine Cour-Thimann, Larry Neal, Pilar Nogués-Marco, William Roberds, Nathan Sussman, Bernhard Winkler, Lars Øksendal, to colleagues from the E.C.B. and the Belgian, Dutch, English, and Italian central banks ECB as well as to participants to presentations at Universidad Carlos III de Madrid, at the University of Warwick, at the Federal Reserve Banks of Atlanta and New York, at the European Central Bank, and at Norges Bank for sharing with us their data and/or their views on earlier drafts. The opinions expressed in this paper do not necessarily reflect those of Norges Bank, Oesterreichische Nationalbank, or the Eurosystem. The usual disclaimers apply.

discount window, available at the discretion of commercial banks, was more or less stigmatized and reserved for use in cases of emergency.

But implementation frameworks also differed in some important respects. This became suddenly evident when the financial crisis hit in 2007/2008. Beforehand, the Federal Reserve had operated exclusively with a handful of dealers in the market for Treasury debt, while the European Central Bank (ECB) traditionally auctioned liquidity to hundreds of large and small universal banks and against a much broader set of collateral. Few people cared about these differences as long as financial markets redistributed central bank liquidity smoothly within the banking system. When the wholesale market froze, however, the Fed had to introduce a number of new lending programs, while (at least in the initial phase of the crisis) the ECB managed to cope with the shock without changing its existing framework. Since then, changes in market functioning and new regulation (in particular, liquidity requirements under Basel III) have raised concerns that in the medium term, the pre-crisis operational frameworks might no longer work as before and would thus need to be adjusted.

This suggests that the microeconomic aspects of monetary policymaking – which macroeconomics and economic policy have long neglected as a merely technical issue – are worth much more attention than they are usually paid. If implementation frameworks differ significantly across countries today, a look back in time uncovers even more important dissimilarities. This raises the question of understanding why implementation frameworks actually look the way they do.

Unfortunately, not much is known about the characteristics of such frameworks in different geographical and chronological contexts. Clearly there is some interaction between the structure of money markets and the practice of monetary policy, but the question has been hardly investigated in a comprehensive manner so far. In order to address it, this paper takes a panel approach. The idea is to systematize our dispersed knowledge on the evolution of money markets and monetary policymaking, to identify regularities, and to propose hypotheses about the relation between the two.

To our knowledge, this research is innovative in at least two respects. On the one hand, we are the first ones to perform a comparative analysis (based on several newly collected datasets) of the microeconomic aspects of monetary policymaking for a relatively large number of countries over a period of nearly two centuries. As our survey starts with the early nineteenth century, we are able to cover the entire history of still existing central banks for all of the countries included in our sample except for the Bank of England, which has a longer history still. On the other hand, we are the first ones to explicitly organize information in a framework of

The Coevolution of Money Markets and Monetary Policy   147

coevolution. Our idea is that there are mutually enforcing processes in the way money markets and monetary policymaking evolve over time: the way the former work not only shapes, but is also shaped by the way the latter works. In our survey of historical evidence, we systematically collect information on both directions of causality.

Our work is at the crossroads of two independent strands of the economic and financial literature. On the one hand, there is the literature on the workings of money markets: it features a wealth of case studies focusing on specific markets in some given periods, but no panel analysis actually exists. On the other hand, there is the literature on monetary policy implementation: it features a number of interesting comparative analyses, but either they provide an only loosely connected collection of individual country portraits (e.g. Holbik 1973; Bank for International Settlements 1997), or they cover a short period of time (e.g. Kneeshaw and Van den Bergh 1989; Borio 1997) or a very limited number of countries (e.g. Goodhart *et al.* 1994; Bindseil 2004). As far as we know, works attempting to bring these two dimensions together are exceedingly scarce – one exception being Forssbæck and Oxelheim (2007), who cover a number of small European countries from 1980 to 2000. Our research breaks new ground not only because it provides a panel analysis of a larger number of developed countries over a very long period, but also because it links these two strands of the literature in a systematic way throughout the analysis.

The remainder is organized as follows. Section 2 sketches a conceptual framework for approaching the question of the coevolution of money markets and monetary policy design. Section 3 constructs quantitative indicators to capture long-term trends and patterns, and presents three newly collected historical datasets. Section 4 concludes.

2 The Coevolution of Money Markets and Monetary Policy: A Conceptual Framework

Coevolution is defined as the influence of closely associated objects on each other in their evolution: changes in A will trigger changes in B, which in turn will trigger changes in A – and so on and so forth, in a continuous loop. The medium- to long-run evolution of money market structures and monetary policy design is a clear case of such reciprocal influence. In what follows, we focus on the channels through which causality works in both directions. First, we ask how the way money markets are structured may impact the design of monetary policymaking. Then, we ask how the way monetary policy is designed may impact the structure of money markets. Finally, we present our approach with respect to this question.

2.1 From Money Markets to Central Banks

A central bank is generally defined as a banking institution whose liabilities (banknotes and deposits) play the role of ultimate medium of exchange (high-powered money) in a given geographical area. This privileged situation is granted to the central bank by its sitting at the center of the payments system. Such a privilege typically does not come without strings attached, as a central bank is often required to be the ultimate banker to the government. In view of this, a central bank's final objectives may be manifold. They may include: preventing disruptions in the payments system (by keeping an efficient financial infrastructure or implementing lending of last resort), protecting the real value of its liabilities (by maintaining convertibility, a foreign exchange target or price stability), supporting government finance (by lending directly to the Treasury or keeping orderly conditions in the government debt market), supporting some particular institutions or sectors considered as strategically important (by providing subsidized loans or preferential credit conditions), and ensuring profitability to shareholders (by farming seigniorage and other operating revenues, which historically often meant running a commercial banking business).

In order to pursue these aims, a central bank typically interacts with the rest of the financial system through the interface of money markets. A money market is generally defined as the locus in which credit assets of short maturity (e.g. up to one year) are exchanged. Because of the particularly short average maturity of a central bank's liabilities, money markets tend to be its preferred domain of operation. Yet many different money markets often coexist, and the central bank will not necessarily be active in all of them. The choice to participate or not in a particular market may depend on different orders of factors. First, it may be dictated by the nature of the central bank's final objectives (e.g. entering the government debt market if political requirements imply so, or the foreign exchange market if a foreign exchange target is set). Second, it may be influenced by the fundamental properties of the underlying asset – viz., its *ex-ante* liquidity (the existence of a sufficiently strong supply and demand) and inherent credit risk (the characteristics of debtors, the opportunity to create supervisory structures, the easiness to seize collateral). Third (and most important), it will be urged by the actual possibility for the central bank to produce significant and durable effects on the financial system – viz., the bank's capacity to effectively influence market prices, and the market's ability to transmit impulses to the wider system and thus serve the bank so as to achieve its ultimate objectives.

The Coevolution of Money Markets and Monetary Policy   149

Once the central bank has selected the money markets in which it will participate, it can proceed to organize its operations. The design of monetary operations depends on market characteristics at a twofold level. On the one hand, the bank's stance towards liquidity provision may be active or passive: it may leave initiative to its counterparties (as is the case with standing facilities) or, alternatively, take initiative on its own (as is the case with open market operations). On the other hand, according to the identity and features of market participants, the bank will decide on the counterparties it wants to interact with. This selection may be relatively neutral (including all or most market participants) or alternatively non-neutral (possibly creating privileged positions for a small group of counterparties, selected according to some particular criteria). The way monetary policy is designed will, in turn, have an impact on the market characteristics on the basis of which it had been formulated.

2.2 From Central Banks to Money Markets

Once a central bank has chosen to enter a given money market, the latter will no longer look the same. Because of the monetary authority's involvement, in fact, crucial changes are bound to take place in the microstructure of the market and, consequently, in the behavior of prices.

In view of its size and its faculty to create high-powered money out of nothing (albeit subject to some constraints), the central bank is not an actor in the money market as any other. In fact, the central bank's participation in a market inevitably enhances the liquidity of the market *ex post* – not only because it establishes a direct channel through which financial assets can be converted into cash, but also because it might encourage further participation via network effects. Moreover, a central bank often has the firepower to become the market-maker of the money markets it participates in – thus modifying their microstructure very radically. The presence of a market-maker impeding complete dry-ups of demand (i.e. a lender of last resort) may provide a money market with a competitive advantage with respect to others; such "subsidization" can be so extreme as to allow for the creation of previously inexistent markets. Thanks to its power, a central bank may be able to impose modifications on the characteristics of market participants (e.g. by refusing to operate with some kinds of counterparties) as well as on the characteristics of the exchanged assets (e.g. by requiring standardization or quality enhancement).

By construction, changes in the microstructure of money markets have a direct impact on price behavior. The market-maker's willingness to buy unlimited amounts at a given bid price (i.e. the existence of a purchase or lending facility) sets a floor to market prices, while its willingness to sell unlimited amounts at a given ask price (i.e. the existence of a selling facility) sets a ceiling. Prices can also be impacted indirectly by the central bank's spot and forward buying and selling operations, or – even in the absence of transactions – by the simple creation of expectations. All of this will decrease the volatility of prices, thus potentially reducing the amount of market risk associated with the given monetary asset.

The relationship between central bank intervention and market success is far from being univocal, though. The complexity of this relationship emerges when money markets with an active central bank are compared to markets without. On the one hand, it is possible that non-participated markets suffer from a relative decline in liquidity and popularity in front of participated ones because of the aforementioned reasons. This might imply that a central bank's involvement in a market may get so heavy, that when policy objectives change and the central bank wants to disengage, the commercial market structure left behind is inadequate and there is a risk of a sudden loss of liquidity. On the other hand, however, the central bank's market power over participated markets may open scope for some sort of "regulatory" arbitrage: in fact, it is also possible that non-participated markets become an ideal outlet for those unable or unwilling to abide with the central bank's requirements, as well as for those looking at price volatility as a positive thing (i.e. generating profit opportunities). As a result, central banks' endeavor to impact money market structure may backfire, as it may not necessarily increase the efficacy of monetary policy itself.

2.3 Conceptual Issues: Sum-Up

The evolution of money markets and that of monetary policymaking are determined by both exogenous and endogenous factors. Money markets may evolve because of changes originating outside the financial system (e.g. increasing or decreasing demand or supply of a given asset as industrial or commercial practices develop). Some of these changes might be country-specific while others international. But money markets may also evolve because of modifications in the operational and regulatory policies adopted by central banks. In turn, monetary policymaking may evolve because of changes originating outside the financial system (e.g. increasing or decreasing importance attached to certain asset classes as political conditions develop), but also because of modifications in the characteristics

The Coevolution of Money Markets and Monetary Policy

of money markets. Assessing precisely the relative weight of exogenous and endogenous factors in triggering evolutionary trends is still an impossible task given the current state of our knowledge. In the light of this, we opt for a descriptive rather than an explanatory approach as a first step into this largely under-researched subject. In what follows, we try to mobilize as much as possible historical information. With the aim of identifying from hard data broad trends and empirical regularities, Section 3 mainly presents quantitative evidence, complemented by qualitative information available from different types of sources. Our goal is to provide an as much as possible inclusive review of the coevolutionary trends that have emerged over the last two hundred years.

3 Quantitative Evidence

To develop a sense of how much the interaction between money markets and monetary policymaking has changed over time and to identify relevant criteria and indicators, it is convenient to start from an obvious but telling example: a basic comparison of the monetary practices of the world's most important central bank today (viz. the Federal Reserve) with those of the world's most important central bank around one hundred years before (viz. the Bank of England).

Before 2008, the Federal Reserve could be sketchily (albeit, under some respects, rather imperfectly) described as a central bank mainly operating (a) in the government bond market (b) by implementing repos (c) on its own initiative (d) with a relatively small number of counterparties (e) while offering a more or less stigmatized standing facility exclusively as an emergency tool, and this (f) with the aim of targeting the uncollateralized interbank market interest rate (g) in order for the latter to basically coincide with the main policy rate – i.e. (h) much lower than the standing facility rate. One century ago, instead, the Bank of England could have been sketchily (but again, quite imperfectly) described as a central bank mainly operating (a) in the acceptance market (b) by discounting assets (c) on the initiative of counterparties, through a standing facility (d) potentially open to a very large number of counterparties (including non-banks) and (e) not stigmatized, (f) with the aim of targeting the acceptance market interest rate (g) in order for the latter to fluctuate freely (h) below but close to the standing facility rate.

This rough "bird's eye" comparison suggests that the design of monetary policy implementation frameworks has been subjected to major changes over the decades. It also allows singling out three main dimensions along which interaction between money markets and central banks can be described: **(1)** The **location** of the interaction, i.e. what is the money market in which the central bank mainly intervenes (government debt market vs. acceptance market) *(a; f)*; **(2)** The **form** of the interaction, i.e. what is the type of financial operation the central bank mainly adopts for intervention (collateralized vs. uncollateralized, repos vs. discounts) *(a; b)*; and **(3)** The **substance** of the interaction, which has several aspects – what are the counterparties to the central bank *(d)*, who takes the initiative in monetary policy operations *(c)*, what are the limits to operations (quantitative restrictions or stigma) *(e)* – which altogether determine the relative position of official bank rates and market rates *(g; h)*. The three dimensions concern both directions of causation in coevolutionary patterns: what they all tell about is always the "reduced-form" outcome of the interaction between central bank preferences and choices, market structures and functioning, and fundamental factors affecting both. This does not in itself allow deducing the underlying supply and demand factors. Still, combined with assumptions and additional information on exogenous factors impacting market development and central bank preferences, it permits getting an idea on causation within the coevolution framework.

All three dimensions lend themselves to quantitative characterization. In order to be useful, quantitative indicators should not only be representative of coevolutionary trends and patterns. They should abstract from institutional details, yet reflect the economic logic underlying monetary intervention and market functioning – thus allowing for reasonable comparisons over time and space. Fortunately, available data allow constructing indicators abiding by these criteria: **(1)** Monetary authorities' main domain of intervention can be assessed by looking at the relative share of each money market instrument within their holdings – i.e. through an analysis of the composition of the asset side of central banks' balance sheets (a *stock variable*); **(2)** The forms of the relationship between markets and banks can be assessed by looking at the type of instruments most often used by the central bank – i.e. through an analysis of the turnover in central banks' operations (a *flow variable*); **(3)** The most substantial aspect of the relationship between markets and banks is price formation, which can be captured by comparing interest rates in the private market with official central bank rates – i.e. though an analysis of the spreads between interbank rates and standing facility rates (a *price variable*). In the end, the three indicators have to be interpreted together to yield a comprehensive picture of the bank-market relationship.

The next three subsections will address these three questions through a panel analysis of each indicator across time and space. The sample includes

The Coevolution of Money Markets and Monetary Policy

a number of big and small countries, situated either at the core of international monetary system or at its periphery. Although we make an effort to provide a reasonably representative overview, our selection criterion is inevitably heuristic. Reflecting long-lasting world financial equilibria, the countries in our sample are mostly located in Western Europe (Austria, Belgium, Britain, France, Germany, Italy, the Netherlands, Norway, and Switzerland), but we also include the United States. Besides the central banks still existing to date (Oesterreichische Nationalbank, Banque Nationale de Belgique, Bank of England, Banque de France, Deutsche Bundesbank, Banca d'Italia, De Nederlandsche Bank, Norges Bank, Schweizerische Nationalbank, and the Federal Reserve), we also cover institutions that provided central banking functions in earlier times (such as Belgium's Société Générale, Germany's Königliche Hauptbank, Preußische Bank, Reichsbank, and Bank deutscher Länder, Italy's Banca di Genova and Banca Nazionale nel Regno d'Italia, as well as the Second Bank of the United States).

3.1 The Location of Interaction: The Central Bank Balance Sheet

The balance sheet of the central bank reflects all its transactions and operations: the issuance of banknotes, purchase and sale of precious metals and foreign exchange, investments, as well as monetary policy operations proper. The composition of the central bank's assets is determined by its ultimate and intermediate objectives: these can include stable exchange rates or the convertibility of its liabilities into some foreign asset, a particular level of short-term interest rates, the quantity of some central bank liability or wider monetary aggregates, support to the government, profitability (notably in the case of privately owned central banks), or the support to some selected sectors or institutions. The central bank will choose its investment assets and the type of operations in order to achieve its objectives.[1] Key characteristics of the assets are risk, maturity, and liquidity; key characteristics of the markets and operations are the possibility to influence or set prices, as well as the importance of the selected asset/market for the broader financial and economic structure – so that policy impulses are

---

[1] In principle, the central bank can manage liquidity conditions also through the liability side of its balance sheet, e.g. through liquidity absorbing repo operations. This is in fact the case in a number of countries with a structural liquidity surplus often due to strong foreign exchange inflows that are sterilized. The phenomenon is however very recent and does not warrant the collection and harmonization of the liabilities for the period under consideration here.

transmitted predictably to other asset prices and the real economy in accordance with the objectives of the central bank.

The use of balance sheet data for assessing central bankers' main domain of intervention does come with a number of caveats. Definitions are not uniform, as they reflect different realities: central bank balance sheets have always been drawn up in the absence of international standards and with accounting rules that vary substantially between countries and over time (Käppeli 1930; Bindseil 2004). Moreover, a high share of a particular instrument in the central bank's portfolio might not necessarily imply that this instrument is particularly important in money market management, but reflect other considerations such as the earning of returns, the subsidization of particular agents, or the transfer of resources to the government. A further complication is due to the fact that central bank reports typically distinguish according to operations, not underlying instruments: advances showing up in the balance sheet may have been granted on marketable securities but also on commercial bills, while discounts may have concerned commercial bills but also Treasury bills. These limitations should be kept in mind when interpreting the following evidence. Despite these caveats, it is nonetheless fair to say that balance sheet data provide an illustrative representation of the broad lines along which interaction between money markets and central banks takes place.

An eternal concern for central banks is the liquidity of their investments. Such a concern, which might seem odd for the sole institutions that can create liquidity at their will, has its roots in the way they have to pursue their monetary policy objectives. As long as central banks aimed to ensure the convertibility of their liquid liabilities (banknotes and deposits) into foreign assets (gold, silver, or foreign exchange) on demand, the bank's portfolio had to be sufficiently liquid to allow a quick reduction of the amount of outstanding liabilities to prevent the exhaustion of reserves of bullion or foreign exchange reserves. In the case of inconvertible fiat currencies there is no threat of a run on foreign reserves, yet the central bank has to be able to adjust the level of its liabilities in order to adjust liquidity conditions in line with its operational target (be it a short term interest rate, an exchange rate, or monetary aggregates: in this setting, the asset portfolio has again to be sufficiently liquid to allow for a precise and timely adjustment of the liquidity position of the banking sector.

Table 4.1 gives the composition of the asset side of the balance sheets of the ten central banks in our sample for seven benchmark years (1835, 1880, 1909, 1928, 1950, 1970, and 1990). The benchmark dates were selected according to three criteria: i) being representative of the period; ii) being as much as

The Coevolution of Money Markets and Monetary Policy

Table 4.1: *Composition of central bank assets (in percentage)*

Austria	1835	1880	1909	1928	1950	1970	1990
Gold, Silver	18	31	54	12	1	32	16
Other foreign assets	0	3	2	54	5	43	41
Discounts	5	25	23	15	31	12	15
Advances	5	4	3	0	0	0	0
Open market operations	0	0	0	0	0	0	18
Other lending to private sector	0	17	10	0	0	0	0
Gov't securities/claims on gov't	69	14	2	8	63	9	0
Securities not specified	2	5	1	0	0	3	7
Other assets	1	2	6	11	0	1	3

Belgium	1835	1880	1909	1928	1950	1970	1990
Gold, Silver	7	20	15	35	29	29	8
Other foreign assets	0	11	14	21	12	46	62
Discounts	6	48	53	25	11	3	4
Advances	8	2	6	1	1	0	0
Open market operations	0	0	0	0	0	0	0
Other lending to private sector	9	0	0	0	0	0	0
Gov't securities/claims on gov't	34	10	9	16	46	20	21
Securities not specified	2	0	0	0	0	0	0
Other assets	35	9	4	2	2	3	5

Britain	1835	1880	1909	1928	1950	1970	1990
Gold, Silver	12	31	36	31	0	0	0
Other foreign assets	0	0	0	0	0	0	0
Discounts	30	3	10	1	1	0	6
Advances	15	11	6	1	0	2	3
Open market operations	5	0	0	0	0	0	0
Other lending to private sector	0	0	0	0	0	0	0
Gov't securities/claims on gov't	30	38	31	60	97	91	58
Securities not specified	4	17	16	6	2	6	26
Other assets	4	0	2	1	0	2	7

(*continued*)

Table 4.1 (*continued*)

France	1835	1880	1909	1928	1950	1970	1990
Gold, Silver	29	53	70	37	10	5	29
Other foreign assets	0	0	0	41	17	27	26
Discounts	41	30	14	5	24	37	0
Advances	12	5	9	3	1	0	0
Open market operations	0	0	0	0	0	0	19
Other lending to private sector	0	0	0	0	0	0	0
Gov't securities/claims on gov't	16	8	6	4	36	7	8
Securities not specified	0	0	0	7	8	17	3
Other assets	3	4	1	3	3	7	14

Germany	1835	1880	1909	1928	1950	1970	1990
Gold, Silver	14	53	30	47	6	60	30
Other foreign assets	0	0	4	1	0	0	0
Discounts	9	32	37	38	24	20	24
Advances	13	5	10	2	8	2	2
Open market operations	0	0	0	0	0	0	34
Other lending to private sector	11	0	0	0	2	0	0
Gov't securities/claims on gov't	34	4	2	1	55	14	4
Securities not specified	0	1	11	2	2	1	0
Other assets	18	5	7	9	3	3	6

Italy	1845	1880	1909	1928	1950	1970	1990
Gold, Silver	20	16	42	22	0	19	11
Other foreign assets	0	0	5	25	12	0	11
Discounts	77	23	21	17	3	1	0
Advances	2	6	6	8	7	8	2
Open market operations	0	0	0	0	0	1	1
Other lending to private sector	0	0	0	0	0	0	0
Gov't securities/claims on gov't	0	12	19	18	76	69	70
Securities not specified	0	13	2	0	0	1	1
Other assets	1	30	6	10	1	1	4

The Coevolution of Money Markets and Monetary Policy

Netherlands	1835	1880	1909	1928	1950	1970	1990
Gold, Silver	46	65	44	57	17	55	35
Other foreign assets	0	0	5	26	26	28	43
Discounts	23	18	19	9	0	2	0
Advances	30	17	21	8	1	0	14
Open market operations	0	0	0	0	0	12	4
Other lending to private sector	0	0	8	0	0	0	0
Gov't securities/ claims on gov't	0	0	0	0	56	0	0
Securities not specified	0	0	3	0	0	0	0
Other assets	0	0	1	0	0	3	5

Norway	1835	1880	1909	1928	1950	1970	1990
Gold, Silver	35	49	42	31	3	1	0
Other foreign assets	0	0	6	9	8	46	53
Discounts	7	30	32	26	0	0	0
Advances	0	0	1	21	0	0	31
Open market operations	0	0	1	0	0	0	0
Other lending to private sector	56	21	2	0	0	1	0
Gov't securities/claims on gov't	0	0	0	0	87	39	13
Securities not specified	0	0	11	5	1	9	0
Other assets	1	0	5	8	1	4	2

Switzerland	1835	1880	1909	1928	1950	1970	1990
Gold, Silver	-	-	39	48	90	51	22
Other foreign assets	-	-	14	22	4	45	70
Discounts	-	-	32	18	3	2	1
Advances	-	-	4	7	1	1	0
Open market operations	-	-	0	0	0	0	0
Other lending to private sector	-	-	0	0	0	0	0
Gov't securities/claims on gov't	-	-	0	0	0	0	0
Securities not specified	-	-	3	2	1	1	5
Other assets	-	-	8	3	1	0	1

(continued)

Table 4.1 (continued)

United States	1831	1880	1909	1928	1950	1970	1990
Gold, Silver	16	-	-	51	46	12	4
Other foreign assets	2	-	-	0	0	0	3
Discounts	63	-	-	20	0	0	0
Advances	0	-	-	0	0	0	0
Open market operations	0	-	-	9	0	0	6
Other lending to private sector	0	-	-	0	0	0	0
Gov't securities/claims on gov't	10	-	-	4	44	70	74
Securities not specified	0	-	-	0	0	0	0
Other assets	9	-	-	16	10	17	14

possible unbiased by cyclical factors (i.e. avoiding boom and bust periods); and iii) being compatible with data availability. Assets are grouped into the following broad categories: foreign assets, which can be decomposed into precious metals (gold, silver) and other foreign assets (bills of exchange, deposits abroad, securities denominated in foreign currencies); monetary policy operations as discounts, advances, and open market operations; and claims on the government, either as direct loans and overdrafts or holdings of government securities. In addition to these components, which are the most important from a monetary policy point of view, balance sheets also include other lending to the private sector (outside monetary policy operations) like mortgage loans, long-term lending to specific financial institutions, unspecified securities, and other assets including real estate, stakeholdings, etc.

Figure 4.1 summarizes the changes in the composition of central bank assets. The following trends emerge. In the 1830s, **foreign assets** consist exclusively of bullion. From a long perspective, all countries report in these years relatively low shares of reserves in total assets. As money market integration improves in the following decades, the share of foreign assets increases everywhere. At the beginning of the twentieth century, foreign bills start to appear in all balance sheets except those of the Bank of England. While holdings are small in absolute terms, they represent an element that is more and more actively used for active exchange rate policy in Austria (Jobst 2009), Belgium (Ugolini 2012), France (Flandreau and Gallice 2005), and Germany (Bopp 1953). This reflects internationally integrated money markets that require central banks to manage the impact

The Coevolution of Money Markets and Monetary Policy 159

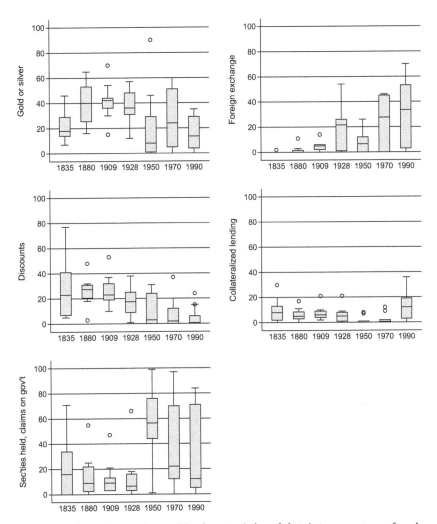

Figure 4.1: Composition of central bank assets (selected dates), in percentage of total assets
Source: Authors' database. For the countries included at the various dates, see Table 4.1.
Note: Each central bank is one observation. For individual country data see Table 4.1. Boxes cover observations between the first and third quartile (inside line being the median), whiskers cover the remaining observations except outside values. Outside values (smaller/larger than the first/third quartile less/plus 1.5 times the interquartile range) are plotted individually.

of short-term capital flows on domestic liquidity: in this context, foreign exchange markets are more liquid and have lower transaction costs than operations in precious metals. In the interwar years the share of foreign exchange increases further to the detriment of gold, as foreign exchange serves more and more as reserve asset in addition to its role as intervention instrument (Eichengreen and Flandreau 2009): the only two exceptions are the anchors of the gold-exchange standard, the Fed and the Bank of England, which hold reserves in gold rather than foreign exchange. Following the break-down of the interwar gold standards, in some countries (e.g. Britain and the United States) gold and foreign exchange reserves were transferred to the Treasury and no longer show up in the central bank's balance sheet. For the majority of countries, total foreign reserves remain relatively high until the 1970s, when an increasing divergence becomes visible. Although some of the divergence is due to different accounting practices (historical costs vs. market value) that began to matter with the end of Bretton Woods, today reserve holdings appear to be much more a function of country size and exchange rate regime, and thus of the need for regular operations in the foreign exchange market (Borio *et al.* 2008).

Domestic monetary operations (as opposed to operations in foreign assets) were long dominated by discounts and advances. In discount operations the central bank buys a financial claim with a short initial or remaining maturity at a discount to its nominal value (the discount rate). In most cases these claims were bills of exchange, sometimes also treasury bills. In advance or lombard operations the central bank grants a loan against some pledged collateral, which are typically securities, sometimes precious metal or goods. The principal difference between the two operations is that discounting is unsecured, i.e. the central bank depends solely on the ability of the issuer to pay, while advances are secured, i.e. in addition to the borrower's ability to pay the central bank also disposes of a pledge that can be sold if the counterparty fails to repay (see Section 3.2). In the first half of the nineteenth century advances can rival with discounts, but rapidly lose importance afterwards. Advances gain again in importance before World War I and during the interwar years. After World War II, patterns appear more idiosyncratic. Open market operations, which in the graph are included alongside advances, only start to appear in the 1920s, the exception being the Bank of England that operated in exchequer bills and East India Company securities to adjust overall liquidity conditions as early as the 1830s (Wood 1939) and then in the 1890s to absorb liquidity (Sayers 1936). The classification here follows official statements given by central banks. In practice, the distinction between advances, open market operations, and security holdings becomes blurry after the 1950s and would require a closer reading of national documentation: in the case of the Fed and the Bank of England, for instance, open market operations appear under the heading "lending to the government" as well as under "other securities". Despite this caveat, it is possible to say that the extensive use of open market operations depends very much on the size and liquidity of underlying markets: thus, it only appears when financial markets are liberalized, and earlier in larger countries, while smaller countries stick longer with traditional discount and/or advance operations (Kneeshaw and Van den Bergh 1989; Borio 1997).

Claims on the government appear mainly driven by geopolitical factors. Central banks came out of the Napoleonic Wars with significant holdings of government debt, which were very slowly reduced over the whole nineteenth century. Remarkably, no major impact of World War I is visible in 1928 (except for Britain), as very large holdings accumulated during the conflict had already been inflated away by then (especially in Austria and Germany). By contrast, the impact of World War II appears much more persistent everywhere. Today, the central banks with relatively large government debt portfolios are those holding relatively few foreign assets (Federal Reserve, Bank of England). It should be noted that this category covers a wide range of operations with very different implications for money markets and monetary policy. On the one hand, central banks have often been obliged to hold government debt as compensation for the note-issuing privilege. Typically these loans were remunerated below market interest rate in order to transfer seigniorage revenue to the Treasury before the introduction of explicit profit sharing arrangements. This was the case e.g. in Austria, Britain, and France. As these loans were long-term, they did not imply any particular involvement of the central bank in government debt markets. On the other hand, though, government debt has also typically served as collateral or investment asset in monetary policy operations. In this case, the main focus is on changing liquidity conditions in the money market, not on influencing the interest expenses of the government in particular. As a result, large holdings after wars might reflect not only past monetization of government deficits, but also the increased breadth and liquidity of the government debt market. Additionally, holdings of government debt can also serve to satisfy the structural demand for banknotes and central bank deposits. Purchases of long-term government debt have the advantage to be low-risk and avoid the costs of lending operations (which have to be frequently renewed). For instance, before 2007 the Federal Reserve provided about two-thirds of the required liquidity against long-term Treasury bonds. In the Euro area much of the structural liquidity demand is catered for through the investment portfolios of the national central banks, again reducing the need for regular liquidity-providing repos. The same is probably true of the securities held by the Bank of England for most of its history (Wood 1939). A positive impact on government finance will however result indirectly from the ensuing increased liquidity of government debt. Before 2008, central banks typically tried to isolate these structural operations from monetary policy, and calibrated purchases so that they did not change asset prices or the yield curve (Board of Governors 2005). Lastly, central banks can operate in the government debt market to influence interest rates more broadly. This is the logic behind the Fed's post-2009 Large Scale Asset Purchase programs (LSAP) that aimed for a general reduction of longer-term market rates rather than the interest rate on government debt alone (Borio and Disyatat 2010). **Other items** are most of the time small and patterns not systematic.

To sum up, our analysis of balance sheet data allows singling out a number of trends in the evolution of the channels through which interaction between money markets and central banks takes place. (i) Foreign exchange markets initially played a relatively small role everywhere, but their importance increased substantially as international market integration developed – country size being a fundamental determinant of central bank involvement into this market. As far as domestic markets are concerned, (ii) government debt markets played a varying role across time and space which was mainly driven by the impact of geopolitical factors on market size, while private debt markets experienced a secular decline: (iii) the discount market peaked in the second half of the nineteenth century and then contracted throughout all of the twentieth century to almost disappear, while (iv) the collateralized loan market contracted during the nineteenth century, partially revived in the first half of the twentieth century, almost disappeared after World War II, and made some comeback in recent decades only. Interestingly, the central banks of large countries appear to have resorted to domestic collateralized lending earlier and more often than those of smaller ones, while the opposite is true for foreign reserves – probably reflecting an international specialization of money markets.

3.2 The Form of Interaction: Uncollateralized vs. Collateralized Lending

Section 3.1 has brought to light a changing importance of uncollateralized vs. collateralized lending by monetary authorities. The two techniques of intervention can be associated to two different concepts of liquidity, corresponding respectively to today's definitions of *liability-side (funding) liquidity*, i.e. the ease with which funding can be obtained, and *asset-side (market) liquidity*, i.e. the ease with which a given asset can be sold

(Holmström and Tirole 2010). In some scholars' view, these two conceptions of liquidity are but the two sides of the same coin (see e.g. Brunnermeier and Pedersen 2009): but this applies only if liability-side liquidity can be exclusively obtained through collateralized loans, access to which is proportional to capital. This is not necessarily always the case, though: when uncollateralized transactions are easily available, funding and market liquidity are not bound to behave accordingly. The reason is that the role of capital as a transmission channel between the two (Brunnermeier and Pedersen 2009) may not be at work: as a matter of fact, access to uncollateralized operations may not be proportional to capital but involve other kinds of (moral) guarantee (Ghatak and Guinnane 1999). This suggests that the two concepts do not perfectly coincide, and that the fact that central banks chiefly provide the one or the other type of liquidity may have important consequences on the overall behavior of the financial system.

The extent to which central bankers embark into the one or the other technique of intervention may be related to the credit risk associated with the two types of operations. In principle, thanks to the double guarantee provided by the borrower and by the collateral, secured transactions should be less risky – in particular if the collateral consists of easily marketable government securities and haircuts are significant. Unsecured lending through the purchase of commercial bills, however, benefits from the additional safety feature provided by the joint moral guarantee of all persons (at least two) who have signed the bill. Unlike marketable securities, moreover, bills are subject to credit risk but not to market risk, as their price at maturity is not liable to vary. As a result, none of the two types of operations is necessarily superior to the other as far as risk is concerned.

In addition, resort to the one or the other form of intervention may be dictated to central bankers by market characteristics. As stated earlier (Sections 2.1 and 3.1), central banks have to keep liquid assets, and *ex-ante* liquidity is a determinant of the choice of the money market in which they intervene. Yet each money market only features one possible operation: by definition, only uncollateralized lending is possible on the discount market, while only collateralized lending is possible on the repo market. As a result, the forms assumed by the market-bank interaction may depend on preexisting structural factors.

Lastly, and most importantly, the choice of the technique of intervention will depend on the preferences of central banks. The latter appear to have changed considerably over time according to evolving institutional environments. Commentators unanimously report that discounting of uncollateralized (but jointly guaranteed) bills of exchange was clearly preferred in the nineteenth century. Reasons seem manifold. First, discounting was deemed to provide more flexibility for the adjustment of overall liquidity. For instance, Niebuhr (1854) argues that bills of exchange were always paid on time, while advances on securities and goods were most difficult to diminish in critical times as borrowers faced declining prices of their collateral assets. In a variation of this argument, Wagner (1873) maintains that continuous backflows from bills falling due could facilitate the granting of new loans to new counterparties, which was useful whenever money markets were not working perfectly. Mecenseffý (1896) and Reichsbank (1910) similarly argue that the central bank might have been forced to prolong advances or face difficulties selling the collateral in the very moment when the liquidity of its portfolio became more important due to a crisis. Bills, on the other hand, were considered to be "self-liquidating", a widespread notion in nineteenth-century banking (Plumptre 1940). The same concern about liquidity can also explain the preference of many central banks for real bills over finance bills, as finance bills needing to be rolled over at maturity rather resemble advances on securities in moments of financial stress. Second, an additional argument in favor of discounting was the possibility for the central bank to derive information on economic activity from the bills submitted to discount (Reichsbank 1910; Roulleau 1914). Central banks were in fact big players in the market. Because of this, they were necessarily concerned about financial stability, and the discounting of bills was thought to provide the possibility to manage the extent of risk taking in the economy. Advances were frequently associated with the financing of stock exchange speculation through margin trading because the overall position of borrowers could not be observed by central bankers, while the origination and distribution of bills were easier to track. By encouraging or discouraging the presentation of certain types of bills for discounting at its discount window, central banks could encourage or discourage particular activities or sectors (Allen 2014).

On balance, discounting was thus perceived as more advantageous in the nineteenth century, and many central banks actively encouraged discount operations. Policies included preferential interest rates and measures to increase the pool of eligible bills by opening branch offices, lowering the minimum nominal amount of eligible bills as well as by reducing the number of signatures required on a bill (most central banks changed from three to two signatures over the course of the century).

Central bankers' attitude seems to have changed following World War I. This prompted a rethinking of the concept of liquidity, which

The Coevolution of Money Markets and Monetary Policy   165

became closer to the modern one – according to which asset- and liability-side liquidity are but the two sides of the same coin (Plumptre 1940; Brunnermeier and Pedersen 2009). Consequently, most central banks started to care less about the relative weight of discounts vs. advances. The long-running opposition of outright purchases vs. secured lending focuses today not on the maturity of outright holdings (i.e. their being "self-liquidating") but on the possibility to sell them in the market if need be (i.e. their "shiftability"): the *ex-ante* liquidity of the markets for those assets potentially used in monetary policy operations is thus a crucial input for the design of open market operations today (Borio 1997). While some central banks (notably, the Fed) keep lending operations to a minimum and operate mostly through outright purchases, others (like the Eurosystem) rely much more on secured lending. Outright purchases expose the central bank fully to credit risk, thus severely limiting the spectrum of assets that qualify for eligibility. The main argument in favor of secured loans is therefore that they can be done on a much broader set of assets without requiring the central bank to analyze credit risk, as the prime responsibility for repayment remains with the counterparty and risk control measures can be limited to keeping a sufficient margin on the collateral. Outright purchases, on the other hand, can be more long-term. This is an advantage insofar as the central bank can reduce the size of operations, limiting operational costs and risks. An additional argument is that long-term outright purchases allow the central bank to earn a term premium. In the end, the relative preferences of central banks seem again related to the structure of the financial system they are operating in. Outright operations in a narrow range of assets require the existence of a sufficient amount of eligible assets, as well as of developed and integrated money markets that can smoothly redistribute central bank liquidity within the banking system and financial markets more broadly. Secured lending operations, on the other hand, give potentially more counterparts direct access to the central bank using a potentially broader and diverse set of assets as collateral (Bindseil and Papadia 2009). This might be more necessary in financial systems that are less well integrated or lack a deep and sufficiently large market in potential assets for outright holdings. The different structure of financial markets in the United States and the euro area and the different choices in monetary policy implementation are thus clearly linked.

Figure 4.2 gives continuous series for the share of advances in total domestic lending between 1815 and 1990. Numbers refer to average or end-of-year holdings. However, as unlike outright holdings of securities, discounts and advances were by statutory rules short-term, with a maturity

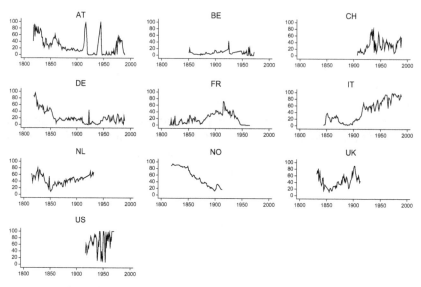

Figure 4.2: Share of advances in domestic lending
Source: Authors' database.

Table 4.2: *Share of advances in domestic lending (advances + discounts)*

	AT	BE	CH	DE	FR	IT	NL	NO	UK
1820	74			71	6		60	91	
1830	51			51	9		60	89	64
1840	34			43	8	11	33	84	36
1850	43	9		30	18	25	22	66	18
1860	38	3		14	16	26	33	52	25
1870	21	3		15	9	13	33	41	38
1880	15	6		17	25	4	44	32	51
1890	16	7		18	33	5	46	20	44
1900	13	10	10	16	40	17	47	26	68
1910	19	12	15	11	34	23	50	19	50

Note: For Norway, mortgage lending is included in domestic lending. War and immediate post-war periods (1914–1919) are excluded from the calculation.

of typically three months or lower, the levels give an approximation of turnover and thus the importance of the two instruments in policy operations. Table 4.2 and Figure 4.3 synthesize available information on all countries by providing averages per decade. This we do only until World War I, as data become exceedingly scarce for the following period.

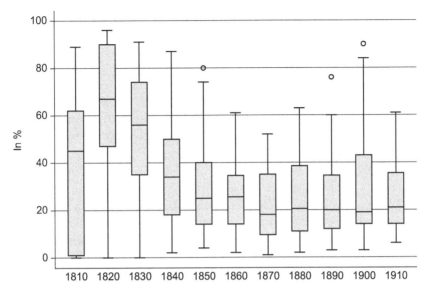

Figure 4.3: Share of advances in domestic lending, averages per decade
Source: Authors' database.
Note: For individual country data, see Table 4.2.

Unlike what was to be expected from contemporaries' preferences, the discounting of bills did not always dominate. With the exception of Banque de France, advances dominated domestic lending in all central banks in the first decades of the nineteenth century. Discounts then increased everywhere at the expense of advances until the 1850s. For the second half of the nineteenth century two groups of countries can be distinguished. On the one hand, in the Netherlands and Britain the share of advances recovers gradually, if not to the levels seen at the beginning of the nineteenth century; also in France it increases notably after the 1880s. On the other hand, in Belgium, Germany, and Austria advances remain stable at low levels between 10 and 20 percent of total lending. If the preference for bills was in fact constant over the nineteenth century, the increase in bill holdings must have reflected a better availability of bills towards the mid of the century. Ziegler (1993) makes this argument for Prussia, where the integration of the Prussian market and the growing importance of trade increased the availability of eligible bills. While the Königliche Hauptbank relied to a large extent on holdings of long-term securities and advances, the statutes of the Preußische Bank (which succeeded the Königliche Hauptbank in 1847) could in a first step limit the share of advances in the cover of the fiduciary note issue to one sixth, and exclude them altogether after 1856 (Ziegler 1993). From the late 1850s onwards the share of advances in domestic lending of the Preußische Bank, later the Reichsbank, fluctuated between a low 10 and 20 percent. After 1880 the Reichsbank, concerned about what it considered a misuse of advances around stock-exchange settlement dates, actively discouraged resort to them by increasing the minimum maturity of loans, thus raising the effective interest rate on very short term loans (Reichsbank 1910). A similar desire to reduce advances in the lending portfolio was voiced by representatives of the Oesterreichische Nationalbank (Mecenseffý 1896).

In other countries like Britain, France, and the Netherlands advances kept a more important role in monetary policy implementation. Bank of England directors seem to have had fewer concerns about liquidity, frequently fixing the rate for temporary advances below discount rate in the 1830s and 1840s (Wood 1939). In the Netherlands, the spread between the interest rate on advances and discounts was most of the time zero after the 1860s (De Jong 1967). The opposite was the case in France, where this spread apparently increased in the 1860s (Bopp 1952). The difference between Germany and Austria on the one hand, and notably Britain and the Netherlands on the other, might reflect differences in the liquidity of securities markets. However, Berlin also hosted a highly developed market for stock exchange loans that was well integrated with the unsecured money market (Prion 1907), thereby limiting the differences between discounts and advances from the point of view of the central bank. A further factor driving the divergence in resort to the discount and advance facilities could be counterparties' preferences. From the counterparties' viewpoint, the main difference between discounts and advances is the maturity of the loan: while in the case of discounts the maturity is determined by the residual maturity of the bill submitted for rediscount, in the case of advances maturity can be set flexibly. This is an advantage, in particular in well-defined periods of temporarily high liquidity demand such as the end of year or quarter (De Kock 1954). A higher share of advances might thus have reflected differences in the structural liquidity deficit and in the amplitude of liquidity demand, which made counterparties access the central bank's lombard facility more often and for greater sums.

Faced with temporary needs for accommodation during World War I, central banks made adjustments in their operational procedures that tended to stay in place after the war – notably increasing the role of Treasury bills in rediscount operations. Commercial banks adopted Treasury bills as secondary reserves, and consequently advances against government securities and rediscounts of Treasury bills became more attractive compared to the classical rediscount of bills of exchange (De Kock 1954). As a result, the traditional link between discounting and the commercial bill market on the one hand, and advances and the market for long-term securities on the other hand, became more blurry – which actually complicates the interpretation of reported figures. Most central banks started to care less about the relative weight of discounts vs. advances. If restrictions on advances persisted in some countries (Germany and Austria), these can be linked to formal constraints on indirect budgetary financing through advances on government debt rather than to the liquidity of the instrument. The newly created Fed applied the same rate for advances and rediscounts. The trend towards indifference between advances and discounts got even stronger after World War II, when some central banks started to report advances and discounts lumped together – as the Bank of England had always done since 1844.

The share of discounts and advances varied widely after World War II. These differences appeared now due less to a preference of the central bank than to the availability of bills in the different countries. Where banking systems relied more on trade bills (notably Belgium, France, and Germany), discounts feature more prominently in the central bank balance sheet, while their role is negligible in the Netherlands and Britain. As bills were originated in specific transactions, moreover, they lent themselves easier to credit allocation. Preferential rates for discounts of certain classes of bills in Belgium, France, and Germany can be read in this context (CEE 1962). By 1990, discounts had almost disappeared from central bank balance sheets in all countries (see Figure 4.1).

To sum up, our analysis of central banks' lending operations allows identifying trends in the evolution of the forms assumed by the bank-market interaction. Not surprisingly, patterns mostly coincide with developments observed through the study of central bank balance sheets (Section 3.1). Collateralized lending was most prominent in the first half of the nineteenth century, when discounting was relatively weak and holdings of government debt important: the two phenomena were linked, as government bonds used to be the most common collateral for secured lending operations. Collateralized lending started to increase again before World War I, and became predominant along the twentieth century. In the meantime, the nature of central banks' collateralized loans changed, as it shifted from secured standing facility lending (advances) to secured open market operations (repos). However, significant deviations from this general trend can be recorded. For instance, unlike in all other countries, in France and Belgium collateralized lending played a marginal role for

3.3 The Substance of Interaction: Market vs. Bank Interest Rates

much of the nineteenth century. Such deviations may have been the outcome of political factors (Ramon 1929; Ugolini 2012).

3.3 The Substance of Interaction: Market vs. Bank Interest Rates

As seen in Section 3.2, discounting and the provision of loans on collateral were the oldest types of monetary policy operations. Both were most often organized as a standing facility, meaning that eligible counterparties of the central bank could use them at their own discretion at any time, while the central bank fixed the general conditions for use. One of the most important parameters to be set by the central bank is the price of liquidity, either expressed as a discount rate (in the case of the purchase of short-term securities) or an interest rate (in the case of collateralized loans). For long periods central banks used to publicly quote a discount rate or "bank rate" that also served as the main indicator for the stance of monetary policy. In most countries this rate applied to the discount of eligible paper. Following its loss of importance in the late twentieth century, some central banks (e.g. Deutsche Bundesbank and Schweizerische Nationalbank) abolished the discount rate in the 1990s. In other countries, the type of the underlying operation changed (in particular after World War II) even if the old name survived: this was the case e.g. for the discount rate of the Federal Reserve, which had since the inception of the Fed been applied to discount and collateralized lending operations alike, and applies exclusively to secured loans since 2002.

A standing facility has a potentially significant impact on market interest rates. Its power derives from the fact that it provides an unlimited amount of liquidity at set conditions. It should be noted that this principal role is independent of whether the rate applies to discounting or advances. *De facto*, however, central banks set more or less restrictive conditions as to the use of the discount facility. These conditions concerned the definition of eligible paper, limits per counterparty, 'moral' restrictions in the sense that counterparties were advised to use the discount facility only to some limited extent, as well as administrative procedures that would add costs to the use of the facility. In addition, most central banks made clear that they could, in principle, always refuse to discount or provide advances without giving reasons (Bindseil 2004). The effective role of standing facilities and thus of the published discount or bank rate crucially depends on these rules and procedures. Changes in the rules repeatedly altered the relationship between the official rate and market rates. A proper understanding of bank rates would thus require detailed knowledge about

The Coevolution of Money Markets and Monetary Policy

practices and how they evolved. An alternative approach is to look at the outcome – i.e. the observed relationship between the official discount rate and market interest rates as well the extent to which the facility was used in order to infer the rules and procedures applied. Market interest rates above the official discount rate are indicators for effective restrictions on the use of the facility. Evidence on the recourse gives indications as to whether the facility was used to satisfy structural or only occasional liquidity demand.

In order to compare official and market rates, first a representative market rate has to be selected among the many rates actually employed in financial contracts. Here, the focus is on rates at which banks invest short-term surplus funds or borrow funds short-term. Where possible, rates should apply to the highest quality counterparties only, in order to avoid differences in credit risk and liquidity premia to pollute the results. The rates are thus most often reference rates, meaning that the rates actually paid might have been higher because they included an individual risk premium. Among different markets available to banks for short-term borrowing and lending, the most liquid market is selected, which is also generally considered the representative market at that time.

In the nineteenth century and until the end of the interwar period, the representative market rate is typically a private discount rate on bills of exchange. While bills of exchange are an instrument with a long tradition (De Roover 1953), for many countries no quotes are available before the 1850s, which might be due either to a hesitancy of traders to report rates (given that usury laws made higher rates illegal) or to the structure of the market itself (which might have lacked standardization: Flandreau *et al.* 2009). When these rates appear, they refer to bills of highest quality, as is evident in terms like "private" or "first class" bills, which means that these bills if any should have been eligible for central bank discounting. Until World War I, in all but the most sophisticated financial markets the open market rate of discount is not only the most representative, but also the only short-term market rate widely published and used as benchmark in money market transactions. Even though the bill market declines after the War, the open market rate retains this role in most countries during the interwar. After World War II, the open market discount rate disappears everywhere. The new benchmark is either the Treasury bill rate, which is used to price also interbank transactions, or an overnight rate for interbank deposits. Following financial liberalization in the 1970s, most countries start to quote rates structured similarly to the London Interbank Offered Rate (LIBOR), which become used as benchmarks and for the pricing of derivatives.

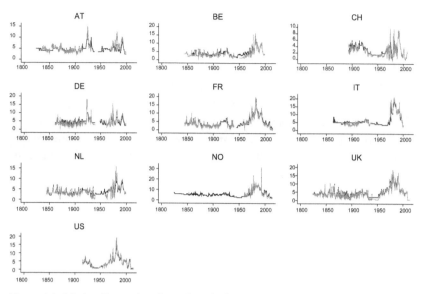

Figure 4.4: Market (in grey) and standing facility interest rates (in black)
Source: Authors' database.

Figure 4.4 plots the official discount rates along with a representative market rate for the ten countries in our sample. Despite significant idiosyncrasies in the design of the standing facilities in the various countries, distinct periods stand out, as becomes evident when looking at average spreads between official and market rates (Figure 4.5) and the number of instances when market rates rose above standing facility rates (Figure 4.6).

In the **first half of the nineteenth century** official rates move very little and mostly lie between 4 and 5 percent. The key feature of this period is that in all countries market rates quote time and again above official rates, meaning that the standing facility was closed and that the central bank did not always serve as liquidity provider of last resort. In other respects, country experiences vary. With the exception of the three years between 1844 and 1847, the Bank of England in principle aimed at a discount rate above market rate in order to keep the provision of liquidity at the standing facility to a minimum and rather adjusted the liquidity position of the market through other channels like open market operations in Indian debt (Wood 1939) or special advances to smooth the end of quarters (King 1936). When demand for discounts increased significantly, however, demand was not satisfied

The Coevolution of Money Markets and Monetary Policy 173

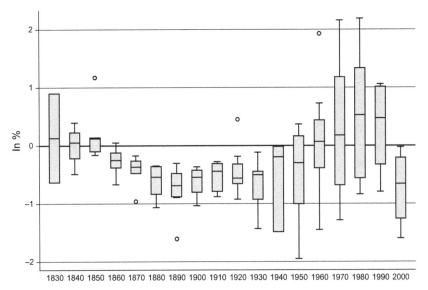

Figure 4.5: Spread between market and standing facility rate in percentage: averages per decade
Source: Authors' database.
Note: For individual country data, see Table 4.3. War and immediate post-war periods (1914–1919 and 1939–1945) are excluded from the calculation.

fully. As the Bank did not (or could not) raise the rate, it instead imposed quantity restrictions (Bignon *et al.* 2012). In Austria, market rates quoted above official rates for extended periods of time, while at the same time the standing facilities were used consistently. This setting suggests that access to the standing facilities was limited to a select group that enjoyed preferential access below market interest rates. From the point of view of the central bank such policy might be optimal as a means to filter out more risky counterparties, as was argued for Austria (Lanier 1998). This was also the case in France (Bopp 1952; Bignon *et al.* 2012). In the Netherlands, access to the discount and advances facilities was hampered by a combination of high costs and fussiness (Jonker 1996), which might explain why market rates moved above official rates occasionally until the 1850s. In Prussia, the Königliche Hauptbank managed its (limited) discount operations restrictively, limiting access and increasing rates whenever liquidity conditions were tight (Niebuhr 1854). As a result and as can be seen in Figure 4.5, market interest rates (where available) tended to fluctuate around and occasionally above the official interest rate.

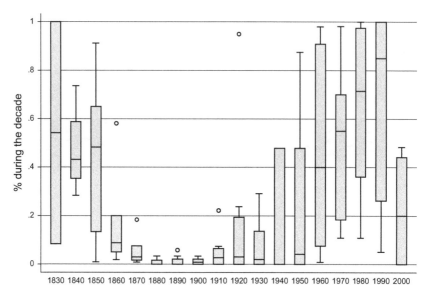

Figure 4.6: Share of months with average market rate above average standing facility rate, averages per decade
Source: Authors' database.
Note: For individual country data, see Table 4.4. War and immediate post-war periods (1914–1919 and 1939–1945) are excluded from the calculation.

Patterns change in the **second half of the nineteenth century**. Also thanks to the repeal of usury laws everywhere, official rates now moved much more frequently, and by the 1860s official rates are the *de facto* upper limit of market rates in all countries covered here. This can be seen in Figure 4.6 from the sharp decline in the number of instances with market rates above official rates between the 1850s and the 1860s. Apparently central banks had eased restrictions on the access to standing facilities sufficiently so that all peaks in demand for central bank money would effectively be accommodated at the standing facility rate. The standing facility rate became the upper bound to the market rate. In Britain the change concerned policy during crises only, as during normal periods market rates had already quoted below the official rate before. By 1857, Bank of England directors acknowledged that demand for central bank deposits was (in the short run) highly inelastic and quantitative restrictions thus useless at best, and would cause panic at worst. Demand should be satisfied in full, while a high bank rate would encourage borrowers to look for alternative sources of liquidity (Wood 1939). In the crises of 1857 and 1866 the Bank of England acted accordingly, and the new

The Coevolution of Money Markets and Monetary Policy 175

doctrine of the lender of last resort was formulated in Bagehot (1873). In France, the evolution in central bankers' attitude followed the very same pattern and timing as in Britain (Bignon *et al.* 2012). Similar changes can be observed on the continent at about the same time. While the Preußische Bank had restricted access to refinancing during the 1847 and 1857 crisis, it acted as a reliable source of refinancing in the crises of 1866, 1870, and 1873 (Tilly 1966; Ziegler 1993). The same is true for its successor, the Reichsbank (Prion 1907; Bopp 1953). Austria is a comparative late-comer. Here the market rate quoted above the official rate quite frequently until as late as the mid-1870s. The stock exchange crisis of 1882 marked the last instance of the market rate surpassing the official rate; in later years the official rate became the effective cap on market rates. In the Netherlands, this was true at least by the early 1870s. Before, the money market was apparently flexible enough to weather the crises of 1857 and 1866 without much support from the Nederlandsche Bank (Jonker 1996).

While the lender-of-last-resort function of the standing facility thus became generalized, below the official rate the behavior of market rates continued to be uneven across national markets, as is evident in the ten-year averages in Figure 4.5. In some countries market rates were most of time close to or equal the official rate, while in other countries market rates quoted on average up to one percentage point below. Short-run patterns looked of course even more different. The importance of the standing facility rate depends on the need of the market to access the facility on a daily basis and thus on the aggregate liquidity position of the banking system. The aggregate liquidity position in turn depends on alternative sources of liquidity. These can be foreign exchange inflows (that in a fixed exchange rate system as the nineteenth-century metallic standards will be automatically converted into domestic money) or operations on the initiative of the central bank (like investments or explicit open market operations); in some instances, high liquidity results from the monetization of government debt. If after taking these alternative liquidity sources into account the system as a whole still suffers from a shortage of liquidity, it is forced to access the standing facility and market rate should quote at the official rate. Often this occurred when the demand for liquidity peaked at the end of the month, quarter, or year (e.g. in Britain: Goodhart 1986). Conversely, a market rate below the official rate implies that there is no aggregate need for liquidity and thus the standing facility need not be used. In fact, however, even though the extent of usage differed, recourse to the standing facility was always positive at all central banks in this period

176 Clemens Jobst and Stefano Ugolini

Table 4.3: *Average spreads between market and standing facility rates in basis points*

	AT	BE	CH	DE	FR	IT	NL	NO	UK	US
1830	90								−63	
1840	40				6		5		−49	
1850	117	−10			12		14		−16	
1860	5	−38		−67	−35		−12		−15	
1870	−18	−34		−96	−48		−26		−40	
1880	−54	−36		−106	−46	−84	−35		−74	
1890	−31	−71	−67	−89	−41	−161	−55		−87	
1900	−37	−54	−55	−103	−60	−100	−37		−48	
1910	−33	−81	−28	−88	−44	−77	−29		−45	
1920	−32	−66	−62	−92	−92	−19	−51		−56	45
1930	−93	−50	−48	−57	−45	−12	−143		−115	−30
1940			−20						−149	−2
1950		−195	−52	−8	29		−96	37	−105	4
1960	44	−145	−36	7	73		−97	193	−39	18
1970	81	−129	−121	126	−55	216	−29	118	−68	65
1980	219		−56	151	−84	53	104	18	−66	133
1990	101			102	−79	51	106	−44	−21	44
2000	−92	−92	−92	−92	−92	−92	−92	−160	−3	−40

Note: War and immediate post-war periods (1914–1919 and 1939–1945) are excluded from the calculation. Countries having adopted the euro have the same value for 2000. These double observations were not considered in Figure 4.5.

(see Sections 3.1 and 3.2). Such recourse, that could be labeled individual recourse (as opposite to aggregate recourse), must reflect some transaction costs that prevented counterparties from accessing the liquidity available in the market at the lower market interest rate (Bindseil 2004). In the case of the Bank of England, special long-standing client relationships existed (Ziegler 1990). On the Continent, central banks entertained business relations with a wide set of clients that would often not access the discount market, typically restricted to banking houses. The maintenance of large branch networks further increased the number of central bank counterparties that had no direct access to the money market. The importance of individual recourse is well evident in the constantly high use of the discount facility in the face of high spreads between market and official rates, notably in Germany (Table 4.3). This alternative motivation for accessing the standing facility is illustrated by the typically much longer maturities of discounts at branch offices (source of structural liquidity) than at the main offices (covering peak demand).

The Coevolution of Money Markets and Monetary Policy 177

Table 4.4: *Percentage of months with average market rates above average standing facility rates*

	AT	BE	CH	DE	FR	IT	NL	NO	UK	US
1830	100								8	
1840	74				42		44		28	
1850	91	1			65		48		13	
1860	58	5		2	12		6		20	
1870	18	2		1	2		4		8	
1880	3	0		0	1	2	0		0	
1890	6	0	0	0	1	0	0		3	
1900	2	0	0	0	3	0	2		3	
1910	7	0	22	0	0	6	0		5	
1920	24	3	0	3	0	19	3		0	95
1930	0	3	2	1	14	16	0		0	29
1940			0						0	48
1950		0	5	0	63		0	88	3	33
1960	95	1	33	52	91		7	98	8	40
1970	70	18	18	84	28	98	43	70	11	68
1980	100		36	100	11	63	98	71	17	95
1990	100			100	5	75	100	31	22	95
2000	0	0	0	0	0	0	0	0	48	40

Note: War and immediate post-war periods (1914–1919 and 1939–1945) are excluded from the calculation. Countries having adopted the euro have the same value for 2000. These double observations were not considered in Figure 4.6.

In modern parlance, the changes happening after the 1850s can be resumed as the establishment of a one-sided interest rate corridor, that in some countries was combined with additional liquidity providing or absorbing operations below the standing facility rate. In principle, this framework remained in place during the interwar. In all countries the discount rate continued to cap market interest rates, even though discount operations lost in importance relative to open market operations. The Bank of England started to keep market rates considerably below its discount rate through open market operations (Sayers 1976). The same role as upper limit to market rates can be observed for France, Austria, and the Netherlands. The newcomer to the central bank world, the Federal Reserve, was an outlier. At its foundation, the Fed conceptualized discount rates as an upper bound along the lines of the Bank of England, but soon market rates quoted above discount rates and continued to do so until 1932. From the beginning, The U.S. discount window was set up in a much more complicated fashion than discount facilities in Europe. The Fed

178   *Clemens Jobst and Stefano Ugolini*

distinguished several types of recourse with different access criteria and administrative procedures (Meltzer 2003). Conditions and rates were set autonomously by the individual Federal Reserve banks, making coordination with open market purchases (as at the Bank of England) very difficult (Meulendyke 1989; Meltzer 2003). During the banking crises of the 1930s, the discount window became increasingly stigmatized. Access to the facility was interpreted as a sign of problems at the individual bank and not of aggregate need for liquidity, a pattern that persisted in the United States at least until the early 2000s. As a result, the discount window was barely used despite its costs being below the level of market interest rates.

After 1945, in many countries the traditional ordering of money market and official rates reversed and market rates started to quote above the discount rate. Data are no longer easy to interpret, as the number of relevant official interest rates multiplied in many countries and money markets became segmented. While in some countries preferential rates had been available for specific kinds of paper (e.g. government securities in collateralized lending) or counterparties (e.g. agricultural cooperatives), before World War II the frameworks were in principle oriented around one interest rate – or, in some cases, two (discount and advances). Now central banks started to operate with four or five standing facilities upwards, each with its own interest rate. The reason for this dramatic change of approach was the introduction of restrictions on the use of the facility within the context of pervasive credit controls during and after the War, and often the introduction of specific rates for different classes of credit. This was the case most notably in France and Belgium, whose central banks operated with a multitude of different rates. Credit controls played a significant role also in the case of Britain (Tucker 2004) as well as in France, the Netherlands, and Belgium (CEE 1962). Individual country experiences were rather idiosyncratic. The German central bank assigned the discount facility a key role after 1948 and until the 1980s. However, already in the 1950s the Bank set individual discount limits calculated as a function of selected liabilities of the banks, thereby changing the discount facility to a much more administrative procedure. In the beginning, foreign exchange inflows limited the need for liquidity from the standing facility, so that the discount rate served as an effective ceiling for market rates. From the mid-1970s onwards, recourse became systematic such that the discount rate became the floor rather than the ceiling for market rates, as banks would typically reduce discount loans to zero before market rates could fall below the discount rate. The role of the marginal borrowing

The Coevolution of Money Markets and Monetary Policy 179

facility was taken over by the advances facility, priced above the discount rate and access to which was most of the time unlimited. The rates thus formed a sort of corridor for the short-term interest rate (Bindseil 2004).

New consensus: corridor. The liberalization of financial markets in the 1980s and the return to market rather than administrative pricing reduced the variety of instruments used across countries. The major reforms of the money market in England in the mid-1990s (Tucker 2004), the introduction of the primary credit facility in the United States in 2002 (Bindseil 2004), and the start of the Eurosystem in 1999 (Galvenius and Mercier 2011) marked the convergence of the major central banks towards a new consensus (Borio 1997). Within this consensus the role of the standing facilities, in most cases a borrowing and a lending facility forming a corridor, is to prevent sharp increases or decreases of the market rate due to unforeseen changes in liquidity demand. According to current practice, the borrowing facility is available against a sufficiently wide range of collateral and not subject to administrative procedures and so, as a successor to the old discount facility, provides again an upper limit to market rates. In normal situations, however, open market operations by the central bank should keep market rates close to the target rate within the corridor and thus well below the borrowing facility rate. Recourse to the facility is accordingly small and not systematic. The main difference to the framework exemplified by the Bank of England before 1914 is thus that nowadays (at least until 2008) central banks effectively neutralize any liquidity shocks through open market operations and reserve averaging, thereby keeping market rates close to target rate, and never forcing (or even letting) the market "into the bank". Yet this very refined system is not without downsides. As banks should be able to obtain all required liquidity at the market rate, use of the borrowing facility implies that the borrowing bank had for some reason no market access. This might be related to timing – if e.g. an unexpected large payment occurs after the interbank market has closed – but could also signal more fundamental liquidity troubles. Consequently, use of the borrowing facility has a tendency to become stigmatized – a problem most notably discussed for the case of the Fed (Armantier *et al.* 2011). When recourse to central bank borrowing is stigmatized, the standing facility rate no longer serves as the upper bound to market rates. If not *de jure, de facto* this is bound to recreate a situation similar to the early-nineteenth-century one, in which the lending-of-last-resort function was not properly provided by central banks. As the 2008 crisis seems to suggest, such dysfunctionalities in the design of the standing facility may engender very costly effects on the overall financial system and require central banks to create new quasi standing facilities – as exemplified by the full-allotment policies of the Fed and ECB during the crisis that might yet suffer from stigma as well.

To sum up, thanks to our analysis of market vs. bank interest rates we are now able to draw a general sketch of the changes in the substance of the market-bank interaction which have taken place over time and space. Positive market-bank spreads frequently occurred in the first half of the nineteenth century, when central banks often rationed credit to a number of counterparties. They basically disappeared around the mid of the century, as soon as usury ceilings were dropped and central banks started to behave as neutral lenders of last resort. They forcefully reappeared after World War I, when a number of preferential conditions for access to central bank liquidity started to be granted to different classes of counterparties. Spreads returned to drop after the 1980s, as central banks generally went back to a more neutral stance with respect to money market participants. Recent attempts at neutrality, however, may have been partly compromised by the sentiment of stigma informally instilled around the discount window. Together with the increasing paucity of the number of counterparties, the creeping stigmatization of standing facility borrowing is a major difference between today's implementation framework and that prevailing in the late nineteenth century.

3.4 Quantitative Evidence: Sum-Up

The results of our quantitative survey suggest that during the last two centuries there were at least four major breaking points, when the interaction between money markets and central banks underwent some substantial transformations. *(1)* In the mid-nineteenth century, the earlier importance of government debt and collateralized loan markets faltered, as the discount market became the predominant channel of interaction between central banks and their counterparties: at around this time, credit rationing disappeared and the official discount rate became the effective upper bound to market rates. *(2)* World War I was a natural watershed, accelerating the rise of foreign exchange markets and the come-back of government debt markets. *(3)* World War II exacerbated such transformations by making wartime credit controls durable: insulation allowed for significant divergences in country experiences and for the creation of a number of privileged positions in the access to central bank liquidity. *(4)* The financial liberalizations of the 1980s and 1990s finally fostered a new convergence of monetary practices around the world, with a general disappearance of discount markets, a relative decline of government debt markets, and a relative rise of foreign exchange and repo markets: like in the late nineteenth century, market rates returned to stay lower than standing facility rates, but – unlike in the late nineteenth century – stigma also came to be attached to the discount window.

The fundamental drivers of the breaks we observed appear to have been exogenous factors: changes in the availability of financial assets (e.g. increasing provision of trade acceptances or government debt), changes in the level of international financial integration (e.g. the late-nineteenth-century globalization or the early-twentieth-century deglobalization), as well as changes in the structural characteristics of the country (e.g. its position within the international monetary system or its level of indebtedness). Driven by these exogenous inputs, money market structures and monetary practices did evolve together.

4 Conclusions

In this chapter, we have surveyed historical information concerning the interplay between money market structures and monetary policy design in Western countries over roughly two hundred years. We have found that the very foundations of the relationship between markets and central banks evolved considerably over time. The money markets that central banks participated in were not always the same; the operational techniques implemented by monetary authorities did vary; and the operational targets of monetary policy also changed. On the one hand, the characteristics of money markets (*ex-ante* liquidity, credit risk, market participation, quality of transmission channels) played a role in determining central bankers' choice of their preferred fields of intervention (the acceptance market, the government debt market, etc.), of their preferred techniques (uncollateralized or collateralized operations), and of their preferred stance (neutral or not). On the other hand, though, the way monetary policy was designed also played a role in determining the relative importance of money markets (the supremacy of the acceptance market, of the government debt market, etc.), their mode of functioning (origination of the one or the other collateral), and their attitude towards monetary authorities (reliance on the lender of last resort, or not). Both directions of causation contributed to determining what monetary policy implementation frameworks looked like over time and space. In the cross-sectional dimension we have seen that, although international trends played a crucial role, significant differences persisted between countries even in periods of convergence. This means that the big, important central banks, that typically dominate policy debates and academic research, are often outliers rather than representative for central banking practices at their time. This is in particular true concerning the role of foreign exchange, the relative importance of government and non-government domestic assets, as well as the reliance on market mechanisms vs. standing facilities in the conduct of monetary policy operations.

Our survey suggests that although implementation frameworks may evolve endogenously, the factors leading to more drastic transformations are rather exogenous in nature. This implies that assessing the actual efficiency of each framework may be much more complicated than it might appear at first sight. Exogenous shocks on money market structures (e.g. commercial openness as a driver of the development of the acceptance market, or government indebtedness as a driver of the development of the Treasury bond market) are bound to impact the degree of optimality of a given monetary policy design. At the same time, though, also exogenous shocks on central bank's policymaking (e.g. political pressure to keep a standing facility for acceptances, or the need to subsidize the government bond market) are bound to impact the degree of optimality of a given money market structure. Approaching these phenomena theoretically in a sensible way appears to be an extremely complex issue. This is even more complicated by the fact that apparently exogenous shocks may not be mutually exogenous. Just to give an obvious example, the economic push leading to the emergence of the government debt market and the political push leading to the emergence of the central bank's management of this market hardly look independent of each other. In order to get a fuller understanding of these important dynamics, a lot of additional research might well be required.

References

Allen, William A. (2014), "Eligibility, Bank Liquidity, Basel 3, Bank Credit and Macro-Prudential Policy: History and Current Issues", Working Paper.

Armantier, Olivier, Eric Ghysels, Asani Sarkar, and Jeffrey Shrader (2011), "Stigma in Financial Markets: Evidence from Liquidity Auctions and Discount Window Borrowing during the Crisis", Federal Reserve Bank of New York Staff Report, 483.

Bagehot, Walter (1873), *Lombard Street: A Description of the Money Market*, 5th edition, London: King.

Bank for International Settlements (1997), "Implementation and Tactics of Monetary Policy", Bank for International Settlements Conference Papers, 3.

Beckhart, Benjamin H. (1932), "Federal Reserve Policy and the Money Market, 1923–1931", in i Benjamin H. Beckhart, James G. Smith, and William A. Brown

The Coevolution of Money Markets and Monetary Policy   183

(eds.), *The New York Money Market*, IV, New York: Columbia University Press, pp. 1–181.

Bignon, Vincent, Marc Flandreau, and Stefano Ugolini (2012), "Bagehot for Beginners: The Making of Lending-of-Last-Resort Operations in the Mid-19th Century", *Economic History Review*, 65:2, pp. 580–608.

Bindseil, Ulrich (2004), *Monetary Policy Implementation: Theory, Past, Present*, Oxford: Oxford University Press.

Bindseil, Ulrich, and Francesco Papadia (2009), "Risk Management and Market Impact of Central Bank Credit Operations", in Ulrich Bindseil, Fernando Gonzalez, and Evangelos Tabakis (eds.), *Risk Management for Central Banks and Other Public Investors*, Cambridge: Cambridge University Press, pp. 271–302.

Board of Governors of the Federal Reserve System (2005), *The Federal Reserve System: Purpose and Functions*, 9th edition, Washington: Federal Reserve System.

Bopp, Karl R. (1952), "Bank of France Policy: Brief Survey of Instruments, 1800–1914", *American Journal of Economics and Sociology*, 11:3, pp. 229–44.

  (1953), *Reichsbank Operations, 1876–1914*, Philadelphia: Federal Reserve Bank of Philadelphia.

Borio, Claudio (1997), "The Implementation of Monetary Policy in Industrial Countries: A Survey", Bank for International Settlements Economic Papers, 47.

Borio, Claudio, Gabriele Galati, and Alexandra Heath (2008), "Foreign Exchange Reserve Management: Trends and Challenges", Bank for International Settlements Papers, 40.

Borio, Claudio, and Piti Disyatat (2010), "Unconventional Monetary Policies: An Appraisal", *The Manchester School*, 78:1, pp. 53–89.

Brunnermeier, Markus K., and Lasse Pedersen (2009), "Market Liquidity and Funding Liquidity", *Review of Financial Studies*, 22:6, pp. 2201–38.

Capie, Forrest, and Alan Webber (1985), *A Monetary History of the United Kingdom, 1870–1982*, I, London: Allen & Unwin.

Caron, Massimiliano, and Luciano Di Cosmo (1993), *I bilanci degli istituti di emissione in Italia, 1894–1990*, Rome: Laterza.

Catterall, Ralph C.H. (1903), *The Second Bank of the United States*, Chicago: University of Chicago Press.

Clapham, John (1944), *The Bank of England: A History*, II, Cambridge: Cambridge University Press.

Communauté Économique Européenne (1962), *Les instruments de la politique monétaire dans les pays de la Communauté Économique Européenne*, Brussels: CEE.

De Jong, Adriaan M. (1967), *Geschiedenis van de Nederlandsche Bank*, Haarlem: Enschedé.

De Kock, Michiel H. (1954), *Central Banking*, 4th edition, London: Staples.

De Mattia, Renato (1967), *I bilanci degli istituti di emissione italiani dal 1845 al 1936*, Rome: Banca d'Italia.

De Roover, Raymond (1953), *L'évolution de la lettre de change du XIIe au XVIIIe siècle*, Paris: Armand Colin.

Eichengreen, Barry J., and Marc Flandreau (2009), "The Rise and Fall of the Dollar (or When Did the Dollar Replace Sterling as the Leading Reserve Currency?)", *European Review of Economic History*, 13:3, pp. 377–411.

Flandreau, Marc, Christophe Galimard, Clemens Jobst, and Pilar Nogués Marco (2009), "The Bell Jar: Commercial Interest Rates between Two Revolutions 1688–1789", in Jeremy Atack and Larry Neal (eds.), *The Origins and Development of Financial Markets and Institutions: From the Seventeenth Century to the Present*, New York: Cambridge University Press, pp. 161–208.

Flandreau, Marc, and François Gallice (2005), "Paris, London and the International Money Market: Lessons from Paribas 1885–1913", in Youssef Cassis and Eric Bussière (eds.), *Paris and London as International Financial Centers*, Oxford: Oxford University Press, pp. 78–106.

Forssbæck, Jens, and Lars Oxelheim (2007), "The Interplay between Money Market Development and Changes in Monetary Policy Operations in Small European Countries, 1980–2000", in David G. Mayes and Jan Toporowski (eds.), *Open Market Operations and Financial Markets*, London: Routledge, pp. 120–52.

Galvenius, Mats, and Paul Mercier (2011), "The Story of the Eurosystem Framework", in Paul Mercier and Francesco Papadia (eds.), *The Concrete Euro: Implementing Monetary Policy in the Euro Area*, Oxford: Oxford University Press, pp. 115–214.

Ghatak, Maitreesh, and Timothy W. Guinnane (1999), "The Economics of Lending with Joint Liability: Theory and Practice", *Journal of Development Economics*, 60, pp. 195–228.

Goodhart, Charles A. E. (1986), *The Business of Banking, 1891–1914*, 2nd edition, London: Gower.

Goodhart, Charles A. E., Forrest Capie, and Norbert Schnadt (1994), "The Development of Central Banking", in Forrest Capie, Charles Goodhart, Stanley Fischer, and Norbert Schnadt (eds.), *The Future of Central Banking, The Tercentenary Symposium of the Bank of England*. Cambridge: Cambridge University Press, pp. 1–261.

Holbik, Karel (ed.) (1973), *Monetary Policy in Twelve Industrial Countries*, Boston: Federal Reserve Bank of Boston.

Holmström, Bengt, and Jean Tirole (2010), *Inside and Outside Liquidity*, Cambridge (Mass.): MIT Press.

Hvidsten, Vetle (2013), "Oversikt over Norges Banks balanseoppstilling, 1817–1945: Konsolidering av delregnskapene", Norges Bank Staff Memo, 2013/6.

Jobst, Clemens (2009), "Market Leader: The Austro-Hungarian Bank and the Making of Foreign Exchange Intervention, 1896–1913", *European Review of Economic History*, 13:3, pp. 287–318.

Jonker, Joost (1996), *Merchants, Bankers, Middlemen: The Amsterdam Money Market during the First Half of the 19th Century*, Amsterdam: NEHA.

Käppeli, Robert (1930), *Der Notenbankausweis in Theorie und Wirklichkeit*, Jena: Fischer.

Kerschagl, Richard (1929), *Die mitteleuropäischen Währungen und Notenbanken*. Vienna: Spaeth & Linde.

King, Wilfred T.C. (1936), *History of the London Discount Market*, London: Routledge.

Kneeshaw, John T., and Paul Van den Bergh (1989), "Changes in Central Bank Money Market Operating Procedures in the 1980s", Bank for International Settlements Economic Papers, 23.

Lanier, Amelie (1998), *Die Geschichte des Bank- und Handelshauses Sina*, Frankfurt am Main: Lang.

Lévy, Raphael-Georges (1911), *Banques d'émission et Trésors publics*, Paris: Hachette.

Lucam, Wilhelm (1861), *Die Oesterreichische Nationalbank und ihr Verhältniss zu dem Staate*, Vienna: Braumüller.

(1876), *Die Oesterreichische Nationalbank während der Dauer des dritten Privilegiums*, Vienna: Manz.

Malou, Jules (1863), *Notice historique sur la Société générale pour favoriser l'industrie nationale établie à Bruxelles, 1823–1862*, Brussels: Decq.

Mecenseffý, Emil (1896), *Die Verwaltung der Oesterreichisch-Ungarischen Bank, 1886–1895*, Vienna: Hölder.

Meltzer, Allan H. (2003), *A History of the Federal Reserve*, I, Chicago: University of Chicago Press.

Meulendyke, Ann-Marie (1989), *U.S. Monetary Policy and Financial Markets*, New York: Federal Reserve Bank of New York.

Niebuhr, Marcus C. N. von (1854), *Geschichte der Königlichen Bank in Berlin: Von der Gründung derselben (1765) bis zum Ende des Jahres 1845*, Berlin: Deckersche Geheime Ober-Hofbuchdruckerei.

Plumptre, Arthur F. W. (1940), *Central Banking in the British Dominions*, Toronto: University of Toronto Press.

Poschinger, Heinrich von (1879), *Bankwesen und Bankpolitik in Preußen*, II, Berlin: Springer.

Prion, Willi (1907), *Das deutsche Wechseldiskontgeschäft*, Leipzig: Duncker & Humblot.

Ramon, Gabriel (1929), *Histoire de la Banque de France d'après les sources originales*, Paris: Grasset.

Reichsbank (1910), *The Reichsbank, 1876–1900*, Washington: National Monetary Commission.

Roulleau, Gaston (1914), *Les règlements par effets de commerce en France et à l'étranger*, Paris: Société de Statistique de Paris.

Sayers, Richard S. (1936), *Bank of England Operations, 1890–1914*, London: King.

(1976), *The Bank of England, 1891–1944*, I, Cambridge: Cambridge University Press.

Tilly, Richard (1966), *Financial Institutions and Industrialization in the Rhineland, 1815–1870*, Madison: University of Wisconsin Press.

Tucker, Paul (2004), "Managing the Central Bank's Balance Sheet: Where Monetary Policy Meets Financial Stability", Bank of England Quarterly Bulletin, Autumn, pp. 359–82.

Ugolini, Stefano (2010), "The International Monetary System, 1844–1870: Arbitrage, Efficiency, Liquidity", Norges Bank Working Paper, 2010/23.

(2012), "The Origins of Foreign Exchange Policy: The National Bank of Belgium and the Quest for Monetary Independence in the 1850s", *European Review of Economic History*, 16:1, pp. 51–73.

Wagner, Adolph (1873), *System der Zettelbankpolitik*, Freiburg: Wagner.

Wood, Elmer (1939), *English Theories of Central Banking Control, 1819–1858*, Cambridge (Mass.): Harvard University Press.

Ziegler, Dieter (1990), *Central Banking, Peripheral Industry: The Bank of England in the Provinces, 1826–1913*, Leicester: Leicester University Press.

(1993), "Zentralbankpolitische 'Steinzeit'? Preußische Bank und Bank of England im Vergleich", *Geschichte und Gesellschaft*, 19, pp. 475–505.

SOURCES

BALANCE SHEETS

Bank	Dates	Source
Austria		
Oesterreichische Nationalbank	1835	OeNB archives
Oesterreichisch-ungarische Bank	1880, 1909	Annual reports, complemented by OeNB archives
Oesterreichische Nationalbank	1928, 1950, 1970, 1990	Annual reports, OeNB
Belgium		
Société Générale de Belgique	1835	Malou (1863)
Banque Nationale de Belgique	1880, 1909, 1928, 1950, 1970, 1990	Annual reports, NBB
Britain		
Bank of England	1835	Parliamentary Report on Banks of Issue (1840), App. 16
	1880	BoE archives
	1909	Lévy (1911); BoE archives
	1928	Käppeli (1930); BoE archives
	1950, 1970, 1990	Annual reports, BoE; BoE archives
France		
Banque de France	1835, 1880	Annual report, BdF
	1909	Lévy (1911)
	1928	Käppeli (1930)
	1950, 1970, 1990	Annual report, BdF
Germany		
Königliche Hauptbank	1835	Niebuhr (1854)
Reichsbank	1880	Reichsbank (1910)
	1909	Lévy (1911)
	1928	Kerschagl (1929)
Bank deutscher Länder	1950	Deutsches Geld- und Bankenwesen in Zahlen 1876–1975
Deutsche Bundesbank	1970	Deutsches Geld- und Bankenwesen in Zahlen 1876–1975
	1990	50 Jahre Deutsche Mark: monetäre Statistiken 1948–1997

Bank	Dates	Source
Italy		
Banca di Genova	1845	De Mattia (1967)
Banca Nazionale nel Regno d'Italia	1880	De Mattia (1967)
Banca d'Italia	1909, 1928, 1950, 1970, 1990	Caron and Di Cosmo (1993)
Netherlands		
De Nederlandsche Bank	1835, 1880	De Jong (1967)
	1909	Lévy (1911)
	1928	Mitteilungen der OeNB
	1950, 1970, 1990	Annual reports, DNB
Norway		
Norges Bank	1835, 1880, 1909, 1928	Hvidsten (2013)
	1950, 1970, 1990	Historical monetary statistics, NB
Switzerland		
Schweizerische Nationalbank	1909, 1928, 1950, 1970, 1990	Historical time series, SNB
United States		
Second Bank of the United States	1831	Catterall (1903)
Federal Reserve System	1928	Kerschagl (1929)
	1950, 1970, 1990	Annual reports, Federal Reserve System

UNCOLLATERALIZED AND COLLATERALIZED DOMESTIC LOANS

Bank	Period	Source	Type of data
Austria			
Oesterreichische Nationalbank	1818–1860	Lucam (1861)	End of year
	1861–1866	Lucam (1876)	End of year
Oesterreichische Nationalbank	1867–1877	Annual reports, OeNB	End of year
Oesterreichisch-ungarische Bank	1878–1918	Annual reports, OeNB	End of year
Oesterreichische Nationalbank	1919–1993	Annual reports, OeNB	End of year
Belgium			
Banque Nationale de Belgique	1851–1913	Annual report 1950, NBB	End of year
	1924–1973	Mitteilungen der OeNB	End of year
Britain			
Bank of England	1832–1840	Parliamentary Report on Banks of Issue (1840), App. 12	End of year
	1841–1847	Parliamentary Report on Commercial Distress, 2nd Report (1847), App. 8	End of year
	1848–1913	BoE archives	Yearly total
France			
Banque de France	1807–1964	Annuaire statistique de la France: résumé rétrospectif (1966)	Yearly total
Germany			
Königliche Hauptbank	1817–1846	Niebuhr (1854)	End of year
Preußische Bank	1847–1875	Poschinger (1879)	Yearly average
Reichsbank	1876–1945	Reichsbank (1910), Deutsches Geld- und Bankenwesen in Zahlen 1876–1975	End of year
Bank deutscher Länder	1948–1957	Deutsches Geld- und Bankenwesen in Zahlen 1876–1975	End of year

Bank	Period	Source	Type of data
Deutsche Bundesbank	1958–1989	Deutsches Geld- und Bankenwesen in Zahlen 1876–1975, Bundesbank	End of year
Italy			
Banca di Genova	1845–1849	De Mattia (1967)	Yearly total
Banca Nazionale degli Stati Sardi	1850–1860	De Mattia (1967)	Yearly total
Banca Nazionale nel Regno d'Italia	1861–1893	De Mattia (1967)	Yearly total
Banca d'Italia	1894–1936	De Mattia (1967)	Yearly total
Banca d'Italia	1937–1990	Caron and Di Cosmo (1993)	Average of end of month
Netherlands			
De Nederlandsche Bank	1814–1913	De Jong (1967)	Yearly average
	1924–1932	Mitteilungen der OeNB	End of year
Norway			
Norges Bank	1819–1913	Historical monetary statistics, NB	End of year
Switzerland			
Sweizerische Nationalbank	1907–1997	Historical times series, SNB	End of year
United States			
Federal Reserve System	1917–1942	Monetary and Banking Statistics (1943)	End of year
	1943–1970	Monetary and Banking Statistics (1976)	End of year

190   *Clemens Jobst and Stefano Ugolini*

MONTHLY INTEREST RATES

Instrument	Period	Source	Frequency of underlying data
Austria			
OeNB discount rate	1824–1999	OeNB	Daily
Shadow interest rate Trieste	1835–1859	Journal des österreichischen Lloyds, Osservatore Triestino, Oesterreichischer Volkswirth, Austria	Weekly
3 month prime bills Vienna	1860–1870	Coursblatt des Gremiums der Börse-Sensale	Weekly
3 month prime bills Vienna	1871–1914	Denkschrift zur Währungsfrage, after 1874 Wiener Zeitung	End of month
3 month prime bills Vienna	1923–1931	Mitteilungen der OeNB	Weekly
Taggeld	1968–1999	OeNB	
Belgium			
NBB discount rate	1851–1914	Annual report 1950, NBB	Weekly
NBB discount rate	1919–1998	NBB	End of month
Antwerp open market	1844–1861	SCOB database	Weekly
Brussels open market	1861–1914	*The Economist*	Weekly
Discount rates at Brussels on first class commercial paper	1920–1936	International Abstract of Economic Statistics	No indication in source
Private discount rate	1937–1939	Fed International Financial Statistics	No indication in source
Argent au jour le jour	1945–1969	NBB	Daily
Rate on banks' deposits of their daily cash surpluses	1970–1998	Eurostat	Daily
Britain			
Bank rate	1824–1835	Clapham (1944)	End of month
Bank rate	1836–1939	NBER MacroHist	Daily
Bank rate	1940–2008	BoE	Daily

The Coevolution of Money Markets and Monetary Policy

Instrument	Period	Source	Frequency of underlying data
Open market rate of discount	1824–1939	NBER MacroHist	Weekly
Prime bank bill rate	1939–1945	Capie and Webber (1985)	End of month
3M T-bills allotment rate	1946–1974	Capie and Webber (1985)	End of month
UK Interbank overnight - middle rate	1975–2013	Thomson Reuters	Daily
France			
Banque de France discount rate	1844–1852	Ugolini (2010)	Weekly
Banque de France discount rate	1852–1940	NBER MacroHist (some observations corrected from *The Economist*)	Daily
Banque de France discount rate	1945–1980	BIS	End of month
Taux directeur sur les pensions de 1 à 10 jours	1980–1989	BIS	End of month
Taux directeur sur les pensions de 5 à 10 jours	1989–1998	BdF	Daily
Open market, Paris	1844–1861	Ugolini (2010)	Weekly
Open market, Paris	1861–1863	*The Economist*	Weekly
Open market, Paris	1863–1940	NBER MacroHist	Weekly
Paris daily rate on private paper	1958–1972	Mitteilungen der OeNB	
Rate for day-to-day loans against private bills	1973–1998	Eurostat	Daily
Germany			
Discount rate Prussian Bank	1861–1875	*The Economist*	Weekly
Discount rate Reichsbank	1876–1938	NBER MacroHist	Daily
Discount rate Bundesbank	1948–1999	Bundesbank BBK01. SU0112	End of month
Open market rate Berlin	1861–1875	*The Economist*	Weekly

(continued)

192 Clemens Jobst and Stefano Ugolini

(*continued*)

Instrument	Period	Source	Frequency of underlying data
Private discount rate, prime banker's acceptances	1876–1939	NBER MacroHist	Daily
Tagesgeld Frankfurt	1959–1999	Bundesbank BBK01. SU0101	Daily
Italy			
Discount rate	1863–1999	BdI statistical database	Daily
Market rate Genoa	1885–1914	*The Economist*	Weekly
Minimum market rate Milan	1927–1935	Bollettino mensile di statistica dell'Istituto Centrale di Statistica del Regno d'Italia	End of month
Minimum market rate Milan	1935–1939	League of Nations, Monthly Bulletin of Statistics	End of month
Interbank rate	1971–1999	International Financial Statistics (IMF), corresponds to "Interbank rates" in the Banca d'Italia Economic Bulletin	Average of daily rates?
Netherlands			
DNB discount rate	1844–1861	Ugolini (2010)	Weekly
DNB discount rate	1861–1913	*The Economist*	Weekly
DNB discount rate	1914–1998	DNB	Daily
DNB discount rate	1914–1998	DNB	Daily
Amsterdam open market	1844–1861	Ugolini (2010)	Weekly
Amsterdam open market	1861–1913	*The Economist*	Weekly
Private discount rate	1920–1936	International Abstract of Economic Statistics	No indication in source
Private discount rate	1937–1939	Fed International Financial Statistics	No indication in source
3M T-bills	1958–1972	Mitteilung der OeNB	

Instrument	Period	Source	Frequency of underlying data
Representative rate on the money market for loans between banks	1973–1981	Eurostat	Daily
Call money guilder market	1982–1998	DNB	Daily
Norway			
Norges Bank discount rate	1818–1965	Historical monetary statistics NB	End of month
Norges Bank marginal rate (various instruments)	1965–2014	Historical monetary statistics NB	End of month
Market rate Christiania	1894–1914	*The Economist*	Weekly
Euro Krone 3M	1959–1986	Historical monetary statistics NB	End of month
NIBOR tomorrow next	1987–2011	NB	Daily
NIBOR 1W	2011–2013	NB	Daily
Switzerland			
Bank rate Geneva	1892–1907	*The Economist*	Weekly
SNB discount rate	1907–1999	Historical times series SNB	Daily
SNB lombard rate/ liqudity shortage financing facility	1907–2007	Historical times series SNB	Daily
Market rate Geneva	1892–1914	*The Economist*	Weekly
Private discount rate	1924–1941	Fed International Financial Statistics	not given in source
Call money	1948–1972	Historical times series SNB	Weekly
Tomorrow next	1972–2007	Historical times series SNB	Daily
United States			
Discount rate New York Fed (average for commercial, agricultural and livestock paper)	1914–1969	NBER MacroHist	Daily

(*continued*)

(*continued*)

Instrument	Period	Source	Frequency of underlying data
Discount rate New York Fed (average on loans to member banks)	1969–2003	Fed H.15m	Daily
Discount rate primary credit	2003–2013	Fed H.15m	Daily
U.S. Commercial Paper Rates, New York City	1857–1953	NBER MacroHist	Daily
Effective Fed funds rate	1954–2013	Fed H.15m	Daily

5

Central Bank Independence in Small Open Economies

Forrest Capie
Cass Business School

Geoffrey Wood
Cass Business School

Juan Castañeda
University of Buckingham

1 Introduction

Central bank independence has for many years now been popular, seen as being not only associated with but actually contributing to low inflation. The modern-day pioneer in establishing an independent central bank with a focus on inflation was New Zealand. There a new central bank constitution was passed into law in 1988, and that constitution gave the central bank the primary objective of low inflation.[1] This was preceded by a considerable amount of work by economists which showed that central bank independence was associated with low inflation, and by some theoretical work which demonstrated that central bank independence would lead to, in the sense of cause, low inflation. There was the occasional partial dissent – Adam Posen (1993), for example, maintained that central bank independence and low inflation were in fact simultaneously produced by the structure of a country's financial system; but no one disputed that there was correlation. The starting point for this paper is a neglected aspect of that body of work; we focus on small open economies.

The reason for doing so is as follows. In a previous study (Capie and Wood, 2014) we argued that crises inevitably compromise central bank independence, as response to the crisis involves changes to the law governing the central bank. This was supported by evidence from several countries and over two centuries. But every country examined was, at least

---

[1] Details of the Act, and on why it was passed, can be found in Wood (1994).

by the standards of the time, large. Why do we consider that small open economies might be different?

At first glance one might expect the finding to hold there too. By their nature such economies are particularly exposed to shocks. Terms of trade shocks have a substantial effect in a small economy. If the exchange rate is fixed they have a fluctuating price level, and if the exchange rate is floating, while a stable price level can be maintained the exchange rate will by its fluctuations affect particular sectors of the economy and produce cries for action by and from politicians. But we nevertheless consider that such economies may be more successful at retaining a stable central bank constitution aimed at maintaining low inflation, and at achieving that low inflation goal.

The argument is straightforward and its essence can be stated briefly. It relies on two propositions. First, the more detailed is a law, the less likely it is to be capable of covering all contingencies. Second, high trust societies function more efficiently than low trust societies because in the former, transactions costs, in the widest sense, are lower. The next section of this paper develops these points to show the argument in full. We then turn to how well our analytical conclusions conform with any patterns there may be in the data. The penultimate section analyses and compares results across several small open economies (New Zealand, Australia, and Spain) and considers our argument in a tentative way in relation to Norway (comparative ignorance limits our capacity to take it further). The final section of the paper comprises an overview followed by a few remarks on whatever policy implications we think can be drawn from our work. There are also three appendices.

But before proceeding further we must dispose of two misconceptions. Fixed and floating exchange-rate regimes are often seen as alternatives, the adoption of which depends on the confidence there is in the monetary authorities of a country to behave properly. They are alternatives in the sense that either one delivers balance of payments equilibrium. A floating exchange rate is more likely to be adopted by a country with a reputation for sound monetary management. A fixed rate is likely to be more appealing to a country seeking to establish such a reputation. For a country with a floating exchange rate there is no exchange rate policy – it looks after itself. An independent monetary policy can be employed. Under truly fixed rates the exchange rate is the target and there is no monetary policy, with monetary conditions determined through the balance of payments.

But Milton Friedman showed that there was an important third type of regime – pegged rates, sometimes called 'fixed-but-adjustable' rates. Under this regime there can be some attempt at monetary policy at the same time as the exchange rate is being targeted. With pegged rates the monetary base has both domestic and foreign components. In some cases this last was effectively implicit in the working of the different exchange equalisation accounts. If capital flows were considered excessive there would be an attempt at sterilising the inflow.[2] Central bank independence is just as likely to prevail when there is an exchange-rate target in place. Such a target is given in a fixed rate regime but could also be employed in a regime of floating rates or of pegged or adjustable. Thus under the gold standard there was an exchange-rate target and a central bank might be entrusted to pursue the policies that ensured the currency was kept at parity. The same was true under Bretton Woods, although as noted there might well be both some monetary policy and some exchange-rate targeting. In fact central banks have mostly been happy with and even preferred exchange-rate targets since they give the banks more obvious power and prestige. (Johnson, 1969)

But nowadays most central banks have an inflation target largely because of a preference for floating rates that evolved after the breakdown of Bretton Woods. Further, there is currently no obvious anchor for the system, no dominant country whose monetary policy others could happily follow.[3]

The second misconception is the far from rare assertion that small open economies are price takers, with the inference that their price level and inflation rate are determined outside their borders. We reject that and agree with Mervyn King, the former Governor of the Bank of England (2003–2013) that, 'you can have whatever inflation rate you want'. It is obvious that a very small and open economy such as New Zealand has been highly successful over the last two decades or so in achieving a low and stable inflation rate of its choice. Similarly, a larger but still relatively small open economy, Canada, has had the same kind of success. And there are others. But as King also remarked it is possible to take the Turkish or Zimbabwean route. A flexible exchange rate allows bad choices as well as good choices to be made.

---

[2] See Fforde (1992) for details of one example of such a regime.

[3] In a previous paper (Capie, Mills, and Wood, 1994) we examined the evidence on central bank independence, first reviewing and comparing previous studies and then extending the work back in time. We recognised, following Friedman, that so-called fixed exchange-rate regimes are seldom truly and rigidly fixed. Rather, in practice they allow some latitude for domestic monetary policy. Looking back into the pegged-rate period found the association between central bank independence and low inflation broadly confirmed.

2 Why Size Matters: Conventions, Trust, and the Role of Law

The claim that 'my country is special' is in general a dubious one. As the late Karl Brunner was inclined to point out when that claim was made, in most countries water usually flows downhill. Nonetheless, although wary of the claim in general, we think it worth taking seriously in the present context. A recent volume, Braude et al. (2013), contains several studies which make this point. Appendix two comprises an overview of this volume: its most useful chapter on Norway we consider later.

So far in this paper we have written as if the only possible, the absolutely inevitable, model of an independent central bank is one established by a central bank law. That is the normal, and sometimes explicit, assumption in this field. That central bank law should, among other things, lay down the objectives the central bank had to achieve, what it had to do if it failed to achieve them, and what possible excuses for failure there were. Further, it might well set out circumstances in which the government of the day could intervene in the operations of the bank by issuing instructions which over-rode the law. It is time to consider whether this law-based (some have called it legalistic) notion of independence is the only possible such notion, or at the least the best one in all circumstances.

First we must make absolutely clear what we mean by independence in the context of central bank law. It is important to emphasise that it is not an absolute concept; the choice is not simply one of independence or not.[4]

Numerous economists have written on central bank independence, but generally paying attention to how to measure some loosely or even undefined notion of independence; little attention was paid to what the term might actually mean. The context was the relationship between degree of independence, somehow measured, and inflation. This relationship was highlighted in two papers by Robert Barro and David Gordon (1983a and b). Their papers show that a politically determined monetary policy will produce high inflation. Hence the recommendation followed – political influence should be removed from monetary policy by giving the central bank 'independence'. There were criticisms of their model, for it showed politicised monetary policy would produce high and steady inflation rather than the fluctuating inflation which is much more commonly seen in practice. This criticism was advanced by Philip Cagan (1986), who

---

[4] We are indebted to Professor Giangiacomo Nardozzi for pointing out to us the importance of doing this.

Central Bank Independence in Small Open Economies 199

went on to show that a desire not to subordinate low unemployment to an inflation objective can, with appropriate lags, lead to the kind of inflation usually observed. But the relationship between too high (and possibly variable) inflation and politically controlled monetary policy survived in theory. All that had changed was the behaviour of the too high inflation that politicised monetary policy was predicted to produce. The question of whether the relationship between low inflation and independence survived in practice remained of interest.

The pioneers in addressing this were Bade and Parkin (1987). Subsequent studies on the lines of their approach were Masciandaro and Tabellini (1988) and Alesina (1989). Bade and Parkin classified central banks into four groups, depending on their estimate of degree of government influence over them. Two types of influence were examined: 'financial type' and 'policy type'. The former refers to the level of government interference in selecting members of the board, the setting of salaries, the determination of budgets, and the distribution of profits. The latter referred to the extent of interference in meetings of the board (or whatever the policy-deciding body is) and whether government has the final decision over policy. Subsequently Capie and Wood (1991, reprinted 2012) reconsidered the issue with a wider range of measures of independence and a longer data period. Broadly speaking the finding of all these papers was unanimous: independence did correlate negatively with inflation, albeit, as Capie and Wood (op. cit.) note, in some countries inflation was low regardless of the status of the central bank.

But none of these studies spent much time on what independence actually meant. Freedom to take policy decisions seemed an obvious concept, and that was taken as being clear and detailed enough for the purpose at hand. In a much earlier paper, however, one which concluded by recommending not central bank independence but a monetary rule as the best guarantee of price stability, Milton Friedman (1962) devoted some time to considering the meaning and inevitable corollary of independence.

Milton Friedman's paper which contained his discussion of central bank independence was it should be noted published in a volume called 'In search of a Monetary Constitution' (a title which has particular resonance in the United States, where that book was published, in view of the importance the US Constitution plays in that country).[5] His paper was

---

[5] The paper may in view of that be interpreted as pointing the way towards recent economic discussion which emphasises the distinction between Common Law, as is usual in but not exclusive to countries with an English legal tradition, and other types of system such as Roman Law.

concerned with institution design. He contrasted two institutions, an independent central bank and a monetary rule, and considered which was likely to be preferable in terms of both retaining political control over monetary policy (essential he maintained in a democracy) and achieving price level stability. To make this contrast he had to make clear what he meant by an independent central bank.

He wrote, 'The device of an independent central bank embodies the very appealing idea that it is essential to prevent monetary policy from being a day-to-day plaything ... of the current political authorities'. (p. 178)[6] Then he went on 'A first step in discussing this notion critically is to examine the meaning of "independence" of a central bank. There is a trivial meaning that cannot be the source of any dispute about the desirability of independence. In any kind of bureaucracy, it is desirable to delegate particular functions to particular agencies'. (p. 179) At this point Friedman gives the example of the Bureau of Internal Revenue as an 'independent bureau' within the US Treasury. As he said, 'This is simply a question of expediency and of the best way of organising an administrative hierarchy'. (p179)

What he called a more basic meaning of independence is that '...a central bank should be an independent branch of government coordinate with the legislative, executive, and judicial branches, and with its actions subject to interpretation by the judiciary'. (p. 179)[7]

That is the meaning which most writers have implicitly applied to the concept of an independent central bank. But as Friedman's examples show, the basic model of a central bank established under law encompasses an enormous range of what might be called independence.

If the central bank is to be independent in the sense in which, say, the judiciary is independent, then it requires a set of instructions to follow just as judges require a set of laws to implement. Further, as is desirable with laws (but not always attained) the instructions must be sufficiently clear that the legislature's intentions are either carried out, or, if they are not, it is clear that they have not been. This manifestly relates to recent discussions of central bank transparency. In our view, 'transparency' in the context of central bank operations must mean clarity in the bank's observable objective; anything else is of no greater interest than the type of coffee served in the bank's staff canteen.

---

[6] All page references to this Friedman article are to the 1968 reprint.
[7] Recently both the European Central Bank (ECB) and the Bank of England have had their actions reviewed by the judiciary, albeit over very different issues. We briefly discuss these incidents below.

2.1 What Instructions?

Here it is useful to return to Friedman's paper, for the context in which he places his discussion of central bank independence leads very straightforwardly to the kinds of instructions that have in recent years been given to 'independent' central banks. He reviews three proposed solutions for the problem of ensuring that so long as government is responsible for money it cannot by debasement abuse that responsibility. He considered the following three solutions: an automatic commodity standard; an independent central bank; and a rule binding the conduct of policy. An automatic standard, such as gold, has tended to develop towards a 'mixed' system with a substantial fiduciary component. Further, it is not now feasible: '...the mythology and beliefs required to make it effective do not exist'. (p. 177)

That point is supported by the well-known quotation often attributed to Ramsay McDonald, the prime minister in the government immediately before that which took the decision, on Britain's leaving the gold standard in 1931: 'No-one told us we could do that'.

The law that establishes the central bank could, for example, say that the bank can conduct monetary policy in any way it likes to achieve any end it wishes; or at perhaps the opposite extreme could say that the bank must conduct policy in a way prescribed by the government to achieve an objective chosen by the government, but that it is independent to choose, for example, the colour of the coats its doormen wear. The model he used in his discussion was one where the bank had a target chosen by the government but was free to operate as it wished to achieve that target.

Note, then, that the basic model of a central bank established under law encompasses an enormous range of what might be called independence. The various attempts to measure independence (of which Capie and Wood's 1994 paper is a particularly wide-ranging one) are all within the basic Friedman framework: they represent developments of it, and are not a body of work independent of and entirely distinct from that framework.

Having set out exactly what we mean by central bank independence, we now go on to develop our argument as to why small open economies may be more successful than most at retaining a stable central bank constitution aimed at maintaining low inflation.[8]

A useful starting point is provided by Ronald Coase's (1937) remarkable and imaginative paper, in which he first assumed the complete absence of

---

[8] We set aside here, as not relevant to the current discussion, why Friedman eventually concluded in favour of a monetary rule.

transactions costs, and explored the consequences of this assumption before relaxing it to show how real world institutions depended for their existence on the presence of such costs. Here we make a different, but analogous, starting assumption.

We assume that we are dealing with a society where a set of conventions has evolved over the years.[9] Because the conventions have evolved, they have arrived at a situation where they are economically efficient. We claim this on the basis of the arguments and evidence that common law evolves thus. (This has been found by for example Mahoney (2001) and by Epstein (2005).) Not only are these institutions efficient, but, we also assume, and this is the novel element we introduce, they have evolved in what we term a 'Virtuous Society' – one where everyone conforms to these conventions, and it is the universal expectation that everyone will conform to them. No-one ever deviates from such behaviour.[10]

In such a society there would be no laws. The conventions evolved – no laws set them out – and no laws are needed to enforce them. The central bank itself would be constrained purely by convention to produce low inflation. No contract would be needed to enjoin that. The central bank would aim at low inflation because of the proven benefits of doing so, and the notion of formal contracts is foreign to the society. In such a society, then, there would be no central bank law because everyone would trust the central bank to deliver low inflation on average, without any law to tell them to do that. (There would still be money. For money's main reason for

---

[9] The best discussions of this evolutionary process which are known to the authors are the Mais Lecture given at Cass Business School by Frederick Hayek shortly before his death – for which reason it regrettably remains unpublished – and Jonathan Sacks's 'Markets, governments, and virtues', of 2002.

[10] The evolution of common and shared norms, institutions, and values in a virtuous society was described by Adam Smith in his 'Theory of Moral Sentiments' (1759, A. Millar, London, and Kincaid and Bell, Edinburgh). By their nature, he maintained, human beings while self-interested are also genuinely social actors. They have sympathy for others and care for them, and so are able to learn from their own personal experience which acts are compatible with the well-being of others and of the society as a whole, and which are harmful and therefore should not be pursued. This, Smith argued, is the very basis of virtue in society. The particular relevance of this to small societies was urged in a subsequent edition. In the 1790 edition (A. Strahan, London and Creech, Bell, and Co., Edinburgh) Smith included a new book, book VI, where he studied 'Virtue'. Section ii therein discusses 'The character of the individual, so far as it can affect the happiness of other people'. There Smith underlines the gradations of affection, care, and attention individuals give to others, with different intensity depending on how near they are to them, starting with family and ending with country and humanity. We are grateful to Professor Pedro Schwartz for bringing to our attention the importance of the changes to the 1790 edition.

existence is the existence of transactions costs. (See e.g. Clower, 1967.) And there would also still be a central bank: see Appendix One.)

Now of course we recognise that whatever might be the situation in some idealised Rousseau-esque society, no such society exists in the world today. But what does exist is a wide range of societies with different degrees of trust. Some states have essentially broken down because they depended not on convention but on the rule of law, and that is largely absent (Somalia, perhaps), while in others crime rates are low, and many, maybe even the majority, of crimes are the result of mental illness or extreme stress. Predatory behaviour and violence for pleasure are both extremely rare.

How might we expect the central bank contract in such a 'high trust' (but not *completely* virtuous) society to be written?

It could be written loosely. That is to say, the preference for low inflation might be expressed in it for convenience, and as a precaution permission to act as Lender of Last Resort in a crisis could be there for the avoidance of doubt when action is urgent, as it is in a crisis.[11] In addition, a tolerance range around which inflation was allowed to fluctuate might be expressed, if economic knowledge (which term we assume for the sake of discussion not to be an oxymoron) allowed that to be done. Otherwise, the only reason for it would be to help people form their expectations. The contract would be free of detailed instructions, since the central bank would be trusted to do the right thing as best it could.

Our argument on the importance of trust has implications for the resilience of central bank independence in the face of shocks. Let us briefly repeat our earlier argument as to why central bank independence seems inevitably to be compromised by a crisis. Central bank independence, we suggested, requires a well-defined contract. It is impossible to write a complete contingent contract. Hence at some time a crisis occurs which is not anticipated in the contract. The contract therefore requires modification, and there is then scope for the government implicitly or explicitly to claim that it has no choice but to interfere with some aspect of the bank's contractual independence. This conclusion was supported by the examples we studied in Capie and Wood (2014). But these examples were from 'normal' societies. Certainly they were not ones where the rule of law had broken down, but nor were they ones where trust is unusually high by the standards of developed nations.

---

[11] For explanation of what is meant by Lender of Last Resort action see Wood (2000).

That particular problem occurs, though, only because the contract was detailed. A contract scarcer in detail would allow a central bank much greater discretion, and thus greater freedom to respond as seemed best to previously completely unforeseen events. The contract would not require updating after a crisis, so there would be no scope for the compromising of independence. These seem to us to be the implications for central bank independence of being in a high trust society. How do these implications bear on the present study? Because, we would argue, of the kind of societies most likely to be high trust.

2.2 High Trust Societies

You may not actively distrust someone you do not know. But trust is much more likely among people who know each other, and have reason for trust. We can imagine groups of people who know each other, and who trust each other as a consequence of regular interactions. These networks can extend, as the groups will not be closed. Each member, or at any rate most, will know individuals outside the group. People who live in a village nowadays will know people outside the village. The network of trust will thus extend, and could extend across the whole society. It would be self-reinforcing because self-rewarding behaviour if it did, because it would reduce the costs of transacting, by for example reducing the amount of pre-contract diligence which it seemed necessary to undertake.

Such a network of interlinked trust groups could not extend across the whole of the United Kingdom, for example. Accordingly, high trust societies will be small societies. And small societies are small economies, and small economies are except by the occasional political quirk (North Korea) inevitably open economies. (We do not assert that small societies are inevitably high trust; rather that high trust societies are inevitably small.)

Hence small open economies, exposed to crises as they are, may nonetheless have central banks which if independent retain that independence through crises. Does the evidence support this conclusion? Or do they lose that independence and revert to high and perhaps variable inflation?

3 What does 'Small and Open' Mean in Practice?

The use of large and small in the international trade literature is usually taken to mean the ability or not to change a country's terms of trade. A large country is defined as one that can change its terms of trade and a small country one that cannot. So, for example, to pick up on a recently

Central Bank Independence in Small Open Economies   205

spotted instance of that view, Dannhauser (2013) writes that the usual
'...assumption of a "small" economy will be maintained, i.e. we abstract
from economies, such as the United States, that have sufficient market
power to influence prices in world markets for internationally traded
goods'. But the definition which that quotation implies might well result
in all countries being classified as small. It is difficult to find a country that
can change its terms of trade in anything more than a very limited range of
products. How much influence does the United States have in world
markets and how many others like her could there be? Similarly, at the
other end of the spectrum a small country that supplied the world with say,
a rare mined metal is likely to have greater influence on world prices than
most other countries. Almost all countries could therefore be categorised as
small in the common international trade sense. It might be more useful in
the present context simply to consider some measure of absolute size on
the grounds that absolute size is what matters in the present context since
it is that, given openness, which determines the importance of shocks of
any given size to the price level. But openness is key. Closed economies can
do as they wish and lose their interest for us in this sense.

3.1 Measuring Openness

How open is open? We turn here to the question of how to measure how
open an economy is. The degree of openness has typically been represented
by the trade/income relationship – the extent of trade in relation to total
output – and usually captured by calculating:

$$\{(X + M)/2\}/Y$$

But there have been many variations around this[12]. For example, Grassman (1980) presented a measure of what he called real openness, with the
ratio defined as volumes of exports (X) and imports (M) adjusted by their
respective price indices:

$$R1 = (XPx + MPm)/NPn + XPx - MPm$$

Where N is domestic output not exported and Pn is the general price level.
   Beenstock and Warburton (1983), however, showed just how greatly
prices mattered in that calculation. If import prices rose the ratio rose

---

[12] We deal only with trade in goods due to data limitations for a considerable part of the
period we cover.

whereas if the non-traded prices rose the ratio fell, and if export prices rose the effect was ambiguous. Moreover, 'most leverage of price movements with respect to R1 will occur through changes in Pm and Pn rather than Px'. They then showed that removing price changes resulted in a substantially different picture of openness for both the United States and the United Kingdom over the century prior to 1980.

It is thus clear that our results might be critically dependent on a particular measure of openness: an unsatisfactory situation. Fortunately, it is possible in the context we are working to reject some openness measures a priori. The argument is as follows. Our concern is with the shocks (crises) which can affect a country from overseas. It does not matter for our purposes whether the shock is purely nominal – a price change only – or a purely real one such as the vanishing of a market for a country's goods (an example is the kind of shock Finland experienced with the collapse of the Soviet Union). Hence we can consider both real and nominal shocks without distinguishing between them, and need not make the 'Grassman Adjustment'.[13] The next stage is therefore to identify the countries we are to call small and open.

3.2 The Data and the Methods

In the spirit of Capie, Mills, and Wood (1994 op. cit.) we consider a long run of data. Observations are for seventeen countries, comprising the current G10 and seven others. This is admittedly a restricted set: there are many economies in the world that it excludes. But we are driven to drawing our data from mature and developed nations by our tests forcing the requirement for long runs of data. That, we should say explicitly, is a compulsion we had no urge to resist – drawing data from a long period covering a good range of political and other institutions, and of historical backgrounds, is highly desirable in all statistical work.

---

[13] It is customary when discussing shocks to distinguish not only between real and nominal shocks, which we maintain we need not do in the present context, but also between permanent and transitory ones and between anticipated and unanticipated ones. We do not make the former distinction either, on the grounds that when the shock actually occurs, and that is usually when any policy response is made, it is not possible to decide whether a shock is permanent or transitory. One might say in objection that some shocks are obviously transitory – a war, for example. But precedent suggests that even in that context transitory can mean up to thirty years. And as for the claim that with modern technology wars will inevitably be short, that may well have been said at the start of the Thirty Years War. Nor does the usual anticipated/unanticipated distinction matter, for it would affect only the timing of any government response.

Central Bank Independence in Small Open Economies   207

The data points are generally every five years, adjusting slightly to omit the years of the First and Second World Wars. Thus, starting at 1890, the points are 1890, 1895,. . ., 1910, 1913, 1919, 1924,. . ., 1938, 1948, 1953,. . ., 2008. We end at 2008 to avoid the financially turbulent following five years.

As well as real GDP, openness, inflation (as measured by a retail price index appropriate to each country), central bank independence, and an index of economic freedom. The central bank independence measure comes from Capie and Wood (1991), and is supplemented where necessary by that produced by Alex Cukierman et al., (1992). We use the latest available index of economic freedom (Prados 2014). These data are in an appendix to the paper, in the above order, in a series of tables. The sources for the other data are given in Appendix three.

Next comes how to decide which economies we regard as small and open. The procedure is as follows. We construct a series of diagrams, one for data up to 1914, one for 1919 to 1938, one for 1953 to 1978, and one for the remainder of our period. Each diagram contains the within-period averages for GDP and for openness for every country in our set. (There are it will be observed five GDP observations and five openness observations averaged for each country in each diagram.)

The diagrams are of four quadrants, constructed as follows. The vertical axis measures GDP, the horizontal measures openness, and their point of intersection is at the median of each series of these two series in the period of the diagram.

It can be seen that for each diagram the small open economies (as compared to the others in the period of the diagram) will lie in the bottom right-hand quadrant. That enables us to produce another table, of small open economies in each five year period, and then to see which, if any, entered or left that group over our data period as a whole. The next section of our paper then explores whatever connection there may be between openness and low inflation, and openness and central bank independence. But first, let us move on to the data.

3.3 The Figures

Before discussing these we simply lay them out in date order.

Our figures are easily read. The horizontal line is the median size of the countries in the figure. The vertical line is the median degree of openness for these same countries. Their intersection gives us four quadrants. Those in the lower right are small and open. Those in the upper left are

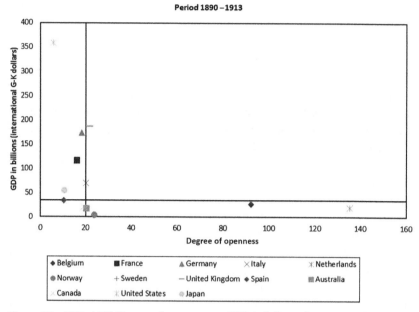

Figure 5.1: 1890–1913 Degree of openness vs GDP in billions (International Geary-Khamis dollars)

large and less open. So, for example, Figure 5.1, which covers the period 1890–1913, shows in the lower right quadrant the two small economies that we normally think of as being very open, Belgium and the Netherlands. The median for openness is twenty on our measure and there is considerable clustering around that. The United States, well known in the nineteenth century as highly protectionist, is one of the least open and by far the largest economy. In this period Norway is both very small and open.

In the following period, the interwar years, as we would expect, the degree of openness has fallen and the median is closer to sixteen on our measure. If anything the United States became more closed with two major tariff hikes in 1922 and 1929. The United Kingdom also has become less open but represents the median. The major factor reducing openness was the collapse of international trade. Nevertheless most countries retain their general positions in the quadrants.

Although in the years after the Second World War there were many moves in the direction of freeing up the international economy it took a long time to have a clear effect. Trade grew faster than output but the measure of openness, the median, was restored to no more than the twenty

Central Bank Independence in Small Open Economies 209

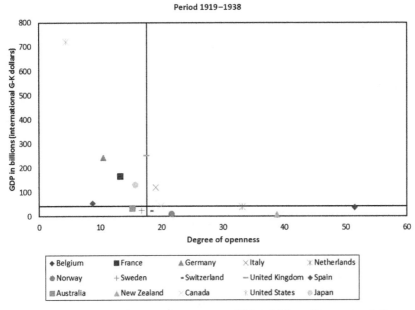

Figure 5.2: 1919 – 1938 Degree of openness vs GDP in billions (International Geary-Khamis dollars)

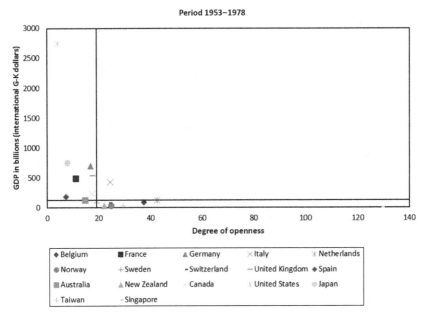

Figure 5.3: 1953 – 1978 Degree of openness vs GDP in billions (International Geary-Khamis dollars)

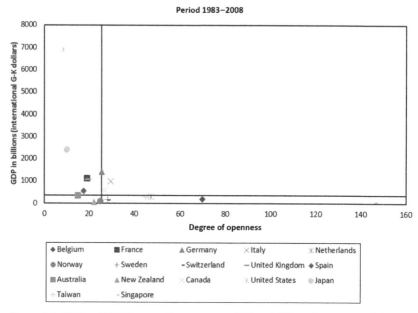

Figure 5.4: 1983 – 2008 Degree of openness vs GDP in billions (International Geary-Khamis dollars)

or so of the pre First World War period. The United States while less protectionist than before continues to appear among the less open economies largely because the external sector is so small in relation to the domestic economy. The main point to make about the period is that there is a greater clustering around the intersection of the medians. Japan makes its appearance as the second largest economy but is relatively closed.

Finally, again as might be anticipated, the period from the 1980s onwards becomes more open, the median rises to more than twenty, and interestingly the clustering lessens. The United States remains stubbornly 'closed'. The small open economies are as before.

The next stage is to examine the relationship, if any, between the degree of openness and inflationary performance. Does good performance depend in some way upon size and/or openness? There already have been some attempts at establishing the connection between openness and inflation. Romer (1993) for example, started from the point that unanticipated monetary expansion leads to real exchange-rate depreciation and observed, uncontentiously, that real exchange-rate depreciation is more damaging the more open is the economy. He then went on to argue that whatever might be the benefits of unanticipated monetary expansion they would be

Central Bank Independence in Small Open Economies 211

lower in more open economies. Therefore, he concludes to explain his finding, the authorities in small open economies have a lower incentive to use unanticipated monetary expansion because of the damage to the real exchange rate.

So while the absence of pre-commitment in monetary policy, that is the absence of central bank independence, generally leads to excessive inflation it does this less, he suggests, in more open economies.

Are our results consistent with his? Tables 5.1–5.4 summarise the data for the small open economies for the four periods already indicated. These show for each country in each period the average size and average inflation

Table 5.1: *Small open economies. Period 1: 1890–1913*

	GDP (average)	Inflation (average)	Central bank independence	Inflation (average, rest of countries)
Belgium	26,541	2.28	Unclassified	1.59
Netherlands	19,339	0.69	NA	
Norway	4,473	3.22	NA	
Sweden	12,399	1.25	Dependent	
Australia	17,622	1.36	NA	

Notes: Central Bank independence as classified by Capie and Wood (1991). GDP in million 1990 International Geary-Khamis dollars

Table 5.2: *Small open economies. Period 2: 1919–1938*

	GDP (average)	Inflation (average)	Central bank independence	Inflation (*) (average, rest of countries)
Belgium	36,172	5.03	Unclassified	2.86
Netherlands	38,710	2.23	NA	
Norway	9,324	3.01	NA	
Sweden	25,004	3.00	Dependent	
Switzerland	22,446	2.07	NA	
New Zealand	7,752	2.03	Unclassified (**)	

Notes: (*) Excluding Germany and thus its deflationary episode of 1924, average inflation would be around 4.5%
(**) The New Zealand Reserve Bank was established in 1933. It was nationalised and became statutory dependent in 1936
Central Bank independence as classified by Capie and Wood (1991). GDP in million 1990 International Geary-Khamis dollars

212   Forrest Capie, Geoffrey Wood, and Juan Castañeda

Table 5.3: *Small open economies. Period 3: 1953–1978*

	GDP (average)	Inflation (average)	Central bank independence	Inflation (average, rest of countries)
Belgium	87,403	2.98	Dependent (*)	5.44
Netherlands	128,914	3.55	Dependent (*)	
Sweden	85,931	4.46	Dependent	
Switzerland	84,912	2.78	Independent (*)	
New Zealand	27,860	5.95	Dependent	
Taiwan	34,134	8.80	NA	
Singapore	8,261	8.48	Dependent (*)	

Notes: Unless indicated, Central Bank independence as classified by Capie and Wood (1991). GDP in million 1990 International Geary-Khamis dollars
(*) Legal Central Bank independence following Cukierman, Webb, and Neyapti (1992). We have adopted 0.50 as the threshold for a central bank to be defined as independent

Table 5.4: *Small open economies. Period 4: 1983–2008*

	GDP (average)	Inflation (average)	Central bank independence	Inflation (average, rest of countries)
Belgium	190,266	2.62	Dependent/Independent (**)	3.55
Netherlands	301,997	2.02	Dependent/Independent (**)	
Sweden	167,153	4.14	Dependent/Independent (***)	
Switzerland	152,208	1.83	Independent (*)	
Taiwan	290,140	1.31	Dependent (*)	
Singapore	70,095	1.95	Dependent (*)	

Notes: Unless indicated Central Bank independence as classified by Capie and Wood (1991). GDP in million 1990 International Geary-Khamis dollars
(*) Legal Central Bank independence following by Cukierman, Webb and Neyapti (1992). We have adopted 0.50 as the threshold for a central bank to be defined as independent (up to 1989)
(**) By 1998 all EMU (Economic and Monetary Union) Member States granted independence to their central banks
(***) The Riksbank was granted independence in 1999

rate across the period. Each table also shows the status of each country's central bank. Additionally, the average rate of inflation for all the other countries is given to allow some comparison.

In the first table the results are mixed. Perhaps for the gold standard years this should be expected. All the countries shown, except Australia, had the institutions that we recognise as central banks. Inflation is low as the average of 1.59% for the rest of the group shows. Both this and the similarity of inflation rates were consequences of the world monetary standard at the time.

Taken across all the periods the results provide support, albeit modest, for Romer's conclusion. Our small open economies with independent central banks do a little better than the average. But it must be emphasised that the inflation in these economies is relatively as well as absolutely low – a stronger finding than that of Romer.

What of central bank independence? Is that more durable in small open economies? Across the whole period dependency is the more common position. But the tables do show central bank independence (or dependence) for our small open economies. Does one relationship or the other emerge as the predominant one? And more important, are there any significant changes in this relationship?

While the results are of course mixed, it does appear that central banks in small open economies do better than the others in terms of retaining their independence. The majority of those that start independent in our data remain so. More important, this is notably the case in the turbulent interwar years of Table 5.2 and as we move from them to the relative stability of the years of Table 5.3.

Independent central banks do appear more likely to remain so in small open economies.

We posited at the outset that high trust societies were likely to function more efficiently than other societies and that high trust was more likely to be found in small open economies. At this point we wish to add tentatively that economic freedom will be found to be greater in these same small open societies; and that better inflation performance should be found in the economies with greater economic freedom. This would remain conjecture were it not for the recent availability of an historical index of economic freedom produced by Leandro Prados. There are some such indexes that cover the second half of the twentieth century. Prados has extended these back to the middle of the nineteenth century. That allows us at least to make a start on testing the hypothesis. All the cautions on the indexes apply as usual.

The main caution to bear in mind in this case is that the indexes of economic freedom are constructed using many of the indicators that we have used implicitly for high trust societies. We would in any case expect freedom to be associated with small open economies and so expect some confirmation of the previous results.

214   *Forrest Capie, Geoffrey Wood, and Juan Castañeda*

Table 5.5: *Changes in statutory independence in small open economies*

	Period 1: 1890–1913	
	Change, year	Direction
Belgium	No	
Netherlands	Yes (1903) (*)	Less independent
Norway	Yes (1892) (*)	Less independent
Sweden	Yes (1897)	More independent
Australia	Established in 1912	

	Period 2: 1919–1938	
	Change, year	Direction
Belgium	Yes (1937)	Less independent
Netherlands	No	
Norway	No	
Sweden	No	
Switzerland	No	
New Zealand	Yes; and nationalised (1936)	Less independent

	Period 3: 1953–1978	
	Change, year	Direction
Belgium	No	
Netherlands	Nationalised, 1948	Less independent
Sweden	No	
Switzerland	No	
New Zealand	Yes	
	1960	Less independent
	1964	More independent
Taiwan	Yes	
	Re-established, 1961	Under the government
	1961	More independent
	1979	Less independent
Singapore	Established 1971	Under the government

	Period 4: 1983–2008	
	Change, year	Direction
Belgium	Yes	
	1993	More independent
	1998	More independent
Netherlands	Yes, 1998	More independent
Sweden	No	
Switzerland	Yes	
	1999	More independent

	Period 4: 1983–2008	
	Change, year	Direction
	2003	More independent
Taiwan	No	
Singapore	No	

Notes: (*) In these cases, permission to buy public debt or an extension of the loans to the government was granted by law.
Sources: Arnone et al (2006) on the OECD countries; Pohl and Freitag (eds., 1994) on the European countries; Swiss National Bank (ed. 2007) several chapters on the origin and evolution of the Swiss National Bank; Linklater (1992), Bell (2004), Hawke (1973) on New Zealand; Shea (1994) on Taiwan; and Sheng-Yi (1990) on Singapore. The statutes of the national central banks were also consulted and accessed via central banks' official websites.

The first step was to examine the rank correlations for economic freedom and inflation in our four sub-periods. The results are not strong but in three of the four sub-periods a negative sign is obtained. That is, if you like, a positive! It is what we expect. The less economic freedom there is the more inflation there is. The relationship is strongest of all in the 1953–1978 period, something to which we return.

We next calculated correlation coefficients for the raw annual data. Again it was for the second half of the twentieth century that the strongest results were found. In fact stronger results were found for both periods: 1953–1978 was -0.875 and 1983–2008 was -0.287. These results are broadly supportive of our earlier position but we would not want to make too much of them. They do raise a number of questions. Our first conjecture at this stage is that the period 1953–1978 was one generally of financial repression with exchange controls in particular being highly restrictive. And with the Bretton Woods arrangements in place together these might explain much of the better inflation performance.

As far as the earlier periods go it could be argued that for the interwar years there was greatly diminished economic freedom and that the mix of hyperinflation and deflation experience distorts the overall results. For the gold standard years again inflation was pinned down and not necessarily closely related to economic freedom.

4 Some Examples of Contracts

In this section we examine the contracts of individual central banks that are of particular interest. These banks all highlight the importance of the circumstances in which central banks gain their independence, and support further our suspicion of the notion of the independent central banker as a deus ex machina who regardless of where he is delivers the desired objective of low inflation.

We start with New Zealand, the country and bank which pioneered the revival of central bank independence in the late twentieth century. One would expect New Zealand to be a relatively high trust society. It is small (the population about half that of London although scattered over an area of land a little bigger than that of Britain), it is isolated, and its population did, with the exception of the fairly small minority, come primarily from a society with a high degree of trust[14]. Does that country have a loosely drawn central bank contract? In fact the answer is an emphatic no. For details of the contract see Capie and Wood (1991, op. cit.) or Wood (1994). But although New Zealand is we maintain a high trust society in general, when the contract was put in place (1989) it was a low trust society as far as monetary policy went. For the preceding government had become notorious for the politicisation of all aspects of economic policy, including monetary policy, and there was strong desire to ensure that could not readily be done again. The contract was drawn tightly and in a way manifestly intended to make government interference in monetary policy not impossible – that would be undesirable in a democracy – but certainly difficult.

Britain is interesting as an example of a society which, while not low trust by any means, did not satisfy the conditions expected to be a high trust one either. It is an 'intermediate' case. The central bank contract there was at least initially comparatively loosely drawn. There was an inflation target, with bands around it, but the only explicit penalty for failure was that the Governor of the Bank had to enter into an exchange of letters with the Chancellor of the Exchequer, in which the Governor explained the failure and what it was proposed to do about it, and to which the Chancellor then replied letting the Governor know if he approved of the proposal for correction. Again, though, note the circumstances. Policy was being taken away from those, the politicians, who were seen as largely responsible for previous failures, and given to a group with clean hands, and which had, indeed, performed well in the central bank capacity of maintaining financial stability, an area of work where it had been untroubled by

---

[14] One of the authors can advance an anecdote to support New Zealand's being a high trust society. Fairly recently one of us (Wood) while working in the New Zealand Treasury took a flight from Wellington to Auckland along with one of his then colleagues. Airport security comprised of the passengers and airport staff greeting each other by name, and enquiring about various developments in respective families. Wood was introduced by his locally known colleague, and accorded the same treatment.

Central Bank Independence in Small Open Economies   217

government. (Further, that the Bank had its contract modified after the recent crisis is we have argued [Capie and Wood, 2014] actually due to the Bank's not making adequate use of its freedom, and only reluctantly using its Lender of Last Resort capacity.)

Australia provides a slightly different example. The Reserve Bank of Australia was founded in 1959 but it had a forerunner in the Commonwealth Bank which had been founded in 1911. There had long been a desire in Australia in the nineteenth century to have an institution similar to the Bank of England. The banking crises of the early 1890s provided a reason and the circumstances were more favourable after Federation in 1901. The Commonwealth Bank is generally reckoned to have been a central bank before the First World War. After 1920 when it had responsibility for the note issue it even more closely resembled the Bank of England. It was 1959 though before the central banking functions were separated from the commercial banking functions. The Reserve Bank nevertheless remained subordinate to the Treasury until the 1980s after which it can be regarded as independent.

The Australian central banking story for the period after the Second World War reads much like that for the United Kingdom. Wartime controls were continued as a means of keeping inflation down, together with the supposed anchor of the pegged exchange rate. Like many other Organisation for Economic Co-operation and Development (OECD) countries Australia enjoyed great prosperity during the 'Golden era' but the seeds were sown in the 1960s for the stagflation of the 1970s. There followed a period until the 1990s during which policy lacked coordination. There was a slow acceptance of the need for monetary discipline. Monetary targeting was adopted after 1976 (and abandoned in 1985). By the late 1980s the Bank was being criticised for allowing an asset bubble to develop, for lacking a clear monetary framework, and being insufficiently independent to carry out monetary policy.

By the early 1990s the requisite independence was acquired, inflation was brought under control and inflation targeting was being followed. (Cornish, 2010) This independence has survived.

Our inclination is to put Australia in the high trust category (in stark contrast to the United States with its rules and litigation). There is co-operation between the Reserve Bank of Australia and the Australian Prudential Regulation Authority (RBA and the APRA) consistent with institutions being more resilient when shocks occur.

The genesis of central banking in Spain follows a very well-established pattern, one by which a government in desperate need of funds could not resort yet again to national or international creditors and opted for establishing a new bank to finance its obligations. The origins[15] of the *Banco de España* are in the last quarter of the eighteenth century, during the Anglo-French war years, when Spain aligned with France and faced extraordinary war payments. To facilitate the access to new borrowing, a new bank, the *Banco de San Carlos*, whose primary function was the redemption of the new public bonds issued to cover war expenses, was given a royal charter. The *Banco de San Carlos* can in fact mainly be viewed as just the *bank of the Government* and it was not until much later that the central bank started to provide other financial services to the economy.

The costs of the Napoleonic war and the run of a succession of budget deficits led to an accumulation of public debt in the balance sheet of the Bank that the State was clearly unable to honour; the Bank was finally liquidated in 1829. A new Bank, *Banco de San Fernando*, was established that was in effect just a continuation of the *Banco de San Carlos* and thus its main function was still to act as the bank of the State. Following what had happened many times before in many other countries (including Britain), in exchange the *Banco de San Fernando* was granted the monopoly of note issue in Madrid. After many travails and different names the bank was finally renamed as the *Banco de España* in 1856.

Even though a private bank, the *Banco de España* remained under the influence of the Government, which appointed the Governor, and its main activity was the provision of credit to the State. Given the weak fiscal position of the State, the need for more borrowing from the Bank continued. With the preparations to join the Latin Monetary Union, Spain launched the Peseta as the national currency in 1868 and adopted a bimetallic monetary system; however, the successive running of both public and trade deficits led to the abandonment of gold (but not silver) convertibility very soon in 1883.

The modernisation of the Bank came as a result of the 1921 Banking Act. Rather than financing the State by purchasing its debt directly, private banks (a select group of them) were given more advantageous credit facilities from the *Banco de España* if they used public bonds as collateral. At the same time, the establishment of new commercial banks was restricted and new supervisory powers were given to the *Banco de España*. The central bank was expected to provide regular lending to the banking

---

[15] For the eighteenth and nineteenth centuries we have mainly followed Tortella's (1994) excellent work on the origins and development of central banking in Spain. More details can be found in Tedde (1988), and Tedde and Marichal (1994).

Central Bank Independence in Small Open Economies 219

sector. And indeed, very soon the Bank had to intervene in the markets and acted as the Lender of Last Resort in the 1931 financial crisis.

After the civil war (1936–1939), with the new 1946 Banking Act the Bank lost almost all its powers and autonomy and became fully dependent on General Franco's government. From 1946 to 1962 the Bank was just an instrument in the hands of a very interventionist government aimed at managing the economy, via the imposition of interest rates and capital and bank controls. With the new 1962 Act the Bank, even though nationalised, resumed some of its lost competences and independence particularly in relation to monetary policy. As a result of three successive new acts (1971, 1980, and 1988) the Bank achieved even more autonomy in relation to the implementation of monetary policy decisions and was given more supervisory powers of both saving and commercial banks.

In 1994, in fulfilment of one of the requisites to join European Monetary Union, the Bank was granted full independence in relation to the implementation of monetary policy and the provision of credit to the Government was prohibited. In 1998 the *Banco de España* joined the European System of Central Banks and the country adopted the euro as the national country and finally delegated its monetary sovereignty on 1 January 1999.

Note then that in the Spanish case the evolution of the Bank of Spain and of its constitution closely reflects what is going on in the country. Initially the creature of government, a succession of wars external and internal, followed by many years of highly centralised, perhaps authoritarian, government led to a central bank which became independent of government ultimately only as a result of external pressures. There was no prospect here of an independent central bank emerging to provide low inflation. It was conferred by a deus ex machina. The political background over-rode openness and size. One can only conjecture whether if allowed enough time the new political culture in Spain would have allowed independence.

Finally but briefly, to the Norwegian experience. Norway is certainly a small economy and by the measures we have used is a very open economy. The Norges Bank Act of 1816 established the Bank as one whose main purpose was issuing the currency, which was convertible into silver. While the governing members were appointed by Parliament, the ultimate authority over the discount rate rested with the Bank. Over the nineteenth century the Bank's commercial activities gradually diminished and it took on responsibility for the banking system though it did not supervise or regulate it, that being done by other bodies.

In 1873 Norway adopted the gold standard and in 1875 joined the Scandinavian Currency Union. In 1892 the Norges Bank Act was revised with the Bank of England as model. Norges Bank then played its part as Lender of Last Resort in the severe financial crisis of 1899. Across the nineteenth century and beyond the Bank's room for independent action was limited. It would have to be classified as dependent.

In 1914 the gold standard was abandoned and then re-established in 1928 before being abandoned again in the Great Depression in 1931. German occupation in wartime paved the way for considerable inflation after the war which in turn reduced the Bank's policy-making authority further. Government took control of interest-rate policy and the discount rate. Nationalisation followed in 1949 and in 1965 a new Act established that interest rates and credit volumes were to be regulated by government. We leave the detailed history and analysis of central bank independence here to those who have all the essential skills, including the ability to read Norwegian. We note only that independence has survived.

5 Conclusions

Low inflation is clearly associated with independent central banks. But why? The Barro and Gordon (1983a) explanation based on the notion of time inconsistency is a common one, and is implicit in Romer's (op.cit.) explanation of why many small open economies have low inflation. Other influences may also matter, however, and this may well be fortunate, as that explanation requires policy makers to have considerable economic knowledge – perhaps more than may actually exist – about economies and how they respond, and how quickly they respond, to policy changes.

We support Romer in his finding of small open economies often being low inflation economies by an explanation additional to and independent of his. Independent central banks tend to be more durable in their independence in such economies because these economies have the option of being, and often are, high trust societies. These allow the writing of simple, and therefore less affected by shocks, central bank contracts, and as Friedman argued many years ago in his pioneering discussion of central bank independence, central banks need a set of instructions and that takes the form of a contract.

This emphasis on the notion that the kind of central bank contract that a society has is in part endogenous to the nature of a society is reinforced by our discussion of four special cases all of which show that contracts depend substantially on the circumstances in which they came about.

Accordingly, we conclude with some confidence that central bank independence is much more likely to be durable in small open economies than in large economies, regardless of the degree of openness of the latter. This can be further tested when banking systems and the central banks at the heart of them have settled down after the recent crisis – but that is still some time off.

Acknowledgements

We are greatly indebted to David Laidler for his comments on an early version of this paper, to J. R. Sargent for his comments on a subsequent draft, to Ali Kabiri for his suggestions of data bases and sources, and to Anandadeep Mandal for assistance with data.

APPENDIX ONE: Free Banking in a High Trust Society?

As so often, some work by Milton Friedman provides an insight into this matter. In his 1960 lectures published as *A Program for Monetary Stability* he discusses (pages 4–9 of the 1983 reprint), whether government should have any role in 'monetary and banking questions. He starts from a '... pure commodity standard, which at first sight seems to require no government intervention'. (p. 4)

He goes on to observe that governments often got involved in such a standard by being assigned or assuming 'the function of stamping the weight or fineness of the metal', although it could be done privately. Keeping such a standard purely metallic, however, involves considerable resource use (see pages 5–6 of the volume for his calculations), so a fiduciary element is introduced. Now, he observes, there is a role for the government to enforce the convertibility contracts. If the currency evolves further, to a purely fiduciary one, then over-issue would lead to a situation where it was once again a 'purely commodity standard', as there was '... no equilibrium price level short of that at which the money value of currency is no greater than that of the paper it contains'. (p. 7) Hence he concludes that there must be an 'external limit' to maintain the value of such a fiduciary currency, because '... competition does not provide an effective limit'.

Note that this conclusion depends crucially on the assumption that without a law to constrain over-issue, it will occur because '... any individual issuer has an incentive to issue additional amounts'. That is the essence of his argument. Individuals are not bound by any convention not to over-issue. This seems to imply that in a high trust, convention based, society, free banking could function – but only in such a society. Whether a Lender of Last Resort would be needed is an interesting additional speculation. Banks would still fail in such a society. Such failures would all be honest mistakes. But that seems to us not necessarily to suggest that there would not be contagion: rational (but not perfectly informed) individuals could fear a failure was the first signal of a common shock.[16]

APPENDIX TWO: Studies of Small Open Economies

Stanley Fischer's introduction to the volume edited by Braude suggests there are ten lessons which central bankers should derive from the recent crisis. One is unexceptionable. In a crisis, do not panic. But otherwise, Fischer's lively introduction does not relate particularly to the kind of economies discussed in the book.

Huw Pill and Frank Smets make three observations relevant to our work: 'malfunctioning' of capital markets has contributed to the length and depth of the current recession, and that dealing with these malfunctions will help recovery; second, that the 'solid anchoring' of inflation expectations was stabilising in the crisis, and that therefore not only should price stability remain the focus of monetary policy but that it is worth considering moving to a target which does not automatically forgive previous target misses; and third that as financial imbalances contributed to the bust as well as the boom, monetary policy should pay heed to monetary and credit aggregates so as to avoid contributing to future imbalances. The second of these points directs attention to how best to anchor price expectations in open economies and to the benefits of doing so, and the third to the problems (as well as benefits) that international capital flows can bring.

On the question of capital flows Jonathan Ostry concludes that controls may occasionally enable the best to be made of a bad job. That far from ringing endorsement can probably be accepted as justifying a few special cases. But what policy response should there be to sudden stops in external capital flows? The lesson he draws is an important one – '... an economy

---

[16] It should be observed that Selgin (1988) and White (1995) differ from this conclusion.

Central Bank Independence in Small Open Economies 223

that follows prudent macroeconomic policies…tends to be in a better relative position to cope with the adverse consequences of a financial crisis'. (p. 213) (As Robert Mundell put it, '… there is no such thing as a bad capital movement only bad exchange-rate systems'.) Again, domestic policies are important in very open economies.

The book contains several case studies of small open economies – Australia, Norway, Israel, and Ireland. The chapter on Norway is perhaps the most instructive of the case studies. There is lots of information on a country and its banking system about which most readers will know little. Of particular interest is the 'flexible inflation target' framework for monetary policy. The policy is very transparent, and forecasts are published in detail – in particular a conditional interest rate forecast is published. This degree of detail and transparency, if well communicated, is surely very helpful in forming and cementing expectations. This opens up discussion of the benefits that may accompany being small – maybe small highly educated democracies do have some special features which affect how their economies behave. This leads us to our discussion of why this may be the case.

In summary, the book reinforces our opening conjecture that in some respects small open economies are 'special'.

APPENDIX THREE

Table 5A.1: *GDP Levels*
(in million 1990 International Geary-Khamis dollars)

	Belgium	France	Germany	Italy	Netherlands	Norway	Sweden	Switz.	UK
1890	20,896	95,074	115,581	52,863	15,070	3,414	8,456	9,389	150,269
1895	22,611	103,021	135,279	52,027	16,015	3,672	9,611	10,861	161,500
1900	25,069	116,747	162,335	60,114	17,604	4,185	11,303	12,649	184,861
1905	27,851	118,336	182,034	69,477	19,953	4,369	12,488	13,543	194,295
1910	30,471	122,238	210,513	85,285	22,438	5,211	15,265	16,177	207,098
1913	32,347	144,489	237,332	95,487	24,955	5,988	17,273	16,483	224,618
1919	25,854	108,800	156,591	105,980	28,049	6,773	17,129	15,707	226,640
1924	35,743	168,474	200,557	107,312	35,561	7,410	20,514	19,631	221,024
1929	40,595	194,193	262,284	125,180	44,270	9,468	25,338	25,466	251,348
1934	38,202	175,843	256,220	121,826	40,078	10,456	28,217	24,642	261,680
1938	40,466	187,402	342,351	143,981	45,593	12,514	33,821	26,785	297,619
1948	42,989	180,611	190,695	142,074	53,804	16,466	44,037	41,768	337,376
1953	51,071	247,223	341,150	204,288	68,652	20,116	50,505	48,001	371,646

(continued)

Table 5A.1 (continued)

	Belgium	France	Germany	Italy	Netherlands	Norway	Sweden	Switz.	UK
1958	58,316	312,966	481,599	265,192	83,701	23,436	59,605	58,732	411,450
1963	72,988	408,090	623,382	371,822	105,686	29,265	76,200	79,370	490,625
1968	90,293	523,967	755,463	482,462	138,627	36,476	95,229	94,272	574,775
1973	118,516	683,965	944,755	582,713	175,791	44,852	114,064	117,251	675,941
1978	133,231	777,544	1,050,404	678,494	201,024	56,173	119,985	111,847	720,501
1983	142,648	852,644	1,119,394	758,360	208,014	64,551	127,742	120,659	755,779
1988	160,632	961,287	1,260,983	880,671	236,824	76,006	145,926	135,709	920,841
1993	175,552	1,048,641	1,350,421	937,303	271,352	86,129	144,709	145,387	955,305
1998	197,587	1,163,069	1,478,795	1,026,365	323,975	106,995	168,815	155,651	1,123,047
2003	219,074	1,298,819	1,572,784	1,107,193	360,759	117,891	194,945	165,515	1,289,685
2008	246,103	1,423,562	1,713,405	1,157,636	411,055	132,365	220,781	190,328	1,446,959

	Spain	Australia	N.Zealand	Canada	US	Japan	Taiwan	Singapore
1890	28,839	13,850	2,497	11,697	214,714	40,556		
1895	30,668	12,066	2,677	12,256	254,552	46,933		
1900	33,164	15,014	3,469	15,887	312,499	52,020		
1905	34,005	17,145	4,457	21,962	390,624	54,170	1,738	
1910	37,633	22,793	5,556	29,225	460,471	64,559	2,509	
1913	41,653	24,861	5,781	34,916	517,383	71,653	2,545	413
1919	43,112	24,488	6,313	34,357	599,130	100,959	3,210	
1924	51,443	31,524	6,943	37,360	713,989	107,766	4,254	
1929	63,570	33,662	7,741	52,199	843,334	128,116	5,028	
1934	62,231	33,810	7,400	40,712	649,316	142,876	5,795	
1938	45,255	40,639	10,365	52,060	799,357	176,051	7,252	
1948	59,970	53,754	12,701	93,121	1,334,331	138,290	4,668	
1953	72,806	66,481	16,084	121,228	1,699,970	216,889	9,029	2,758
1958	94,829	82,351	20,957	149,021	1,859,088	303,857	12,923	3,485
1963	130,477	103,413	25,749	185,041	2,316,765	496,514	18,534	4,848
1968	185,747	134,913	29,095	242,703	2,983,081	813,984	30,423	7,123
1973	266,896	172,314	37,177	312,176	3,536,622	1,242,932	53,284	13,108
1978	332,597	196,184	38,097	376,894	4,089,548	1,446,165	80,608	18,245
1983	361,902	218,539	42,955	409,246	4,433,129	1,706,380	111,545	27,695
1988	431,389	274,737	46,435	510,815	5,512,845	2,107,060	175,747	36,491
1993	485,899	314,360	49,627	529,921	6,146,210	2,428,242	248,023	55,404
1998	568,115	390,635	57,449	629,755	7,413,357	2,558,595	334,622	77,549
2003	686,076	461,200	69,243	746,491	8,431,121	2,686,224	391,261	93,910
2008	797,927	531,503	77,840	839,199	9,485,136	2,904,141	479,645	129,521

Sources: Data from the original A. Maddison dataset (at the *Groningen Growth & Development Centre* website)

Central Bank Independence in Small Open Economies

Table 5A.2 *Inflation (year on year rate of growth of CPI, %)*

	Belgium	France	Germany	Italy	Netherlands	Norway	Sweden	Switz.	UK
1890	3.45	0.00	2.74	3.56	1.06	NA	2.56	NA	0.00
1895	−2.44	−1.04	−1.35	−0.56	−3.37	0.00	1.35	0.00	−1.15
1900	12.66	1.06	1.32	0.46	2.38	11.84	1.19	0.00	4.55
1905	2.56	0.00	3.80	0.11	0.00	0.00	2.38	1.19	0.00
1910	2.22	1.03	2.22	2.77	2.75	1.15	0.00	2.13	1.05
1913	−4.76	0.00	0.00	0.20	1.30	3.09	0.00	−0.99	−1.01
1919	NA	20.24	37.24	1.51	8.83	6.90	15.79	8.66	10.05
1924	16.33	10.68	−100.00	3.52	0.90	9.92	−1.90	2.94	−0.53
1929	6.38	3.01	1.01	1.60	−0.93	−4.76	−0.99	0.00	−1.11
1934	−6.17	−10.08	2.60	−5.16	0.00	0.00	0.00	−1.23	0.00
1938	3.57	12.59	1.23	7.68	2.33	3.00	2.08	0.00	1.20
1948	14.39	42.43	5.46	5.88	3.54	−0.61	1.32	2.96	7.61
1953	0.00	−2.07	−1.96	1.95	0.00	2.04	1.01	−0.99	3.05
1958	0.93	8.95	1.87	4.79	1.73	5.36	3.51	1.90	3.20
1963	1.77	5.01	2.54	7.52	3.82	3.08	3.01	3.48	1.89
1968	3.33	5.31	2.17	1.27	3.69	3.53	2.25	2.17	4.65
1973	8.11	8.49	7.21	10.37	7.99	7.02	7.02	8.77	9.10
1978	3.73	9.72	2.74	12.45	4.05	7.87	9.94	1.34	8.30
1983	3.38	9.29	3.26	14.99	2.83	8.48	9.18	2.73	4.59
1988	2.15	3.08	1.01	4.95	0.71	6.73	5.94	1.95	4.91
1993	3.31	2.07	4.44	4.20	2.06	2.44	4.63	3.19	1.59
1998	0.91	0.27	0.94	1.80	1.92	2.27	−0.27	0.02	3.43
2003	1.51	2.16	1.05	2.46	2.14	2.48	1.92	0.64	2.89
2008	4.49	1.00	2.63	3.23	2.49	3.77	3.44	2.43	3.97

	Spain	Australia	N. Zealand	Canada	US	Japan	Taiwan	Singapore
1890	1.05	0.00	NA	1.22	0.00	4.70	(1900 on)	(1963 on)
1895	1.88	−3.45	−1.72	−1.65	−3.85	1.14		
1900	3.43	−5.00	1.79	8.09	0.00	3.86	12.82	
1905	−2.37	5.08	6.90	2.15	0.00	14.98	4.85	
1910	−1.43	3.08	1.85	2.47	0.00	4.04	8.20	
1913	2.55	8.45	1.79	−12.99	2.41	3.87	−3.23	
1919	6.62	7.22	7.22	13.00	14.86	13.44	24.23	
1924	5.81	0.00	0.00	0.00	0.20	0.00	6.90	
1929	1.06	0.91	0.91	0.00	0.00	−1.09	0.95	
1934	6.40	0.00	0.00	0.00	3.35	2.74	2.30	

(continued)

226 Forrest Capie, Geoffrey Wood, and Juan Castañeda

Table 5A.2 (continued)

	Spain	Australia	N. Zealand	Canada	US	Japan	Taiwan	Singapore
1938	13.73	2.04	2.04	2.22	−1.86	14.94	5.61	
1948	7.64	8.71	7.81	15.65	7.77	83.43	562.94	
1953	8.12	4.14	4.50	−1.75	0.75	6.65	12.99	
1958	11.76	1.37	4.59	2.30	2.73	−0.36	1.50	
1963	7.69	0.62	1.94	1.60	1.21	7.47	0.59	2.21
1968	4.95	2.74	4.32	4.27	4.20	5.15	6.02	0.71
1973	11.58	9.64	8.25	5.49	6.23	11.65	24.05	26.28
1978	20.09	7.92	12.11	9.14	7.66	4.14	7.65	4.72
1983	12.10	10.15	7.37	8.37	3.22	1.81	−1.19	1.04
1988	5.40	6.12	4.97	4.14	4.08	0.70	1.10	1.52
1993	4.65	1.25	0.86	2.12	2.95	1.16	4.63	2.29
1998	2.27	0.86	1.27	1.12	1.56	0.67	2.11	−0.27
2003	3.10	2.73	1.75	4.48	2.28	−0.25	−0.06	0.49
2008	4.13	4.35	3.96	2.10	3.84	1.38	1.26	6.61

Notes: Own calculations of inflation based on data on the price level from Mitchell's *International Historical Statistics* volumes: On Africa, Asia and Oceania, 2003; The Americas, 1998; and Europe 1998, unless indicated. Updated from the mid-1990s onwards from the IMF's *World Economic Outlook* (April, 2013) database (accessed online), as well as other national statistics offices. See exceptions and further details on the series and sources below.

Further notes: Belgium data updated from 1994 onwards from the IMF. Germany: CPI data from the Statistisches Bundesamt and the German Institute for Statistics (Destatis). Updated from the IMF data from 2008. France (Global Financial Data). Italy, from the Italian National Institute of Statistics (ISTAT). The Netherlands: (1880–1900) from Mitchell's, (1901 onwards) from the Dutch national bureau of statistics (CBS). For the United Kingdom we have used the Retail Price Index: (1) (1880 to 1987) from O'Donoghue's 'Consumer price inflation since 1750', in Economic Trends no. 604, March 2004 and (2) (1988–) from the Office for National Statistics. For Spain (1850 to 2000) prices data corresponds to (1) the GDP deflator as estimated by Prados' (2003) and (2) the CPI (2000 onwards) from IMF. For New Zealand: (1) (1891 to 1907) prices corresponds to Mitchell's wholesale prices, then CPI prices; (2) 1994 on from IMF. Canada (Global financial Data): (1848–1912) wholesale prices and CPI from 1914 onwards. For the United States: (1) From 1913 onwards from the US Bureau of Labor Statistics Consumer Price Index; (2) for earlier periods data from the Historical Statistics of the United States; (3) From 2010 onwards: IMF. For Japan: (1880–1922), Mitchell's wholesale prices; (1923–1946) RPI in Tokyo. From 1994 on from IMF, Global Insight and Nomura database. Taiwan: (1900–1903) from Global Financial Data; (1904–1993) from Mitchell's and from 1994 onwards the IMF. Singapore: (1961–1979) from Mitchell's and from 1980 onwards the IMF.

Central Bank Independence in Small Open Economies

Table 5A.3 *Degree of Openness (%) ((X + M)/2/Nominal GDP) × 100*

	Belgium	France	Germany	Italy	Netherlands	Norway	Sweden	Switz.	UK
1890	*(1913 on)*	15.81	17.19	16.35	103.36	22.54	22.50	*(1929 on)*	22.74
1895			15.88	17.24	116.45	22.37	20.50		20.18
1900		14.83	17.37	19.64	134.15	22.44	20.28		20.07
1905			18.03	21.23	143.71	24.80	20.13		20.96
1910		17.88	19.47	23.83	158.33	24.68	17.26		23.71
1913	92.17		21.67	23.18	155.75	26.31	20.16		24.29
1919	NA	21.20	NA	26.95	41.39	28.09	18.63		18.03
1924	68.95	16.95	NA	22.78	39.30	24.14	16.93		24.03
1929	NA	12.31	18.39	21.38	39.45	21.72	18.07	24.15	20.72
1934	38.49	7.15	7.28	11.47	20.51	16.71	14.31	14.05	12.59
1938	46.90	8.59	5.98	12.70	25.28	17.57	16.04	16.48	12.60
1948	32.54	7.02	NA	17.15	29.66	21.51	15.26	22.41	15.92
1953	27.12	9.43	16.67	18.58	44.33	24.97	17.81	21.50	17.74
1958	30.17	9.22	16.12	18.59	45.47	25.12	18.51	21.86	15.67
1963	36.06	10.33	14.38	23.04	47.39	22.64	18.75	23.83	15.40
1968	39.92	10.81	16.89	26.37	43.53	26.02	18.54	24.48	16.43
1973	48.43	14.80	17.02	29.26	46.64	28.22	22.20	25.59	18.66
1978	48.02	15.98	19.68	36.91	41.20	24.30	23.15	27.72	22.10
1983	63.92	18.17	24.58	35.40	50.40	25.91	27.41	26.03	20.62
1988	59.12	17.22	24.07	30.67	42.02	22.79	24.56	27.01	19.59
1993	55.08	16.00	18.12	30.93	40.28	23.61	22.92	23.07	19.43
1998	69.92	19.95	22.70	36.91	48.23	25.75	30.14	26.71	19.81
2003	78.48	20.50	26.90	19.66	45.58	23.75	29.15	28.24	18.24
2008	92.66	22.79	37.03	23.84	57.16	28.42	35.77	36.88	20.07

	Spain	Australia	N. Zealand	Canada	US	Japan	Taiwan	Singapore
1890	9.74	15.63	*(1931 on)*	15.53	6.35	6.20	*(1961 on)*	*(1957 on)*
1895	9.44	23.48		18.00	5.80	8.04		
1900	11.26	24.23		21.39	6.11	9.86		
1905	10.96	20.25		20.24	5.55	12.79		
1910	10.04	20.56		19.05	4.82	12.27		
1913	11.36	18.62		20.93	5.35	14.20		
1919	10.69	16.88		28.25	6.97	14.88		
1924	9.47	15.62		22.16	4.90	15.35		
1929	9.09	15.71		20.29	4.61	15.53		
1934	5.78	13.42	43.18	14.68	2.84	18.37		
1938	NA	14.49	34.48	14.55	2.89	14.43		
1948	3.35	23.26	27.91	19.19	3.52	2.15		
1953	2.15	17.98	25.33	16.52	2.99	9.45		
1958	6.32	13.62	23.02	14.21	3.25	8.80		157.97
1963	7.95	12.60	19.91	14.03	3.20	8.17	16.51	138.10
1968	9.14	11.68	19.17	17.04	3.59	8.13	19.93	102.86
1973	10.29	11.04	19.05	18.21	4.90	8.49	37.56	103.09

(continued)

228 *Forrest Capie, Geoffrey Wood, and Juan Castañeda*

Table 5A.3 (*continued*)

	Spain	Australia	N. Zealand	Canada	US	Japan	Taiwan	Singapore
1978	10.78	12.00	20.53	21.32	6.64	8.84	43.58	143.75
1983	15.05	11.80	23.11	20.32	6.20	11.39	42.85	139.40
1988	14.08	12.98	18.44	21.79	7.22	7.61	45.32	156.96
1993	14.08	14.49	23.32	24.82	7.60	6.93	35.35	135.40
1998	20.12	16.18	21.86	33.69	9.05	8.52	41.03	129.66
2003	20.55	15.22	21.44	27.97	8.58	9.91	44.35	145.92
2008	21.68	19.41	24.54	31.32	11.88	15.03	61.62	169.57

References

Alesina, A. (1989) 'Politics and business cycles in industrial democracies', *Economic Policy*, 8, April, pp. 55–98

Bade, R., and M. Parkin (1987) 'Central Bank laws and monetary policy', University of Western Ontario Department of Economics Discussion Paper

Barro, R., and R. J. Gordon (1983a) 'A positive theory of monetary policy in a natural rate model', *Journal of Political Economy*, 91(4), pp. 589–610

 (1983b) 'Rules, discretion, and reputation in a model of monetary policy', *Journal of Monetary Economics* 12 (1), July, pp. 101–121

Beenstock, M., and P. Warburton (1983) 'Long-term trends in economic openness in the United Kingdom and the United States', Oxford Economic Papers, pp. 130–35

Braude, J., Z. Eckstein, S. Fischer, and K. Flug (eds.) (2013) *The Great Recession: lessons for central bankers,* MIT Press: Cambridge, Mass.

Cagan, P. (1986) 'Conflict between short and long run objectives', in Colin Campbell, and William Dougan (eds.), *Alternative monetary regimes,* Johns Hopkins University Press: Baltimore

Capie, F. (2010) '*The Bank of England 1950s to 1979'. Studies in Macroeconomic History Series.* Cambridge University Press: Cambridge and New York

Capie, F. and G. Wood (1991) 'Central Banks and Inflation: an historical perspective – part 1, pp. 27–46, *Central Banking,* Vol.2, Autumn

Capie, F. H., T. S. Mills, and G. E. Wood (1994) 'Central bank independence and inflation performance: an exploratory data analysis', in Pierre Siklos (ed.), *Varieties of Monetary reforms: Lessons and experiences on the road to Monetary Union,* Kluwer Academic Publishers: Dordrecht

Capie, F., and G. Wood (2014) 'Can central bank independence survive a crisis?', in Owen Humpage (ed.), *Current Federal Reserve Policy Under the Lens of Economic History: Essays to Commemorate the Federal Reserve System's Centennial,* Cambridge University Press: New York

Clower, R. (1967) 'A reconsideration of the microfoundations of monetary theory', *Western Economic Journal*, 6(1), pp. 1–8

Coase, R. (1937) 'The nature of the firm', *Economica*, 4(16), pp. 386–405

Cornish, S. (2010) *The Evolution of Central Banking in Australia*, Reserve Bank of Australia: Sydney

Cukierman, A., S. Webb, and B. Neyapti (1992) 'Measuring the independence of central banks and its effect on outcomes', *World Bank Economic Review*, 6(September), pp. 439–458

Dannhauser, J. (2013) 'The euro – the story of a suboptimal currency', in Philip Booth (ed.), *The euro – the beginning, the middle and the end*, Institute of Economic Affairs: London

Epstein, R. A. (2005) *Free markets under siege: Cartels, politics, and social welfare*, Hoover Institution Press: Stanford

Fforde, J. (1992) *The Bank of England and public policy, 1941–1958*, Cambridge University Press: Cambridge

Friedman, M. (1962) 'Should there be an independent monetary authority?' in Leland B. Yeager (ed.), *In search of a Monetary Constitution*, Harvard University Press: Boston, Mass.

Grassman, S. (1980) 'Long-term trends in openness of national economies', Oxford Economic Papers 32 (1), pp. 123–33

Hawke, G. R. (1973) *Between governments and banks. A history of the Reserve Bank of New Zealand*. Government Printer: Wellington

Johnson, H. (1969) The case for floating exchange rates, Hobart Paper No. 46, Institute of Economic Affairs: London.

Mahoney, P. G. (2001), 'The common law and economic growth: Hayek might be right', *The Journal of Legal Studies*, 30(2), pp. 503–25

Masciandaro, D., and G. Tabellini (1988) 'Monetary regimes and fiscal deficits: a comparative analysis', in Hang-Sheng Cheng (ed.), *Monetary policy in the Pacific basin countries*, Kluwer Academic: Boston, Mass.

Mundell, R. (2000) 'A re-interpretation of the twentieth century', Lionel Robbins Lectures, London School of Economics, (January)

Posen, A. (1993) 'Why central bank independence does not cause low inflation: there is no institutional fix for politics', in Richard O'Brien (ed.), *Finance and the International Economy*, Oxford University Press: New York

Prados, L. (2014) 'Economic Freedom in the Long Run: Evidence from OECD Countries (1850-2007)'. Working Papers in Economic History (14-02). Instituto Figuerola. Universidad Carlos III de Madrid.

Romer, D. (1993) 'Openness and Inflation: Theory and Evidence', Quarterly Journal of Economics, 108(4) 869–903

Sacks, J. (2002) 'Markets, Governments and Virtues', in F. H. Capie and G. E. Wood, *Policy Makers on Policy*, Routledge: London

Selgin, G. (1988) *The Theory of Free Banking: Money Supply under Competitive Note Issue*, Rowman and Littlefield: Lanham, MD

Singleton, John (2011) *Central Banking in the Twentieth Century*, Cambridge University Press: Cambridge

Tedde, P. (1988) *El banco de San Carlos*. Alizanza Editorial: Madrid.

Tedde, P., and C. Marichal (eds.) (1994) 'La formación de los bancos centrales en España y America Latina (Siglos XIX y XX)', (Vol. I. España y México). *Serie de Estudios de historia Económica Num.* 29. Banco de España: Madrid

Tortella, G. (1994) 'Spanish banking history, 1782 to the present', in Manfred Pohl and Sabine Freitag (eds.), *Handbook on the History of European Banks*, European Association for Banking History, Edward Elgar: London, pp. 865–91

White, L. (1995) *Free Banking in Britain; Theory, Experience, and Debate, 1800–1845*, Institute of Economic Affairs: London

Wood, G. (1994) 'A pioneer bank in a pioneers' country', *Central Banking*, V(1), Summer, pp. 59–76

(2000) 'The Lender of Last Resort reconsidered', *Journal of Financial Services Research*, 18(2/3), December, pp. 203–28

Statistical Sources

Arnone, M., B. Lorens, and J. F. Segalotto (2006) 'Measures on central bank autonomy. Empirical evidence for the OECD, developing and emerging market economies', IMF working Paper 228

Bell, S. (2004) *Australia's Money Mandarins. The Reserve Bank and the Politics of Money*. Cambridge University Press: Port Melbourne

Capie, Forrest, and G. Wood (1991) 'Central banks and inflation: an historical perspective. Part I'. *Central Banking*, 1(2), pp. 27–46

Cukierman, A., S. Webb and B. Neyapti (1992) 'Measuring the independence of central banks and its effects on policy outcomes'. *The World Bank Economic Review*, 6 (3), pp. 353–98

Linklater, J. (1992) *Inside the Bank: The role of the Federal Reserve Bank of Australia in the economic, banking and financial system*, Allen and Unwin: St. Leonards, NSW, Australia

Hawke, G. R. (1973) *Between governments and banks. A history of the Reserve Bank of New Zealand*, Government Printer, Wellington

Mitchell, B. R.: 'International historical statistics'. Several volumes (Europe; Africa, Asia & Oceania; The Americas)

Pohl, M. and S. Freitag (eds.) (1994) *Handbook on the history of European banks*, Edward Elgar and European Association for Banking History: Cheltenham and Vienna

Prados, L. (2003) *El progreso económico de España (1850–2000)*, Fundación BBVA: Bilbao.

Shea, J. D. (1994) 'Taiwan. Development and structural change of the financial system', in H. Patrick and Y.C. Park (eds.), *The Financial Development of Japan, Korea and Japan*, Oxford University Press: New York

Sheng-Yi, L. (1990) *The Monetary and Banking Development of Singapore and Malaysia*. Singapore University Press: Singapore

Swiss National Bank (ed.) (2007) *The Swiss National Bank: 1907–2007*, Swiss National Bank: Zurich

6

Fighting the Last War

Economists on the Lender of Last Resort

Richard S. Grossman
Wesleyan University, Middletown, Connecticut and CEPR

Hugh Rockoff
Rutgers University, New Brunswick, New Jersey and NBER

1 Introduction

In this paper we trace the evolution of lender of last resort (LOLR) doctrine – and its implementation – from the nineteenth century through the panic of 2008. There are, of course, many excellent histories of lenders of last resort, including, Bordo (1990), Humphrey (1989, 1992), Goodhart (1999), Capie and Wood (2006), Kindleberger and Aliber (2011), and Bignon, Flandreau, and Ugolini (2012). Inevitably, we will cover many of the same experiences and ideas as these authors, but we hope to draw attention to some patterns in the way ideas about the LOLR have emerged from historical experience that have not received as much attention as we believe they should.

In the next section we define a LOLR and identify some of the important controversies surrounding the topic. In Section 3 we recount the evolution of the Bank of England as LOLR and in Section 4 the evolution of LOLRs in other countries. Section 5 discusses the evolution of the theory of LOLR, focusing especially on Bagehot's *Lombard Street*. Section 6 discusses the Great Depression and Section 7 the contributions of R.G. Hawtrey, Milton Friedman and Anna J. Schwartz, and Ben Bernanke to the theory of the LOLR. In Sections 3–7, our focus is on the provision of money to calm a financial panic that is already underway. In Section 8 we address "rescue operations": bailouts of individual firms with the idea of preventing a financial panic from starting. Section 9 discusses the subprime crisis and Section 10 concludes.

We are indebted to the participants in our session, and especially to our designated discussant Charles Goodhart, for many helpful comments and criticisms.

2 The Lender of Last Resort: Definitions and Controversies

What is a lender of last resort? Economists have offered many definitions. Thomas Humphrey (1992, 571) put it this way: "The term 'lender of last resort' refers to the central bank's responsibility to accommodate demands for high-powered money in times of crisis, thus preventing panic induced contractions of the money stock." In *Manias, Panics, and Crashes*, Charles P. Kindleberger and Robert Z. Aliber (2011) tell us, however, that "[t]he idea is that the lender of last resort can and should forestall a run by depositors and other investors from real assets and illiquid financial assets into money by supplying the amount of money that is needed to satisfy the demand."

At the heart of both definitions is the notion of a "run" or "panic" and the damage it can do. The classic banking panic was characterized by a sudden widespread fear that "hard cash" (i.e., specie when there was a metallic monetary standard, fiat currency when there was not) would not be available when needed, leading holders of bank notes or deposits to try to withdraw their funds as quickly as possible. The potential for a damaging run is inherent in fractional reserve banking: since banks only hold cash accounting for a portion of deposits, if all depositors demand their cash at once only a fraction can be paid. Diamond and Dybvig (1983) is the first in a long line of papers analyzing the inherent instability of the banking system within a formal model.

The two definitions of the LOLR differ, however, in terms of the range of events that would warrant intervention. Humphrey, evidently, would limit the LOLR's actions to a relatively narrow swath of the financial sector, perhaps to just the banking sector, and would focus on the goal of maintaining the stock of money. Kindleberger and Aliber's definition goes beyond the familiar case of commercial bank depositors attempting to convert deposits into cash. Their "real and illiquid financial assets" would include real estate, stocks and bonds, reserves of raw material, and so on. For Kindleberger and Aliber, a collapse of farm prices or a crash on the stock market might require action by a LOLR. The range of markets and institutions that should be protected remains one of the fundamental controversies in the theory of the LOLR.

The "contagion of fear" (Friedman and Schwartz 1963, 308) that ignites a run might be based on bad economic news, such as the decline of a key agricultural price or the failure of an important company that endangered the soundness of the banking system. Alternatively, it might be based on a false rumor that, for example, an unsuccessful speculation had put an important segment of the financial sector at risk. In the classic analogy someone yells "fire" in a crowded theater and everyone rushes to the exit hoping that they won't be consumed by the fire. The panic may have a factual basis (someone may have detected the start of a potentially damaging electrical fire) but it might be based on an unfounded rumor (the person who yelled fire was mistaken).

There is no doubt that financial crises, especially banking panics, have been associated with severe economic contractions. Why panics cause so much distress, however, is still a matter of controversy. In some cases the inability to complete transactions – to pay workers or suppliers of raw materials for example – clearly depressed economic activity in the short-run (James, McAndrews, and Weiman 2013). Monetarists point to contractions in the money stock produced by decreases in the money multiplier as the main causal channel (Friedman and Schwartz 1963, Cagan 1965). Note that Humphrey's definition expressly stresses the role of the LOLR in preventing contractions in the stock of money. In response, Keynesians have pointed to waves of pessimism that depress investment spending (Temin 1976). And Bernanke (1983) argued that banking panics could depress economic activity by raising the cost of financial intermediation.

Typically, we think of the central bank as the institution making more money available during a panic; however, Kindleberger and Aliber's definition, rightly in our view, leaves open the institutional identification of the LOLR because other institutions have often played this role, including governments, individual or groups of private banks, and wealthy individuals. In the recent American crisis both the Treasury and the Federal Reserve played important roles in meeting the crisis, and private banks such as Bank of America and JPMorgan Chase were brought into the policy response. Kindleberger and Aliber (2011, 311) would go even further, suggesting that a legislative action, for example the repeal of the Sherman Silver Purchase Act in 1893, should be counted as LOLR operations.

The money that the LOLR can make available in a crisis depends on the underlying monetary regime. At one extreme is a major country with a central bank that creates fiat money. In the event of a bank run the central bank can print whatever amount is needed no matter how large the demand. The central bank may worry that money creation will lead to inflation or an asset price bubble, but not that it will run out of money. At the other extreme is a country on the gold standard where the central bank's reserves are limited to its holdings of gold. In those circumstances, the central bank must husband its reserves. A rumor that the central bank itself is running short of reserves may intensify a crisis.

Once a run on the banking system is underway, the experts agree that the LOLR needs to step in and bring it to a halt. The only disagreement is over the terms on which additional funds should be made available. Some traditional theorists, Walter Bagehot in particular, suggest that the LOLR should set stiff terms: interest rates should be high and no compromise should be made on the quality of the collateral required. Kindleberger and Aliber (2011, 224–225), on the other hand, suggest that it is wrong for the LOLR to be so exacting, and that the important thing is for the LOLR to stop the crisis before it spreads.

Perhaps the most significant disagreement is over whether the LOLR can and should intervene to prevent panics from developing in the first place. Historically, panics have often been precipitated by the failure of an important financial institution. If the LOLR could have stepped in and "rescued" the failing institution before it had a chance to fail, it might have prevented the ensuing panic. The question then becomes how widely the LOLR should roam in its search for firms in need of rescue. Should it provide assistance only to solvent banks, as Bagehot implied, or should it rescue the insolvent as well? Should it stick to banks, financial institutions in general, or should it rescue any business or government agency that it believes is so "systematically important," to use the currently fashionable term, that its failure might trigger a financial panic?

3 The Evolution of the Bank of England as LOLR

Although the Bank of England was the first institution in the world to act as LOLR on a consistent basis, its evolution into that role was neither direct nor quick. The Bank was granted a charter as England's first limited liability joint stock bank in 1694 in return for a substantial loan to the crown. The charter was renewed nine times between 1697 and 1844, typically in return for a fresh loan or an improvement in the terms of its outstanding loans (Broz and Grossman 2004). With the passage of the second rechartering act (establishing its third charter) in 1708, the Bank was granted an exception to the law prohibiting firms of more than six persons from operating a bank, effectively giving it a monopoly on joint stock banking in England and Wales, a privilege that persisted into the nineteenth century.

Despite its quasi-public character as the government's banker and privileged position as England's only joint stock bank, the Bank of England was universally regarded as a private institution with limited responsibility beyond its shareholders. Nonetheless, Ashton (1959, 112) asserts that the Bank expanded its discounts during eighteenth-century stringencies, and Lovell's (1957) statistical analysis of the period 1758–1798 demonstrates that the Bank *did* expand its discounts in response to both the level and change in the level of commercial bankruptcies.

One factor that may have complicated the Bank's willingness and ability to function as LOLR was its responsibility to maintain the rate of exchange between the pound and gold, that is, adherence to the gold standard. This requirement gave the Bank an incentive to conserve its gold holdings at the precise moment when, as LOLR, it should have been lending freely. This conflict seemed to impair the Bank's actions as a LOLR during the crisis of 1793, when, according to Baring (2007 [1797], 7–8), "...the Directors caught the panic; their nerves could not support the daily and constant demand for guineas (i.e., gold); and for the purpose of checking that demand, they curtailed their discounts." Thus, the Bank reduced its lending and discounting in order to preserve its gold holdings (Clapham, 1945, I, 261). The failure of the Bank to act as LOLR led the government to take on that role by issuing Exchequer bills to merchants on the security of commodities of all kinds (Thomas 1934, 26).

The conflict between the Bank's evolving role as LOLR and its commitment to maintain gold convertibility arose again during the crisis of 1797. Contrary to the Bank's 1694 charter, which forbade it from lending to the government without the consent of Parliament, Chancellor of the Exchequer William Pitt tapped the Bank for funds by discounting Treasury Bills. The continual borrowing led the Bank's gold reserve to fall from over £6 million in 1795 to about £1 million in 1797. With the outbreak of crisis in February 1797, the government issued an order prohibiting the Bank – against its wishes – from redeeming its notes in gold. The suspension of the gold standard would last until 1821.

Although, the Bank of England's reaction to the crisis of 1793 was tentative, Bagehot (1924 [1873], 52) describes the response to the crisis of 1825 as more sure-footed:

The way in which the panic of 1825 was stopped by advancing money has been described in so broad and graphic a way that the passage has become classical. "We lent it," said Mr. Harman [a former governor], on behalf of the Bank of England, "by every possible means and in modes we had never adopted before; we took in stock on security, we purchased Exchequer bills, we made advances on Exchequer bills, we not only discounted outright, but we made advances on the deposit of bills of exchange to an immense amount, in short, by every possible means consistent with the safety of the Bank, and we were not on some occasions over-nice. Seeing the dreadful state in which the public were, we rendered every assistance in our power." After a day or two of this treatment, the entire panic subsided, and the 'City' was quite calm.

Despite the Bank's activism in 1825, its behavior in 1836 was again timid. As financial pressure increased in 1835, the Bank decided not to make advances on bills that had been endorsed by note-issuing joint-stock banks. This was no doubt partly a consequence of the Bank's displeasure that the 1833 rechartering act had eliminated its monopoly on joint stock banking in London. During the summer of 1836, the Bank further decided to reduce substantially the amount of its holdings of bills accepted by the major merchants in Anglo-American trade (Collins 1972, 52). Upon a deputation from the Bank of Liverpool, the Bank of England relaxed its policy, and again agreed to permit the discounting of American bills drawn against the actual transfers of goods.

The Bank of England became much less hesitant to act as LOLR in subsequent crises, particularly those following the enactment of the Bank Charter Act of 1844, called Peel's Act after Prime Minister Sir Robert Peel. In theory, this legislation should have made it more difficult for the Bank to act as LOLR. Among its other provisions, the law split the Bank into two departments: the Issue Department, which was to assume responsibility for the note issue (and, hence, maintaining convertibility into gold); and the Banking Department, which was to carry on the rest of the Bank's business. The Act permitted the Bank to issue £14 million in notes backed by securities, the so-called "fiduciary issue." Any additional notes beyond the fiduciary issue were to be backed one-for-one by gold, thus hampering the Bank's ability to expand the note issue – in the absence of a corresponding increase in the gold reserve – in times of crisis. And, in fact, opponents of the Act, including Thomas Tooke and John Fullarton, raised this objection during the debate over the legislation. Fullarton argued that an increase of notes should be permitted in time of emergency, warning that the arrangement ". . .must have the very effect of disabling [the Bank of England] for the performance of what has hitherto been considered the duty of the Bank in time of difficulty and pressure" (Fetter 1965, 187–191).

Economists on the Lender of Last Resort

Peel understood the constraints of the new law and privately acknowledged that it might be necessary to suspend the Act in time of emergency. A new pattern emerged following the law's passage in 1844: during the crises of 1847, 1857, and 1866, the Government encouraged the Bank to violate Peel's Act by exceeding its fiduciary limit and, in return, sent the Bank a letter promising that it would introduce a bill in Parliament indemnifying the Bank for any violations of the law: such a law was enacted in 1857, but was not needed during the crises 1847 or 1866.

The rigidity in the law regarding the quantity of notes issued can be seen as a protection against an overexpansion of the note issue. Peel, however, believed that would be possible for the Bank to act as LOLR despite the law. Following the crisis of 1847 Peel, now in opposition, congratulated the Government on their handling of the crisis:

My confidence is unshaken that we are taking all the precautions which legislation can prudently take against the recurrence of a monetary crisis. It *may* recur in spite of our precautions, and if it does, *and if it be necessary* to assume a grave responsibility for the purpose of meeting it, I daresay men will be found willing to assume such responsibility (Andréadès 1966 [1909], 329n).

Thus, in Peel's view, the LOLR should be constrained in its note issue in normal times, but should have the flexibility to expand its note issue during an emergency.

The second half of the nineteenth century saw three crises in Britain that highlight the distinction between a LOLR operation and a bailout and the difficulties faced by policy makers in navigating them. Financial upheavals of 1866, 1878, and 1890 were each centered on a key and – to use modern terminology – systematically important financial institution: Overend, Gurney, and Company; the City of Glasgow Bank; and Baring Brothers, and Company.

Overend, Gurney had its origins in a firm of Norwich wool merchants, which eventually became established country bankers. The company later merged with a firm of London bill brokers and grew to such status, according to the *Times* of London (May 11, 1866), that it could, ". . . rightly claim to be the greatest instrument of credit in the Kingdom." The relationship between Overend, Gurney, and the Bank of England had long been hostile and, when Overend collapsed in 1866 leading to widespread panic, it appealed to the Bank of England for assistance. The Bank denied the request on the grounds that the firm did not have adequate security; however, the Bank did increase its discounting activities, in line with its role as LOLR. It is unclear whether the City of Glasgow Bank – which failed largely due to fraud – approached the Bank of England, but it did request assistance from the association of Scottish bankers, which denied the request on the grounds that bank's affairs were well beyond repair.

The Baring crisis erupted in 1890 when Baring Brothers, an old established firm of merchant bankers, failed. Baring had long been London's leading lender to Latin America, particularly Argentina and Uruguay. When Argentina's land boom collapsed leading to a run on its banking system, the market for Baring's substantial portfolio of Latin American debt securities dried up. The threat of an international run on Baring would also have called Britain's commitment to the gold standard into question, and so when Baring's directors approached the Bank of England with a request for assistance, the Bank reacted with alacrity. The Bank immediately ordered an audit in order to determine whether, given enough time, Baring's currently illiquid assets would be sufficient to eventually pay off its liabilities. Convinced that it was – and accompanied by an assurance from the government that it would also absorb some of the cost of the liquidation of Baring, should it not prove true – Bank of England governor William Lidderdale set about assembling subscribers to a guarantee fund which would be called on if the Bank-supervised liquidation of Baring's assets was not sufficient to meet its liabilities. Lidderdale placed the Bank of England's name at the top of the list for £1 million and set about coaxing, cajoling, and, in some cases, even threatening potential subscribers. All of this was done before news of Baring's difficulties became public. By the time the story became known, the guarantee fund was already fully subscribed and no panic materialized. The Baring rescue surely spared Britain a banking crisis and, potentially, a run on the pound.

The Baring Crisis was by no means the first time that the Bank of England had provided funds for individual firms. In 1801 the Bank had lent to Hibberts, Fuhr, & Purrier on guarantees from thirteen firms including Baring Brothers & Co. In 1836–1837 the Bank loaned to several firms that had run into difficulties while financing trade with the United States. Aid was provided to Sir James Esdaile, Esdaile, Grenfell, Thomas & Co. on the guarantee of several private bankers. Aid was also provided to the three W's – Wiggin, Wildes, and Wilson – for a time, although they were eventually allowed to fail. And aid was provided to W. & J. Brown & Co., which received a total of almost £2,000,000, about £5.6 billion in today's money using GDP as the inflator (www.measuringworth.com). Still it was the relief of Baring in 1890 that brought the Bank's practice of lending to individual firms to arrest an incipient panic clearly into focus.[1]

4 Lenders of Last Resort Elsewhere in the Nineteenth and Early Twentieth Century

Other central banks acted as LOLR during the nineteenth century, although none had as much time to grow into this role as the Bank of England. In 1890 the Bank of Japan – just eight years after its establishment – provided liquidity during a stock market crisis, preventing the collapse of a large number of banks (Tamaki 1995, 66–67). Under the leadership of Governor Jacques Lafitte, the Banque de France – which had only been established in 1800 – loaned freely during the crisis of 1818 acting as "an intuitive lender of last resort." This mantle was, however, only temporary, since, "[t]hereafter, the Bank of France forgot the lesson..." When a downturn in the textile industry led to a financial crisis ten years later, the Bank responded by restricting its lending. The crisis was only stemmed after syndicate of twenty-six Paris banks stepped in to provide funds (Kindleberger and Aliber 2011, 204–205). The Banque was consistent in this attitude for many years, refusing to intervene during the failures of the Crédit Mobilier in 1868 or the Union Générale in 1882. It did, however, provide a loan for the Paris Bourse in 1882 (White, 2007). And it did intervene when the Comptoir d'Escompte was on the point of failure in 1889 by authorizing a large loan on behalf of the Banque and persuading several large banks to guarantee the loan (Hautcoeur, Riva, and White 2013). Kindleberger and Aliber (2011, 218) argue that the Comptoir d'Escompte was bailed out not because of any change of heart by the Banque, but because it was thought that a second large bank failure within the span of seven years might have destroyed the credibility of the French financial system. According to Plessis (1995, 11), during the late nineteenth and early twentieth century the Banque de France considered itself to be in competition with the large deposit banks, although it was

...willing 'to help Trade and Treasury' by making capital available to them – in so far as it could. On an *ad hoc* basis, it helped banks with temporary difficulties (such as Société Générale in early 1914), but had no intention of fully taking on the role of lender of last resort.

---

[1] This paragraph is based on Hidy (1946).

LOLR facilities emerged rapidly in response to worldwide financial crisis of 1857, sometimes by central banks acting alone, other times in concert with governments. Although many major commercial centers were hard hit during this crisis, the disruption was especially severe in Hamburg. As an important center for trade between Scandinavia, northern Germany, Britain, and the Americas, the expansion in the issue of Hamburg bills of exchange in the years leading up to the crisis left it particularly vulnerable when the crisis struck (Wirth 1874, 373). Hamburg's government, after debating whether to increase its note issue, with the potential consequence of a depreciation of its silver-backed currency, created a new bank to discount mercantile trade bills. This new bank was funded with securities deposited by the Treasury, as well as government-borrowed silver.

By contrast, the Bank of Prussia refused to lend the required silver during the crisis. Assistance came from Austria, which was on an inconvertible paper standard and was thus happy to lend 10 million marks *banco* (the securities deposited by the Treasury accounted for 5 million marks *banco*) at interest. The arrival of the train carrying the silver (*Silberzug*) from Austria is said to have calmed the crisis almost immediately (Ahrens 1986; Flandreau 1997, 750; Kindleberger and Aliber 2011, 237).

Elsewhere in northern Europe, governments and central banks responded vigorously to the crisis of 1857. The Denmarks Nationalbank unilaterally extended the maturity on all Hamburg bills it held by three months and the quantitative limit on its note-issue was abolished. Sweden and Norway contracted large state loans to tide the markets over the crisis (Jensen 1896, 380; *Times* of London, December 7, 1857). And the Nederlandsche Bank undertook the role of LOLR during the 1857 crisis by "lending freely at a penalty rate," as Bagehot's advice would later be formulated: the Bank raised its discount rate sharply (from between 3 and 4 percent to 7 percent), and discounted freely against good collateral. As it noted in its annual report on the year:

We decided to enlist all our forces in an effort to allay the crisis; (...) while we did increase the interest rate, we equally let it be known far and wide that we did not lack in strength and that anyone who could pledge good collateral might count on the support of our institution (Vanthoor 2005, 48–49).

In subsequent crises, the focus shifted from governments to central banks. In Finland, the government acted as LOLR during the late 1870s and early 1880s, when the state took the unusual action of approving loans to the banks in order to alleviate their liquidity problems – a role it reprised during a crisis at the turn of the century. It was the Bank of Finland, however, that rescued Kansallis-Osake-Pankki in the early 1890s and provided selective support to banks during the 1931 crisis (Herrala 1999; 7–12; Capie, Goodhart, Fischer, and Schnadt 1994, 137). Norges Bank (1899) and Sweden's Riksbank (1897) also adopted the role of LOLR later in the nineteenth century (Capie, Goodhart, Fischer, Schnadt 1994, 124, 147). Taking on this role may have been facilitated by the fact that both of these banks were developing a clearing system among domestic banks around this time, allowing them to directly affect the level of reserves.

The Banca d'Italia, established in 1893, developed into a LOLR shortly after the turn of the twentieth century, adopting Bagehot's principle of lending freely during the crisis that struck in 1906 – going so far as to refer to Bagehot by name in its 1907 Report and Accounts. After having taken a similar action in 1910, the Bank's annual report stated: "At that particular time, what was important to the Italian business community was not so much to obtain funds at reasonable conditions, but to know that credit was still available for good risk transactions. And the Bank did not fail to provide this type of credit" (Wood 2000, 208–209).

A set of private institutions took on the role of LOLR in the United States during the nineteenth century: the bank clearing house. Clearing houses of one sort or another have existed at many times and in many places; they are institutions that provide a central location where representatives of individuals or firms can meet to settle claims against one another, thus reducing the time, effort, and cash necessary to do so. For example, if A owes B 10 and B owes C 10, the debts can be cleared with one payment from A to C, rather than two payments (A to B and B to C). If A owes B 10, B owes C 10, and C owes A 10, the account can be settled with no payment whatsoever, rather than three individual payments of 10.

American bank clearing houses settled a variety of claims during the nineteenth century, including banknotes, checks, drafts, and bills of exchange. They also set rules for the behavior of member banks, including limiting deposit rates and setting prices of claims to be traded. Unlike the central banks discussed earlier, American bank clearing houses were entirely private, owned by the banks themselves. The New York clearing house was officially formed in 1853, although Albert Gallatin – who had been Secretary of the Treasury under presidents Jefferson and Madison– had suggested the formation of clearing houses as early as 1831. Clearing houses were subsequently formed in Boston (1856) and Philadelphia (1858). Clearing houses were not only established in large banking centers, but also in smaller banking markets including Topeka, Kansas, and St. Joseph, Missouri (Cannon 1900; 1910).

Clearing houses took on special importance during crises (Gorton 1985, 280–281; Cannon 1900, 1910; Timberlake 1984). At the outbreak of a panic the clearing house would authorize the issuance of clearing house loan certificates, a sort of reserve currency. A bank facing a shortfall of cash could apply to the clearing house loan committee for certificates, against which the bank would submit a portion of its securities portfolio as collateral. Certificates were issued with maturities of from one to three months, carried an interest charge, and were issued in large denominations. These could then be used in place of cash in the clearing, allowing banks to keep more cash on hand to satisfy depositors' demands.

American clearing houses worked, in some ways, like the Bank of England during crises, creating liquidity in the form of loan certificates during emergencies. The loan certificates were the joint obligations of the members of the clearing house, so that if the security posted as collateral was not sufficient to redeem the loan, the liability fell upon the surviving members of the clearing house. Like the Bank of England, the clearing houses issued additional liquidity on the security of collateral, and discounted the collateral as warranted.

The operations of the clearing houses differed from the Bank of England in a number of important respects. Because the clearing houses were private institutions, operating without any government supervision, regulation, or public responsibilities, they did not require legislative approval to increase the supply of money or reserves beyond some government-imposed limit. The Bank of England, although a private, profit-making institution, had a legal obligation to maintain a certain level of gold reserves.[2] Despite their purely private nature, clearing house members were nonetheless willing to offer – at least temporarily–credit to insolvent banks. They may have done this because, as financial market participants themselves, they were attuned to the destructive potential of systemic risk.

---

[2] The exact nature of the Bank of England's status vis-à-vis the institutions of government varied across time. Speaking of the Bank in 1781, the Prime Minister Lord North said that it was "…from long habit and usage of many years…a part of the constitution" (Clapham 1945, I, 174). On the other hand, according to Sayers (1976, 14) Sir Otto Niemeyer commented more than a century later that "it was a Treasury tradition that when the Permanent Secretary [of the Treasury] visited the Bank of England, about once in 12 months, he took a taxi because he was not quite sure where the Bank was." To which Sayers adds: "picturesque hyperbole, but indicative."

Second, at least in earlier crises, the clearing houses created liquidity only in the form of large-denomination clearing house loan certificates, which were used solely for inter-bank clearing, unlike Bank of England notes which served both as reserves and also as a circulating medium. In the later crises of 1893 and 1907, however, American clearing houses went even further, issuing small denomination loan certificates, which circulated among the public. These issues amounted to approximately $100 million, or 2.5 percent of the total outstanding money stock, in 1893 and $500 million, or about 4.5 percent of the money stock, in 1907 (Gorton 1985, 282). The issuance of a "private" currency without official sanction soon attracted the attention of the government. Following the crisis of 1907, the Aldrich-Vreeland Act (1908) confined the power to authorize the issue of emergency currency to the Secretary of the Treasury.

Finally, clearing houses differed markedly from Bagehot's ideal of a LOLR in their willingness and ability to micro-manage banking affairs during crises. Clearing houses often directed loans from healthy banks to ailing banks during periods of financial turbulence. Banks that were in poor condition were usually not allowed to fail during crises, but were expelled for failing to repay loans after the panic had ended, generally leading to their failure (Gorton 1985). Thus, although the clearing house fulfilled the classical role of the LOLR, it also appears to have instituted elements of a bailout, by directing credit to ailing institutions, and added the powers of a regulator, with the authority to discipline poorly behaving banks.

5 The Lender of Last Resort: The Idea Takes Shape

The theory of the LOLR developed in response to the financial crises outlined in the previous sections, but the theory, it must be said, did not progress rapidly. The ideas of theorists writing decades ago, in a few cases writing more than a century ago, still appear relevant and are still debated by today's experts. In the following sections we describe the evolution of thinking about the LOLR. We focus first on ideas about what should be done once a panic has begun; what should be done once the forest fire is well underway and flames are leaping from tree to tree; after that we look at "rescue operations" intended to prevent individual failures from igniting panics, that is, how to spot the burning tree struck by lightning that if left unattended might set the whole forest ablaze.

5.1 From Adam Smith to Henry Thornton

As usual Adam Smith is a good place to start a review of economic doctrines. In the *Wealth of Nations* Smith points out that even in his day the Bank of England played a unique role in supplying credit to merchants, especially during times of stress in financial markets. The Bank, according to Smith,

> ...upon several different occasions, supported the credit of the principal houses, not only of England, but of Hamburgh and Holland. Upon one occasion, in 1763, it is said to have advanced for this purpose, in one week, about 1,600,000£; a great part in bullion. I do not, however, pretend to warrant either the greatness of the amount or the shortness of the time. (Smith 1981[1776], II.ii.85, 320).[3]

The failure of the Ayr Bank in Scotland was a pivotal moment in the Crisis of 1772. Smith may well have been aware of many of the details. According to Checkland (1975, 130-131), in a last desperate effort to avoid bankruptcy the Ayr Bank sent a delegation, which included the Duke of Buccleuch – a shareholder who was being advised by Smith (Smith had been his tutor) – to negotiate a loan from the Bank of England. The Bank of England offered £300,000, but the terms were so stiff that the Ayr Bank refused the loan. Shortly after, the Ayr Bank closed its doors, accelerating the panic: a Lehman Brothers moment.

These manoeuvers clearly read like LOLR operations. Smith's opinion, although admittedly discerned by reading between the lines, appears to be that the role of LOLR "goes with the territory." The Bank of England was given special privileges which led to its becoming England's dominant financial institution, in exchange for which it was expected to support the government and the merchant community in their times of need. It must be admitted, however, that Smith did not address the key issue, or at least what for us would be the key issue: whether this arrangement was a good thing (Rockoff 2013, 320-321).

The term "lender of last resort" was first used, it is commonly held, by Sir Francis Baring (1797) in "Observations on the establishment of the Bank of England." The French Revolution had provoked financial crises in 1793 and 1797. The 1793 crisis affected the British country banks, but the

---

[3] Estimates of this sum in today's dollars would range from £190 million pounds using a retail price index as the inflator to £17.3 billion using the share of GDP (www.measuringworth.com).

1797 crisis, triggered by a (quickly repulsed) French invasion of Wales, was a larger crisis that produced a suspension of gold payments by the Bank of England as well as many interior banks, although apparently not by the Scottish banks. Baring used the French legal term for a court of last appeal, *denier resort*, and seems to have used it much like Smith, as a description of the economic facts of life: once a loan request had been turned down by everyone else, the last resort was the Bank of England. Baring offered three recommendations for meeting the current difficulties: a prohibition on the issue of demand notes and deposits by the country banks (notes or deposits paid at a later date were permissable), making the notes of the Bank of England legal tender, and limiting the total note issue of the Bank of England.

Henry Thornton (1802) provided what appears to be one of the first clear statements of the case for a LOLR.[4] The crisis of 1793 was relieved in part, Thornton (1807, 40) tells us, by the issue of exchequer bills – government bills that merchants could obtain by pledging private securities.

That fear of not being able to obtain guineas, which arose in the country, led, in its consequences, to an extraordinary demand for bank notes in London; and the want of bank notes in London became, after a time, the chief evil. The very expectation of a supply of exchequer bills, that is, of a supply of an article which almost any trader might obtain, and which it was known that he might then sell, and thus turn into bank notes, and after turning into bank notes might also convert into guineas, created an idea of general solvency.

This was certainly a LOLR operation, but one carried out by the Treasury, not the Bank of England. In 1797 the Bank, according to Thornton (1807 [1802], 59–78), reduced its note issue in response the crisis to protect its reserve, but in so doing increased the severity of the crisis. The right thing to do was to increase its note issue during a panic.[5] Thornton also saw danger from overexpansion of the Bank of England's note issue during the Napoleonic suspension. At the end of his masterpiece Thornton (1807 [1802], 248–249) offered a prescription for the Bank of England to follow – both in normal times and in panics – that even now would be considered sound advice for a central bank.

---

[4] See Hetzel (1987) for a detailed study of Thornton.

[5] Thornton (1807 [1802], 78) took the Bank to task for acting "according to what seems likely to have been the advice of Dr. A. Smith in the case." However, as we indicated earlier, Smith did not provide a clear statement of what he thought the Bank of England should do in financial crises. Thornton's criticism, rather, is based on deductions from some of Smith's conclusions in other contexts.

To limit the total amount of paper issued, and to resort for this purpose, whenever the temptation to borrow is strong, to some effectual principle of restriction; in no case, however, materially to diminish the sum in circulation, but to let it vibrate only within certain limits; to afford a slow and cautious extension of it, as the general trade of the kingdom enlarges itself, to allow of some special, though temporary, increase in the event of any extraordinary alarm or difficulty, as the best means of preventing a great demand at home for guineas, and to lean to the side of diminution, in the case of gold going abroad, and of the general exchanges continuing long unfavourable, this seems to be the true policy of the directors of an institution circumstanced like that of the Bank of England.

5.2 Bagehot's *Lombard Street*

Britain suffered financial crises in 1810, 1815, 1819, 1825, 1837, 1839, 1847, 1857, and 1866. But it was the crises of 1825, 1847, 1857, and 1866 that provided the raw material for what is still the most influential text on the LOLR: Bagehot's *Lombard Street* (1924 [1873]). Bagehot thought that the crises of 1793 and 1797 lay too far in the past to provide much instruction, that the crises of 1815 and 1819 occurred during the restriction of gold payments and therefore raised a different set of issues, and that the crises of 1837 and 1839, although severe, did not "terminate in a panic."

Bagehot's policy prescription, what is often referred to as "Bagehot's rule," was "that in time of panic it [the Bank of England] must advance [lend] freely and vigorously to the public out of the reserve." This plan, however, was subject to two important qualifications: "First, that these loans should only be made at a very high rate of interest" and "Secondly, that at this rate these advances should be made on all good banking securities, and as largely as the public ask for them" (Bagehot 1924 [1873], 187–188).

In a recent series of lectures Ben Bernanke put it this way:

He [Bagehot] had a dictum that during a panic central banks should lend freely to whoever comes to their door; as long as they have collateral, give them money. Central banks need to have collateral to make sure that get their money back, and that collateral has to be good or it has to be discounted. Also, central banks need to charge a penalty interest rate so that people do not take advantage of the situation; they signal that they really need the money by being willing to pay a slightly higher interest rate. If a central bank follows Bagehot's rule, it can stop financial panics. (Bernanke 2013, 7).

To fully understand Bagehot's rule, it is necessary to understand the institutions that Bagehot took for granted. Bagehot was prescribing for a particular patient, and did not warrant that his medicine, and the dosage he recommended, would provide a satisfactory outcome in all patients. The most important of these institutions was the gold standard. Adherence to the gold standard had become an article of faith accepted by the business community and most other segments of the community, and maintaining the gold standard was perhaps the highest priority for monetary policy. Bagehot fully supported Britain's commitment to gold and opposed bimetallism when it became an issue in the 1870s. "England," Bagehot wrote, "has a currency now resting solely on the gold standard, which exactly suits her wants, which is known throughout the civilized world as hers, and which is most closely united to all her mercantile and banking habits" (Bagehot 1877, 5, 613). A fiat money regime was also well known to Bagehot: after all, that regime had prevailed in Britain from 1797 to 1819 when specie payments were suspended as a result of the Napoleonic Wars. Bagehot specifically rejected basing his prescription for the LOLR on the financial crises that had occurred during those years because "the problems to be solved were altogether different from our present ones" (Bagehot 1924 [1873], 190).

The Bank of England was the holder of the main reserve of gold. The joint stock banks and other participants in the money market looked to the Bank of England to provide them with gold when necessary and so held minimal reserves. Bagehot believed, moreover, that the Bank of England itself often held an inadequate reserve, and it was part of his purpose to persuade the Bank to make every effort to maintain a reserve commensurate with its responsibilities.

It was possible, Bagehot understood, to imagine alternative institutional arrangements. In an oft-quoted passage Bagehot appears to have endorsed the theoretical superiority of free entry in banking.

But it will be said – What would be better? What other system could there be? We are so accustomed to a system of banking, dependent for its cardinal function on a single bank, that we can hardly conceive of any other. But the natural system – that which would have sprung up if Government had let banking alone – is that of many banks of equal or not altogether unequal size (Bagehot 1924 [1873], 66).

But Bagehot goes on to argue that turning the clock back and starting over with a free banking system was unwise if not impossible. People trusted the current system, and trust was a valuable form of what today would be called "social capital" that took a long time to accumulate. So Bagehot's goal was to make the existing institutions work better, not to propose some alternative set of institutions that might work better, if they could be adopted at all, only after a long transition period.

Bagehot's first qualification to his rule, that emergency loans be made at high interest rates, followed in part from the dependency of the British banking system on the Bank of England's limited reserves. High interest rates during a panic would discourage merchants from borrowing simply to fortify their own reserve positions, thus reducing the reserve at the Bank of England. Since the public followed the Bank of England's reserve and was alarmed when it fell to low levels, it was important to protect the reserve even during a panic.

The rate should be raised early in the panic, so that the fine may be paid early; that no one may borrow out of idle precaution without paying well for it; that the banking reserve may be protected as far as possible (Bagehot 1924 [1873], 187–188).

The case for raising the rate of interest during the panic was especially strong during a panic in which an "internal drain" (i.e, gold flowing from the banking system to the public) was combined with an "external drain" (i.e, gold flowing abroad). Bagehot believed that internal drains and external drains tended to arrive at the same time (Mints 1945, 191). And Bagehot was insistent that when that happened the right medicine was a high rate to end the outflow of gold combined with liberal lending. Here is Bagehot's (1924 [1873], 56) recommendation.

Before we had much specific experience, it was not easy to prescribe for this compound disease [an external drain combined with an internal drain]; but now we know how to deal with it. We must look first to the foreign drain and raise the rate of interest as high as may be necessary. Unless you can stop the foreign export, you cannot allay the domestic alarm . . . Very large loans at very high rates are the best remedy for the worst malady of the Money Market when a foreign drain is added to a domestic drain.

Although it is clear that Bagehot believed that a high rate was especially important in the face of an external drain, it would be a mistake to think that he recommended a high rate only in the case of an external drain. In summarizing his rule, Bagehot (1924 [1873], 188) recommended a high rate during panics without a further qualification that a high rate would be appropriate only when an external drain was present. A second consideration is that Bagehot approved of the Bank's handling (after a bad start) of the Panic of 1825, a panic that Bagehot (1924 [1873], 54) regarded as "entirely internal." At the height of the panic in December 1825 the Bank of England raised the Bank Rate from 4 percent to 5 percent, the legal maximum.

Sometimes, as in the quote from Bernanke, Bagehot's high rate is described as a *penalty* rate, a term that Bagehot himself did not use. If penalty is being used simply as a synonym for high, Bagehot's prescription, obviously, is unchanged. Bagehot, as we showed earlier, explained his high rate as a *fine* for excessive timidity. However, some writers who have used the term penalty have suggested that Bagehot meant a rate that was higher than the very high market rates that prevailed, typically, during financial panics. But as Goodhart (1999) and Bignon, Flandreau, and Ugolini (2012) show, this is going too far. Bagehot thought of his rate in instrumental terms: one that would be recognized as high by pre-crisis standards and that was high enough to discourage hoarding of reserves.

Under a fiat standard the urgent need to protect the reserve that so concerned Bagehot would disappear. There might still be reasons to lend at a high rate, for example to discourage borrowing for the purpose of speculative investments, or in the event of an external drain to protect the reserve of foreign currency. It is clear, however, that the accumulation of a large gold reserve, or the transition to a fiat standard, would alter the costs and benefits of raising rates during a panic. It is not at all clear, therefore, that Bagehot would have recommended a high rate for a central bank in the midst of a financial crisis under these circumstances. As we will see below, Friedman and Schwartz thought that the Federal Reserve had made a mistake in keeping its lending rate too high during the Great Contraction when the Federal Reserve, although adhering to the gold standard, had what Friedman and Schwartz considered an abundance of reserves.

Similarly, Bagehot's recommendation that the Bank of England lend only against good collateral was based on another important feature of the existing economic landscape: almost all of the securities circulating in the marketplace would be good under ordinary circumstances. The Bank of England could provide general relief by insisting on good collateral and only a very few potential borrowers would be excluded. Bagehot (1924 [1873], 188) put it this way.

The amount of bad business in commercial countries is an infinitesimally small fraction of the whole business. That in a panic the bank, or banks, holding the ultimate reserve should refuse bad bills or bad securities will not make the panic really worse; the 'unsound' people are a feeble minority, and they are afraid even to look frightened for fear their unsoundness may be detected.

What if a speculative boom had proceeded so far that a substantial amount of securities were suspect? What if the unsound firms were not a "feeble minority" but rather a substantial minority? The costs and benefits of insisting on good collateral would be altered and the benefits of lending to some potential borrowers who lacked good collateral would be higher.

Under a fiat standard, moreover, the costs of accepting weak collateral would be lower because there would be no need to sell securities to replenish the reserve. Again it is not at all clear that under these alternative institutional arrangements Bagehot would have insisted that lending be limited to amounts that could be backed by good collateral. If the unsound people were more than a "feeble minority" it might be necessary to lend to some of them to calm a panic.

Bagehot's concept of LOLR, it is important to note, did not include other modes of rescuing the banking system, namely bailing out individual institutions or more drastic rescue measures, such as nationalizing the banking system (Grossman 2013, chapter 4). Capie (2002, 310) illustrates how a LOLR would work in theory (and often did work in practice) if it followed Bagehot's prescriptions religiously.

The mechanism can be thought of as the central bank with a discount window that is of frosted glass and is raised just a few inches. Representatives of institutions could therefore appear at the window and push through the paper they wanted discounted. The central bankers would return the appropriate amount of cash, reflecting the going interest rate. The central banker does not know, nor does he care, who is on the other side of the window. He simply discounts good quality paper or lends on the basis of good collateral.

The identity, creditworthiness, and importance of the borrower are completely irrelevant to the process – the LOLR merely lends against sound collateral. We will return to the theory and practice of rescue operations later.

6 The Great Depression and the Absence of a LOLR in the United States

The Dow Jones Industrial Average started 1928 at 200. By September 1929, it had reached 380, the final leg of the bull market of the roaring twenties. But it soon began to fall, and on October 28 (Black Monday) and October 29 (Black Tuesday) lost over 25 percent of its value. The stock market crash drastically altered expectations and ushered in a decline in spending on consumer durables (Romer 1990). The Federal Reserve Bank of New York reacted to the immediate effects of the crash by supplying additional funds to New York banks so that they could make loans to securities brokers and dealers. But it did not address the macroeconomic trends set in motion by the stock market crash. During the following three years the American banking system suffered from wave after wave of bank failures. According to Friedman and Schwartz (1963, 299),

Economists on the Lender of Last Resort 251

"More than one-fifth of the commercial banks in the United States ... suspended operations because of financial difficulties."[6] The stock of money (M2) fell by 35 percent between 1930 and 1933. To be sure, the monetary base rose, but not nearly enough to reverse the decline in the stock of money and other quantitative measures of credit created by the banking system.

Many explanations have been put forward for the failure of the Federal Reserve to act as LOLR, all of which probably highlight some part of the full story. Friedman and Schwartz (1963, 412-416) argue that a lack of effective leadership was key. Benjamin Strong, the governor of the Federal Reserve Bank of New York and a dominant figure in the early years of the Federal Reserve System, had recognized that a banking panic called for aggressive open market purchases. But Strong died in 1928, and no one with the same grasp of the problem and a similarly forceful personality emerged to take his place. The governors of the other Federal Reserve branch banks, moreover, had secured an increase in the membership of the Open Market Committee, reducing the potential for decisive action. Temin (1989) and Eichengreen (1992), on the other hand, stress the constraints, real and psychological, imposed by the gold standard. And Wheelock (1991) and Meltzer (2003) argue that flawed policy doctrines hampered the Federal Reserve. The Federal Reserve tended to rely on borrowed reserves – what Meltzer calls the "Riefler-Burgess doctrine" after the developers of the theory – and nominal interest rates as indicators of monetary policy: Low bank borrowing and low nominal rates signify that monetary policy was easy. Since borrowing and nominal rates were low in the early 1930s, the Federal Reserve assumed that it was doing all it could to abort the slide.

One could also ask whether outside experts on banking and finance pressured the Federal Reserve to change course. Some did, but opposition to Federal Reserve policy was a minority cause. Perhaps the weightiest outside expert was O.M.W. Sprague, the author of the classic *History of Financial Crises under the National Banking System* (1910). Had he campaigned for a vigorous response to the Depression by the Federal Reserve, especially if he had been joined by a chorus of other experts, he might have made a difference. But Sprague never saw any part of the banking failures of 1930–1933 as a financial crisis requiring LOLR action. The problem may have been that the developments that defined a financial panic in earlier

---

[6] Some of these banks were reopened after the emergency had passed; in some cases without major changes in their balance sheets, and in others after major reorganizations.

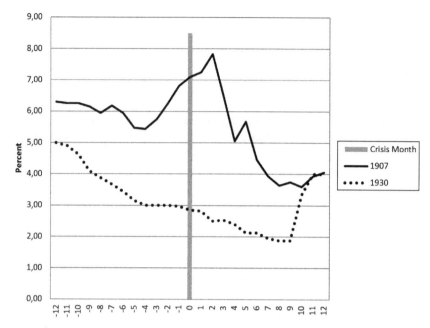

Figure 6.1. The commercial paper rate in 1907 and 1930
Note. The data is monthly. The crisis month in 1907 was October when the Knickerbocker Trust suspended. In 1930 it was December when the Bank of United States failed.
Source. The NBER macrohistory data base. (www.nber.org/databases/macrohistory/rectdata/13/m13001a.dat accessed January 2014).

crises, and that Sprague had discussed at length in his classic, were absent in 1930–1933 (Rockoff 2012). In 1907 for example, as shown in Figure 6.1, the commercial paper rate rose sharply at the same time that the banking crisis in New York was ignited by the failure of the Knickerbocker Trust Company; nothing like that happened in November 1930 when Caldwell and Company failed or in December 1930 when the Bank of United States failed. In retrospect economists have identified these failures as important, but an economist looking to short-term interest rates to measure the temperature of the money market would not have identified them as such.

The banking crises of the 1930s came to a head with the wave of "bank holidays" announced by state and local governments during the interregnum between the election of President Roosevelt in November 1932 and his assumption of office in March 1933. Once in office Roosevelt took several actions that ended the crisis. First, he turned the mounting tide of state and local bank holidays into a national bank holiday. During the holiday, the Roosevelt Administration explained, banks would be inspected and sound banks would be allowed to reopen. The Administration also announced legislation creating federal deposit insurance. These reforms – which were neither LOLR operations nor bailouts of individual firms, but something more dramatic – seem to have quieted the storm and there were few bank failures in the United States during the remainder of the 1930s.

In the wake of this colossal meltdown a number of important financial reforms were introduced. Some were aimed at strengthening the banking system and making future panics unlikely. These included the separation of commercial banking from investment banking, the creation of the Securities and Exchange Commission to regulate securities brokers and insure that investors had accurate information about the securities they were buying, and the regulation of interest on bank deposits, among others.[7] Other reforms were aimed explicitly at strengthening the capacity of the Federal Reserve to act as LOLR. The Board of Governors was made the dominant division of the system to prevent conflicts between the regional banks and the Board from thwarting effective action. The Federal Reserve, moreover, was given legal authority to lend to non-member banks and in "exceptional and unusual circumstances" to non-banks.

The Great Depression may have begun in the United States – not all scholars agree on this point – but it soon emerged in Europe. The Europeans were suffering from some of the same problems as the United States. Falling farm prices, for one thing, undermined European banks with a strong presence in agricultural areas just as they did in the United States. But it is also likely that the fears generated by the stock market crash on Wall Street and the bank failures in other parts of the United States simply jumped over international boundaries. In May 1931 the Kreditanstalt, the largest private bank in Austria failed. The panic spread quickly to Germany. The Danatbank, one of the largest German Banks, failed on July 13th and German banks were closed on the 14th and 15th. The pressure then hit Britain. In August, John Maynard Keynes recommended a major devaluation. In September, Britain left the gold standard, ending a connection that had been established after the end of the Napoleonic wars. Many other countries, particularly those in the British Empire, followed Britain off gold and established a relationship between their own currency and the

---

[7] These reforms left the banking system more stable, but also more constrained and less competitive. The rollback of this regulation contributed to financial instability that emerged in the 1970s and 1980s. Grossman (2010, 251–259).

pound. As a result the world was effectively divided into two blocs: a sterling bloc led by Britain and a gold bloc led by the United States.

Various attempts based on international cooperation were made to stop the downward spiral in Europe, but for political reasons – after all this was happening only a decade after the end of World War I – they proved insufficient (Kindleberger and Aliber 2011, 240–246). When the Kreditanstalt's difficulties were revealed, the Austrian government turned to the League of Nations, which then turned to the Bank for International Settlements. Credits from a number of countries were arranged, but these were soon exhausted. When the run shifted to Germany credits were arranged from the Bank of England, the Bank of France, and the Federal Reserve Bank of New York, but again not in sufficient amounts to quell the panic. When the run shifted to Britain private and government credits were arranged, but again in insufficient amounts. When New York experienced an external drain of gold, the Federal Reserve Bank of New York raised its discount rate, probably stanching the drain but further undermining the economy.

The appropriateness of monetary policy during the remainder of the Great Depression continues to be a matter of debate. In the United States after 1933 the stock of money rose at a fairly rapid rate except during the "recession within the depression" of 1937–1938. The outbreak of World War II produced a radically different monetary policy. The federal government ran large deficits to finance the war effort and the Federal Reserve froze the prewar interest rates on government bonds, buying any bonds not taken by the private sector at the prewar price. Between 1930 and 1933 the stock of money fell by 11.7 percent per year; between 1933 and 1941 it rose by 8.3 percent per year; and between 1941 and 1945 it rose by 17.6 percent per year, doubling in four years.

The Federal Reserve entered the postwar era with its powers as LOLR greatly enhanced for several reasons, although for the better part of the next half century, these powers would not be called upon: (1) as noted earlier, reforms during the 1930s had centralized power within the Federal Reserve Board, giving it increased authority to deal with incipient panics; (2) a chastened Federal Reserve had learned important lessons about the danger of allowing banks to fail. To be sure, the rise to dominance of Keynesian economics meant that the potential for monetary policy to influence the macro-economy was downplayed. Nevertheless, there was an understanding that permitting the fear of bank failures to spread among depositors had been a mistake; and (3) the United States had accumulated large stocks of gold, and under the Bretton Woods system the U.S. dollar had become the hegemonic currency. There was little danger that a fear of running out of reserves would prevent the Federal Reserve from halting a potential panic.

7 The Impact of the Great Depression on the Doctrine of LOLR

The Great Depression produced some rethinking of the role of the central bank as LOLR. This rethinking was more limited than might be expected. Bagehot's *Lombard Street* still remained the touchstone in discussions of the doctrine of LOLR. Here we briefly review three of the most important contributions that reflected the impact of the Great Depression: R.G. Hawtrey's (1932) *The Art of Central Banking*; Friedman and Schwartz's (1963) *A Monetary History of the United States*; and Ben Bernanke's "Nonmonetary effects of the financial crisis in the propagation of the great depression" (1983).

7.1 R.G. Hawtrey: *The Art of Central Banking*

Although Francis Baring deserves credit for first describing the Bank of England as the dernier resort, it was R.G. Hawtrey's *The Art of Central Banking* (1932) that propelled the English term "lender of last resort" into the mainstream of economic discussion. A Google Ngram (Figure 6.2) shows that specific phrase "lender of last resort" first came into widespread use in the 1930s. And a search of Google Books and JSTOR (where the term also emerges in the 1930s) suggest that Hawtrey's (1932) *The Art of Central Banking* was important in popularizing the term.

Indeed, Hawtrey's book was a milestone in the development of the theory of the LOLR. Hawtrey, like Bagehot, saw the need for the LOLR to lend freely in a financial panic, although on good collateral. Hawtrey

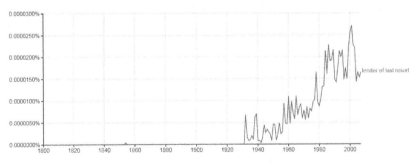

Figure 6.2. A Google Ngram of "Lender of Last Resort," 1800–2008.
Source. Google Ngram Viewer. https://book.google.com/ngrams. Accessed August, 2014.

thought that central banks in his day could attack a panic more easily than the Bank of England in Bagehot's time because they could issue fiat currency in denominations the public would find acceptable, something that, in practice, the Bank of England had been prevented from doing in the nineteenth century. But the Crisis of 1931, Hawtrey thought, was something new. International withdrawals were of such magnitude that they could drive countries off the gold standard. The Austrian government had addressed the problem of internal panic when it guaranteed the deposits of the Kreditanstalt, and the German government had done likewise when it guaranteed the deposits of the Danatbank. But the problem of external drains could not be addressed in this way (Hawtrey 1932, locations 3828–3870). The events of 1931, in short, were like a run on an individual bank, but instead were "a run on the entire banking system of a country" (Hawtrey 1932, locations 3936–3942). What was needed, Hawtrey argued, was an international LOLR (Hawtrey 1932, locations 3942–3947). This idea appears to be new, or at least given a decisive boost, by Hawtrey (de Boyer des Roches and Solis Rosales 2011). Finding or creating an institution that could become the international LOLR, Hawtrey warned, would not be easy. The Bank for International Settlements was, as far as Hawtrey could see, the best existing candidate. But turning it into an effective international LOLR would require changes in both the balance sheet of the Bank for International Settlements and its leadership.

7.2 Friedman and Schwartz: A Monetary History of the United States

Banking panics play a central role in Friedman and Schwartz's *A Monetary History of the United States*. Several of the panics – in 1873, 1893, 1907, and 1931 – were associated with severe economic contractions. During these earlier crises there was no central bank in the United States. What little LOLR actions there were, were carried out by the U.S. Treasury, private banks and clearing houses, and private individuals.

But while Bagehot, Hawtrey, and others saw the need for the central bank to maintain gold payments, Friedman and Schwartz now emphasized maintenance of the stock of money. Their analysis followed from a model of the economy based on the demand for and supply of money. The demand for money was determined by GDP and the proportion of GDP that people wanted to hold as money, which in turn was a function of interest rates, expected inflation, and other variables – the quantity theory of money. The supply of money was determined by the amount of high-powered money and the money multiplier. The latter, in turn, was a function of the deposit-currency ratio of the public and the deposit-reserve ratio of the banking system, with the supply of money rising when either of these determinants rose.

In this framework there is a straightforward interpretation of a banking panic. When people fear the safety of their bank deposits they withdraw cash from banks, leading to a decline in the deposit-currency ratio and hence the money supply falls. Banks could attempt to increase their liquidity by, say, refusing to renew loans: the deposit-reserve ratio would also tend to fall. If the amount of high-powered money did not change during the panic, the stock of money would fall and, with it, GDP. This framework then, provides a clear set of symptoms to look for in a banking panic: a decline in the deposit-currency ratio, a decline in the deposit-reserve ratio and, hence, if no offsetting actions are taken, a decline in the stock of money.

Table 6.1 shows what happened to these quantities in 1873, 1884, 1890, 1893, 1907, the major crises under the national banking system, and 1931, the first under the Federal Reserve. The panic years are marked in bold. In each case, except for the mild panic in 1890, there was a decline in the stock of money in the panic year or the following year: 1.8 percent from 1873 to 1874, 6.5 percent from 1892 to 1893, 3.4 percent from 1907 to 1908, and 6.2 percent from 1930 to 1931. These decreases were exceptional – the stock of money normally rose – and driven mainly by decreases in the money multiplier.

Figure 6.3, based on Friedman and Schwartz's monthly data, shows what happened in 1931. The pattern is similar to the earlier panics: the deposit-currency ratio drops precipitously after the failure of the Bank of United States, the trigger for the crisis.[8] The deposit-reserve ratio also falls, although not as precipitously, and there may have been a slight downward trend in the ratio before the banking crisis.

The establishment of the United States Postal Savings System in 1910 provides another variable that measures the presence of fear about the safety of deposits in commercial banks. Figure 6.4 plots the amount of postal savings, showing that the financial panic began at the end of 1930. It resembles the famous hockey stick, with the bend at the end of 1930. In short, whether we use the determinants of the stock of money or postal savings as metrics, it is correct to view the crises of 1930–1933, and

---

[8] More on this failure later.

Richard S. Grossman and Hugh Rockoff

Table 6.1. *Monetary statistics for seven financial crises*

Year	Month	High-powered money	Deposit-reserve ratio	Deposit-currency ratio	M2	Percent change in M2	Percent change in real GDP
		Billions	Ratio	Ratio	Billions	Percent	Percent
1873	February	0.78	4.63	1.94	1.62	2.45	8.19
1874	**February**	**0.80**	**3.88**	**2.03**	**1.59**	**−1.80**	**1.80**
1875	February	0.78	4.82	2.12	1.70	6.28	−0.18
1883	June	1.18	5.96	2.28	2.81	8.03	2.73
1884	**June**	**1.19**	**5.54**	**2.28**	**2.76**	**−1.65**	**−1.66**
1885	June	1.23	4.54	2.64	2.84	2.68	0.35
1890	June	1.37	6.32	3.40	3.91	9.75	9.27
1891	**June**	**1.43**	**6.05**	**3.36**	**4.02**	**2.75**	**1.18**
1892	June	1.53	5.90	3.81	4.47	10.66	4.97
1892	June	1.53	5.90	3.81	4.47	10.66	4.97
1893	**June**	**1.51**	**6.05**	**3.25**	**4.19**	**−6.54**	**−5.98**
1894	June	1.57	4.87	3.78	4.22	0.87	−4.86
1907	June	2.82	8.87	5.84	11.61	6.66	2.54
1908	**June**	**3.08**	**6.98**	**5.53**	**11.23**	**−3.37**	**−11.44**
1909	June	3.14	7.48	6.45	12.57	11.34	6.98
1929	June	7.10	13.16	10.74	45.91	0.14	5.87
1930	June	6.91	12.90	11.31	45.31	−1.31	−8.89
1931	**June**	**7.30**	**11.67**	**9.66**	**42.59**	**−6.20**	**−6.60**
1932	June	7.79	10.44	5.95	34.48	−21.13	−13.81
1933	June	7.94	8.39	5.08	30.08	−13.63	−1.27
2006	June	838	62.8	8.2	6,812	5.08	2.63
2007	June	851	67.7	8.6	7,245	6.17	1.76
2008	**June**	**864**	**72.2**	**9.0**	**7,705**	**6.16**	**−0.29**
2009	June	1,771	8.2	8.9	8,419	8.86	−2.81
2010	June	2,028	6.7	8.7	8,588	1.99	2.50
2011	June	2,656	4.8	8.4	9,089	5.67	1.59
2012	June	2,642	5.6	8.5	9,946	9.00	2.29
2013	June	3,218	4.5	8.5	10,635	6.70	2.20
2014	June	3,985	3.7	8.4	11,341	6.43	NA

Source and *Notes.* Monetary Statistics: Friedman and Schwartz (1963, table B3, 799–804). The first observation following the panic is shown in bold. High-Powered money is a synonym for the monetary base. Real GDP: Samuel H. Williamson, "What Was the U.S. GDP Then?" Measuring Worth, 2014 URL: www.measuringworth.org/usgdp/. Real GDP is an annual series. The last column shows percentage changes from the previous annual observation. Data for 2006 to 2014 is from Federal Reserve Bank of St. Louis, Fred Economic Data.

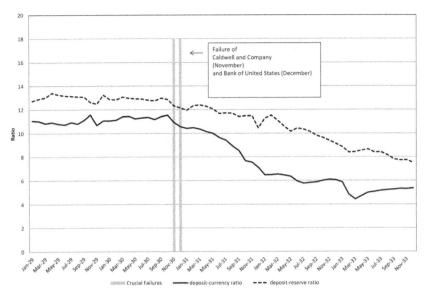

Figure 6.3. The deposit-reserve ratio and the deposit-currency ratio in the Great Contraction, 1929–1933
Source. Friedman and Schwartz (1963, table B3, 799–804).

especially the crisis of 1930–1931, as the same sort of malady that had hit the economy in 1873, 1893, and 1907.

Friedman and Schwartz then offer, implicitly, an alternative to Bagehot's rule. The central bank should inject sufficient high-powered money into the banking system to offset the decline in the deposit-reserve and deposit-currency ratios and maintain the stock of money. If velocity was affected presumably they would support a further increase in the amount of high-powered money to offset any decline in velocity.

Friedman and Schwartz (1963, 407) did argue, however, that even a policy based solely on Bagehot's rule would have produced far better results than the policy actually followed. Here is how they put it.

The actions required to prevent monetary collapse [in the early 1930s] did not call for a level of knowledge of the operation of the banking system or of the workings of monetary forces or of economic fluctuations which was developed only later and was not available to the Reserve System. On the contrary, as we have pointed out earlier, pursuit of the policies outlined by the System itself in the 1920's, or for that matter by Bagehot in 1873, would have prevented the catastrophe. The men who established the Federal Reserve System had many misconceptions about monetary theory and banking operations. It may well be that a policy in accordance with their understanding of monetary matters would not have prevented the decline in the stock of money from 1929 to the end of 1930. But they understood very well

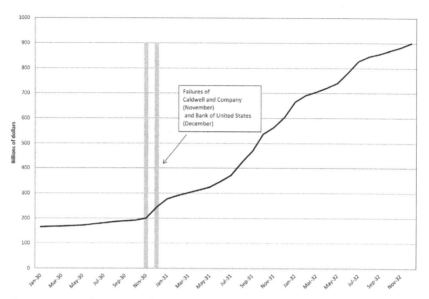

Figure 6.4. Postal savings in the United States, Monthly, January 1930 – December 1932
Source. Friedman and Schwartz (1970, table 1, 24–26, column 6).

the problem raised by a panic attempt to convert deposits into currency, and provided ample powers in the Act to deal with such a panic. There is little doubt that a policy based solely on a thorough perusal of the hearings preceding the enactment of the Federal Reserve Act and a moderately informed understanding of them would have cut short the liquidity crisis before it had gone very far, perhaps before the end of 1930.

Allan H. Meltzer's recent history of the Federal Reserve reinforces Friedman-Schwartz on this point. In his final summary of policy in the 1930s Meltzer (2003, 729) writes that:

Bagehot's work was known at the time. Senior officials referred to him but they did not follow his advice. They tried to protect the gold reserve, and at crucial times did not function as a system.

The difference between Bagehot and Friedman-Schwartz can be seen in particular with respect to interest rates and open market operations. Recall that Bagehot, with one eye always on the Bank of England's reserve, recommended high interest rates even during an internal drain. But when criticizing Federal Reserve policy in 1931 Friedman and Schwartz (1963, 395) go in the opposite direction.

Economists on the Lender of Last Resort 261

> True, during the height of the internal and external drain in October, it [the Federal Reserve] permitted its discounts and its bills bought to rise sharply. But this was at the initiative of the member banks, in spite of sharp rises in the rates on both, and was a result of the desperate situation of member banks because of the double drain. As we have seen, even after the height of the crisis, the New York Bank reduced bill buying rates only gradually and kept them above market rates, so bills bought declined rapidly. The System took no active measures to ease the internal drain, as it could have done through open market purchases.

Evidently, Friedman and Schwartz concluded that given the abundant reserves of the Federal Reserve, and the possibility that formal legal restraints would have been lifted if they had asked for it, the need to protect the Federal Reserve's gold reserve should have been ignored in favor of increasing the stock of money.[9]

In the ensuing decades Bagehot's idea of calming panics by lending, and Friedman and Schwartz's idea that the stock of money had to be prevented from falling remained fundamental to thinking about the LOLR. Perhaps the most intense debate was about how aggressively the central bank should turn to LOLR actions. The aggressive view is exemplified by Kindleberger and Aliber's *Manias, Panics, and Crashes* (2011), which argues that market economies often go off the rails, and need government intervention to get them up and running again. Although it is somewhat unfair to reduce this wide ranging essay to a simple formula, it is not unfair to draw the conclusion that the social costs of untreated financial crises were often extremely high and that central banks should therefore err on the side of intervention. Anna Schwartz, in a well-known essay entitled "Real and pseudo-financial crises," took the other side, arguing that asset price bubbles could be allowed to burst and insolvent financial firms be allowed to fail without endangering the payments mechanism, the latter being the appropriate object in need of protection by the LOLR

7.3 Ben Bernanke and the Cost of Financial Intermediation

There have been many criticisms of the Friedman and Schwartz interpretation of the Great Depression, as well as many defenses. The criticism, or more accurately the addition, with the most resonance for the doctrine of the LOLR is Bernanke (1983), who argues that there was more to the financial side of the Great Depression than the decline in the stock of money. The failure or near failure of many financial institutions ruptured

---

[9] On this point also see Nelson (2013).

long-term relationships between lenders and borrowers, increasing the "cost of credit intermediation." Potential borrowers who could not go to the institution they had long depended on might (after a time consuming search) find another lender with sufficient reserves to make a loan, but the borrower could not then offer adequate proof of his or her character and commitment to fulfilling long-term financial contracts. The trust between borrower and lender that had been built up over a long period of time was missing. In effect, the cost of financial intermediation had risen. The potential borrower might make up for the lack of trust by offering collateral. But the decline in asset prices produced by the Depression made it hard to collateralize new loans. The persistence of the Great Depression in this analysis reflected the time it took to rebuild borrower-lender relationships shattered by the initial financial crisis.

The implication of Bernanke's analysis for the LOLR was that simply maintaining or increasing the stock of money, although a good thing to do, was not enough. The increased demand for money produced by the financial crisis might be fully slaked, and yet the economy would not be able to recover because important borrower-lender relationships had been severed. Therefore, it was important for the LOLR to preserve important lending institutions, and to funnel credit to borrowers who could not utilize their normal sources of credit. In the 2008 crisis as we will show below, Bernanke followed through on this vision by creating the Term-Asset Backed Loan Facility, for borrowers cut off from their traditional sources of credit. Eventually, the Facility lent about $70 billion (Nelson 2013, 76–77).

8 Rescue Operations

Bagehot's main concern was what the Bank of England should do once a panic was underway. He recognized the existence of a stage preceding the full-blown panic that he referred to as an "incipient panic" when financial markets were anxious and a panic was likely. In those circumstances he thought that the Bank of England needed to be especially vigilant about protecting its reserve because it would be needed when incipient panic turned to actual panic. Bagehot never explains how to distinguish an incipient panic, when the right policy was for the Bank to conserve its reserve, from an actual panic, when the right policy was to lend the reserve freely. He appears to have thought that it would be obvious (Rockoff 1986). But was there nothing that the central bank could do except to keep its powder dry? In 1890 during the famous Baring Crisis, discussed in greater detail in Section 3, the Bank of England famously took action to prevent a panic from starting. Baring, an important investment bank, was on the verge of insolvency as a result of poor investments in Argentina. A consortium of lenders, which included the Rothchilds, was organized by the Bank of England to guarantee Baring's liabilities, successfully forestalling a panic. Clearly the Bank and other leading firms feared a panic if Baring was allowed to go under, but *would* there have been a panic if the firm had been allowed to go under?[10]

Indeed, whether the failure of a single firm could trigger a panic in the absence of fundamental strains in the financial system remains an unsettled question. On the one hand, many explanations for panics stress the build-up of distortions in the financial system, an emphasis which suggests that the failure of a particular firm is merely an epiphenomenon. Once a panic becomes inevitable, it cannot be stopped merely by rescuing a single firm. If one firm is rescued, another will fail and start the panic. Some examples of theories that emphasize the build-up of distortions are Calomiris and Gorton (1991), Reinhart and Rogoff (2009), and Schularick and Taylor (2012), or to take an older example, Mitchell (1941). We don't mean to go to the extreme of suggesting that these authors would completely discount a role for individual failures, merely that their analyses stress the build-up of fundamental strains rather than idiosyncratic events.

On the other hand, another class of explanations for panics stresses the inherent instability of a fractional reserve banking system. In that view a dramatic event can produce a cataclysmic banking contraction even when distortions are absent. Banks promise to pay cash on demand. But banks only hold a fractional reserve because on an ordinary day only a small percentage of depositors will want cash. But if alarm about the liquidity of the bank takes hold, there will be a run on the bank, and the bank will be forced to break its promise to its depositors. If fear about all the banks takes hold, a full-blown panic will result.

Diamond and Dybvig (1983) provide the first formal model of a fragile banking system prone to runs. Their initial effort has produced a large literature extending, modifying, and criticizing their original model. In the Diamond-Dybvig model government policies such as deposit insurance or

---

[10] There are, of course, many examples of troubled financial institutions being bailed out by the government because of the perceived cost of permitting the firm to fail. Among the earliest bailouts on record are those of Australia's Bank of New South Wales in 1826, the Banque de Belgique in 1838–1839, and Cologne's A. Schaaffhausen Bank in 1848.

a commitment to freeze deposits in the event of a run can prevent panics from occurring. Some of the difficulties that can arise in models of this type are illustrated by Ennis and Keister (2009), who show that although the most efficient policy ex ante is for the central bank to commit to a policy of freezing all deposits in the event of a panic, the most efficient policy ex post is to allow exceptions to the freeze for people in need. Knowing that this policy will actually be followed may increase the probability of run. Goodhart and Huang (2005) model the rescue choice itself, and illustrate the trade-off between the cost, in terms the increase of moral hazard created by the rescue of a large financial institution, and the benefit from reducing the risk of a financial panic.

The two approaches – fundamental distortions and inherent fragility – are not, of course, mutually exclusive. It may be true that distortions built up in the economy are bound to produce a severe contraction, and yet it may still be possible that additional random events determine whether a panic is added to the contraction. There may be a fire in a crowded auditorium, which may result in many people being overcome by smoke, but it is still possible to imagine two outcomes. In one, someone rises quietly, politely asks their neighbors to excuse them, and begins walking toward the exit, leading to an orderly evacuation. In the other, someone yells fire, a panic ensues, and the crush of people trying to leave magnifies the damage done by the fire.

In any case, the idea that the failure of a large bank can start a panic, although often questioned, remains an important folk theorem for financial historians. Bagehot, for one, believed that the financial system in his day was inherently fragile and that the failure of an important financial firm could trigger a panic.

Such accidental events [that trigger panics] are of the most various nature: a bad harvest, an apprehension of foreign invasion, the sudden failure of a great firm which everybody trusted, and many other similar events, have all caused a sudden demand for cash (Bagehot 1924 [1873], 118).

The Baring crisis (1890) is the iconic example of successful intervention to prevent a potentially damaging failure. The astute American expert on financial crises, O.M.W. Sprague (1909, 401), noted that the practice of central banks had been broadened by the Baring Crisis to include the rescue of banks that were "not hopelessly insolvent" in order to prevent crises. The Bank of England's response to the Baring episode, to reiterate, did not fit the mold of classical LOLR operations described by Bagehot for three reasons. First, the Bank of England acted proactively; typically, LOLRs provide liquidity only *after* a crisis emerges. Second, the Bank of England's response involved providing a guarantee, rather than actual liquidity: in this sense, the Bank's actions were more like an ex post provision of deposit insurance, guaranteeing Baring's liabilities. Finally, the Bank did not act alone. It was the main organizer of the rescue, but because it was not the sole participant – and also had an explicit government commitment as a fiscal backstop – it was able to do so while at the same time limiting its potential loss on the operation. Although Bagehot's formulation did not exclude the possibility of a syndicated rescue, it did not envision it. But, as Sprague noted, it was practice that had changed, not theory. Economists have never enunciated a clear prescription of how a central bank should respond to the information that a large financial institution was about to fail.

The failure of the Bank of United States in December 1930 plays an important role in Friedman and Schwartz's history of the Great Depression. This failure, they argue, was of special importance because it was the first large bank in New York to fail during the Great Contraction, and possibly because its name misled some people into believing that it was sponsored by the federal government, although in fact it was an ordinary commercial bank chartered by the state of New York. As shown in Figure 6.3, both the deposit-reserve ratio of the banking system and the deposit-currency ratio declined after the failure, thus accelerating the decline in the stock of money.

In a long footnote in *A Monetary History* Friedman and Schwartz (1963, 309) described the efforts to save the bank. The plan was to merge the bank with several others in New York and to inject $30 million provided by the clearing house banks. It would not have been the sort of emergency lending described by Bagehot in *Lombard Street*, but it would have been similar to the rescue organized by the Bank of England in the Baring Crisis and in earlier crises. In *A Monetary History* Friedman and Schwartz (1963, 310 n. 9) provide only hints as to why the plan fell apart. They report a recollection by one of the participants, Jackson Reynolds, the President of First National Bank and of the Clearing House Association, who thought that the effects of the closure would be "local." And they report the recollection of another participant that the representatives of the Clearing House were concerned about the Bank of the United States' real estate investments. In modern parlance the beliefs were that the bank was not "systemically important" and not solvent.

In some of his popular writings and most importantly in his 1980 TV series, "Free to Choose," Friedman went further in pointing to the failure of the Bank of United States as the trigger for the crisis and in identifying the reasons why it was allowed to close. He began Episode Three, "Anatomy of a Crisis," his story of the Great Depression, with scenes in which he is filmed looking up at the building that was the former home of the Bank of United States.[11] This was where the crucial event occurred, Friedman tells the viewer, which turned a recession that was already severe because of the stock market crash into a crisis.[12] He goes on to explain that the bank served mainly Jewish merchants on the Lower East Side of New York, the famous starting point for many poor Jewish immigrants. Anti-Semitism, Friedman suggested, was the reason why the Clearing House failed to rescue of the Bank of United States. Rumors, fuelled by anti-Semitism, he added, may even have contributed to the runs on the bank that had so weakened it that a rescue was necessary. In the end, Friedman and Schwartz (1963, 355) noted that the bank had paid well when it was liquidated and that it was therefore probably a good candidate for a rescue.

Friedman's contentions about the role of anti-Semitism have been vigorously challenged and defended (Temin 1976, 90–93, Lucia 1985, Friedman and Schwartz 1986b, O'Brien 1992, and Trescott 1992). Although Friedman and Schwartz evidently believed that Bank of United States should have been rescued because its failure had disastrous effects and because it was in fact a sound bank, they do not state explicitly, as far as we can tell, what they think should have been done if in fact the bank had been clearly insolvent.

There were many important potential failures in the post-war period. Some were allowed to go to bankruptcy without a government-sponsored bailout, and yet these failures did not produce financial panics. The failure of Equity Funding Corporation of America in 1973 and of Drexel Burnham Lambert in 1990 are examples. Perhaps these failures did not have systemic effects because the dominant narratives about them in the business press stressed corruption and made them appear to be outliers. In any case, the belief based on the reactions to the failure of the Bank of United States in 1930 or the Knickerbocker Trust Company in 1907, and earlier examples, was that the failure of an important firm *could* trigger a damaging panic and led to several government rescues.

In June 1970 the Penn Central Railroad declared bankruptcy. There was a widespread fear that the failure of Penn Central to make good on its borrowings in the commercial paper market would ignite a panic. The

---

[11] www.youtube.com/watch?v=SWVoPrntBso.

[12] The book that accompanied the television series, Friedman and Friedman (1980, 80–82), gives a starring role to the failure of the Bank of United States.

Federal Reserve took several actions designed to prevent a panic, including open market purchases to increase the stock of money. Friedman (1970) was critical of this rescue operation. In his view, there was little danger of a banking panic. Failures of industrial firms, in Friedman's view, were distinctly different from failures of financial firms, and only the latter could precipitate a panic. As long as the payments system was protected by a LOLR or deposit insurance there was no need, in his view, to bail out an industrial firm. In 1974, however, there was a major bankruptcy within the banking system: Franklin National Bank. The Federal Reserve provided an emergency loan and later the Federal Deposit Insurance Company stepped in as receiver. In this case, Friedman (1974) was more sympathetic to the need for government action, but at the same time he expressed confidence that there was no danger of a financial panic because the presence of deposit insurance would prevent the sort of contagion of fear that undermined the banking system in 1931–1933.

In 1984 Continental Illinois, the nation's eighth largest bank, failed because of losses on investments in energy loans made by Penn Square Bank of Oklahoma. The Federal Reserve and Federal Deposit Insurance Company cooperated in creating a bailout plan that included replacement of the bank's management. Friedman and Schwartz (1986a) thought that the bailout had been handled well, and used it as an example of the ongoing danger of contagion that created a need for government involvement in banking. Thus, it would appear that Friedman and Schwartz had moved to the position that the potential failure of large institutions within the banking system needed to be addressed by the authorities in a way that would minimize the danger of a panic-inducing bankruptcy. A fire department was needed, but not every fire needed to be extinguished; only those that threatened to ignite a major conflagration.[13]

9 The Subprime Crisis

It has become commonplace for journalists to describe to the sub-prime mortgage crisis as the "worst financial crisis since the Great Depression" (Grossman 2013, 137). Google Trends shows a sharp increase in media references to "Great Depression" following the failure of Lehman Brothers in September 2008 (Eichengreen 2012, 289). Journalists are not alone in this regard. When Christina Romer asked President Obama's chief of staff

---

[13] See Nelson (2013) for a further description of Friedman's ideas about the LOLR and the extent to which they were implemented after the crisis in 2008.

Rahm Emanuel why she, an economic historian, was chosen to chair the president's Council of Economic Advisers rather than someone with more of a policy background, Emanuel replied: "You're an expert on the Great Depression, and we really thought we might need one."[14]

The similarities of the sub-prime crisis with the Great Depression were not lost on chairman of the Federal Reserve at the time the crisis erupted, Ben Bernanke. Bernanke, as discussed earlier, had written extensively on the Great the Depression prior to becoming chairman of the Federal Reserve (Bernanke 2000).[15] In 1992, as a member – although not yet chair – of the Fed's Board of Governors, Bernanke spoke at the ninetieth birthday celebration for Milton Friedman who, along with Anna Schwartz, famously wrote about how misguided Federal Reserve policy had worsened the Great Depression. In his remarks, Bernanke addressed Friedman and Schwartz directly: "You're right, we did it. We're very sorry. But thanks to you, we won't do it again."[16] Thus, it is clear that at the very highest levels of the Federal Reserve and the executive branch, there was little doubt about the severity of the crisis and a strong awareness of the consequences of inaction.

The sub-prime crisis, like the majority of financial crises during the last 200 years, resulted from the collapse of a boom-bust economic cycle (Fisher 1932, 1933, Minsky 1982, Calomiris and Gorton 1991, Reinhart and Rogoff 2009, Kindleberger and Aliber 2011, and Schularick and Taylor 2012). The boom had a number of causes, among them expansionary fiscal policy (i.e., three tax cuts along with increased spending to fund wars in Afghanistan and Iraq) and excessively loose monetary policy. The situation was made worse by wholly inadequate regulation and supervision, particularly of the sub-prime mortgage market and the new funding instruments used to speed the flow of funds to low quality mortgages. The collapse of house prices left a large volume of mortgages under water, a number of home-owners unable to service their debts, and many intermediators holding distressed – often denoted "toxic" – assets. The value of these assets were dubious, threatening many institutions, including banks, investment banks, as well as institutions such as insurance giant American International Group which had insured a substantial amount of toxic assets.

---

[14] http://newscenter.berkeley.edu/2011/10/11/romer-talk-offers-young-academics-solace-sense-and-secrets/

[15] And, in its wake, penned a series of lectures on the Federal Reserve and the crisis (Bernanke 2013).

[16] www.federalreserve.gov/BOARDDOCS/SPEECHES/2002/20021108/

On the one hand, the extraordinary relief efforts included actions well beyond those envisioned by Bagehot. Through a variety of programs falling under the main category of the Troubled Asset Relief Program (TARP), the Treasury, with assistance from the Federal Reserve, purchased preferred stock, equity warrants, and provided asset guarantees to a variety of financial institutions.[17] Another segment of the TARP program provided funds to restructure General Motors and Chrysler. In addition, the amount of deposits covered by the Federal Deposit Insurance Corporation was raised to $250,000 from $100,000.

On the other hand, some of the programs established under the auspices of the Federal Reserve were similar in spirit to those prescribed by Bagehot, providing credit for money market mutual funds in danger of being unable to meet depositor withdrawals, issuers of commercial paper, primary dealers (broker-dealer counterparties to the Federal Reserve in Open Market Operations), to depository institutions (through the Term Auction Facility), and by lending out high-quality Treasury securities from the System Open Market Account against collateral deemed good (although less credit-worthy than Treasury securities), much as exchequer bills had been used to quell the panic in 1793. In addition, the Federal Reserve provided currency swap lines with international central banks, in order to avoid a shortage of dollars on international markets. To quote a central banker from a previous century, the Fed "... lent it by every possible means and in modes [...] never adopted before and ... [was] not on some occasions over-nice."[18]

The defining moment in the crisis was the failure of Lehman Brothers on September 15, 2008. The U.S. economy had already contracted and an atmosphere of near panic prevailed in financial markets. But the failure of Lehman Brothers precipitated a full blown financial panic and accelerated the decline in the economy. Why did the failure of Lehman Brothers have major consequences? Partly, it was the characteristics of Lehman Brothers itself. A large and once highly regarded Wall Street investment bank, its failure naturally undermined confidence in the financial system as a whole. If Lehman Brothers could not be trusted, who could be? It was also partly due to the order in which the crisis events had occurred. Other firms had gotten into trouble and had received aid. In March 2008 the Federal Reserve provided financing to help JPMorgan Chase acquire the troubled

---

[17] These initiatives included the Capital Assistance Program, the Capital Purchase Program, the Community Development Capital Initiative, the Asset Guarantee Program, and the Targeted Investment Program.

[18] See page 236

270   *Richard S. Grossman and Hugh Rockoff*

investment bank, Bear Stearns. In July the Federal Reserve Board and the Treasury authorized lines of credit for the Federal National Mortgage Association (Fannie Mae) and the Federal Home Loan Mortgage Corporation (Freddie Mac). On September 7 Fannie Mae and Freddie Mac were essentially nationalized. But on September 15 Lehman Brothers, another troubled investment bank, was allowed to fail, while American International Group, which had sold credit protection against a large volume of now toxic assets, was bailed out by the Federal Reserve in return for a nearly 80 percent share in the company. These apparently contradictory decisions raised questions about the willingness or the ability of the government to act as LOLR, and may well have been the final precipitant of the panic. Andrew Ross Sorkin (2009, 535) put it this way in his detailed history of the financial crisis.[19]

They offered a safety net to Bear Stearns and backstopped Fannie Mae and Freddie Mac but allowed Lehman to fall into chapter 11, only to rescue AIG soon after. What was the pattern? What were the rules? There didn't appear to be any, and when investors grew confused – wondering whether a given firm might be saved, allowed to fail, or even nationalized – they not surprisingly began to panic.

There has been some debate about why Lehman Brothers was allowed to fail. The Federal Reserve has maintained that it lacked the legal authority to rescue Lehman Brothers because Lehman was insolvent; Lehman Brothers simply lacked securities that could adequately collateralize sufficient loans. On the other hand, more than a few observers have suggested that political considerations also played a role. As the crisis progressed the government came under increasing pressure to end what appeared to the public to be simply handouts to the richest Americans. Shortly before the collapse of Lehman Brothers, Treasury Secretary Henry Paulson purportedly told Ben Bernanke and Timothy Geithner "I can't be Mr. Bailout" (Sorkin 2009, 282).[20] But the question for the future is whether Lehman should have been bailed out, and in what circumstances in general, if any, should apparently insolvent institutions be rescued.

---

[19] Anna Schwartz made a similar argument (Ryssdal 2009).

[20] That said, the first version of the bailout bill that Paulson sent to Congress was 840 words long, would have authorized $700 billion in spending to buy toxic assets, and made the Secretary of the Treasury immune from oversight by the courts or Congress. The text of the proposal read, in part, "Decisions by the Secretary pursuant to the authority of this Act are non-reviewable and committed to agency discretion, and may not be reviewed by any court of law or any administrative agency." www.nytimes.com/2008/09/21/business/21draftcnd.html?_r=1

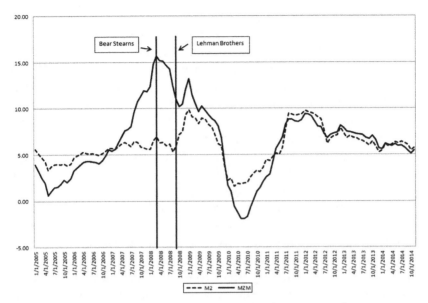

Figure 6.5. Percentage change in monetary aggregates from a year earlier.
Note. M2 is the narrower monetary aggregate similar to the aggregate chosen by Friedman and Schwartz. MZM (money with zero maturity) excludes various time accounts but includes money market funds.
Source. Federal Reserve Bank of St. Louis, Fred Economic Data.

For Friedman and Schwartz (1963) the stock of money was the crucial variable. As can be seen in Figure 6.5, the growth rate of M2 (Friedman and Schwartz's preferred measure of the stock of money) decelerated after the collapse of Bear Stearns and Lehman Brothers. The rate of change of money with a zero maturity (MZM) actually became negative. However, this was despite a massive increase in the amount of high-powered money by the Federal Reserve. In the year following the failure of Lehman Brothers the St. Louis Fed's estimate of the adjusted monetary base rose by 66 percent. The Federal Reserve was certainly responding in the direction approved by Friedman and Schwartz, even if they were not able to keep the monetary aggregates completely on track. Whether even more could have been done is a worthwhile question, but one that will have to be addressed in another paper.

It did not take long for the crisis to stimulate discussion and policy recommendations. The major legislative response to the crisis was the Dodd–Frank Wall Street Reform and Consumer Protection Act, an 848-page, 360,000-plus word law enacted in 2010. This law's provisions, too numerous to outline here and not completely finalized, include measures to coordinate financial stability oversight, provide for orderly liquidation of failing financial institutions, increase oversight of securities transactions, and establish more stringent consumer protections. There have been numerous complaints from the financial sector that the regulatory burden of Dodd-Frank is too heavy, although it is far too soon to know if benefits the stability-enhancing and consumer protection provisions outweigh the regulatory burdens.

In the wake of the crisis Goodfriend (2012) drew attention to the large discretionary power exercised by the Federal Reserve and the Treasury during the crisis and suggested that Congressional approval be required for large scale "bridge loans" to financial intermediaries or for purchase of private securities. Meltzer (2013, 413) pointed out that the Federal Reserve has never followed Bagehot's advice and announced the LOLR policies it intended to follow during the next crisis. Meltzer's recommendation is that the Federal Reserve announce which types of collateral it would accept in emergencies, and impose capital requirements that would rise (up to a limit) with the size of the institution. One is entitled, however, to be skeptical and to question whether any announced policy that would lead to costs being imposed on politically influential sectors could be adhered to in the midst of a crisis, particularly if it was felt that the failure of a particular firm could substantially worsen a crisis that was already underway. The claim that it will be "another Lehman Brothers" is a potentially powerful argument. Gary Gorton (2012), on the other hand, has suggested that because each crisis is unique and arrives so suddenly that it is impossible to follow rules announced before the crisis hits. Some guidelines might be possible – don't try to liquidate financial institutions during a panic is his suggestion – but he is skeptical about the possibility of announcing credible policy rules.

Another mechanism for reducing the likelihood – and potential impact – of a crisis is through enhanced shareholder liability. This can be achieved by turning debt holders into equity participants when capital levels fall to a predetermined level through contingent convertible securities (Cocos), as suggested by Flannery (2010). Historically, enhanced shareholder liability has been achieved by issuing "uncalled liability." For example, in nineteenth-century Britain, shares were typically issued with a stated nominal share value, only a portion of which was paid in at issue. Thus a £50 share in a firm might have been issued with only £40 paid-in, meaning that shareholders could be called upon to pay in an additional £10 in the case of failure or, more generally, at the discretion of the management

(Jefferys 1946). Grossman and Imai (2013, 141) note that uncalled liability was more common and extensive in sectors where leverage was high and the physical assets were either meager or inaccessible to creditors.

In the United States during the nineteenth century, bank shares were frequently issued with "double liability." Under double liability, when a bank failed, shareholders would not only lose the total amount that they had invested in the shares, but would also be liable for an amount equal to the value that shares had been worth at their initial offering. In some states, shareholders were liable for twice the initial value of the shares (i.e., so-called "triple liability"); in other states, shareholder liability was unlimited (Grossman 2001, 2007). Flannery (2010), White (2010), and Grossman and Imai (2010) have suggested that the liability of shareholders in financial institutions be raised, thus increasing the incentive of shareholders to monitor banks while allowing the Fed and FDIC to protect other stakeholders. Despite these and other suggestions, no consensus has emerged about the best way forward.

10 Conclusions

The theory of the LOLR has evolved in response to financial crises. Typically, economists look back at the most recent crisis – and occasionally the one or two before that – in order to formulate guidelines that would have prevented that crisis, and that they hope might prevent the next one. That was true for Adam Smith, who studied the crises of 1763 and 1772, Henry Thornton, who studied the crises of 1793 and 1797, Walter Bagehot, who studied the crises of 1825, 1847, and 1866, Friedman and Schwartz, who studied the crises of 1873, 1893, 1907, and 1930, and Ben Bernanke, who studied the banking crises of the 1930s. Alas, this program has not led to rapid progress. In most branches of economics, the literature cited is primarily of recent vintage; but when it comes to the LOLR, Bagehot's *Lombard Street*, first published in 1873, still reigns supreme. Economists, it turns out, are like generals, always fighting the last war: as we have seen, economists have begun, tentatively, to come up with guidelines based on the most recent crisis that will provide government officials with new and better ways to handle financial panics. Clearly, more rethinking of the LOLR doctrine is needed. In the meantime, policymakers will need to make do with the older plans of Thornton, Bagehot, Friedman and Schwartz, Bernanke, et. al. Perhaps there is no general rule to follow and central banking in financial crises will remain, as R.G. Hawtrey suggested, an art rather than a science.

References

Ahrens, Gerhard 1986. *Krisenmanagement 1857: Staat Und Kaufmannschaft in Hamburg Während Der Ersten Weltwirtschaftskrise.* Hamburg: Verlag Verein für Hamburgische Geschichte.

Andréadès, Andreas Michael 1966 [1909]. *History of the Bank of England, 1640–1903.* New York: August M. Kelley.

Ashton, T. S. 1959. *Economic Fluctuations in England, 1700–1800.* Oxford: Clarendon Press.

Bagehot, Walter 1891 [1877]. *Some Articles on the Depreciation of Silver and on Topics Connected with It.* London: H. S. King & Co. Reprinted in *The Works of Walter Bagehot.* Ed. Morgan Forrest. Vol. 5. Hartford: The Travelers Insurance Co.

    1924 [1873]. *Lombard Street: A Description of the Money Market.* 14th ed. London: William Clowes and Sons, Limited.

Baring, Sir Francis 2007 [1797]. Observations on the establishment of the Bank of England; and on the paper circulation of the country. In *The Lender of Last Resort.* Eds. Forrest H. Capie and Geoffrey E. Wood. London: Routledge.

Bernanke, Ben 1983. Nonmonetary effects of the financial crisis in the propagation of the great depression. *American Economic Review* 73(3)(June): 257–276.

    2000. *Essays on the Great Depression.* Princeton, NJ: Princeton University Press.

    2012. Some reflections on the crisis and the policy response. Speech delivered at "Rethinking Finance," a conference sponsored by the Russell Sage Foundation and the Century Foundation. April 13 ed. New York.

    2013. *The Federal Reserve and the Financial Crisis.* Princeton NJ: Princeton University Press.

Bignon, Vincent, Marc Flandreau, and Stefano Ugolini. 2012. Bagehot for beginners: The making of lender-of-last-resort operations in the mid-nineteenth century. *Economic History Review* 65(2)(05): 580–608.

Bordo, Michael D. 1990. The lender of last resort: Alternative views and historical experience. *Federal Reserve Bank of Richmond Economic Review* 76(1): 18–29.

Broz, J. Lawrence, and Richard S. Grossman 2004. Paying for privilege: The political economy of Bank of England Charters, 1694–1844. *Explorations in Economic History* 41(1): 48–72.

Cagan, Phillip 1965. *Determinants and Effects of Changes in the Stock of Money, 1875–1960.* New York: National Bureau of Economic Research.

Calomiris, Charles W., and Gary Gorton 1991. The origins of banking panics: Models, facts, and bank regulation. In *Financial Markets and Financial Crises.* Ed. R. Glenn Hubbard, 109–173. A National Bureau of Economic Research Project Report; Chicago and London: University of Chicago Press.

Cannon, James Graham 1900. *Clearing-Houses; Their History, Methods and Administration.* New York: D. Appleton and Company.

    1910. *Clearing Houses.* Washington: Government Printing Office.

Capie, Forrest 2002. The Bank of England as a mature Central Bank. In *The Political Economy of British Historical Experience, 1688–1914.* Eds. Donald Winch and Patrick O'Brien, 295–318. Oxford: Oxford University Press.

Capie, Forrest, Charles Goodhart, Stanley Fischer, and Norbert Schnadt 1994. *The Future of Central Banking: The Tercentenary Symposium of the Bank of England*. Cambridge: Cambridge University Press.

Capie, Forrest, and Geoffrey Edward Wood 2006. *The Lender of Last Resort*. New York: Routledge.

Checkland, S. G. 1975. *Scottish Banking: A History, 1695–1973*. Glasgow: Collins.

Clapham, John H. 1945. *The Bank of England: A History (2 volumes)*. Cambridge: Cambridge University Press.

Cline, William R., and Joseph E. Gagnon 2013. Lehman died, Bagehot lives: Why did the fed and treasury let a major wall street bank fail. *Institute for International Economics: Policy Brief* (September): 1–13.

Collins, Michael 1972. The Langton papers: Banking and Bank of England policy in the 1830s. *Economica* 39(153): 47–59.

de Boyer des Roches, Jerome, and Ricardo Solis Rosales 2011. R. G. Hawtrey on the national and international lender of last resort. *European Journal of the History of Economic Thought* 18(2)(05): 175–202.

Diamond, Douglas W., and Philip H. Dybvig 1983. Bank runs, deposit insurance, and liquidity. *Journal of Political Economy* 91(3): 401–419.

Eichengreen, Barry, 1992. *Golden Fetters: The Gold Standard and the Great Depression, 1919–1939*. New York and Oxford: Oxford University Press.

2012. Economic history and economic policy. *Journal of Economic History* 72(2): 289–307.

Ennis, Huberto M., and Todd Keister. 2009. Bank runs and institutions: The perils of intervention. *American Economic Review* 99(4): 1588–1607.

Fetter, Frank W. 1965. *Development of British Monetary Orthodoxy, 1797–1875*. Cambridge: Harvard University Press.

Fisher, Irving 1932. *Booms and Depressions: Some First Principles*. New York: Adelphi.

1933. The debt-deflation theory of Great Depressions. *Econometrica* 1: 337–357.

Flandreau, Marc 1997. Central Bank cooperation in historical perspective: A skeptical view. *Economic History Review* 50(4): 735–763.

Flannery, Mark J. 2010. Stabilizing large financial institutions with contingent capital certificates. CAREFIN Research Paper No. 04/2010. Available at SSRN: http://ssrn.com/abstract=1798611.

Friedman, Milton 1970. *Interview with Milton Friedman, Penn Central Bankruptcy*. Sound recording 53. Ed. Rose D. Friedman. Instructional Dynamics, Online Archive of California.

1974. *Interview with Milton Friedman: Franklin National*. Sound recording 146. Ed. Rose D. Friedman. Instructional Dynamics, Online Archive of California.

Friedman, Milton, and Rose D. Friedman 1980. *Free to Choose: A Personal Statement*. 1st ed. New York: Harcourt Brace Jovanovich.

Friedman, Milton, and Anna J. Schwartz 1963. *A Monetary History of the United States, 1867–1960*. Princeton: Princeton University Press.

1970. *Monetary Statistics of the United States: Estimates, Sources, Methods*. New York: Columbia University Press.

1986a. Has government any role in money? *Journal of Monetary Economics* 17(1)(01): 37–62.

1986b. The failure of the Bank of United States: A reappraisal: A reply. *Explorations in Economic History* 23(2)(04): 199–204.

Goodfriend, Marvin 2012. The elusive promise of independent central banking: Keynote speech. *Monetary and Economic Studies* 30(11): 39–54.

Goodfriend, Marvin, and Robert G. King 1988. Financial deregulation, monetary policy, and central banking. *Federal Reserve Bank of Richmond Economic Review* 74(3): 3–22.

Goodhart, Charles A. E. 1999. Myths about the lender of last resort. *International Finance* 2(3)(11): 339–360.

Goodhart, Charles A. E., and Haizhou Huang 2005. "The lender of last resort." *Journal of Banking & Finance* 29(5): 1059–1082.

Gorton, Gary 1985. Clearinghouses and the origin of central banking in the United States. *Journal of Economic History* 45(2): 277–283.

2012. *Misunderstanding Financial Crises: Why We Don't See Them Coming*. New York: Oxford University Press.

Grossman, Richard S. 2001. Double liability and bank risk taking. *Journal of Money, Credit and Banking* 33(2): 143–159.

2007. Fear and greed: The evolution of double liability in American banking, 1865–1930. *Explorations in Economic History* 44(1): 59–80.

2010. *Unsettled Account: The Evolution of Banking in the Industrialized World since 1800*. Princeton: Princeton University Press.

2013. *WRONG: Nine Economic Policy Disasters and What We Can Learn from Them*. New York: Oxford University Press.

Grossman, Richard S., and Masami Imai 2010. Contingent capital and risk taking: Evidence from Britain' banks 1878–1912. Vox.eu, September 7, 2010. www.voxeu .org/article/liability-and-excessive-risk-taking-historical-evidence-britain-s-banks.

2013. Contingent capital and bank risk-taking among British banks before the First World War. *Economic History Review* 66(1): 132–155

Hautcoeur, Pierre-Cyrille, Angelo Riva, and Eugene N. White 2013. Can moral hazard be avoided? The Banque de France and the Crisis of 1889. Prepared for the Carnegie-Rochester-NYU conference on public policy, mimeo.

Hawtrey, R. G. 1932 *The Art of Central Banking*. London, New York, etc.: Longmans, Green and Co. Kindle Ebook edition.

Herrala, Risto 1999. Banking crises versus depositor crises: The era of the Finnish Markka, 1865–1998. *Scandinavian Economic History Review* 47(2): 5–22.

Hetzel, Robert L. 1987. Henry Thornton: Seminal monetary theorist and father of the modern central bank. *Federal Reserve Bank of Richmond Economic Review* 73(4): 3–16.

Hidy, Ralph W. 1946. Cushioning a crisis in the London money market. *Bulletin of the Business Historical Society* 20(5): 131–145.

Humphrey, Thomas M. 1992. Lender of last resort. In *The Palgrave Dictionary of Money & Finance.*, Eds. Peter Newman, Murray Milgate, and John Eatwell. Vol. 2, 571–573. London and Basingstoke, United Kingdom: The Macmillan Press Limited.

1989. Lender of last resort: The concept in history. *Federal Reserve Bank of Richmond Economic Review* 75(2): 8–16.

James, John A., James McAndrews, and David F. Weiman 2013. Wall Street and main street: The macroeconomic consequences of New York bank suspensions, 1866–1914. *Cliometrica* 7(2)(05): 99–130.

Jefferys, James B. 1946. The denomination and character of shares, 1855–1885. *Economic History Review* 16(1): 45–55.

Jensen, Adolph 1896. A history of banking in the Scandinavian nations. In *A History of Banking in All the Leading Nations, Volume 4*, 1–412. New York: Journal of Commerce and Commercial Bulletin.

Kindleberger, Charles Poor 1984. *A Financial History of Western Europe*. London: Allen and Unwin.

Kindleberger, Charles Poor and Robert Z. Aliber 2011. *Manias, Panics and Crashes: A History of Financial Crises*. Basingstoke: Palgrave Macmillan.

Lovell, Michael C. 1957. The role of the Bank of England as lender of last resort in the crises of the eighteenth century. *Explorations in Entrepreneurial History* 10(1): 8–20.

Lucia, Joseph L. 1985. The failure of the Bank of United States: A reappraisal. *Explorations in Economic History* 22(4)(10): 402–416.

Meltzer, Allan H. 2013. What's wrong with the Fed? What would restore independence? *Cato Journal* 33(3): 401–416.

2003; 2009. *A History of the Federal Reserve*. Chicago: University of Chicago Press.

Minsky, Hyman P. 1982. *Can 'It' Happen Again?* New York: M.E. Sharp.

Mints, Lloyd W. 1945. *A History of Banking Theory in Great Britain and the United States*. Chicago, Ill.: University of Chicago Press.

Mitchell, Wesley C. 1941. *Business Cycles and Their Causes*. A new edition of Mitchell's Business cycles: part III. Berkeley and Los Angeles: University of California Press.

Nelson, Edward 2013. Friedman's monetary economics in practice. *Journal of International Money and Finance* 38(11): 59–83.

O'Brien, Anthony Patrick 1992. The failure of the Bank of the United States: A defense of Joseph Lucia: A note. *Journal of Money, Credit, and Banking* 24 (3)(08): 374–384.

Plessis, Alain 1995. The Bank of France from the early 20th century to the 1950s. In *The Evolution of Financial Institutions and Markets in Twentieth-Century Europe*. Youssef Cassis, Gerald D. Feldman, and Ulf Olsson. Aldershot, Hants and Brookfield, VT: Scolar Press, 9–19.

Reinhart, Carmen M., and Kenneth S. Rogoff 2009. *This Time Is different: Eight Centuries of Financial Folly*. Princeton and Oxford: Princeton University Press.

Rockoff, Hugh. 1986. Walter Bagehot and the theory of central banking. In *Financial Crises and the World Banking System.*, Eds. Forrest H. Capie and Geoffrey E. Wood, 160–180. New York: Macmillan Press, Ltd.

2012. Bagehot, Sprague, Friedman and Schwartz and the Great Depression. In *Internationale Studien Zur Geschicte von Wirtschaft und Gesellschaft*, Ed. Karl Hardach. Vol. 2, 945–972. Frankfurt am Main: Peter Lang.

2013. Adam Smith on money, banking, and the price level. In *Oxford Handbook of Adam Smith*. Eds. Christopher J. Berry, Maria Pia Paganelli, and Craig Smith, 307–332. Oxford: Oxford University Press.

Romer, Christina D. 1990. The Great Crash and the onset of the Great Depression. *The Quarterly Journal of Economics* 105(3): 597–624.

Ryssdal, Kai 2009. Interview with Anna J. Schwartz. In Marketplace, Taking Stock: Lessons from History. June 9. [database online]. Available from www.marketplace .org/topics/business/taking-stock/taking-stock-lessons-history (accessed May 29, 2013).

Sayers, R.S. 1976, *The Bank of England 1891–1944*. Cambridge: Cambridge University Press.

Schularick, Moritz, and Alan M. Taylor 2012. Credit booms gone bust: Monetary policy, leverage cycles, and financial crises, 1870–2008. *American Economic Review* 102(2)(04): 1029–1061.

Schumpeter, Joseph Alois 1954. *History of Economic Analysis*. New York: Oxford University Press.

Schwartz, Anna J. 1986. Real and pseudo-financial crises. In *Financial Crises and the World Banking System.*, Eds. Forrest H. Capie, Geoffrey E. Wood, 11–40. New York: St. Martin's Press.

Smith, Adam 1981 [1776]. *An Inquiry into the Nature and Causes of the Wealth of Nations*, Eds. R. Campbell, A. Skinner. Indianapolis, Indiana: Liberty Fund.

Sorkin, Andrew Ross 2009. *Too Big to Fail: The Inside Story of How Wall Street and Washington Fought to Save the Financial System from Crisis–and Themselves*. New York: Viking. Kindle edition.

Sprague, O. M. W. 1909. The proposal for a central bank in the United States: A critical view. *Quarterly Journal of Economics* 23(3): 363–415.

1910. *History of Crises Under the National Banking System*. U. S. 61st cong., 2d sess. senate. doc. 538. Washington: Govt. Print. Off.

Tamaki, Norio 1995. *Japanese Banking: A History, 1859–1959*. Cambridge: Cambridge University Press.

Temin, Peter. 1976. *Did Monetary Forces Cause the Great Depression?* 1st ed. New York: Norton.

1989. *Lessons from the Great Depression: The Lioncel Robbins Lectures for 1989*. Lionel Robbins lectures. Cambridge, Mass.: MIT Press.

Thomas, Samuel Evelyn 1934. *The Rise and Growth of Joint Stock Banking*. London: Sir I. Pitman and Sons, Ltd.

Thornton, Henry 1807 [1802]. *An Enquiry into the Nature and Effects of the Paper Credit of Great Britain (1802)*. The Google Books Edition ed. Philadelphia: James Humphreys.

Timberlake, Richard H. 1984. The central banking role of clearinghouse associations. *Journal of Money, Credit and Banking* 16(1): 1–15.

Trescott, Paul B. 1992. The failure of the Bank of the United States, 1930: A rejoinder. *Journal of Money, Credit, and Banking* 24(3)(08): 384–399.

U.S. Department of the Treasury. 2013. The Financial Crisis Five Years Later: Response, Reform, and Progress, September 2013, www.treasury.gov/connect/blog/Documents/ FinancialCrisis5Yr_vFINAL.pdf

Vanthoor, Wim 2005. *The King's Eldest Daughter: A History of the Nederlandsche Bank, 1814–1998*. Amsterdam: Boom.

Wheelock, David C. 1991. *The Strategy and Consistency of Federal Reserve Monetary Policy, 1924–1933*. Studies in monetary and financial history. Cambridge England; New York: Cambridge University Press.

White, Eugene N. 2007. "The Crash of 1882 and the Bailout of the Paris Bourse." *Cliometrica* 1(2):115–144.

    2010. *Rethinking the Regulation of Banking: Choices or Incentives?* Rutgers University, Mimeo, December.

Wirth, Max 1874. *Geschichte Der Handelskrisen.* Frankfurt am Main: J. D. Sauerländer's Verlag.

Wood, Geoffrey 2000. The lender of last resort reconsidered. *Journal of Financial Services Research* 18(2/3): 203–227.

7

A Century and a Half of Central Banks, International Reserves, and International Currencies

Barry Eichengreen
University of California, Berkeley

Marc Flandreau
Graduate Institute of International and Development Studies, Geneva

1 Introduction

In an insightful survey written several years ago, Claudio Borio, Gabriele Galati and Alexandra Heath of the Bank for International Settlements reflected on trends in foreign reserve management.[1] They noted that central banks' portfolio management strategies and standards had become increasingly aligned with those of the private asset management industry. Central banks, they concluded, were increasingly concerned with profitability along with other, more traditional motives. Their portfolio managers used many of the same standards and strategies as private fund managers. At the same time that reserve managers sought to balance returns with liquidity and safety, the authors went on, they also exhibited greater transparency and organizational transformations aimed at strengthening internal decision-making. While these trends were visible for their population of central banks, there was also, the authors noted, significant cross-sectional variation in central bank practice.

With the passage of time, these trends have only been reinforced, inasmuch as the financial crisis of 2007 forced central banks to expand their balance sheets further. A related development since 2007 has been the multiplication of foreign exchange swap agreements, principally between

University of California, Berkeley and Graduate Institute of International and Development Studies, Geneva, respectively.

[1] Borio et al. (2008). The benchmark year for their study is 2006. The study resulted from an ad hoc survey of twenty-eight central banks covering 80 per cent of total reserve management.

A Century and a Half of Banks, Reserves, and Currencies   281

the U.S. Federal Reserve System and other central banks, enabling those central banks to extend dollar repo lines to banks and firms and further heightening the importance of managing currency exposures.[2]

In this paper we provide a historical perspective on central bank foreign reserve management, spanning the 150-plus years since the middle of the nineteenth century. Compared to today, the issues surrounding the holding of foreign assets by banks of issue, as central banks were known, were so simple then as to appear almost rudimentary. Until the late nineteenth century, foreign exchange reserves were a minor component of central bank balance sheets. National banks of issue, most of which were privately owned, government-chartered companies, held their international reserve assets principally in the form of bullion warehoused either domestically or abroad. This so-called "reserve" of gold or silver bullion was a guarantee of the value of the banknote circulation. It was a zero-interest-yielding asset, essentially dead weight for the central bank's profit and loss account.

Information on the reserve was deemed of great importance, although not all central banks were forthcoming about their holdings. It was thought to be necessary and desirable to impose regulatory requirements on what could be held as reserves, and where they could be held. The historical image, if we contrast it with modern practice as portrayed by Borio et al. (2008), is not of revenue-seeking asset managers engaging in transactions on international capital markets as part of their search for revenue, but rather of institutions connected to the external sector and other central banks solely through fluctuations in their bullion reserve and the rules of convertibility.

We argue in this paper that this traditional story is too simple. Central banks already possessed some policy room for maneuver even when reserves were held wholly or principally in specie and gold standard rules tied the note circulation to the bullion reserve (Eichengreen and Flandreau 1997 is our distillation of the point). There was an evolution in the reserve management practices in the course of the late nineteenth and twentieth centuries away from holding the reserve entirely in bullion toward holding also foreign exchange reserves and using them to intervene on foreign exchange markets. The result was to transform the ways in which central banks were connected to the global economy over this *longue durée*.

---

[2] Paralleling this, the Federal Reserve has played an important role in shoring up dollar liquidity over and above its normal operations with U.S. financial institutions, including by lending directly to the U.S. subsidiaries of foreign financial institutions.

Although several previous studies have sketched the selected aspects of this story, much remains to be done in terms of tying successive periods together and illuminating longer term economic and institutional developments. Ideally, one would want a consistent panel of central bank balance sheets spanning a long historical period. Unfortunately, much of the relevant data has been lost or remains cloistered in the archives. Some is still regarded as too sensitive to release; other data have been selectively weeded or destroyed. Still, recent literature has made headway in shedding additional light on specific aspects of the long-run history of foreign exchange reserves. This permits us to attempt a systematic narrative account of the subject.

We emphasize three themes. The first theme traces the evolution of the principal reserve assets: sterling before 1914, the rise of the dollar as a competing reserve currency in the 1920s, the retreat of sterling and then the dollar in the 1930s, and finally the persistence of sterling as a reserve asset followed by the dominance of the dollar after World War II. This familiar narrative emphasizes the persistence of reserve currency status (put another way, the advantages of incumbency) but also the scope for challenges (often underestimated) by new reserve units.[3] We provide more detail and nuance on these aspects in what follows.

Our second theme emphasizes the rise of active reserve and portfolio management. The evolution we trace highlights the decades leading up to World War I as a key period when central banks accumulated foreign exchange reserves and began using them, via intervention in the foreign exchange market, in pursuit of a range of objectives. The central banks of Belgium, Austria-Hungary, Portugal, Spain and France emerge as key players in this period.

The interwar years were then a second period of innovation. Additional central banks moved from following relatively mechanical gold standard rules and holding limited foreign exchange reserves, largely in a form linked to the currency of denomination of their governments' foreign borrowings, to more active management of their reserve portfolios.[4] This

---

[3] Again, this is a narrative to which we have contributed in our own work: see Eichengreen and Flandreau (2009) and Eichengreen (2011).

[4] In the earlier period, before 1913, holding foreign reserves in the same currency as foreign borrowings were denominated was a way of hedging foreign exposures and smoothing debt service payments. In the 1920s, these earlier motives survived but were joined by the effort to maximize a combination of safety and return on the portfolio, in a manner reminiscent of modern mean-variance optimization. Or, rather, modern mean-variance of optimization is reminiscent of this earlier central bank practice.

A Century and a Half of Banks, Reserves, and Currencies   283

approach then suffered a setback in the 1930s, when financial volatility spiked and central banks experienced large balance-sheet losses. Not unexpectedly, similar practices were then suppressed after World War II, when capital flows and the international use of national currencies other than the dollar was strictly controlled.

But with the progress of financial and capital account liberalization in the second half of the twentieth century, the earlier trend toward active portfolio management reasserted itself. Recent decades then saw a third key period of transformation when central banks moved further in the direction of active foreign reserve management, adopting practices that resembled those of private financial institutions.

Our third theme is the influence of politics.[5] This link is evident before World War I in the dominance of sterling in the foreign exchange holdings of Britain's formal and informal empires (Mclean 1976). It is evident in the 1920s, when the Bank of England under Montagu Norman and the Federal Reserve System under Benjamin Strong competed in creating spheres of influence for sterling and the dollar (Chandler 1958). It is evident in the 1960s, when liquidation of dollars by the Bank of France reflected the aspirations of the French Republic to reassert its geopolitical influence in the face of American dominance as well as familiar doubts about whether the dollar would hold its value. The question raised by this final theme is whether and how geopolitical considerations might now affect the reserve holding behavior of central banks going forward.

2 The Early History of Central Bank Reserves

The starting point for our narrative is the mid-nineteenth century, when "reserves" (or, more precisely, the "reserve") meant coins and bars made of precious metal.

2.1 Reserves Equal Bullion

The practice of holding reserves grew naturally out of central banks' role as banks of issue. In more economically advanced countries, early modern monetary systems rested on legal tender laws that recognized coins made of gold and/or silver bullion as instruments for settling debts. To the extent

---

[5] As we explain later, this is another traditional theme in the literature on foreign exchange reserve management practices, although we give it a somewhat different spin in what follows.

that a bank of issue was allowed to issue notes without legal tender status, such notes were claims on specie. A critical element, therefore, was ensuring their quality by guaranteeing their convertibility. Convertibility meant that notes could be redeemed at the central bank's window and were thus as good as gold (bullion). For this to work, the central bank had to make good on that commitment. This is the standard explanation for how central banks came to hold reserves in the form of gold and silver.

Rules determining the requisite quantity differed across countries. In Britain and other countries following its example, a fixed amount of free issue was authorized, beyond which every banknote had to be fully backed by reserves (these were countries with so-called fiduciary systems). Alongside there were systems where a maximum ratio of circulation to reserves was specified (so-called proportional systems). There could be further constraints. For example, the 1874 Spanish Law under which the Bank of Spain secured a monopoly of note issue stated that notes could not exceed four times bullion reserves and five times paid-in capital. Martín-Aceña, Martínez-Ruiz and Nogués-Marco (2011) show that in practice this last constraint was the one that bound.

As a result, the asset side of the balance sheet of a typical national bank showed the "reserve" (essentially bullion), a "portfolio" of short-term bills of mainly domestic instruments, and finally other investments such as domestic government and mortgage debts. The liability side showed capital, deposits, retained earnings, profits and the value of outstanding banknotes. Contemporary analysis (e.g. Juglar 1862) suggested that those liabilities should be compared to the reserve to gauge the strength or willingness of the central bank to deliver on its commitments.

An implication of holding reserves in bullion was that central banks, even when they transacted with one another or intervened on the foreign exchange market, transacted with one another mainly in specie. Examples of this were instances of central bank swap lines and credits through which central banks lent reserves to one another (Eichengreen 1992, Flandreau 1997, 2004). Central banks exchanged bullion against bills in domestic currency. Merchant banks stood between the principals and undertook the exchange of, say, francs for sterling.

2.2 The Mystery of Bullion

Reliance on bullion was a technology for delegating authority to the central bank while still maintaining control of its actions. There was no consensus on alternative metrics, beyond the reserve, for measuring central bank

A Century and a Half of Banks, Reserves, and Currencies 285

performance. Specifically, there was no consensus on measuring prices: in the early nineteenth century it was felt that commodity prices were too volatile for index numbers of such prices to constitute a proper target for monetary policy.[6] Ricardo's attacks on the Bank of England during the inconvertible paper currency period that coincided with the French Wars illustrate the concern of early political economists and policy makers about the prospect of a central bank running monetary policy in the absence of proper rules.

Thus, the central bank's mandate was to target the value of the domestic currency in terms of an asset (gold or silver) whose price was readily observable and free of manipulation. The convertibility rule was a monetary policy target (preserving the external value of the currency) similar, in essence if not in methods and objectives, to modern inflation targeting.[7] In practice the target was met by requiring the central bank to buy or sell bullion against notes at prescribed prices. That this target produced stable exchange rates when two or more central banks adopted it was incidental.[8]

This characterization is consistent with the famous British monetary policy debates of the first half of the nineteenth century, with counterparts in other countries, insofar as these can be interpreted as disputes about the optimal contract for central bankers (see Fetter 1965). One view, associated with the Currency School, was that monetary and banking systems would be most resilient if money creation was tied to specie reserves. Members of this school essentially sought to transform the central bank into a currency board and supported the introduction of quantitative targets.

This was opposed by members of the Banking School, who favored a more flexible monetary policy attuned to the liquidity needs of the banking and financial system. As a result, a compromise, Peel's Act, was reached in 1844. This created in the Bank of England an Issue Department separate from a Banking Department. The former was in charge of issuing notes in amounts matching the bullion reserve, after allowing for an unbacked

---

[6] As is evident from the *Bullion Report* and Ricardo's writings. It was not until Fisher (1922) that a measure of consensus regarding the measurement of inflation emerged. See Flandreau (2008) for a survey of historical disputes regarding the proper benchmark of currency depreciation.

[7] Bordo and Kydland (1995) prefer to think of this as a monetary policy rule rather than a target. Given the scope for exceptions (through, inter alia, temporary suspension) we prefer the present terminology.

[8] Just as the tendency for two countries to both pursue explicit inflation-targeting regimes to enjoy relatively stable exchange rates vis-à-vis one another (Eichengreen and Taylor 2004) is incidental.

fiduciary issue of £14 million, while the latter was responsible for discounting bills, i.e. providing short-term secured loans to bankers, to the shadow banking system (leveraged bill brokers like Alexanders and Gurneys), and select commercial customers (Sayers 1976).

The puzzle is why central banks were still reluctant to hold – and were sometimes prevented from holding – foreign exchange reserves. Foreign exchange markets in this period were far from primitive. The practice of holding foreign exchange bills and trading them in distant foreign exchange markets had been routine in banking circles since the Commercial Revolution of the fifteenth and sixteenth centuries. Every financial center of consequence had an active market for bills denominated in foreign currency. It was not unusual for private banks to accept payment in foreign exchange, which yielded positive interest whereas the nominal return on bullion was zero. Since the overwhelming majority of early central banks were privately owned, one would expect the profit motive to have prevailed.

One explanation for why foreign exchange could not be counted toward the statutory reserve is that central banks faced stiff resistance from other banks fearing competition. Central banks were tolerated as necessary sources of market liquidity during crises, but they were not welcome competitors. The example of the Second Bank of the United States, which faced opposition from banking circles and, not incidentally, engaged in the practice of selling foreign exchange to customers, illustrates the point (Bordo, Humpage and Schwartz 2007). Put simply, central banks may have been prevented from including foreign exchange in their portfolios because dominance of this market was a valued prerogative of other banks.

Another explanation is that holding foreign-currency-denominated claims required acquiring information about foreign correspondents, foreign signatures, etc., something that was not the comparative advantage of central banks, in contrast to Rothschilds and Morgans, which could rely on family links and personal connections abroad. That the problem was one of expertise explains why, as indicated earlier, central banks turned to leading private banks (like Rothschild and Morgan) to assist them in market interventions as soon as they went beyond the comparatively simple task of managing a bullion reserve and ascertaining the quality of the financial instruments they discounted and took as collateral.

A third answer is that policy makers remained reluctant to give central banks discretion over risk taking, given their responsibility for the convertibility of the currency. Problems associated with investments in foreign exchange would indeed develop in the interwar years and result in major losses for central banks, in some sense vindicating these earlier concerns.

Contemporaries did not want the central bank taking excessive risk that might jeopardize the value of the currency of which it was the custodian. Profitability was therefore sacrificed in the interest of transparency, security and predictability.

2.3 The Belgian Exception

An innovator from this point of view was the National Bank of Belgium (Conant 1910, Ugolini 2011, 2012). Founded in the aftermath of the 1847–1848 crisis with the goal of stabilizing the Belgian franc, the National Bank engaged from the beginning in the practice of holding foreign exchange reserves. For accounting purposes. its foreign exchange reserves were kept separate from its specie reserve and reported along with domestic bills. When its charter was renewed in 1872, however, the statute was modified, allowing the Bank to hold foreign exchange as part of the official reserve.

The creation of the National Bank exhibited the interplay of competing interests and a general reluctance on the part of powerful discount banks to allow the new bank to compete. Ugolini (2012) describes the "gentleman's agreement" between the government and the Bank, which had the Bank accepting, beyond its obligation to convertibility, a second informal mandate of keeping market interest rates at low levels. Belgium had two active foreign exchange markets, Brussels and Antwerp, that acted as hubs in the European money market. Interest rates were sensitive to changes abroad because of pervasive arbitrage business, resembling the modern carry trade, in which investors shifted from low- to high-return assets (De Cecco 1990, Flandreau 2004). If one wanted to prevent the depreciation and increase in yields on Belgian francs that followed increases in yields abroad, the central bank had to sell foreign exchange and buy francs. But for this to happen, it had to accumulate foreign exchange in the first place. Hence, the modification in its statute.

Ugolini describes the National Bank's reserve portfolio in 1851–1853 as dominated by French francs, British pounds, Dutch guilders and three German currencies (the Hamburg mark banco, Frankfurt guilder and Prussian thaler). While the identity of these currencies is not unexpected, the proportions in which they were held is striking. By far the most important foreign asset was the French franc, reflecting the fact that Belgium and France shared the same specie standard.[9] French francs were

---

[9] Technically, Belgium was silver based, while France was bimetallic. However, Belgium's silver franc was patterned after the French silver franc.

288   *Barry Eichengreen and Marc Flandreau*

the foundation of the National Bank of Belgium's foreign exchange portfolio and were held throughout. The proportions in which other currencies were held were adjusted in response to changes in yields. Interestingly, the pound sterling was only a minor reserve asset and wholly absent from the Bank's portfolio for much of the period.

The National Bank also limited the diversification of its reserve portfolio. From the mid-nineteenth century it committed not to hold inconvertible currencies in its investment portfolio (although such currencies could be posted as collateral by borrowers from the Bank).[10] From 1872, when the Bank was first permitted to include foreign exchange in the reserve, its charter still excluded inconvertible currencies, referring to "valeurs commerciales sur l'étranger, payables en numéraire" ("foreign trade bills, payable in specie"). This illustrates how contemporaries saw guaranteeing the value of the currency in terms of bullion and the holding of inconvertible currencies in the reserve as mutually incompatible.

3 Europe's Lombard Street Moment

For many years, Belgium was praised by economists but without followers. When Japanese policy makers decided to otherwise pattern the statutes of the Bank of Japan after those of the Bank of Belgium, they conspicuously avoided authorizing the inclusion of foreign exchange within the official reserve, even when doing so was recommended in Count Matsukata's expert report in 1882 (Schiltz 2006). However, toward the end of the nineteenth century, and despite the continued ban from the banknote "reserve," foreign exchange nonetheless managed to infiltrate the portfolios of central banks.

3.1 The Rise of Official Reserves before World War I

As described by Lindert (1969), the years leading up to World War I saw a remarkable expansion of the practice of holding foreign exchange reserves. By 1910, the ratio of foreign exchange to gold held by official institutions (including foreign deposits from large holders of foreign reserves such as the Russian government) reached roughly 1:4.[11] In the overwhelming majority of cases, this occurred not by including foreign exchange in statutory reserves but through the accumulation of a separate portfolio.

[10] Ugolini (2011), p. 9.
[11] The figure includes governments.

A *Century and a Half of Banks, Reserves, and Currencies* 289

The dispersion of individual foreign exchange holdings was enormous. Some countries like Britain still did not hold foreign exchange. At the other extreme was the Bank of Japan, now emulating rather than shunning the Belgian example, whose ratio of foreign exchange to gold reserves reached 1:1 circa 1909, a remarkable evolution given that those reserves were not part of the statutory gold reserve and had thus been accumulated despite the absence of any legal requirement or institutional incentive.[12]

The accumulation of foreign exchange reserves centered on the handful of currencies that Lindert labels "key currencies," in descending order of importance: the British pound, the French franc and the German mark, which had exhibited stability in terms of gold (suggesting that the explicit rules that the Bank of Belgium had formulated were implicitly adhered to in other places). These currencies had special status in the international monetary system in that they were traded in the largest number of foreign exchange markets and were most liquid as a result. Analysis of interest rate differentials supports the view (often expressed by contemporaries) that the use of these currencies by institutional investors (public and private) in turn fed back on the liquidity of these currencies in a virtuous circle (Flandreau and Jobst 2005, 2009).

3.2 The Politics of Key Currencies

The rise of key currencies, described here, was supported by a combination of market forces, institutions and, not least, politics. Global trade expanded rapidly in the 1840s and 1850s. Traders made arrangements with correspondent bankers in leading centers where drawing facilities (which provided the ability to source trade credit and deposit receipts) were cheap and reliable. Correspondents securitized the resulting credits as "acceptances" and assisted with their placement and distribution. Money market funds were established to invest in these instruments, giving rise to a large shadow banking system. London and Paris were the leading centers in this process.

The crisis triggered by the failure of an important constituent of this shadow banking system, Overend & Gurney, in 1866 resulted in a liquidity

---

[12] Its balance sheet in late 1909 showed 221 million yen in gold and ingots but a slightly larger amount (242 million yen) held in foreign exchange, including bills and remunerated foreign deposits with correspondents (Lévy 1911, p. 257); The circulation of notes was 352 million, so that the cover ratio strictly defined (monetary liabilities relative to bullion reserves) stood at only 62 per cent.

crisis in London. The crisis was resolved by the Bank of England, which temporarily suspended the convertibility of notes into gold and distributed cash to all who could post adequate collateral. Because the resumption of convertibility was widely anticipated, this action addressed immediate liquidity needs without endangering the exchange rate. The episode heralded the subsequent rise of international currencies subject to complex commitments, rules and options (Bordo and Kydland 1995, Flandreau and Ugolini 2013).

An important document highlighting the political dimension of these arrangements is the circular that the British Foreign Secretary addressed to all diplomatic representatives a few days after the outbreak of the crisis. This asked British agents abroad to convey the message that British authorities were prepared to go to "the utmost of its means" (or, to paraphrase Mario Draghi, to do "whatever it took") to support the money market. The circular characterized the episode as a liquidity crisis and emphasized that the market was sound, its principal participants solvent (Overend & Gurney notwithstanding). When making reference to the generous lending policy of the Bank of England, it emphasized that the policy of the Bank was fully endorsed by Her Majesty's Government, which would secure parliamentary support for further measures if need be.[13] This powerful message signalled unambiguously that when the soundness and continuity of the London market were at stake, the British authorities would not be constrained by formalities.

A second factor supporting the rise of key currencies was the growth of overseas lending. The final decades of the nineteenth century saw an enormous increase in bond flotations on behalf of foreign and colonial borrowers in London, Paris and Berlin. Bonds issued in these centers on behalf of overseas borrowers were predominantly denominated in the currency of the lending country (Flandreau and Sussman 2005). This was a matter of convenience and tradition; it appealed to the domestic clientele of retail investors. When governments and private parties borrowed in, say, London, they incurred a sterling-denominated liability. It thus made sense for their agent, the central bank, to hold sterling-denominated assets as

---

[13] The Circular went on to state: "The Bank of England is prepared to extend relief to the utmost of its means, to all cases which are justly deserving of its support; while Her Majesty's Government, in full reliance on the eventual sanction of Parliament, if it should be necessary to go beyond the law as it now stands, have signified to the Bank of England their permission to hold itself free from the observance of the ordinary limitations on its issues, if the exigencies of the time require such an extraordinary measure" (Patterson 1870).

insurance. These could then be lent to the principals in the event of liquidity problems affecting their ability to meet their interest obligations. In the same way that the growth of foreign trade and foreign exchange reserve holdings went together, the growth of foreign lending and the holding of exchange reserves complemented one another.[14]

Again, political factors supported the connection. While H.M. Government generally took a hands-off policy toward overseas lending, the French and German governments actively promoted such lending as a means of strengthening diplomatic alliances.[15] They were happy to see capital flow to potential allies and for those allies, through their central banks, to in turn hold balances in foreign exchange in Paris and Berlin.

One significant rival to sterling was the French franc, as we saw in the case of Belgium; the same was true in the cases of a number of members of the Latin Union (Switzerland for example). In the years following the Overend & Gurney crisis, Paris as a financial center grew on the back of France's expanding trade and foreign capital exports, low interest rates and abundant gold reserves (Cameron 1961), the last of which enabled the Bank of France to set a narrower gold bid-ask spread than the Bank of England (Flandreau 2004). It almost seemed as if France and the franc were poised to threaten the dominance of sterling.

Thus, the international monetary and financial system might have developed in a rather different direction in the absence of the Franco-Prussian War and the Paris Siege, which disrupted payments and led to a moratorium on the payment of French bills, dealing a blow to Paris' international financial aspirations. Another blow was the extended period of inconvertibility resulting from Germany's adoption of the gold standard and abandonment of the silver standard. In response, the Bank of France set out to stabilize the gold price of the franc. As Bagehot remarked,

The note of the Bank of France has not indeed been depreciated enough to disorder ordinary transactions. But any depreciation, however small — even the liability to depreciation without its reality — is enough to disorder exchange transactions. They are calculated to such an extremity of fineness that the change of a decimal may be fatal, and may turn a profit into a loss. Accordingly London has become the sole great settling-house of exchange transactions in Europe,

---

[14] We give examples of this self-insurance behavior later.
[15] We qualify this view of the British authorities' so-called "hands-off policy" in some respects in Section IV.

292   *Barry Eichengreen and Marc Flandreau*

instead of being formerly one of two. And this pre-eminence London will probably maintain, for it is a natural pre-eminence. The number of mercantile bills drawn upon London incalculably surpasses those drawn on any other European city; London is the place which receives more than any other place, and pays more than any other place, and therefore it is the natural clearing-house.[16]

Thus, those who held sterling bills payable in London knew that, in times of crisis, such bills would always be cashable at the Bank of England, which thereby guaranteed their liquidity. They understood from their response to the Overend & Gurney crisis that officials would ensure, to the best of their ability, that banknotes remained convertible into gold. Sterling was liquid and secure. The readiness with which sterling bills could be cashed made them as good as gold. Indeed, the interest they threw off made them superior. In a famous passage in *Lombard Street* (1873), Bagehot described this mechanism as accounting for the ascent of sterling as the world currency.

The whole liability for such international payments in cash is thrown on the Bank of England. No doubt foreigners cannot take from us our own money; they must send here value in some shape or other for all they take away. But they need not send cash; they may send good bills and discount them in Lombard Street and take away any part of the produce, or all the produce, in bullion. It is only putting the same point in other words to say that all exchange operations are centering more and more in London.

It is important to recall that Bagehot was not just a journalist but also a propagandist for the Liberal Party. He was involved in the political battle aimed at pushing the Bank of England to adopt a more active role in dealing with crises.[17] His claim that London was destined to dominate deliberately neglected the fact that any currency backed by a strong commitment to ensure its stability and liquidity could become a "key currency." Thus, Bagehot did not anticipate, or at least did not wish to acknowledge, that by opening the door to the possibility of substituting for gold another asset with a higher return, sterling might eventually have to contend with competition from not just the French franc but also with the German mark, both of which were found in substantial amounts in the portfolios of official institutions on the eve of World War I. According to Lindert (1969), "while greater balances were held in London than in any other international financial center, a larger share was held in France and

---

[16] Bagehot (1873) pp. 33–35.

[17] This was a theme of *Lombard Street*, which actually led to a dispute with Hankey, a director of the Bank of England, who feared this would encourage moral hazard.

A Century and a Half of Banks, Reserves, and Currencies   293

Germany than has been generally realized. The frequent portrayal of London as the major reserve center before WWI exaggerates somewhat."[18]

4 Pre–World War I Motives for Accumulating Foreign Exchange Reserves

Explanations of the accumulation of foreign reserves have emphasized rising entanglements between politics and money management. Because the export of capital had significant implications for the management of sterling, from the 1890s onward the Bank of England played an increasingly important role in colonial finance. Through Crown Agents and London brokers and via its influence over colonial governments, the Bank sought to restrain capital exports when money was tight and, conversely, to provide inducements to borrow when it was abundant. The ability to follow such still unconventional open market interventions intended to increase the effectiveness of official discount rate changes was evidently a product of Empire – of the leverage which London political and monetary authorities had over overseas borrowers (Sayers 1976, Sunderland 2004).

The result was a close relation with Empire, which de Cecco (1974) served to highlight. In de Cecco's account, this connection resulted from the happy coincidence of the need to manage the convertibility of sterling on a "thin film of gold" with the structural position of the less developed countries under Britain's influence. Members of its formal and informal empires borrowed from London in sterling and warehoused the receipts there. This was convenient since their sterling could be drawn on to service debt and pay for imports. It was also rational from the standpoint of hedging exposures, since sterling balances in London served as an effective hedge against sterling-denominated debts.[19] De Cecco gives a special place to India, emphasizing "the basic importance of India as the main stabilizing element." Through its London deposits, India (and other less advanced

---

[18] Lindert (1969). See also Bloomfield (1963, p. 93). Lindert does not appear to have noted the fact that a substantial part of such holdings could be acquired in domestic money markets. That said, recent work by Flandreau and Gallice on the balance sheet of Banque de Paris et des Pays-Bas, France's largest investment bank and an important repository of foreign exchange deposits from the Russian Government and central bank, shows that this bank recycled its large liabilities (which at one point doubled the size of its balance sheet) through heavy investment in sterling bills. If this pattern was general (if it extended also to other investment banks), then official foreign deposits in francs and marks would have been themselves dependent on private sterling deposits, thus qualifying Lindert's qualification (Flandreau and Gallice 2005).

[19] For more on this see Subsection b in Section IV.

294 *Barry Eichengreen and Marc Flandreau*

countries like Japan) permitted London to act as an intermediary in the short-term capital market.[20]

4.1 Self-Insurance

Another motive for accumulating gold reserves is illustrated by the case of Russia, which was, along with Japan and India, one of the principal holders of foreign exchange in the pre-1914 period. Domestic opposition criticized the maintenance by Russia of short-term deposits in Paris at 2 per cent when the Bank of France's lending rate was 3 per cent and the Paris market was lending to Russia at 4 per cent (Flandreau 2003). In response, the Russian authorities emphasized the perils of the political conditionality to which Russia would be subject if forced to borrow in an emergency. Self-insurance was therefore advisable. The argument thus anticipated on the modern interpretation that saw the accumulation of Chinese reserves in the late 1990s as a response to the Asian crisis (see Aizenman and Lee 2005).

In one of the rationalizations he provided for his government's extensive holding of foreign exchange, Finance Minister Sergei Witte clearly referred, in the language of his time, to the risks of "political conditionality" in a situation of sudden stops:

Generally, needs resulting from political events are unpredictable and when they occur, absolutely urgent. From [which] we can see that, if we did not have [foreign exchange] reserves, we would see ourselves, in such a circumstance, [having] either to sacrifice political interest or to borrow at any price. But then experience shows that states, like individuals, are often offered loans at attractive prices when they have not use for them, while by contrast, regardless of their solvency, they sometimes just can't find resources at an affordable price, when they need [them] urgently. In such situations, the lack of a pecuniary reserve might cause to the State a political prejudice.[21]

Thus, when it comes to the insurance motive for holding foreign reserves (as an alternative to recourse to International Monetary Fund or European Stability Mechanism assistance), there is little new under the sun.

---

[20] But the same argument might be made without reference to India's trade position, in the same fashion as in the monetary approach to the balance of payments, it is the demand for money that drives the current account. Because the predominance of sterling was so important to the British dominions, efforts to shore up the cash position of London were supported by British political authorities, who encouraged the regions under their influence, to hold sterling balances. This provided for the defense of the London market and the rest followed. For a recent study of the organic link between Indian finance, the London money market and Empire see the recent book by Sunderland (2013).

[21] Quoted in Flandreau (2003), p. 46. See this reference for more details on this policy.

4.2 Interest-Rate Smoothing

Studies for Belgium, Austria-Hungary and France point in addition to the utility of foreign exchange reserves as an instrument for smoothing interest rate fluctuations. Historical evidence is indicative of widespread concern over sharp changes in interest rates (Conant 1910, Patron 1910, Einzig 1931, White 1933, Kauch 1950, Bordo and McDonald 2012). Sudden increases in interest rates were unpopular and triggered protests because they were perceived as "depress[ing] business, reduc[ing] trade and production and provok[ing] urban unemployment and possibly unrest" (Reis 2007). A further complaint was that sharp changes in interest rates, especially in the upward direction, had an adverse impact on the price of government bonds.

Fortunately, the gold standard left some room for intervening in the foreign exchange market to smooth such fluctuations. Because shipping gold between markets entailed costs, exchange rates were only fixed up to the cost of shipping gold. Pushing the exchange rate down toward the gold export point created the expectation that it would revert toward the middle of the band; this expectation of subsequent appreciation in turn led investors to accept lower interest rates (Keynes 1930, Eichengreen and Flandreau 1997). Such interest rate effects appear to have been the main reason for the Bank of Belgium's policy of holding foreign reserves and intervening in the foreign exchange market. That its intervention was successful (as manifested in the fact that the secured interest rate on Belgian francs was often lower than rates in other leading markets) encouraged emulation.

One prominent emulator was France. Contamin (2003) shows how interest-rate-smoothing motives explain why the Bank of France began acquiring sterling assets in the Paris foreign exchange market from private banks around the turn of the century. Because sterling paper was the most liquid instrument and was held by all internationally-active banks, liquidity shocks in the London money market that forced the Bank of England to raise its discount rate put pressure on the Bank of France. To prevent this, the Bank of France conducted countercyclical interventions buying sterling when the banks were selling and vice versa (Flandreau and Gallice 2005).

The behavior of the Austrian-Hungarian central bank was not dissimilar. Along with Japan, India and Russia, the Austro-Hungarian bank was one of the key holders of foreign exchange in this period. Von Mises 1909, Einzig (1931), Flandreau and Komlos (2006) and Jobst (2009) describe its foreign exchange policy. It was hailed by interwar economists like Keynes (1930) as an exemplar of successful monetary management for the way it relied on the foreign exchange market and in particular on forward-market intervention in order to avoid having to continually adjust its interest rate to foreign levels.

Flandreau and Koulos (2006) shows that this was done using a range of sophisticated instruments that included forwards and foreign exchange repurchase agreements. When British interest rates rose, the Austro-Hungarian central bank let the florin depreciate against the pound while intervening to push it up in the forward market, thus compensating invest-ors in florins for the lower interest rates and preventing further fluctuations. According to Jobst (2009), for most of the period, the Austro-Hungarian bank was the main participant in the market for foreign exchange, making its operations influential and credible.

4.3 Carry Trades

A third motive for investing in, or borrowing, in foreign exchange reserves may be described using the modern expression "carry trade." This is a trading strategy that relies on the observed failure of the currency of the country with the lower interest rate to appreciate over time so as to eliminate deviations from open interest parity. Central banks repeatedly attempted to exploit this inefficiency, borrowing currencies bearing low interest rates in order to invest in others bearing higher rates. Reis (2007) describes how the Bank of Portugal borrowed in London at relatively low interest rates. In order to avoid a drain on its gold reserves, it sold drafts on London at a discount (the equivalent of receiving deposits in sterling), in effect borrowing foreign reserves. Once the draft was sold, the Bank could invest the proceeds in Portugal, where interest rates were higher. Drawing foreign exchange permitted it to avoid curtailing credit (as would have been the case if bullion had been sold, since cover ratio rules would have become binding, forcing a reduction in the money supply).[22]

Martinez-Ruiz and Nogués-Marco (2014) suggest that the Bank of Spain did something similar in periods of domestic stringency such as 1882 and 1889–1891, when it borrowed foreign exchange from the Banque de Paris et des Pays-Bas instead of using its reserves. Foreign bills paid 3.25 per cent

---

[22] The technique of drawing in London to invest in Portuguese securities might be described as an early case of the carry trade, this time however implemented by monetary authorities themselves.

A Century and a Half of Banks, Reserves, and Currencies   297

at a time when Spanish interest rates were around 5 per cent. Thus, so long as the exchange rate remained stable, borrowing foreign exchange was profitable. Given the high interest rates that characterized so-called "peripheral" countries and may have resulted either from credibility or from liquidity problems in the periphery (as argued by Bordo and Flandreau 2003), similar central bank-led carry trades must have been considerable elsewhere as well and ought to retain the attention of future researchers.[23]

5 The Rise and Fall of Genoa

The 1920s and 1930s were pivotal decades for foreign reserve management by central banks. The period saw the rise and fall of the so-called gold exchange standard. The idea of replacing the gold standard with a gold exchange standard, building on pre-war experience with key currencies, was fully articulated at the Genoa Conference in 1922.[24] The Financial Commission of the conference, presided over by British Chancellor of the Exchequer Sir Robert Horne, considered remedies for the perceived dangers of global deflation. The war and its aftermath had seen considerable monetary creation: return to the pre-war order implied "tapering" and, by implication, deflation and associated pressures, including unemployment. This was not an appetizing prospect for Western powers haunted by the specter of the Bolshevik Revolution.

Along with this general concern with the future of Western capitalism were specific British concerns that reestablishing a gold standard along pre-war lines would make it difficult for London to regain its position as a financial center. Forced to adopt austerity measures, Britain would have to discourage capital exports and the provision of trade finance to foreign customers, opening the door to new competition from the United States.

This is how the Genoa Conference was led to reimagine the pre-war gold standard as having sowed the seeds of a superior gold exchange standard now to be implemented (Nurkse 1944, p. 29). The key innovation lay in the attempt to systematize how foreign exchange reserves were handled and codifying earlier ad hoc practices. Resolution 9 of the report of the Financial Commission declared that the aim of the convention would be to

---

[23] See also Mitchener and Weidenmier (2015).

[24] The League of Nations was prominently involved in promoting the gold exchange standard, and we owe to the League's de facto chief economist Ragnar Nurkse the first post-mortem of the system (Nurkse 1944; see also Fior 2008 and Biltoft 2014).

"centralize and coordinate the demand for gold, and so avoid those wide fluctuations in the purchasing power of gold which might otherwise result from the simultaneous and competitive efforts of a number of countries to secure metallic reserves." Resolution 11 stated that the "maintenance of the currency at its constant gold value must be assured by the provision of an adequate gold reserve of approved assets, not necessarily gold."[25]

It may be an exaggeration to speak of a "Genoa Order" because, like so many other expert recommendations of the time, the agreements of the members of the Financial Commission fell to pieces subsequently. That said, many of the ideas had an enduring impact. The effect of Genoa was visible in financial stabilization programs adopted under the auspices of the League of Nations in the 1920s. In Austria, Danzig, Hungary, Bulgaria, Estonia and Greece, League of Nations "packages" included newly created or reorganized central banks with statutes that authorized them to hold foreign exchange as a component of their reserves (League of Nations 1932, Clavin 2013).

5.1 The Mlynarski Dilemma

The gold exchange standard envisaged at Genoa had inherent contradictions, including one that came to be known later as the "Triffin dilemma," after the Belgian economist Robert Triffin (1947), who leveled the same critique against the dollar-based Bretton Woods System. In the 1920s and 1930s the argument was identified with Feliks Mlynarski, the Polish-born economist and affiliate of the Financial Committee of the League of Nations, who pointed to it in Mlynarski (1929). Under the gold exchange standard, Mlynarski noted, the gold supply problem was simply replaced by the confidence problem. This confidence problem would inevitably arise when foreign exchange reserves grew large relative to the gold stocks of the key-currency central banks, exposing the latter to the equivalent of a bank run. But it could arise even earlier as a result of instability on the London and New York markets and associated policy uncertainty, as events would soon reveal.

Austrian stipulations regarding which currencies the central bank could hold provide a case in point. Austrian statute stated that foreign currencies held as reserves would have to be not just convertible but also stable and liquid. The statutes adopted in the 1920s permitted investment in inconvertible currencies but allowed only "foreign currencies which have not undergone any violent fluctuation of exchange" to be counted as part of

[25] Nurkse (1944), p. 28.

A Century and a Half of Banks, Reserves, and Currencies 299

the cash reserve (Kisch and Elkin 1928, pp. 163–164). This was both a weakening and a continuation of the logic pioneered by Belgium some 70 years earlier when inconvertible currencies were shunned as components of the reserve but admitted as collateral.

The emphasis of Austrian lawmakers on "currencies which have not undergone any violent fluctuation of exchange" suggests that foreign exchange accumulation was not conceived as asset diversification but as an indirect way of holding gold. By the 1920s the architects of central bank statutes could look to many examples of how convertibility promises could and had been broken.[26] Hence only countries with the strongest commitment to convertibility could aspire to the status of reserve centers. The result was a hierarchical international monetary order. As envisaged in the Genoa Report, certain of the participating countries would come to "establish a free market in gold and thus become gold centers." These special countries would peg their currencies to gold, whereas the rest of the world in turn would peg to those currencies. The Bretton Woods System after World War II in which the dollar was pegged to gold while other currencies were pegged to the dollar was a lineal descendent of the Genoa order.

The contrasting composition of reserves in different countries illustrates the implications. In late 1929, at the height of the gold exchange standard, the proportion of foreign exchange in the reserves of twenty-four countries that did not produce a key currency stood at 37 per cent.[27] In contrast, the Bank of England held foreign exchange equal to only 11 per cent of its combined gold and foreign exchange holdings (and foreign exchange holdings were not allowed to be included in the statutory reserve). The typed forms on which the Bank of England recorded its foreign exchange holdings listed only two foreign exchange entries: "French franc securities" and "dollar investments." (And the fact that they were typed suggests that the recorders did not expect this to change.) Dollar investments, moreover, made up fully 99 per cent of Bank of England's foreign exchange as of late 1929.[28] The Federal Reserve, for its part, held negligible quantities of

---

[26] A case in point was that of Serbian bonds. Serbian bonds had been issued in francs before World War I with the understanding that this meant gold francs, although bond covenants were not explicit about this matter. After the war, the Serbian authorities had taken advantage of the depreciation of the French franc to reimburse the bonds in paper francs, leading bondholders to litigate (Wälde 2004).

[27] Nurkse (1944) p. 235.

[28] Sayers (1976), 349ff. Archive of the Bank of England. The very limited role of the French franc as a reserve currency in this period is further documented, for other countries, by Eichengreen and Flandreau (2009).

foreign exchange. This, then, was a profoundly asymmetric system, again anticipating Bretton Woods. In the republic of currencies, some currencies were more equal than others.

5.2 The Leverage Cycle

A powerful pro-cyclical dynamic was built into this system. During expansions, non-key currency central banks happily accumulated sterling and dollars, allowing them to expand their money supplies, while the key currency countries did nothing to contract theirs. During contractions, when doubts might arise about the stability of key currencies, there was a tendency to flee to gold. Non-key-currency countries would present their foreign exchange and demand gold from reserve-currency central banks in return, putting pressure on the reserves of the latter and, in turn forcing them to raise interest rates. The central banks of the key-currency countries were thus in no position to play a countercyclical role like that of the Federal Reserve System starting in 2008. The result was not unlike the leverage cycle emphasized by Geanakoplos (2009), where improvements in the quality of collateral led to increases in leverage and credit, although central banks rather than commercial banks were at the center of this particular story.

The dilemmas of the gold exchange standard were evident in the behavior of the largest of all non-key currency central banks, the Bank of France, which had not entirely given up hope of regaining its pre–World War I status. The presence of its currency in the ledgers of the Bank of England and the books of Paul Einzig suggest that some took this possibility seriously.[29] Since such ambitions required following the example of the United States and Britain, the stabilization law of 1928 therefore defined reserves as comprising solely gold, although the Bank of France also held very large amounts of foreign exchange beyond the statutory gold reserve (Bouvier 1989, Mouré 2002).[30]

Holding reserves exclusively in gold was the hallmark of a key-currency country. At the same time, accumulating sterling and dollars was tempting, for it promised financial returns. Torn between these objectives, the Bank of France alternated between accumulating foreign exchange and seeking to liquidate its holdings. After having held at one point nearly half of

---

[29] See Einzig (1931) and, further, Myers (1936).
[30] For a view emphasizing Gallic incompetence and malice, see Johnson (1997) and Irwin (2012).

A Century and a Half of Banks, Reserves, and Currencies

world's foreign exchange reserves, the Bank ended up incurring large losses when Britain abandoned the gold standard in 1931 before French central bank could dispose of its sterling (Accominotti 2009).

5.3 Market Liquidity as a Two-Edged Sword

The Bank of France's losses were not unique, Belgium and the Netherlands being other cases in point. Gone now were the dull days of the nineteenth century when the bulk of Western foreign exchange transactions took place within the narrow margins of the gold points. Even then there had been excitement in markets for so-called "peripheral" currencies, such as the Austro-Hungarian florin in the 1870s or the Argentine peso in the 1890s. But these problems were essentially limited to the local market (Vienna and Buenos Aires respectively). In addition, the forward market existed to provide hedging instruments that investors could use to protect themselves (Flandreau and Komlos 2006).[31]

But now the markets developed further, as did the risks. Atkin (2005) argues that the expansion of trading on the foreign exchange market in centers like London was the proximate source of the rise of exchange rate volatility. Traders there would periodically line up on one or the other side of the market. Variations over short intervals could be substantial. These variations increased the value of immediate settlement services, providing the basis for the growth of the telegraphic transfers that increasingly dominated the market. This transformation also enabled commercial banks, with their networks of foreign branches, to participate in a market previously dominated by investment banks. This evolution also increased the demand for hedging and generalized the availability of forward exchange instruments (Einzig 1937) and foreign exchange options (Mixon 2009). A consequence was that shorting currencies became easier. Not for the last time, financial development proved to be a two-edged sword from the point of view of financial stability.

Central banks ignored this at their peril. Foreign exchange market intervention was frequent in the 1920s (Chlepner 1927, Van der Vee and Tavernier 1975, Blancheton and Maveyraud 2009). Central banks intervened to prepare the market for loans, to counter speculation and to push

---

[31] The experience of Russia in the early 1890s also provides evidence that foreign exchange markets were by no means irrelevant: the development in Berlin of a forward market had led Russian authorities to launch their famous "ruble bear squeeze" to discourage speculation against the Russian currency (Raffalovich 1891).

the exchange rate toward their targets. Intervention took the forms of standing orders in the spot market, sales and purchases on the forward market and quasi "currency repos," the combination of spot sales and forward repurchases, or vice versa, as in the case of Austria's "Kostdevisen" (Einzig 1937, Eichengreen and Flandreau 2009, p. 409). Bank of France Governor Emile Moreau's memoirs describe how in 1926 foreign exchange trader Léon Verdier was loaned to the Bank of France by a commercial bank to organize a foreign exchange department to handle these operations (Moreau 1954, p. 103).[32]

5.4 Fiscal Implications

A complication, which will also be familiar to observers of the modern scene, was the interaction of treasuries and central banks over foreign exchange policy. During World War I, treasuries increased their control of foreign exchange markets. The long-run goal was in principle a "retreat" of political supervision, but governments remained reluctant to surrender all authority to the central bank, which was in the majority of cases still a private institution. Exchange control had become part of the standard arsenal of economic policy. At a minimum, treasuries continued to monitor developments in this area.

Until de facto stabilization of the franc in 1926, which led to the creation of a foreign exchange department, as noted earlier, the Bank of France needed the agreement of the Treasury in order to intervene in the foreign exchange market and was regularly prevented from doing so. Intervention took a hybrid form involving the Bank of France, the Treasury (which held foreign exchange as a result of earlier foreign loans) and private banks, where the latter executed the actual interventions. Only in 1926 was a framework established enabling the Bank to purchase foreign exchange, and even then the Treasury retained power of authorization.

The Treasury was reluctant to surrender authority in part because it shared the profits from investing in foreign securities (Mouré 2002). The same mechanism came into play in reverse when the Bank of France suffered losses in the sterling crisis of 1931 and had to be recapitalized by the Treasury (Accominotti 2009). Similar conflicts help to explain the subsequent creation of Exchange Equalization Accounts in Great Britain, United States, Switzerland, Netherlands, Belgium, France and other

---

[32] Until that date, the Bank of France operated through Lazards in New York. See Blancheton and Maveyraud (2009).

A *Century and a Half of Banks, Reserves, and Currencies* 303

countries where the consequences of exchange rate uncertainty were now dealt with directly by the fiscal authorities. Governments used technical pretexts to justify the transfer of responsibility. Economists emphasized instead that the exchange rate, being a matter of general interest, should be managed by the government.[33]

The modern debate on the fiscal effects of asset purchases thus has a twentieth century precedent in this dispute over the management of foreign exchange reserves. The lesson policy makers derived from the 1930s was that the stakes of reserve and exchange rate management were too high for the policy to be delegated to central bankers. Thus, we see here the roots of modern practice in countries like the United States, where monetary policy is the domain of the central bank but foreign exchange policy is the responsibility of the treasury, with all the resulting tensions and contradictions.

5.5 The Sterling Area

Whereas previous authors argued that it was not until after World War II that the dollar overtook sterling as the leading reserve currency, more recent research, including our own (Eichengreen and Flandreau 2009) has shown that already in the 1920s the dollar challenged sterling as a reserve currency. The newly created Federal Reserve System worked actively to create a liquid market in internationally accepted dollar credits (Eichengreen and Flandreau 2012). U.S. commercial banks were authorized to branch abroad for the first time by the provisions of the Federal Reserve Act. This helped them to develop a market in dollar denominated bonds (Chitu, Eichengreen and Mehl 2012). Investment banks like J.P. Morgan were enlisted to sell the U.S. tranche of stabilization loans under the Dawes Plan to retail investors in the United States. London was by no means ready to abandon this market, although current-account problems led, the Treasury and Bank of England to embargo foreign capital calls at various points in the 1920s, encouraging borrowers to look elsewhere.

The 1931 sterling crisis was a defining moment. It conferred large losses on holders of sterling (official as well as private) and cooled attitudes toward holding foreign exchange. Yet the effects of the crisis on the international status of sterling were paradoxical. Sterling's depreciation, after the sharp

---

[33] Others argued that treasuries, being subjected to even less public scrutiny and disclosure than central banks, were in a better position to outsmart the market. See Polejina (1939), Pumphrey (1942) and Howson (1980).

304 *Barry Eichengreen and Marc Flandreau*

initial drop, was not disorderly, and investors soon began betting on sterling's appreciation. There was a notable absence of bank failures and liquidity problems in London. Another casualty of the sterling crisis was the credibility of the dollar's peg to gold (Accominotti 2009). Given the clouds over other currencies, including the dollar and the currencies of the gold bloc, it remained attractive to peg to sterling, which in turn strengthened the incentive to hold sterling balances. Amidst the general retreat from foreign exchange reserves, sterling actually managed to strengthen its position, now principally in the Dominions and Sterling Area.[34]

The Sterling Area provided a favorable combination of stability and flexibility. Channeling the views of the Banking School, the British financial system remained biased towards expansion while at the same time offering facilities to back-stop the currency and deal with crises. This attractive package was embraced where there were powerful banking constituencies with vested interests in the prosperity of the City (as in the Dominions) and in Scandinavia where the lessons of the interwar period were already digested, leading to the understanding that there were other, better focal points for central bankers than the price of gold (Jonung 1979).

As summaries of these developments, Figures 7.1 through 7.3 show Hirschman-Herfindahl indices for holdings of gold and foreign exchange by various countries (where an index of 1 means zero diversification: the lower the index, the higher the diversification). At one end of the spectrum were countries skeptical of the benefits of diversification in the early 1920s and still in the 1930s. For them, the gold exchange standard was a short-lived and not very happy episode of diversification. At the other end were the countries that joined the Sterling Area; they had been early reserve diversifiers well before the Sterling Area was formed.

6 Bretton Woods and After

The Bretton Woods System, as we have seen, was a lineal descendent of the gold exchange standard envisaged in Genoa. The key currency, now the

---

[34] Encouraging the creation of central banks was another mechanism for repatriating New York deposits to London. Canada was a case in point. While Canadian banks customarily relied on New York for foreign exchange services, the creation of the Bank of Canada and its cajoling by the Bank of England led this institution to hold the bulk of its reserves in London, although it was initially pointed out that the British suggestion that the Bank of Canada should hold its reserves in gold and foreign exchange, "without specifying any minimum in gold, and at a time when the devaluation of major currencies had made holding their assets hazardous" (Cain 1996 pp. 350–351). For the official British view on the subject, see Curtis (1934).

A Century and a Half of Banks, Reserves, and Currencies

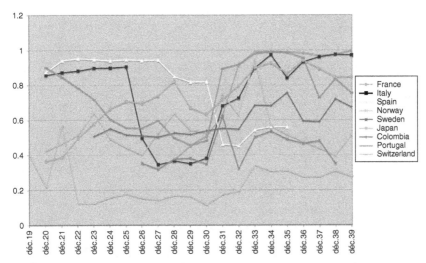

Figure 7.1. Herfindahl-Hirschman Indices for External Assets (Gold+FX): Various Countries
(H-H is computed as sum of squared shares in total external reserves)
Source: Authors' computations from Authors' Database

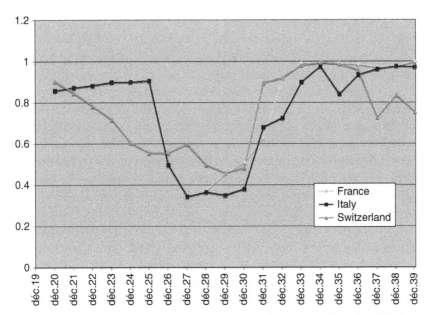

Figure 7.2. Herfindahl-Hirschman Indices for External Assets (Gold+FX): Gold Bloc
Source: Authors' computations from Authors' Database

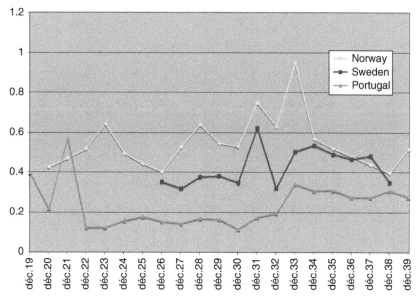

Figure 7.3. Herfindahl-Hirschman Indices for External Assets (Gold+FX): Sterling Countries
Source: Authors' computations from Authors' Database

dollar, was convertible into gold (now exclusively for official foreign holders), while other currencies were convertible into dollars, and central banks other than the Federal Reserve were encouraged to hold their reserves not just in gold but in key currency form. Key currency form meant dollar form, since only the dollar was freely traded in deep and liquid markets open to international investors, official as well as private.

The system in practice was not as simple or uniform as implied by the capsule description of the preceding paragraph. Much as in the earlier gold standard era, different countries used different instruments and intermediaries to intervene in the foreign exchange market. An example is Belgium, which operated a dual or two-tier foreign exchange market for much of the period, buying and selling foreign exchange at the official price (par value) to finance transactions on current account but allowing agents to transact at a market-determined "free rate" for permitted capital account transactions. At the same time, the National Bank adjusted policy to limit the differential between the free and official rates and hence the scope for arbitrage.

Another example was Canada, which operated a floating exchange rate from 1950 to 1962. Not free floating, however; the Canadian authorities regularly adjusted policy in response to exchange rate movements and, in

A Century and a Half of Banks, Reserves, and Currencies 307

extreme instances, intervened in the foreign exchange market (Bordo, Gomes and Schrembi 2010).

This system was subject to the same contradictions as its 1920s predecessor, in the form of the Triffin née Młynarski dilemma. The decision for reserve managers was in what proportions to hold gold and dollars. Once U.S. foreign monetary liabilities exceeded U.S. gold reserves in the early 1960s, the incentive was to shift from dollars to gold to avoid 1931-like capital losses on the former. This in turn threatened to precipitate the very crisis and collapse of the system that reserve managers and other policy makers presciently feared.

Or so goes the textbook story. The reality was more complex. First, in the aftermath of World War II, the vast majority of global foreign exchange reserves – as much as 85 per cent – were in fact in the form of sterling. This accounts for the relatively high value of the Hirschman-Herfindahl Index coming immediately following the war (see figure 7.4).[35] The disproportion reflected less the attractions of sterling in the 1930s (see Section IV) than the accumulation of balances by Britain's Commonwealth, Empire and allies during World War II, which they acquired to help finance their joint war effort. At the war's conclusion, overseas sterling was more than £3.5 billion, nearly six times the British government's gold and dollar reserves.[36]

The majority of these balances were, necessarily, blocked. That is, they could be sold only to finance imports from other members of the Sterling Area if at all (Shannon 1950, Schenk 1994). Moral suasion was applied to foreign governments and central banks. Starting in October 1946, the British government signed a series of agreements with non-Sterling Area countries that permitted only newly earned sterling (not existing balances) to be freely converted into dollars.

These arrangements then gave way to a set of four formalized arrangements designed to maintain the usefulness of sterling, and therefore its reserve currency role, while at the same time preventing wholesale liquidation. Members of the Sterling Area were free to use sterling to settle payments among themselves, subject only to local controls on capital account transactions. Similarly, sterling held by so-called Transferable Account economies was not convertible into U.S. dollars or any other

---

[35] The HH index is computed as above. the normalized version adjusts the raw series for changes over time in the number of currencies included in the index.

[36] And nearly a third of U.K. GDP. Overseas liabilities fall to half the government's gold and dollar reserves if the hard currency provided by the American loan agreement is included.

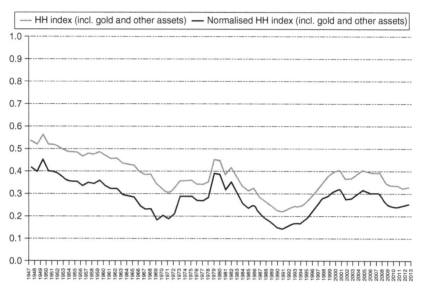

Figure 7.4. Herfindahl-Hirschman Indices for External Assets (Gold+FX): World
Source: Authors compilations from Authors' Database

currency, although countries with Transferable Accounts were free to use sterling to transfer payments among themselves as well as with members of the Sterling Area. American Account economies (the United States and other mainly Western Hemispheric members of the dollar bloc) were able to negotiate more far-reaching concessions: they were free to convert their sterling into dollars and to use it to settle payments among themselves as well as with members of the sterling area. At the other extreme, so-called Bilateral Account countries could use sterling to settle payments with another country only with the express permission of the Bank of England.[37] The nature of these arrangements reflected both the perceived danger of conversion (members of the Sterling Area with a historical allegiance to Britain were thought unlikely to engage in such practices, but Bilateral Account countries were a different matter), as well as the negotiating leverage of the foreign countries in question (as with the very different treatment of American Account and Transferrable Account countries).

Interest rates on these British liabilities were artificially suppressed insofar as the demand for sterling reserves was supported by these blocking measures. Although central bank reserve portfolios were still dominated by sterling as late as the Korean War, to see this as the persistence of a

---

[37] Schenk (1994), pp. 8–9.

A Century and a Half of Banks, Reserves, and Currencies 309

sterling-centered international monetary system would be a misapprehension. Sterling balances were a dead weight on central bank reserve portfolios, which managers would have shed had they been able to do so, not an active element in the monetary system.

The dollar was not subject to analogous restrictions. Already the key source of global liquidity, after 1953 it overtook sterling as the largest component of central bank reserve portfolios. The immediate postwar dollar shortage – the difficulty that other countries, especially in Europe, had in attempting to earn dollars – was overcome by the 1949 devaluations (Kindleberger 1950, Eichengreen 1993). Thereafter the accumulation of dollar reserves proceeded apace. Restrictions on the use of sterling balances were progressively relaxed, and central banks engaged in their orderly liquidation. "Group Arrangements" were negotiated in 1966, 1968 and 1977, under which central banks pledged lines of credit to limit the impact of flight from sterling. Responding to pressure from other central banks, the United Kingdom agreed in 1968 to guarantee the dollar value of 90 per cent of the reserves of other countries, with the goal of forestalling flight from sterling.

The result, as Schenk (2010) describes, was the relatively orderly decline of sterling as a reserve currency, albeit not without periods of turbulence and even crises along the way. But the key point for present purposes is that central bank reserve managers were constrained in optimizing the share of sterling in their portfolios as late as the 1970s by this combination of regulatory restraints, policies and politics. They were not able to engage in active reserve management.

In the absence of other alternatives, the key decision in the 1950s and 1960s, the latter especially, was the proportions in which to hold dollars and gold. Here too there were constraints: contemporaries were aware of the collective action problem whereby a decision by one central bank to convert dollars into gold might provoke a run on U.S. gold reserves that collapsed the Bretton Woods gold-dollar system. Moral suasion was used to encourage central banks to maintain their dollar balances. Geopolitics – the U.S. commitment to defend its Western German ally against aggression from the east – was invoked to encourage compliance by the Bundesbank and the Federal Republic. A gold pooling arrangement was negotiated under which other governments (those of Belgium, France, Germany, Italy, the Netherlands, Switzerland and the United Kingdom), acknowledging their collective interest in a solution, agreed to reimburse the United States for a portion of its gold losses.[38] The gold pool did not survive France's withdrawal in 1967. But it put off the day of reckoning.

---

[38] The gold pool is described and analyzed by Eichengreen (2007).

These measures were designed to support the operation of the system while a successor was under negotiation. There was the agreement to create Special Drawing Rights to supplement dollar reserves in 1968, but their issuance was too little, too late. There was discussion of a Substitution Account to retire dollar balances in the portfolios of central banks and replace them with SDR-like instruments, but no action was taken. The result was a continued increase in the share of dollars in the portfolios of central banks, not just in the latter part of the 1960s but as late as 1977, when the share of dollar reserves peaked at close to 80 per cent of global foreign exchange reserves. The ascent of the dollar was not interrupted, to the surprise of contemporaries, by the collapse of the Bretton Woods System in 1971–1973. As Hori (1986) described, "after adjusting for factors which affect the currency composition of global exchange reserves but which are unrelated to changes in countries' currency preferences, there was no large-scale diversification out of dollars into other currencies during the period under review by groups of countries. In the 1970s the adjusted proportion of dollar holdings in their foreign exchange reserves remained virtually unchanged..." Indeed the dollar's subsequent ascent de-diversification was strikingly steady if Eurodollars are included along with conventional dollar reserves (again, see Figure 7.4).

An important force supporting the dollar in the post–Bretton Woods period was the absence of alternatives. Britain had chronic economic and financial problems; the final liquidation of sterling as a reserve currency began around 1970 and was complete by 1976, the occasion of yet another sterling crisis (Burk and Cairncross 1992). After 1972 the deutchmark was a more important component of reserve portfolios than sterling, but that was not saying much. The German authorities resisted rapid international-ization of their currency, fearing that foreign demand might somehow undermine domestic inflation control (Tavlas 1990). Starting in 1970 they introduced a higher reserve ratio on the growth of German banks' liabil-ities to nonresidents as a way of discouraging foreign holdings of deutsch-marks. This was then followed in 1972 by a cash deposit requirement of 40 per cent on most types of new credits by nonresidents to German nonbanks (where the cash deposit, held by the Bundesbank, did not bear interest). Variants of this measure remained in place through 1974. In addition, from mid 1972 through early 1974 the federal government permitted nonresidents to purchase fixed-interest deutschmark securities only with prior authorization.

Similarly, the Japanese authorities resisted yen internationalization, fearing that the financial liberalization it entailed might constrain their

A Century and a Half of Banks, Reserves, and Currencies 311

conduct of industrial policy.[39] The capital account of the balance of payments remained strictly controlled; upon joining the OECD in 1964, Japan maintained exceptions ("reservations") to 18 items in the organization's Code of Liberalization. Throughout the 1970s, the finance ministry retained the authority to order the modification or cancellation of overseas lending and cross-border issuance of securities, both domestically and abroad, when it judged that the transaction would have an adverse impact on the economy.[40] When the Japanese finally turned to financial liberalization in the 1980s, the result was an asset bubble, a bust and a banking crisis, which hardly enhanced the yen's attractions as a reserve unit.[41]

Markets in other currencies, meanwhile, were too small and/or illiquid to much change this global picture. Consequently, to the extent that there was active reserve management in this period, it was reserve management at the margin. There were only limited opportunities to diversify out of dollars in favor of other currencies. The story of continuing dollar dominance is less first mover advantage, incumbency or persistence (as the point is variously put) than the failure of policy makers in other countries to offer alternatives.

The creation in 1999 of the euro, a currency with the scale, stability and liquidity necessary to function as a first-class reserve unit, had the capacity to transform this state of affairs. But Figure 7.4 shows that this does not translate in a rise in overall diversification. Starting in 2010, the Eurozone descended into crisis. It is not inconceivable that Europe will draw a line under its crisis and that the euro will reclaim its place as a first-class international and reserve currency. But neither does this prospect seem eminent.

The other runner in this race is the Chinese renminbi. Chinese policy makers are serious about internationalizing their currency and enhancing its attractions as an international unit of account, means of payment and store of value, all preconditions for making it a more attractive form of international reserves. While they are making progress, they also face challenges. Currency internationalization requires capital account liberalization, and capital account liberalization is a process fraught with risks and difficulties. Successful currency internationalization also requires the maintenance of economic and financial stability; currently, doubts about

---

[39] For details see Bakker and Chapple (2002).
[40] Details are in Aramaki (2006).
[41] For an overview see Taguchi (1992).

this center on the country's shadow banking system. Successful currency internationalization requires developing the deep and liquid financial markets; currently, Chinese financial markets remain illiquid by the standards of the United States.

Finally, attracting foreign investors, official as well as private, requires convincing them that contract enforcement is reliable and that China abides by rule of law. Those foreign investors will want to see, inter alia, an independent central bank and independent financial regulator. In other words, China still has a lot of work to do before the renminbi has the capacity to change the picture in Figure 7.4.

7 Conclusion

The reserve management practices of central banks increasingly resemble those of private financial institutions. This resemblance manifests itself in seminars and training programs that offer official reserve managers tuition in portfolio optimization techniques. The World Bank runs a Reserve Advisory Management Program to advise national officials in investment policy, guidelines and strategic asset allocation "to control risks...while earning a competitive market return."[42] Global banks run conferences to educate reserve managers in private sector techniques, while at the same time advertising their availability to book the resulting trades.

Around the world, central bank reserve managers report investing in a wider range of non-traditional currencies, such as Australian and Canadian dollars, and riskier assets, including even equities (Pringle and Carver 2013). But investing in equities, even equity indices, is perceived as risky, and the majority of central banks remain reluctant to go too far down this road. The installed base of Canadian and Australian dollars and other nontraditional reserve currencies is small.

In sum, reserve managers aspire to diversify and trade more actively but are constrained by the limited availability of assets to trade and add to their portfolio. Age-old problems of risk, responsibility and liability, which had led in the nineteenth century to efforts to restrict the "investment mandate" of central banks, still linger. Trading and diversification still occur only on the margin, and the effect of the subprime crisis has been to highlight the resulting shortage of safe assets into which official reserve managers can diversify.

---

[42] Quoted from the RAMP website (http://treasury.worldbank.org/sip/htm/ramp_africa .html).

A Century and a Half of Banks, Reserves, and Currencies 313

The emergence of meaningful rivals to the dollar, whether the euro and the renminbi or something else, and experience with investing in alternatives to fixed-income securities, whether equities or something else, may change this situation over time. But the history of central bank reserve management has also involved disappointments. That history leaves open the question of whether the transition will go smoothly or, like the Bank of France with its portfolio of foreign assets in 1931, reserve managers will learn the hard way about the risks of their strategy.

References

Accominotti, Olivier (2009), "The Sterling Trap: Foreign Reserves Management at the Bank of France, 1928–1936," *European Review of Economic History* 13(3), pp. 349–376.

(2012), "London Merchant Banks, the Central European Panic, and the Sterling Crisis of 1931," *Journal of Economic History* 72 (1), pp. 1–43.

Aizenman, Joshua and Jaewoo Lee (2005), "International Reserves: Precautionary vs. Mercantilist Views, Theory and Evidence," IMF Working Paper no. 05–198 (October).

Aramaki, Kenji (2006), "Sequencing of Capital Account Liberalization: Japan's Experiences and their Implications to China," *Public Policy Review* 2, pp. 177–231.

Atkin, John (2005), *The Foreign Exchange Market of London: Development since 1900*, London: Routledge.

Bagehot, Walter (1873), *Lombard Street. A Description of the Money Market*, London: King.

Baillie, Richard and Young-Wook Han (2002), "Central Bank Intervention and Properties of the 1920s Currency Markets," unpublished manuscript, Michigan State University and City University of Hong Kong (April).

Bakker, Age and Bryan Chapple (2002), "Advanced Country Experiences with Capital Account Liberalization," Occasional Paper no. 214, Washington, D.C.: IMF (September).

Biltoft, Carolyn (2014), "Theorizing the Gaps: Ohlin, Manoilescu and Nurske," in Erik S. Reinert (ed.), *The Handbook of Heterodox Economics*, London: Edward Elgar.

Blancheton, Bertrand and Samuel Maveyraud (2009), "French Exchange Rate Management in the 1920s," *Financial History Review* 16 (02), pp. 183–201.

Bloomfield, Arthur (1958), *Monetary Policy under the International Gold Standard*, New York: Federal Reserve Bank of New York.

(1963), "Short-term Capital Movements under the Pre-1914 Gold Standard," Princeton Studies in International Finance no. 11, International Finance Section, Department of Economics, Princeton University.

Bordo, Michael D. and Marc Flandreau (2003) "Core, Periphery, Exchange Rate Regimes and Globalization." In Michael D. Bordo, Alan M. Taylor and Jeffrey G. Williamson, *Globalization in Historical Perspective*, Chicago: University of Chicago Press and NBER, pp. 417–472.

314   *Barry Eichengreen and Marc Flandreau*

Bordo, Michael D. Tamara Gomes and Lawrence L. Schembri (2010), "Canada and the IMF: Trailblazer or Prodigal Son?" *Open Economies Review* 21 (2), pp. 309-333.

Bordo, Michael D., Owen Humpage and Anna J. Schwartz (2007), "The Historical Origins of US Exchange Market Intervention Policy," *International Journal of Finance and Economics* 12, pp. 109-132.

Bordo, Michael D. and Finn E. Kydland (1995), "The Gold Standard as a Rule," *Explorations in Economic History* 32 (4), pp. 423-464.

Bordo, Michael and Ronald McDonald (2012), *Credibility and the International Monetary Regime: A Historical Perspective*, Cambridge: Cambridge University Press.

Borio, Claudio, Gabriele Galati and Alexandra Heath (2008), "FX Reserve Management: Trends and Challenges," BIS Papers no. 40 (May).

Bouvier, Jean (1989), "A propos de la stratégie d'encaisse (or et devises) de la Banque de France de juin 1928 à l'été 1932," in J. Bouvier (ed.), *L'historien sur son métier*, Paris: Editions des Archives Contemporaines.

Burk, Kathleen and Alex Cairncross (1992), *Goodbye, Great Britain: The 1976 IMF Crisis*, New Haven: Yale University Press.

Cain, P.J. (1996), "Gentlemanly Imperialism at Work: the Bank of England, Canada, and the Sterling Area, 1932-36," *Economic History Review*, pp. 336-357.

Cameron, Rondo (1961), *France and the Economic Development of Europe 1800-1914*, Princeton: Princeton University Press.

Chandler, Lester (1958), *Benjamin Strong, Central Banker*, Washington, D.C.: Brookings Institution.

Chitu, Livia, Barry Eichengreen and Arnaud Mehl (2012), "When Did the Dollar Overtake Sterling as the Leading International Currency? Evidence from the Bond Markets," NBER Working Paper no. 18097 (May).

Chlepner, B. S. (1927),"La dépréciation et la stabilisation du Franc belge," *Revue d'Economie Politique* XLI, pp. 5-39.

Clavin, Patricia (2013), *Securing the World Economy: The Reinvention of the League of Nations, 1920-1946*, Oxford: Oxford University Press.

Conant, Charles (1910), *The National Bank of Belgium*, Washington, D.C.: National Monetary Commission.

Contamin, Rémy (2003), "Interdépendances financières et dilemme de politique monétaire: La Banque de France entre 1880 et 1913," *Revue économique* 54 (1), pp. 157-179.

Curtis, C. A., (1934), "The Canadian Macmillan Commission," *Economic Journal* 44 (173), pp. 48-59.

De Cecco, Marcello (1974), *Money and Empire: The International Gold Standard*, London: Allen & Unwin.

(1990) "Introduction" in M. De Cecco (ed.), *L'Italia e il sistema finanziario internazionale, 1861-1914*, Laterza: Roma-Bari, 1990.

Durré, Alain and Philippe Ledent (2014), "Escaping the Macroeconomic Trilemma: The Belgian Two-Tier Foreign Exchange System under Bretton Woods," *European Review of Economic History* 18 (1), pp. 49-56.

Eichengreen, Barry (1992), *Golden Fetters: The Gold Standard and the Great Depression, 1919-1939*, New York: Oxford University Press.

(1993), *Reconstructing Europe's Trade and Payments: The European Payments Union*, Ann Arbor: University of Michigan Press.

A Century and a Half of Banks, Reserves, and Currencies   315

(2007), *Global Imbalances and the Lessons of Bretton Woods*, Cambridge, Mass.: MIT Press.

(2011), *Exorbitant Privilege: The Rise and Fall of the Dollar and the Future of the International Monetary System*, New York: Oxford University Press.

Eichengreen, Barry and Marc Flandreau (1997), "Introduction," in Barry Eichengreen and Marc Flandreau (eds.), *The Gold Standard in Theory and History*, second edition, London: Routledge.

(2009), "The Rise and Fall of the Dollar (or When Did the Dollar Replace Sterling as the Leading International Currency?)," *European Review of Economic History* 13 (3), pp. 377–413.

(2012), "The Federal Reserve, the Bank of England, and the Rise of the Dollar as an International Currency, 1914–1939," *Open Economies Review* 23(1), pp. 57–87.

Eichengreen, Barry and Alan Taylor (2004), "The Monetary Consequences of a Free Trade Area of the Americas," in Antoni Esevadeordal, Dani Rodrik, Alan Taylor and Andres Velasco (eds.), *Integrating the Americas: FTAA and Beyond*, Cambridge, Mass: David Rockefeller Center on Latin American Studies, Harvard University, pp. 189–226.

Einzig, Paul (1931), *The Fight for Financial Supremacy*, London: Macmillan.

(1937), *The Theory of Forward Exchange*, London: Macmillan.

Fetter, Frank (1965), *Development of British Monetary Orthodoxy, 1797–1875*, Cambridge, MA: Harvard University Press.

Fior, Michel (2008), *Institution globale et marchés financiers. La Société des Nations face à la reconstruction de l'Europe, 1918–1931*, Paris: Peter Lang.

Fisher, Irving, (1922), *The Making of Index Numbers: A Study of Their Varieties, Tests, and Reliability*, New York: Houghton Mifflin.

Flandreau, Marc (1997), "Central Bank Cooperation in Historical Perspective: A Sceptical View," *Economic History Review* 50 (4), pp. 735–763.

(2003), "Crises and Punishment: Moral Hazard and the Pre-1914 International Financial Architecture", *Money Doctors: The Experience of International Financial Advising 1850–2000*, London: Routledge, pp. 13–48.

(2004), *The Glitter of Gold. France, Bimetallism, and the Emergence of the International Gold Standard, 1848–1873*, Oxford: Oxford University Press.

(2008), "Pillars of Globalization: A History of Monetary Policy Targets, 1797–1997," in A. Beyer and L. Reichlin (eds.), *The Role of Money and Monetary Policy in the 21st Century*, Frankfurt: ECB, pp. 208–243.

Flandreau, Marc and François Gallice (2005), "Paris, London and the International Money Market: Lessons from Paribas 1885–1913," in Y. Cassis and E. Bussiere (eds.), *London and Paris as International Financial Centres in the Twentieth Century*, Oxford: Oxford University Press, pp. 78–106.

Flandreau, Marc and Clemens Jobst (2005), "The Ties that Divide: A Network Analysis of the International Monetary System, 1890–1910," *Journal of Economic History* 65 (4), pp. 977–1007.

(2009) "The Empirics of International Currencies: Network Externalities, History and Persistence," *Economic Journal* 119 (537), pp. 643–664.

Flandreau, Marc and John Komlos (2006), "Target Zones in Theory and History: Credibility, Efficiency, and Policy Autonomy," *Journal of Monetary Economics* 53 (8), pp. 1979–1995.

Flandreau, Marc and Nathan Sussman (2005), "Old Sins: Exchange Clauses and European Foreign Lending in the 19th Century," in Barry Eichengreen and Ricardo Hausmann (eds.), *Other People's Money: Debt Denomination and Financial Instability in Emerging Market Economies*, Chicago: University of Chicago Press, pp. 154–189.

Flandreau, Marc and Stefano Ugolini (2013), "Where it All Began: Lending of Last Resort and Bank of England Monitoring during the Overend, Gurney Panic of 1866," in Michael D. Bordo, and William Roberds (eds.), *The Origins, History, and Future of the Federal Reserve: A Return to Jekyll Island*, Cambridge: Cambridge University Press.

Geanakoplos, John (2009), "The Leverage Cycle," *NBER Macroeconomics Annual* 24, pp. 1–66.

Hatase, Mariko and Mari Ohnuki, 2009, "Did the Structure of Trade and Foreign Debt Affect Reserve Currency Composition? Evidence from Interwar Japan," *European Review of Economic History* 13(3), pp. 319–347.

Horii, Akinari (1986), "The Evolution of Reserve Currency Diversification," BIS Economic Paper no. 18 (December).

Howson, Susan (1980), "Sterling's Managed Float: The Operations of the Exchange Equalization Account, 1932–1939", Princeton Studies in International Finance, No 46.

Irvin, Douglas (2012), "The French Gold Sink and the Great Depression," *Cato Papers on Public Policy* 2, pp. 1–56.

Jobst, Clemens (2009), "Market Leader: The Austro-Hungarian Bank and the making of foreign exchange interventions, 1896–1913," *European Review of Economic History* 13, pp. 287–318.

Johnson, H. C. (1997), *Gold, France and the Great Depression, 1919–1932*, New Haven: Yale University Press.

Jonung, Lars (1979), "Knut Wicksell's Norm of Price Stabilization and Swedish Monetary Policy in the 1930s," *Journal of Monetary Economics* 5, pp. 45–496.

Juglar, Clément (1862), *Des crises commerciales et de leur retour périodique en France, en Angleterre et aux États-Unis*, Paris: Guillaumin.

Kauch, P. (1950), *La Banque nationale de Belgique: 1850–1918*, Bruxelles: Banque Nationale de Belgique.

Kesner, R. M. (1977), "Builders of Empire: The Role of the Crown Agents in Imperial Development, 1880–1914," *Journal of Imperial and Commonwealth History* 5 (3), pp. 310–330.

Keynes, John Maynard (1930), *A Treatise on Money*, London: Macmillan.

Kindleberger, Charles (1950), *The Dollar Shortage*, Cambridge, Mass.: MIT Press.

Kisch, C. H. and W. A. Elkin (1928) *Central Banks. A study of the Constitutions of Banks of Issue, with an Analysis of Representative Charters*. London: Macmillan.

League of Nations (1932), *Monetary and Central Bank Laws* (Edited by Paul Singer), Geneva: League of Nations.

Lévy, Raphaël-George, (1911), *Banques d'émission et trésors publics*, Paris: Hachette.

Lindert, Peter (1969), "Key Currencies and Gold, 1900–13," Princeton Studies in International Finance No. 24, International Finance Section, Department of Economics.

Martín-Aceña, P., E. Martínez-Ruiz, and P. Nogués-Marco, (2011), "Floating against the Tide: Spanish Monetary Policy, 1870–1931," in Anders Ögren and Lars F. Øksendal (eds.), *The Gold Standard Peripheries: Monetary Policy, Adjustment and Flexibility in a Global Setting*, Basingstoke: Palgrave Macmillan, pp. 145–173.

Martinez-Ruiz, Elena and Pilar Nogués-Marco, (2014), "Tipo de cambio, política monetaria y controles de capital: la gestión del trilema en España, 1880–1975," Madrid: Banco de España-Estudios de Historia Económica (forthcoming).

Mclean, Donald (1976), "Finance and 'Informal Empire' Before the First World War," *Economic History Review* new ser. 29, pp. 291–305.

Mitchener, Kris J. and Marc D. Weidenmier, (2015), "Was the Classical Gold Standard Credible on the Periphery? Evidence from Currency Risk", *The Journal of Economic History*, 75, pp. 479–511.

Mixon, Scott (2009), "The Foreign Exchange Option Market, 1917–1921" unpublished manuscript, Société Générale Corporate and Investment Banking (January).

Młynarski, Feliks (1929), *Gold and Central Banks*, London: Macmillan.

Moreau, Emile (1954), *Souvenirs d'un gouverneur de la Banque de France: histoire de la stabilisation du franc, 1926–1928*, Paris: Génin.

Mouré, Kenneth (2002), *The Gold Standard Illusion: France, the Bank of France, and the International Gold Standard, 1914–1939*, Oxford: Oxford University Press.

Myers, Margaret (1936), *Paris as a Financial Center*, London: P.S. King.

Nurkse, Ragnar (1944), *International Currency Experience*, Geneva: League of Nations.

Patron, Maurice (1910), *The Bank of France and its Relation to National and International Credit*, Washington: Government Printing Office.

Patterson, Robert H. (1870), "On Our Home Monetary Drains, and the Crisis of 1866," *Journal of the Statistical Society of London* 33 (2), pp. 216–242.

Polejina, Vladimir, 1939, *Les Fonds d'égalisation des changes, pratique et théorie* Paris: P. Bossuet.

Pringle, Robert and Nick Carver (2013), *RBS Reserve Management Trends 2013*, London: Central Banking Publications.

Pumphrey, Lowell M. (1942), "The Exchange Equalization Account of Great Britain, 1932–1939: Exchange Operations," *American Economic Review* 32 (4), pp. 803–816.

Raffalovich, Arthur (1891), *Le marché financier*, Vol. 1, Paris: Guillaumin.

Reis, Jaime (2007) "An 'Art', not a 'Science'? Central Bank Management in Portugal under the Gold Standard, 1863–871," *Economic History Review*, new ser. 60 (4), pp. 712–741.

Sayers, Richard (1976), *The Bank of England 1891–1944, Vol. 3 Appendices*, Cambridge: Cambridge University Press.

Schenk, Catherine (1994), *Britain and the Sterling Area: From Devaluation to Convertibility in the 1950s*, London: Routledge.

(2010), *The Decline of Sterling: Managing the Retreat of an International Currency*, Cambridge: Cambridge University Press.

Schiltz (2006), "An 'Ideal Bank of Issue': the Banque Nationale de Belgique as a Model for the Bank of Japan," *Financial History Review* 13 (2), pp. 179–196.

Shannon, H. A. (1950), "The Sterling Balances of the Sterling Area, 1939–49," *Economic Journal* 60 (239), pp. 531–551.

Sunderland, David (2004), *Managing the British Empire: The Crown Agents, 1833–1914*, Woodbridge: Boydell Press.

(2013), *Financing the Raj The City of London and Colonial India, 1858–1940*, London: Routledge.

Taguchi, Hiroo (1992), "On the Internationalization of the Japanese Yen," in Takatoshi Ito and Anne Krueger (eds.), *Macroeconomic Linkage: Savings, Exchange Rates and Capital Flows*, Chicago: University of Chicago Press, pp. 335–357.

Tavlas, George (1990), "On the International Use of Currencies: The Case of the Deutsche Mark," IMF Working Paper no. 90/3 (January).

Triffin, Robert (1947), "National Central Banking and the International Economy," *Postwar Economic Studies* 7, pp. 46–81.

Ugolini, Stefano (2011) "Foreign Exchange Reserve Management in the 19th Century: The National Bank of Belgium in the 1850s," Working Paper 2010/22, Norges Bank Bicentenary Project.

(2012) "The Origins of Foreign Exchange Policy: the National Bank of Belgium and the Quest of Monetary Independence in the 1850s," *European Review of Economic History* 16, pp. 51–73.

Van der Wee, H. and K. Tavernier (1975), *La Banque Nationale de Belgique et l'histoire monétaire entre les deux guerres mondiales*, Brussels.

Von Mises, Ludwig (1909), "The Foreign Exchange Policy of the Austro-Hungarian Bank," *Economic Journal* 19, pp. 201–211

Wälde, Thomas (2004), "The Serbian Loans Case: A Precedent for Investment Treaty Protection for Foreign Debt," in V. V. Veeder (ed.), *International Investment Law and Arbitration*, London: Cameron May, pp. 383–424.

White, Harry Dexter (1933), *The French International Accounts 1880–1913*, Cambridge, Mass.: Harvard University Press.

8

Central Banks and the Stability of the International Monetary Regime

Catherine Schenk
University of Glasgow

Tobias Straumann
University of Zurich

1 Introduction

An international monetary regime can be defined as a set of rules and arrangements underpinned by expectations that provide two global public goods: international currencies and external stability (Bordo and Schwartz 1999, Dorrucci and McKay 2011). Its main function is to facilitate economic and financial integration between the nations that are part of the international monetary regime. Eichengreen (1996, p. 1) describes it as "the glue that binds national economies together." This paper deals with how this glue has bound national economies together throughout the last 200 years. Specifically, we focus on the role of central banks in shaping the broad trends from the commodity standards of the nineteenth century to the present mixed regime of floating and managed exchange rates. This story is not easy to capture, partly because the law usually left no formal role for central banks in the determination of exchange rate regimes. They were charged with maintaining internal price stability, issuing currency and promoting well functioning financial and money markets, but the choice of regime itself tended to be statutory and political, leaving the delivery of the exchange rate system as an adjunct to central banks' responsibility for domestic price stability. Therefore, officially, there was no major turning point in the history of the international monetary regime in which a central bank formally made a crucial difference. For example Britain's return to the gold standard in 1819 was decided by the Parliament, and it was the government that suspended the gold standard in 1914. After the war, again the government decided to bring sterling back to the pre-war parity in 1925 and suspended the gold standard again in 1931.

319

France's decision to limit silver coinage in the 1860s was taken by the government, not the central bank. As in Britain, the suspension of the gold standard in 1914, the resumption of convertibility in the 1920s and the devaluation in the 1930s were all government affairs. In Germany, the decision to adopt the gold standard after the Franco-Prussian War was taken before the Reichsbank was even founded. After 1949 the Bundesbank retained a powerful stance in restraining domestic inflation, but the Snake, the European Monetary System and the Euro were the result of decisions taken by the government, in some cases against the advice of the Bundesbank. In the United States, the Federal Reserve was irrelevant when in April 1933 President Roosevelt decided to devalue the dollar. Subsequently, the main architect of the Bretton Woods system was Harry Dexter White of the Treasury, not Fed Chairman Marriner S. Eccles, and the accord was made legally effective by Congress. The timing of the end of the gold convertibility in August 1971 appears to have been mainly determined by President Nixon and his hawkish Treasury Secretary John Connally. This insight emphasizes the distinction between strategic and operational responsibilities under the different forms of international monetary system. While the strategic choice of regime may have rested with the government, the operational details and implementation of that decision was usually delegated to central bankers. This enhanced their *informal* influence even where the formal legal position may have suggested that they were mere functionaries in the system.

The subordinate role in choosing the exchange rate regime does not imply that central banks were irrelevant throughout the history of international monetary regimes. The way they managed the regime proved essential for international financial and monetary stability. Central bankers shared particular characteristics that made them the guardians of expertise about monetary matters. First, they often had the closest relationships with the constituents of the foreign exchange market in the form of banks and other financial institutions because of their roles as discounters and supervisors. Moreover, in most countries they were not subject to the political cycles of democratic regimes and so spanned government tenures in a way that lifted them above immediate political pressures. Being unaccountable directly to parliaments or voters also created opportunities for personal and private cooperation and communication, which facilitated their actions compared to democratically accountable politicians. In times of crisis, central bankers were frequently able to meet quickly and resolve obstacles expeditiously in ways that political actors were not able to achieve. The historical record also reveals frequent episodes of conflict between central banks and governments over the priority of price stability over growth with attendant implications for the exchange rate regime.

As it is nearly impossible to capture all sides of the complex interaction between central banks and the international monetary regime, we focus on a question that appears to be particularly relevant in the wake of the recent financial crisis. We ask under what historical circumstances central banks have been successful in preserving the two main elements of an international monetary regime – international currencies and external stability – over the last 200 years. Our focus is on the history of the leading central banks in the Western Hemisphere since the end of the Napoleonic Wars and of the Bank of Japan since 1973. The choice is selective, but can be justified by the fact that these central banks were more crucial for the international regime and became models for the non-Western world, starting in the nineteenth century.

The most obvious answer to our question is that much depends on the personalities who led the central banks. A famous example is the history of the Federal Reserve in the interwar years. Benjamin Strong has been said to be an able man who died too early, while George Harrison did not have the grandeur to deal with the extraordinary crisis of the early 1930s (Friedman and Schwartz 1963). We take a different approach. Our main insight is that legal constraints on their powers pushed central bankers into a rather weak position so that they have had little effective influence on the crucial factors that have determined their success in managing the international monetary system during most of the past 200 years. This is not to say that personalities have not mattered at all or that no policy mistakes were made. But as a rule, central bankers acted within their mandate and in accordance with a broad consensus when making decisions. Episodes of failure are rather mistakes than a clear sign of incompetence.

The first factor that determined the influence of central banks is the type of exchange rate regime. Under a fixed exchange rate regime, central banks have fewer tools and a narrower range of operations than under a floating regime. This is particularly relevant in the event of severe financial crises. The second factor is central bank independence, which determines to what extent central banks have to be subservient to short-term domestic political interests. The more independent they are, the higher the probability that they can give priority to the international monetary regime, thus stabilizing expectations. The third factor is the degree of economic policy divergence among the core countries. Capital controls may give central banks more time to cushion international tensions, but they do not solve underlying imbalances. The same is true for central bank cooperation.

Table 8.1: *Comparison of international monetary regimes*

	Central bank independence	Economic policy convergence
Fixed exchange rate regimes		
Classical gold standard	+	+
Interwar gold standard	+	−
Bretton Woods system	−	−
Floating exchange rate regimes		
1973–1979	−	−
1979 to the present	+	−

It can be useful to overcome temporary disturbances, but is to no avail if national agendas contradict the requirements of international stability.

We also observe that under a fixed exchange rate regime international economic policy divergence is by far the most important factor determining central bank performance. Regardless of the degree of their independence, central bankers fail in their attempts to preserve international monetary stability or, still worse, reinforce the collapse of the system by their actions, when core countries pursue divergent economic policies. Under a floating exchange rate regime, by contrast, central bank independence seems to be the crucial variable. Equipped with full instrument independence, central banks have the power to stabilize the international monetary system even when national economic policies diverge. Table 8.1 shows our argument about the role of central banks in a stylized form. The interwar gold standard and the Bretton Woods system were not sustainable, because the leading economic powers pursued divergent economic policies, and the floating exchange rate regime from 1973 to 1979 was unstable because of the lack of central bank independence to cope with the exogenous shocks of this era. By contrast, the classical gold standard and the floating exchange rate regime from 1979 to the present can be considered stable regimes, either because there was an international consensus (classical gold standard) or because central banks were independent (1979 to the present).

In the following sections, we will put more flesh on the bones of our argument. Section 2 describes the era of the classic gold standard, which was the first international monetary regime where central banks played an important role. Until this time, "the banks of note issue" had been secondary, since the system of "international bimetallism" (Flandreau

Stability of the International Monetary Regime   323

2004) was decentralized and based on privately owned and transacted bullion. The classic gold standard was a stable regime because it combined central bank independence and economic policy convergence. To be sure, there were attacks on the gold standard and rudiments of divergence, especially in the United States, but they never became strong enough to destroy the political and institutional foundations of the international monetary system.

The next two sections deal with the interwar gold standard and the Bretton Woods system. Both systems proved inconsistent as the economic policies of the great powers diverged. The degree of central bank independence varied throughout the period. It was quite high between the end of the First World War and the beginning of the Great Depression, while after 1945 central banks were almost everywhere subordinated to the ministry of finance or the treasury. Possibly, the Fed could have done a better job in the 1930s when large parts of the banking system were collapsing, or it would have contained inflation in the 1960s, had it been more independent. Yet, as we will argue, the systemic flaws were too fundamental to be papered over by a different monetary policy. Central bank cooperation was reinforced, but proved inadequate in the wake of growing international imbalances.

Section 5 analyses the experiences since 1973, which have been mixed. In the first period, lasting from 1973 to 1979 the system was unstable. Governments had abandoned fixed exchange rates without embracing the advantages of the floating exchange rates and giving central banks the mandate to curb inflation. The regime was also inconsistent as states wavered between ameliorating unemployment and containing inflationary expectations. Things changed after 1979 when the Fed, the British government and the members of the newly founded European Monetary System increased their determination to restrain inflation. The era of the Great Moderation promoted the reputation of independent central banks in achieving relatively full employment, sustained economic growth with price stability. In the wake of the financial crisis of 2007–2009 the record looks less impressive than before 2007. However, we will argue that even from today's perspective the glass is half full, not half empty. The chapter ends with a short conclusion.

2 Central Banking under the Classical Gold Standard

Between the end of the Napoleonic Wars (1815) and the outbreak of the First World War (1914) most Western countries had a fixed exchange rate regime based on a gold, silver or bimetallic standard. Economic historians distinguish between two eras. The first era, lasting from 1815 to 1873, was characterized by so-called international bimetallism, whereas the years between 1873 and 1914 were dominated by the classic gold standard. During the gold standard era, silver standards continued to exist only in China, India and some Central American economies, while the bimetallic standard remained only a de jure regime but was de facto abandoned.

The time between 1815 and 1914 was also the period when most industrialized countries set up "banks of issue" (Table 8.2). The forerunners had been the Swedish Riksbank (1668), the Bank of England (1694) and the Banque de France (1800). An important milestone was the establishment of the Prussian Bank in 1847, which in 1876 was transformed into the Reichsbank to unify the German currency and deliver the rules of the gold standard in the German Empire. The State Bank of the Russian Empire was founded in 1860. The Bank of Japan, the first central bank outside Europe, opened in 1882, but had a rival in the Yokohama Specie Bank, which managed metallic reserves and international transactions. Japan only joined the gold standard in 1897 after a war indemnity in gold was won from the Chinese government. The United States lacked a central bank until 1913, which impeded the coherence of national monetary policy. The United States formally joined the gold standard in 1900, finally giving up the fight for silver based on the silver mines of Nevada.

Central banks did not play a vital role prior to the advent of the classical gold standard. A short digression into the inner workings of the international regime before 1873 is needed in order to understand why. The regime consisted of three different groups. Britain, the heartland of the industrial revolution and the rising center of the world economy, was the head of the gold group, in association with its dominions and colonies. Outside of the British Empire only Brazil, Portugal and Turkey were also on the gold standard by the mid-nineteenth century. It is important to note that prior to the classical gold standard the pound sterling and the London market were not yet as predominant as they would be after the 1870s (Ugolini 2010). The silver group was bigger, but had no strong financial center or lead central bank. It comprised Austria, Prussia and the other German states, the Netherlands and the Scandinavian countries. Outside of Europe, Asia was firmly on silver (China, India and Japan) while in the Americas only Mexico opted for this standard. The strong position of silver in Asia was a result of the sustained drain of American and European silver to the developed industrial centers in the Far East since the sixteenth century. The third group was on a bimetallic standard, with France at its

Stability of the International Monetary Regime

Table 8.2: *The origins of central banks**

Year	Country	Name	Motivation
1668	Sweden	Sveriges Riksbank	Finance war
1694	United Kingdom	Bank of England	Finance war
1782	Spain	Banco de España	Finance war
1800	France	Banque de France	Manage public debt, generate seignorage
1811	Finland	Suomen Pankk	Monetary sovereignty
1814	Netherlands	Nederlandsche Bank	Promote economic growth
1816	Austria	Österreichische Nationalbank	Manage public debt as a result of war finance
1816	Norway	Norges Bank	Economic crisis in Denmark prompts monetary reform
1818	Denmark	Danmarks Nationalbank	Restore stability in aftermath of war finance
1846	Portugal	Banco de Portugal	Restore credibility to previous monetary regime
1847	Prussia	Bank of Prussia	
1850	Belgium	Banque nationale de Belgique/Nationale Bank van België	Reform prompted by banking crises
1860	Russia	State Bank of the Russian Empire	
1876	Germany	Reichsbank	Consolidation of previous note issuing authorities following unification
1882	Japan	Bank of Japan	Part of modernization of Meiji regime
1893	Italy	Banca d'Italia	Consolidation of previous note issuing authorities following unification
1907	Switzerland	Schweizerische Nationalbank/Banque nationale suisse	Elimination of note issuing authority
1911	Australia	Commonwealth Bank of Australia	Creation of a single note issuing authority
1913	United States	Federal Reserve System	Creation of lender of last resort and other banking related functions

Sources: Goodhart, Capie and Schnadt (1994), Siklos (2002).

Note: *The list is confined to central banks of today's OECD countries. There were also new central banking institutions on the Netherlands Antilles (established 1828), in Indonesia (1828), Bulgaria (1879), Romania (1880) and Serbia (1883).

center and Belgium, Italy and Switzerland as its associates. In the mid-1860s, the group formalised rules concerning the silver content of the 5-franc coin by constituting the Latin Monetary Union. In 1868, Greece and Spain joined. The United States was also on a bimetallic standard from 1792 to 1862, when in the course of the Civil War the dollar began to float. Contrary to the textbook predictions that bimetallism breeds instability, the early nineteenth century bimetallic standard proved robust and durable, partly through the management of central banks (Friedman 1990, Velde 2000, Flandreau 2002).

Alhough there were three distinct groupings, it is appropriate to speak of one regime, because it succeeded in providing the two essential public goods of any international monetary system: international currencies and external stability. From 1803, the bimetallic group legally stabilized the price ratio between gold and silver (1:15.5). It did so by absorbing the metal that was in oversupply, while releasing the other metal that was scarce. In this careful balancing act, the Banque de France succeeded very well and the ratio between gold and silver remained very stable from 1803 to the early 1870s when the system of international bimetallism collapsed (Friedman 1990, Flandreau 2004). In particular, the system was elastic enough to absorb the monetary supply shocks following the discovery of gold in Australia and California in the late 1840s and the discovery of silver in Nevada in the late 1850s. But central banks were not essential for the operation of international bimetallism because a large part of the bullion stock was in private hands and payments in gold and silver were still very common, even across borders to offset payment imbalances between trading firms, banks and investors. In 1860, the Banque de France held only 14 percent of total specie supplies in France which made up more than three quarters of the money supply M1 (Flandreau 2004, p. 4).

Although they were not supporting pillars of the international monetary regime, central banks underwent an important transformation prior to 1873. Probably the most important innovation was their new role as lenders of last resort. In the first half of the nineteenth century even the most experienced institution at the time, the Bank of England, still made serious mistakes by rationing credit during financial crisis, thus magnifying negative effects. In the 1850s and 1860s, however, the Bank of England, the Banque de France and other central banks such as Norges Bank began to understand better how to deal with financial panics (Calomiris 2011, Bignon et al. 2012, Eitrheim et al. 2016). Bagehot's 1873 *Lombard Street* provoked considerable debate across Europe about the role of lender of last resort and the terms and conditions under which central banks could lend to financial institutions. Another important development before 1873 was the British discussion about rules vs. discretion under a metallic standard. Historic milestones were the bullionist debates following the suspension of convertibility in 1797, the controversy between the banking and the currency schools after the restoration of the gold standard in 1821, the Bank Act of 1833 that made Bank of England notes legal tender and the Bank Act of 1844 which gave the Bank of England the monopoly of note issue.

The co-existence of different metallic standards came to an end in the early 1870s. The crucial event was the Franco-Prussian War of 1870/1871. With fresh gold reserves from its war indemnity from France, the newly founded German Empire decided to abandon the silver standard in favor of the gold standard. In retaliation for German unilateralism, France reacted by suspending its role as moderator of the international bimetallic regime. As a result, the price of silver relative to gold began to decline, prompting the European silver group to adopt the gold standard. France and the United States, driven by the advantages of network effects, soon followed (Gallarotti 1995, Flandreau 1996, Meissner 2005). By the late 1870s the transition to a mono-metallic gold standard was completed, leaving relatively few low income economies such as Mexico, India and China retain the silver standard. A new era had begun and central banks became important in the management of the international monetary regime.

First and foremost, central banks managed a much larger share of gold than before 1873, and they acted as the institution that took responsibility for maintaining convertibility between gold and notes. The shift to the gold standard thus brought a nationalization and centralization of the international monetary regime and, based on their monopoly, central banks became ever more skilful in expanding their room to maneuver. Seen from today, however, they were not yet conducting a modern monetary policy.[1] They also differed with respect to their mandates and instruments. The Bank of England was an exception rather than the rule in terms of its statutory independence and range of responsibilities. One essential difference was the importance of the banking business. While the Bank

---

[1] Sayers (1976, p. 1) observes: "The term 'central bank' had been creeping into public discussion in the second half of the nineteenth century but had not yet any settled concept behind it. (...). At the end of the nineteenth century, however, 'central bank' meant scarcely more than a single bank distinguished from others by unique public responsibilities eclipsing its commercial interests."

of England had only a few branches outside London and faced strong competition by private banks in London, the Banque de France and the Reichsbank had a dense web of subsidiaries that provided a substantial share of normal banking services. Another difference was the variation in gold and silver reserves. The Banque de France possessed a huge share of global gold reserves, providing a strong shield against external shocks and widening their room to maneuver, whereas the Bank of England had a rather small gold cushion. The Bank of England also used the discount rate as the main policy instrument, while the Banque de France did not (Contamin 2003, Morys 2013).

All in all, the core central banks succeeded in preserving stability, mainly because of the high degree of credibility of the monetary regime. Private-sector agents expected that central banks would always keep their commitment to safeguarding convertibility, except in well justified exceptional circumstances. This set in motion a virtuous circle between strong credibility and monetary autonomy in the short-run which helped run the system like a target zone (Bordo and Flandreau 2003, Bordo and MacDonald 2012). When the exchange rate fell toward the lower limit (gold point), central banks were not immediately forced to raise interest rates; investors drove the exchange rate back to par, expecting that the central bank would ultimately react. In anticipating a tightening of monetary policy, short-term capital movements replaced the reaction and allowed "automatic" stabilisation or at least gave the central bank some breathing space. Of course, the principle of convertibility acted as a constraint. Nevertheless, the notion that monetary policy was purely on autopilot has no historical foundation.

There were several opportunities for central bankers to enlarge their active management of the system. In good times, they increased the level of metallic and foreign exchange reserves well above the legal minimum in order to pursue an accommodative stance in times of crisis. They also used their holdings of bonds and bills to sterilize capital inflows (Øksendal 2012, Ögren 2012, Ugolini 2012). Another way to dampen the shocks to the financial and monetary system was to deploy so-called "gold devices" such as delaying capital movements or to demand a fee to introduce further frictions into capital flows. Some central banks, especially the Austro-Hungarian bank, became quite skillful in using foreign exchange intervention to avoid interest rate spikes emanating from the Bank of England (Flandreau and Komlos 2006, Jobst 2009). The Bank of Belgium, the pioneer of foreign exchange management in the 1850s, also used this policy (Ugolini 2012) and it was an inspiration for the Bank of Japan. Finally, many peripheral countries never introduced specie convertibility (Morys 2013).[2]

The classic gold standard enjoyed such a high degree of credibility partly because it was shielded from domestic politics and partly because the core countries pursued similar economic policy goals. Among the core countries the level of public debt was manageable, the public spending ratio to GDP was below 20 percent and wages and prices were relatively flexible. Furthermore, the costs of adjustment were passed on to those parts of society that had the least political rights (Eichengreen 1996). In the nineteenth century suffrage was quite limited in most Western countries and governments in Europe were mainly concerned with internal and external security and property rights. A consensus that the state was responsible for the economic welfare of populations had begun to develop, but was not well established until the end of the century. This left most monetary authorities relatively free to pursue deflationary policies in order to maintain a metallic standard. The combination of exchange rate stability and free capital movements was the chosen combination, at the expense of a fully independent monetary policy.

The second factor promoting credibility was the relatively underdeveloped state of economic theory. True, early versions of price level targeting were developed in the beginning of the nineteenth century, and towards the end of the nineteenth century several economists, notably Knut Wicksell and Irving Fisher, devised well developed frameworks that explained the relationship between monetary policy and the business cycle (Laidler 1999, Burdekin et al. 2012). They showed that the gold standard was not the best framework for monetary policy. But these ideas remained marginal before 1914. Accordingly, the public and voters were not aware of the power central banks were exerting over the business cycle. Monetary policy was not yet politicized.

Thirdly, there were fewer massive exogenous shocks during the pre-1914 decades. Revolutions and wars as well as financial panics were frequent and serious, but not comparable to the First World War, the Bolshevik Revolution or the Great Depression. The most serious European war between

---

[2] Morys (2013, p. 221): "If peripheral countries modified the 'English' gold standard to suit their needs, this probably entails a wider lesson for the functioning of the Classical Gold Standard. There was not only one gold standard but a variety of gold standards. Peripheral countries apparently followed a version different from the one pioneered by England. Perhaps it is precisely this institutional flexibility which explains why the Classical Gold Standard remains to this day the longest-ever system of fixed exchange-rates."

1815 and 1914 was the Franco-Prussian war of 1870/1871.[3] It lasted less than one year (from July 1870 to May 1871), with Germany and France counting 45,000 and 139,000 dead and 90,000 and 143,000 wounded soldiers respectively. In comparison, during the First World War more than nine million soldiers died and about seven million civilians lost their lives. The revolutions of 1848 shattered existing social orders, but did not undermine property rights in the long run. In contrast, Bolshevik Russia eradicated the noble and bourgeois elites, socialized all means of production and defaulted on all external debts. The Great Depression of 1929–1933 paralyzed the two largest economies of the world, the United States and Germany, for more than three years, with real GPD declining by a third and unemployment rising to more than 20 percent. The only crisis of the nineteenth century that came near the catastrophe of the 1930s was the panic of 1837 in the United States. And as Calomiris (2011, p. 106) argues, financial panics after 1850 were harmless relative to the crises in the late twentieth and early twenty-first centuries, because banks maintained high equity-to-assets and liquidity ratios.

A fourth explanation explaining the persistence of the gold standard highlights the importance of international emergency measures. Central banks repeatedly shipped gold or silver across frontiers to help contain a financial panic, especially in 1890 and 1907. The 1890 sovereign debt crisis focused in Latin America nearly brought down the great London finance house of Barings (Mitchener and Weidenmier 2008, Flores 2011) and threatened to push Britain off the gold standard. Argentina issued bonds payable in gold or in sterling in London, but was not itself on a metallic standard. After investing borrowed funds in infrastructure projects, the government found itself unable to service these debts in an environment of inflation and a depreciating peso. The resolution of the crisis required emergency central bank cooperation. Barings was rescued by the Bank of England, which arranged gold loans from the Banque de France and Russia's central bank. Likewise, in 1906–1907, heavy US borrowing drained gold from the Bank of England, but a damaging rise in interest rates was avoided through loans from the Banque de France and the German Reichsbank (Toniolo 2005, p.15). These early examples of central bank cooperation show how central bankers could perceive themselves as a

---

[3] The most important political events between 1815 and 1914 were: Revolutions: 1830 and 1848, wars: Crimean War (1853–1856), US Civil War (1861–1865), Austro-Prussian War (1866), Franco-Prussian War (1870–1871), the Spanish-American War (1898), the Boer War (1899–1902), Balkan Wars (1912-1913).

Stability of the International Monetary Regime 331

collective group with common interests in preserving the stability of the international monetary system.

Of course, all explanations have their weaknesses. First, even in countries with a full-fledged democracy for male voters since 1848, as in France and Switzerland, the metallic standard was not challenged by the public. Second, central bankers were absolutely aware that raising interest rates would hurt the economy (Morys 2013). Third, shocks were maybe not as big as during the first half of the twentieth century, but they had the potential to destroy the international monetary regime. Reinhart and Rogoff identify twenty-four banking crises in high and middle income countries during the period of high capital mobility from 1880–1914 (Reinhart and Rogoff 2009. pp. 344–345).[4] And fourth, the concerted interventions by central bankers were a response to exceptional strains rather than a key function of the everyday operation of the gold standard. For the most part central banks acted in their own national interest with little spirit of coordination for its own sake (Flandreau 1997).

Nevertheless, despite these objections, it is clear that historical circumstances provided a strong basis for the credibility of the classical gold standard. Central banks were only successful in managing the international monetary system because the classical gold standard was compatible with the political environment, both domestically and internationally. This is not to say that there was no threat to stability (Bordo and Capie 1993, pp. 5–6; Bordo and Schwartz 1999, pp. 160–161; Eichengreen 1996, pp. 41–42). But it would be wrong to argue that the collapse of the classical gold standard was inevitable in 1914.

3 Central Banks and the Collapse of the Interwar Gold Standard

During the interwar years, central banks struggled to sustain the gold-based international monetary regime that was reconstructed after the war. In the 1920s most governments pursued a concerted effort to return to "normal" by restoring the gold value of their currencies. Starting in 1931, the gold exchange standard collapsed, and subsequently central banks in Britain, France, Germany and the United States lost their independence. However, as we will argue, their responsibility for the Great Depression has

---

[4] Major financial crises between 1815 and 1914 were: In Britain: 1825, 1836–39, 1847, 1857 and 1866. In France: 1818, 1840, 1848 and 1851. In the United States, the most important financial panics are the following: 1819, 1837, 1857, 1873, 1884, 1893, 1896, 1907 and 2011.

been overemphasized. They made mistakes, but the fundamental problem was that the international monetary regime was not compatible with the dynamics of both international and domestic politics (Ritschl and Straumann 2010). Central banks had full instrument independence, but centrifugal forces proved much too strong.

Ex ante, things were not looking as bad as they did ex post. The postwar stabilization after 1918 was a direct consequence of the contingent gold standard rules and resembled what happened after the Napoleonic Wars and the American Civil War. The debate after 1918 echoed in many ways the Bullionist debate more than a hundred years earlier, when English politicians, bankers and economists debated the pros and cons of convertibility. But there was an important difference to earlier periods. The interwar gold standard was the result of repeated international conferences that brought government officials and central bank governors together to discuss the redesign of the international monetary system. The delegates at the Genoa International Economic Conference in 1922 explicitly recommended that central bank cooperation was a vital aspect of a prospective new gold standard and that this should be institutionalized in a convention or "entente."[5] This new focus on central bank independence and cooperation to manage the international monetary system particularly reflected the views of the Governor of the Bank of England Montagu Norman, and Benjamin Strong, first Governor of the Federal Reserve Bank of New York, who together promoted close relations and cooperation. In Britain, Norman joined with the UK Treasury to push the inexperienced Chancellor of the Exchequer Winston Churchill to return speedily to the gold standard in 1925 . The enhanced prominence of these key central bankers helped to promote the role of central banks in the global system.

The interwar gold exchange standard launched a new era of central banking outside Europe. The First World War prompted a surge of state-building that included a desire to have national central banks as part of the apparatus of independent policy-making. Central banks were also an important tool to operate the interwar gold exchange standard. Governor Montagu Norman of the Bank of England promoted a network of central banks modeled on the Bank of England that could cooperate to deliver "orthodox" policies aimed at monetary and exchange rate stability. His vision was supported by the Financial Committee of the League of Nations, which sent missions to a range of central European states in the mid-1920s

---

[5] Papers relating to International Economic Conference, Genoa, April–May 1922, London: HMSO, p. 60.

Stability of the International Monetary Regime 333

as part of the general spirit of creating a coordinated international monetary system. Sir Otto Niemeyer and other officials from the Bank of England toured a range of emerging markets to advise on monetary policy, "sound money" and to promote the establishment or reform of independent central banks. His advice was sometimes controversial, for example in Australia where his recommendations of austerity to restore exchange rate stability and to allow the national debt to be serviced were greeted with indignation (Attard 1992, p. 82). Many Western Hemisphere states looked to the United States and Edwin Kemmerer of the Federal Reserve Bank toured a range of countries from 1917–1931 advising on the organization of central banks, including Colombia, Chile, Ecuador, Bolivia and Peru (Singleton 2011. p. 60). Table 8.3 shows a range of central banks designed by the League of Nations and Bank of England advisers. In the end, these central banks lasted much longer than the international monetary system that they were designed to deliver.

The restored international monetary system was a haphazard inconsistent adoption of a pegged gold exchange standard, which relied more on sterling and other national currencies as foreign exchange reserves. Exchange rates tended to reflect political targets rather than economic realities. Thus, sterling was pegged at the pre-war parity despite significant changes in Britain's global economic standing. The French franc was stabilized at a greatly devalued rate compared to 1900, prompting inflationary pressures and the accumulation of reserves. Politics over-rode economic reality and central bankers who were left managing the system were unable to fend off market pressures that led ultimately to a global banking and financial crisis in 1931, ironically just after the founding of the Bank for International Settlements seemed to be fulfilling the central bank association that was the "dream of Genoa" (Toniolo 2005, p. 20 quoting Bank of England's Charles Addis in 1929).

When the cost of maintaining the international system became too high in the contagious financial crisis of the 1930s, the mood shifted radically and states abandoned the struggle to fight the market and suspended the gold standard. The international system was swiftly fragmented into currency and trade blocs. The interwar gold standard failed to provide the two global public goods in times of crises: international currencies and external stability. In 1931 there was a shortage of liquidity, and currencies tumbled off the gold standard one after another. Germany introduced capital controls in the summer of 1931, and Britain took sterling off gold in the autumn of the same year. The United States followed in the spring of

Table 8.3: *Central banks and international missions in the interwar period*

Countries	Year	Mission	Outcome
South Africa	1920	Sir Harry Strakosch	South African Reserve Bank
Austria	1923	League of Nations	Austrian National Bank
Poland	1923	League of Nations	Reorganised National Bank into central bank
Free State of Danzig	1923	League of Nations	Bank of Danzig
Hungary	1924	League of Nations	National Bank reorganized into central bank
Czechoslovakia	1926	League of Nations	National Bank of Czechoslovakia
Estonia	1927	League of Nations	National Bank reorganized into central bank
Bulgaria	1928	League of Nations	National Bank reorganized into central bank
Greece	1928	League of Nations	Central Bank of Greece
Australia	1930	Sir Otto Niemeyer	Commonwealth Bank reorganized into central bank?
New Zealand	1930	Sir Otto Niemeyer	Central Reserve Bank of NZ 1934
Brazil	1931	Sir Otto Niemeyer	Bank of Brazil reorganized into central bank
Canada	1933	Lord Macmillan, Sir Charles Addis	Bank of Canada
India	1933	Sir Ernest Harvey, W.H. Clegg	Central Reserve Bank of India
El Salvador	1934	F.F.J. Powell	Central Reserve Bank of El Salvador
Argentina	1935	Sir Otto Niemeyer	Central Bank of Argentine
China	1935	Sir Frederick Leith-Ross	Currency reform: sterling/dollar peg
Egypt	1936	Sir Otto Niemeyer	National Bank of Egypt reorganized into central bank

1933, France in the fall of 1936. The experiment with a deliberately constructed specie based system had failed.

Why were central banks not able to prevent the regime from collapsing? They certainly made several mistakes, not only from today's perspective, but also in the eyes of critical contemporaries such as Fisher or Keynes. Especially the Fed could have done more to contain the banking panics of the 1930s. Instead of pursuing an expansionary monetary policy to stabilise the money supply, it concentrated on keeping the monetary base constant (Friedman and Schwartz 1963, Meltzer 2003). Admittedly, the US banking system was particularly weak due to the high share of unit banking, but there is no doubt that the Fed could have done more to mitigate the negative macroeconomic consequences of the banking crises in the early 1930s (Carlson and Mitchener 2009, Calomiris 2011). Certainly central banks bore some of the responsibility.

Yet, it would be too easy to put all the blame on the shoulders of central bankers. In the United States the Fed was arguably following one of its main rules, namely to preserve convertibility. In Germany, Hans Luther was perhaps not the best central banker in German history, but he had little room to manoeuver once a run on the German currency developed in the challenging political and economic climate (James 2013, p. 213). Open credit lines provided by France, the United Kingdom or the United States may have made a crucial difference, but central bankers were inhibited by political obstacles from offering substantial credits to Germany. And once the German crisis escalated, sterling quickly followed, pushed on by domestic political stalemate over government spending and taxation that undermined credibility in the ability of politicians to restore prosperity. The combination of an overvalued currency, the political costs of austerity and a drain of foreign reserves as a result of the international liquidity crisis forced the government to suspend the gold standard in September 1931. From then, it was only a matter of time until the United States and France devalued their currencies as well.

Furthermore, not only central bankers, but most politicians were in favor of prioritising nominal exchange rate stability. Even after the suspension of the gold standard the authorities remained conservative with respect to any regime change and their preference was usually in favour of stable or pegged exchange rates. During the interwar economic crisis, centre-right politicians as well as Social Democrats and trade union officials were reluctant to abandon the gold standard, even though the monetary straitjacket reinforced the slump (Eichengreen and Temin 2000). The most notorious example is the slow dissolution of the Gold Bloc in the 1930s. Most independent observers predicted that it was a futile exercise to maintain the existing parity after the United Kingdom and the United States left the gold standard in September 1931 and April 1933 respectively. But France together with Belgium, Italy, the Netherlands, Poland and Switzerland defended their deflationary policies within a Gold Bloc until the domestic political support had crumbled in the mid-1930s (Feinstein, Temin and Toniolo 1997). Even after the interwar gold standard collapsed in the 1930s, both governments and central banks in many countries aimed to minimise exchange rate fluctuations because floating was believed to introduce uncertainty and transactions costs harmful to trade. In June 1933 the Bank of England, Banque de France and the Fed agreed to try to stabilize the gold price of their currencies but they were over-ridden by President Roosevelt's desire to retain domestic monetary policy sovereignty (Feinstein, Temin and Toniolo 1997). From 1933, therefore, the international monetary system came to look more like a prototype of the Bretton Woods system than a system of freely floating exchange rates. Sterling broke the peg to gold in September 1931, but most of Britain's main suppliers of food and raw materials retained their peg to sterling as part of the sterling bloc. Only in Sweden was there serious consideration of abandon the peg for price level targeting, but the Riksbank was very reluctant to adopt the proposals made by Swedish economists (Berg and Jonung 1999, Straumann and Woitek 2009).

In the interwar period, central bankers no doubt made monumental mistakes in policy that aggravated the Great Depression, but they were operating in difficult circumstances. They were responsible for maintaining the international monetary system, while governments failed to address the roots of imbalances, namely the conflict between the former war powers and domestic instability. There were many reasons for why the political environment had changed relative to the era of the classical gold standard. By 1920, universal suffrage had become the norm in Western countries and the trauma of the First World War altered expectations about the responsibilities of the state for welfare. At the same time greater fiscal debt and price instability strengthened the reorientation towards domestic policy goals and the importance of monetary policy sovereignty. The Allied powers had different interests with respect to German reparations, with the United States reluctant to adopt the role of the leader (Kindleberger 1973). Faced with these severe contradictions, central banks failed to stabilize the international monetary regime, but this was likely an impossible task. In the process several lessons were learned about the need for greater coordination that influenced the post-Second World War settlement.

4 Central Bank Cooperation and the End of the Bretton Woods System

Immediately after the Second World War, central bankers were not key to the design and strategic management of the international monetary system, although they retained operational responsibilities. As the Bretton Woods system evolved, central bankers devised ways to cooperate in order

Stability of the International Monetary Regime   337

to overcome weaknesses in the pegged exchange rate system, thus gaining back some of the lost ground. By the end of the 1960s, however, international imbalances had become too large to be ameliorated by central bank cooperation. Once more, central banks faced increasingly powerful diverging national interests among governments that meant that the international monetary regime had become incompatible with the political environment.

With hindsight, it is hard to understand why after 1945 the world went back to a system of fixed exchange rates. Similar to the period after the disastrous conflict of 1914–1918, there was a broad consensus that stable exchange rates offered the best prospect for global recovery. The damaging political as well as economic effects of the apparent "currency wars" of the 1930s prompted a return to the doctrine of stable exchange rates after the interregnum of the Second World War. The Bretton Woods system was based on a consensus built during the war that international capital markets were dangerous to orderly global integration, that international trade liberalization was the primary means to ensure sustained economic growth and that stable exchange rates encouraged economic cooperation and reduced transactions costs (Schenk 2010; Chwieroth 2010). Importantly, the blueprint for Bretton Woods was not led by central banks but by Treasury officials in the United Kingdom (John Maynard Keynes) and United States (Harry Dexter White). This reflects the heightened political atmosphere in which the two main allied nations developed their plans for the postwar monetary system. The failure of economic cooperation and coordination in the interwar period and the damaging flows of hot money that characterized the European financial crisis of 1931 were to be avoided through a managed stable exchange rate with convertibility of currencies for current account purposes but a sustained reliance on capital controls to protect national monetary independence.

Rather than focusing on the mainly self-interested actions of national central banks established during the gold standard eras, this new system created a distinctive specialist international monetary institution to monitor stable exchange rates. The International Monetary Fund (IMF) was designed to provide the international economic cooperation that was essential to a lasting world peace, in contrast to US isolationism and European economic nationalism of the 1930s. Central bankers were excluded from the formal governance of the system, which was led by the Executive Board of the IMF – itself made up of nominees from among state bureaucracies. But, as we shall see, the flaws in the system led to a new role for the Bank for International Settlements to provide supporting apparatus that drew central bankers back to the core of the international monetary system.

Formally, all core countries were part of the system between 1947 and 1973; only Canada in the 1950s really experimented with a floating exchange rate at this time, although the commitment to a free float is debated (Siklos 2009; Helleiner 2005). But while the Bretton Woods regime may have been based on a common set of rules, there was hardly any year in which these rules were followed by all major members. There were frequent adjustments in the values of international currencies against the dollar that undermined the credibility of the system (e.g. devaluation of all European currencies 1949, DM revaluation 1961, sterling devaluation 1967, franc devaluation 1969, DM float 1969). Within the Bretton Woods regime, regional or currency-based systems emerged as it became clear that the comprehensive international payments system based on convertible currencies would be delayed indeterminately. Among European states the European Payments Union provided a clearing system based on gold and dollars from 1950–1958 that facilitated a form of convertibility of European currencies. Current account convertibility, the cornerstone of the original Bretton Woods framework of multilateralism, was only achieved at the end of 1958 for most European currencies (Kaplan and Schleiminger, 1989).

At the same time, the United Kingdom was the centre of the sterling area group of countries from 1945–1972, which pooled their foreign exchange reserves at the Bank of England and operated exchange controls against the dollar in return for freer access to the London capital market (Schenk, 2010). These countries included major primary product producers such as Australia, New Zealand and South Africa as well as oil producers in the Middle East such as Kuwait, Iraq and Persian Gulf States. British colonies such as Hong Kong, Singapore, Malaysia, Nigeria and Ghana, Kenya and Tanganyika operated currency boards linked to sterling. French colonies and former colonies in Africa operated currency boards based on the franc and formed the Franc Area. The Bank of England had as its primary responsibility the maintenance of the pegged exchange rate and the management of the foreign exchange reserves.

Controlled capital markets and pegged exchange rates focused attention on defending balance of payments equilibrium during the building of comprehensive welfare states in many European countries and the liberalization of trade flows. Germany's interwar experience of hyperinflation meant that the Bundesbank was particularly averse to inflation and pressed its influence over the government to restrain any risk to price stability.

Stability of the International Monetary Regime

At the same time the Bundesbank vigorously resisted adjusting the DM exchange rate to combat inflationary pressure, seeking instead to put pressure on domestic economic policy, but it was over-ruled by the West German government in the early 1960s (Neumann 1999, pp. 297–298). The Bank of England was also wedded to the importance of a stable exchange rate as the foundation of the international financial leadership of the City of London as well as a constraint on successive government's tendency toward inflationary growth policy. This led to a series of sometimes heated battles between the Bank of England and the government (Schenk 2004). Central bankers tended to be strong advocates of exchange rate stability both because they believed this led to more orderly international markets and because fixed rates exercised discipline over government economic policy.

Flaws in the operation of the IMF created opportunities for central bankers to reassert their influence over the governance of the international monetary system. It took much longer to establish the conditions for freeing up exchange controls than had been anticipated at the Bretton Woods conference in 1944. Current account convertibility was generally delayed for twelve years beyond the inauguration of the IMF, so the system of multilateral payments designed at Bretton Woods could not come into practice. Borrowing from the IMF was also restrained initially by the alternative flow of Marshall Aid from 1947 and then by uncertainty about the conditionality that might be imposed on the economic policy of debtor governments. The IMF Executive Board and staff became a large bureaucratic organization focused on annual inspections of each member country's exchange controls and lacked the spontaneity and flexibility to deal with the periodic crises that threatened the pegged exchange rate regime. Meanwhile, G10 central bank governors met monthly at the Bank for International Settlements in Basel, Switzerland to discuss issues of mutual interest informally. This provided an alternative forum for the exchange of information about foreign exchange market intervention and coordinated support among central banks (Toniolo 2005; Schenk, 2010). Without being exposed to public scrutiny in their discussions or publicity for their operations, the Board of Governors of G10 (plus Switzerland) central banks were able to respond more nimbly to strains in the system.[6] There were two main routes through which the central bankers at Basel co-operated; lines of credit and the Gold Pool.

---

[6] Countries included Sweden, United Kingdom, France, Belgium, Netherlands, Italy, United States, Canada and Japan.

340   *Catherine Schenk and Tobias Straumann*

In March 1961, when the fixed US$ gold price of $35/oz came under pressure, the Federal Reserve Bank benefited from bilateral loans and sales of gold organized through the BIS. Three months later a more concerted line of credit (peaking at $904 million) was offered to support the Sterling exchange rate and a second support scheme was organized in the summer of 1963 ($250 million) (Toniolo 2005, pp. 382–383). The subsequent easing of market pressure and quick repayment of the arrangements persuaded central bankers that through concerted cooperation they could defend the international monetary system from attack by speculators. Sterling was a particular beneficiary of these schemes (Schenk, 2010), but other currencies including the Italian Lira were also supported through successive lines of credit organized quickly (sometimes overnight by telephone) among central bankers. In addition, and sometimes in concert, the US Federal Reserve engaged in substantial bilateral swaps with a range of central banks in Europe and beyond to provide extra liquidity, beginning in 1962 with a $50 million swap line with the Banque de France. By 1978 the Fed's swap network had grown to a total of $30 billion (Toniolo 2005, p. 387). What is particularly important about these networks of cooperation to support the international monetary system is that they did not require parliamentary approval and were not always made public in the way that inter-governmental loans were required to be.

As the international monetary system came under increasing pressure, the focus of attack was on sterling and the arrangements to support that currency were enhanced (Schenk 2010, chapter 8). In June 1966 the Bank of England negotiated a "Group Arrangement" of swap credits for up to $600 million from other G10 central banks at Basel. The facility was under-used and easily renewed in March 1967. But this time the entire amount was drawn in the crisis that preceded the devaluation of sterling in November 1967. A second "Group Arrangement" in 1968 (known as the Basel Agreement) became much more public and the terms of the credit were more onerous. This time, the Bank of England's creditor central banks required the British government to negotiate agreements with major sterling holders to maintain the ratio of sterling in their reserves. This could only be achieved through a guarantee of the dollar value of these reserves. An elaborate network of thirty-four bilateral Sterling Agreements was quickly concluded in order for the Bank of England to claim the $2 billion line of credit. Although at its height the British drawing was only $600 million, the psychological effect of this cushion of credit was believed to have quietened the market and restored credibility to the sterling exchange rate until the summer of 1972. While central banks did not have a statutory role in the operations and support for the international monetary system, it was clear that they established institutional frameworks that allowed it to survive through the 1960s.

The second major effort of coordination among G10 central banks was initiated by the IMF and government Treasuries. Concerned about the diverging market price of gold from the fixed price, the British and American governments developed a plan in 1961 for G10 central banks to cooperate to stabilize the London gold market. Toniolo (2005; pp. 375–381) relates how central bankers were initially reluctant to engage in "fixing" the market, but were eventually persuaded by the Americans, who arguably had the most to lose from a break in the gold value of the dollar. Each participating central bank earmarked an agreed amount of gold to be used by the Bank of England to intervene in the London market. In the first few years the scheme worked fairly well and deals were modest, but as confidence in the US dollar waned after the devaluation of sterling in November 1967, sales of gold escalated and the pool suspended operations in March 1968. Thereafter, the market price of gold was allowed to diverge from the fixed \$35/oz and the underpinning of the Bretton Woods system was fatally weakened.

Central bankers' various schemes to prop up the Bretton Woods pegged exchange rate system ultimately failed. In the early 1970s, under Chairman Arthur Burns, the US Fed persisted with expansionary monetary policy to counteract unemployment, increasing the pressure on the balance of payments and exposing the divergence of internal and external stability (Meltzer, 2010). During the early months of 1971, the US President Nixon and his Secretary of the Treasury John Connally came to view the support of the dollar price of gold as an unbearable burden on the American economy (Schenk, 2010). The so-called Nixon Shock of August 1971 suspended the convertibility of the US dollar to gold and threatened import surcharges if surplus countries did not revalue their currencies. Despite this dramatic departure from the Bretton Woods system, the renewed commitment to adjusted pegged exchange rates through the Smithsonian Agreement in December of 1971 demonstrates the tenacity with which governments of the G10 sought to avoid floating exchange rates. Within six months, however, the markets had tested the credibility of the new parities. From August to December 1971, despite the growing consensus among professional economists, policy-makers and central bankers clung to the pegged exchange rate regime, going through considerable contortions to replace it at different exchange rates under the Smithsonian Agreement.

This patch on the system was short-lived with the float of sterling in June 1972 and of European currencies and the Yen in February/March 1973. Even the float of sterling was only meant to be temporary until a (defendable) new equilibrium rate could be found; it was chosen because the government did not think that another pegged rate would be credible (Schenk 2010). The members of the IMF only formally embraced the new mixture of floating and managed exchange rates system in 1976.

Once again, the system had proved incompatible with the political environment. In the late 1960s the postwar social and political consensus came to an end in many countries, not only on the university campuses, but also in the wage agreements between employers and workers. Expansionary monetary policies and the lack of wage restraint reinforced each other and resulted in higher inflation expectations, thus bringing instability and a loss of confidence in the dollar. One major destabilizing political factor was the escalation of the war in Vietnam which lessened the US government's commitment to price stability. With divergent national economic policy priorities and goals, the float of most core currencies against the dollar ushered in a decade of instability punctuated by commodity and asset price shocks through the 1970s.

5 The Shift to Floating Exchange Rates and the Rise of Central Banks

The end of the Bretton Woods system launched a new era in the history of the international monetary regime. Its main feature has been the mixture of floating and managed exchange rates. Many countries, notably the United States, the United Kingdom and Japan, abandoned their fixed exchange rate regime in 1973 and since then have aimed at stabilizing domestic inflation. By contrast, France, Germany and most other members of the European Union (EU) have delegated their monetary sovereignty to the European Central Bank (ECB), while the euro itself is a floating currency. Many countries in East Asia, most notably China, have tried to keep their exchange rate stable against the dollar to foster export-led growth and have accumulated foreign exchange reserves as insurance against future crises. Still others have alternated between floating and pegged exchange rate regimes (Klein and Shambaugh 2010).

The post-1973 international monetary regime is perhaps best characterized as a dollar standard, because the US currency has remained the dominant unit of account, the preferred means of settlement and the most popular reserve currency. The Euro has not become a serious challenge to the dollar yet. The incomplete institutional foundation for the single European currency remains a threat to international monetary stability for the time being. The euro crisis of 2010 revealed the fragility of the system and the asymmetric effects to which a collection of diverse states in a single monetary union are prone. It has required considerable political will to overcome the crisis and ensure that the single currency solution continued. Eurosystem members have created a rescue fund (European Stability Mechanism) and have laid the basis for a banking union. But the architecture is still fragile. In order to become a serious alternative to the dollar, the euro needs to have more integrated financial markets, fiscal policy coordination and more flexibility of factor markets.

In more recent times, the Chinese Renminbi has been identified as a potential new rival for the dollar. But, as with the euro, it seems premature to predict its imminent supremacy since this would require the Chinese government to liberalize the capital account, which entails financial and political risks. Therefore the Chinese authorities have chosen a stepwise approach by establishing off-shore trading platforms and enhancing bilateral trade payments using the Chinese currency while preserving capital controls to insulate the domestic monetary and financial system from external shocks. Meanwhile the People's Bank of China has grappled with intense domestic monetary strains posed partly by its pegged rate policy during the 2000s when enormous balance of payments surpluses threatened price stability through internal and external capital controls. Thus, despite the seismic shocks to the global financial system, the ascendency of the dollar persisted.

The dollar standard went through two distinctive phases. The first phase, lasting from 1973 to 1979, was characterized by a high degree of instability. Inflation rates within the core diverged considerably; West Germany and Japan restoring price stability after the first oil shock, while France, the United Kingdom and the United States gave priority to full employment over price stability. As a result, exchange rates became very volatile. Outside the G7, other groups of countries were set adrift by the float of the dollar in the 1970s, prompting a more stratified global system.[7] Developing economies faced particular obstacles to adopting floating exchange rates with relatively thin local foreign exchange markets and

---

[7] G7 included United States, Japan, Canada, United Kingdom, Germany, France and Italy.

vulnerability to seasonal instability due to dependence on primary product production. Also, the "seal of approval" (Bordo and Rockoff 1996) identified for peripheral states in the classic nineteenth century that enhanced their ability to borrow in global capital markets appeared to persist for emerging and developing economies a century later. As a result, many countries continued to peg their exchange rates to the dollar as a commitment mechanism. When pegging to a depreciating dollar became uncomfortable in the inflationary era of the 1970s, some opted for adjustable pegs or pegged to trade weighted baskets (Schenk and Singleton 2015).

The second phase started in the late 1970s when the United States, the United Kingdom and a series of other OECD countries began to rein in inflation regardless of the short-term cost to employment. As a result, exchange rate volatility decreased, and the international monetary system gained in stability. The era of the Great Moderation from the 1980s to 2008 achieved consistently low inflation rates in most of the industrialized world and the financial and currency crises that punctuated this stability had mainly regional effects, although these were at times severe. The success of macroeconomic policies in the 1980s and 1990s encouraged the member states of the European Economic Community (EEC) – since 1992 the EU – to move inexorably toward monetary union by introducing the euro in 1999 (Mourlon-Druol 2012).

During the 1990s, a consensus emerged that countries should adopt either a "hard peg" that had strong credibility through a currency board of currency substitution, or they should freely float their exchange rate (Fischer 2001). This bi-polar view reflected the repeated failures to defend pegged rates against market attack and the mixed record of experiments with sterilized intervention in foreign exchange markets. Direct operations by central banks in the foreign exchange market alone seemed to have at best short term effects; to be more effective they required buttressing monetary policies. In the same period, however, financial and currency crises in emerging markets stretching from Mexico in 1994 to the Asian Financial Crisis of 1997, the Rouble crisis of 1999 and the Argentinian crisis of 2002 pushed most of these countries to resort to floating exchange rates. In particular, the collapse of Argentina's currency board cast doubt on the bipolar solution. Indeed, the IMF argued in 2011 that emerging markets with pegged exchange rates were more vulnerable to currency and financial crises. With little theoretical support for intermediate regimes, emerging market economies were urged to follow the United States in a free float, but most exhibited a so-called "fear of floating" (Calvo and Reinhart 2002). While many claimed to float, in fact the incidence of

Stability of the International Monetary Regime

Table 8.4: *IMF de facto classification of exchange rate regimes for emerging markets for 2009*

Emerging markets with freely floating exchange rate	Emerging markets with manage floating exchange rate	Emerging markets with pegged exchange rate
Brazil	Columbia	Hungary
Chile	Peru	Qatar
Korea	Czech Republic	United Arab Emirates (UAE)
Mexico	Egypt	China
Philippines	Russia	
Poland	India	
South Africa	Indonesia	
Turkey	Malaysia	
	Thailand	
	Malaysia	

Source IMF 2009
Note: no classification for Taiwan.

intervention and capital controls were more prevalent in practice (Reinhart and Rogoff 2004). Meanwhile, wide fluctuations in exchange rates among core countries such as the United States, Japan and Europe threatened to have damaging consequences for smaller countries.

Among emerging markets, the share of countries that have a pegged or a managed floating exchange rate is still far higher than the share of countries with a freely floating exchange rate. According to the IMF de facto classification for the year 2007, ninety-eight had a pegged exchange rate,[8] four a crawling peg, fifty-six a floating exchange rate and only sixteen a freely floating exchange rate (Table 8.4). By 2009 the IMF analysis based on de facto regimes (rather than de jure) determined that economies with a formal pegged rate regime had a better record for inflation. But growth performance was better with an intermediate system, for example by not adopting a strict bilateral peg to another currency.

Some scholars have interpreted the persistence of stable exchange rates among emerging markets as a sign of a revived Bretton Woods system (Dooley, Folkerts-Landau and Garber 2004). The accumulation of dollar reserves among Asian countries as a result of undervalued pegs against a depreciating dollar since 2000 is compared to the similar surpluses accumulated by rapidly growing Japanese and West German economies in the

---

[8] Including regional agreements like the West African Economic and Monetary Union.

1960s. Due to cheap imports from Asia, inflationary pressure in the United States declined, leading the Fed to keep real interest rates at a historic low. Asian central banks suffered from the low US yields, but were willing to accept them as long as the growth strategy was seen as vital for political and social stability. Whether this mutual dependence between Asia and the United States justifies speaking of a revived Bretton Woods system, is open to debate. But the behavior of Asian countries strongly confirms the impression that the dollar standard can be considered an international monetary regime from 1980, based on structural relations, rather than a "non-system" of exchange rate regimes.

What role have central banks played in this new international monetary system? As for the period between 1973 and 1979, most of them either proved helpless in containing price and exchange rate volatility or at worst reinforced the fragility of the system. Lacking statutory independence (except in a few countries like Western Germany and Switzerland) they were subject to the political business cycle which resulted into high and persistent inflation. In particular, the Fed focused almost exclusively on domestic issues, causing frequent plunges and reversals in the real value of the dollar that increased the fragility of the international financial system. Overall, the 1970s were one of the low points in the history of modern central banking. The combination of political dependence and international policy divergence made it impossible for them to stabilize the monetary system.

Towards the end of the decade the situation began to change. The successful reduction of inflation in the mid-1970s by the Bundesbank and the Swiss National Bank became the template for other countries to restore price stability (Bernanke et al. 1999). In this process central banks seized the moment to reaffirm their position vis-a-vis their governments. Notably, the Fed experienced a comeback under Paul Volcker (formerly Under Secretary of the Treasury for Monetary Affairs) who used his tenure as chairman to operate an aggressive monetary policy that successfully cut inflation in the United States and contributed to wider systemic stability. His determined and successful actions also strengthened the independent status of the central bank. Alan Greenspan, Volcker's successor from 1987, allowed real interest rates to decline further in an environment of stable inflation and reduced business cycle volatility. When Greenspan's successor Ben Bernanke took office in February of 2006, he was quickly confronted with the global financial crisis of 2007–2009 and its repercussions. The Fed provided a range of lifelines to prevent the financial system from collapsing, pushed the federal funds rate to the zero lower

Stability of the International Monetary Regime 347

bound and initiated several rounds of quantitative easing. So far, it has been successful in preventing a severe depression coupled with deflation. And most importantly, central bank independence, though questioned by some members of Congress, is still in place.

The reemphasis on domestic policy goals and the abandonment of managed exchange rates marked a turning point for relations between central banks and governments in all core countries (Cukierman 1992). The move to inflation targeting in the early 1990s reinforced the trend for central banks to become legally independent from the government. This institutional innovation shields them from domestic political concerns and aims to promote longer term focus on stable prices (Berger et al. 2001). In a more flexible exchange rate regime, central banks in the main industrialized countries have thus enhanced their independent influence over markets. At the same time, however, their role in the international monetary system has been marginalized as their range of policy targets has been reduced. Nevertheless, a keen awareness of the interdependence of national economic policies means that institutional independence from their national governments has not resulted in an absence of international cooperation among central bankers. The backbone of central bank cooperation has continued to be the Board of Governors of the BIS. It has served as the major institutional forum for central banks to develop relationships which allow a coordinated response to changes in the international monetary system and has adapted to the shifting complexion of international economic relations. With the rise of emerging market economies such as China, Brazil and Russia as important players, the BIS Board of Directors was expanded to twenty-one members in 2005. Among the original members the central bank Governors of Belgium, France, Germany, Italy, the United Kingdom and the United States (plus an extra representative from each of these countries) continue to have a seat, but they are joined by an additional nine elected governors of other central banks. This expansion makes the organization more representative, but it has also altered the practical nature of the meetings, the informality and traditions of the cooperative structures in place since the financial crisis of 1931.

Other multilateral and bilateral cooperative institutions for central banking operate alongside the BIS. Bilateral cooperation through central bank swaps continues to be an important element of the management of the international monetary system. For example in December 2007 the Federal Reserve authorized bilateral swap facilities with fourteen central banks to sustain liquidity when there were strains in global short term dollar funding markets. The dollar swap lines were predominantly used by

348   *Catherine Schenk and Tobias Straumann*

the ECB, Swiss National Bank and the Bank of England in 2008–2009.[9] In a multilateral forum, central bank governors meet alongside finance ministers at the regular G7 summits that began in the late 1970s, prompted by a desire to moderate "excessive" volatility and "disorderly" exchange rates that were blamed for "adverse implications for economic and financial stability". At each summit the participants reassert their commitment to market determined exchange rates but also signal their determination to "cooperate as appropriate".[10] Central bank governors are also sometimes named as alternate representatives at the IMF Board of Governors (Bodea and Huemer 2010). But the effectiveness of central bank operations in stabilizing exchange rate dynamics has been controversial.

Many countries also choose to intervene in exchange markets from time to time to stabilize nominal rates and central banks have an operational role in this task. Mostly, the intervention is sterilized to insulate the domestic monetary base and a consensus emerged in the 1990s that such sterilized intervention was generally ineffective, although there have been exceptions where the market accepted that the interventions signaled future changes in economic policy and fundamentals. After a substantial appreciation of the US dollar against the DM in 1984, for example, there was a coordinated intervention by the Bundesbank, the Federal Reserve System and the Bank of Japan in early 1985. This was followed by a series of large and well publicized interventions in the late 1980s and early 1990s by G5 central banks to moderate fluctuations of the core industrialised countries' currencies as part of the Plaza Agreement of 1985 and the Louvre Accord of 1987 (Dominguez 1998; Sarno and Taylor 2001). From the early 2000s, however, central banks in the main industrialised countries withdrew from foreign exchange intervention.

Central banks in emerging market economies have tended to intervene more in exchange markets to dampen volatility, curb speculation or to influence the level of exchange rate during the 2000s (Mohanty and Bat-el Berger 2013; Menkhoff 2013). In the wake of the 2008 global financial crisis the priority of domestic economic stabilization resulted in rapid monetary expansion in the United States and other industrialized economies as they sought to avoid the deflationary spiral of the 1930s Great Depression. This introduced a new era of uncoordinated monetary policies and exchange rate instability that created negative externalities for many emerging market economies that have suffered from appreciating nominal

---

[9] www.federalreserve.gov/newsevents/reform_swaplines.htm.

[10] Quotations from the 2013 G7 Ministers and Governors' statement.

exchange rates as the dollar depreciated. Because nominal exchange rate changes can affect domestic prices, central banks in emerging market economies have thus intervened in foreign exchange markets to support their inflation targeting. The asymmetric onus of adjustment between the USA and emerging market economies has in turn led to new calls for reform of the international monetary and financial architecture.

Surveying the period since 1979, the international monetary regime has so far delivered the two public goods – international currencies and external stability – for most of the time, and central banks have contributed to international monetary stability, although the system has been quite heterogeneous and gone through different crises. The crucial variable has been the independence of central banks, which has enabled them to preserve price stability against the short-term interests of the government and to take extraordinary measures in times of crisis. The other variable, the degree of international policy convergence, seems to have been less relevant since 1979. There were times when the core nations pursued different policy goals, but the international monetary system was not threatened by this divergence, thanks to the floating exchange rate regimes in the core countries. Of course, our overall positive assessment of what central banks have achieved over the last few decades may be premature. At the time of writing, the negative consequences of the global financial crisis are still not digested.

6 Conclusion

This survey has discussed the question of how central banks in the core economies contributed to the stability of the international monetary system. Our hypothesis is that the combination of three variables answers this question: the exchange rate system, the degree of international policy convergence and the extent of central bank independence. Under a system of fixed exchange rates central banks can play a constructive role only when there is a high degree of international policy convergence, while central bank independence is secondary. By contrast, under a system of floating exchange rates central bank independence is the crucial variable, while the degree of international policy convergence is less important.

We have traced the historical development from the nineteenth century when the management of national currencies emerged as an important policy instrument and central banks were required to operationalize the gold standard in most countries, which proved to be quite stable. The underlying reason was that from the 1870s to 1914 core countries adhered to the same liberal principles and central bankers were able to use their room of manoeuver in a constructive way thanks to this strong liberal consensus. Fixed exchange rates in the twentieth century, however, were not sustainable due to the lack of common goals and interests. Central banks were not able to overcome the centrifugal political as well as economic forces in the 1920s and the 1960s, even though they were independent in the first period and collaborated extensively in the latter one.

Subsequently, the system of floating exchange rates in the 1970s proved unstable because most central banks, notably the Fed, the Bank of England and the Banque de France, were not independent. They were subject to short-term considerations of the cabinet, political parties and lobbying groups. In the late 1970s, following the German and Swiss example, governments began to free central banks from their political dependence. As a result, the international monetary system became much more stable. Since then, central banks have played a pivotal role in preserving the two public goods any international monetary regime is supposed to provide: international currencies and external stability – perhaps more than ever in history. Central banks also managed to prevent the system from collapsing during the severe financial crisis of 2007–2009. They could draw on the range of operations to prop up the fixed exchange rate system deployed in the 1960s, such as bilateral swap network, with the BIS having an important role in bringing central bankers together to exchange views and information confidentially. In contrast to the 1930s, the international monetary order among core economies has not broken down, although the longer term extent and impact of spillover effects on emerging market economies remains unresolved.

Accordingly, praising or blaming central bankers for the functioning of the international monetary system misses the core fact that crucial levers were often outside their reach. While exercising some informal power through their responsibility for operationalizing the decisions of governments over the form of the international monetary system and occasionally influencing the decisions more directly, central banks have generally played a supportive rather than leading role. They have been able to exploit their particular characteristics, such as their technical expertise, their close links with the private sector and their ability to take agile and sometimes secretive action. In the end, however, politics and institutions decide whether or not central banks are able to play a constructive role.

References

Attard, B., 1992. "The Bank of England and the Origins of the Niemeyer Mission, 1921–30," *Australian Economic History Review* 32, pp. 66–83.

Berg, Claes and Jonung, Lars, 1999. "Pioneering Price Level Targeting: The Swedish Experience 1931–1937," *Journal of Monetary Economics* 43(3), pp. 525–551.

Berger, H., J. de Hann and S.C.W. Eijffinger, 2001. "Central Bank Independence: An Update of Theory and Evidence," *Journal of Economic Surveys* 15(1), pp. 3–40.

Bernanke, Ben, Laubach, Thomas, Mishkin, Frederic and Posen, Adam, 1999. *Inflation Targeting: Lessons from the International Experience.* Princeton N.J.: Princeton University Press.

Bignon, Vincent, Flandreau, Marc and Ugolini, Stefano, 2012. "Bagehot for Beginners: The Making of Lender-of-Last-Resort Operations in the Mid-Nineteenth Century," *Economic History Review* 65(2), pp. 580–608.

Bodea, C. and Huemer, S., 2010. "Dancing Together at Arm's Length? The Interaction of Central Banks with Governments in the G7," *European Central Bank Occasional Paper* 120.

Bordo, Michael D. and Capie, Forrest, 1993. "Introduction," in Michael D. Bordo and Forrest Capie, *Monetary Regimes in Transition*, Cambridge and New York: Cambridge University Press, pp. 1–12.

Bordo, Michael D. and Flandreau, Marc, 2003. "Core, Periphery, Exchange Rate Regimes, and Globalization," in Michael D. Bordo, Alan M. Taylor, and Jeffrey G. Williamson (eds.), *Globalization in Historical Perspective*, Chicago: The University of Chicago Press, pp. 417–472.

Bordo, Michael D., Humpage, O.F., and Schwartz, A.J., 2010. "US Foreign Exchange Market Intervention during the Volcker-Greenspan Era," *NBER Working Paper* 16345.

Bordo Michael D. and Kydland, Finn E., 1995. "The Gold Standard As a Rule: An Essay in Exploration," *Explorations in Economic History* 32(4), pp. 423–464.

Bordo, Michael D. and MacDonald, Ronald, 2012. *Credibility and the International Monetary Regime: A Historical Perspective, Studies in Macroeconomic History*, Cambridge and New York: Cambridge University Press.

Bordo, Michael D. and Rockoff, Hugh, 1996. "The Gold Standard as a "Good Housekeeping Seal of Approval," *The Journal of Economic History* 56(02), pp. 389–428.

Bordo, Michael D. and Schwartz, Anna, 1999. "Monetary Policy Regimes and Economic Performance: The Historical Record," in John Taylor and Michael Woodford (eds.), *Handbook of Macroeconomics*, Volume 1 A, pp. 149–234.

Burdekin, Richard C.K., Mitchener, Kris, and Weidenmier, Marc D., 2012. "Irving Fisher and Price-Level Targeting in Austria: Was Silver the Answer?," *Journal of Money*, Credit and Banking 44(4), pp. 733–750.

Calomiris, Charles, 2011. "Banking Crises and the Rules of the Game," in Geoffrey Wood, Terence Mills and Nicholas Crafts (eds.), *Monetary and Banking History: Essays in Honour of Forrest Capie*, Routledge, pp. 88–132.

Calvo, G.A. and Reinhart, C.M., 2002. "Fear of Floating," *Quarterly Journal of Economics* 117 (2), pp. 379–409.

352 Catherine Schenk and Tobias Straumann

Capie, Forrest, Stanley Fischer, Charles Goodhart and Norbert Schnadt, 1994. *The Future of Central Banking: The Tercentenary Symposium of the Bank of England*, Cambridge and New York: Cambridge University Press.

Carlson, Mark and Mitchener, Kris, 2009. "Branch Banking as a Device for Discipline: Competition and Bank Survivorship during the Great Depression," *Journal of Political Economy* 117(2), pp. 165–210.

Chwieroth, J.M., 2010. *Capital Ideas: The IMF and the Rise of Financial Liberalization*, Princeton: Princeton University Press.

Contamin, Rémy, 2003. "Interdépendances financières et dilemme de politique monétaire. La Banque de France entre 1880 et 1913," *Revue économique* 54 (1), pp. 157–180.

Cukierman, Alex, 1992. *Central Bank Strategy, Credibility, and Independence: Theory and Evidence*, Cambridge, MA: The MIT Press.

De la Torre, A., A. Ize and S. Schmukler, 2011. *Financial Development in LAC: The Road Ahead*, Washington, DC: World Bank.

Dominquez, K.M., 1998. "Central Bank Intervention and Exchange Rate Volatility," *Journal of International Money and Finance* 17(1), pp. 161–190.

Dooley, Michael P., David Folkerts-Landau and Garber, Peter. "The Revived Bretton Woods System," *International Journal of Finance and Economics* 9(4), pp. 307–313.

Dorrucci, Ettore, and McKay, Julie, 2011. "The international monetary system after the financial crisis," *Occasional Paper Series* 123, European Central Bank.

Eichengreen, Barry and Hausmann, Ricardo, 1999. *Other People's Money: Debt Denomination and Financial Instability in Emerging Market Economies*, Chicago: The University of Chicago Press.

Eichengreen, Barry and Temin, Peter, 2000. "The Gold Standard and the Great Depression," *Contemporary European History* 9(2), pp. 183–207.

Eichengreen, Barry, 1992. *Golden Fetters. The Gold Standard and the Great Depression 1919-1939*, Oxford and New York: Oxford University Press.

  1996. *Globalizing Capital: A History of the International Monetary System*, Princeton: Princeton University Press.

Einaudi, Luca, 2001. *European Monetary Unification and the International Gold Standard (1865-1873)*, Oxford and New York: Oxford University Press.

Eitrheim, Øyvind, Klovland, Jan Tore, and Øksendal, Lars Fredrik, 2016 (forthcoming). *A Monetary History of Norway*, 1816-2016, Cambridge and New York: Cambridge University Press.

Feinstein, Charles, Peter Temin and Gianni Toniolo, 1997. *The European Economy between the Wars*, Oxford and New York: Oxford University Press.

Fischer, Stanley, 2001. "Exchange Rate Regimes: Is the Bipolar View Correct?," *Journal of Economic Perspectives* 15(2), pp. 3–24.

Flandreau, Marc, 1996. "The French Crime of 1873: An Essay on the Emergence of the International Gold Standard, 1870-1880,"*The Journal of Economic History, Cambridge University Press* 56(04), pp. 862–897.

  1997. "Central Bank Cooperation in Historical Perspective: A Sceptical View," *Economic History Review* 50(4), pp. 735–763.

  2002. "'Water Seeks a Level'": Modeling Bimetallic Exchange Rates and the Bimetallic Band," *Journal of Money, Credit and Banking* 34(2), pp. 491–519.

Stability of the International Monetary Regime

2004. *The Glitter of Gold: France, Bimetallism and the Emergence of the International Gold Standard 1848-1873*, Oxford and New York: Oxford University Press.

Flandreau, Marc and James, Harold, 2003. "Introduction," in Marc Flandreau, Carl-Ludwig Holtfrerich and Harold James (eds.), *International Financial History in the Twentieth : System and Anarchy*, Cambridge: Cambridge University Press, pp. 1–17.

Flandreau, Marc, and Komlos, John, 2006. "Target Zones in Theory and History: Credibility, Efficiency, and Policy Autonomy," *Journal of Monetary Economics* 53(8), pp. 1979–1995.

Friedman, Milton and Schwartz, Anna, 1963. *A Monetary History of the United States, 1867-1960*, Princeton: Princeton University Press.

Friedman, Milton, 1990. "Bimetallism Revisited," *Journal of Economic Perspectives* 4(4), pp. 85–104.

Gallarotti, Giulio, 1995. *The Anatomy of an International Monetary Regime: The Classical Gold Standard 1880-1914*, Oxford and New York: Oxford University Press.

Ghosh, A.R., Ostry, J.D., and Tsangarides, C., 2010. "Exchange Rate Regimes and the Stability of the International Monetary System," *Occasional Paper* 270, Washington D.C.: International Monetary Fund.

Grauwe, Paul De, 2012. "The Governance of a Fragile Eurozone," *Australian Economic Review* 45 (3), pp. 255–268.

Gros, Daniel and Thygesen, Niels, 1992. *European Monetary Integration*, London: Longman.

Helleiner, Eric, 2005. "A Fixation with Floating: The Politics of Canada's Exchange Rate Regime," *Canadian Journal of Political Science* 38(01), pp. 23–44.

Irwin, Douglas A., 2010. "Did France Cause the Great Depression?," *NBER Working Paper* 16350, September.

James, Harold, 2012. *Making the European Monetary Union: The Role of the Committee of Central Bank Governors and the Origins of the European Central Bank*, Cambridge (Mass.): Harvard University Press.

2013. "The 1931 Central European Banking Crisis Revisited," in Hartmut Berghoff, Jürgen Kocka and Dieter Ziegler (eds.), *Essays in Modern German and Austrian Economic History*, edited by. Cambridge: Cambridge University Press, pp. 119–132.

Jobst, Clemens, 2009. "Market leader: the Austro-Hungarian Bank and the making of foreign exchange intervention, 1896–1913," *European Review of Economic History* 13(3), pp. 287–318.

Kaplan J. and Schleiminger, G., 1989. *The European Payments Union; Financial Diplomacy in the 1950s*, Oxford: Clarendon Press.

Kindleberger, Charles P., 1973. *The World in Depression, 1929-1939*, Berkeley: University of California Press.

Klein, Michael W. and Shambaugh, Jay C., 2010. *Exchange Rate Regimes in the Modern Era*, Cambridge (Mass.) and London: The MIT Press.

Kleivset, Christoffer, 2012. "From a Fixed Exchange Rate Regime to Inflation Targeting. A Documentation Paper on Norges Bank and Monetary Policy, 1992–2001," *Norges Bank Working Paper* 13.

Laidler, David, 1999. *Fabricating the Keynesian Revolution: Studies of the Inter-war Literature on Money, the Cycle, and Unemployment*, New York and Cambridge: Cambridge University Press.

Meissner, Christopher M., 2005. "A New World Order: Explaining the International Diffusion of the Gold Standard, 1870-1913," *Journal of International Economics* 66 (2), pp. 385–406.

Menkhoff, L., 2013. "Foreign Exchange Intervention in Emerging Markets: A Survey of Empirical Studies," *The World Economy* 36(9), pp. 1187–1208.

Meltzer, Allan H., 2003. *A History of the Federal Reserve, Volume 1, 1913-1951*, Chicago: University of Chicago Press.

 2010. *A History of the Federal Reserve, Volume 2, Book 1, 1951-1969*, Chicago: University of Chicago Press.

Mitchener, Kris and Weidenmier, Marc D., 2008. "The Baring Crisis and the Great Latin American Meltdown of the 1890s," *The Journal of Economic History* 68(02), pp. 462–500.

Mohanty, M.S. and Berger, Bat-el, 2013. "Central Bank Views on Foreign Exchange Intervention," *Bank for International Settlements Papers* 73.

Morys, Matthias, 2013. "Discount Rate Policy under the Classical Gold Standard: Core versus Periphery (1870s–1914)," *Explorations in Economic History* 50(2), pp. 205–226.

Mourlon-Druol, Emmanuel, 2012. *A Europe Made of Money: The Emergence of the European Monetary System*, Ithaca: Cornell University Press.

Neumann, Manfred J., 1999. "Monetary Stability: Threat and Proven Reponse," in Deutsche Bundesbank (ed.), *Fifty Years of the Deutsche Mark*, Oxford: Oxford University Press, pp. 260–306.

Ögren, Anders, 2012. "Central Banking and Monetary Policy in Sweden during the Long Nineteenth Century," in Lars Fredrik Øksendal and Anders Ögren (eds.), *The Gold Standard Peripheries: Monetary Policy, Adjustment and Flexibility in a Global Setting*, Basingstoke: Palgrave Macmillan.

Øksendal, Lars Fredrik, 2012. "Freedom for Manouevre. The Gold Standard Experience of Norway, 1874–1914," in Lars Fredrik Øksendal and Anders Ögren (eds.), *The Gold Standard Peripheries: Monetary Policy, Adjustment and Flexibility in a Global Setting*, Basingstoke: Palgrave Macmillan.

Reinhart, Carmen and Rogoff, Kenneth, 2004. "The Modern History of Exchange Rate Arrangements: A Reinterpretation," *The Quarterly Journal of Economics* 119(1), pp. 1–48.

 2009. *This Time Is Different: Eight Centuries of Financial Folly*, Princeton: Princeton University Press.

Ritschl, Albrecht, 2013. "Reparations, Deficits, and Debt Defaults," in Nicholas Crafts and Peter Fearon (eds.), *The Great Depression of the 1930s: Lessons for Today*, Oxford: Oxford University Press, pp. 110–139.

Ritschl, Albrecht and Straumann, Tobias, 2010. "Business Cycles and Economic Policy, 1914-1945", in Stephen Broadberry and Kevin O'Rourke (eds.), *The Cambridge Economic History of Modern Europe*, Volume 2, Cambridge and New York: Cambridge University Press, 2010, pp. 156–180.

Sarno, L. and Taylor, M.P., 2001. "Official Intervention in the Foreign Exchange Market: Is It Effective and, if so, How Does It Work?," *Journal of Economic Literature* 39(3), pp. 839–868.

Sayers, Richard S., 1976. *The Bank of England, 1891-1944*, Volume 1, Cambridge: Cambridge University Press.

Schenk, Catherine, 2004. "The New City and the State in the 1960s," in Ranald Michie and Philip Williamson (eds.) *The British Government and the City of London in the Twentieth Century*, Cambridge: Cambridge University Press, pp. 322–339.

2010. *The Decline of Sterling: Managing the Retreat of an International Currency, 1945–1992*, Cambridge: Cambridge University Press.

Siklos, Pierre L., 2002. *The Changing Face of Central Banking: Evolutionary Trends Since World War II*, Cambridge: Cambridge University Press.

2009. "Not Quite as Advertised: Canada's Managed Float in the 1950s and Bank of Canada Intervention," *European Review of Economic History* 13(03), pp. 413–435.

Singleton, John, 2011. *Central Banking in the Twentieth Century*, Cambridge: Cambridge University Press.

Singleton, John and Schenk, Catherine, 2015. "The Shift from Sterling to the Dollar 1965-76: Evidence from Australia and New Zealand," *Economic History Review* 68(4), pp. 1154–1176.

Straumann, Tobias and Woitek, Ulrich, 2009. "A Pioneer of a New Monetary Policy? Sweden's Price-Level Targeting of the 1930s Revisited," *European Review of Economic History* 13(02), pp. 251–282.

Straumann, Tobias, 2010. *Fixed Ideas of Money: Small States and Exchange Rate Regimes in Twentieth-Century Europe*, Cambridge and New York: Cambridge University Press.

Swoboda, Alexander, 1986. "Credibility and Viability in International Monetary Arrangements," *Finance and Development* 23, pp. 15–18.

Toniolo, Gianni, 2005. *Central Bank Cooperation at the Bank for International Settlements, 1930-1973*, Cambridge and New York: Cambridge University Press.

Ugolini, Stefano, 2010. "The International Monetary System, 1844–1870: Arbitrage, Efficiency, Liquidity," *Working Paper* 2010/23, Norges Bank.

2012. "The Origins of Foreign Exchange Policy: The National Bank of Belgium and the Quest for Monetary Independence in the 1850s," *European Review of Economic History* 16(1), pp. 51–73.

Velde, François, and Weber, Warren E., 2000. "A Model of Bimetallism," *Journal of Political Economy* 108(6), pp. 1210–1234.

Wicker, Elmus, 1996. *The Banking Panics of the Great Depression*, New York: Cambridge University Press.

9

The International Monetary and Financial System

A Capital Account Historical Perspective

Claudio Borio
Bank for International Settlements

Harold James
Princeton University

Hyun Song Shin
Bank for International Settlements

When during the liquidity crisis of 1931 one European market after the other sustained sweeping withdrawals of short-term balances, the dangers involved in superabundance of international short-term lending became strikingly apparent. It was then felt that measures might have been taken to moderate the increasing indebtedness if the stupendous growth of liabilities had been known at the time. 4th BIS Annual Report, 1934.

1 Introduction[1]

There is one history of the international monetary and financial system (IMFS) that is about current accounts. It is the most popular and influential. It goes back to at least David Hume's view of the gold specie standard (Hume (1752)). It sees the economic havoc in the interwar years through the eyes of the transfer problem (Keynes (1929a,b), Ohlin (1929a,b)). It identifies a systematic contractionary bias in the global economy because of an asymmetric adjustment problem: deficit countries are forced to retrench while surplus countries are under no pressure to expand (Keynes (1941)). It traces the 1970s woes and Latin American crisis to the recycling

---

Paper prepared for the Norges Bank conference, 5–6 June 2014

[1] We would like to thank Angelika Donaubauer for excellent statistical support. The views expressed are our own and not necessarily those of the BIS.

The International Monetary and Financial System 357

of oil exporters' surpluses (Lomax (1986), Congdon (1988)). It argues that a saving glut, reflected in large Asian current account surpluses, was at the root of the Great Financial Crisis that erupted in 2007 (Bernanke (2005, 2009), Krugman (2009), King (2010)). And it is front and centre in G20 discussions, heavily preoccupied with global imbalances – a short-hand for current account imbalances.

There is a parallel history that is about capital accounts. It is less popular and, in large part, still to be written. It highlights the role of the mobility of financial capital in the gold standard (Bloomfield (1959), De Cecco (1974)). It sees the economic turmoil of the interwar years through the lens of large cross-border flows (Schuker (1988)). It focuses on biases and asymmetries that arise from countries' playing the role of bankers to the world (Triffin (1960), Kindleberger (1965), Despres et al. (1966)). It argues that a financial surge, unrelated to current accounts, was at the origin of the Great Financial Crisis (Borio and Disyatat (2011), Shin (2012)). It laments the peripheral attention that the G20 pay to financial, as opposed to current account, imbalances.

Of course, these two views should be reconcilable. After all, the current and capital accounts are part of the same balance-of-payments identity. And our sharp distinction between the two histories is intentionally stylised. At times narratives diverge, but at others they intersect or even merge (e.g., Obstfeld (2010, 2012)).

That said, the lens matters. It matters for the analysis. To focus on current accounts means zeroing in on the good markets – on output and expenditures – as well as on net capital flows. To focus on the capital account means zeroing in on asset markets as well as on gross capital flows and the corresponding stocks. In fact, most international finance macro models nowadays are about current accounts and net flows, as the residual to consumption and investment decisions. And the lens matters also for policy. Central banks have far less influence on the current account than on the capital account: monetary and financial stability policies – what central banking is all about – are fundamentally about changes in asset prices, portfolios and balance sheet positions.

This paper fits in this second, parallel history of the IMFS. Its premise is that in a highly globalised economy financial markets hold sway and the most serious macroeconomic problems arise from financial system breakdowns – systemic financial crises. These cannot be understood by focusing on current accounts alone. In fact, in some important respects, current accounts may be a distraction. The Achilles heel of the IMFS is not so much a contractionary bias that reflects an asymmetric current account adjustment problem, what might be termed a propensity to generate "excess saving"; rather, it is its propensity to amplify the financial booms and busts – financial cycles – that generate crises, what might be termed its "excess financial elasticity" (Borio and Disyatat (2011), Borio (2014a)). Surges and collapses in credit expansion, be these through banks – "banking gluts" – or securities markets, are key ingredients (Shin (2012, 2013)), typically alongside equivalent surges and collapses in asset prices, especially property prices (Drehmann et al. (2012)).

Moreover, once we focus on the system's excess financial elasticity we need to look beyond the capital account. For one, the decision-making units, be these financial or non-financial, often straddle borders. The residence principle that defines the boundary for the national accounts, and hence also for the balance of payments, is inadequate: we need to consider the consolidated income and balance sheet positions of the relevant players. In addition, the currencies underpinning financial and real transactions, in which goods and services are invoiced and, above all, assets are denominated, are often used outside national boundaries. Some currencies play a huge role in the IMFS, most notably the US dollar – a point fully understood by those steeped into international monetary system issues, but often overlooked in standard macroeconomic models used to examine spillovers and coordination questions. Finally, it is not so much the international component of the balance sheet position of a country that matters, but how it fits into the overall balance sheet of the economy. Financial and macroeconomic vulnerabilities can be properly assessed only in that context.

In this paper we illustrate these points by examining two historical phases of special interest: the interwar years and the period surrounding the recent Great Financial Crisis. Both phases featured high financial market integration globally and hence illustrate perfectly our arguments.

The rest of the paper is organised as follows. Section 2 lays out the main analytical reference points; it does so briefly, as they have been discussed in more detail elsewhere. Section 3 revisits the interwar years, while Section 4 recalls the more recent experience.

2 Analytical Reference Points

Two analytical reference points anchor our discussion: the excess financial elasticity hypothesis and the inadequacy of the national accounts boundary to capture the complex web of financial transactions that can give rise to serious macroeconomic vulnerabilities. Consider each in turn.

The excess financial elasticity hypothesis

Financial crises are not like meteorite strikes from outer space. They resemble volcanic eruptions or earthquakes: they reflect the sudden and violent release of pressure that has built up gradually over time. The pressure takes the form of protracted financial booms, which often straddle business cycle fluctuations until they become unsustainable, thereby sowing the seeds of their subsequent demise. The build-up of such financial imbalances gives rise to endogenous boom-bust processes, or "financial cycles" (Borio (2013a)). Systemic banking crises typically occur towards their peak and usher in the bust phase; the subsequent recessions are especially deep and the recoveries weak (e.g., Drehmann et al. (2012)).

The most characteristic hallmark of these cycles is the surge and collapse in credit expansion (e.g., Drehmann et al. (2011), Aikman et al. (2011), Jordá et al. (2011a), Drehmann and Tsatsaronis (2014)), typically alongside equivalent fluctuations in asset prices, especially property prices (Drehmann et al. (2012)). And because as credit expansion proceeds retail funding lags behind, a growing share of the financing comes from wholesale funding, such as non-core bank deposits, often from international sources (Borio and Lowe (2004), Shin and Shin (2010), Borio et al. (2011), Hahm et al. (2013)).

We do not have a full understanding of the forces at work. But a key mechanism involves the self-reinforcing interaction between loosely anchored perceptions of value and risk as well as attitudes towards risk, on the one hand, and liquidity or financing constraints, on the other. In modern terminology, the "price of risk" moves highly procyclically, amplifying financial and economic fluctuations (e.g., Borio et al. (2001), Danielsson et al. (2004), Adrian and Shin (2010)). It is this interaction that imparts considerable inertia to the process.

Borio and Disyatat (2011) and Borio (2014a) use the term "excess financial elasticity" to denote the property of an economic system that generates the build-up of financial imbalances. They focus, in particular, on the inability of the financial and monetary regimes to constrain those imbalances. Think of an elastic band that stretches out further but, at some point, inevitably snaps back. So used, the term "elasticity" takes root way back in the history of economic thought, when it denoted the elasticity of credit (e.g., Jevons (1875)).

Financial and monetary regimes matter greatly. Liberalised financial systems weaken financing constraints, thereby providing more room for the build-up of financial imbalances. Indeed, the link between financial liberalisations and subsequent credit and asset price booms is well documented.[2] And so do monetary policy regimes that do not directly respond to that build-up. This was true for the gold standard, in which central banks kept interest rates relatively stable unless the external or internal convertibility constraints came under threat. And it is also true of regimes focused on near-term inflation control: the authorities have no incentive to tighten policy as long as inflation remains low and stable. It is no coincidence that the build-up of financial imbalances is all the more likely following major positive supply-side developments (Drehmann et al. (2012)): these put downward pressure on inflation while at the same time providing fertile ground for financial booms, as they justify the initial optimistic expectations – a source of what Kindleberger (2000) called the initial "displacement."

What is the role of the IMFS in all this? The IMFS can amplify the excess elasticity of domestic policy regimes (Borio (2014a)) through their interaction internationally.

Financial regimes interact. For one, mobile financial capital across currencies and borders adds an important external (marginal) source of finance – hence the outsize role of external credit in unsustainable credit booms (e.g., Avdjiev et al. (2012)). And when exchange rates are flexible, it can induce overshooting in exchange rates, through familiar channels (e.g., Gyntelberg and Shrimpf (2011), Burnside et al. (2011), Menkhoff et al. (2012)). In fact, these channels are analogous to those that result in unsustainable asset price booms in a domestic context. More generally, in an integrated financial world risk perceptions and attitudes spread across assets classes through the forces of arbitrage and become embodied in risk premia. This explains, for instance, why proxies for the global price of risk, such as the popular VIX index, are closely correlated with global pricing of assets as well as capital and credit flows (Forbes and Warnock (2012), Rey (2013)) – what Rey has termed the "global financial cycle."

And also *monetary* regimes interact. They can spread easy monetary conditions from core economies to the rest of the world, thereby increasing the risk of unsustainable financial imbalances. They do so *directly*, whenever currency areas extend beyond national jurisdictions. Think, in particular, of the huge international role of the US dollar. Policy in international-currency countries has a more direct influence on financial conditions elsewhere. More importantly, they do so *indirectly*. If exchange

---

[2] In the post-war period, the link first became evident following the experience of liberalisation in the Southern Cone countries of Latin America in the 1970s (Diaz-Alejandro (1985), Baliño (1987)).

The International Monetary and Financial System 361

rates are fixed, such as under the gold standard, the transmission is immediate. But even when they are flexible, the transmission can take place through resistance to exchange rate appreciation, ie through the interplay of policy reaction functions (e.g., McKinnon (1993)).[3] Policymakers in the rest of the world keep policy rates lower than otherwise and/or intervene and accumulate foreign currency reserves. For instance, there is ample evidence that since the early 2000s at least EMEs and advanced small open economies have kept interest rates below what traditional benchmarks for purely domestic conditions would suggest (Hofmann and Bogdanova (2012)) and that the US federal funds rate helps to explain these deviations (Taylor (2013), Gray (2013), Spencer (2013) and Takats (2014)).

This explains the choice of the two episodes examined in this paper. Both relate to historical phases in which financial markets have been highly integrated and in which monetary regimes have paid little attention to the build-up of financial imbalances, regardless of the exchange rate regime. The rationale is consistent with the similar financial and economic fluctuations that punctuated also the classical gold standard, especially in the periphery, including Norway (e.g., Goodhart and De Largy (1999), Gerdrup (2003)).

Measuring capital flows: which boundary?

Once the focus is on financial instability and its macroeconomic costs, current accounts fade into the distance.

This is true from a behavioural standpoint. To be sure, large current account deficits may well increase the costs of systemic banking crises. And, by definition, they reflect a situation in which domestic demand far exceeds domestic output – a possible symptom of unsustainable expansions. But, historically, some of the most disruptive banking crises have erupted in the wake of financial booms that took hold in countries with large current account surpluses.[4] Think of Japan in the 1980s-early 1990s and, as we will discuss later, the United States in the 1920s. Moreover, as we write, a major financial boom has been underway for several years in China.[5]

---

[3] For a discussion of the limited insulation properties of exchange rate flexibility, see Borio et al. (2011) and for a formalisation of some of these channels, see Bruno and Shin (2013).

[4] See also Jordá et al. (2011b) and Gourinchas and Obstfeld (2012), who find a strong link between credit growth and banking crises, but little link between these and current account positions.

[5] For a development of this argument, and also a critique of the view linking current account surpluses to a saving glut and low real interest rates, see Borio and Disyatat (2011).

Equally, current accounts fade into the distance from a measurement or accounting perspective (Borio and Disyatat (2011)). By construction, current accounts and the net capital flows they represent reveal little about financing. They capture changes in net claims on a country arising from trade in *real* goods and services and hence *net* resource flows. But they exclude the underlying changes in gross flows and their contributions to existing stocks – all the transactions involving only trade in financial assets, which make up the bulk of cross-border financial activity. As such, current accounts tell us little about the role a country plays in international borrowing, lending and financial intermediation, about the degree to which its real investments are financed from abroad and about the impact of cross-border capital flows on domestic financial conditions. They are effectively silent about the intermediation patterns that trigger banking distress.[6]

Moreover, even gross capital flows and the corresponding stocks tell only part of the story. To see this, and the more pervasive distortions that well-meaning simple analytical devices can have in our thinking, it is worth stepping back and consider national income accounting 101.

The measurement of capital flows is traditionally based on the boundaries established by national income accounting. The purpose of the national income boundary is to measure aggregate output within a well-defined boundary of an "economic territory." The measurement rests on the residence principle. An economic entity (a firm, say) is deemed to be resident in the economic territory if it conducts its principal economic activity within its boundaries. The national income accounts further classify the activity into sectors and subsectors according to the nature of the activity.

The boundary of the economic territory for national income accounting often coincides with the national border, but need not do so. The principle of measurement is based on residence, rather than nationality. So, even if a firm is headquartered elsewhere, as long as the firm conducts its business

---

[6] Borio and Disyatat (2011) argue that the misleading focus on current accounts reflects the failure to distinguish sufficiently clearly between saving and financing. Saving, as defined in the national accounts, is simply income (output) not consumed; financing, a cash-flow concept, is access to purchasing power in the form of an accepted settlement medium (money), including through borrowing. Investment, and expenditures more generally, require financing, not saving. Financial crises reflect disruptions in financing channels, in borrowing and lending patterns, about which saving and investment flows are largely silent.

The International Monetary and Financial System 363

within the boundary, it is counted as part of the aggregate activity of the territory concerned.[7]

In the benchmark international finance macroeconomic models, the boundary defined in national income accounting also serves two other roles, as it conveniently permits aggregating all actors within the boundary.

First, the national income boundary is often taken to define the *decision-making unit*. Thus, the residents within the boundary are aggregated into a representative individual whose behaviour is deemed to follow an aggregate consumption function. In particular, the balance sheet of the decision-making unit is defined by the boundary set by national income accounting. The balance of payments and capital flows are defined by reference to the increases in assets and liabilities of those inside the boundary against those outside. Since the models typically further assume that assets and liabilities are perfect substitutes, they end up considering only net capital flows, ie current accounts. Thus, capital inflows are defined as the increase in the liabilities of residents to non-residents, where the measurement is taken in net terms, as the change in assets minus that in liabilities. The assumption of a representative agent makes this restriction even more natural.

Second, in simple economic models, the national income boundary is also assumed to define the currency area associated with a particular currency. As a result, the real exchange rate between two national income territories is defined as the ratio of the prices between the two economic territories. The nominal exchange rate, in turn, is defined as the price of one currency relative to another. Thus, implicitly, monetary policy by the central bank within the boundary affects the residents within the boundary itself in the first instance. To the extent that monetary policy has spillover effects, they may be captured either through the current account and trade balances, or through capital inflows and outflows measured in residence terms.

To recap, the boundary of an "economic territory" in international economics serves three roles. First, it is the boundary relevant for national income accounting. Second, it is the boundary that defines the decision-making unit, including its balance sheet. Third, it is the boundary that distinguishes domestic currency from foreign currency.

The triple coincidence between the three roles of the national income boundary is a convention followed in simplified economic models. It is not

---

[7] The recent working paper of the Irving Fisher Committee (BIS (2012)) gives an introduction to the conceptual distinctions in measurement of international financial positions.

364   *Claudio Borio, Harold James, and Hyun Song Shin*

a logical consequence of the measurement of output or of the underlying financial transactions. It probably reflects the fact that these models were formulated and refined in an era when capital flows were not as central as they have become subsequently, and the simplification has served a useful purpose. That said, the triple coincidence between the three notions of economic boundaries was a reasonable approximation only in a relative brief phase in the immediate post-war period.

The reason is simple. For one, decision-making units straddle national boundaries. In a world in which firms increasingly operate in multiple jurisdictions, consolidated income and balance sheet data are more informative. For, it is these units that decide where to operate, what goods and services to produce at what prices and how to manage risks. Importantly, it is these units that ultimately come under strain. Nationality, which reflects the consolidated balance sheet of firms, rather than residence, often sets the more relevant boundary.[8] Indeed, the BIS consolidated banking statistics were created in the 1970s precisely to address this shortcoming (McGuire and Wooldridge (2005), Borio and Toniolo (2008)). In addition, as noted, international currencies are actively used well beyond the boundary of the currency jurisdiction[9]. And the intersection between the nationality of the players and the currencies they use is what matters most to understand currency and funding exposures, vulnerabilities and the dynamics of financial distress.

With these analytical reference points in mind, it is now time to consider in more detail the experience in the interwar years and around the Great Financial crisis.

3 Interwar Experience

In the interwar story, the current account imbalance gives only a partial picture. While the German current account deficit and the US surplus attracted an enormous amount of attention at the time and since, the financial flows and the round-tripping between Germany and its neutral neighbours, the Netherlands and Switzerland, were largely beneath the

---

[8] "Nationality" in this context generally relates to the country where the company is headquartered. There may be different criteria to decide to which country to assign a decision-making unit, but the principle of consolidation is not affected by this.

[9] For instance, McCauley, McGuire and Sushko (2014) report that more than 80 percent of the dollar bank loans to borrowers resident outside the United States were booked outside the United States.

The International Monetary and Financial System 365

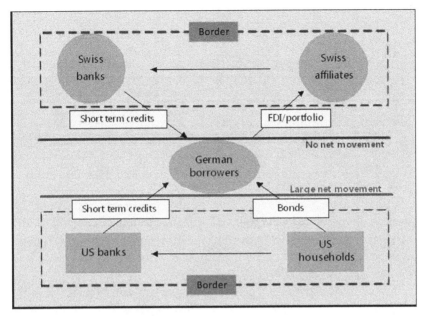

Figure 9.1 The geography of capital flows in the interwar years

radar screen for public policy. Their implications only became clear after a major financial crisis in 1931, in which foreign short term credits in Germany were frozen. Foreign borrowing by the German private and public sectors occurred in foreign currencies, with dollar denominated bonds and credits from the United States and sterling denominated bonds and credits from the United Kingdom. German agents also accumulated foreign currency claims in other countries, above all in the small neutral neighbours, and these sums then were relent to German corporations. In the lead-up to the financial crisis, as German capital flight accelerated, it was financed in part by drawing on credit lines of US and UK banks. As a result, in 1931, there were net gold inflows to France, Switzerland and the Netherlands (of $771 m.), and gold outflows from Germany but also from the United States and the United Kingdom (Allen and Moessner (2013)). A schematic version of the 1920s flows is given in Figure 9.1.

It is in the 1920s that the phenomenon of excess financial elasticity appeared in its modern form. Although in the classical (pre-1914) gold standard regime financial instability was a feature of many countries on the periphery – including the United States – the core countries of the gold standard, Great Britain, France and also Germany, were comparatively stable and after 1873 did not experience systemic crises. That relative

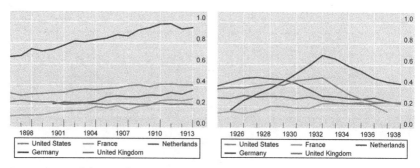

Figure 9.2 Bank loans relative to GDP. Ratios 1896–1913 (left), 1924–1938 (right).
Source: Taylor/Schularick dataset

stability was admired by the National Monetary Commission in the United States after the panic of 1907, attributed to differing European institutional arrangements and held to be a reason for instituting a European-style central bank (Mitchell (1911)).

The contrast between the generally modest pre-war fluctuations at the core and the post-war emergence of an outsize cycle is dramatically evident from comparative data on bank loans. Before the war, bank loans relative to GDP grew gradually in all countries (Figure 9.2 left-hand panel); and even the sharp crisis of 1907 provided only a brief interruption to the trend. By contrast, some, but not all, countries experienced very substantial bank gluts (or excess financial elasticity) in the 1920s, with a collapse in the Great Depression. There is little sign of such a glut in France or Great Britain, but the cycle is very noticeable in the Austrian, German and American cases, and also in the Netherlands and in Switzerland (which is not included in the Taylor/Schularick dataset).

The data on long term bank lending for fourteen countries collected by Taylor and Schularick was used to test the relationship between expansion of bank lending in the pre–Great Depression period (1924–1929) and output declines in the Great Depression (1929–1932). There is a significant difference between the treated group (larger than median GDP declines) and control (smaller than median GDP declines). Those countries with a large decline in GDP during 1929–1932 had a larger increase in loans before 1929. The severity of the Great Depression as measured conventionally by output, industrial production or unemployment was thus significantly greater in the countries with the gluts. In the view of Accominotti and Eichengreen (2013) the flows were chiefly driven by the outsize cycle in the principal exporting country, the United States.

The gluts were linked through capital flows, but it is important to note that they were not necessarily correlated with current account positions.

The International Monetary and Financial System 367

The United States, with a substantial surplus, and Germany, with a substantial deficit, both saw large credit and property price booms (Figure 9.2 right-hand panel).[10] By contrast, France, with a large surplus, and Britain, with trade deficits, did not experience the phenomenon (same figure). Germany and the United States were linked by a substantial gross capital flow, both in the form of bond issues and in bank lending. Financial fragility played a major role in the build-up of vulnerability, and then in the propagation of crisis.

The choice of currency regime alone does not explain the interwar pattern. France and Great Britain returned to the gold standard, the former at a rate conventionally thought to be undervalued and the latter at an overvalued rate as policymakers sought to restore the pre-1914 parity. Banks in both countries engaged in international lending, and some of the relatively small London merchant banks were heavily engaged in South America and Central Europe, and consequently faced illiquidity or even insolvency threats in the Great Depression (Accominotti (2014)). But the segmentation of British banking into merchant banks and clearing banks meant that there was no general glut, and no generalised banking crisis after the Central European collapse in the summer of 1931. Thus attempts to explain interwar weakness primarily in terms of the gold standard and its constraints (Temin (1989), Eichengreen (1992), Eichengreen and Temin (2010)) build on the argument about asymmetric adjustment (Keynes (1941)); but they miss a central element in the vulnerability of the interwar IMFS.

A key distinction between the pre-1914 world and that of the restored gold standard or gold exchange standard in the 1920s was the centrality of bond financing before the First World War, in contrast with the rise of bank credit afterwards. The most common explanation of the 1920s peculiarity lies in the preoccupation with normalisation, a return to peacetime normality. With normality, there was an expectation that bond yields would fall. Consequently, short-term bank financing was regarded as an attractive way of bridging the interim before the normalisation, and the return of lower yields and thus less expensive financing. In addition, the increased prominence of bank credit was driven by the financial reconstruction of European countries (especially in Central Europe) after wartime and post-war inflation and hyper-inflation. The promise of a restoration of pre-war conditions was the ground for the initial optimism

---

[10] For a more detailed discussion of the credit boom in the United States, see (e.g., Persons (1930), Robbins (1934), Eichengreen and Mitchener (2003)).

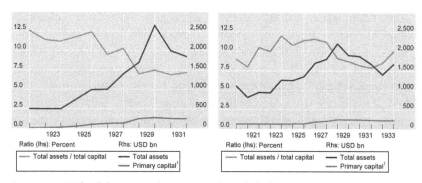

Figure 9.3 US bank leverage. Chase National Bank (left), National City Bank (right).
Sources: Banks' financial statements (provisional)
(1) Capital, surplus and undivided profits

or "displacement", in Kindleberger's terminology, that generated the flows which pushed the banking glut.

The principal creditor country, the United States, experienced considerable financial innovation, with a new market for foreign bonds developing as a supplement to the older market for domestic bonds (Flandreau et al. (2009)). In addition, while the traditional issuing houses (notably J.P. Morgan) were very cautious about the burgeoning European market, new, innovative and pushy houses such as the Boston bank Lee Higginson saw an opportunity to win market share. Figure 9.3 provides some examples of the expansion of the balance sheet and the assets of large internationally active US banks. By contrast, there was much less innovation in the creditor countries that did not experience the glut.

For the debtor countries, financial innovation offered a return to a past that seemed to have been destroyed by the War and its legacy. In the course of the inflation, German bank capital had been destroyed; and in the stabilisation of the mid-1920s, banks began with severely reduced levels of capital relative to the pre-war position. They found it expensive to raise new capital, and their new lending in consequence occurred on a very thin capital basis. They also found it much harder than before the War to attract retail deposits, and they funded lending in consequence with interbank credit – both from domestic sources and from international borrowing. The external source of finance drove the German expansion. It was only at the height of the credit boom that bank loans relative to GDP reached pre-war levels (which were high in an international comparison). Paradoxically, this reflection on catch-up offered one ground for creditors to believe that their claims might be secure (Balderston (1993)).

The vulnerability was increased by the persistence of a German pre-war tradition of thinking of the central bank as a lender of last resort. That

The International Monetary and Financial System 369

represented the most fundamental flaw in the domestic policy regime. The safety net provided by the Reichsbank allowed a thinner capital basis, and gave a misguided confidence to both the banks and their creditors (James (1998)). While the banks appeared to have no liquidity constraints, the central bank in the post-stabilisation world after 1924 was constrained by the convertibility requirements of the gold standard.

The expansion of borrowing by Central European banks occurred in an informational or statistical fog (BIS (1932, 1934)). While the extent of bond financing was quite well known, because bond issues were managed publicly, the extent of foreign borrowing was not appreciated. The bimonthly and then monthly bank balance sheets, whose publication was required by law in Germany, do not distinguish between foreign and domestic liabilities: although they do give figures for different terms or duration of borrowing. The Reichsbank's assessment of the size of short-term debt in early 1931 on the eve of the crisis was thus one quarter lower than it should have been (Schuker (1988), p. 57). It was only after the reversal of flows, and the inability to make foreign exchange payments after the summer of 1931, that the extent of the commercial short-term bank indebtedness became known, and statistical overviews could be prepared. The initial assessment of the extent of Germany's short-term debt was presented in August 1931 by the Wiggin-Layton committee (Wiggin (1931)); but the estimates rose further in the course of the following months (Special Advisory Committee (1931)).

While the government banking and regulatory authorities knew about the phenomenon, they were thus ignorant of its extent. The ignorance casts some doubt on a theory that explains the large expansion of international credit in terms of a well-defined and deliberate strategy on the part of the borrowers. It has been suggested that reparations debtors (and above all Germany) tried to build up their foreign debt liabilities in order to engineer a payments crisis in which the claims of reparations creditors and commercial and bank creditors would come into conflict. According to this logic, when the debt level approached the point of unsustainability, a crisis would be triggered in which the commercial creditors would assert the priority of their claims, and in consequence press for the cancellation or radical reduction of the reparation burden (Ritschl (2002)). The argument was laid out in the following way: "Schacht [the President of the German central bank] appeared to be letting German banks run up their short-term liabilities to correspondent institutions in Britain and American so that the latter, fearing for their own liquidity, would entreat their governments to go easy in the next reparations round." (Schuker (1988), p. 46)

This argument was certainly accepted by some of the lenders, and became a way of boosting creditor confidence. A politically well-connected British banker, Reginald McKenna of the Midland bank, made the observation that "under pressure of circumstances when political and commercial forces are in the exchange market with marks to get foreign currencies [to service debt], in practice the commercial would always get priority and success and leave the political in the lurch. [...] Each bank will act as a clearing house of marks against sterling for its own customer. Each trade operation sets in motion its own demand and offer of one of the two currencies. There would be a private arrangement within the walls of the bank to clear these against each other before the balance of demand was released to the open exchange market." (Johnson (1978), pp. 307–308)

The international flow of capital followed a complex web of linkages, often through decision units that straddled borders. The tangled connections of Germany, a major borrower in the 1920s, and its immediate neighbours, the Netherlands and Switzerland, provide a powerful illustration. Especially in the immediate aftermath of the First World War, many German companies, including banks as well as non-financial corporations, acquired stakes, or formed close relations with, banks in the Netherlands and Switzerland. There was an initial outflow of funds in building these external relationships. The Dutch and Swiss companies were then used as vehicles to borrow money, which was relent to Germany, often to the parent company. International credit could be leveraged up in a foreign country, and the resulting capital inflow could in turn be leveraged up in the recipient country. Within Germany, a substantial discussion of the phenomenon of capital flight began even while US money was still flooding into Germany (James (1986)).

The motivation for the development of the outward flow from Germany was complex. Originally, one reason may have been tax advantages from buying a foreign subsidiary and running substantial operations through it. Initially, many of the fiscal advantages were related simply to saving stamp duty and stock exchange taxes in Germany. A second reason was that the wartime neutrality of the Netherlands and Switzerland meant that companies there had been used to camouflage German ownership during the First World War. But in the 1920s, a third reason was probably the decisive one: borrowing through a non-German corporation substantially reduced the cost of credit, as a carry trade developed with interest rates in the United States and in the neutrals substantially lower than in Germany.

One of the best known examples of this sort of operation was the financial company IG Chemie (Internationale Gesellschaft für Chemische Unternehmungen AG), incorporated in Basel in 1928 under the control of

The International Monetary and Financial System 371

the giant German chemical company IG Farben. One year later, in 1929, after a capital increase to CHF 290 million, IG Chemie became one of the largest Swiss corporations. Its explicit purpose was to build up international acquisitions for the parent company, above all in Norway and the United States as well as in Switzerland itself. The Swiss driver of the business was an "IG Consortium" run by a small Swiss private bank, Eduard Greuter, whose principal had already been working with one of the predecessor companies of IG Farben, the Metallgesellschaft, before the First World War, operating a company named "Metallwerte" that was a sort of predecessor of IG Chemie.

After the War, Greuter's business consisted almost entirely in providing money for Germany. In 1929 the Greuter bank borrowed from IG Farben in order to launch IG Chemie: the German company provided about 70 percent of the funds. A small part of the capital came from the large Swiss banks, which supplied much more extensive credit to IG Farben. Representatives of the two largest Swiss banks sat on the board of the new company, where they were given by unusually high compensation (four times that of board members for the big Swiss banks). The *Neue Zürcher Zeitung* commented in the summer of 1929: "The complicated and opaque construction of the Basel holding company can only be understood in terms of the need for capital by the Frankfurt firm, which cannot itself raise capital directly." (König (2001)). For the German authorities, the main goal seemed to be reduction of IG Farben's tax liability, but a Finance Ministry note concluded that "such transactions cannot be stopped if the mobility of international capital is not interfered with." (James (1986), p. 299). In 1930 the Polyphonwerke concluded a similar transaction, as did the synthetic textile company Vereinigte Glanzstof-Fabriken AG. So too did a state owned company, the Prussian electricity works.

The circular character of some of this lending is obvious. Direct lending to German industrial, commercial or agricultural business from Switzerland and the Netherlands amounted to no less than 45 and 67 percent, respectively, on July 28, 1931, when the credits were frozen, while for the United States these direct loans represented a much smaller proportion, 28 percent. The prominence of Switzerland and the Netherlands as intermediaries is revealed by the calculation that corporations and individuals in these countries held 32.2 percent of Germany's short-term debt and 29.2 percent of the long-term debt (Statistisches Reichsamt, (1932), Schuker (1988), p. 117).

The rundown during the financial crisis in German banks and in Swiss banks occurred in parallel. There was substantial capital flight, as the economic situation worsened and as the fragile political stability of Germany was eroded. Such operations involved repaying German loans from

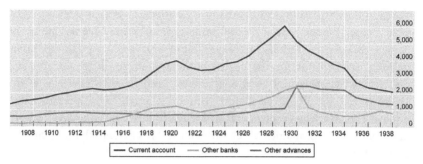

Figure 9.4 Swiss Bank assets 1906–1938
Sources: Statistisches Handbuch des schweizerischen Geld-und Kapitalmarktes 1944; Das schweizerische Bankwesen, vol 1953, 1973 and 1992.

Swiss banks; German banks also saw their deposits fall and, in addition, liquidated some of their foreign holdings. By the time the banking crisis hit in July 1931, the Wiggin-Layton Committee's estimate was that the short-term foreign assets of German banks had contracted by 40 percent. Swiss bank claims against other banks contracted by a similar amount, 52 percent, over the course of 1931 (Figure 9.4).

The movements of funds out of Germany occurred well before the major US banks started to cut credit lines. It was only on June 23, 1931, for instance that the Bankers Trust Company cut the credit line of Deutsche Bank. On July 6, only a week before the failure of a large German bank, the Guaranty Trust Company announced immediate withdrawals. These outside banks, unlike the insiders involved in the intricate German-Netherlands-Switzerland loop, were relatively ill-informed, and also probably reluctant to trigger a panic in which they were bound to lose their a substantial part of their assets.

There has been a considerable controversy about the extent to which the German banking crisis was a banking crisis or a general currency and political crisis set off by the German government's desperate reparations appeal of June 6, 1931. The latter case is made by Ferguson and Temin (2003). However, a look at the positions of individual banks suggests that the withdrawals were not made equally from all German banks; those with a weak reputation suffered the most dramatic outflows (see also James (1984); Schnabel (2004)). Thus the Darmstädter- und Nationalbank (Danat), the bank with the most vulnerable reputation, suffered an almost complete collapse of the bulk of its short term deposits (between 7 days and 3 months maturity); there was also a run on the more solid Deutsche Bank und Disconto Gesellschaft, but of a significantly less complete character (Figure 9.5, left hand panel) and (Figure 9.5, right hand panel).

Withdrawals from banks meant that the banks demanded more discounting facilities at the central bank; but the Reichsbank refused because it was

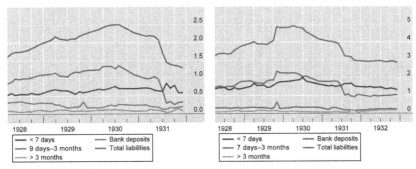

Figure 9.5 German bank deposits 1928-32. Darmstaedter (left), Deutche-Disconto (right). In billions of Reichsmark. Source: Die Bank

under pressure from the Bank of England and the Federal Reserve Bank of New York to restrict its credit in order to stem the developing run on the German currency. The central bank no longer had the currency reserves it would have needed in order to satisfy the demand for foreign currency that arose in the course of credit withdrawal. The Reichsbank no longer had operational freedom, but was tied under the gold exchange standard system into a network of agreements and dependent on the willingness of other central banks to engage in swaps or other forms of support.

In short, the fragility that had built up in the banking glut was a major cause of the reversal of confidence, and of the major financial crisis that hit central Europe in the summer of 1931. Ostensibly, excess financial elasticity was at work.

4 The Great Financial Crisis

We can trace similar forces behind the recent Great Financial Crisis. As is well known, the crisis in the United States was preceded by a major financial boom. Credit and property prices surged for several years against the backdrop of strong financial innovation and an accommodative monetary policy.

By comparison with other credit booms, much of the credit expansion was financed from purely domestic sources. As Figure 9.6 suggests, in keeping with the usual pattern, external credit (dotted lines and shaded areas) did outpace purely domestic ones (solid line). But the fraction of external funding as measured by the balance of payment statistics was low compared to, say, the credit booms in Spain or the United Kingdom roughly at the same time.

Even so, this aggregate picture conceals the key role that foreign banks, especially European Banks and cross border flows more generally played in this episode. Indeed, the subprime crisis illustrates well the importance of

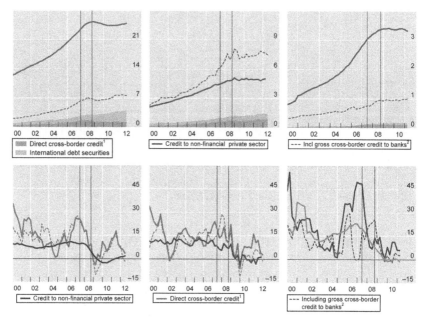

Figure 9.6 Credit booms and external credit: selected countries. United States (left), United Kingdom (middle), Spain (right). Upper panel: Stocks at constant end-Q1 2001 exchange rates, in trillions of US dollars. Lower panel: Year-on-year growth, in per cent. The vertical lines indicate crisis episodes end-Q2 2007 and end-Q3 2008. For details on the construction of the various credit components, see Borio et al (2011).[1] Estimate of credit to the private non-financial sector granted by banks from offices located outside the country.[2] Estimate of credit as in superscript (1) plus cross-border borrowing by banks located in the country. Source: Borio et al (2011).

drawing the correct boundary for analysis for capital flow analysis. In particular, European global banks sustained the shadow banking system in the United States by drawing on dollar funding in the wholesale market to lend to US residents through the purchase of securitised claims on US borrowers (Shin (2012)).

Figure 9.7 is a schematic that illustrates the direction of flows. It shows that European global banks intermediate US Dollar funds in the United States by drawing on wholesale dollar funding (for instance, from money market funds in the United States) which are then reinvested in the securities ultimately backed by mortgage assets in the United States. Capital first flows out of the United States and then flows back in. In this way, the cross-border flows generated by the European global banks net out, and are not reflected as imbalances in the current account.

In the run-up to the crisis, money market funds in the United States played the role of the base of the shadow banking system, in which

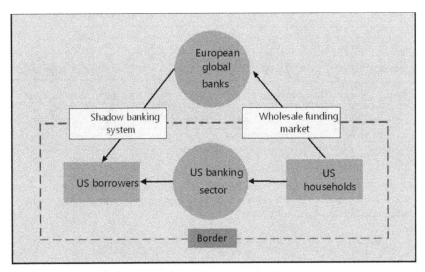

Figure 9.7: European banks in the US shadow banking system. Source: Shin (2012).

wholesale funding is recycled to US borrowers via the balance sheet capacity of banks, especially European banks.

Figure 9.8, taken from the IMF's Global Financial Stability Report of September 2011, quantifies their role. It shows the amount that banks, classified by nationality, owed US prime money market funds based on the top 10 by size, representing US$755 billion of approximately US$1.66 trillion total prime money market fund assets. As a rule of thumb, 80 percent of the money market fund assets were the obligations of banks and 50 percent of European banks.

The netting of gross flows shown in the schematic in Figure 9.7 is reflected in the items that make up the US gross capital flows by category. Figure 9.9, taken from Shin (2012), shows the categories of capital flows for the United States from the annual data published by the US Bureau of Economic Analysis. Positive quantities (and bars) indicate gross capital inflows (the increase in claims of foreigners on the United States), while negative quantities indicate gross capital outflows (the increase in the claims of US residents on foreigners).

The grey shaded bars indicate the increase in claims of official creditors on the United States. This includes the increase in claims of China and other countries accumulating foreign exchange reserves. While official flows are large, private sector gross flows are larger still. The negative bars before 2008 indicate large outflows of capital from the United States (principally through the banking sector), which then re-enter the country through the purchases of non-Treasury securities.

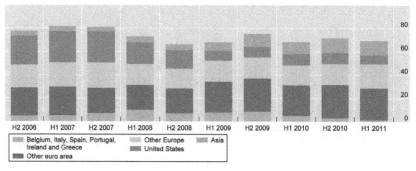

Figure 9.8 Amount owned by banks to US prime money market funds. By nationality of borrowing bank; stacked from bottom; in per cent of total. Sources: IMF, Global Financial Stability Report, Oct 2011; Fitch.

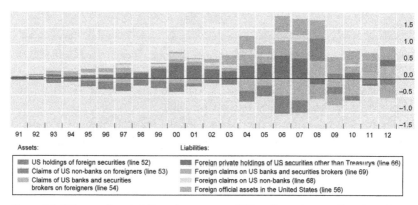

Figure 9.9 US annual capital flows by category. USD trillion. Source: Shin (2012); US Bureau of Economic Analysis.

The schematic of the "round-trip" capital flows through the European banks in Figure 9.7 is useful in interpreting gross flows. European banks' US branches and subsidiaries drove the gross capital outflows through the banking sector by raising wholesale funding from US money market funds and then shipping it to headquarters. Under the residence principle in the national income and balance of payment accounts, foreign banks' branches and subsidiaries in the United States are treated as US banks in the balance of payments, as the balance-of-payments accounts are based on residence, not nationality.

The gross capital flows into the United States in the form of lending by European banks via the shadow banking system no doubt played a pivotal role in influencing credit conditions there in the run-up to the subprime crisis. However, since the Eurozone had a roughly balanced current account while the United Kingdom was actually a deficit country, their collective current account positions (net capital flows) vis-à-vis the United States did not reflect the influence of their banks in setting overall credit conditions in the country.

Moreover, the episode illustrates clearly the interaction between the nationality of the banks and the foreign currency in which they operated. Policymakers at the time were caught completely by surprise by the US dollar funding squeeze on European institutions. Why was their need for US Dollars so large? The account given earlier provides an explanation. More generally, the BIS international banking statistics reveal that combined US dollar assets of European banks reached some $8 trillion in 2008, including retail and corporate lending as well as holdings of US securities – Treasury, agency and structured products (Borio and Disyatat (2011)). Of this amount, between $300 and $600 billion was financed through foreign exchange swaps, mostly short-term, against the pound sterling, euro and Swiss franc. Estimates indicate that the maturity mismatch ranged between $1.1 to as high as $6.5 trillion (McGuire and Von Peter (2009)). Hence the surprising funding squeeze that hit these banks' (and others') US dollar positions, and the associated serious disruptions in foreign exchange swap markets – the so-called US dollar shortage (Baba and Packer (2008)). US money market funds played a key role. In particular, the Lehman Brothers failure stressed global interbank and foreign exchange markets because it led to a run on money market funds, the largest suppliers of dollar funding to non-US banks, which in turn strained the banks' funding (Baba et al. (2008), (2009)). The role of the US dollar as the currency that underpins the global banking system is undiminished. In a recent paper, McCauley, McGuire and Sushko (2014) report that more than 80 percent of the dollar bank loans to borrowers resident outside the United States have been booked outside the United States.

To sum up, the role of European banks during the US subprime mortgage crisis illustrates well the importance of drawing the right boundary in international finance. Capital flows are traditionally viewed as the financial counterpart to savings and investment decisions, in line with the narrative of capital flowing "downhill" from capital-rich countries with lower rates of return to capital-poor countries with higher returns (e.g., Lucas (1990)). From this perspective, the focus is typically on net capital flows, since that is what counts for funding a country's borrowing requirements. However, in the case of European banks intermediating US dollar funding, the boundary defined for national income accounting is traversed twice, so that the usual net flows do not capture the activities of the financial intermediaries engaging in the maturity transformation in the mortgage market. And the institutions' consolidated balance sheet, covering also their operations in the United States, provides valuable additional information. If the objective is to gauge credit conditions and overall financial vulnerability, the current account was of very limited use. Rather than the global savings glut, a more plausible culprit for subprime lending in the United States was the "global banking glut."

The shortcomings of the often assumed "triple coincidence" between the national income boundary, decision-making balance sheet and the currency area have again become evident since then (Shin (2013)). In this case, the symptom has been the rapid pace of bond issuance by emerging market borrowers in offshore locations since 2010. And, once again, this is happening as several of their countries of origin have been experiencing strong financial booms ((Caruana (2014a), Borio (2014a)). The amount outstanding of international debt securities of private sector borrowers has displayed a yawning gap between the total measured by the nationality of the borrower (based on the location of the headquarters of the borrower) and the total by residence. As of the end of 2013, outstanding international debt securities of private sector borrowers from emerging economies stood at 0.97 trillion dollars by residence of issuer and 1.73 trillion dollars by nationality of issuer, implying a gap of $758 billion.[11]

Moreover, the currency composition of offshore corporate bond issuance by emerging market firms has been tilted towards the US dollar (McCauley, Upper and Villar (2013)). As a result, emerging market borrowers have become sensitive to US dollar funding conditions and interest rates even though they may be remote from the United States geographically.

If the proceeds of the borrowing are sent to headquarters through an explicit capital account transaction, the balance of payments accounts would show a capital inflow in the form of greater external liabilities of the headquarters to its overseas subsidiary. Misleadingly, this may be recorded as FDI. However, if the multinational firm chooses to classify the transaction as part of trade flows in goods and services - for instance through the practice of "over-invoicing" where the value of exports are inflated – then the traditional balance of payments account would not capture the flow as an increase in the liabilities of the headquarter's unit.

Figure 9.10 also illustrates the impact of such transactions on the domestic financial system of the recipient economy if the proceeds are held as

---

[11] www.bis.org/statistics/secstats.htm

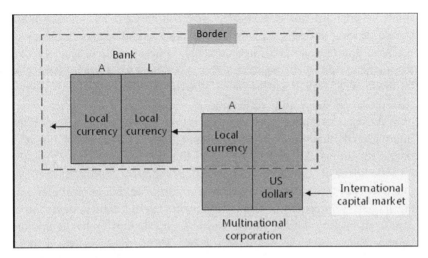

Figure 9.10 Offshore borrowing by multinational corporation

short-term financial claims in local currency. On a consolidated basis, the multinational firm has a currency mismatch on its balance sheet, with dollar liabilities in its overseas subsidiary and local currency assets at headquarters. One motivation for such a currency mismatch may be to hedge currency risk on cash flow denominated in US dollars, but another motivation would be the speculative one of positioning the company's balance sheet to benefit from the appreciation of the local currency against the dollar. In practice, hedging and speculation may be difficult to distinguish, even ex post. Whatever the motivation, the local currency financial assets held by the firm will then be on-lent by intermediaries thereby impacting the overall financial conditions in the local economy (Shin (2013), Turner (2014)).

5 Conclusion

As we have learnt once more in the wake of the Great Financial Crisis, finance and macroeconomics are inextricably linked. And what is true domestically is also true internationally. In the current historical phase, both real and financial markets are highly integrated globally, just as they were almost uninterruptedly for many decades until the Great Depression. The need to develop new analytical frameworks to think about the interaction between finance and macroeconomics in a domestic context inevitably extends to the global stage.

This calls for a reversal in the prevailing perspective. One should not ask what the real side of the equation means for its financial counterpart, but what the financial side means for its real counterpart. The starting point should be what happens in financial asset markets rather than in the goods markets, domestically and internationally. Otherwise, there is a risk that the financial side will be neglected. This is precisely what has happened for far too long. There is a need to redress the balance. Through the alternative lens, the world looks quite different.

In this paper we have taken some steps in this direction, focusing on the international dimension. We have highlighted three points. First, in a financially integrated global economy, the IMFS tends to amplify the "excess financial elasticity" of national economies, raising the risk of financial crises with huge macroeconomic costs. Second, current accounts are largely uninformative about these risks; the relevant information is contained in the capital accounts and in their relationship to the broader balance sheets of the relevant economies. Third, there is a need to go beyond the resident/non-resident distinction that underpins the balance-of-payments and to consider the consolidated balance sheets of the decision-making units that operate across borders, including the currencies of denomination. Put differently, the single boundary that sets the "economic territory" in standard international finance macroeconomic models, in which residence defines who produces and consumes, its financial assets and liabilities and, often, the currency of denomination, is badly inadequate.

The experiences of the interwar years and of those surrounding the Great Financial Crisis illustrate these points nicely. In both cases, financial surges and collapses within and across national borders were at the root of the historic financial crises. Current account positions did not provide a useful pointer: surges occurred in both surplus and deficit countries. And in both cases, understanding the build-up of vulnerabilities requires looking beyond the capital account to what decision-making units operating in multiple jurisdictions were doing – banks and non-financial corporates in the interwar years, and, above all, the nexus between European banks and US money market funds in the US sub-prime crisis. Moreover, since then non-financial corporations in EMEs have been taking on substantial external debt that is not captured by residence-based statistics – potentially another source of significant vulnerability.

This analysis has major implications for central banks. Given their primary responsibility for monetary and financial stability, central banks inevitably end up under the spotlight once the focus shifts to asset prices, balance sheets and financial crises. Focus shifts to asset prices, balance sheets and financial crises. As long as the focus is on current accounts,

The International Monetary and Financial System

central banks' role is necessarily more peripheral. This is not the place to expand on what all this means for policy (e.g., Borio (2013b, 2014a,b), Caruana (2012 and 2014b)). There is little doubt, however, that policy frameworks should be strengthened to incorporate more systematically financial surges and collapses. And in a highly globalised world, ways should also be found to take proper account of policy spillovers, both on other countries and on aggregate conditions.

References

Accominotti, O (2014): "London merchant banks, the Central European panic and the Sterling crisis of 1931", *Journal of Economic History*.

Accominotti, O and B Eichengreen (2013): "The mother of all sudden stops: capital flows and reversals in Europe, 1919–1932", *CEPR Working Paper*.

Aikman, D, A G Haldane, and B Nelson (2011): "Curbing the credit cycle", final version published in *The Economic Journal*, vol. 125, Issue 585, pages 1072–1109, June 2015. Cf. also the Voxeu Policy Portal on 17 March 2011.

Allen, W A and R Moessner (2013): "The liquidity consequences of the euro area sovereign debt crisis", *BIS Working Papers*, no 390, First published October 2012, revised March 2013.

Avdjiev, S, R McCauley and P McGuire (2012): "Rapid credit growth and international credit: Challenges for Asia", *BIS Working Papers*, no 377, April.

Baba, N, R McCauley and S Ramaswamy (2009): "US dollar money market funds and non-US banks", *BIS Quarterly Review*, March, pp. 65–81.

Baba, N and F Packer (2008): "Interpreting derivations from covered interest parity during the financial market turmoil of 2007–08", *BIS Working Papers*, no 267, December.

Baba, N, F Packer and T Nagano (2008): "The spillover of money market turbulence to FXswap and cross-currency swap markets", *BIS Quarterly Review*, March, pp. 73–86.

Balderston, T (1993): *The origins and course of the German economic crisis: November 1923 to May 1932*, Berlin: Haude & Spener.

Baliño, T (1987): "The Argentine banking crisis of 1980", *IMF Working Papers*, no WP/87/77.

Bank for International Settlements (BIS) (1932): *2nd BIS Annual Report*, Basel.

(1934): *4th BIS Annual Report*, Basel.

(2012) "Residency/local and nationality/global views of financial positions", *IFC Working Paper* no 8, Irving Fisher Committee on Central Bank Statistics, www.bis.org/ifc/publ/ifcwork08.htm

Bernanke, B (2005): "The global saving glut and the U.S. current account deficit", the Sandridge Lecture, Richmond, 10 March.

(2009): "Financial reform to address systemic risk", Speech at the Council on Foreign Relations, Washington, D.C, 10 March.

Bloomfield, A I (1959): *Monetary policy under the international gold standard, 1880–1914*, New York: Federal Reserve Bank of New York.

Borio, C (2013a): "The financial cycle and macroeconomics: what have we learnt?", *Journal of Banking & Finance*, vol. 45(2014), pp. 182–198. Also available as *BIS Working Papers*, no 395, December.

(2013b): "On time, stocks and flows: understanding the global macroeconomic challenges", *National Institute Economic Review*, August. Slightly revised version of the lecture at the Munich Seminar series, CESIfo-Group and Süddeutsche Zeitung, 15 October 2012, which is also available in *BIS Speeches*.

(2014a): "The international monetary and financial system: its Achilles heel and what to do about it", *BIS Working Papers*, no 456, August [a slightly revised version of a paper prepared for a keynote lecture at the Festschrift in honour of Niels Thygesen.]

(2014b): "Monetary policy and financial stability: what role in prevention and recovery?", *BIS Working Papers* no 440, February. Forthcoming in *Capitalism and Society*.

Borio, C and P Disyatat (2011): "Global imbalances and the financial crisis: link or no link?", *BIS Working Papers* no 346, May. Revised and extended version of "Global imbalances and the financial crisis: Reassessing the role of international finance", *Asian Economic Policy Review*, vol. 5, 2010, pp. 198–216.

Borio, C, C Furfine, and P Lowe. 2001. "Procyclicality of the financial system and financial stability: issues and policy options" In *Marrying the macro- and micro-prudential dimensions of financial stability, BIS Papers* 1 (March): pp. 1–57.

Borio, C and P Lowe (2004): "Securing sustainable price stability: should credit come back from the wilderness?", *BIS Working Papers* no 157, July.

Borio, C, R McCauley and P McGuire (2011): "Global credit and domestic credit booms" *BIS Quarterly Review*, September, pp. 43–57.

Borio, C and G Toniolo (2008): "One hundred and thirty years of central bank cooperation: A BIS perspective" in C Borio, G Toniolo and P Clement (eds) *The past and future of central bank cooperation*, Studies in Macroeconomic History Series, Cambridge: Cambridge University Press.

Bruno, V and H Shin (2013): "Capital flows and the risk-taking channel of monetary policy", *BIS Working Papers* no 400, December.

Burnside, C, M Eichenbaum and S Rebelo (2011): "Carry trade and momentum in currency markets", *Annual Review of Financial Economics*, vol. 3, pp. 511–535.

Caruana, J (2012): "International monetary policy interactions: challenges and prospects", Speech at the CEMLA-SEACEN conference on "The role of central banks in macroeconomic and financial stability: the challenges in an uncertain and volatile world", Punta del Este, Uruguay, 16 November.

(2014a): "Global liquidity: where it stands, and why it matters", IMFS Distinguished Lecture at the Goethe University, Frankfurt, Germany, 5 March.

(2014b):"Global economic and financial challenges: a tale of two views", lecture at the Harvard Kennedy School in Cambridge, Massachusetts, 9 April.

Congdon, T (1988): *The debt threat: the dangers of high real interest rates for the world economy*, Oxford: Basil Blackwell.

Danielsson, J, H Shin and J Zigrand (2004): "The impact of risk regulation on price dynamics", *Journal of Banking and Finance*, vol 28, pp. 1069–1087.

De Cecco, M (1974): *Money and empire: the international gold standard*, Oxford: Blackwell.

The International Monetary and Financial System   383

Despres, E, C Kindleberger and W Salant (1966): *The dollar and world liquidity: a minority view*, Washington D.C.: Brookings Institution.

Diaz-Alejandro, C (1985): "Good-bye financial repression, hello financial crash", *Journal of Development Economics*, vol 19, pp. 1–24.

Drehmann, M, C Borio and K Tsatsaronis (2011): "Anchoring countercyclical capital buffers: the role of credit aggregates", *International Journal of Central Banking*, vol 7(4), pp. 189–239.

(2012): "Characterising the financial cycle: don't lose sight of the medium term!", *BIS Working Papers*, no 380, June.

Drehmann, M and K Tsatsaronis (2014): "The credit-to-GDP gap and countercyclical capital buffers: questions and answers", *BIS Quarterly Review*, March.

Eichengreen, B (1992): *Golden fetters: the gold standard and the great depression, 1919–39*, Oxford: Oxford University Press.

Eichengreen, B and K Mitchener (2003): "The Great Depression as a credit boom gone wrong", *BIS Working Papers*, no 137, September.

Eichengreen, B and P Temin (2010): "Fetters of gold and paper", *Oxford Review of Economic Policy*, vol 26(3), pp. 370–384.

Ferguson, T and P Temin (2003): "Made in Germany: the German currency crisis of 1931", *Research in Economic History*, 21, pp. 1–53.

Flandreau, M, Flores, Gaillard, Nieto-Parra (2009): "The end of gatekeeping: underwriters and the quality of sovereign bond markets, 1815–2007", *NBER Working Paper* no 15128.

Forbes, K and F Warnock (2012): "Capital flow waves: surges, stops, flight and retrenchment", *Journal of International Economics*, vol 88(2), pp. 235–251

Gerdrup, K R (2003): "Three episodes of financial fragility in Norway since the 1890s", *BIS Working Papers*, no 142, October.

Goodhart, C and P De Largy (1999): "Financial crises: plus ça change, plus c' est la même chose", *LSE Financial Markets Group Special Paper*, no 108.

Gourinchas, P-O and M Obstfeld (2012): "Stories of the twentieth century for the twenty-first", *American Economic Journal: Macroeconomics*, vol 4(1), pp. 226–265.

Gray, C (2013): "Responding to the monetary superpower: investigating the behavioural spillovers of US monetary policy", *Atlantic Economic Journal*, vol 41(2), pp. 173–184.

Gyntelberg, J and A Schrimpf (2011): "FX strategies in period of distress", *BIS Quarterly Review*, December, pp. 29–40.

Hahm, J-H, H Shin and K Shin (2013): "Noncore bank liabilities and financial vulnerability", *Journal of Money, Credit and Banking*, vol 45(1), pp. 3–36.

Hofmann, B and B Bogdanova (2012)): "Taylor rules and monetary policy: a Global Great Deviation?", *BIS Quarterly Review*, September, pp. 37–49.

Hume, D (1752): *Political Discourses*, Edinburgh: Kincaid and Donaldson.

James, H (1984): "The causes of the German banking crisis of 1931", *Economic History Review*, vol 38, pp. 68–87.

(1986): *The German slump: politics and economics 1924–1936*, Oxford: Oxford University Press

(1996): *International monetary cooperation since Bretton Woods*, Washington, D.C. and Oxford: IMF and Oxford University Press.

(1998): "Die Reichsbank 1876 bis 1945", in Deutsche Bundesbank (ed), *Fünfzig Jahre Deutsche Mark: Notenbank und Währung in Deutschland seit 1948*", Munich: C.H. Beck, pp. 29–89.

(2001): *The end of globalization: lessons from the Great Depression.* Harvard: Harvard University Press.

Jevons, W (1875): *Money and the mechanism of exchange,* New York: D. Appleton and Co.

Johnson, E (1978): *Collected writings of John Maynard Keynes XVIII, activities 1922–1932, the end of reparations,* Cambridge: Royal Economic Society.

Jordá, O, M Schularick and A Taylor (2011a): "When credit bites back: Leverage, business cycles and crises", Federal Reserve Bank of San Francisco Working Paper Series 2011–27.

Jordá, O, A Taylor and M Schularick (2011b): "Financial crises, credit booms, and external imbalances: 140 years of lessons", *IMF Economic Review,* vol 59, pp. 340–378.

Keynes, J M (1929a): "The German transfer problem", *Economic Journal,* vol 39, pp. 1–7.

(1929b): "The reparations problem: a discussion. II. A rejoinder", *Economic Journal,* vol 39, pp. 179–182.

(1941): "Post-war currency policy", memoranda reproduced in D Moggridge (ed) (1980): *The collected writings on John Maynard Keynes, vol 25, Activities 1940–1944, Shaping the post-war world: the Clearing Union,* MacMillan/Cambridge University Press.

Kindleberger, C (1965): "Balance-of-payments deficits and the international market for liquidity", *Princeton Essays in International Finance,* no 46, May.

(2000): *Manias, panics and crashes,* Cambridge: Cambridge University Press, 4th edition.

King, M (2010): Speech delivered to the University of Exeter Business Leaders' Forum, 19 January.

König, (2001): *Interhandel: Die schweizerische Holding der IG Farben und ihre Metamorphosen – eine Affäre um Eigentum und Interessen (1910–1999),* Zurich: Chronos.

Krugman, P (2009): "Revenge of the glut", *The New York Times,* 1 March.

Lomax, D (1986): "The developing country debt crisis", London: Macmillan.

Lucas, R (1990): "Why doesn't capital flow from rich to poor countries?", *American Economic Review* 80 (May), pp. 92–96.

Ma, G and R McCauley (2013): "Global and euro imbalances: China and Germany", *BIS Working Papers,* no 424, September. Forthcoming in M Balling and E Gnan (eds), *50 years of money and finance: Lessons and challenges,* Vienna and Brussels: Larcier.

McCauley, R, P McGuire and V Sushko (2014): "Global dollar credit: links to US monetary policy and leverage", paper prepared for the 59th Panel Meeting of Economic Policy, April 2014.

McCauley, R, C Upper and A Villar (2013): "Emerging market debt securities issuance in offshore centres", *BIS Quarterly Review,* September, pp. 22–23.

McGuire, P and P Wooldridge (2005): "The BIS consolidated banking statistics: structure, uses and recent enhancements", *BIS Quarterly Review,* September.

McGuire, P and G von Peter (2009): "The US dollar shortage in global banking and the international policy response", *BIS Working Paper*, no. 291, October.

McKinnon, R (1993): "The rules of the game: International money in historical perspective", *Journal of Economic Literature*, vol 31(1), pp. 1–44.

Menkhoff, L, L Sarno, M Schmeling, and A Schrimpf (2012): "Currency momentum strategies", *Journal of Financial Economics*, vol 106(3), pp. 660–684.

Mitchell, W C (1911): "The Publications of the National Monetary Commission", *Quarterly*.

Obstfeld, M (2010): "Expanding gross asset positions and the international monetary system", Remarks at the Federal Reserve Bank of Kansas City symposium on "Macroeconomic Challenges: The Decade Ahead", Jackson Hole, Wyoming, 26–28 August.

(2012): "Does the current account still matter?", *American Economic Review*, vol 102(3), pp. 1–23.

Ohlin, B (1929a): "The reparation problem: a discussion", *Economic Journal*, vol 39, June, pp. 172–183

(1929b): "Mr. Keynes' views on the transfer problem. II. A Rejoinder from Professor Ohlin", *Economic Journal*, vol 39, pp. 400–404.

Persons, C (1930): "Credit expansion, 1920 to 1929, and its lessons", *Quarterly Journal of Economics*, vol 45(1), pp. 94–130.

Rey, H (2013): "Dilemma not trilemma: the global financial cycle and monetary policy independence", paper presented at the Federal Reserve of Kansas City Economic Policy Symposium "Global Dimensions of Unconventional Monetary Policy", Jackson Hole, 22–24 August.

Ritschl, A (2002): *Deutschlands Krise und Konjunktur 1924–1934: Binnenkonjunktur, Auslandsverschuldung und Reparationsproblem zwischen Dawes-Plan und Transfersperre*, Berlin: Akademie Verlag.

Robbins, L (1934): *The Great Depression*, New York: Macmillan.

Schnabel, I (2004): "The twin German crisis of 1931", *Journal of Economic History*, vol 64, pp. 822–871.

Schuker, S (1988): "American 'reparations' to Germans, 1919-33: Implications for the Third World debt crisis", *Princeton Studies in International Finance*, no. 61, July.

Shin, HS (2012): "Global banking glut and loan risk premium", *Mundell-Fleming Lecture, IMF Economic Review*, vol 60(2), pp. 155–192.

(2013): "The second phase of global liquidity and its impact on emerging economies", Keynote address at the Federal Reserve Bank of San Francisco *Asia Economic Policy Conference*, 3–5 November.

Shin, HS and K Shin (2010): "Procyclicality of monetary aggregates", *NBER Working Paper* no 16836, February.

Special Advisory Committee (1931): *Report of the Special Advisory Committee, issued at Basle*, 23 December.

Spencer, M (2013): "Updating Asian 'Taylor rules'", *Deutsche Bank, Global Economic Perspectives*, 28 March.

Statistisches Reichamt (1932): "Die deutsche Auslansverschuldung", *Wirtschaft und Statistik*, August, pp. 490–493.

Takats, E (2014): "How does US monetary policy affect policy rates in emerging market economies?", *BIS Quarterly Review*, March, pp. 6–7.

Taylor, J (2013): "International monetary policy coordination and the great deviation", *Journal of Policy Modelling*, in press.

Temin, P (1989): *Lessons from the Great Depression*, Cambridge: MIT Press.

Triffin, R (1960): *Gold and the dollar crisis; the future of convertibility*, Yale University Press: New Haven.

Turner, P (2014): "The global long-term interest rate, financial risks and policy choices in EMEs" *BIS Working Papers*, no 441, February.

Wiggin, A (1931): *Report of the Committee Appointed on the Recommendation of the London Conference 1931*, Basel, 18 August.

10

Central Banking

Perspectives from Emerging Economies

Menzie D. Chinn
University of Wisconsin and NBER

[T]o the gods we are as flies to wanton boys
–William Shakespeare, *King Lear*

1 Introduction

In May 2013, market perceptions that the Federal Reserve would soon take steps to rein in quantitative easing measures led to sharp reversals in capital flows to emerging markets. The decision to taper – or at least the market perception of the decision – was roundly criticized, and perhaps the most vociferous criticisms were delivered by emerging market central bank policy makers. And yet, equally vociferous complaints had been leveled, often by critics at those same institutions, at the implementation of unconventional monetary policies. Consider the recent speech by Raghuram Rajan, Governor of the Reserve Bank of India:

> [T]he current environment is one of extreme monetary easing through unconventional policies. In a world where debt overhangs and the need for structural change constrain domestic demand, a sizeable portion of the effects of such policies spillover across borders, sometimes through a weaker exchange rate. More worryingly, it prompts a reaction. Such competitive easing occurs both simultaneously and sequentially, [so that] ... [A]ggregate world demand may be weaker and more distorted than it should be, and financial risks higher. To ensure stable and sustainable growth, the international rules of the game need to be revisited. (Rajan, 2014)

It would be tempting to dismiss these criticisms as opportunistic attempts to lay blame for emerging market turmoil elsewhere. However, I believe it's more appropriate to view these complaints as a manifestation of the unenviable position that a typical emerging market central bank policy makers is in. Emerging market economies are typically small, in economic

388 *Menzie D. Chinn*

terms, relative to a global economy that is dominated by developments in the core advanced economies. So, while the international trilemma – the fact that a country cannot simultaneously pursue full monetary autonomy, exchange rate stability, and financial openness – constrains all economies, the degree to which the constraints bind is much more pronounced in emerging market economies.[1] For instance, a decision by the Fed to raise the policy rate drags up interest rates around the globe. Corresponding decisions in a given emerging market seldom have a similar effect, except for the very largest of the emerging markets, and even then only occasionally.[2]

This asymmetry is of course not new. Consider the consequences of the decision by advanced economy central bankers to raise policy rates during the mid-1990s, after several years of negative real interest rates. At that time, similar complaints were lodged, and it's not unreasonable to at least partly trace the financial crises in Latin America and subsequently in East Asia to the cycle in core country policy interest rates.

The issue of size is not the only complication for emerging market central bankers. The other key factors include the underdevelopment or distortion of the financial sector, along many dimensions. Historically, banks in emerging markets have been subject to financial repression, government policies that regulated interest rates, or required holdings of government debt. More recently, with the advent of domestic financial liberalization in many countries, problems arising from financial repression have given way to boom-bust cycles and the accompanying cyclical costs.

Another problem more endemic to emerging market economies, at least historically, has been the inability of governments to issue sovereign debt denominated in domestic currency that is then traded internationally – that is, "original sin" – and relatedly the pro-cyclical behavior of fiscal policy. As these characteristics recede, the task of macroeconomic stabilization may become easier; however, there is no guarantee that recent trends will continue.[3]

---

[1] I have taken the distinction between advanced economies and all others as fairly sharp. As the discussant has pointed out, the extent of the gap is up for debate. Some have pointed to the Eurozone periphery countries as akin to emerging market economies, unable to issue debt in their own currencies, and possessed of procyclical fiscal policies.

[2] One exception is China. Given its large economic weight in terms of production, and its role as a source of saving flows, it's possible for its policy actions to move international asset prices. See Fratzscher and Mehl (2013), and Chinn (2014).

[3] Ashoka Mody observes that the gap between emerging market and Eurozone periphery countries in terms of financial underdevelopment and original sin might not be particularly large.

Central Banking: Perspectives from Emerging Economies 389

Viewed against this backdrop, the perspectives of central bankers in emerging markets make sense. In this paper, I characterize emerging market central bank behavior, looking backward in time, and then focusing on the recent evolution of behavior.

The first section reviews the international trilemma (also known as the "impossible trinity") to describe the international constraints faced by emerging market central bank policy makers. Second, I describe the evolution of monetary policy over time, with specific reference to the recent adoption of inflation targeting, and examine how the different types of flexible inflation targeting regimes actually implemented address some, but not all, of the special concerns facing emerging markets. The next section addresses the motivation for the marked accumulation of reserves over the past two decades, a special attribute of emerging market economies. I end with some conjectures regarding the future of monetary policy in emerging markets.

2 The International Trilemma

2.1 The Historical Context

In this examination, I focus on the set of emerging market economies as of 2014 – a set variously defined by the international financial institutions (IMF, World Bank) or other commercial organizations as encompassing about forty countries. However, it's useful to observe that the set of emerging markets has evolved over time, and the emerging markets of 1880 are in many cases the advanced economies of 2014. In other words, it would be wrong to think that the problems encountered by today's emerging market economies were not previously of importance. However, the economies of the periphery in the 1880s faced a world where the gold standard defined monetary policy. The problems posed by rigid exchange rate arrangements are still relevant for some emerging market economies, but those instances are rare, so I will defer to others on that subject.[4]

In the post–World War II era, the newly independent countries faced a world emerging from global conflict, with a newly established framework for international trade and finance. A wide variety of arrangements for monetary policy existed, but one defining characteristic, shared with advanced economies, was the essential lack of separation between the fiscal

---

[4] See in particular Bordo (1981, 2005).

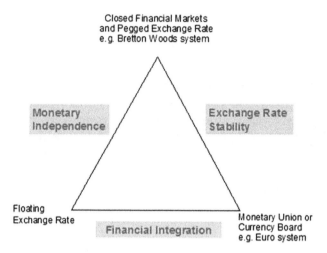

Figure 10.1: The trilemma of international finance

authority and the monetary authority. As a consequence, an apt characterization would be that the monetary policy largely served as a means of financing government deficits.

The breakdown of the Bretton Woods system marked a period of heightened choices for emerging market central banks. Fixed exchange rates, while still the norm, were no longer necessarily the default option, even for emerging market economies. Hence, this marks the point of departure for this analysis.

2.2 The Choices

The international trilemma – the thesis that a country can simultaneously choose any two, but not all, of the three goals of monetary independence, exchange rate stability, and financial integration – is illustrated in Figure 10.1. Each of the three sides of the triangle – representing monetary independence, exchange rate stability, and financial integration – represents a goal. Clearly, it is not possible to be simultaneously on all three sides of the triangle. For instance, the top point, labeled "closed capital markets" is associated with monetary policy autonomy and a fixed exchange rate regime and the absence of financial integration.[5]

---

[5] See Obstfeld, Shambaugh, and Taylor (2005) for further discussion and references dealing with the trilemma.

Countries have adopted different arrangements aimed at achieving combinations of two out of the three policy goals. The Gold Standard delivered capital mobility and exchange rate stability; the Bretton Woods system provided monetary autonomy and exchange rate stability. The fact that different economies have opted for different combinations indicates that policy authorities trade off certain goals as economic conditions evolve.[6]

Greater monetary independence allows policy makers to stabilize the economy through monetary policy without being subject to other economies' macroeconomic outcomes, thus potentially insulating the economy. However, in a world with price and wage rigidities, the resulting room for discretion means that policy makers might manipulate output movement, thus leading to increasing output and inflation volatility. On the other hand, monetary independence could permit a monetary authority to pursue an alternative nominal anchor that might simultaneously overcome the time inconsistency problem and preserve the option of pursuing countercyclical monetary policy.[7]

Alternatively, price stability could potentially be achieved through exchange rate stability; such stability could also mitigate interest rate and exchange rate uncertainty, thereby lowering the risk premium. The trade-off is that greater levels of exchange rate stability could deprive policy makers of the option of using the exchange rate as a shock absorber. Prasad (2008) argues that exchange rate rigidities would prevent policy makers from implementing appropriate policies consistent with macroeconomic reality, implying that they would be prone to cause asset boom and bust by overheating the economy. Hence, the rigidity caused by exchange rate stability could not only enhance output volatility, but also cause misallocation of resources and unbalanced, unsustainable growth.

The third goal, financial openness, has been, and remains, hotly debated. On the one hand, more open financial markets could lead to greater economic growth by encouraging greater efficient resource allocation,

---

[6] Aizenman et al. (2010) have statistically shown that external shocks in the last four decades, namely, the collapse of the Bretton Woods system, the debt crisis of 1982, and the Asian crisis of 1997–1998, caused structural breaks in the trilemma configurations.

[7] Examination of the trilemma usually takes the constraint on monetary policy as being imposed on short run interest rates. There is some "wiggle room" associated with the fact that long term interest rates can, for a variety of reasons, be partly delinked from short rates. See Ito (2013); a contrary view, see Obstfeld (2014).

392 *Menzie D. Chinn*

enhancing risk sharing, and supplementing domestic savings.[8] On the other hand, financial liberalization exposes economies to potentially destabilizing cross-border capital flows, and attendant boom-bust cycles (Kaminsky and Schmukler, 2002).[9]

2.3 The Emerging Market Economies Stand Apart

Aizenman et al. (2010) develop a set of the trilemma indices that measure the degree to which each of the three policy choices is implemented. The monetary independence index (MI) is based on the inverse of the correlation of a country's interest rates with the base country's interest rate. The index for exchange rate stability (ERS) is the inverse of exchange rate volatility, measured as the standard deviations of the monthly rate of depreciation (based on the exchange rate between the home and base economies). The degree of financial integration is measured with the Chinn-Ito (2006, 2008) capital controls index (KAOPEN).[10]

The evolution of the trilemma indices for different income-country groups is displayed in Figure 10.2. For the advanced economies (Figure 10.2A), financial openness experienced a discrete upward shift after the beginning of the 1990s, while the extent of monetary independence declined. At the end of the 1990s, measured exchange rate stability rose significantly. These trends reflect the introduction of the euro in 1999.

The experience of the emerging market economies presents a stark contrast (Figure 10.2B). First, exchange rate stability declined rapidly from the 1970s through the mid-1980s. After some retrenchment around early 1980s (in the wake of the debt crisis), financial openness resumed its ascent from 1990 onwards.[11] For the developing economies (Figure 10.2C),

---

[8] Although as Obstfeld (2013) notes in his survey, the benefits in practice of complete or near complete openness are difficult to discern, empirically.

[9] See Aizenman et al. (2013) for a discussion of how differing combinations of exchange rate stability, monetary autonomy, and financial openness affect inflation levels, and output and inflation volatility.

[10] More details on the construction of the indexes can be found in Aizenman et al. (2010, 2013), and the indexes are available at http://web.pdx.edu/~ito/trilemma_indexes.htm. There is substantial disagreement regarding the extent to which de facto capital control measure the extent of actual insulation of monetary policy; see Klein (2012), and Klein and Shambaugh (2013).

[11] In these figures, the emerging market economies are defined as the economies classified as either emerging or frontier during 1980–1997 by the International Financial Corporation. For those in Asia, emerging market economies are "Emerging East Asia-14" defined by Asian Development Bank plus India.

Central Banking: Perspectives from Emerging Economies

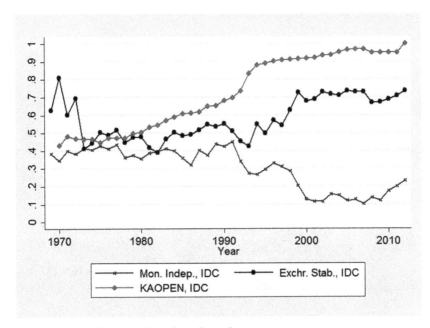

Figure 10.2A: Trilemma indices for industrial countries

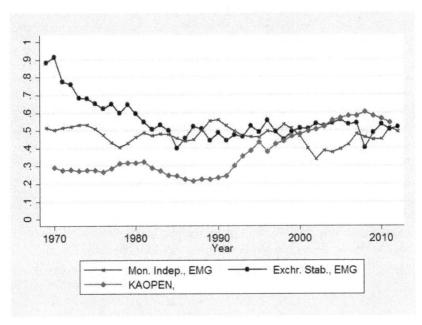

Figure 10.2B: Trilemma indices for emerging market economies

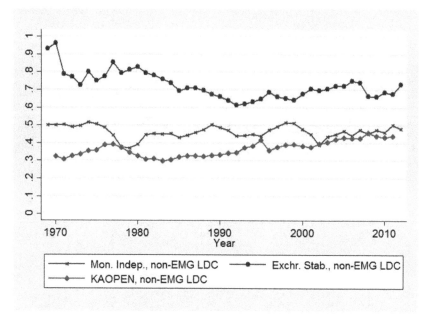

Figure 10.2C: Trilemma indices for less developed countries

exchange rate stability declined less rapidly, and financial openness trended upward more slowly. In both cases though, monetary independence remained more or less trendless.

Interestingly, for the emerging market economies, the indices suggest a convergence toward the middle ground, even as discussion of the disappearing middle of intermediate exchange rate regimes rose in prominence. This pattern suggests that policy makers in these economies have been aiming for moderate levels of both monetary independence and financial openness while maintaining higher levels of exchange rate stability. In other words, they have been leaning against the trilemma over a period that coincides with the accumulation of sizable foreign exchange reserves, on the part of several key countries.

For developing economies, exchange rate stability has been the goal most aggressively pursued throughout the period. In contrast to the experience of the emerging market economies, financial openness has not been expanding for the non-emerging market developing economies, as a group.

One way to interpret the differential responses of emerging market and developing country is to consider the diverging perceptions regarding exchange rates. For advanced economies, with well-developed financial markets and the means to hedge exchange rate risk, exchange rates serve

Central Banking: Perspectives from Emerging Economies

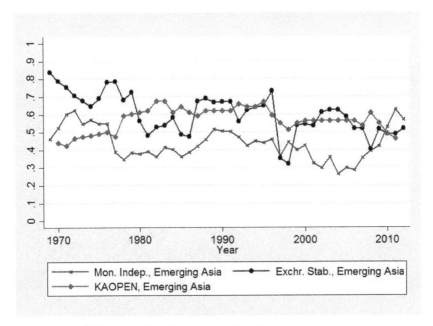

Figure 10.3A: Trilemma indices for emerging East Asia

the textbook function of shock absorbers in an aggregate demand framework. For less developed countries, exchange rates are perceived as *sources* of financial and macroeconomic instability (by way of tradables prices and expected asset returns). Emerging market economies have developed over time sufficiently efficient financial markets so that the perception of exchange rates has shifted away from being a source of shocks and toward that of shock absorber. The convergence toward greater exchange rate flexibility makes sense in that context.

Some observations regarding Emerging Asia merit additional discussion.[12] Figure 10.3A shows that for these economies, this sort of convergence is not a recent phenomenon. Since as early as the early 1980s, the three indexes have been clustered around the middle range. However, for most of the time, except for the Asian crisis years of 1997–1998, exchange rate stability seems to have been the most pervasive policy choice. In the post-crisis years in the 2000s, the indices diverged, but seem to have re-converged in the recent years.

---

[12] In these figures, the sample of "Asian Emerging Market Economies" include Cambodia, China, Hong Kong, India, Indonesia, Rep. of Korea, Malaysia, Philippines, Singapore, Thailand, and Vietnam.

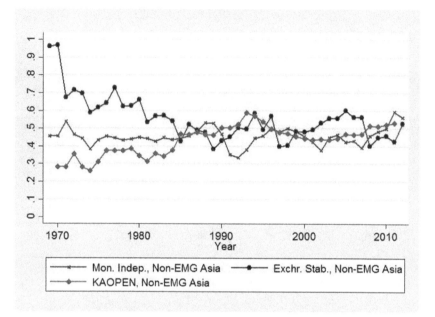

Figure 10.3B: Trilemma indices for developing East Asia

This characterization does not appear to be applicable to non-emerging market economies in Asia (Figure 10.3B) or to non-Asia emerging market economies (Figure 10.3C). For non-EMG economies in Asia or non-Asian developing economies, convergence in the trilemma configurations seems to be the case in the last decade.

One aspect not directly incorporated into the measurement of the trilemma is the accumulation of foreign exchange reserves. As long as capital openness is less than complete, there remains scope for controlled reserve accumulation/decumulation.

To the extent that external imbalances (private capital flows and current account balances) manifest in changes in official reserves, this has implications for monetary policy. Foreign exchange reserves are on the asset side of the balance sheet, so changes in reserves must result in corresponding changes in central bank liabilities (high powered money) in the absence of sterilization operations. Increases in money base will typically lead to increases in the money supply – once again in the absence of sterilization procedures such as bank reserve ratio increases.

Note sterilization is impossible if financial openness is complete. That's because infinite capital inflows or outflows would overwhelm any such attempts at sterilization. In practice, almost no country is completely open,

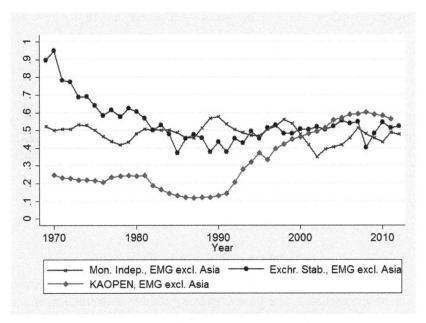

Figure 10.3C: Trilemma indices for Non-Asia emerging market economies

as capital controls – or the threat of the imposition of such controls – is always present. And prudential regulations mean that the financial system incorporate a fair share of nontradable assets so that not all yields are equalized.[13]

Why do emerging market countries accumulate these reserves? There are a variety of reasons, and indeed Ghosh, Ostry, and Tsangarides (2012) argue that the importance of these motivations have varied over time; detailed discussion of this issue is reserved for Section 4. For the moment, I'll merely note that incomplete financial integration allows for controlled foreign reserve accumulation and decumulation, and thus reserves are important to track as part of an individual country's choices regarding the trilemma.

Aizenman, Chinn, and Ito (2011) find that Asia, especially those economies with emerging markets, behave differently from other groups of economies; the middle-ground convergence took place earlier for this

---

[13] See Ito and Chinn (2007) for a discussion of political risk as a source of covered interest differentials. Chinn and Dooley (1997) examine the implications of nontradable assets due to banking system segmentation.

group, as opposed to all emerging market economies. In addition, the group of Asian emerging market economies stands out from the others with their sizeable and rapidly increasing amount of foreign reserve holding.

The Aizenman, Chinn, and Ito measure of monetary independence describes how domestic short term interest rates depend on – or more properly fail to correlate to – interest rates in a key foreign country. However, it doesn't specify how those interest rates are determined, so it is an incomplete description of the conduct of monetary policy. To further explain the evolution of monetary policy in emerging markets, the determinants of central bank policy rates are examined.

3 Describing Monetary Policy

3.1 Monetary Autonomy, to What End?

The international trilemma defines the tradeoffs between short term monetary policy, exchange rate policy, and the degree of financial openness broadly defined, at an instant. But the existence of a tradeoff is not sufficient to define what monetary regime is actually implemented. This is an important point. Aizenman et al. (2013) find that greater monetary independence is associated with lower output volatility, while greater exchange rate stability implies greater output volatility. Greater monetary autonomy is associated with a higher level of inflation while greater exchange rate stability and greater financial openness with a lower the inflation rate.

This characterization leaves out part of the story, because it lumps together countries that might be implementing very different monetary policy frameworks, even while enjoying some monetary autonomy. And choices regarding those different frameworks arise partly because emerging market central banks face additional constraints in addition to those imposed by the international trilemma.

To organize concepts regarding the policy frameworks that have been applied in emerging markets, I rely on the taxonomy of Stone and Bhundia (2004). This taxonomy is based on the clarity of and transparency of the nominal anchor adopted.

- Monetary nonautonomy: the central bank does not issue its own currency
- Exchange rate peg: the central bank sets the value of the home currency relative to another, usually with the allowance for adjustments.
- Weak anchor: no nominal anchor is defined.

Central Banking: Perspectives from Emerging Economies 399

- Money anchor: a monetary aggregate is used as the nominal anchor.
- Full-fledged inflation targeting: the central bank aims for an explicit inflation goal.
- Implicit price stability anchor: the central bank pursues policies that target a given inflation rate, without explicit statement of that goal.
- Inflation targeting lite: the central bank pursues a broad inflation objective, but incorporates a role for the exchange rate.

The selection of one or the other of these regimes depends on the context.[14] For instance, the prevalence of a weak anchor regime – essentially one where monetary policy under discretion uses a variety of economic indicators to guide policy – seems somewhat mysterious until one considers the conditions in many emerging markets before the 1980s. Montiel (1991) sums up the situation:

In developing countries ... the menu of assets available to private agents is very limited. Organized securities markets in which the central bank can conduct open market operations simply do not exist in many countries. By and large, individuals can hold currency as well as demand and time deposits issued by the banking system, and they can borrow from commercial banks. ... [O]rganized equity markets are small or nonexistent. Capital controls and prohibitions on the holding of foreign exchange limit the extent to which foreign assets may be held by domestic residents, although parallel markets for foreign currency often emerge in response to such regulations, thereby allowing private agents to circumvent official controls, at least in part. Finally, even in the case of those assets and liabilities available to individuals such as demand or time deposits and bank credit, official restrictions typically determine the interest rates paid and charged by financial institutions.

In other words, the characteristics of emerging market financial systems – the absence of deep equity and particularly bond markets – meant that the monetary transmission mechanism worked perhaps as strongly through credit as much as monetary channels.

As a consequence, monetary policy in emerging market economies, particularly before the 1990s, relied on an eclectic mix of money and/or credit stock targeting, and/or varying types of exchange rate pegs, bands, or managed floats. Monetary policy typically worked in tandem with fiscal policy to fulfill various goals with respect to growth, inflation, external balances, and reserves accumulation, which changed over time.

---

[14] Mishkin (1999) lays out a slightly different taxonomy: exchange rate targeting, monetary targeting, inflation targeting, and monetary policy with an implicit but not explicit nominal anchor.

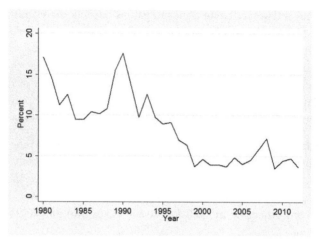

Figure 10.4. Median inflation rate for emerging market economies
Source: IMF, World Economic Outlook (October 2014).

In practice, monetary policy tended to be procyclical. One key reason for this outcome was the high degree of fiscal procyclicality.[15] Kaminsky, Reinhart, and Vegh (2005) documented the cyclicality in the monetary policy of a broad set of countries covering both emerging market and advanced economies. When fiscal policy resulted in deficits greater than the maximum amount of seignorage, then rapid inflation was the typical outcome; some of this phenomenon is hinted at in Figure 10.4, which shows the evolution of the median inflation rate in emerging market economies.

As a consequence of price instability, the search for nominal anchors gained strength during the 1980s. Entering the 1990s there was a growing recognition that nominal anchors in the absence of central bank independence would be ineffectual. The East Asian crises of 1997 further reinforced the belief in nominal anchor via hard pegs, given the perceived fragility crawling and adjustable pegs.

While the advent of inflation targeting in New Zealand can be marked to the beginning of the 1990s, some form of inflation targeting only became a commonplace policy framework in emerging market economies near the end of the decade, starting in Europe by way of Poland in January 1998, East Asia in April of that year (Korea), and Latin America in June 1999

---

[15] Talvi and Vegh (2005).

Central Banking: Perspectives from Emerging Economies 401

(Brazil).[16] The move to targets or rules based policies is closely associated with the move to autonomous or independent central banks.

In order to characterize the conduct of monetary policy since the late 1990s, it's useful to estimate reaction functions for monetary policy – essentially variants of the Taylor rules – for those countries that declared adherence to full-fledged inflation targeting, as well as those that did not.[17]

Obviously, not all central banks pursued inflation targeting, but even those that did not seemed to react to inflation and output, suggesting that they might have adhered to what Stone and Bhundia refer to as inflation targeting lite. And those that indicated that they followed inflation targeting sometimes reacted to other variables. That is, even for some inflation targeting central banks, the exchange rate and foreign exchange reserves exerted measurable effects on central bank decisions regarding the policy rate.

Aizenman et al. (2011) examine the behavior of emerging market inflation targeters Brazil, Columbia, the Czech Republic, Hungary, Israel, Korea, Mexico, Peru, the Philippines, Poland, and Thailand (see Figure 10.5 for inflation targets), and non-inflation targeters of Argentina, Indonesia, Jordan, Malaysia, and Morocco, over the period from 1989 to 2006. They find in a panel setting that self-proclaimed inflation targeters do respond to the output and inflation gaps. Interestingly, the coefficient on the output *growth* gap (defined as HP filter deviations from trend growth) is typically small and statistically insignificant. On the other hand, the inflation rate does enter, usually with a short run coefficient of approximately 0.22–0.29. That means, given the partial adjustment mechanism assumed, a long run coefficient of between 1.4 and –1.7. That is a one percentage point increase in inflation induces a 1.4–1.7 percentage point increase in the policy rate.

They also find that emerging market inflation targeting central banks tend to lean against the wind when it comes to exchange rate changes; a 1 percent depreciation in the real effective exchange rate leads to a long run interest rate hike of 0.4 percentage points.[18]

---

[16] Israel is an early adopter, beginning in 1992. In addition, one can find earlier dates if one considers implicit inflation targets.

[17] One could imagine alternative reaction functions. Mehrotra and Sanchez-Fung (2011) argue that hybrid functions incorporating nominal income targets fit better for several of the nominally inflation targeting countries.

[18] Stone and Bhundia (2004) term a regime that augments inflation and output gap based reaction function with a responsiveness to exchange rates "inflation targeting lite," while Goldstein (2002) terms this "managed floating plus."

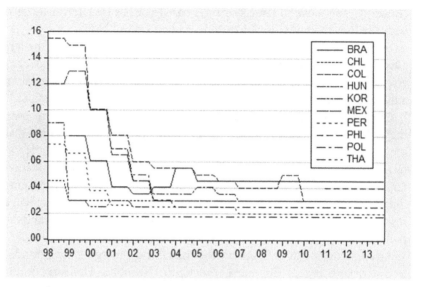

Figure 10.5: Inflation targets in selected countries

The contrast with the non-inflation targeting countries is marked. In a specification including real exchange rate depreciation, the long run impact of a one percentage point inflation rate increase is 0.6. The tendency to lean against exchange rate depreciation is slightly more pronounced – each percentage point depreciation leads to a 0.5 increase in the policy rate in the long run (the short run impact does differ quantitatively and statistically, though). Another difference is that non-inflation targeters tend to react strongly to reserve accumulation. A 1 percent increase in foreign exchange reserves is associated with a 0.26 percentage point decrease in the policy rate.

One key distinction from advanced economy IT policies is that the output *growth* gap is not an economically or statistically significant determinant of the policy rate. In fact, the output growth gap is not important for the non-IT countries.

Commodity exporting inflation targeters behave somewhat differently than non-commodity exporters. Commodity exporters respond more strongly to inflation, as well as exchange rate changes, than do non-commodity exporters. I come back to this point in Section 3.3.

A more recent study by Ostry, Ghosh, and Chamon (2012) obtains similar results through 2010, although for a slightly different specification. They find that inflation targeters respond to the extent of the real exchange rate deviation, rather than the real exchange rate depreciation.

Central Banking: Perspectives from Emerging Economies 403

3.2 Inflation Targeting – or Not – After the Crisis

Do the same characterizations still apply to the inflation targeting regimes during and after the global financial crisis and its aftermath? In order to examine this question, I examine a set of countries slightly larger than Aizenman, Hutchison, and Noy did, and over the slightly longer 1998–2013 period.

The IT emerging market countries include Brazil, Chile, Columbia, Hungary, Korea, Mexico, Peru, Philippines, Poland, and Thailand.[19] The non-IT emerging market sample is heterogeneous, and includes Argentina, Bulgaria, China, Estonia, Indonesia, India, Lithuania, Malaysia, Russia, Singapore, South Africa, and Turkey.

The baseline specification is:

$$i_{it}^{policy} = \beta_0 + \beta_1 \pi_{it} + \beta_2 \hat{y}_{it} + \beta_3 \Delta q_{it} + \beta_4 \Delta res_{it} + \rho i_{it-1}^{policy}$$

Where π is 4 quarter CPI inflation, $\hat{y}$ is the output gap, q is the real exchange rate,[20] res is log foreign exchange reserves. β_1, $\beta_2 > 0$, and $\beta_3 > 0$ if the central bank leans against the wind with respect to the real exchange.[21] The lagged interest rate is included to account for the tendency of central banks to smooth the policy rate (see the data appendix for details).

Depending on the specification, β_3 or β_4 or both might be suppressed. Note that this specification imposes a constant target inflation rate (as well as equilibrium real interest rate).

The results of estimating the Taylor rule for the official inflation targeters are reported in Table 10.1; results for non-inflation targeters in Table 10.2.[22] The results in columns 1–3 in Table 10.1 confirm that inflation targeting countries respond to inflation; the coefficient on

---

[19] No distinction is made between different levels of credibility and inflation targeting (see Carare and Stone, 2006).

[20] In principle, the deviation of the real exchange rate from a trend is more appropriate (see for instance Chinn and Dooley, 1998). However, the results using the HP deviations fail to exhibit significant coefficients in any specification.

[21] The channels by which reserves could induce a movement in the policy rate are multiple. It could be that reserves are accumulated in response to exchange rate deviations from trend (e.g., Ostry, Ghosh, and Chamon, 2012), or reserves feed into money and credit stocks which then induce a tighter monetary policy. Notice that the sign on the coefficient is ambiguous.

[22] Estimates using OLS, with fixed country and time effects.

404 *Menzie D. Chinn*

Table 10.1: *Taylor Rule Regressions, Inflation Targeters, 1998Q1–2013Q4*

	Dependent variable: Policy interest rate					
	[1]	[2]	[3]	[4]	[5]	[6]
Output gap	0.208***	0.201***	0.205***	0.196***	0.184***	0.196***
	(0.064)	(0.063)	(0.062)	(0.069)	(0.067)	(0.067)
Inflation	0.184**	0.195***	0.186**	0.265***	0.289***	0.265***
	(0.072)	(0.073)	(0.071)	(0.076)	(0.073)	(0.076)
Inflation target				−0.043	−0.050	−0.043
				(0.125)	(0.125)	(0.126)
Exchange rate		0.023			0.038	
depreciation		(0.024)			(0.027)	
Reserve change			−0.011			−0.001
			(0.021)			(0.019)
Lagged dependent	0.693***	0.691***	0.692***	0.634***	0.634***	0.638***
variable	(0.064)	(0.064)	(0.064)	(0.090)	(0.089)	(0.090)
Fixed eff.	Yes	Yes	Yes	Yes	Yes	Yes
Time fix. eff	Yes	Yes	Yes	Yes	Yes	Yes
Individuals	10	10	10	10	10	10
Adj-R sq	0.89	0.89	0.89	0.91	0.91	0.91
N	627	627	627	519	519	519

Notes: OLS estimates (robust standard errors in parentheses). *(**)[***] indicates significance at the 10%(5%)[1%]. Sample: Brazil, Chile, Colombia, Hungary, Korea, Mexico, Peru, Philippines, Poland, Thailand. For columns 4–6, sample pertains to time period for which inflation targets are available.

inflation is typically statistically significant, with the implied long run value of about 0.6. Since we have data on announced inflation targets (see Figure 10.5), one can also estimate:

$$i_{it}^{policy} = \delta_0 + \beta_1 \pi_{it} + \delta_1 \pi_{it}^{target} + \beta_2 \hat{y}_{it} + \beta_3 \Delta q_{it} + \beta_4 \Delta res_{it} + \rho i_{it-1}^{policy}$$

Where $\delta_1 < 0$.

The results corresponding to this specification are reported in columns 4–6. They also indicate the monetary authority responds positively to inflation, with the central bank tightening in response to rising inflation, in the long run about 0.7–0.8 percentage points for each percentage point increase in inflation.

In contrast to the findings in Aizenman, Hutchison, and Noy, inflation targeting central banks respond to the output gap (with a long run

Central Banking: Perspectives from Emerging Economies 405

Table 10.2: *Taylor Rule Regressions, Non-Inflation Targeters, 1998Q1–2013Q4*

	Dependent variable: Policy interest rate					
	[1]	[2]	[3]	[4]	[5]	[6]
Output gap	−0.024	0.012	−0.010	0.051	0.051	0.030
	(0.089)	(0.087)	(0.088)	(0.128)	(0.127)	(0.130)
Inflation	0.194***	0.214***	0.202***	0.250***	0.263***	0.273***
	(0.053)	(0.054)	(0.052)	(0.072)	(0.071)	(0.070)
Exch. depr.		0.152***			0.114*	
		(0.049)			(0.066)	
Res. change			−0.052***			−0.130
			(0.022)			(0.095)
Lagged depvar	0.700***	0.682***	0.693***	0685***	0.676***	0.672***
	(0.065)	(0.066)	(0.065)	(0.090)	(0.090)	(0.089)
Fixed eff.	Yes	Yes	Yes	Yes	Yes	Yes
Time fix. eff	Yes	Yes	Yes	Yes	Yes	Yes
Individuals	12	12	12	8	8	8
Adj-R sq	0.79	0.79	0.79	0.80	0.80	0.80
N	715	715	715	477	477	477

Notes: OLS estimates (robust standard errors in parentheses). *(**)[***] indicates significance at the 10%(5%)[1%]. Broad sample: Argentina, Bulgaria, China, Estonia, Indonesia, India, Lithuania, Malaysia, Russia, Singapore, Turkey, and South Africa. Narrow sample: China, Indonesia, India, Malaysia, Russia, Singapore, Turkey, and South Africa.

coefficient of about 0.5–0.7). The results differ in part because of the definition of the gap variable differs (they use *growth* gaps).[23]

Over the entire sample, inflation targeting central banks do not appear to respond to external factors, in accord with priors regarding a full-fledged inflation targeting regime (although the response to exchange rate depreciation is borderline significant (at the 17 percent) in column [5]). Unlike the findings of Aizenman, Hutchison, and Noy, commodity exporters do not exhibit a substantially different responsiveness to exchange rate changes. Hence, at first glance, the inflation targeters appear to live up to their name.[24]

In Table 10.2, the results of the non-inflation targeters are reported, first for a larger sample of fourteen emerging market economies (columns 1–3),

---

[23] If the first difference of the output gap – approximately the same as the HP defined growth gap – is used, then the estimated output coefficient becomes statistically insignificant.

[24] These results contrast with Mohanty and Klau (2004), who examined the behavior of inflation targeters on a country by country basis.

406   *Menzie D. Chinn*

and for a narrower sample of eight (columns 4–5). Monetary authorities respond fairly strongly to inflation – in the long run, as strongly as in the inflation targeting sample. Somewhat surprisingly, there is no marked response to the output gap. On the other hand, these central banks do appear to lean against the wind when it comes to the real exchange rate. In the long run, central banks raise the policy rate by one-third to one-half a percentage point in response to a 1 percent depreciation.

A fair characterization of emerging market central bank monetary policy is that several countries have adopted – and retained – inflation targeting. As Rose (2014) has shown, these inflation targeting regimes have proven remarkably durable, even in the face of the 2008 financial crisis and ensuing global downturn.

One caveat to this characterization is that while the framework has remained in place where instituted, it has not necessarily remained unchanged; Rose alludes to the fact that inflation targeting has survived exactly because it has been implemented in a flexible fashion.

The estimates of the parameters in the reaction functions over time confirms this point. The estimates have changed, particularly with respect to the exchange rate. Table 10.3 presents results for the Taylor rule, estimated over two subsamples, 1998–2007, and 2008–2013.

The responsiveness to output deviations declines in economic and statistical terms. The long run impact post-crisis is about half of what was exhibited in the pre-crisis period, while the degree of interest rate smoothing increases. More interestingly, the results indicate that in the period up to 2007, inflation targeting central banks did seem to respond to exchange rates (in line with Aizenman et al. 2011). Over the 2008–2013 period, central banks appear to respond to reserve accumulation by raising rates.[25]

No such correspondingly large change is apparent in the non-inflation targeting group, with respect to output gaps, inflation rates, or exchange rate changes.

3.3 Some Macro Factors not Addressed by Inflation Targeting

While inflation targeting has not been adopted on a wholesale basis, a flexible inflation targeting framework does seem to characterize the monetary policy of a number of prominent emerging market economies.

---

[25] Instrumenting reserve changes with the US policy interest rate and lags in the rate and accumulation to account for endogeneity yields the same positive coefficient. Admittedly, these instruments might not be adequate to fully address reverse causality.

Central Banking: Perspectives from Emerging Economies 407

Table 10.3: *Taylor Rule Regressions, Inflation Targeters, over Time*

	Dependent variable: Policy interest rate					
	1998–2007			2008–2013		
	[1]	[2]	[3]	[4]	[5]	[6]
Output gap	0.359***	0.342***	0.362***	0.051***	0.048**	0.046**
	(0.130)	(0.127)	(0.127)	(0.020)	(0.020)	(0.019)
Inflation	0.332**	0.385***	0.333***	0.046	0.048	0.044
	(0.099)	(0.097)	(0.100)	(0.031)	(0.031)	(0.031)
Infl. target	−0.028	−0.032	−0.029	−0.107	−0.105	−0.083
	(0.170)	(0.169)	(0.169)	(0.250)	(0.250)	(0.246)
Exch. depr.		0.072*			0.005	
		(0.044)			(0.009)	
Res. change			0.004			0.015*
			(0.025)			(0.008)
Lagged depvar	0.533***	0.524***	0.533***	0.870***	0.870***	0.876***
	(0.113)	(0.111)	(0.113)	(0.046)	(0.046)	(0.045)
Fixed eff.	Yes	Yes	Yes	Yes	Yes	Yes
Time fix. eff	Yes	Yes	Yes	Yes	Yes	Yes
Individuals	9	9	9	9	9	9
Adj-R sq	0.89	0.89	0.89	0.96	0.96	0.96
N	295	295	295	221	221	221

Notes: OLS estimates (robust standard errors in parentheses). *(**)[***] indicates significance at the 10%(5%)[1%]. Sample: Brazil, Chile, Colombia, Hungary, Korea, Mexico, Peru, Poland, Thailand.

Moreover, even countries that have not adopted inflation targets appear to respond to inflation rates.

That being said, it is not clear that inflation targeting constitutes the most appropriate policy framework for most, let alone all, emerging markets. Some key issues include the extent and importance of exchange pass through, the prevalence of supply and terms of trade shocks, and the susceptibility to asset bubbles.[26]

Exchange rate pass through

One aspect of most emerging market economies is their relatively greater trade openness. Exports and imports, expressed as a ratio to GDP, is typically higher than in the core advanced economies such as the G-7. At

---

[26] This section draws heavily on Frankel (2011). In addition, Anand and Prasad (2010) notes that the optimal target price index changes when one incorporates into the analysis financial frictions in the form of credit constrained consumers.

the same time, because imports to emerging markets tend to be denominated in foreign currencies, and exports in foreign currency, exchange rate pass through into domestic prices is usually higher than it is in the G-7 economies. Consequently, exchange rate changes have proportionately larger impacts on wide swaths of a typical emerging market economy.

As noted in the previous section, inflation targeting narrowly defined, doesn't mean that the monetary authority won't respond to exchange rate changes. However, the effect is indirect, and it's only by virtue of the impact of exchange rates on aggregate prices that the exchange rate matters.

However, it's plausible that the central bank should care about the extent of exchange rate changes, not only because it potentially affects the price level, but additionally because it has ramifications for the relative price of tradables and nontradables.

Terms of trade shocks

Relatedly, when the terms of trade deteriorate for reasons other than exchange rate changes – for instance as a consequence of an oil price increase – there is a likelihood of a feed through into the price level and domestic inflation. This implies that the response of the central bank under inflation targeting will be to tighten monetary policy by raising interest rates; however, in terms of demand management, this doesn't make sense, as it makes policy more contractionary at exactly the times that one would want a more expansionary policy.

Supply shocks

This is not a problem specific to emerging markets, but is perhaps more pronounced, especially if such shocks dominate output fluctuations. Aguiar and Gopinath (2007) point out that the cycle is the trend in most emerging market economies, so supply shocks are more important. Then positive supply shocks exert downward pressure on prices, which prompt interest rate declines. In the absence of distortions in the financial system, this procyclicality might not be too problematic. However, if feedback loops associated with collateral constraints are in force, then these policies are likely to exacerbate financial boom-bust cycles.

3.4 Macroprudential Issues and Inflation Targeting

This point regarding boom-bust cycles leads to the issue of monetary policy and the threat of asset bubbles. Since this topic applies to advanced economies as well as emerging market economies, the issues are relatively well known. The positive feedback loops that led to the boom-bust cycle in asset prices

Central Banking: Perspectives from Emerging Economies 409

during the 2000s were, in retrospect, not dealt with adequately by flexible inflation targeting focused on goods prices (see Chang, 2013, for a discussion of the challenge of financial frictions to the case for inflation targeting).

These concerns are of even greater importance in emerging markets where capital inflows are large relative to the size of the domestic financial markets, and regulatory infrastructure even less well developed. The degree of asymmetric information is likely more pronounced in these economies. The additional constraints imposed by these other international financial linkages – what Obstfeld (2014) terms the financial trilemma – are of great importance.

Currency mismatches and original sin
One of the characteristics of emerging market economies is that the government is typically constrained to borrowing in foreign currencies when accessing international markets. In addition, most domestic firms are typically only rarely able to issue debt in domestic currency terms; rather they will issue debt in foreign currency (if available). Cross border borrowing from the international banking system is often denominated in foreign currency terms because it is substantially cheaper.[27]

As a consequence, domestic firms – including banks – often build up mismatches on their balance sheets that exhibit currency mismatches that can lead to insolvency should there be rapid and large changes in currency values. For instance, if liabilities are in US dollars, but assets in domestic currency, then a large devaluation (or depreciation) can lead to insolvencies of a breadth sufficient to pose a systemic risk. This leads to ambiguous implications for observed central bank behavior: it means a lean against the wind policy, particularly for large changes. On the other hand, it suggests that excess rigidity can lead to insufficient hedging against exchange rate risk.

3.5 Inflation Targeting and Prerequisites

One complicating factor is the procyclical behavior of the fiscal authority in many emerging market economies, at least traditionally. Typically, governments have raised spending when tax revenues were high and borrowing in international markets relatively easy. However, those times are exactly the times when on aggregate demand management terms one would like a restrained fiscal policy. On the other hand, fiscal policy

---

[27] See Eichengreen, Hausmann, and Panizza (2007) for an explication of the distinctions between original sin and currency mismatch (as well as debt intolerance). See Cespedes, Chang, and Velasco (2004) for an examination of the importance of balance sheet effects.

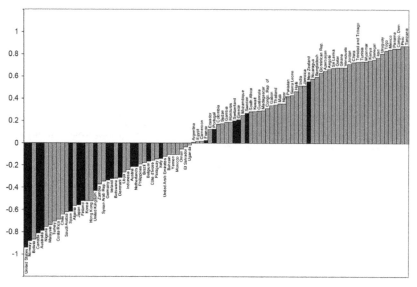

Figure 10.6: Fiscal Procyclicality, 2000–2009
Source: Frankel, Végh, and Vuletin (2013).

has tended to be relatively tight when the economy has receded, as revenues decline and international sources of lending dry up as perceived risk rises. Fiscal deficits can be run as long as the central bank has been willing to finance the deficit by way of monetization. It's exactly the presence of such conditions that elicited the skepticism by Masson et al. (1997) that inflation targeting would be implemented widely.[28]

This procyclicality of fiscal policy has been well documented (Talvi and Vegh, 2005).[29] In a sample extending from 1960 to 1999, Frankel, Vegh, and Vuletin (2013) show that almost no emerging market or less developed countries exhibited countercyclical fiscal policy.[30] However, since 2000, several emerging market countries have graduated from procyclical to countercyclical fiscal policy, as shown in Figure 10.6. Bergman and Hutchison (2015) argue that this decline in procyclicality is partly due to the implementation of fiscal rules.

Coulibaly (2012) contends that the increasing popularity and success of inflation targeting – either in its explicit form or as one of several

---

[28] Relatedly, there is the concern that the level of institutional development is not sufficient to support inflation targeting; see Mishkin (1999).
[29] Originally circulated in 1998.
[30] See also Ilzetzki and Vegh (2008).

Central Banking: Perspectives from Emerging Economies 411

important goals – is partly due to the changing conditions, including less pronounced fiscal procyclicality. Lower government debt burdens and less short term external debt also count.

If the trend toward more countercyclical fiscal policy and favorable debt burdens remain in place, then two offsetting forces will be in place. On the one hand, inflation targeters will be better able to hit their targets in a benign macroeconomic environment. On the other hand, the need for a nominal anchor based on inflation becomes less pronounced. That is, the optimal tradeoff between inflation targeting – that aims to overcome time consistency problems – and alternative monetary frameworks that are motivated by minimizing cyclical fluctuations, evolves over time. Nonetheless, inflation targeting and countercyclical fiscal policy should be viewed primarily as complements, insofar as the latter facilitates the former.

4 Reserve Accumulation and Self-Insurance

One of the central differences between the central bank policy in the advanced economies and the emerging market economies is the marked buildup of reserves, particularly since the East Asian financial crises of 1997–1998. China, the world's largest holder of foreign exchange reserves, currently held nearly $4 trillion of reserves in March 2014, accounting for approximately 30 percent of the world's total. As of the first quarter of 2014, the top 10 reserve holders were all emerging market or developing economies, with the exceptions of Japan and Switzerland. The eight developing economies, including China, Korea, the Russian Federation, and Taiwan, held approximately 60 percent of world foreign exchange reserves. These developments have contrasted sharply with those applying to the advanced economies. As illustrated in Figure 10.7, advanced economies – which happen to be fairly financially open – have not accumulated a lot of foreign exchange reserves relative to GDP. The relatively closed non-advanced economies (which include developing as well as emerging market economies) have accumulated lots of reserves, and that trend has continued over time.

Why have emerging market economies accumulated such large stocks of reserves? Various motivations have been forwarded, ranging from the traditional motivations – coverage of shocks to trade flows – to mercantilism, and self-insurance against capital account shocks. Ghosh, Ostry and Tsangarides (2012) attempt to decompose emerging market reserve accumulation into component parts. Their analysis yields the decomposition displayed in Figure 10.8.

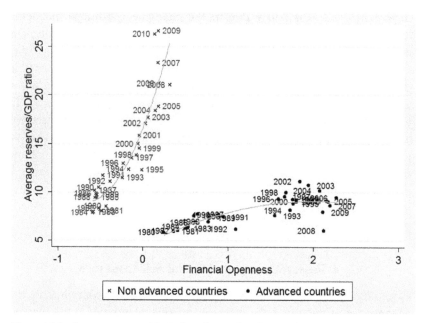

Figure 10.7: Average reserves/GDP for advanced and non-advanced countries
Source: Bussière, Chen, Chinn and Lisack (2015).

Their analysis suggests that some of the reserve accumulation is motivated by maintaining sufficient funds to cover shocks to trade flows, and only a small (but measurable) proportion to mercantilist motives. However, an important driver of recent reserve accumulation in this group of countries is self-insurance against capital account shocks, such as those that might arise due to a sudden stop.

Even in the absence of sudden stops, the vagaries of international capital markets make caution the preferred course. Consider the consequences of the expansionary monetary policies undertaken by the United States from 2008 onward. In addition to driving the overnight rate driven to zero, the Fed undertook quantitative easing – purchases of long term Treasury securities and Agency mortgage backed securities – that were perceived to have caused large spillovers to emerging market economies.

There is merit in these perceptions. Chinn (2013) surveys studies, including those by Fratzscher, Lo Duca, and Straub (2013), that indicate a substantial depreciation of the dollar, and increase in outflows to emerging market economies, as a consequence of unconventional

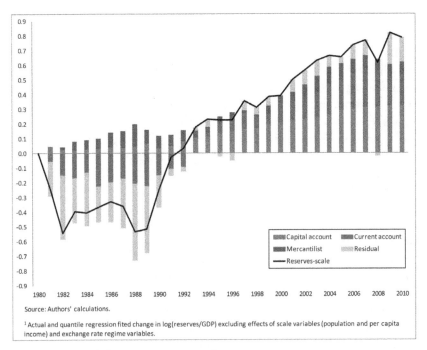

Figure 10.8: Fitted changes in reserves, and components
Source: Ghosh, Ostry, and Tsangarides (2012).

monetary policies, particularly QE2. The increase in the Fed balance sheet is also shown to have ambiguous effects on exchange rates in the largest emerging market economies of Brazil, Russia, India, and China.[31] The corresponding displeasure at the Fed's suggestion of a taper in the large scale asset purchases suggests that there were substantial spillover effects.[32]

It's important to recall that a similar pattern of capital flow surges occurred during a previous episode of Fed easing – namely the drop in interest rates during the 1990–1991 recession, and the eventual tightening of policy in 1994. At that time, there was substantial discussion of push and pull factors in capital flows to emerging markets. Then, as now, push factors due to depressed advanced country yields

---

[31] Other studies include Chen et al. (2012), IMF (2013a,b).
[32] For assessments of the impact of the taper, see Lim et al. (2014), Eichengreen and Gupta (2015), and Aizenman et al. (2014).

414   *Menzie D. Chinn*

was important (Calvo et al., 1993; Fernandez-Arias, 1996; Dooley, Fernandez-Arias and Kletzer, 1996).

In this sense, the emerging market central bank view that in a world of high capital mobility, it is eminently rational to build up reserves to guard against financial crises of the sort that afflicted East Asia and Latin America during the 1990s. The consensus in the literature certainly tends to buttress the view that countries with an insufficient level of reserves experienced more serious currency and financial crises – see for instance Flood and Marion (2001), Berg and Pattillo (1999), Reinhart and Kaminsky (1999), Gourinchas and Obstfeld (2012), Catao and Milesi-Ferretti (2013), and Obstfeld (2013).

Further confirmation comes from the most recent episode of global financial stress. It appears to be the case that the accumulation of foreign reserves protected countries from the negative shock. In particular, Bussiere, Chen, Chinn, and Lisack (2015) find that the foreign reserves to short term debt variable two years prior to the global crisis is positively and significantly correlated with the real GDP growth deviation from the trend; the coefficient from the full specification with control variables is 0.73.[33] Hence, a doubling of the reserves to debt ratio is associated with a 0.4–0.5 percentage point faster growth rate. This result is robust to the exclusion of outliers and small countries.[34]

Moreover, Bussiere et al. observe that a larger depletion of reserves during the crisis is associated with a stronger rebound. This seems once again to confirm countries' increasing appetite for reserve assets as a means of self-insurance.

The pace of reserve accumulation has slowed down in the last couple of years. There are several competing stories about the recent "flattening-out" in reserve accumulation. First, it is possible that, once a country reaches its pre-crisis level of reserves, it slows the pace of foreign reserve accumulation, since holding large reserves incurs opportunity costs and possibly large risks associated with valuation effects. Second, the deceleration of foreign reserve accumulation might reflect a change of policy priority with regard to monetary autonomy, exchange rate stability and financial openness in the wake of the 2008–2009 financial crisis. Lastly, if foreign reserve accumulation tails off, it might be because of the

---

[33] The results are robust to using alternative measures of economic performance. Using the deviation from the World Economic Outlook forecast, we obtain a similar estimate of 0.62.

[34] See also Dominguez, Hashimoto, and Ito (2012) for similar results for a smaller set of countries.

Central Banking: Perspectives from Emerging Economies 415

stabilization of the underlying macroeconomic variable – short-term debt as argued by Bussiere et al. (2015) – that foreign reserves are accumulated to cover.[35]

5 Some Conjectures Regarding the Future

Policy makers in emerging market economies face a variety of challenges that differ from those facing their counterparts in advanced economies. These include less developed financial markets, relatedly a susceptibility to rapid reversals in capital in- and out-flows, a minimal ability to influence global markets, an inability to borrow internationally in domestic currency, and finally procyclical fiscal policies. On top of these conditions is the fact that the economies are typically relatively small in economic terms so that the international trilemma binds more strongly.

In fact, Rey (2013) argues that increased financial globalization means that the trilemma has reduced in practice to a dilemma – essentially, insulation from world capital markets via capital controls is not feasible. There is some empirical basis for the idea that capital controls in many instances fail to insulate (e.g., Forbes et al., 2014). Hence, core country monetary policies drive periphery country monetary policies, regardless of exchange rate regimes.

There is also something to the view that flexible exchange rates do not provide complete insulation. Nonetheless, Klein and Shambaugh (2013) provide evidence that floating regimes (and to a lesser extent capital controls, particularly if they are durable and extensive) do provide greater monetary autonomy than fixed regimes.

How have policy makers addressed the challenges of the trilemma? After experimenting with a wide range of monetary and exchange rate policies over the 1960s through the 1980s, numerous central banks have implemented various forms of inflation targeting – usually incorporating a role for exchange rates. Thus far, no country that has implemented formal inflation targeting (either by the IMF or other criterion) has exited inflation targeting, leading Rose (2014) to conclude that inflation targeting has proved to be a remarkably durable framework, surviving even the global financial crisis.

---

[35] Results obtained from estimating VECM's lend support to this last interpretation. That is, with the "flattening-out" of short-term debt after the financial crisis, the demand for foreign reserves will tend to decline.

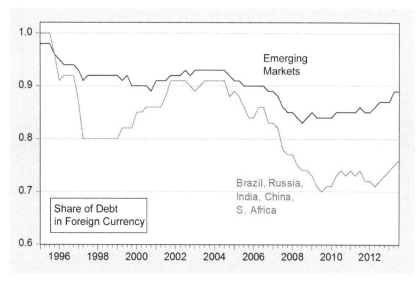

Figure 10.9. Share of debt in foreign currency
Source: IMF, *Global Financial Stability Report* (April 2014), figure 2.3.5, p. 73.

One way to look at this success is that for certain countries, the tradeoff between the usefulness of a nominal anchor to overcome time inconsistency problems and countercyclical stabilization has been favorable to the former. For others, it has not. For those in the latter group, the costs of failing to respond to terms of trade shocks and the need for self-protection have outweighed the time inconsistency concerns.

Other conditions have changed, also altering the calculus. The extent of original sin has declined over the past decade, particularly for certain countries. This decline is shown in Figure 10.9. That development suggests that the exchange rate might figure less prominently in central banks' calculations. Working in the other direction, Hausmann and Panizza (2010) argue the reduction in original sin has been modest.

Emerging-market-ness is a temporary phenomenon, and the emerging market economies of today will eventually graduate to advanced country status. At that juncture, the tradeoff will likely again change. On the other hand, some developing countries will move into the emerging market category, and then confront the same choices. In other words, the emerging market economies – and their particular set of concerns – will always be with us.

Acknowledgments: Paper presented at the Norges Bank, bicentenary project conference "Of the Uses of Central Banks: Lessons from History," 5–6 June 2014, Oslo. I thank Luis Catao, Barry Eichengreen, Hiro Ito,

Maury Obstfeld, Eswar Prasad, Mark Stone, and the discussant Ashok Mody, for extremely helpful comments. However, all remaining errors are solely my responsibility. I thank Joshua Aizenman and Hiro Ito for allowing me to draw on joint work, Ilan Noy for sharing data on inflation targets, and Jélan Passley and Yi Zhang for assistance in collecting data. Faculty research funds of the University of Wisconsin are gratefully acknowledged.

References

Aguiar, Mark, and Gita Gopinath, 2007, "Emerging Market Business Cycles: The Cycle Is the Trend," *Journal of Political Economy* 115: 69–102.

Aizenman, Joshua, Benici Mahir, and Michael Hutchison, 2014, "The Transmission of Federal Reserve Tapering News to Emerging Financial Markets," *NBER Working Paper* No. 19980.

2011, "Surfing the Waves of Globalization: Asia and Financial Globalization in the Context of the Trilemma," *Journal of the Japanese and International Economies* 25: 290–320.

2010, "The Emerging Global Financial Architecture: Tracing and Evaluating New Patterns of the Trilemma Configuration," *Journal of International Money and Finance* 29(4): 615–641.

Aizenman, Joshua, Michael Hutchison, and Ilan Noy, 2011, "Inflation Targeting and Real Exchange Rates in Emerging Markets," *World Development* 39(5): 712–724.

Aizenman, Joshua, Menzie Chinn, and Hiro Ito, 2013, "The 'Impossible Trinity' Hypothesis in an Era of Global Imbalances: Measurement and Testing," *Review of International Economics* 21(3): 447–458.

Anand, Rahul, and Eswar Prasad, 2010, "Optimal Price Indices for Targeting Inflation Under Incomplete Markets," *NBER Working Paper* No. 16290.

Berg, Andrew, and Catherine Pattillo, 1999, "Are Currency Crises Predictable? A Test," *IMF Staff Papers* 46(2): 107–138.

Bergman, U. Michael, and Michael Hutchison, 2015, "Economic Stabilization in the Post-Crisis World: Are Fiscal Rules the Answer?" *Journal of International Money and Finance* 52: 82–101.

Bordo, Michael D., 2005, *The Gold Standard and Related Regimes: Collected Essays.* Cambridge University Press.

1981, "The Classical Gold Standard: Some Lessons for Today," *Federal Reserve Bank of St. Louis Review* (May): 2–17.

Bussière, Matthieu, Gong Cheng, Menzie Chinn, and Noëmie Lisack, 2015, "For a Few Dollars More: Reserves and Growth in Times of Crises," *Journal of International Money and Finance,* 52:127–145.

Calvo, Guillermo A, Leonardo Leiderman, and Carmen M. Reinhart, 1993, "Capital Inflows to Latin America: The Role of External Factors," *IMF Staff Papers* 40: 108–151.

Carare, Alina, and Mark R. Stone, 2006, "Inflation Targeting Regimes," *European Economic Review* 50(5): 1297–1315.

Catao, Luis, and Gian-Maria Milesi-Ferretti, 2013, "External Liabilities and Crises," *IMF Working Paper* 13/113 (Washington, D.C.: International Monetary Fund, May).

Cespedes, Luis, Roberto Chang,, and Andres Velasco, 2004, "Balance Sheets and Exchange Rate Policy," *American Economic Review* 94: 1183–1193.

Chang, Roberto, 2013, "Rethinking Monetary Policy After the Crash," paper presented at conference "Setting Up the Monetary Policy Framework: What Role for Financial Sector Considerations?" Graduate Institute of International and Development Studies, Geneva, October 2013.

Chen, Qianying, Andrew Filardo, Dong He, and Feng Zhu, 2012, "International Spillovers of Central Bank Balance Sheet Policies," in *Are Central Bank Balance Sheets in Asia Too Large?* BIS Papers No. 66 (October), 230–274.

Chinn, Menzie, 2014, "Global Supply Chains and Macroeconomic Relationships in Asia," in *Global Supply Chains and Trade in Value Added*, edited by Benno Ferrarini and David Hummels (Asian Development Bank): 249–286.

2013, "Global Spillovers and Domestic Monetary Policy: The Impacts on Exchange Rates and Other Asset Prices," *BIS Working Paper* No.436 (Basel: BIS, December).

Chinn, Menzie, and Hiro Ito, 2008, "A New Measure of Financial Openness," *Journal of Comparative Policy Analysis* 10(3): 307–320.

2006, "What Matters for Financial Development? Capital Controls, Institutions and Interactions," *Journal of Development Economics* 61(1): 163–192.

Chinn, Menzie, and Michael Dooley, 1998, "Monetary Policy in Japan, Germany and the United States: Does One Size Fit All?" in *Japanese Economic Policy Reconsidered,* edited by Craig Freedman (London: Edward Elgar, 1998): 179–217.

1997, "Asia-Pacific Capital Markets: Measurement of Integration and the Implications for Economic Activity," in *Regionalism versus Multilateral Trading Arrangements*, edited by Takatoshi Ito and Anne O. Krueger (Chicago: Chicago University Press for NBER, 1997): 169–196.

Chinn, Menzie, and Shang-Jin Wei, 2013, "A Faith-based Initiative: Do We Really Know that a Flexible Exchange Rate Regime Facilitates Current Account Adjustment?" *Review of Economics and Statistics* 95(1): 168–184.

Coulibaly, Brahima, 2012, Monetary Policy in Emerging Market Economies: What Lessons from the Global Financial Crisis?. *FRB International Finance Discussion Paper*, (1042).

Dominguez, Kathryn M.E., Yuko Hashimoto, and Takatoshi Ito (2012) "International Reserves and the Global Financial Crisis," *Journal of International Economics* 88(2): 388–406.

Dooley, Michael, Eduardo Fernandez-Arias, and Kenneth Kletzer, 1996, "Is the Debt Crisis History? Recent Private Capital Inflows to Developing Countries," *The World Bank Economic Review* 10(1): 27–50.

Eichengreen, Barry, and Poonam Gupta, 2015, "Tapering Talk: The Impact of Expectations of Reduced Federal Reserve Security Purchases on Emerging Markets," Emerging Markets Review 25: 1–15.

Eichengreen, Barry, Ricardo Hausmann, and Ugo Panizza, 2007, "Currency Mismatches, Debt Intolerance, and the Original Sin: Why They Are Not the Same and Why It Matters," in *Capital Controls and Capital Flows in Emerging Economies: Policies, Practices and Consequences*, edited by Sebastian Edwards (Chicago: University of Chicago Press): 121–170.

Fernandez-Arias, Eduardo, 1996, "The New Wave of Private Capital Inflows: Push or Pull?." *Journal of Development Economics* 48(2): 389–418.

Flood, Robert P., and Nancy Peregrim Marion, 2001, "Holding International Reserves in an Era of High Capital Mobility." *Brookings trade forum.* Vol. 2001. No. 1. (Brookings Institution Press).

Forbes, Kristin, Marcel Fratzscher, and Roland Straub, 2014, "Capital Controls and Macroprudential Measures: What are They Good for?" *CEPR Discussion Papers* No. 9798 (London: January).

Frankel, Jeffrey, 2011, "Monetary Policy in Emerging Markets: A Survey," in *Handbook of Monetary Economics,* edited by Benjamin Friedman and Michael Woodford (Elsevier: Amsterdam).

Frankel, Jeffrey, Carlos Végh, and Guillermo Vuletin, 2013, "On Graduation from Fiscal Procyclicality," *Journal of Development Economics* 100(1): 32–47.

Fratzscher, Marcel, and Arnaud Mehl, 2013, "China's Dominance Hypothesis and the Emergence of a Tri-polar Global Currency System," *The Economic Journal* 124 (581): 1343–1370.

Fratzscher, Marcel, Marco Lo Duca, and Roland Straub, 2013, "On the International Spillovers of US Quantitative Easing," *Discussion Papers of DIW Berlin 1304,* (Berlin: German Institute for Economic Research).

Fry, Maxwell, 1998, "Assessing Central Bank Independence in Developing Countries: Do Actions Speak Louder than Words?" *Oxford Economic Papers* 50(3): 512–529.

Ghosh, Atish R., Jonathan Ostry, David Tsangarides, and G. Charalambos, 2012, Shifting Motives: Explaining the Buildup in Official Reserves in Emerging Markets since the 1980s," *IMF Working Paper* No. 12/34 (Washington, D.C: IMF, January).

Goldstein, Morris, 2002, *Managed Floating Plus* (Washington, D.C.: Peterson Institute).

Gourinchas, Pierre-Olivier, and Maurice Obstfeld (2012), "Stories of the Twentieth Century for the Twenty-first," *American Economic Journal: Macroeconomics* 4(1): 226–65.

Hausmann, Ricardo, and Ugo Panizza, 2010, "Redemption or Abstinence? Original Sin, Currency Mismatches and Counter-Cyclical Policies in the New Millennium," *Center for International Development Working Paper* No. 194 (Cambridge: Harvard, February).

Ilzetzki, Ethan, and Carlos A. Végh, 2008, "Procyclical Fiscal Policy in Developing Countries: Truth or Fiction?," *NBER Working Paper* No. 14191.

IMF, 2013a, "Unconventional Monetary Policies – Recent Experience and Prospects," (Washington, D.C.: IMF, April 18).

2013b, "Unconventional Monetary Policies – Recent Experience and Prospects – Background Paper," (Washington, D.C.: IMF, April 18).

Ito, Hiro, 2013, "Monetary Policy in Asia and the Pacific in the Post, Post-Crisis Era," paper prepared for 36th Pacific Trade and Development (PAFTAD) Conference "Financial Development and Cooperation in Asia and the Pacific," November 19–21, 2013.

Ito, Hiro, and Menzie Chinn, 2007, "Price-based Measurement of Financial Globalization: A Cross-Country Study of Interest Rate Parity," *Pacific Economic Review* 12(4): 419–444.

420   *Menzie D. Chinn*

Kaminsky, Graciela L., Carmen M. Reinhart, and Carlos A. Végh, 2005, "When It Rains, It Pours: Procyclical Capital Flows and Macroeconomic Policies." *NBER Macroeconomics Annual 2004*, Volume 19. (Cambridge: MIT Press): 11–82.

Kaminsky, Gracia, and Sergio L. Schmukler, 2002, "Short-Run Pain, Long-Run Gain: The Effects of Financial Liberalization. *IMF Working Paper* No. 0334 (Washington, D.C.: International Monetary Fund, October).

Klein, Michael W., 2012, "Capital Controls: Gates versus Walls," *Brookings Papers on Economic Activity* 2012(2): 317–367.

Klein, Michael W., and Jay Shambaugh, 2013, "Rounding the Corners of the Policy Trilemma: Sources of Monetary Policy Autonomy," *NBER Working Paper* No. 19461.

Lim, Jamus Jerome, Sanket Mohapatra, and Marc Stocker, 2014, "Tinker, Taper, QE, Bye? The Effect of Quantitative Easing on Financial Flows to Developing Countries," *Background Paper for Global Economic Prospects 2014* (Washington, D.C.: World Bank).

Masson, Paul R., Miguel A. Savastano, and Sunil Sharma, 1997, "The Scope for Inflation Targeting in Developing Countries," *IMF Working Paper* No. 97/130.

Mehrotra, Aaron, and José R. Sánchez-Fung, 2011, "Assessing McCallum and Taylor Rules in a Cross-Section of Emerging Market Economies," *Journal of International Financial Markets, Institutions and Money*, 21(2): 207–228.

Mishkin, Frederic S., 1999, "International Experiences with Different Monetary Policy Regimes," *Journal of Monetary Economics* 43(3): 576–606.

Mohanty, Madhusudan, and Marc Klau, 2004, "Monetary Policy Rules in Emerging Market Economies: Issues and Evidence," *BIS Working Paper* No. 149 (Basel: Bank for International Settlements).

Montiel, Peter J., 1991, "The Transmission Mechanism for Monetary Policy in Developing Countries," *IMF Staff Papers* 38(1): 83–108

Obstfeld, Maurice, 2014, "Trilemmas and Tradeoffs: Living with Financial Globalization," *mimeo* (Berkeley, May 15).

2013, "Never Say Never: Commentary on a Policymaker's Reflections," *mimeo* (UC Berkeley, November).

Obstfeld, Maurice, Jay C. Shambaugh, and Alan M. Taylor, 2005, "The Trilemma in History: Tradeoffs among Exchange Rates, Monetary Policies, and Capital Mobility," *Review of Economics and Statistics* 87 (August): 423–438.

Ostry, Jonathan D., Atish R. Ghosh, and Marco Chamon, 2012, "Two Targets, Two Instruments: Monetary and Exchange Rate Policies in Emerging Market Economies," *IMF Staff Discussion Note* SDN/12/01 (February 29).

Prasad, Eswar S., 2008, "Monetary Policy Independence, the Currency Regime, and the Capital Account in China." in *Debating China's Exchange Rate Policy*, edited by Goldstein, M. and N. R. Lardy (Washington, D.C.: Peterson Institute for International Economics).

Rajan, Raghuram, 2014, "Competitive Monetary easing – Is It Yesterday Once More?" Speech at the Brookings Institution, (Washington, D.C., April 10).

Reinhart, Carmen M., and Graciela L. Kaminsky, 1999, "The Twin Crises: The Causes of Banking and Balance-of-Payments Problems," *American Economic Review* 89(3): 473–500.

Rey, Helene, 2013, "Dilemma not Trilemma: The Global Financial Cycle and Monetary Policy Independence," prepared for the 2013 Jackson Hole Meeting.

Rose, Andrew, 2014, "Surprising Similarities: Recent Monetary Regimes of Small Economies," *Journal of International Money and Finance* 49(Part A): 50-27.

Shambaugh, Jay C., 2004, "The Effect of Fixed Exchange Rates on Monetary Policy," *The Quarterly Journal of Economics* 119(1): 301–352.

Stone, Mark R., and Ashok J. Bhundia, 2004, "A New Taxonomy of Monetary Regimes," *IMF Working Paper* No. 04/191.

Talvi, Ernesto, and Carlos A. Végh, 2005, "Tax Base Variability and Procyclical Fiscal Policy in Developing Countries," *Journal of Development Economics* 78(1): 156–190.

Data Appendix

DATA FOR SECTION 2:

Monetary Independence (MI)

The extent of monetary independence is measured as the reciprocal of the *annual correlation* of the *monthly interest rates* between the home country and the base country. Money market rates are used.[36]

The index for the extent of monetary independence is defined as:

$$MI = 1 - \frac{corr(i_i, i_j) + 1}{2}$$

where i refers to home countries and j to the base country. By construction, the maximum and minimum values are 1 and 0, respectively. Higher values of the index mean more monetary policy independence.[37]

The base country is defined as the country that a home country's monetary policy is most closely linked with as in Shambaugh (2004). For the countries and years for which Shambaugh's data are available, the base countries from his work are used, and for the others, the base countries are

---

[36] The data are extracted from the IMF's *International Financial Statistics* (60B...ZF...). For the countries whose money market rates are unavailable or extremely limited, the money market data are supplemented by those from the Bloomberg terminal and also by the discount rates (60...ZF...) and the deposit rates (60L...ZF...) series from *IFS*.

[37] The index is smoothed out by applying the three-year moving averages encompassing the preceding, concurrent, and following years ($t - 1$, t, $t+1$) of observations.

422   *Menzie D. Chinn*

assigned based on the IMF's *Annual Report on Exchange Arrangements and Exchange Restrictions (AREAER)* and the *CIA Factbook*.

Exchange Rate Stability (ERS)

To measure exchange rate stability, annual standard deviations of the monthly exchange rate between the home country and the base country are calculated and included in the following formula to normalize the index between zero and one:

$$ERS = \frac{0.01}{0.01 + stdev(\Delta(\log(exch\_rate)))}$$

Single year pegs are dropped because they are quite possibly not intentional ones. Higher values of this index indicate more stable movement of the exchange rate against the currency of the base country.

Financial Openness/Integration (KAOPEN)

The Chinn and Ito (2006, 2008) *KAOPEN* is based on *de jure* information regarding restrictions in the IMF's *Annual Report on Exchange Arrangements and Exchange Restrictions (AREAER)*. *KAOPEN* is the first standardized principal component of the variables that indicate the presence of multiple exchange rates, restrictions on current account transactions, on capital account transactions, and the requirement of the surrender of export proceeds (see Chinn and Ito, 2008).

The Chinn-Ito index is normalized between zero and one. Higher values of this index indicate that a country is more open to cross-border capital transactions.

Data for Section 3.2 drawn primarily from IMF, *International Financial Statistics*.

Interest rates are overnight call money rates. Turkey rate is from St. Louis Fed, Hungary is from ECB, and China is from Trading Economics.

Inflation is four quarter CPI growth rates, measured in log differences. Chile and China is from OECD Main Economic Indicators via St. Louis Fed.

Inflation targets are annual, and drawn (except for Chile) from a data set provided by Ilan Noy (database of Aizenman et al. 2011). Original sources are central banks.

Output gap is calculated as Hodrick-Prescott filtered log GDP, seasonally adjusted using ARIMA X-12 (if necessary). In order to mitigate the

Central Banking: Perspectives from Emerging Economies

end-point problem, output is extended by forecasting out six quarters using an ARIMA (1, 1, 1) before applying the HP filter.

The real exchange rate is the log CPI deflated trade weighted exchange rate. Rates for Argentina, Estonia, India, Indonesia, Lithuania, Peru, Thailand, and Turkey are broad CPI deflated indices from BIS.

Reserves are international reserves excluding gold.

11

The Evolution of the Financial Stability Mandate

From Its Origins to the Present Day

Gianni Toniolo
LUISS, CEPR and Duke University (emeritus)

Eugene N. White
Rutgers University and NBER

1 Introduction

Financial stability remained a goal, of course.
  –Ben Bernanke (2013)

In his somewhat wistful discussion of the Great Moderation of 1984–2007 for the centennial of the Federal Reserve, Ben Bernanke (2013) conceded that "financial stability did not figure prominently in monetary policy discussions during these years" as many economists and central bankers had concluded that "the details of the structure of the financial system could be largely ignored when analyzing the behavior of the broader economy." The Federal Reserve's and most other central banks' financial stability mandate was often a secondary consideration for much of this period when control of inflation was of foremost importance. Since the Crisis of 2008, central banks have been given broad, new or renewed, mandates to guarantee financial stability. The objective behind these mandates is to prevent another financial meltdown, but there is little agreement about how to select and implement the appropriate policy instruments. While there is a vast historical literature on the issue of price stability that has informed the development of policies to carry out the price stability mandate, there are large gaps in our knowledge of financial stability policies in the past. In this paper, we provide a historical overview of the evolution of the "financial stability mandate" or FSM. Surveying its development from the emergence of modern central banks through the Great Moderation, we offer some general lessons.

The Evolution of the Financial Stability Mandate

As the behavior of policy makers during the Great Moderation demonstrated, price stability and financial stability are often treated as separable in "ordinary times," with regulation and supervision of financial institutions and markets frequently conducted outside of central banks. A commonly shared view, similar to that prevailing a century earlier, was that the best guarantee of financial stability that a central bank could provide was long-term price stability (Bordo and Schwartz, 1995; Bordo and Wheelock, 1998). If a financial crisis – an "extraordinary" event– erupted, the central bank should step in, as Bagehot (1873) recommended, and act as a lender-of-last-resort (LOLR), providing liquidity to the market. Central bank responses to the 1987 stock market and the dot. com crashes are near textbook examples of this approach, with its emphasis on containment through liquidity provision that enables solvent firms to withstand a panic and preserves the payments and settlement systems (Mishkin and White, 2014). What is missing from this approach and what the Crisis of 2008 highlighted, is that regulation and supervision create financial systems that may moderate or amplify panic-inducing shocks. For the most part, we will leave questions of LOLR, which treats financial stability in "extraordinary" times to others in this conference volume and focus on financial stability policies – regulation and supervision – deployed during "ordinary" times with the aim of reducing the frequency and magnitude of crises.

In this paper, we investigate the origins and growth of the FSM with an eye to improving policy makers' understanding of why central banks and policy regimes in the past succeeded or failed to meet their FSM. Two issues inform this chapter (1) whether supervision should be conducted within the central bank or in independent agencies and (2) whether supervision should be rules- or discretion/principles-based? We focus on the history of six countries, three in Europe (England, France, and Italy) and three in the New World (United States, Canada, and Colombia) to highlight the essential developments in the FSM. While there was a common evolutionary path, the development of FSM in each individual country was determined by how quickly each adapted to changes in the technology of the means of payment and their political economy, including their disposition towards competitive markets and openness to the world economy.

Our historical approach permits us to provide an important perspective on the newly relevant FSM. Mandates for price stability and full employment have been broad, perhaps even vague, leaving central banks considerable discretion to define precise measures of their performance. The same is certainly true for the FSM.[1] For financial stability to be a separate goal from price stability and full employment, Ricardo Reis (2013) points out that there must be a measurable definition of financial stability and the trade-offs with these other goals must be recognized so that a policy action may be contemplated when prices are stable and the economy has met its growth objective but financial instability is a threat.[2]

In the next part, Section 2, we provide a definition of the FSM and the issues that arise from this definition. Our survey begins in Section 3 with the nineteenth century when FSM concerned itself with the convertibility of banknotes into coin. The challenge of deposit banking to the FSM is examined in Section 4. Section 5 covers the transitional years from World War I to the Great Depression when the problem of disentangling the payments mechanism from large systematically important banks – SIFIs – to use an anachronistic term led some countries to rescue insolvent institutions. Section 6 examines financial repression from the 1930s to the 1970s, when the shock of the depression and the echoes of World War II induced countries to provide an explicit or implicit guarantee to all banks while they imposed heavy regulation either to fund wars or channel resources to favored industries. In Section 7, we cover the era of globalization and deregulation beginning in the 1970s through the 1990s, when driven by international capital flows and growing crises, financial repression collapsed. Although much of the regulatory structure of the previous period was abandoned, the explicit and implicit guarantees remained in place, leaving us with today's unresolved dilemma. We end our survey in Section 7 by examining the issues

---

[1] The Swiss National Bank's (2014) task is to "contribute to the stability of the financial system," where "a stable financial system can be defined as a system whose individual components – financial intermediaries and the financial market infrastructure – fulfill their respective functions and prove resistant to potential shocks." The European Central Bank (2014) seeks financial stability, defined as: "a condition in which the financial system – intermediaries, markets and market infrastructures – can withstand shocks without major disruption in financial intermediation and in the effective allocation of savings to productive investment." The Norges Bank (2014) is charged to promote "financial stability and contribute to robust and efficient financial infrastructures and payment systems." The Financial Services Act of 2012 gave the Bank of England a statutory objective of protecting and enhancing the stability of the financial system of the United Kingdom. Under the Bank's "Core Purposes," the bank is committed to sustain financial stability whose purpose is to maintain three vital functions of the financial system (1) the payments mechanism, (2) financial intermediation, and (3) insuring against and dispersing risk.

[2] Borio (2011) argues that it may not be possible to attain all of these objectives simultaneously, presenting the central bank with a dilemma.

surrounding the internationalization of bank supervision. We touch briefly on the renewal of the FSM after the 2008 crisis.

Although the term FSM is of recent coinage, its purpose has remained basically the same over time: a protection of the payments and settlements system. Problems arise when attempts are made to use the supervisory regime for other purposes – serving macroeconomic policy or special interests. Several basic findings emerge from our selective historical survey: (1) Supervision can only be as effective as the regulatory structure it is mandated to enforce. It is necessary to support regulation but it has only limited scope in substituting for a flawed structure that requires reform to keep pace with financial innovation of the payments and settlement system. (2) Given that financial innovation moves ahead of regulatory updating, supervision cannot be simply rules-based and must have a discretionary component, especially for treating large systemically important financial institutions. However, excessive reliance on supervisory discretion cannot replace a poor regulatory regime and often leads to inappropriate forbearance. (3) Initially, when competition in the payment's system was strong, as in the United States, independent supervisory agencies pursuing rules-based supervision were established; but when there was limited competition in the provision of the payments and settlements system, supervision was implicitly or explicitly given to the central bank. When regulation became a tool for monetary policy, notably in times of financial repression, central banks gained increased supervisory authority. This shift often accompanies increased discretion and reduced transparency. (4) Most supervisory regimes successfully managed financial systems, except when they were hit by macro-systemic shocks, which they were not designed to offset. These types of shocks overwhelmed the supervisors' capacity to achieve their FSM and often produced a regime shift that tried to address the regulatory/supervisory deficiencies.

2 The FSM in Ordinary and Exceptional times

In our historical overview, we argue that the financial stability sought by various monetary and financial regimes is best described, in its narrowest and most precise definition, as protection of the "means of payment," or the "settlements systems." This definition broadly fits both a FSM in ordinary times and the LOLR function of the central bank in crises, thus harmonizing these two policy activities. In a spirited, critical survey of central bank intervention, Anna Schwartz (1987) argued that crises that merited LOLR operations were liquidity crises that threatened the payments mechanism. Other interventions were inappropriate because they essentially rescued insolvent rather than illiquid institutions, wastefully transferring resources and creating moral hazard. Her conclusions followed the classical Thornton-Bagehot school that the LOLR should discount freely to anyone having good collateral at a high rate to channel funds to illiquid financial institutions in order to halt a panic. An even stronger position has been taken by Marvin Goodfriend and Robert King (1988) who argue that discounting to selected banks is inherently distortionary and open market operations is the only instrument required to halt a liquidity crisis. At the other end of the spectrum is the position of Charles Goodhart (1985, 2011a) who has argued that the LOLR should provide funds to illiquid and insolvent banks because it is impossible to distinguish between them in a crisis and bank failures sever valuable customer relationships, impeding recovery. Many central banks have adhered to this position, particularly in the last crisis, leading to legislative reactions, like the Dodd-Frank Act of 2010. These arguments about what is the appropriate role for a LOLR are, of course, arguments about how narrowly or how broadly the FSM should be in ordinary times and will inform how we trace the development of the FSM through history.

In reviewing the history of the agencies that have carried out the FSM, we have in mind the question whether the authority for regulation and supervision should be independent of or located in the central bank. Factors that have bearing on this question are the importance of information acquired through supervision for a central bank's success as LOLR, how redistributive trade-offs should be decided, transparency and political oversight, and whether supervision policies should be rules-based or discretion-based. While we will see how these questions were answered over time, it is worthwhile to note here that there is little contemporary consensus about who the regulator should be. Martin Feldstein (2010) has recently argued that a central bank should control the supervision of all large bank holding companies. Casting a wider but still limited net, favored by some central banks, Alan Blinder (2010) has recommended that the central bank supervise "all systemically important institutions."[3] Implicit in this design for the FSM is the granting of broad discretionary powers to the central bank. These approaches alarm Luigi Zingales (2009) who is concerned they would concentrate too much authority. Instead, he

---

[3] Defining "systemically important institutions, Blinder (2010) states "the definition is clearly *subjective* and *not* numerical. Thus, a handful are the *systemically important financial institutions* that are too big to be allowed to fail messily."

The Evolution of the Financial Stability Mandate 429

recommends that there be three agencies, each with its own goals – a central bank for monetary policy, a regulatory agency for supervisory policy, and a consumer protection agency – to induce transparency and allow for the evaluation of trade-offs in the political arena.

Furthermore, in today's debates about the FSM, the potential trade-offs between financial stability, price stability and full employment/growth receive scant attention. Yet, it is precisely the difficulty of addressing how to handle these trade-offs that weakened the effectiveness of financial stability policy over time, creating conditions that increase the threats that the FSM seeks to avoid. In its simplest form, this may be seen by considering the basic functions of money as defined by any standard textbook: money serves as a unit of account, a means of payment and a store of wealth. Problems that arise when money is difficult to use as a unit of account are rare in the modern world, arising mostly when hyperinflations create obstacles to determine the relative price of goods over even the shortest of time spans. The core difficulty in the search for financial stability is the fact that by guaranteeing the safety of the means of payment, there is a danger that a monetary authority will (be pressured to) guarantee certain stores of wealth. If one could restrict guaranteeing the means of payment simply to ensuring the safe and accurate crediting and debiting of accounts, then these two functions of money might be completely separable and the execution of the mandate might be straightforward. Instead, because stores of wealth are defined as money, – currency and deposits, for example – both the public's perception of the goal of financial stability and the ability of the monetary authorities to clearly define the goal can be muddled and conducive to crises.[4]

In pursuit of financial stability, the monetary authorities may begin by very narrowly defining the means of payment and tightly regulating its issue, as was the case when banknotes began to supplement coin as a means of payment in the nineteenth century. By setting regulations and incentives for stakeholders, the government influences the risk-return choices made by financial institutions, economic growth and the vulnerability of the regime to financial crises. Supervision is deemed necessary as there is an asymmetry in banking between management and other insiders on the one hand and shareholders and those funding the bank with

---

[4] The temptation to broadly define financial stability is exemplified in the calls to guarantee almost all classes of financial assets. One example is the argument to treat investment funds with more than $100 billion as systemically important and potential candidates for bailouts, Morgenson (2014).

deposits and borrowed funds on the other. Consequently, some agency may be delegated the responsibility for forcing increased disclosure, examining banks for compliance with the rules, and disciplining them.

If the rules for such a system are carefully drawn and the system well-monitored, a regime may credibly guarantee the means of payment; but there are two inherent problems. First, those holding the protected means of payment, for example banknotes, would tend to regard it as a means to insure their wealth in this form. Second, if the supply of the means of payment is sufficiently constrained, it will fail to satisfy the demand for a low cost means of payment by a growing economy. The result will be financial innovation to provide an alternative means of payment. The public will hold wealth in new and old forms of means of payment, but shocks will induce them to shift to the guaranteed form of wealth holding, creating runs and perhaps panics, with the regime losing its credibility, as the public is aggrieved to have lost some wealth. Consequently, there will be a demand for a new regime that guarantees the expanded means of payment. If the guarantee of the means of payment is not carefully circumscribed in the new regime, more wealth will be guaranteed. This mission creep poses a threat to the task of securing financial stability, as it will induce moral hazard and create a potential for politically divisive future wealth transfers to make good on its guarantee.

3 The Protection of Banknotes and the Origins of the FSM

3.1 England

The Bank of England was founded in 1694 as a privileged bank of issue with the expressed purpose of providing a loan of £1.2 million to the Crown in wartime. Oversight or supervision was provided by Parliament which imposed regulations on its total note issue. Collateral requirements protected the value of the currency and high minimum denominations kept notes out of the hands of the less financially literate public to protect against counterfeiting. The weekly task of verifying the accounts of the Bank – its notes issued, reserves, securities, and capital – fell to the Commissioners of Stamps and Taxes. Other banks, usually partnerships, operating without the privilege of note issue, were not the subject of regulation or supervision.

After the banking crisis of 1825, Parliament passed the Act of 1826 that ended the Bank of England's monopoly of joint-stock banking, permitting the establishment of banks with more than six partners, outside of London

The Evolution of the Financial Stability Mandate 431

(Grossman, 2010). These partnerships – note-issuing joint stock unlimited liability banks – were not subject to any balance sheet regulations or requirements to file or publish financial data. Their only obligation was to submit an annual return, including the name of the bank, place of business and names of all partners and two officers in whose name the firm could be sued. Competition increased when the Bank Charter Act of 1833 permitted the formation of joint stock banks in London where they were not allowed to issue banknotes and were notably exempt from the reporting requirements.

The Bank Charter Act of 1844 began the centralization of note issue in England and Wales by forbidding new banks of issue (The Bank Charter Act of 1844). Although the Stock Banking Act (1844) established a banking code for England, it was repealed by, a series of acts between 1855 and 1857 that allowed banks to be formed with limited liability under company law. This arrangement with no explicit supervision became the basic legal framework that would govern English banking into the early twentieth century. One key feature was added by the Companies Act of 1879, which created "reserve liability," requiring half of banks' uncalled capital be available in the event of bankruptcy (Grossman, 2010, pp. 182–183).

Given that note issue had been de facto centralized in the Bank of England and the FSM focused on the convertibility of banknotes, there was relatively little concern for the supervision of other financial institutions. The Joint Stock Banking Companies Act of 1857, Section XIV specified that "No appointment of inspectors to examine into the affairs of any banking company shall be made by the Board of Trade, in pursuance of the Joint Stock Companies Act, 1856, except upon the application of one-third at least in number and value of the shareholders in such a company" (Wordsworth, 1859). No supervision was legally specified for the Bank of England though Bignon, Flandreau and Ugolini (2012) have shown the Bank of England maintained extensive files that enabled it to distinguish the quality of paper presented by discount houses.[5]

3.2 France

Although the Banque de France was founded in 1800, we begin our examination of France in the middle of the nineteenth century with two defining events: the de facto monopolization of note issue by the Banque

---

[5] Other nineteenth century banks maintained similar filing systems for the same purpose.

432 *Gianni Toniolo and Eugene N. White*

de France in 1848 and the establishment of free and largely unregulated entry into the non-issuing banking business with the passage of the Commercial Code in 1867. The first made the Banque de France the guarantor of banknotes as a means of payment, while the second allowed a rapid development of the banking industry.

Until 1848, the Banque de France was the dominant but not the only bank of issue in France.[6] The crisis of that year led the government to concentrate the privilege of issue with the Banque. Coin continued to be the dominant means of payment; as late as 1880, coin constituted 65 percent of the means of payment, with banknotes and deposits dividing the remainder. Convertibility of banknotes into coin was ensured by the Banque's large gold reserves; and circulation was limited by high minimum denominations, similar to the Bank of England.

Until 1867, any firm, including banks that wished to form a limited liability corporation (société anonyme, SA) was subject to the Commercial Code of 1807 and had to follow a tortuously long review process, ending with a decision of the Conseil d'Etat. The new code in 1867 removed the discretionary power of the government and opened the doors to free entry. A wave of incorporation ensued and by 1898, there were 1,169 banks and insurance companies that had incorporated as SAs (Freedeman, 1993). There were modest minimum capital requirements and periodic reporting for all firms but few other limitations. The result was a competitive and diverse financial industry.

In 1877, the Banque de France began to report a quarterly review of its outstanding discounts and advances, providing the managers of the Banque with some surveillance of the industry, though it was primarily used to protect the Banque from bad loans. The absence of a supervisory authority, inside or outside of the central bank, to obtain information or examine banks well into the twentieth century is captured by a 1929 survey of French banking:

It is difficult to define the precise limits of the activity of the big deposit banks ... No law determines these, and sources of information are few and insufficient ... Those things which it would be most interesting to know and which must influence the future of the company ... remain the secret of the board of directors and of the management. The balance sheets are obscure, as each bank prepares them on a different plan, which it modifies at will. In the balance sheet the most dissimilar items are united. (Beckhart and Willis, 1929, p. 574).

---

[6] See Leclercq (2010) for a recent description of the structure and operations of the Banque de France.

The Evolution of the Financial Stability Mandate 433

Like the Bank of England, the Banque de France was seen as fulfilling its FSM by guaranteeing the convertibility of its notes into coin.

3.3 Italy

Prior to the Italian political unification (1861) banks of issue were found in the Kingdom of Sardinia, the Grand Duchy of Tuscany (a second one being established immediately after the unification), the Duchy of Parma, the Pope's State (in Bologna and Rome), with the Kingdom of the Two Sicilies having two banks. As in other European countries, the establishment of banks of issue, with powers of discount and deposit, was seen as a financial innovation aimed at modernizing a backward financial system. In addition, the banks were regarded as useful subscribers to government bonds. After unification, the Sardinian (Piedmontese) bank, denominated Banca Nazionale nel Regno, became the dominant bank of issue with about 65 percent of the outstanding circulation.

Similar to the pattern established elsewhere in Europe, the banks of issue were private-public companies, regulated and supervised by governments that issued charters, set minimum capital requirements, prescribed reserve ratio, and dictated the rules for the convertibility under a bimetallic system (which soon however became a de facto gold standard). Supervision was entrusted to a government commissioner who sat on the banks' boards and whose approval was needed for major decisions, including changes in the discount rate and the creation of new branches. For Prime Minister Cavour, founder of the basic institutions of the Kingdom of Italy, the FSM mandate dictated that banks of issue "must be governed with the strictest prudence as their most stringent obligation is to be always solvent, with assets much higher than liabilities, in order to be always in such condition as to be able to honor their convertibility pledge in the case of notes and deposits" (Rossi and Nitti, 1968, p. 2074). Cavour believed that the government should exercise discretionary oversight of the central bank because of the potential disruptive threat of crises that made "useless the most stringent [legal] precautions."

Although Cavour included the guarantee of deposits in his view of the FSM, the dominant component of means of payment in Italy at mid-century were coins. Coins accounted for 80 percent of the means of payments with notes taking a little less than 10 percent and deposits a little more than 10 percent in 1861. This structure of the means of payment began to change very rapidly with the advent of easy incorporation for commercial banks – they remained virtually free from regulation and

434   *Gianni Toniolo and Eugene N. White*

supervision. The Civil Code of 1865 did not treat banks differently from other "commercial" companies, and the Commercial Code of 1882 defined bank operations as "acts of commerce," subject only to a monthly delivery of certified statement of their accounts to local Courts.[7]

Unlike Britain and France, the development of banking in Italy occurred largely under a suspension of convertibility that lasted from 1866 to 1883 inducing more regulations and supervision to restrain the issue of inconvertible banknotes.[8] In the wake of the banking crisis of 1873, the Banking Act of 20 April 1874 imposed new regulations on the issue of banknotes and on investments by the banks of issue. The six banks of issue became subject to supervision by the Minister of Finance whose representatives participated in the board meetings and enjoyed inspection powers (Galanti, D'Ambrosio and Guccione, 2012). Following a long-simmering banking crisis of the early 1890s the Banking Act of 1893 merged four banks of issue into the Banca d'Italia, which became the dominant bank of issue and discount.[9] The 1893 Act (Toniolo 1990; Polsi, 2001; Toniolo 2013) set a maximum limit to outstanding circulation, tightened regulation of the discount business, forbade banks of issue from real estate mortgage operations and controlled deposits and interest payments. Already supervising the savings banks, the Ministry of Agriculture, Industry and Commerce was given supervisory authority over the banks of issue, in consultation with the Treasury. The general manager of the Banca d'Italia was to be approved by the government, no bank official could be also a member of parliament, and the state supervised the printing of banknotes (Negri 1989, pp. 81–84). The fact that the Banca d'Italia was created in response to a severe banking crisis impressed upon policy makers and the management of the new bank the idea that financial stability should be one of its main missions. As the banking crisis of 1907 would show, the Banca d'Italia had become aware that it had a de facto FSM. It therefore sought to acquire information about the operations of individual commercial banks,

---

[7] The exception to this very liberal regulatory regime were land banks, specializing in securitized credit to agriculture, first regulated in 1866 and more systematically in 1869. The first comprehensive banking legislation was approved by Parliament in 1888, covering savings banks. These institutions were placed under the supervision of the Minister of Industry and Agriculture who could fine directors and dissolve the board.

[8] Banknote denominations were smaller in Italy than in England or France, which may have been the result of the suspension of convertibility, leading to an absence of coin. This phenomenon also occurred in Britain during the suspension of convertibility from 1797 to 1821.

[9] The two banks of issue in the former Southern Kingdom of the Two Siciles retained issuing rights until 1926

The Evolution of the Financial Stability Mandate 435

availing itself of its branch network and information from its own lending and discount operations.

To sum up, in the nineteenth century, in Great Britain, France and Italy as in most other European countries, there was no institution formally endowed with a FSM. The government directly regulated and inspected the monopoly or dominant banks of issue primarily because of their role in the payments system; but with the exception of savings banks, other credit institutions were not perceived by legislators as different from any other commercial company or having a potential to destabilize the financial system. Although Britain had a limited banking code, a general commercial code sufficed for France and Italy, leading to development of universal banking, with mergers and branching forming very large banks by the end of the nineteenth century.

3.4 The United States

New World banking stood in contrast to Old World banking in that multiple banks of issue were the norm, leading to the formation of specific agencies for supervision. In the United States, federalism paved the way for the creation of competitive banks of issue. Although many of the newly independent states began by chartering a single bank (Schwartz, 1947), it became common for legislatures to offer numerous new charters, supplying the United States with substantial banking capital, which by some measures exceeded that provided in Europe (Sylla, 1998).

Price stability was anchored by the Coinage Act of 1792 that established a bimetallic system and banks were legally obliged to ensure the convertibility of their banknotes into coin. Empowered by their size and extensive branching networks, both the First and Second Banks of the United States (1791–1811 and 1816–1836) accepted a FSM, where they returned the banknotes of state-chartered banks promptly for collection, to increase state banks' liquidity and limit their loan expansion. At the same time, state banks with liquidity problems were provided with loans. Supervision of the First and Second Banks was conducted by the Secretary of the Treasury who could demand weekly statements, which were not available to the public or Congress. (Robertson, 1968). Whether the First and Second Banks interventions with state banks had a measureable effect on the financial system has been a subject of debate (Fenstermaker and File, 1986; Perkins, 1994), but the failure to renew both banks' charters put an end to this early American experiment in central banking.

After 1836, the FSM devolved completely to the states, which led to the establishment of the first explicit, agencies for bank supervision. While Congress or a state legislature might directly supervise a single or even a few banks, the competitive nature of the banking system and public concerns about potential corruption led to the creation of independent, specialist agencies to monitor compliance with regulations. Financial stability could thus be viewed as a separate issue from price stability. The years from 1836 to 1864 were period of experimentation by the states to protect the means of payment. Two experiments were the Safety-Funds and Free Banking (Rolnick, Smith and Weber, 2000). Supervision in the modern sense of delegating oversight responsibility to a public agency first appeared in the United States with the Safety-Fund System devised by New York in 1829 and copied by other states. These systems provided mutual guarantee funds aimed at protecting banknote holders and depositors from loss. Supervisors monitored banks but failed to control risk taking, leading to the demise of some systems and the restriction of others to the protection of note holders (Golembe and Warburton, 1958; Golembe, 1960; Calomiris, 1990). More successful and widespread were the free banking systems first implemented by Michigan (1837) and New York (1838). These laws permitted free entry with banknote issue, backed by state bonds, held in segregated accounts that were sold to compensate banknote holders in the event of failure. These provided a high degree of protection for banknote holders (Rockoff, 1975; Rolnick and Weber, 1983). To limit the financial illiterates' use of banknotes, the First Bank set a high minimum denomination of $5. While the state systems tended to follow this example, the democratizing impulse in the United States sometimes led to lower denominations (Bodenhorn, 1993).

The shock of the Civil War disrupted the banking systems of several states, giving the federal government an opportunity to intervene. The success of the New York version of free banking informed the writing of the National Bank Act of 1864, establishing a banking regime that would endure until 1913. The 1864 Act provided for free entry, a uniformly-designed and uniformly bond-backed currency issued by the individual national banks, plus regulations governing minimum capital, reserve requirements, and loans and double liability for shareholders. The act also created the Office of the Comptroller of the Currency (OCC), whose name reflects the initial overwhelming concern for ensuring that the national banknotes issued by each individual bank had the proper bonds set aside to protect them in the event of a bank failure. The Comptroller was empowered to obtain frequent reports from national banks and dispatch

The Evolution of the Financial Stability Mandate 437

examiners to ensure compliance with regulations (White, 1983). Supervision was largely rules-based; and while it became more formalized over time, it represented a continuity with the earlier, smaller state efforts. Examiners and the Comptroller could privately reprimand banks for what they viewed as excessive risks, but the only true sanction was to close a bank down.

3.5 Canada

While influenced by both British and particularly Scottish banking with widespread branching, Canada followed the American pattern of detailed statutory regulation of banks that had the right to issue banknotes. Beginning with the passage of the Dominion Act in 1871, commercial banks were given ten year charters subject to renewal, thereby forcing a regular re-examination of supervision.

Although Canada may be considered to have a generally competitive commercial banking system, entry was tightly controlled and a special act of Parliament was required for a bank charter, with a high minimum paid-in capital. Like American national banks, their shareholders were subject to double liability. In 1871, there were twenty-eight banks, declining, primarily due to mergers, to ten banks in 1935. These ten banks had extensive national branching networks, making them large geographically diversified institutions, another contrast with the United States (Allen et al., 1938). Canadian chartered banks had broad commercial and investment banking and brokerage powers, but mortgage lending was prohibited.

In this period, the FSM aimed at the protection of the means of payment, limited to currency, which came in two forms: Dominion notes and banknotes of the chartered banks, with the latter constituting the largest share. The issue of Dominion notes was tightly controlled, with a ceiling on the issues that could be created with a fractional reserve of gold and securities and above that a 100 percent reserve was required. This well-protected currency was issued in denominations over $10,000 for interbank transactions and under $5 for hand-to-hand transactions. Similar to United States and European countries, the minimum denomination for banknotes was set in relatively high in 1881 at $5. Banks were required to redeem their notes in gold coin or Dominion notes. In the event of insolvency, banknotes had first lien on a bank's assets, a strong protection given that a bank's issue was limited to be a maximum of its paid-in capital.

When the Bank Act was revised in 1891 a Bank Circulation Redemption Fund was established and endowed with funds equal to 5 percent of the

438   *Gianni Toniolo and Eugene N. White*

average circulation of banks. The fund was not intended to guarantee banknotes, for which there were other protections, including double liability, but to ensure that notes of failed banks could be redeemed at par without delay, while liquidation was completed (Allen et al., 1938). To protect this redemption fund, the Canadian Bankers Association (privately organized in 1891) began regular supervision of banks. The Bank Act of 1900 then gave the Association, which was then incorporated by a special act of Parliament, oversight of the issue and destruction of bank notes. In the event of a bank suspension, the Association was given the authority to appoint a curator for the suspended bank. Commenting on this supervision, Willis and Beckhart (1929) wrote:

> All the banks are contributories to this fund and in case of the failure of a bank and subsequent depletion of the fund the remaining banks are obliged to restore the fund. Thus every bank has an interest in the regularity of the note issues of every other bank, and it is important that there should be some control by a properly authorized body of the printing and distribution of notes to the banks and their destruction.

3.6 Colombia

Although considered an economic laggard, compared to the United States or Canada, the history of regulation and supervision of banking reveals some common New World attributes. Free banking arrived in Colombia in 1865 after the Civil War that brought to power a new liberal government that produced a federalist constitution in 1863 for the United States of Columbia. Under the Banking Law of 1865, the Colombian states were granted the authority to set bank regulations. Typically, banks were simply subject to the commercial code that applied to all firms and there was free entry, plus some minimal regulations. By 1880, there were approximately forty chartered banks of issue in Colombia. Political volatility and the fluctuating prices of tobacco and coffee, led these banks to concentrate on short-term credits, so that they could quickly wind down their operations and withdraw notes from circulation in response to a shock. Nevertheless, banks had to suspend payment twice in response to crises (White, 1998b).

The Civil War in 1885 ended the experiment in free banking, when the new government in Bogotá suspended convertibility of the note issue of the Banco Nacional, its fiscal agent and made its notes legal tender, eliminating the privilege of note issue for all other banks. Continued political instability and the financial needs of the government led to an expansion of the Banco Nacional's note issue, its liquidation, and a direct issue of currency by the

The Evolution of the Financial Stability Mandate   439

government. Inflation soared during the War of a Thousand Days (1898–1903), and the remaining banks shrank. Peace brought the establishment of a new monopoly bank of issue, the Banco Central and put the peso on the gold standard in 1907. With note issue tied to the gold reserves of the Banco Central, other banks were left largely unregulated and unsupervised. In 1918, a new banking law reaffirmed the wide powers of banks, enumerating them at length; these included the authority to serve as investment banks, hold stocks and bonds, develop and organize railroads, canals and industry, and handle contracts for public service (White, 1998b). Thus, while Colombia had started with a system similar to the United States and Canada, it transited to one more familiar in Europe.

4 The Challenge of Deposit Banking to Financial Stability

The financial stability of both European banking regimes, where there was a monopoly bank of issue, and American banking regimes were there were competitive banks of issue were gradually undermined by the growth of deposits Deposit banking had a long history, but as Dunbar (1929) pointed out, it had long been restricted to the large and well-informed customers of banks.[10] Given the limited quantity of coin and the restrictions on the volume and denomination of banknotes, it is not surprising that deposits began to emerge as a substitute means of payment in the late nineteenth century with economic expansion and rising incomes. The public began to lay "claim upon the sympathy and guardianship of the legislature" (Dunbar, 1929) to expand the FSM. How this evolution played out in different countries depended heavily on their banking structure. Moving beyond Bagehot's policy recommendations, the failure of major financial institutions were managed with lifeboats in Europe, with a growth of supervision in Italy.

4.1 The United Kingdom

The Act of 1844 protected the means of payment but at a price. Curzio Giannini (2011) has described the system, as showing "excessive zeal":

---

[10] Cavour held a different view and believed that deposits had a higher risk of creating instability as they were on average large and in hands of few people. The contrast with Dunbar is similar to the division between those who see panics arising from the withdrawals of the uninformed versus the informed. For the stability of the system, Cavour deemed supervision of banks of issue necessary for the protection of both notes and deposits (Rossi and Nitti, p. 1848)

The combination of ceilings on issue, reserve requirements, separation between issue and rediscount operations, as well as financial reporting obligations (the Bank of England was required to publish a fortnightly statement of account) created a framework of draconian restrictions, the purpose of which, as we have seen, was to reduce banknotes to a mere surrogate of precious metal, with no identity of their own." (p. 86).

Limiting the creation of the means of payment led to an expansion of the financial system through deposit banking, as non-issuing banks were subject to few restrictions. Banking crises then took the form of panics to convert deposits into notes and coin – presenting a direct challenge to the FSM in extraordinary times. In 1847, the failure of a number of provincial banks provoked a liquidity crisis. Discounting liberally, the Bank of England saw its reserves drop. Rather than see the Bank cut off credit to the market the Chancellor of the Exchequer sent the Governor of the Bank a letter inviting him to continue to discount at 8 percent, promising that the government would send a bill of indemnity to Parliament if the currency in circulation exceeded the legal limits. Issuance of this "Treasury letter" calmed the panic and did so again in 1857 and 1866. Recent research (Bignon, Flandreau and Ugolini, 2012) has confirmed that the Bank of England did not take full advantage of Treasury letters until after 1866 and rationed credit during crises, exacerbating them. At this point, the Bank of England became, in the view of most writers, a true LOLR, placing the interests of the banking system ahead of those of its shareholders.

In addition to the growth of deposit banking, the wave of mergers concentrated the banking industry in the last quarter of the nineteenth century, creating large institutions that posed a new problem. When Overend Gurney failed in 1866, it was a very large bank with wide-ranging activities. Its insolvency occasioned a liquidity crisis and the Bank followed what became Bagehot's recommended policy rule. Yet, when Baring Brothers failed in 1890, liquidity was supplied to the market by the Bank; but a lifeboat rescue was also constructed, in cooperation with the central banks of France and Russia, to prevent the collapse of Barings from creating a greater shock. In modern terms, Barings was regarded as a "systemically important financial institution," a "SIFI." At the outset, the Chancellor of the Exchequer, George Goschen thought that the crisis of 1866 would appear to be a "trifle" if Barings collapsed in run; and he offered a Treasury letter to the Bank. The letter was declined on the grounds that it signalled weakness. When the demand for liquidity surged, the Bank reached an agreement with the government to absorb half of any losses from the

The Evolution of the Financial Stability Mandate

Bank's holdings of Barings bills, while the Governor assembled banks to provide a £17 million lifeboat rescue for Barings. The panic ended, but the process of liquidating Barings was drawn out until the mid-1890s. While the Bank was praised for its prompt action, it was also attacked in *The Economist,* setting out the moral hazard peril for the whole of the banking system (Clapham, 1966). Nevertheless, there was no effort by the Bank of England to develop a policy of supervision in response to this crisis and there was no legislation forthcoming from Parliament.

4.2 France

As in the United Kingdom, in France, there was no policy or institutional change in the FSM in response to the trends in the banking industry arising from the expansion of deposit-funded commercial banks. The collapse of the large Union Générale and other smaller banks in 1882 presented the Banque with the question of how to intervene. Although it may have been influenced by political considerations, the Banque and the government decided to let these banks fail, while providing liquidity to the general market (White, 2007). But, the imminent collapse of the Paris Bourse – the Lyon Bourse was allowed to go under – was halted by the formation of a lifeboat operation, where the big banks intermediated a loan from the Banque to the Bourse. A shutdown of the Bourse threatened the means of settlement for the securities market – thus the Banque expanded its implicit FSM mandate to prevent a broader crisis (White, 2011).[11] However, the fallout from the bank insolvencies contributed to the sharp recession of the next several years.

The next time a large and a more highly connected bank was on the brink of failure, the Banque intervened. In 1889, a run on the Comptoir d'Escompte was feared would lead to a banking panic. At the prompting of the Minister of Finance, the Banque organized a lifeboat operation to rescue the Comptoir. The Banque supported the market by providing additional liquidity based on sound collateral, even as it took over all of the assets of the insolvent Comptoir as collateral for a loan (Hautcoeur, Riva and White, 2014). The depositors of the Comptoir were promised payment in full and an orderly liquidation was allowed to proceed, and shareholders were given a deal to recapitalize the bank, with the directors suffering significant losses. In modern terms, a resolution mechanism was

---

[11] The Bourse was primarily a forward market with twice monthly clearing and settlement periods that created high temporary demands for liquidity.

442   *Gianni Toniolo and Eugene N. White*

devised to guide the process. When a bank, the Société de Dépôts et Comptes Courants, failed in 1891 it was provided a similar rescue. While there was no other large bank failure before World War I, the Banque had shifted its policy and appeared ready to protect the deposits of "SIFIs," though perhaps not smaller banks. However, there was no change in the supervisory regime for the next forty years. As seen in Beckhart and Willis report in 1929 above, there was no movement to impose new regulations on the banking industry or efforts to set up a supervisory authority to monitor and discipline these banks. When the Governor of the Banque was interviewed for the American National Monetary Commission in 1910, he forcefully told his audience that in crises abundant credit had been and would only be provided for the highest quality collateral, omitting any reference to the lifeboat operations that had been deployed in 1882, 1889 and 1891 (Aldrich, 1910).

4.3 Italy

In Italy, the shift to deposit banking occurred much more rapidly than in France. Notes rapidly replaced coins but deposits grew even faster, accounting for approximately 45 percent of the means of payment in 1893, contributing to the instability of the Italian banking system that experienced five major banking crises, coinciding with international crises, 1866, 1873, the early 1890s, the early 1920s and 1931.

In the early 1890s, seeing a danger of contagion from the real estate sector to the financial sector, the government insisted with the banks of issue to act as LOLRs to *both* large construction companies and banks. Concerned about profitability, the largest bank of issue, the Banca Nazionale nel Regno argued that these banks had already stepped in to provide liquidity to the real estate sector that had previously relied on now departing foreign capital and that the extraordinary note issue requested by the government should not be subject to a supplementary tax of 2 percent instead of the normal 1 percent. Prime Minister Crispi refused to rescind the tax and therefore the banks of issue did not provide liquidity. This episode reflects the fact that policy makers already viewed banks of issue as having the power to halt financial crises, though they still behaved as private institutions, and the government felt that it could only apply moral suasion to induce the banks to act. Ultimately, the government-mandated merger of three banks of issue into the Banca d'Italia (which also took over the liquidation of a fourth bank of issue) in 1893 tackled these problems; although by "inheriting" the bad assets of the previous banks,

The Evolution of the Financial Stability Mandate 443

the new central bank was saddled with illiquid assets that it took almost a decade to liquidate.

The Banca d'Italia's first crisis management took place in 1907 with the collapse of the Società Bancaria Italiana (SBI), the country's third largest bank. The Banca organized a rescue of SBI, inducing the two largest commercial banks to share in its liquidation (Bonelli, 1971). As in the case of France, a resolution mechanism for insolvent banks was in place before the advent of a formal regulation-supervision system. No contagion ensued and fallout to the real economy was minimal, with the Banca d'Italia providing liquidity and engineering a loan from the Treasury. Throughout the crisis the lira remained within the gold points. This episode parallels the Bank of England's 1890 intervention in the Barings Crisis and the Banque de France's actions in 1889. As in these cases, there was no change in the Italian FSM for ordinary times, although the mandate for extraordinary times had expanded to rescue SIFIs.

4.4 The United States

Until the 1860s, banknotes and capital were the primary sources of funding for banks. However in the second half of the century, the share of banknotes plummeted and banks became more leveraged. Deposits became the dominant source of funding for banks and the bank-generated means of payment. Two factors played key roles. First, while the 10 percent tax on state banknotes imposed in 1865 induced many banks to join the National Banking System, the revision of state banking codes in the 1880s encouraged new banks to take out state charters, funding their operations by issuing deposits (White, 1983, 2013). Secondly, the 1864 Act had imposed various regulations limiting the issue of national banknotes, most importantly tying them to the dwindling supply of U.S. government bonds. Consequently, national banks as well as state-chartered banks turned to deposit creation to grow, expanding the means of payment, outside of the "safety net."

Conditioned by regulation, the evolving American banking system had a greater potential for financial instability. The almost universal prohibition on branch banking created thousands of small relatively undiversified single office banks that were very sensitive to local economic shocks. Coupled with reserve requirements that induced country banks to hold deposits in city banks, the need to clear checks, collect payments and make investments produced huge interbank deposits that could be withdrawn in the event of a liquidity shock. "Competition in laxity" between federal and state governments served to further reduce reserve, capital and loan regulations, with some banks engaging in "regulatory arbitrage," switching charters to gain regulatory advantage. As part of this development, states created their own supervisory authorities (White, 1983).

These weaknesses appear to have been mitigated by the imposition of double liability on the shareholders of national banks and many state banks, inducing them to more closely monitor management and shut down several unprofitable banks before they became insolvent. Losses to depositors from failed banks were relatively modest. For national banks, they totalled $44 million for the period 1865–1913, a fraction of 1 percent of a year's GDP (White, 2013). Nevertheless, regulatory choices reflected trade-offs with growth. Grossman (2001, 2007) has documented that states that favored stability over growth were more likely to choose double or triple liability than single liability for the shareholders of state-chartered banks.

To many contemporaries, the most lamentable characteristic of the American banking was its banking crises, more frequent than those experienced by other industrializing nations. In the absence of a central bank, the LOLR was partially filled by the clearing houses in large cities. These institutions issued clearing house loans certificates, providing more liquidity; but ultimately, many panics could only be stopped by a costly suspension of payments by the banks (Friedman and Schwartz, 1963). These crises were primarily liquidity events – generated by a panic-driven search for a safe means of payment rather than widespread insolvencies of financial institutions. The panics of the early 1890s and 1907, appearing ever larger and more costly, were followed by three responses – changes in bank supervision, state deposit insurance schemes, and calls for a central bank. All of these implicitly or explicitly recognized that protecting the means of payment had to include deposits.

At the federal level, the OCC intensified its efforts at supervision. Instead of yearly surprise examinations for each bank, two examinations per year became the norm. These examinations became more thorough and the Comptroller issued new instructions to examiners to challenge boards of directors. At the state level, bank superintendents were appointed in states that had lacked them and examinations increased in number and vigor (Barnett, 1911; Jaremski and Michener, 2014). The focus of these examinations was no longer the relatively limited role initially envisioned to ensure that banknotes were protected but a broader one, more concerned with the general solvency of a bank to protect its depositors.

In spite of its very mixed experience, the antebellum idea of deposit insurance re-emerged; it became a favored remedy of bankers in rural

The Evolution of the Financial Stability Mandate 445

states dominated by small single office banks that found it hard to assure their customers of the safety of their deposits. Between 1886 and 1933, bills were introduced to Congress to establish a system of deposit insurance. Given their narrow constituency at the federal level, these failed (Calomiris and White, 1994). However, at the state level, the Panic of 1907 induced seven states to establish mutual guarantee systems for state-chartered banks (White, 1983; Calomiris 1990). Nevertheless, difficulties with moral hazard and adverse selection plagued these state funds, which wound down over the next two decades. Instead, the key innovation for financial stability was the passage of the Federal Reserve Act in 1913.

4.4 Canada

In Canada, the stability provided by the diversified nationwide branching banks helped to prevent any major banking crisis before 1914, even as deposits became an increasingly important component of the means of payment. Nevertheless, there was concern because deposits were outside of this safety net, though double liability added some protection. Between 1900 and 1935, eight banks failed with a capital of about C$9 million. Shareholders were assessed and paid C$3.6 million, which was sufficient to cover depositors' claims in all but three banks. In those three banks, depositors lost slightly over $2 million, with losses to other creditors totaling $15 million (Allen et al., 1938).[12]

As, in the other cases, Canada's FSM in this era focused on protection of currency. Supervision was conducted through the Canadian Bankers Association rather than an explicit agency as in the United States. The small number of banks perceived an interest in mutual supervision, as did the clearing houses in the American cities. While Parliament showed increased concern for depositors, no attempt was made to give them the same guarantee as banknote holders. Depositors had to rely on the market incentives, amplified by the imposition of double liability of shareholders to protect them.

4.5 Colombia

The political upheavals in Colombia in the twenty years prior to the First World War hindered economic growth. After the inflationary issues of

---

[12] By comparison, losses to depositors and other creditors in the larger U.S. national banking system totaled $44 million from 1865 to 1913 (White, 2013).

446   *Gianni Toniolo and Eugene N. White*

paper money, a new regime for price stability was legislated in 1907. Yet, although the peso had been tied to gold, a monopoly of note issue was conceded to a single bank, and broad powers given to the banking industry, Colombia did not fully enjoy the prosperity of this period. Banking remained limited, and questions about how the growth of deposit banking might threaten bank stability were not raised. Only with the boom of First World War and Colombia's radical reforms in 1923 did the country begin to rapidly develop a modern banking sector.

5 Central Banks and the Shock of the First World War

The First World War had two effects on the evolution of the FSM. First, to cope with the huge initial shock and financial crises, there were innovative responses. Their success gave a green light to the use of increased discretion to supervisors. The second effect arose from the need to transfer resources from the public to the state. The magnitude of this transfer and the degree to which banks facilitated it entangled state finance and the balance sheets of the banks, intertwining the solvency of the state with that of the banking system. While the leading central banks had previously balanced their public purposes with private profitability, the war emphasized the pre-eminence of the former, shifting them towards completely public institutions.

Although military plans were well-developed at the outbreak of the war, relatively little attention had been given to financial contingency plans (Horn, 2002). As payments and settlements systems were threatened by banking and stock market panics and the international finance system edged towards collapse, policy makers recognized that financial stability was essential to the war economy. Finance Ministers co-opted their central banks to address the shocks and direct the war economy, entrusting them with new tasks and discretionary authority. Besides an accommodative monetary policy, central banks managed moratoria on payments and exchange rates, underwrote and led consortia for the issue of government bonds, served as government paymasters, and dealt with requisitioned assets.

5.1 The United Kingdom

During the Great War, the Bank of England became a close collaborator of the Treasury. The Bank of England briefly tried to manage the crisis at the outbreak of the war by traditional means, raising the discount rate briefly

The Evolution of the Financial Stability Mandate

to 10 percent, but the convertibility of banknotes was quickly suspended, as were the Bank Acts that set limits on the outstanding circulation (Horn, 2002). The liquidity crisis that hit the London remittance houses threatened to spread to the money market, prompting the introduction of a bank holiday from August 3 to 7 (Sayers, 1976). According to Brown (1940), the main aim of the moratorium was to safeguard "the strength of Great Britain as a creditor nation (which would have not been) possible without suspending temporarily the basic operations of international finance."

Controls during World War I were relatively minimal and fiscal policy was governed by the "McKenna Rule," where the objective was to raise enough tax revenue to pay for ordinary peacetime expenditures plus interest on war loans. However, bond finance with low interest rates maintained by the Bank of England led to rapid inflation, as the pound was allowed to float (Broadberry and Howlett, 2005). In the 1920s the deflationary policy for the return to gold hit the banks not because they were directly financing the government but because they were imperiled by their credits to industry. The old industries of the First Industrial Revolution – textiles, iron, steel and coal – had expanded during the war and now had excess capacity. The Bank of England intervened, departing from its narrowly defined pre-war role. Sayers (1976) explained this change as "partly to help the cotton industry, partly to keep the question away from politics, but more especially to relieve certain of the banks from a dangerous position."

Resistance to radical downsizing in textiles and shipbuilding took the form of collusion to raise prices, which surprisingly found support among Liberal, Conservative and Labor politicians alike who emphasized the destructive side of competition. Aid did not come directly from the government but the Bank of England and the Bankers Industrial Development Corporation (BIDC) established in 1929, which Hannah (1983) has argued was an attempt to prevent direct government intervention. The BDIC's most prominent venture was the formation of the Lancashire Cotton Corporation in 1929 to reorganize the industry and scrap inefficient mills. The Bank of England also supported the formation of the National Shipbuilders Security Ltd. for similar purposes (Bowden and Higgins, 2004) World War I had pushed the Bank of England to become a guarantor of the financial system and by extension industrial stability. Yet, while the Bank provided credits to support an industrial policy, there was no change in its supervision of financial institutions and its formal FSM.

5.2 France

World War I forced the government to use discretionary authority to confront the unexpected crisis at the outset of the war and find the means to fund its extraordinary costs. French wartime finance did not co-opt the banking system, which appears to have insulated banks from the postwar shocks that created banking crises in other countries.

Increasing geopolitical uncertainty rattled markets and during the late Spring of 1914, rumors circulated that Société Générale was in a precarious state, leading to substantial withdrawals of deposits (Horn, 2002). In response, the Ministry of Finance issued a communiqué on June 7, reassuring the public about the state of the bank–an innovation in communication. Accommodating liquidity demands, the Banque of France expanded discounts, while quickly raising its discount rate from 3.5 to 6 percent. After Austria's declaration of war on Serbia and fearful of a run on the franc, the Banque suspended convertibility of its notes on July 31 and began to issue small denomination, 5 and 20 francs notes. To halt a banking panic, a partial moratorium of withdrawals from deposit and current accounts was announced on August 2nd, lasting until January 1, 1915.[13] As the threat of a panic was ended, the Banque cut the discount rate to 5 percent on August 20 where it would remain until 1920.

Chastened by the suspension, deposits did not recover and the public shifted to buying short-term government debt. The share of deposits in the means of payment shrank between 1910 and 1920, and coin disappeared. The banks' role in finance declined, as government financing accessed the bond market directly, assisted by the Banque de France, which kept the interest rate on the *bons de la Defense Nationale* pegged at 5 percent. Meanwhile French enterprise relied heavily on self-financing (Feinstein, Temin and Toniolo, 2008, p. 21). Banks did not regain their 1914 level of deposits in real terms until 1928 and total loans fell from 33.4 percent of national income in 1913 to 18.6 percent in 1926. As loans shrank, banks increased liquidity by buying the *bons*; their very short maturities ensured that banks' balance sheets were not imperilled as they might have been if they had been buying long-term bonds in an inflationary environment.

---

[13] Société Générale asked for line of credit from the Banque for 80 million francs in September 1914 but it was refused then and again in February 1915 on the grounds that it had a weak balance sheet. What is unclear is whether the bank was insolvent and if so, was there forbearance in closing the bank. Some critics believed that the general provision of more liquidity probably saved Société Générale and other weak institutions (Blancheton, 2014).

The banks were thus not tied to government finance and their solvency was not dependent on the government's solvency. Combined with their wartime downsizing, there was no banking crisis immediately after World War I – and hence no need to reconsider the FSM.

After the war, the government's optimistic plans for reconstruction were supported by bond-financed deficit spending, where if the public failed to buy the bonds, there was recourse to the Banque, leading to inflation. Although the Banque de France provided credits to the banks so that they would buy government debt, banks did not over-expand in the perilous early postwar years (Bouvier, 1988). Bank's role in reconstruction was also limited by the establishment in 1919 of Crédit National, a semi-public institution that issued bonds to finance long-term investment. Lescure (1995) concludes that the banking sector did not keep pace with the growth of the economy in the postwar inflationary years from 1917 to 1926, although the largest banks expanded their branching networks. The end result was that the underlying regulatory and supervisory regime remained unchanged.

5.3 Italy

With the outbreak of World War I, novel discretionary power was used by the Italian authorities, and the role of the Banca d'Italia, which had accepted *de facto* responsibility for financial stability in 1907, expanded. Even though Italy had remained neutral, in August 1914, a run on deposits prompted the Banca d'Italia to act to prevent financial panic. A law providing for a moratorium on the withdrawal of deposits was drafted by the Banca and rushed through Parliament by the government.

At the same time the Banca d'Italia increased the provision of liquidity to the financial system, and acquired, through its branch system, more information about the solvency of individual banks. Yet, there were no legal grounds for the Banca d'Italia to demand that the banks disclose private information. It was gathered informally and by moral suasion, to which smaller banks more readily agreed. Behind the scenes, Prime Minister Salandra wrote Bonaldo Stringher, the Banca d'Italia's general manager, "If information cannot be privately gathered, do not hesitate to use any other means, *even by ordering an inspection* [our italics], which the banks, though private, cannot refuse given the advantages they draw from the present moratorium" (Toniolo 1989, p. 21). Salandra thus articulated a clear justification for supervision, based on the special advantages extended by the state to the banks that gave the authorities the right to request disclosure of private information and supervise the banks.

450   *Gianni Toniolo and Eugene N. White*

The efforts to supply the Italian army were assisted by the Banca d'Italia. When the First National Loan was issued in 1915 and the public failed to take the whole issue, the Banca stepped in to purchase the remainder. Afterwards the Banca continued to support bond prices and offered liberal discounting, enabling banks to extend credits to war industries. The central bank soon became directly involved in industrial finance. In 1914, the Consortium for Industrial Finance was created to lend on easy terms to industry, continuing its assistance in the immediate postwar period. Although it was funded by private capital, it was governed and financed by the Banca d'Italia. In general, the war increased the close collaboration between the government and the bank, which continued in the years after the armistice.

The postwar slump hit Italian industry and its banks hard. The heart of Italy's problem was excess capacity in heavy engineering sectors, such as shipbuilding. Not only did banks provide credits and invest in this industry's securities, they had interlocking shareholdings and directorships with large industrial companies. The crisis erupted when one of the largest conglomerates, Ansaldo, had its parent bank, the Banca di Sconto, commissioned the construction of ships at a time when demand for tonnage was sharply declining. The government executed a *de facto* take over of Ansaldo, while the Banca d'Italia was given the task of liquidating the Banca di Sconto. It was kept on life-support with liquidity provided by the Banca d'Italia and a guarantee from the newly-formed Mussolini government, until it was merged with another bank (Gigliobianco, Giordano and Toniolo, 2009, pp. 54–55; Guarino and Toniolo, 1993).

In response to the postwar financial crisis, a new banking act was prepared with the assistance of the Banca d'Italia. Although opposed by many economists and the Association of Limited Liability Companies who claimed that it would increase moral hazard and infringe upon the basic freedoms of individuals and firms, the Bank Act was passed in 1926, giving the Banca d'Italia a monopoly of note issue, sanctioning the *de facto* situation. In addition, there were new rules for the authorization of new banks and new branches by existing banks. The law also prescribed minimum capital/deposit ratios, credit ceilings for individual clients and disclosure rules. Supervision was handed to the Banca d'Italia rather than to the Ministry of Finance. (Guarino, Toniolo, Gigliobianco and Santonocito, 1993).

The short time between the Bank Act of 1926 and the banking crisis of 1931 did not allow the Bank of Italy to gain much experience and set up a supervisory structure. It was, however, able to prevent the mismanagement of a large number of "Catholic banks" from developing into panic.

The Evolution of the Financial Stability Mandate   451

Inspections were carried out, capital requirements were imposed, and mergers were ordered. In spite of this success, the Bank Law of 1926's design reflected the regulatory needs of the pre-1913 banking system and did not take into account the changes in the universal banks portfolios that had taken place during and after the war, leaving them with large industrial holdings (Toniolo, 1995).

5.4 The United States

As in all countries, World War I presented two challenges. The first, at the war's outset was the banking panic and stock market crash. Although the Federal Reserve was not yet operational, the Aldrich-Vreeland Act of 1908 had established a procedure to inject additional currency that mimicked the clearing houses methods of issuing loan certificates but reached a greater number of banks (Friedman and Schwartz, 1963). A stock market collapse, precipitated by Europeans dumping their holdings of American securities, heightened the demand for gold, threatening the dollar. A crisis was averted by the Secretary of the Treasury shutting down the New York Stock Exchange, thus blocking these transactions, until the European demand for war materiel turned the balance of payments in favor of the United States (Silber, 2008). Thus, both the means of payment and settlement were threatened, with the latter resolved by unprecedented action of discretion by the Treasury that would foreshadow the management of 1930s crisis. The granting of discretionary authority to the president was codified in the 1917 Trading with the Enemy Act.

The second challenge to the stability of the banking system arising out of World War I was the use of the banks as vehicles for the sale and absorption of government war debt. Banks were induced by a public campaign and the availability of credit at the new Federal Reserve banks to lend to their customers to buy war bonds. Although they added U.S. bonds to their portfolios, this indirect method of finance was more important. Fortunately, U.S. involvement in World War I was not as great as the European belligerents and the nation was able to quickly wind down its military operations and produce budget surpluses that ensured that banks' link to government revenue requirements was eliminated. However, many banks in rural areas failed after the collapse of the postwar international commodity boom.

Although the Federal Reserve Act of 1913 gave the Fed the power to provide additional liquidity to the banking system, Fed officials realized that there was a new challenge for the FSM because it was not so simple to

452 *Gianni Toniolo and Eugene N. White*

draw a line between protecting currency and deposits. In describing the function of examination for the Federal Reserve banks, Burgess (1927) emphasized that its purpose was to "prevent too constant or too large use of borrowing facilities" by a member bank, recognizing a moral hazard problem that had led hundreds of banks to become dependent on discount loans by the mid-1920s. He offered a pointed example: rural banks loaded with doubtful farm paper that brought their good paper to the discount window. If they failed, the good discounted paper would remain with at a Federal Reserve Bank, leaving depositors with little for their claims. Burgess concluded that "The Reserve Bank must consider not only the safety of its loan, but the interests of the depositors" (Burgess, 1927).

This soul-searching indicated an inclination towards discretion-based supervision. During the post–World War I downturn, some regional Reserve Banks, notably Atlanta began to roll over discounts whose repayment might have caused banks to fail. The hope was that by granting extensions, banks would recover their solvency as the economy improved (White, 2015). Other than showing more discretion in examinations, implementing a change in the FSM was another matter. Apart from jawboning, the central bank had no formal policy instruments to reduce the riskiness of a bank. Complicating matters further were the presence of multiple regulatory agencies – the Fed, the OCC and the state superintendents – that engaged in competition in laxity, inducing regulatory arbitrage (White, 1983).

5.5 Canada

In the absence of a central bank, Parliament responded to the crisis at the outbreak of the war by passing the Finance Act of 1914 that enabled the Minister of Finance to provide Dominion notes against approved securities to both chartered banks and savings banks and permitted the Government in Council to allow the banks to suspend redemption of Dominion notes in gold and establish a general moratorium (Royal Commission, 1933). These actions augmented the discretionary authority of the government, although they did not immediately alter the FSM that focused on the protection of banknotes.

Modest measures were undertaken to increase oversight; and in 1923, chartered banks were required to provide monthly reports to the Minister of Finance and to conduct annual audits with two approved auditors, selected by a bank's shareholders, plus a special annual report provided to the Minister of Finance and the directors of the banks. Ironically, shortly

The Evolution of the Financial Stability Mandate

after this new legislation was passed, the Home Bank failed in 1923, leaving initial losses of $11 million, far exceeding any previous single bank failure. Concerned about this large failure, the Canadian Bankers Association advanced a "dividend" of 25 percent to depositors before liquidation of the Home Bank was complete. While this was an extraordinary action, it basically represented an extension of the Redemption Fund. However, at the same time, the Government of Quebec used a $15 million off-balance sheet line of credit to assist the merger of the Banque Hochelaga with the Banque Nationale by taking over the former's questionable assets and slowly liquidating them to prevent a failure and a fire sale.

Kryzanowski and Roberts (1993, 1999) have argued that beginning in 1923, there was an implicit guarantee from the Canadian government of all deposits, operating through the Canadian Bankers Association or the government's arrangement of mergers of failing institutions. In contrast, Carr, Mathewson and Quigly (1995) claim that only solvent banks were merged and depositors still suffered losses in failed banks. While this debate focuses on how to value bank assets during an economic decline and how to interpret stock premia paid in mergers, there was a clear shift in public expectations as reflected in the testimony of a former Minister of Finance to the commission investigating the Home Bank's failure: "Under no circumstances would I have allowed a bank to fail during the period in question . . . If it had appeared to me that the bank was not able to meet its public obligations, I should have taken steps to have it taken over by some other bank or banks, or failing that, would have given it necessary assistance under the Finance Act, 1914" (quoted in Kryzanowski and Roberts, 1993, p. 366).

The legislative response to the Home Bank, which did not wait for the decennial cycle of Bank Act revision, was the 1924 Bank Act Amendment that created the office of Inspector General, which the Select Standing Committee described as having the aim to "better protect the interests of depositors and prevent similar occurrences in the future." While depositors were given no explicit guarantee, the inspector-general, an officer of the Ministry of Finance, was empowered to carry out yearly examinations and could ask the Canadian Bankers Association to appoint a curator if the bank appeared to be insolvent.

5.6 Colombia

During World War I, Colombia experienced a boom in its exports of coffee and bananas. Hit by a temporary postwar slump, the boom revived in the

454   *Gianni Toniolo and Eugene N. White*

years 1919–1920, with exports doubling but imports increasing five-fold. The collapse in 1920–1921 caused a fiscal crisis for the government and threatened many banks with failure.

As part of a general plan of economic reform to stabilize the economy and attract foreign capital, The Colombia Congress invited an American mission, headed by Edwin Kemmerer, professor at Princeton University, to visit the country and provide advice on how to reform the banking and monetary system. Conducting missions in several Latin American countries, Kemmerer advised the adoption of an improved system of American regulation and supervision. Eight of Kemmerer's ten recommendations were adopted, with Ley 45 of 1923 creating a single supervisory authority, the Superintendencia Bancaria

In this new regime, entry was in principle free but subject to oversight by the Superintendencia; and branching was permitted. Concerned about leverage, Kemmerer added a capital ratio of 15 percent of liabilities. Banks had to submit five yearly call reports to the Superintendencia and they were subject to twice yearly examinations. The superintendent had the authority to levy fines on banks that violated regulations, sue bank directors, and take possession of insolvent banks, deciding whether they should be rehabilitated or liquidated.

Kemmerer also set up a new central bank the Banco de la República, modelled on the Federal Reserve System but where all banks were members. However, the agricultural elite were disappointed by Kemmerer's mandated limits on long-term lending. To meet their demands, an agricultural mortgage bank, the Banco Agrícola Hipotecario was created in 1924. Half the capital was provided by the central government and half by the public and local and state governments. Subject to the Superintendencia's oversight, this bank offered mortgage loans with maturities of up to twenty years. In 1927, private shareholders were bought out and the bank was nationalized, becoming an instrument for indirectly channeling credit to a special sector.

Having reformed its fiscal and financial systems, Colombia gained access to world capital markets and experienced an extraordinary boom in the 1920s. Foreign capital flowed in funding public and private ventures, and the banking system rapidly expanded. The reports of the Superintendencia reveal a deep concern about risky loans that soon turned bad and were not written off. By the late 1920s, the independent superintendent found himself in conflict with the Banco de la República, whose swelling gold reserves had led it to increase its discounting to member banks so that they could expand and the Banco Agrario Hipotecario (White, 1998b).

The Evolution of the Financial Stability Mandate   455

Behind these events, there appears to have developed an implicit guarantee for depositors that had not been manifest before 1923. With a central bank and supervisory agency working in close cooperation, failing banks were rescued. With only thirteen national and five foreign banks in 1929, the loss of even a single bank was perceived as a potential threat to stability. One notable example was the failure in 1924 of the Banco Dugand of Barranquilla. When this bank began losing deposits, the Banco and Superintendencia engineered an assisted takeover by the Banco de Colombia. This approach to closing an insolvent bank in a concentrated industry resembled the late nineteenth century interventions of the Bank of England and the Banque de France and the Banca d'Italia in 1907.

6 The Great Depression and After: Supervision under Financial Repression

By 1930, only two of the three central banks in this study – in the United States and Italy – had been given formal supervisory authority. The Great Depression and the Second World War changed this picture: not only did the other central banks become bank regulators but controls on international capital movements, introduced in the thirties and strengthened in the wartime, resulted in the a "nationalization" of financial markets, enabling the state to intervene more deeply in managing credit flows, resulting in a system characterized by financial repression. Bank regulation was turned into tool for the management of credit flows, interest rates, and international capital mobility.

6.1 The United Kingdom

The United Kingdom's experience in World War I and the troubled interwar years paved the way for greater intervention during World War II, when the government, anxious to contain inflation and channel credit to war industries, imposed a broad program of controls and rationing that continued after the war (Broadberry and Howlett, 2005). In addition to using controls to limit inflation, the Bank of England became directly involved in industrial finance after World War II. One vehicle was the Financial Corporation for Industry (FCI) and the Commercial Finance Corporation (CFC) whose objectives were to provide financing to companies that found it difficult to raise external finance, with the Bank subscribing the largest share of their capital and providing advances. (Capie, 2010).

After World War II, the Bank of England was tasked with enforcing the Treasury's interest rate targets and controls on bank loans. Taking office as the Chancellor of the Exchequer in 1950, Hugh Gaitskell explained that the Bank of England should "give [banks] direct instructions about the level of advances, with perhaps some guidance as to the particular borrowers who should be cut," subject to the stipulation "there should be no increase in the rate at which the Government borrows short-term" (Wood, 2005, p. 299).

Subordination of the Bank of England to the Treasury was formalized when it was nationalized in 1946. Although the government intended to include details of bank regulation in the nationalization bill this was successfully resisted by the Bank. Instead, of the "iron hand" of the Treasury supervising the banks, the Bank used its "velvet glove," relying on persuasion of the small group of cartelized clearing banks that dominated British finance (Capie, 2010). Consequently, the Bank felt no need to develop a supervisory organization within the bank itself and eschewed economic and statistical analysis. Supervision depended more on the "Governor's eyebrows" than a set of formal rules or principles.

Furthermore, the 1946 Act did not give the Bank a mandate with specific objectives; its tasks were implicitly understood. Basically the Treasury set policy and the Bank conducted the day-to-day operation. Sayers (1958) summed this arrangement as the fundamental business of a central bank is to control the commercial banks to support monetary policy as directed by the state." Capie (2010) describes banking supervision as "distinctly low key – to the point of invisibility. There were no formal mechanisms of control, and neither was there any statutory provision for oversight of the banking system." The 1946 Act allowed the bank, with Treasury authorization, to give directions to banks but; this power was not used and the bank preferred to discuss problems and issue private warnings. In the Bank of England's 1957 submission to the Radcliffe Committee, it stated that there was "no formal control over other banks and no duty of inspection" (Capie, 2010).

Characterized as "stop-go," British macroeconomic policy in the 1950s and 1960s fostered growth with budget stimuli and cheap money until an exchange rate crisis forced an abrupt contraction. Key tools were credit controls, such as "hire-purchase" restrictions introduced in 1952 whose terms were set by the Bank of England. By 1968, the Bank's authority may be seen in the complex of set of ten interest rates and maturities that the clearing banks agreed to for customers (Capie, 2010). These were largely eliminated in 1970 by the Act for Competition and Credit Control (CCC) that aimed at promoting efficiency and competition.

The Evolution of the Financial Stability Mandate 457

Although there was no statutory obligation, Capie (2010) argues that the Bank took on the responsibility for financial stability after the Second World War. The Bank closely monitored the city, chiefly through the Principal of the Discount Office, but this became increasingly difficult after CCC initiated a deregulation. The first postwar threat to financial stability came from the secondary or "fringe" banking sector, which had grown up in the late 1950s and early 1960s by borrowing on wholesale money markets and lending primarily on real estate. These banks were buoyed by the expansionary policies of 1971–1973 and the CCC's deregulation. When the economy slowed, the fringe banks found themselves facing large losses and withdrawals. Responding to this collapse, the Bank of England provided temporary liquidity with losses shared out in successive lifeboats. Some banks went into liquidation, while others were reorganized. The total cost was estimated to be approximately £1.2–£1.3 billion, with the Bank of England absorbing 10 percent (Capie, 2010).

However, the informal discretion-based *cum* moral suasion approach to discipline remained; and when there were proposals to bring the licensing and supervision of all deposit-taking institutions under a comprehensive system, the Bank of England resisted. The Banking Act 1979 bowed to the Bank and set up a two-tier structure of supervision for the recognized and fringe institutions with prudential criteria that remained informal. This arrangement was soon collapsed in the wake of the failure of another bank, Johnson Matthey, in 1984 (Capie, 2010).

6.2 France

Between October 1929 and September 1937, 670 banks failed, 276 were joint-stock banks and the remainder partnerships. In these troubled years, there were banking crises in 1931 and 1934 when the Banque de France had to provide additional liquidity to the market. Most of the failing institutions were small banks, though there were some important regional banks: the Banque Adam in Boulogne, the Banque d'Alsance-Lorraine, the Banque Renauld in Nancy, and the Banque Carpenay in Grenoble. One large bank, the Banque Nationale de Credit (BNC) failed, but it was apparently the only bank that received assistance from the Banque de France and the government (Lescure, 1995). Although details of this intervention are somewhat obscure, it was provided with sufficient liquidity to survive and then was liquidated and recapitalized as the Banque National pour le Commerce et l'Industrie. Thus, it resembled the rescue of the Comptoir d'Escompte in 1889. The secondary literature indicates that mergers and takeovers were often encouraged to prevent losses to depositors.

The depression in France, a period of sharp deflation, was a systemic shock to the banking system, leading the government to implicitly become its guarantor, signified by the state's takeover of the Banque de France in 1936, effectively nationalizing it. Reflecting the Popular Front's philosophy of "republican corporatism" to ensure that decisions made were representative of the nation's economic and social interests, shareholders' elected members on the governing board were reduced to two in twenty, with the remainder appointed by either various government agencies or professional associations. This approach to control was then fully expanded under the Nazi-dominated Vichy regime (Monnet, 2012).

Formal supervision did not come from the creation of specific government institutions to monitor, examine and discipline banks – an American-style model that had evolved from having multiple banks of issue – but from a corporatist model, arising from the drive to reorganize the banking industry and channel credit flows. Persisting until the last quarter of the twentieth century, the state-directed banking system, allocating funds through financial repression, began under the Vichy regime. Banks came under the supervision of the Comission Bancaire, created by the Banking Act of 1941, to ensure that they complied with the rules imposed by the new regime. To provide the occupying Germans with the means to buy war materiel, occupation payments were imposed on France, paid for by money creation by the Banque de France. Seeking to minimize the inflationary potential of this action, the government imposed wage, price and interest rate controls and tried to absorb the monetary increase by massive bond sales. To support this activity, banks' bond portfolios swelled (Occhino, Oosterlinck and White, 2008).

Postwar French governments did not attempt to return to a market-based financial system but took over and expanded the institutional architecture begun under Vichy. In 1945, the Banque de France was formally nationalized and the Commission de Contrôle des Banques (Commission Bancaire) was reorganized and expanded. Headed by the Governor of the Banque and operating under its aegis, the Commission had four other members, the president of the Financial Section of the Council of State, the head of the Treasury Department, a representative of the Bankers' Association, and a representative of the trade unions. To complete this system, the largest commercial banks were nationalized in 1945.

For the nationalized banks the Comission Bancaire acted with the National Credit Council, in place of shareholders, to set policy for the

The Evolution of the Financial Stability Mandate   459

banks, wielding considerable discretionary authority. Smaller banks were left in private hands but the state had authority over the allocation of and terms of credit. State financial institutions were divided into five groups: the postal savings system, savings banks (caisses d'épargnes), cooperative banks (caisses mutuelles); most of them affiliated with the Caisse Nationale de Crédit Agricole, the banques populaires, and the Banque française du commerce extérieur. These institutions had their collected funds allocated almost exclusively by the state. The French State took the role of inter-mediary, with a complex web of regulation governing commercial banks, insurance companies, finance companies and brokerages to distribute loans to households and firms.

For the period 1945–1963, fiscal deficits were largely financed through the banking system (Melitz, 1982). Issues of Treasury bonds were modest but state agencies dominated the market and their issues were placed with financial institutions. The Treasury decided the level and structure of interest rates, with the Caisse de Dépôts de Consignations ensuring that the rates stay on target. As rates were kept low in real terms there was excess demand for new issues and a queue for who would obtain funds beginning with the Treasury and ending with private firms.

State finance and banking were so intertwined that the solvency of the state and the financial system were not separate questions. For at least three decades after 1945, the FSM in a broad sense did not exist as it was assumed that capital controls and government direction would guarantee stability. Financial repression in France left no clear lines of delegation of authority over financial institutions and markets. Melitz's 1982 description of the confused authority over monetary policy is equally applicable to the complementary authority for financial stability:

Exactly who the monetary authorities are is somewhat of a question since there is no tradition of central bank independence in the country, and the ministers of the Economy and Finance ... clearly have a large hand in monetary policy. Yet the weight of the Bank of France and the general power and prestige of the civil service is such that the ministers do not rule monetary policy alone. Monetary power may be said to be essentially divided between the Bank of France, these ministers, and to some extent also, the Treasury and some of the high officials in several of the satellite credit agencies in the sphere of the government.

The persistence of financial repression directing the flow of funds is striking. In 1960, the Treasury-directed financial institutions collected 53.2 percent of funding and offered 45.6 percent of credits. Although its funding sources fell to 38.0 percent by 1980, the state's control of credit reached 60.8 percent of all financing. By 1993, it still collected 27.5 percent

460   *Gianni Toniolo and Eugene N. White*

of funds and directed 48.1 percent of credits (Plihon, 1995). When inflation threatened, credit rationing was reinforced by a program of *encadrement du crédit* that set individual ceilings on the growth of credit for banks. First applied in 1958, it was repealed once inflation fell, then it was reimposed in 1963–1965, 1968–1970, and finally in 1972–1987 (Monnet, 2014), The rigid controls that had developed after 1945 began to slowly decline in response to three factors: the fiscal difficulties of the state, the breakdown of the Bretton Woods System's capital controls, and European economic integration.

6.3 Italy

The slump in industrial output that began in 1930 and consequent sharp declines in manufacturing and utility companies' stock prices damaged the portfolios of the three largest banks, leaving them illiquid and perhaps insolvent. When foreign deposits withdrawals accelerated in 1931, swift and secret lending by the Banca d'Italia with the backing of the government avoided a crisis like those of Germany and Austria, where universal bank-dominated financial structures were similar to that of Italy. The government took de facto control of the major banks and overhauled Italy's banking system. Bailed-out banks were then supplied liquidity deemed sufficient to operate as "ordinary" commercial banks (i.e., limited to short term borrowing and lending), and they were forbidden to hold equities of non-financial companies. The banks' industrial interests were taken over by the state, which created special ad hoc vehicles that led to the establishment in 1933 of the Istituto per la Ricostruzione Industriale (IRI), a state holding company that operated until the early 1990s.

As a result of the 1931 bailout, the three main banks fell under the indirect control of the state, while the fourth largest bank (the Banca Nazionale del Lavoro) was directly controlled by the government as were all long-term credit institutions. Government influence was exerted on savings banks, whose boards were appointed by local authorities and heads by the central government, which also owned the Cassa Depositi e Prestiti that received vast inflows of postal savings to invest in public works and state bonds. Only a handful of small private banks and the tightly regulated local cooperative banks were not under the central government's influence.

Firmly in control, the fascist government revised the regulatory and supervisory system in the Bank Act of 1936, which, amended in 1947, remained the defining bank law until 1993. By minutely regulating and repressing the financial sector the law sought to obtain financial stability.

The Evolution of the Financial Stability Mandate   461

It ensured a strict separation between long and short-term credit and between investment and credit institutions. The Treasury was given broad regulatory and supervisory powers over the financial system, which, in turn, delegated supervision to the Banca d'Italia. The Bank Act of 1936 set up an Inspectorate for the Safeguarding of Savings and for Credit Activity, reporting to a committee of ministers, headed by the Prime Minister. This inspectorate was given regulatory and supervisory authority over the banking system. Given explicit tasks to prevent crises and credit allocation, the Inspectorate was headed by the Governor of the Banca d'Italia and it never operated separately from central bank. (Guarino and Toniolo, 1993).

6.4 United States

During the Great Depression and its aftermath, the FSM changed dramatically in the United States, primarily because the banking panics of 1930, early 1931, late 1931 and most importantly 1933 eliminated the belief of most legislators and much of the public that the banking system was inherently stable and the means of payment could be protected by a combination of guarantees for currency and market incentives for deposits. The panics drove a vast shrinkage of deposits that was only halted on March 5, 1933 by the President's declaration of a bank holiday. What followed was the implicit assumption of responsibility for the solvency of all reopened banks by the government. Instead of guaranteeing a well-defined financial instrument – all currency – the government guaranteed the banks.

This shift was accomplished by the means the government chose to reopen the banks. On March 9, 1933, Congress passed the Emergency Banking Act of 1933, giving the Treasury, the Fed and the OCC extraordinary discretionary authority to reopen or close banks. Silber (2009) commented that this act, four days after the declaration of a bank holiday "combined with the Federal Reserve's commitment to supply unlimited amounts of currency to reopened banks, created de facto 100 percent deposit insurance." In a prelude to legislation that would follow later, the act gave the president the power to regulate all banking functions and transactions in foreign exchange, enabled the OCC to take control of any bank with impaired assets and appoint a conservator, let the Secretary of the Treasury provide capital to any bank via the Reconstruction Finance Corporation or make direct loans, and gave the Fed the power to issue emergency currency not backed by gold. Supervision was expanded and with vast discretion delegated to the regulators.

A sequential opening of banks began, with teams of examiners and auditors visiting closed banks (Friedman and Schwartz, 1963). Those that were judged to be clearly solvent were immediately re-opened, those whose position was unclear required further examination and those determined to be insolvent were liquidated. In essence, this was first "stress test" conducted by the government through all the supervisory agencies. Although we do not know, how the examiners carried out this operation, they probably erred on the side of caution and only opened banks considered clearly solvent. These actions appear to have sufficed to give the public an implicit guarantee for their deposits, and led to the re-depositing of much of the currency that had fled the banks.

The New Deal in banking as codified in the Banking Acts of 1933 and 1935, as well as changes instituted by bank supervisors, ended an era of competition. Entry was now subject to regulatory discretion, and branching barriers reaffirmed, protecting existing banks. Regulation Q banned interest on demand deposits and put ceilings on savings and time deposits rates. Commercial banks' range of products was limited, most notably by the Glass-Steagall Act that split commercial and investment banking. Senator Carter Glass, a true believer in the real bills doctrine and head of the Senate banking committee, insisted that separation of commercial and investment banking be included in the 1933 law and obtained it in exchange for establishing the Federal Deposit Insurance Corporation (FDIC) that Representative Henry Steagall, chairman of the House Banking and Currency Committee, had demanded at the behest of small bank lobby (Calomiris and White, 1994).

Deposit insurance was initially conceived of as protecting only small accounts, but was slowly expanded to cover most deposits in commercial banks over the next three decades, thanks to lobbying by the banking industry (White, 2007). What had been offered as a mutual guarantee system, paid for by bank premia gradually came to look like universal deposit insurance, with an implicit government guarantee. This shift enlarged the FSM, making the regulatory agencies and ultimately the taxpayer guarantors of bank deposits. It appeared to be a costless shift to the public, as the bank failures ceased. Yet, this development was deceptive because the massive banking collapse of the early 1930s had eliminated all weak institutions. Furthermore, the scramble for liquidity during the banking panics had led banks to replace loans with cash and bonds. Yet, some changes increased risk in the future. The 1930s collapse of the capital markets and wartime efforts led regulators to encourage banks to make more long-term loans, increasing the maturity mismatch.

To meet the broadened FSM, the practice of bank supervision was transformed. Before the collapse, bank examiners followed a general rules-based approach, where they priced a bank's marketable assets at market prices, and promptly closed banks that they deemed to be insolvent. If these practices had been followed during the Great Depression's deflation and asset-price volatility there would have been even more numerous bank closures. Instead, market discipline was abandoned and supervisory discretion replaced mark-to-market rules (White, 2013). Assets were valued at what they would fetch in normal times, not the current crisis; forbearance to close a currently insolvent institution became a supervisory option. These actions were further justified in the name of protecting bank depositors–acknowledging the expansion of the FSM. The establishment of the Federal Deposit Insurance Corporation (FDIC) created a third federal supervisory agency, signalling this shift. With its explicit mandate to insure banks, the FDIC sought to restrain banks from taking risks that would draw on its guarantee fund.

During World War II, bank credit was diverted to purchase government bonds, and bank portfolios were transformed, with bonds' share of total assets exceeding the share for loans (White, 1992). During the war, the Federal Reserve kept yields under a very low ceiling to ensure a cheap source of funds for the government, but this meant that after the war, interest rates would have to rise when wartime controls were lifted. Considering the size of banks' U.S. bond holdings, the losses could have been considerable, threatening bank solvency. Only in 1951, were interest rates permitted to rise after the negotiation of the Treasury-Fed Accord.

By the 1960s, the FSM had been transformed – in the mind of the public and of Congress – from protecting a narrowly defined means of payment to the prevention of bank failures. This change can be seen in the oversight of the federal agencies by Congress. Very few banks had failed during the 1950s and this became the expected norm. In 1964, when a tiny Texas bank with $3.7 million in assets failed, the Comptroller of the Currency was summoned to Congress for questioning. When two more banks failed in 1965, the House Banking and Currency Committee discussed whether the OCC ought to be dissolved, with the task of supervising all federal insured banks being transferred to the Secretary of the Treasury (White, 1992). The FSM mandate had been expanded, with inflated expectations for supervision, and the measurement of supervisory agencies' success became "zero tolerance" for bank failures, a task that was facilitated by financial repression.

Canada

Even though Canada suffered a monetary contraction approximately equal to that in the United States in the 1930s, economists south of the border (Friedman and Schwartz, 1963; Bordo, Redish and Rockoff, 2011) have argued that the absence of large bank failures and banking panics in Canada during was due to the strength of the large diversified Canadian banks. However, some research indicates that the solvency of the Canadian banking system was compromised but government intervention prevented a U.S. style disaster. Kryzanowski and Roberts (1993) find that for the period 1929–1940, nine of the ten Canadian banks had several insolvent years.[14] None of these banks were closed, indicating forbearance. Notably, in October 1931, Orders-in-Council mandated that banks value securities at their book value or market value as of August 31, in spite of GAAP accounting rules. If there was not implicit deposit insurance in the 1920s, it was certainly adopted early in the Great Depression.

The 1933 Royal Commission began the overhaul of the banking system. In an Addendum to the 1933 Royal Commission's Report, Sir Thomas White recognized deposits as a "medium of exchange," attributing their fluctuation to decisions of banks to make loans and "confidence or lack of confidence, in the financial stability of the nation." Created in 1935, the Bank of Canada (Bordo and Redish, 1987) began to accumulate supervisory authority and became ultimately the sole bank of issue. The Bank obtained some of the Minister of Finance's supervisory authority, gaining the power to require inspections of chartered banks first upon demand, then on a regular basis in 1936. In addition, the Bank received the monthly reports that were sent to the Minister who took over the power to appoint a curator for suspended banks from the Canadian Bankers Association.

Buying government debt, the Bank of Canada played an important role in financing Canada's war effort during World War II. After the war, the Bank of Canada was conscripted to channel the flow of credit. An Act of Parliament in 1944 established a subsidiary, the Industrial Development Bank (IDB) to stimulate investment in Canadian businesses, with the Governor of the Bank as its CEO. Its early mission was to assist small industrial enterprises to convert from military production to peace-time operations. Its role was expanded in 1952 to offer financing and advice to companies in the commercial airlines industry and eventually all industries

---

[14] For the debate on this issue, see Carr, Mathewson and Quigley (1995) and Kryzanowski and Roberts (1999).

The Evolution of the Financial Stability Mandate 465

across Canada. In 1975, the IDB was renamed the Federal Business Development Bank, and began to provide venture capital.

By the 1960s, the Bank of Canada was not viewed as an independent institution by the government. After conflict with the prime minister over lowering interest rates, the Governor of the Bank resigned, leading to a Royal Commission on Banking and Finance. Its report recommended reduced financial repression and greater regulation of the near-banks that had been competing with the commercial banks. Although no commercial banks failed, there were numerous failures of trust, mortgage and savings companies with losses to their customers. Thus, when the Bank Act of 1967 created the Canada Deposit Insurance Corporation (CDIC), it covered banks and these new institutions. Originally, insurance was limited to $20,000 per account; this was raised to $60,000 in 1983 and then $100,000 for each eligible deposit account to per depositor in 2005. The FSM was thus expanded to include financial institutions that had slipped around the regulations that constrained commercial banks and cover most deposits.

6.5 Colombia

The collapse of export prices and the termination of foreign lending drove the Colombian economy into a deep recession in 1929. To remain on the gold standard, the Banco de la República kept interest rates high but did not restrict access to its lending facility. By providing massive liquidity to the banks, the central bank prevented a banking collapse and the contraction of financial intermediation was orderly, although like Canada, numerous branches were closed. The support of the government and the central bank gave the public assurance that their deposits were protected.

Following Britain, Colombia abandoned the gold standard in 1931, permitting the central bank to cut interest rates and increase credits to the government. While the resulting reflation eased conditions somewhat, banks found their shrunken portfolios filled with mortgages whose payments were in arrears or in default. Although the exact condition of the banking industry has not been accurately assessed, the Superintendencia may have exercised forbearance to prevent the closure of troubled banks. To ease the condition of debtors, new legislation in 1932 allowed them to repay their loans in cash or depreciated government bonds. To offset the losses to the banks, the government promised to buy up to 25 percent of the bonds that banks received, writing off the rest of the bad loans.

Although the banking system had been cleansed of bad loans, it was weakened. When the economy began to recover, the banks were unwilling to expand credit, leading to intense criticism from the public and the government. The attempt by Kemmerer to keep banks limited to lending on "real bills" and the shock of the depression ensured that banks shied away from longer term credits. The Superintendencia that had been a bastion of this liberal regime shifted to promote direct intervention in the financial system.

Cut off from credit and buffeted by the fall in coffee prices, the coffee growers induced the government to create the Caja de Crédito Agrario in 1931, supervised by the Superintendencia. With the government providing a quarter of its capital for it, the Caja provided loans up to two years. In 1932, its operations were expanded to include five year industrial loans, and it was rechristened the Caja de Crédito Agrario, Industrial y Minero. The reports of the Superintendencia praised this new bank for expanding credit faster than all the other banks combined. The Superintendencia that had been a bastion of the liberal regime shifted to promote direct intervention in the financial system. In 1932, a new mortgage bank, the Banco Central Hipotecario was founded on a similar model; in 1939 the Institute de Crédito Territorial was organized to make loans for low cost housing for the poor; and to promote industrial development, the Institute de Fomento Industrial was created in 1940. To provide more resources to these quasi-governmental banks, a postal savings system was established in 1937.

The increasing role of the government to redirect credit gained a further boost in World War II when the demand for Colombia's exports produced a new boom, threatening another round of inflation. To soak up savings, the government issued national defense bonds, requiring forced subscriptions. Viewing the market as unable to allocate resources, the superintendent outlined a policy with three goals: (1) credit was to be democratized with a banking office established in each town, (2) the government would direct loans, and (3) interest rates would be controlled, with the lowest rates for the sectors that the government gave top priority. Given the influx of wartime dollars, leading to a monetary expansion the commercial banks also expanded under the government's aegis, focusing on import-substituting industrialization.

In the new post–World War II environment, Colombia's financial institutions were reshaped to foster the government's vision of growth. Although it took until 1973 for the Banco de la República to be nationalized, the Treasury began to dominate the bank beginning in 1931 when the Treasury Minister was mademember of the Banco's governing board. With its resources bolstered by its acquisition of the Stabilization Fund, the central bank began to grant development credits in the 1950s. Financing from the central bank and other banks supported import-substituting industrialization backed by tariffs and a system of licensing imports. Commercial banks were drafted into this system by laws focusing their investment.

Supervision was largely focused on increasingly complex regulations to channel credit and bank failures were administered to ensure flows of funds were not endangered. When the large Banco Popular, a bank mandated to have 55 percent of its loans in small industry, failed the Treasury decided to bail it out and recapitalize it, guaranteeing its deposits. To provide funding for the huge loss all government ministries were forced to reduce their spending for the year by 7 percent. However, when two small commercial banks failed in 1966 and 1967, they were not accorded the same consideration. They were liquidated, and although the depositors were paid in full, they had a long wait to receive payment.

7 Deregulation and the Globalization of Banking

Beginning in 1959, when European currencies became convertible for current account transactions, there was a steady growth of the Eurodollar market that contributed to the relaxation of controls on international capital and ultimately, to the re-internationalization of financial markets. After the collapse of Bretton Woods, floating exchange rates, inflation, and international capital flows helped to undermine national systems of financial repression resulting in market-driven financial systems (Padoa-Schioppa and Saccomanni, 1994). Mastering macroeconomic management in this new environment enhanced central banks' visibility and respect, yielding them greater independence from national treasuries (Borio and Toniolo, 2008).

7.1 The United Kingdom

The deregulatory impulse, beginning with the 1970 act moved the United Kingdom in the direction of a market-driven financial system. Nevertheless, British financial institutions continued to lag behind foreign competitors and London appeared to have lost its place as a center of world finance. In a major reform, the "Big Bang" of 1986, abolished fixed commissions and the distinctions between stock jobbers and stock brokers, and moved the London Stock Exchange to electronic, screen-based trading. Dismantling its system of financial repression, London experienced spectacular growth as a minimally regulated financial center.

Beyond the Bank of England's largely informal oversight, supervision was conducted by self-regulating industry groups overseen by the Financial Intermediaries, Managers and Brokers Regulatory Association (FIMBRA) which was recognized as a self-regulatory organization. Yet, the government retained oversight by the creation of an independent governmental supervisory authority in 1985, the Securities and Investments Board, to which the Chancellor of the Exchequer delegated some statutory regulatory powers. However, a series of scandals in the 1990s and the collapse of Barings Bank in 1995 ended the self-regulatory approach, terminating recognition of FIMBRA; and the Securities and Investments Board expanded its operations. Its name was changed to the Financial Services Authority (FSA) in 1997, and it was given additional powers under the Financial Services and Markets Act of 2000. Operating with considerable autonomy, the FSA drew its funding from fees and fines and was governed by a management that was selected by the Treasury. The scope of the FSA was broad, covering most aspects of universal banking. It was charged with maintaining confidence in the financial system, promoting financial stability, consumer protection and a reduction in financial crime. It followed a principles-based rather than a rules-based regulation.

Failing to anticipate the spectacular collapse of Northern Rock in 2008, the FSA was pilloried for its weak enforcement and abolished in 2012. In its place, the Prudential Regulation Authority was set up within the Bank of England, taking responsibility for financial stability and supervision of banks, building societies, credit unions, insurers, and investment companies. The remaining financial services, including asset managers and financial advisors were placed under the supervision of the Financial Conduct Authority, outside of the Bank of England.

7.2 France

Beginning in the 1960s, the French state began to reduce its role as a financial intermediary and regulator, increasing the independence of state enterprises and banks, while trying to balance its budget. Reforms gave banks and other institutions more control over their interest rates and balance sheets, yet the state retained wide-ranging powers of regulation and continued to direct substantial flows of credit.

Financial problems arising from the oil price shock of 1974 caused the state to take increased control of the banking sector. In an effort to revive the French economy and stabilize exchange rates in the late 1970s, the government devised a system of bank loan subsidies to spur investment

The Evolution of the Financial Stability Mandate   469

and exports. To manage inflation, the *encadrement du crédit* was reintroduced in 1972, strengthening the government's authority to ration credit and protect bank financing (Bertrand et al. 2007). Melitz (1982) commented, "In fact, the commercial banks are so secure in the current arrangements that they do not hold any capital market assets at all for their protection."[15]

Integration into the European Union (EU) posed a challenge for the repressed French financial system. With the formation of the European Monetary System (EMS) in 1979, the slow growing French economy created a problem for the franc that was supposed to remain within a tight band set by the EMS. When the franc weakened in early 1981, the government raised the intervention rate above 20 percent but kept bond rates lower. Interest rates on term deposits jumped and banks then saw profits collapse in a funding squeeze (Melitz, 1982). The election of a Socialist government in 1981 led to the nationalization of all domestic commercial banks with deposits above one billion francs in 1982. Nationalization spelled the temporary end to liberalization and a continuation of the *encadrement du credit*. The new Socialist government began an expansionary policy, strengthened by capital controls. Pressure was now put on the banking sector to support weak or failing industries, with new loan schemes to preserve jobs and firms. Interest rates ceased to allocate capital and the banks began to accumulate nonperforming loans. The failure of this effort led to a major policy reversal. The *encadrement du credit* was abolished and subsidized loans were phased out. Monetary policy switched to conventional central bank methods of setting legal reserve requirements and interest rates. Capital controls were fully eliminated by 1991. Between 1986 and 1990, 10 percent of the banks with 20 percent of deposits were privatized. A second wave of privatizations, de-nationalizing the major banks and state enterprises, occurred in 1993. These reforms finally shifted the French financial sector towards a market based system, reducing the role of the Treasury's network. The Act of 1941 was finally repealed in 1984, and the Commission Bancaire was reorganized as an administrative body in the Banque de France to examine, monitor and sanction banks with the Banque providing staff and resources (Banque de France, December 2004).

Although the emerging privatized French banks gained control over their balance sheets, they remained subject to political influence, notably Crédit Lyonnais suffering huge losses beginning in 1991. The bank was

---

[15] Melitz (1982) noted that official regulations did not permit banks to hold any open position in foreign currencies.

470 Gianni Toniolo and Eugene N. White

bailed out in 1994 with the injection of new capital and the removal of bad loans from its balance sheet to a bad bank, where losses were absorbed by the Treasury (*The Economist*, April 7, 1994). Crédit Lyonnais was fully privatized in 1999, but problems with assets in the good bank resurfaced in 2001. In 2003, it was bought by Crédit Agricole, which reorganized the bank.

The approach of monetary union and the formation of the European Central Bank (ECB) began to transform the Banque de France and the system of regulation and supervision. Legislation in 1993 reformed its statutes, giving the Banque de France policy independence. In 1999, the Banque became a part of the European System of Central Banks, "Eurosystème," whereby it implemented the monetary policy decisions adopted by the ECB's Board of Governors. Regulation and supervision remained in French hands, with increased authority over a broad range of institutions granted in 1999. The Comité de Réglementation Bancaire et Financière was charged with the general regulation for all credit institutions, while the Commission Bancaire handled supervision. Although some limited protection for depositors had existed before, through the Association Française des Banques, a formal government institution for deposit insurance arrived with the advent of monetary union.

In the wake of the financial crisis of 2008, the French Prudential Supervisory Authority (Autorité de Contrôle Prudentiel (ACP) was organized in 2010 as an independent administrative authority under the auspices of the Banque de France, merging the Banking Commission, the Mutual Insurance Supervisory Authority (ACAM) and the Credit Institutions and Investment Firms Committee (CECEI). The ACP is not a legal entity and its President is the Governor of the Banque de France; however it has financial independence, receiving funds from contributions of regulated institutions. It cannot issue regulations but it has the power to monitor and issue sanctions. Supervision of financial markets remains separate under the Autorité des Marchés Financiers.

7.3 Italy

After World War II, the Bank Act of 1936 was modestly revised in 1947. The Inspectorate was suppressed and all its supervisory powers given directly to the Bank of Italy. No major changes were in the regulatory and supervisory architecture until the early 1990s. What did change were the priorities and objectives of the regulator, the Bank of Italy, reflecting changes in government policy and the international environment. For the nearly fifty years after the Bank Act of 1946, the elaborate post-war credit-policy tools offered an institutional and administrative framework to implement the government's industrial policies via credit allocation (Hogdman, 1973; Forsyth, 1997).

The underlying rationale for these "industrial policies" was that the market had failed to efficiently allocate resources over the long run. It was more or less explicitly assumed that governments possessed more reliable information about the longer term growth prospects. In France, such policy was conducted within the framework of a formal economic plan (Monnet, 2012). In Italy the main tool used to direct credit for reconstruction, industrialization, or the reduction of geographic income disparities was the so called *credito agevolato* (subsidized sub-prime credit) whereby banks were directed to provide credit at below market rates to a number of "strategic" recipients. The state would then pay credit institutions the difference between market and subsidized interest rates. An inter-ministerial committee was in charge of deciding credit allocation priorities. To facilitate this allocation after the passage of the Bank Act of 1947, there was a "fast-growing secondary legislation, mainly rules set by the Bank of Italy. The vast panoply of instruments at the Bank of Italy's disposal included: authorization of loans; authorization to issue bonds; caps on interest rates; reserve requirements; rules on the composition of the banks' bond portfolios. Moral suasion was also largely used" (Barbiellini, Gigliobianco, and Giordano, 2012). At the same time, the central bank made sure that the banks, most of which remained under the direct or indirect control of the state, maintained a prudent stance in credit creation, thereby promoting the stability of the system. The Bank of Italy, therefore, had to walk a tight rope between guarding its independence as prudential regulator and facilitating the implementation of the government's credit policy directives (Cotula, 2000).

This dual mandate was facilitated by the Bretton Woods international monetary regime, which imposed controls on short term capital movements, insulating Italian and other continental banks (Hodgman, 1973) from external shocks. By the 1980s, the postwar Italian regulatory and supervisory regime began to lose its underpinnings, as the Bank of Italy gained more independence in monetary policymaking, and looser controls on capital movements progressively undermined government-led credit allocation. Increased competition in the financial sector also arose from the integration of markets in the emerging European Union: regulatory changes were introduced to abide by European directives and the so-called Basel soft laws.

The Italian banking system, sometimes defined as "petrified forest," was increasingly unable to serve the credit needs of an ever more market-oriented economy. Recognition of this untenable position was finally recognized in a major legislative overhaul 1993 that took into account the new rules under the European Union and globalization of financial markets. The Bank Act of 1993 set in motion a process of privatization and mergers for both state-owned banks and savings institutions that picked up speed during the decade.

7.4 The United States

Erosion of the New Deal's Banking regime was slow, giving the appearance of a durable financial stability by protecting established financial intermediaries from competition by entry, mergers, branching and interest rate controls. As inflation began to rise in the late 1960s, it wreaked havoc on the New Deal regime. Attempting to protect the regulated institutions and channel flows of credit, particularly to the housing industry, Congress first strengthened regulations and then unevenly deregulated. The result was a complete collapse of the Savings and Loan industry and a partial collapse of the banking industry in the late 1970s and early 1980s. (White, 2000). While banks and savings and loans failed in large numbers, depositors were protected by the FDIC. The FSM was significantly widened in 1984 with the failure of Continental Illinois of Chicago, the sixth largest bank in the United States – which was deemed "too big to fail." Having purchased massive oil loans from an Oklahoma bank that also failed, Continental was exposed to a run as much of its funding was not FDIC-insured. The Federal Reserve, the FDIC, and the OCC stepped in to quell the run, with the FDIC purchasing the bank's problem loans, and assuming its debts, giving all creditors protection. This new FSM doctrine was used to bail out failing banks in Texas and the Northeast in the latter half of the 1980s.

The elimination of many high risk banks and the tightening of regulatory standards virtually eliminated all bank failures by the mid-1990s. At the same time, the collapse of the financial intermediaries provoked a dismantling of much of the New Deal regulatory regime. To ensure that banking services did not vanish in the wake of numerous failures, states and the federal government eased the long-standing rules on branching, culminating in the granting of full nationwide branching in 1997. The barriers to universal banking also fell; and in 1999 the Gramm-Leach Bliley Act permitted holding companies to combine commercial banking, investment banking, and insurance.

The Evolution of the Financial Stability Mandate   473

Although capital requirements had been raised in 1981, a major change in how federal supervisors approached implementation was made in 1991 with the passage of the Federal Deposit Insurance Corporation Improvement Act. Before this act, supervisors had followed the precedent set during the Great Depression and exercised considerable discretion in the examination of banks and forbearance in deciding whether to close a bank or keep it in operation in the hopes that it would recover. The experience of the banking debacle of the 1980s led Congress to shift to a rules-based policy with the 1991 Act. A clear set of rules was created specifying exact remedies that were to be undertaken when capital ratios fell below certain levels, leaving supervisors with much less discretion in the hope that a repeat of the large losses of the 1980s could be avoided.

By the turn of the century, the absence of bank failures gave the impression that the new regulatory and supervisory strictures, coupled with the formation of larger more diversified banks, had done their job. What was unexpected by most observers was how the change in the supervisory regime would contribute to the next crisis in 2008. Given a rules-based system that, by necessity, depended on accounting definitions, banks would conform and supervisors would be able to demonstrate that it worked. When a bank was found to be deficient in some capital measure, it was forced to meet the rules. Formal compliance was attained, but banks conducted a growing off-balance sheet business, beyond the rules of 1991, embodying higher risks and higher returns to enterprising management. Furthermore, the old problems of "competition in laxity" among the multiplicity of federal and state regulators allowed some bankers to pursue "regulatory arbitrage" and find the weakest set of regulatory constraints. Finally, there had been no change deposit insurance or the doctrine of too-big-to-fail that encouraged moral hazard.

7.5 Canada

Given the system of financial repression, new competition for Canadian banks sprung up on the fringe with the trust and mortgage companies. These fast-growing intermediaries were outside of the supervisory safety net. Although two of these institutions, the Commonwealth Trust Company and the Security Trust Company had failed in 1970 and 1972, there was no change in the supervisory regime. However, as Canada gradually open up to international markets and deregulated its repressed financial system, the sharp recessions of the early 1980s caused twenty-two trust and mortgage companies to fail between 1980 and 1987.

474   *Gianni Toniolo and Eugene N. White*

In response, the Estey Commission conducted an enquiry into these failures, highlighting the need to ensure a sound approach to handling the risks associated with the financial marketplace. In 1987, acting on the commission's recommendations, Parliament passed the Financial Institutions and Deposit Insurance Amendment Act and the Office of the Superintendent of Financial Institutions Act. This legislation created a deposit insurance fund and joined the Department of Insurance and the Office of the Inspector General of Banks to form the Office of the Superintendent of Financial Institutions (OSFI), which was given the powers to supervise and regulate all federally regulated financial institutions, providing a more comprehensive approach to supervision. Yet, a new wave of trust and mortgage company failures occurred in the early 1990s, prompting a new act, the 1996 Bill C-15, which clarified OSFI's prime responsibilities to minimize losses to depositors and shareholders, and to contribute to public confidence in the Canadian financial system. While the OSFI was not given a mandate specifically to prevent failures; it was directed to promote sound business practices to reduce the risk that financial institutions will fail. The mandate stressed the importance of early intervention to achieve OSFI's objectives.

7.6 Colombia

The boom years for Colombia ended with the shutdown of international capital markets in the wake of the Mexican debt crisis of 1982. Economic conditions led to a sharp deterioration in the portfolios of most financial intermediaries that had rapidly expanded during the 1970s. The problem, as in other countries, was that rising inflation was frustrating the government's efforts to direct credit, even as it devised new schemes to channel credit, notably the National Development Plan of 1971. The regulation of interest rates was now the key instrument in development strategy, but the complicated interest rate structure could not guarantee that resources would be allocated to meet targeted goals. New financial intermediaries appeared to compete with those closely controlled by the government. To bring these institutions under government oversight, the Superintendencia Bancaria expanded its operations but strained under the increasingly complex government regulations and limited resources.

A crisis erupted in 1982 when a number of financial institutions tied to the Grupo Colombia, appeared on the brink of collapse. The flight of depositors then led the Superintendencia to take control of the bank. When faced with the insolvency of the Banco del Estado, the government decreed a state of economic emergency on October 8, 1982 and authorized the government to nationalize failing financial institutions, replacing their management and adding to their capital with credits from the Banco de la República. Over the next three years, these powers were increased to handle the massive bad loans in bank portfolios.

In 1985, a deposit insurance fund, the Fondo de Garantías de Instituciones Financieras, was created. Although all banks had to subscribe to the fund, it was supplied with resources from a new windfall in coffee revenues. Instead of closing banks, the Fondo nationalized them by buying their assets for one centavo and replaced their capital. As the banks slowly recovered under government control, the government dismantled the system of financial repression in favor of a liberalized banking system. The Ley 45 of 1990 gave banks a wide range of powers, along the lines of universal banking. The banking sector was opened to foreign competition with Venezuelan banks purchasing many nationalized banks, followed by American, Spanish, Dutch, and German banks. Colombia banks responded with a wave of mergers. At the same time the Superintendencia revised its operations, bringing its approach to supervision more in line with the international norms (White, 1998b).

8 The Internationalization of Bank Regulation

After 1971, central bank cooperation in macroeconomic and monetary issues lost the role it played in upholding the stability of the Bretton Woods system and began to follow *ad hoc*, divergent, regional arrangements. At the same time, after two decades of financial stability, bank failures and financial crises reappeared, bringing regulation and supervision back to the front of the central banks' agenda and made financial stability the focus of central bank cooperation, as capital mobility increased the risk of international contagion of banking crises. This new problem highlighted the inherent tension between the need to find common international ground for prudential regulation, to avoid a race to the bottom in regulatory competition and the fact that legislation remained in the hands of national states. Over the years, tentative solutions consisted in attempts at to develop a system of internationally accepted "soft laws" to be "suggested" for adoption by individual states. Central banks became the main players in this process due to their expertise in a field that most politicians found esoteric and due to the strong links that had been developed among governors over the previous decades (Borio and Toniolo, 2008).

476   *Gianni Toniolo and Eugene N. White*

8.1 The Basel Committee on Bank Supervision (BCSC)

From the late 1950s onward a market emerged in Europe for short-term deposits and credits denominated in a currency different from that of the country in which the deposit-taking and credit-giving bank was located (Schenk, 1998; Battilossi, 2000; Toniolo, 2005). Since most deposits were denominated in dollars, the term Eurodollars was coined. At first central bankers took a benign neglect attitude with respect to the Eurodollar market. In a 1967 meeting of central bank experts, it was declared that "its undesirable side effects could be readily checked by ad hoc measures given the sophistication reached by central bank policies both in the field of domestic cooperation and in domestic matters" (quoted in Toniolo, 2005, p. 461). By the end of the 1960s, however, the Euro-currency market had reached such proportions that central banks began to intervene to control its effects on domestic monetary aggregates.

In 1973–1974, however, two events began to focus the attention of central banks on the unintended effects of capital market liberalization on financial stability. The first was the oil crisis of 1973, which raised the question about "the ability of the international banking system to recycle the flow of funds from oil producers (creditors) to oil importers (debtors). The second was the collapse of Bankhaus Herstatt in June 1974" (Goodhart 2011b, p. 11). The two events raised the issues of the international banking system's efficiency and stability at a time when it was required to perform new crucial functions.

After several decades of relative financial autarky, central bankers and market participants alike faced the difficult process of learning how to operate in a liberalized and more competitive environment and how to price risk. According to Goodhart (2011b, p. 32ff.) the Herstatt crisis acted as a catalyst for revising risk assessment. *The Economist* (3 August 1974) even wondered about a "World banking crisis?" and worried about increasing risk premia particularly for smaller banks and banks from weaker countries. These events led central bankers' to formally establish the Group de Contact as the Basel Committee for Bank Supervision (BCBS) (Goodhart, 2011b).

The creation of the BCBS, which first met in Basel in February 1975, was a landmark episode in the history of bank regulation, making it a key item in the agenda of central bank cooperation. The BCBS included the G-10 governors and Switzerland, with Luxembourg holding a special seat. Membership included officials from the bank supervisory agencies if they were not part of the central bank. The Committee met for two days three or four

The Evolution of the Financial Stability Mandate 477

times a year at the Bank for International Settlement in Basel, which provided support, and the first three BCSB chief secretaries, came from the BIS staff (Goodhart, 2011b, p. 60).

The members of the BCBS regarded themselves as advisors to the central bank governors who had the responsibility of lobbying their domestic constituencies in order to obtain supporting legislation passed by national parliaments. In practice, however, each delegate came to the negotiating table aware of the interests involved and the possible room for maneuver in his or her country. As described by Kapstein (2008), international cooperation within the BCBS could be seen as "two-level game" diplomacy *à la* Putnam (1988) where negotiators must strike deals not only with each other but also with their domestic policy makers, which in their turn must keep into account the relevant interests involved. Given the large number of countries involved, some of them with more than one regulatory agency, the domestic interests concerned, and each country's idiosyncratic law-making process, one may wonder how the BCSC produced any significant cooperation in the two decades, up to the Basel II agreement. Two factors are likely to have contributed to its success in this period. The first is that not all the international players were of equal importance. The banking systems of the United States, and the United Kingdom were larger and more global; and when these two countries acted in concert, they could exercise a leadership role to manage the international part of the two-level game. The second factor for the success of the BSCS is to be found in the highly technical nature of the discussion and the familiarity of the committee members both with each other and with the matters at hand. Over time, BSCS members got to know each other well, both personally and in terms of their domestic concerns, making it easier to reach common resolutions. Even so, given the enormous macroeconomic, political and institutional challenges to cooperation, the results achieved in the 1970s and 1980s "took many observers by surprise" (Kapstein, 2008, p. 126).

8.2 From the Concordat to Basel I

At its first meeting in February 1975, the BCBS selected four topics for future study and consideration: (i) the relation between banks and foreign exchange brokers, (ii) the responsibility for supervision of banks' overseas branches, subsidiaries and joint ventures, (iii) the support and rescue operations, and (iv) the definition of capital and its role (Goodhart, 2011b, pp. 96–97). In the following years, the issue of cross border supervision and balance sheet consolidation, came to the fore, leading to the so-called Concordat, the first milestone in regulatory cooperation.

In the late 1970s the BCBS worked on improving the rules for the supervision of cross-border banks. These rules were eventually merged into a single code under the name of Concordat. According to Goodhart (2011b, p. 102), "the (Concordat) title first surfaces in the archives of the BCBS in late 1979 ... it was coined ... to indicate a set of understandings between sovereign parties, but without being based on a common legal authority or being legally binding." This framework would later be known as "soft law."

The crisis of Banco Ambrosiano in 1982 and so-called "Bank of Credit and Commerce International (BCCI) affair" in 1991 led to discussions within the BSBC about the need to revise of the Concordat. The two cases posed a key question of how to supervise a non-bank holding company, registered in Luxembourg, controlling international affiliates in several countries. After surveying the national supervisory authorities, the BSBC issued *Minimum standards for the supervision of international banking groups and their cross-border establishments* in May 1992 (Goodhart, 2010), which was distributed to supervisory agencies in BCBS member and non-member countries. Based on this reports findings, the Concordat was eventually revised. Goodhart (2011b, p. 113) summarized the accomplishment: "The continuing exercise of the Concordat showed the work of the BCSC to best advantage. The basic principles involved, that every banking establishment should be supervised and that parental (home) should do so on the basis of consolidated accounts, were largely uncontroversial and incontrovertible. What was needed was attention to detail, patient negotiation, and advocacy at high level. The BCBS had these qualities."

If two relatively minor bank failures led to the definition of principles for the supervision of international banks, the first "systemic crisis" of the postwar re-focused the attention of regulators on "the international financial architecture." The crisis came to a head in August 1982 when Mexico declared it was unable to service its debt, mostly owned to North American banks. Contagion affected most Latin American countries and threatened the very survival of some large U.S. intermediaries. When the Mexican debt crisis erupted, the BCBS had been bogged down in the discussion of measures and criteria for capital adequacy; but now . The pace of decision-making was accelerated.(Goodhart, 2010, p. 154) This development took a dramatic turn when U.S. president Reagan asked the Congress for additional IMF funding to provide liquidity to distressed Latin American

The Evolution of the Financial Stability Mandate   479

economies, thereby indirectly supporting U.S. banks, some of which were close to bankruptcy, Congress asked for capital ratios to be raised unilaterally. The banking community voiced its fears that such measures would put the industry at competitive disadvantage vis-à-vis foreign banks. To maintain level international playing field, Paul Volker flew to Basel in 1984 on a mission to revive negotiations about capital adequacy. Reaching an agreement, however, proved to be difficult as both measures and standards of capital adequacy reflected the peculiarities of each country's financial systems, and accounting practices (Kapstein, 2008, p. 131). For another three years it seemed that agreement would be impossible to make. The standstill was broken in 1987 when the United States and the United Kingdom announced a bilateral agreement on bank capital adequacy, threatening lesser players with being marginalized. In December 1987, the BCBS announced an agreement on a proposal for international convergence of capital measures and standards, which came to be known as the Basel Accord (later nicknamed Basel I).

8.3 Basel II

The Basel Accord was received with scathing criticism. Most commentators charged that the "Accord's approach to risk management was too crude and hardly reflected best practices" already adopted by the leading money centers (Kapstein, 2008, p. 132). Critics from the private sector argued that it would lead to a credit crunch, a charge repeated thereafter against every measures aimed at increasing banks' capital. A number of scholars argued that, contrary to its stated objectives, the Basel Accord and its subsequent revisions would have a pro-cyclical impact, increasing systemic risks, as intermediaries would move along the risk/return line in order to compensate for higher capital requirements (Friedman and Kraus, 2011). Even though other scholars held the opposite opinion (Aghion and Kharroubu, 2013), there were urgent callas for revision.

By the early 1990s, controls on capital movement, steadily reduced in the 1980s, had almost entirely disappeared in the developed market economies and global credit expansion followed. Both Western intermediaries and regulators felt increasingly confident about their risk management techniques. Soon, however, the second Mexican crisis (1995) and the ensuing contagion focused attention on the global risks posed by the banking systems of emerging markets. In response, the BCBS drafted an agreement in 1997 called *Core Principles for Effective Banking Supervision*. The *Core Principles* "were designed as a model for banking supervision

480   *Gianni Toniolo and Eugene N. White*

regardless of the specifics of individual banking systems" (Borio and Toniolo, 2008). In subsequent years, they were adopted by a large number of supervisors worldwide. The Asian crisis provided a new stimulus to review and strengthen the Basel principles and their dissemination. The result was the June 2004, the BCBS agreement on *International Convergence of Capital Measurement and Capital Standards. A Revised Framework*, better known in short as Basel II (BCBS, 2004). Designed to rein in bank risks in both advanced and emerging economies, Basel II was based on three pillars: (i) Minimum capital requirements, (ii) Supervisory review process, and (iii) Market Discipline.

8.4 The European Banking Union

At the time of finalizing this survey, a European Banking Union (EBU) transferring regulatory and supervisory authority from member states to the European Union was in the process of formation. As in most of the cases discussed in this chapter, it was a financial crisis that exposed the need for changes in the existing national banking regimes and created the political conditions for their implementation.[16] When the financial crisis that started in 2008 turned into a sovereign debt crisis in 2010, it revealed a link between the stability of each member country's banking system and the market's assessment of their government's default probability. This situation has led to a partial "re-nationalization" of the national banking systems within the Eurozone, with banks of one country unwilling to lend to those of another, undermining the financial foundations of the European Union's single market. Many observers attached a high probability to the end of the euro. The crisis also exposed some weaknesses of the European Central Bank's position that "surprised many observers with its large purchase of the debt of distressed governments" (Eichengreen, et al., 2011, p. 48). Soon, it was realized that emergency measures were no substitute for structural reforms to correct the weaknesses of the original design of the European Monetary Union.

To complete the EU's economic and monetary union, the European Council initiated a European banking union (EBU) in June 2012. Next, in October 2012, the Council decided to create a Single Supervisory

---

[16] The role of the crisis in shaping the new rules was officially acknowledged: "Since the crisis started in 2008, the European Commission has worked hard to learn all the lessons from the crisis and create a safer and sounder financial sector (...) so that future taxpayers will not foot the bill when banks make mistakes" (European Commission, 2014)

The Evolution of the Financial Stability Mandate 481

Mechanism, with federal supervisory authority entrusted to the European Central Bank (Barucci and Messori, 2014). The Banking Union also included a Single Recovery and Resolution Mechanism and the Single Deposit Guarantee Scheme. Because of the complexity of the issues and the cumbersome EU decision-making process, details are still being hammered out in 2014–2015; but the creation of a banking union has proceeded relatively swiftly, reflecting the perception that the crisis threatened the survival of the monetary union.

The transfer and allocation of supervisory authority to the ECB has focused on three issues: (1) the division of responsibilities between the ECB and the national supervisory bodies, (2) the possible conflict of interest within the ECB between its monetary and regulatory tasks, and (3) the problem that arises from the EU Treaties that make the ECB's decisions binding on members of the monetary union but not countries outside of the monetary union, even though all EU states participate in the single market.

For supervision, a formula has been devised that allocates 130 of the largest banks to the ECB, leaving the smaller ones to national authorities. In addition, the ECB has been granted discretionary authority to request oversight of any additional bank. Erection of a federalized system of bank supervision, poses potential problems for the EU, as evidenced in our narrative by the historical experience of the United States and to a lesser degree Canada, where competition in laxity between regulators and regulatory arbitrage has weakened the effectiveness of regulation and supervision (Nieto and White, 2013). Whether the added discretionary authority of the ECB and other features can overcome the dangers inherent when there are plural supervisors will only be adequately tested by the next crisis.

The debate on the pros and cons of conferring supervisory powers on a central bank resurfaced in the creation of the EBU, although the ECB's Statute had already granted it the power to "perform specific tasks concerning policies relating to prudential supervision of credit institutions."[17] Those in favor of allocating supervisory authority to a central bank believe that it is essential for a central bank's LOLR function to have the fullest possible access to financial intermediaries' private information that is gathered by supervision. Those in favor of separating supervision from the monetary authority are concerned that a combination creates a conflict of interest where supervision may be compromised in the interests of

---

[17] Art. 22.2 of the ECB Statute

monetary policy or vice versa (Zingales, 2009; Bini Smaghi, 2014).[18] Recognizing this potential problem, the Supervisory Board was made largely but not entirely independent of the ECB's Governing Council, its policy making body. Again it is too early to say whether this arrangement will mitigate of the conflict of interest when monetary and supervisory authorities are combined.

The problem arising from the presence of monetary union member and non-member countries within the EU was addressed by making membership in the EBU compulsory for nations using the euro. Membership remains voluntary for countries in the EU but outside of the monetary union. However, the Banking Union's effectiveness may be seriously undermined as the UK, home to the largest financial center and a number of systemically important intermediaries, will almost certainly not join the EBU.

In December 2013, EU finance ministers "laid out a blueprint for a new agency backed by a 55 billion-euro industry-financed resolution fund," (Blumberg, 2014) that would hand most decisions on resolution to a board of EU authorities and national representatives. However, by the end of 2014, a final decision had not yet been taken on the details of the Single Resolution Mechanism (the central authority for resolving failing intermediaries). The thorny issue of a bail-in of failing financial institutions–how losses should be borne by shareholders, bond holders, and possibly depositors, rather than taxpayers has not been resolved. Bail-in provisions represent, in part, a return to solutions of previous banking regimes, notably double or extended shareholder liability, for the resolution of bank failures. While the post-crisis political climate favors large bail-in provisions, this approach may not be the most effective way of fighting a systemic crisis, as was evidenced in the 1930s.

Unsurprisingly, the creation of a EBU is proving a complex technical, legal and political undertaking reflecting not only the magnitude of the institutional overhaul for the European Union but also the need to devise solutions for many of the same problems that institution builders struggled with in previous eras.

9 Conclusion

The histories of supervision in our six countries highlight patterns that are likely to be common in other European and New World countries.

---

[18] Ioannidou (2005) provides empirical evidence of how the Federal Reserve's supervision of banks was compromised in comparison with the FDIC and the OCC.

The Evolution of the Financial Stability Mandate   483

We observe the following evolution of supervision. Before World War I, the FSM was understood to protect the convertibility of banknotes into coin, anchored by a gold or bimetallic standard, requiring clearly delineated rules governing the issue of currency. The underlying assumption was that currency stability would also guarantee financial stability. In our three European countries that restricted and later monopolized the issue of bank notes, supervision was conducted directly, with parliaments setting the rules and the executive branch of government and/or parliament, monitoring of issuing banks. Typically in the New World, where there was a competitive note issue, two outcomes were observed. In Canada where large branching banks were encouraged and a concentrated banking industry developed, supervision could be managed by cooperation among the small number of banks, with modest direct government oversight and no central bank. In the United States, where regulation spawned a fragmented system of unit banks, independent agencies were delegated the task of supervision, complicated by a federal political system that created multiple agencies. Although Colombia began with competitive banks of issue, the need of the state to control seigniorage in a highly unstable political environment led it move to the European model.

By the end of the nineteenth century, all countries had defined their FSM; but the strict rules governing bank note issue contributed to the growth of deposit banking, leaving a key component of the means of payment potentially unstable. This problem was further complicated by mergers, branching, and financial diversification that created "systemically important banks" – SIFIs – in Europe and Canada whose insolvency could threaten the broader banking and financial system. These issues were first addressed by the execution of the FSM in extraordinary times by expanding the LOLR function as defined by Bagehot to include the rescue of insolvent SIFIs in Europe before 1913 and Canada afterwards. These countries were grappling with a perennial dilemma: how to maintain a competitive market-driven banking system and prevent large failures from disrupting the payments and settlements system without engendering moral hazard. However, in ordinary times, there were only modest or minimal changes in supervision, as there was resistance to an expansion of the FSM.

The enhanced role of governments in the economy during World War I brought central banks and governments into closer cooperation, with the former subordinated to the latter. The Great Depression and World War II forced the financial system to accept the government's direction of financial flows and the government to accept the need to prop up the financial system when subjected to large systemic shocks. Laws introducing stringent anti-competitive regulatory and supervisory regimes were introduced in every country, together with administrative controls on capital movements. The end result of the new regulatory regimes was financial repression in all countries and an extension of the FSM to the protection of established banks and other financial institutions from failure. Supervision shifted from rules-based to discretion-based systems that accommodated financial repression. Under such a broad FSM, banking systems enjoyed systemic stability.

Beginning in the 1970s, the end to international capital controls and the slow and partial dismantling of national systems of financial repression led to a growing series of bank failures, arising primarily from new financial institutions competing in the unregulated "fringe" of banking. Deregulation driven by increasing international competition in banking, demands to finance growth and a growing consensus on the market's intrinsic stability, created incentives to take risk by the established banks and their competitors in the 1980s. The failure of discretion-based supervision, in some countries, and more widespread forbearance, led to the adoption of a more rules-based supervision again with new or expanded agencies inside and outside of central banks. The globalization of finance, with the diffusion of cross-country banking, exposed the inconsistency of home-based regulation and supervision and the dangers of a regulatory race to the bottom. The Basel Accords represented an attempt at international coordination of the domestic drives to ramp up regulation and supervision of market-based banking by promoting "soft laws" aimed at producing a level field regulatory environment.

The problems we face after the Crisis of 2008 are, in general terms, no different than the problems faced at the beginning of the twentieth century. In extraordinary times, liquidity must be provided during a crisis and an orderly process established for liquidating (resolving) failed SIFIs without bailing them out; while in ordinary times, the FSM and the institutions that receive the mandate must be credibly defined to protect the means of payment and settlement and ensure they grow and evolve to support the economy's financing needs. Now as in the past, the transition from extraordinary to ordinary circumstances is a complex process requiring discretion.

From the long-run perspective of our selected six countries, we saw that problems arose when supervision was bent to serve allocative policies. We also observed that supervision can support regulation but it cannot fix a flawed structure that requires reform to keep pace with financial

The Evolution of the Financial Stability Mandate 485

innovation of the payments and settlement system. Financial innovation regularly moves ahead of regulatory updating so that supervision cannot be simply rules-based and must have a discretionary component, especially for treating large systemically important financial institutions. Nevertheless, there is an important balance to be achieved, as excessive reliance on supervisory discretion often leads to inappropriate forbearance. Independent supervisory agencies were created for competitive financial systems where transparent rules-based supervision was established. However, when competition was limited by market developments or efforts of the state to channel the flow of funds, supervision was given to the central bank, with less transparency and more discretion being exercised. Our case studies reveal that most supervisory regimes successfully managed financial systems in ordinary times, sometimes preventing a troubled institution from generating a systemic crisis, but were less capable of dealing with extraordinary macro-systemic shocks, which they were not designed to confront. When macro-systemic shocks overwhelmed supervisors' capacity to meet the FSM, the shocks led to regulatory/supervisory regime shifts that primarily addressed past deficiencies, rather than focusing on reforms to ensure the stability of a continually innovating financial system.

References

Aghion, Philippe and Enisse Kharroub (2013) "Cyclical Macroeconomic Policy, Financial Regulation and Economic Growth," BIS Working Paper No. 434.

Aldrich, Nelson (1910) *Interviews on the Banking and Currency Systems of England, Scotland, France, Germany, Switzerland and Italy* Washington, D.C.: National Monetary Commission.

Allen, Arthur M., Sidney R. Cope, Leslie J. H. Dark, and Henry J. Witheridge (1938) *Commercial Banking Legislation and Control* London: Macmillan and Co.

Alfredo, Gigliobianco, Claire Giordano, and Gianni Toniolo (2009) "Innovation and Regulation in the wake of Financial Crises in Italy (1880s–1930s)," in A. Gigliobianco and G. Toniolo (eds.) *Financial Market Regulation after Financial Crises: The Historical Experience* Roma: Banca d'Italia, pp. 45–74.

Bagehot, Walter (1873) *Lombard Street: A Description of the Money Market* London: H.S. King.

Banca d'Italia (1908) *Adunanza generale ordinaria degli azionisti* Banca d'Italia: Roma.

Bank of England (2013) "The Strategy for the Bank's Financial Stability Mission, 2013–2014" www.bankofengland.co.uk/about/Documents/strategy1314.pdf.

Banque de France (2004) "The Commission Bancaire," Fact Sheet No. 132, December.

Barbiellini Amidei Federico, Alfredo Gigliobianco, and Claire Giordano (2012) "Credit Policy and Economic Development in Post-WWII Italy," in H. Bonin, N. V. Haueter, A. Gigliobianco, and H. James (eds.) *Public Policies and the Direction on Financial Flows. Studies in Banking and Financial History* Bucarest: EABH.

486   *Gianni Toniolo and Eugene N. White*

Barbiellini, Amidei, Federico Giordano, and Claire Giordano (2012) "Regulatory Responses to the 'Roots of all Evil': The Re-shaping of the Bank-industry-Financial Market Interlock in the U.S. Glass-Steagall and the Italian 1936 Banking Acts," Banca d'Italia (mimeo).

Barnett, George E. (1911) *State Banks and Trust Companies Since the Passage of the National-Bank Act* Washington, D.C.: National Monetary Commission, Government Printing Office.

Barucci, Emilio and Marcello Messori (eds.) (2014) *Towards the European Banking Union. Achievements and Open Problems* Bagno a Ripoli: Passigli.

Battilossi, Stefano (2000) "Financial Innovation and the Gold Ages of International Banking: 1890–1931 and 1958–81," *Financial History Review* 7:2 (October), pp. 141–176.

Beckhart, B. H. and H. P. Willis (1929) *Foreign Banking Systems* New York: H. Holt and Company.

(1933) Report of the Royal Commission (Macmillan Commission), *Banking and Currency in Canada* Ottawa: J.O. Patenaude.

Bernanke, Ben S. (2013) "A Century of US Central Banking: Goals, Frameworks, Accountability," *Journal of Economic Perspectives* 27:4 (Fall), pp. 3–16.

Bertrand, Marianne, Antoinnette Schoar, and David Thesmar (2007) "Banking Deregulation and Industry Structure: Evidence from the French Banking Reforms of 1985," *Journal of Finance* 62:2 (April), pp. 597–628.

Bignon, Vincent, Marc Flandreau, and Stefano Ugolini (2012) "Bagehot for beginners: The Making of Lender-of-Last Resort Operations in the Mid-Nineteenth Century," *Economic History Review* 65:2, pp. 580–608.

Blancheton, Bertrand (2014)"Les improvisations financières de la guerre de 1914–1918 en France. Les enjeux de la liquidité," Cahiers du GREThA, (January) No. 2014-03.

Blinder, Alan S. (2010) "How Central Should the Central Bank Be," *Journal of Economic Literature* 48:1 (March), pp. 123–133.

Blumberg (2014), *Europe's Banking Union* (October 28), www.bloombergview.com/quicktake/europes-banking-union.

Bodenhorn, Howard (1993) "Small Denomination Banknotes in Antebellum," *America Journal of Money Credit and Banking* 25:4 (November), pp. 812–827.

Bonelli, Franco (1971) *La crisi del 1907. Una tappa dello sviluppo economico italiano* Torino: Fondazione Einaudi.

(1991) *La Banca d'Italia dal 1894 al 1913. Momenti della formazione di una banca centrale* Laterza: Roma-Bari.

Bordo, Michael D. and Angela Redish (1987) "Why Did the Bank of Canada Emerge in 1935?" *Journal of Economic History* 47, pp. 405–417.

Bordo, Michael D. and Anna J. Schwartz (1995) "The Performance and Stability of Banking Systems Under 'Self-Regulation': Theory and Evidence," *Cato Journal* 14:3 (Winter), pp. 453–479.

Bordo, Michael D. and David C. Wheelock (1998) "Price Stability and Financial Stability: The Historical Record," *Federal Reserve Bank of St.Louis Review* 80:5 (September), pp. 41–62.

Bordo, Michael D., Angela Redish and Hugh Rockoff (2011) "Why Didn't Canada Have a Banking Crisis in 2008 (or in 1930, or 1907, or...)?" NBER Working Paper 17312.

Borio, Claudio (2011) "Implementing a Macroprudential Framework: Blending Boldness and Realism," *Capitalism and Society* 6:1 (August), pp. 1–23.

Borio, Claudio and Gianni Toniolo (2008) "One Hundred and Thirty Years of Central Bank Cooperation: A BIS Perspective," in Borio Claudio, Piet Clement, Gianni Toniolo (eds.) *Past and Future of Central Bank Cooperation* Cambridge: Cambridge University Press, pp.16–76.

Bouvier, Jean (1988) "The Banque de France and the State from 1850 to the Present Day," in Toniolo, Gianni (ed.) *Central Banks' Independence in Historical Perspective* New York: De Gruyter, pp. 73–104.

Bowden, Sue and David M. Higgins (2004) "British Industry in the Interwar Years," in Roderick Floud and Paul Johnson (eds.) *The Cambridge Economic History of Modern Britain* Cambridge: Cambridge University Press, pp. 374–402.

Broadberry, Stephen and Peter Howlett (2005) "The United Kingdom during World War I: Business as Usual?," in Stephen Broadberry and Mark Harrison (eds.) *The Economics of World War I* Cambridge: Cambridge University Press, pp. 206–234.

Brown, William Arthur (1940) *The International Gold Standard Reinterpreted 1914–34* Cambridge: National Bureau of Economic Research.

Burgess, W. Randolph (1927) *The Reserve Banks and the Money Market* New York: Harper & Brothers.

Calomiris, C. W. (1990) "Is Deposit Insurance Necessary? A Historical Perspective," *Journal of Economic History* 50:2 (June), pp. 283–296.

Calomiris, C. W. and G. Gorton (1991) "The Origins of Banking Panics: Models, Facts and Bank Legislation," in Hubbard, R.G. (ed.) *Financial Markets and Financial Crises* Chicago: University of Chicago Press.

Calomiris, C. W. and E. N. White (1994) "The Origins of Federal Deposit Insurance," in Claudia Goldin and Gary D. Libecap (eds.) *The Regulated Economy: A Historical Approach to Political Economy* Chicago: Chicago University Press.

Capie, Forrest (2010) *The Bank of England, 1950s to 1979* Cambridge: Cambridge University Press.

Cardarelli, Sergio (2009) "Il ruolo degli istituti di emissione nella concezione crispina," in Aldo G. Ricci and Luisa Montevecchi (eds.) *Francesco Crispi. Costruire lo Stato per dare forma alla Nazione*," Atti del convegno tenuto all'Archivio Centrale dello Stato il 27 novembre 2001 nel centanario della morte di Crispi, Mibac: Roma.

Carr, Jack, Frank Mathewson, and Neil Quigley (1995) "Stability in the Absence of Deposit Insurance: The Canadian Banking System, 1890–1966," *Journal of Money Credit and Banking*, 27:4 (November), Part 1, pp. 11337–11158.

Cesarano, Francesco, Giulio Cifarelli, and Gianni Toniolo (2012) "Exchange Rate Regimes and Reserve Policy: The Italian Lira 1883–1911," *Open Economies Review*, 23:2, pp. 253–275.

Clapham, J. H. (1966) *The Bank of England: A History* Cambridge: Cambridge University Press.

Cotula, Franco ed., (2000) *Stabilità e sviluppo negli anni Cinquanta. Politica bancaria e struttura del sistema finanziario* Roma-Bari: Laterza.

Dunbar, Charles F. (1929) *The Theory and History of Banking* New York: Knickerbocker, 5th Revised Edition.

The Economist (3 August 1974).

Eichengreen, Barry, Robert Feldman, Jeffrey Liebman, Jurgen von Hagen, and Charles Wyplocz (2011), *Public Debt: Nuts, Bolts and Worries* International Center for Monetary and Banking Studies – CEPR: Geneva and London.

European Central Bank (2014) "What is Financial Stability," www.ecb.int/pub/fsr/html/index.en.html.

European Commission (2014) *Banking Union: Restoring Financial Stability in the Eurozone* Memo (Brussels).

Feinstein, Charles H., Peter Temin and Gianni Toniolo (2008) *The World Economy between the Wars* Oxford: Oxford University Press.

Feldstein, Martin (2010) "What Powers for the Federal Reserve?," *Journal of Economic Literature* 48:1 (March), pp. 134–145.

Fenstermaker, J. V. and J. E. Filer (1986) "Impact of the First and Second Banks of the United States and the Suffolk System on New England Bank Money 1791–1837," *Journal of Money Credit and Banking* 18:1 (February), pp. 28–40.

Fernandez-Bollo, Édouard (2013) "Structural Reform and Supervision of the Banking Sector in France," *OCED Journal: Finance Market Trends* 2:1, pp. 31–38

Forsyth, Douglas and Ton Iotermans eds., (1997) *Regime Changes: Macroeonomic Policy and Financial Regulation in Europe from the 1930s to the 1990s* Providence, RI: Berghahn Books.

Freedeman, Charles (1993) *The Triumph of Corporate Capitalism in France, 1867–1914* Rochester: University of Rochester Press.

Friedman, Jeffrey and Wladimir Kraus (2011), *Engineering the Financial Crisis: Systemic Risk and the Failure of Regulation* Philadelphia: University of Pennsylvania Press.

Friedman, Milton and Anna J. Schwartz (1963) *A Monetary History of the United States, 1863–1960* Princeton: Princeton University Press.

Galanti, Enrico, Raffaele D'Ambriosio and Alessandro V. Guccione (2012) *Storia della legislazilazione bancaria, finanziaria e assicurativa dall'Unità d'Italia al 2011* Marsilio: Venezia.

Galassi, Francesco and Mark Harrison (2005)"Italy at War, 1915–1918," in Stephen Broadberry and Mark Harrison (eds.) *The Economics of World War I* Cambridge: Cambridge University Press, pp. 276–309.

Gigliobianco, Alfredo, Claire Giordano, and Gianni Toniolo (2009) "Innovation and Regulation in the wake of Financial Crises in Italy (1880s–1930s)," in A. Gigliobianco and G. Toniolo (eds.) *Financial Market Regulation after Financial Crises: The Historical Experience* Rome: Banca d'Italia, pp. 45–74.

Golembe, Carter H. (1960) "Deposit Insurance Legislation of 1933: An Examination of Its Antecedents and Its Purposes," *Political Science Quarterly* 75:2(June), pp. 181–200.

Golembe, Carter H. and Clark Warburton (1958) "Insurance of Bank Obligations in Six States During the Period, 1829–1866," (Washington, D.C.: Federal Deposit Insurance Corporation.

Goodfriend, Marvin and Robert King (1988) "Financial Deregulation, Monetary Policy, and Central Banking," Federal Reserve Bank of Richmond Working Paper 88-01.

Goodhart, Charles (1985)*The Evolution of Central Banks. A Natural Development?* London: The London School of Economics STICERD.

(2010) "How Should We Regulate Bank Capital and Financial Products? What Role for Living Wills?" *Revista de Economia Institucional*, 12:23, pp. 85–109.

The Evolution of the Financial Stability Mandate 489

(2011a) "The Changing Role of Central Banks," *Financial History Review*, 18:2 (August), pp. 135–154.

(2011b) *The Basel Committee on Banking Supervision: a history of the early years, 1974–1997* Cambridge University Press, Cambridge

Grossman, Richard S. (2001) "Double Liability and Bank Risk Taking," *Journal of Money, Credit and Banking* 33:2, Part I (May), pp. 143–159.

(2007) "Fear and Greed: The Evolution of Double Liability in American Banking, 1865–1930," *Explorations in Economic History* 44:1 (January), pp. 59–80.

(2010) *Unsettled Account: The Evolution of Banking in the Industrialized World Since 1800* Princeton: Princeton University Press.

Guarino, Giuseppe, Gianni Toniolo, (1993) *La Banca d'Italia e il Sistema Bancario, 1919–1936* Roma-Bari: Laterza.

Hannah, Leslie (1983) *The Rise of the Corporate Economy* London: Methuen.

Hautcoeur, Pierre-Cyrille, Angelo Riva, and Eugene N. White (2014) "Floating a Lifeboat: The Banque de France and the Crisis of 1889," *Journal of Monetary Economics* 65(July).

Hogdman, Donald (1973) *Credit Controls in Western Europe: An Evaluative Review* Boston: Federal Reserve Bank of Boston.

Horn, Martin (2002) *Britain, France and the Financing of the First World War* Montreal and Kingston: McGill-Queen's University Press.

Ioannidou, Vasso, P. (2005)"Does Monetary Policy Affect the Central Bank's Role in Bank Supervision," *Journal of Financial Intermediation* 14:1 (January), pp. 58–85.

Jarmeski, Matthew and Kris James Mitchener (2014) "The Evolution of Bank Supervision: Evidence from U.S. States," NBER Working Paper 20603.

Kapstein, Ethan B. (2008), "Architects of Stability? International Cooperation among Financial Supervisors" in Borio Claudio, Piet Clement and Gianni Toniolo (eds.) *Past and Future of Central Bank Cooperation* Cambridge: Cambridge University Press, pp.113–152

Kryzanowski, Lawrence and Gordon S. Roberts (1993) "Canadian Banking Solvency, 1922–1940," *Journal of Money Credit and Banking* 25:3 (August), pp. 361–376.

(1999) "Perspectives on Canadian Bank Insolvency During the 1930s," *Journal of Money Credit and Banking* 31:1 (February), pp. 130–136.

Leclercq, Yves (2010) *La Banque supérieure: La Banque de France de 1800 à 1914* Paris: Editions Classiques Garnier.

Lescure, Michel (1995) "Banking in France in the Inter-war Period," in Charles Feinstein (ed.) *Banking Currency and Finance in Europe Between the Wars* Oxford: Oxford University Press, pp. 314–336.

Lorenzo, Bini Smaghi (2014) "Monetary Policy and Supervision: Moral Hazard and Conflicts of Interest?," in E. Barucci and M. Messori (eds.) *Towards the European Banking Union. Achievements and Open Problems* Bagno a Ripoli: Passigli, pp. 55–61.

Luzzatto, Gino (1963) *L'Economia Italiana dal 1861 al 1914* Milano: Banca Commerciale Italiana.

Melitz, Jacques (1982) "The French financial system: Mechanisms and Questions of Reform," Annales de l'INSEE No. 47–48 (July–December), pp. 361–387.

Mishkin, Frederic S. and Eugene N. White (2014) "Unprecedented Actions: The Federal Reserve's Response to the Global Financial Crisis in Historical Perspective," NBER Working Paper No. 20737, (December).

Monnet, Eric (2012)"Politique monétaire et politique du credit en France pendant les Trente Glorieuses, 1945–1973, (PhD thesis, Ecole des Hautes Etudes en Sciences Sociales, Paris School of Economics).

(2013) "Financing a Planned Economy, Institutions and Credit Allocation in the French Golden Age of Growth (1954–1974), (Berkeley Economic History working paper No. 2).

(2014) "Monetary Policy with Interest Rates: Evidence from France's Gold Age (1948–1973) Using a Narrative Approach," *American Economic Journal: Macroeconomics* 6:4, pp. 137–169.

Morgenson, Gretchen (2014) (January 12), "Bailout Risk, Far Beyond The Banks," *New York Times*.

Negri, Guglielmo (1989), *Giolitti e la nascita della Banca d'Italia* Roma-Bari: Laterza.

Nieto, Maria J. and Eugene N. White (2013) "Will Bank Supervision in Ohio and Austria Be Similar? A Transatlantic View of the Single Supervisory Mechanism." (March 22) www.voxeu.org.

Nitti, Gian Paolo and Ernesto Rossi (1968) *Banche, Governo e Parlamento negli stati Sardi. Fonti documentarie (1843–1861)*, Vol. II Torino: Fondazione Einaudi,

Norges Bank (2014) "Mandate and Core Responsibilities," www.norges-bank.no/en/about/mandate-and-core-responsibilities/.

Occhino, F., K. Oosterlinck, and E. N. White (2008) "How Much Can a Victor Force the Vanquished to Pay? France Under the Nazi Boot," *Journal of Economic History* 68:1 (March), pp. 1–45.

Padoa-Schioppa, Tommaso and Fabrizio Saccomanni (1994) "Managing a Market-Led Global Financial System," in Peter Kenen (ed.) *Managing the World Economy: Fifty Years after Bretton Woods* Washington, D.C.: Peterson Institute, pp. 235–268.

Perkins, Edwin J. (1994) *American Public Finance and Financial Services, 1700–1815* Columbus: Ohio State University.

Plihon, Dominique (1995) "L'Évolution de l'Intermédiation Bancaire (1950–1993)," Bulletin de la Banque de France No. 21 (Septembre), pp. 131–159.

Polsi, Alessandro (2001) *Stato e Banca Centrale in Italia. Il governo della moneta e del sistema bancario dall'Ottocento a oggi* Roma-Bari: Laterza.

Reis, Ricardo (2013) "Central Bank Design," *Journal of Economic Perspectives* 27:4 (Fall), pp. 17–44.

Robertson, Ross M. (1968, 1995) *The Comptroller and Bank Supervision: A Historical Appraisal* Washington, D.C.: Office of the Comptroller of the Currency.

Rockoff, Hugh (1975) "Varieties of Banking and Regional Development in the United States, 1840–1860," *Journal of Economic History* 35:1, pp. 160–181.

Rolnick, Arthur J. and Warren E. Weber (1983) "New Evidence on the Free Banking Era," *American Economic Review* 73:5 (December), pp. 1080–1091.

Rolnick, Arthur J., Bruce D. Smith, and Warren E. Weber (2000) "The Suffolk Bank and the Panic of 1837," *Federal Reserve Bank of Minneapolis Quarterly Review* 24:2, pp. 3–13.

The Evolution of the Financial Stability Mandate 491

Royal Commission (Macmillan Commission) (1933) *Report: Banking and Currency in Canada* Ottawa: J.O. Patenaude.

Sayers, Richard S. (1958) *Central Banking after Bagehot* Oxford: Oxford University Press.

(1976) *The Bank of England 1891–1944* Cambridge: Cambridge University Press.

Schenk, Catherine R. (1998) *The Origins of the Eurodollar Market in London, 1955–1963* Amsterdam: Elsevier.

Schwartz, Anna J. (1947) "The Beginning of Competitive Banking in Philadelphia, 1782–1890," *Journal of Political Economy* 55:5 (October), pp. 417–431.

Schwartz, Anna J. (1987) "Real and Pseudo-Financial Crises," in Anna J. Schwartz, Michael D. Bordo, and Milton Friedman (eds.) *Money in Historical Perspective* Chicago: Chicago University Press.

Silber, William (2008) *When Washington Shut Down Wall Street: The Great Financial Crisis of 1914 and the Origins of America's Monetary Supremacy* Princeton: Princeton University Press.

(2009) "Why did FDR's Bank Holiday Succeed?" *Economic Policy Review* 15:1 (July), pp. 19–30.

Smith, Adam (1776, 2008) *The Wealth of Nations* Oxford: Oxford University Press.

Swiss National Bank (2014) "Financial Stability: The SNB Mandate," www.snb.ch/en/iabout/finstab.

Sylla, Richard (1998) "U.S. Securities Markets and the Banking System, 1790–1840," Federal Reserve Bank of St. Louis Review (May/June), pp. 83–98.

Thornton, H. (1802) *An Enquiry into the Nature and Effects of the Paper Credit of Great Britain*, Edited by F. A. Hayek. Fairfield: August M. Kelley.

Toniolo, Gianni (1989) *La Banca d'Italia e l'economia di guerra, 1914–1919*, Laterza: Roma-Bari.

(1990) *An Economic History of Liberal Italy, 1850–1918* London: Routledge.

(1995) "Italian Banking, 1919–1939," in Feinstein Charles (ed.) *Banking, Currency and Finance in Europe Between the Wars* Clarendon Press: Oxford, pp. 296–314.

(2005) *Central Bank Cooperation at the Bank for International Settlements, 1930–1973* Cambridge: Cambridge University Press.

(2013) "An Overview of Italy's Economic Growth" in ID (ed.) *The Oxford Handbook of the Italian Economy since Unification (2013)* Oxford University Press (dicembre 2012, in via di pubblicazione).

White, Eugene N. (1983) *The Regulation and Reform of the American Banking System, 1900–1929* Princeton: Princeton University Press.

(1992)*The Comptroller and the Transformation of American Banking, 1960–1990* Washington, D.C.: Comptroller of the Currency.

(1998a) "Banking and Finance in the Twentieth Century," in Stanley Engerman and Robert Gallman (eds.) *Cambridge Economic History of the United States* Cambridge: Cambridge University Press.

(1998b) *The Evolution of Banking Regulation in Twentieth Century Colombia* Bogotá: Superintendencia Bancaria.

(2000) "Banking and Finance in the Twentieth Century," in Stanley L. Engerman and Robert E. Gallman (eds.) *The Cambridge Economic History of the United States:*

492   *Gianni Toniolo and Eugene N. White*

The Twentieth Century Vol. 3, Cambridge: Cambridge University Press, pp. 743–802.

(2007) "Legacy of Deposit Insurance: The Growth, Spread, and Cost of Insuring Financial Intermediaries," in Michael D. Bordo, Claudia Goldin, and Eugene N. White (eds.) *The Defining Moment: The Great Depression and the American Economy in the Twentieth Century* Chicago: Chicago University Press, pp. 87–124.

(2011), "Implementing Bagehot's Rule in a World of Derivatives," in Geoffrey Wood, Terence Mills, and Nicolas Crafts (eds.) *Monetary and Banking History: Essays in Honour of Forrest Capie* Oxford: Routledge, pp. 72–87.

(2013) "'To Establish a More Effective Supervision of Banking: How the Birth of the Fed Altered Bank Supervision," in Michael D. Bordo and William Roberds (eds.) *The Origins, History and Future of the Federal Reserve: A Return to Jekyll Island* Cambridge: Cambridge University Press, pp. 7–54.

(2015) "Protecting Financial Stability in the Aftermath of World War I: The Federal Reserve Bank of Atlanta's Dissenting Policy," NBER Working Paper w21341.

White, Lawrence J. (2009) "The Role of Capital and Leverage in the Financial Markets Debacle of 2007–2008," *Mercatus on Policy*, 37, (February), pp. 1–3.

Wood, John H. (2005) *A History of Central Banking in Great Britain and the United States* Cambridge: Cambridge University Press.

Wordsworth, Charles Favell Forth (1859) *The New Joint Stock Company Law of 1856, 1857, and 1858* London: Shaw and Sons.

Zingales, Luigi (2009) "A New Regulatory Framework," www.Forbes.Com (March 31).

12

Bubbles and Central Banks

Historical Perspectives

Markus K. Brunnermeier
Princeton University, NBER, CEPR, CESifo

Isabel Schnabel
University of Bonn, MPI Bonn, CEPR, CESifo

1 Introduction

There is a long-standing debate regarding the role that monetary policy should play in preventing asset price bubbles. In the years before the recent financial crisis, the Federal Reserve and most other central banks were reluctant to use monetary policy as an instrument for tackling asset price bubbles. However, in light of the huge costs of the crisis, many observers speculate whether these costs could have been avoided or at least reduced if central banks had taken into account the evolution of asset prices in their monetary policy. The debate gathered momentum in the aftermath of the crisis as it was feared that historically low interest rates and nonconventional monetary measures would give rise to new asset price bubbles and thereby plant the seeds for a new crisis.

There exist a number of different views concerning the role of monetary policy with regard to asset price bubbles. Bernanke and Gertler (1999, 2001) argue that asset prices should play a role in monetary policy only insofar as they affect inflation expectations. In this regard, the components of price indices used by policy makers play a decisive role. Typically, asset prices are not explicitly included in these price indices. However, real estate

We thank Stephanie Titzck, Christian Wolf, and especially Sarah Heller and Simon Rother for excellent research assistance. We are also grateful for comments received from participants in the two conferences on the project "Of the Uses of Central Banks: Lessons from History" in Geneva and Oslo, in the SUERF conference in Vienna, and in the Econometric Society Meetings in San Francisco, as well as in seminars at the CESifo in Munich, the Center for Financial Studies/Institut für Bankhistorische Forschung, and the European Central Bank. We would especially like to thank our discussants, Andrew Filardo and Gary Gorton.

prices are indirectly taken into account through rents. Consequently, Goodhart (2001) argues that the whole debate could be solved if asset prices were given a larger weight in the inflation target. In contrast, others take the view that asset price developments should not be targeted by monetary policy at all. For example, the Fed's declared policy prior to the subprime crisis was to "clean up the mess," i. e., to mitigate the consequences of bursting bubbles rather than try to detect and prevent asset price bubbles (Greenspan, 1999, 2002).

Several arguments have been brought forward to support the belief that monetary policy should not react to asset price bubbles. First, bubbles cannot be identified with confidence. A deviation from the fundamental value of an asset could be detected only if the asset's fundamental value was known. Second, monetary policy instruments are said to be too blunt to contain a bubble in a specific market. In particular, while hikes of the policy rate – if large enough – may in fact deflate a bubble, this comes at the cost of substantial drops in output and inflation (Assenmacher-Wesche and Gerlach, 2008). These costs may well outweigh the benefits of bursting the bubble. Third, bubbles appear to be a problem especially in combination with unstable financial institutions or markets. Therefore, bubbles should be tackled by financial regulation rather than monetary policy. Overall, these arguments resonate closely with the "divine coincidence" of standard New Keynesian models (Blanchard and Galí, 2007): If inflation is stable, then output will be at its natural level, so there is no need to give any extra attention to asset prices and potential bubbles.

This view has been forcefully opposed by the Bank for International Settlements (BIS). Several prominent BIS economists have argued that monetary policy should "lean against the wind," i.e., try to prevent the buildup of bubbles by reacting early on to upward-trending asset prices (Cecchetti et al., 2000; Borio and Lowe, 2002; White, 2006). Although they recognize the difficulties associated with the identification of bubbles, proponents of this policy approach argue that a passive role is not optimal. As in other decision problems under uncertainty, policy makers should rely on a probabilistic approach. To underpin these arguments, some point to the fact that many observers detected the recent housing bubble in the United States well before it burst.

Moreover, the expected costs of bursting bubbles are said to outweigh the costs of early intervention. Such costs include, for example, the risk of new bubbles after a cleaning approach has been taken. The reason is that such a policy is asymmetric, which tends to raise the price level and risks creating the next bubble (the famous "Greenspan put").

Bubbles and Central Banks: Historical Perspectives 495

Finally, proponents suggest that financial regulation as a means to avoid or counter asset price bubbles may not be fully effective in all circumstances. This regards the timing as well as the scope of interventions. With respect to timing, financial regulation may prove to be procyclical rather than countercyclical. Concerning the scope, regulation may be undermined by regulatory arbitrage. Monetary policy could be a more effective tool since it also reaches the shadow banking system. Indeed, the central bank may not even need to *directly* adjust monetary policy; instead, it could use verbal communication to dampen bubbles – in effect, "talk down" the market.

In the run-up to the recent financial crisis, the Fed and other central banks largely followed the Greenspan view of a monetary policy that did not try to prevent the emergence of bubbles. Instead, they "cleaned up the mess" when the crisis broke, just as they had done after the dot-com bubble burst in 2000. In fact, they had considered the ex-post cleanup operation quite successful. Of course, they ignored the fact that the dot-com bubble had been largely financed by equity and not by debt as the subprime bubble had been. However, the recent crisis has shown quite plainly the huge costs that can arise from bursting asset price bubbles. The theoretical links between (bursting) bubbles, financial crises, and the associated macroeconomic fallout are discussed in detail in Brunnermeier and Oehmke (2013). Overall, the recent crisis experience tilted the view toward more intervention, and the old consensus (Greenspan view) has seemingly shifted to a new consensus closer to the BIS view (see, e.g., the speeches by Jeremy Stein, former member of the Board of Governors of the Federal Reserve System, February 7, 2013 and March 21, 2014). The new debate therefore centers more on the question of how to react to asset price bubbles. Most people agree that the newly created macroprudential instruments can serve this purpose. The question, however, is whether this is sufficient or whether monetary authorities should explicitly consider asset price distortions in their decisions.

This paper attempts to shed new light on this debate by taking a historical perspective. We document the most prominent asset price bubbles from the past 400 years, characterizing the types of assets involved, the holders of assets, policy environments during the emergence of bubbles, the severity of crises, and policy responses. By the very nature of our approach, we cannot present any definitive policy conclusions. Rather, we try to identify typical characteristics of bubbles and illustrate the inescapable trade-offs at the heart of the "leaning versus cleaning" debate. In particular, we link the severity of crises to certain features of bubbles and to the subsequent policy response.

Our overview of bubbles is inevitably selective. We typically learn about bubbles that either were not tackled and burst or that were tackled by mistake, resulting in severe crises. In order to deal with this selection problem, we also searched for bubbles that did not result in severe crises because these are most likely to be instructive regarding effective ex-ante policy measures. Although we cannot hope to remove the selection problem from historical reporting, this may help mitigate it.

The paper will proceed in Section 1 by describing our selection of crises and by providing an overview of the twenty-three identified bubble episodes, including the types of assets and economic environments. Section 2 tries to link the severity of crises to the described characteristics of bubble episodes. Section 3 then develops a number of hypotheses regarding the effectiveness of various policy responses. These hypotheses are then discussed informally by providing illustrative supporting or contradicting evidence from individual bubble episodes. Section 4 concludes by summarizing our results and deriving some policy implications. The appendix contains a detailed overview of the twenty-three crises on which our analysis is based.

2 An Overview of Bubble Episodes

2.1 Selection of Bubble Episodes

Our analysis focuses on twenty-three famous bubble episodes from economic history. In order to identify these episodes, we started from the full sample of crises in the seminal book by Kindleberger and Aliber (2011), *Panics, Manias, and Crashes: A History of Financial Crises.* We reduced the sample by only considering episodes that were related to an asset price boom. Hence, an overheated economy would not be described as a bubble if no particular bubble asset was involved. For example, the Panic of 1819, which is sometimes called America's first great economic crisis, can be traced to an overheated economy that included overtrading and speculation in nearly all kinds of assets. Other crises, such as the Panic of 1907, evolved mainly because of other factors, such as an unsound banking sector. We also had to keep the size of our sample manageable and therefore excluded episodes that were very similar to included episodes but for which less material was available. In other cases, bubble episodes seemed closely related to previous crises or did not provide additional insights. Moreover, some episodes had to be removed because too little secondary literature could be found on them. We did not drop episodes merely because the crises were not severe enough. Rather, such crises may be the most interesting for us because they could point toward effective policies for dealing with a crisis. Nevertheless, the listing in Kindleberger and Aliber already has a selection

Bubbles and Central Banks: Historical Perspectives   497

bias in the direction of severe crises, which we could not avoid. This limitation should be kept in mind when interpreting our sample of crises. We complemented the sample by adding some important bubble episodes that are not covered in Kindleberger and Aliber's book: namely, the Chicago real estate boom of 1881–83, the Norwegian crisis of 1899, and the Australian real-estate bubble in the early 2000s.

Our selection leads to a sample of twenty-three bubble episodes, listed in Table 12.1 and spanning almost 400 years. The table in the appendix contains a detailed overview of all bubble episodes considered. The first bubble is the Tulipmania of 1634–37, and the most recent ones are the U.S. subprime housing bubble and the Spanish housing bubble. The table in the appendix starts by giving a brief overview of the respective bubbles

Table 12.1: *Overview of sample of bubble episodes*

	Event	Time	Place
1	Tulipmania	1634–37 (crisis: Feb. 1636)	Netherlands
2	Mississippi bubble	1719–20 (crisis: May 1720)	Paris
3	Crisis of 1763	1763 (crisis: Sept. 1763)	Amsterdam, Hamburg, Berlin
4	Crisis of 1772	1772–73 (crisis: June 1772)	England, Scotland
5	Latin America Mania	1824–25 (crisis: Dec. 1825)	England (mainly London)
6	Railway Mania	1840s (crises: April/Oct. 1847)	England
7	Panic of 1857	1856–57 (crisis: Oct. 1857)	United States
8	Gründerkrise	1872–73 (crisis: May 1873)	Germany, Austria
9	Chicago real estate boom	1881–83 (no crisis)	Chicago
10	Crisis of 1882	1881–82 (crisis: Jan. 1882)	France
11	Panic of 1893	1890–93 (crisis: Jan. 1893)	Australia
12	Norwegian crisis of 1899	1895–1900 (crisis: July 1899)	Norway
13	U.S. real estate bubble	1920–26 (no crisis)	United States
14	German stock price bubble	1927 (crisis: May 1927)	Germany
15	U.S. stock price bubble	1928–29 (crisis: Oct. 1929)	United States
16	"Lost decade"	1985–2003 (crisis: Jan. 1990)	Japan
17	Scandinavian crisis: Norway	1984–92 (crisis: Oct. 1991)	Norway
18	Scandinavian crisis: Finland	1986–92 (crisis: Sept. 1991)	Finland
19	Asian crisis: Thailand	1995–98 (crisis: July 1997)	Thailand
20	Dot-com bubble	1995–2001 (crisis: April 2000)	United States
21	Real estate bubble in Australia	2002–04 (no crisis)	Australia
22	Subprime housing bubble	2003–10 (crisis: 2007)	United States
23	Spanish housing bubble	1997–2012 (crisis: 2007)	Spain

and their wider context. Then it lists the major characteristics of these bubbles, such as the type of assets, their holders and their financiers, and the "displacement" that presumably triggered the bubble. The table then describes the economic environment accompanying the origins of the bubbles. We specifically consider expansive monetary policy, the occurrence of lending booms, foreign capital inflows, and financial deregulation. These four factors are typically said to accelerate the emergence of bubbles. The table also collects indicators regarding the severity of crises, focusing on three aspects: the severity of the recession, the occurrence of a banking crisis, and spillovers to other countries. Most importantly, the table displays various types of policy reactions. The final line of the table lists the sources.

One word of caution about nomenclature is necessary here. We are using the word "bubble" in a rather broad (and somewhat sloppy) sense here. Our data are not sufficiently rich to have any chance of truly identifying deviations of prices from fundamental values. Therefore, the word "bubble" here merely refers to the fact that the asset price movement was considered excessive – rightly or wrongly – by market participants and that the result was often (but not always) a sharp price decrease when the bubble burst.

2.2 Characteristics of Bubbles

The list shows that bubbles historically occurred in many different asset classes, ranging from commodities (such as tulips, sugar, or grain) to financial assets (especially stocks and bonds), real estate (land as well as residential and commercial building sites), and infrastructure projects. Bubbles in commodities were present especially in the earlier part of the time span examined in our sample. The nineteenth century saw many bubbles in the area of infrastructure, such as railroads and canals. In contrast, bubbles in securities and real estate emerged throughout our sample period.

With respect to the holders of bubble assets, we are particularly interested in whether the assets were held by specific groups of society or by large parts of the population. When assets are held by specific groups, such as specialized traders or wealthy individuals, wealth effects of bursting bubbles on consumption and investment are likely to be smaller than when assets are held widely and constitute a large share of agents' wealth. We also analyze whether assets were held directly by financial institutions, which could amplify a crisis owing to fire sales or margin calls. Regarding the financing of bubble assets, a crucial aspect is the importance of debt financing because this raises the probability of spillovers to other parts of

Bubbles and Central Banks: Historical Perspectives 499

the economy. Virtually all bubbles in our sample were financed by debt to a large degree. Two noteworthy exceptions are the Chicago flat craze and the dot-com crisis, which were to a large extent financed by equity, as will be discussed in more detail later. In addition, we are interested in whether banks were involved in the financing of the bubble assets because this increases the likelihood of a banking crisis.

Bubbles are typically triggered by some type of "displacement," an exogenous shock that significantly changes expectations and fuels a bubble (see Kindleberger and Aliber, 2011). Examples are technological innovations (such as railways or the emergence of the New Economy), financial innovations (e.g., futures, acceptance loans, or securitization) or deregulation (opening new business opportunities), and political events (like the beginning or end of a war). This displacement frequently happens in specific sectors and channels funds into specific uses. It is often accompanied by euphoria and extrapolative expectations, making people believe that the upward movement of prices will continue forever.

2.3 Economic Environment

The second section of the appendix table characterizes the economic environment in which the bubbles emerged. The overall picture is familiar and confirms standard results from the literature. We see that most of the identified crises emerged when the stance of monetary policy was expansive. For earlier periods, when central banks either did not exist or were more similar to private banks, the issuance of bank notes by private banks often had an expansionary effect on money supply in the early phase of a bubble episode. An example is the Latin American Mania in England in 1824–25, when country banks issued large volumes of small-denomination banknotes (Neal, 1998, p. 55). Another example is the Gründerkrise, when some federal states in Germany broadened the rights of money emission for certain banks. In other cases, such as the crisis of 1857 or the panic in Australia in 1893, gold discoveries caused an expansion of the money supply and spurred optimistic expectations. Although we cannot make any causal statements here, our observations are in line with evidence by Bordo and Landon-Lane (2013), who show that "loose" monetary policy has a positive impact on asset prices, especially in periods of asset price booms.

Similarly, the overwhelming share of bubbles was accompanied by a lending boom, which appears to be an almost universal feature of asset price bubbles. This expansion of credit was frequently related to financial innovation. For example, before the crisis of 1882, forward securities trading at the Paris and the Lyon exchanges were financed through a system of "reports": To purchase a security, the investor could make a down payment and borrow the rest from a stockbroker ("agent de change"). The broker himself borrowed money in the call market from banks, caisses, and individuals for one day and expected to roll over the loan each day, a structure that proved to be vulnerable in a crisis. Other examples of financial innovations entailing the rapid expansion of credit are "swiveling" (the use of fictitious bills of exchange to create credit) before the crisis of 1772, the invention of the acceptance loan before the crisis of 1763, or the securitization of mortgages in the run-up to the U.S. subprime crisis. Reversely, not all lending booms lead to asset price bubbles, as they may also lead to a more general overheating of the economy rather than to exaggerations in a particular asset market. Hence, lending booms appear to be (almost) a necessary, but not sufficient, condition for the occurrence of asset price bubbles.

In some cases, bubbles seem to have been fueled by capital inflows from abroad. In more than half of the bubble episodes, not only domestic but also foreign investors participated in the buying frenzy. Examples are found throughout the period considered in this study. The Railway Mania in England during the 1840s was fueled by massive foreign investments in the railway system. Similarly, prior to the Panic of 1857, the United States received large capital inflows, mainly from England but also from Germany and France. Nearly half of about $400 million in outstanding railroad bonds in the mid-1850s was financed by foreign investors; following net investment outflows of $3 million in 1849, net inflows grew to $250 million in the crisis year 1857 (Riddiough and Thompson, 2012, p. 4, and sources therein). Foreign capital also played a considerable role during the Panic of 1893 and the German stock price bubble of 1927. Often, the bursting of bubbles leads to a redirection of capital flows, spurring new asset price booms in other regions. Examples are the Scandinavian and Asian asset price bubbles after the bursting of the Japanese bubble, as well as the dot-com bubble and the U.S. subprime housing bubble after the Asian crisis.

Finally, bubbles often occur during phases of financial deregulation. Examples are the Gründerkrise of 1872–73, when the reform of stock corporation law led to a surge in the foundation of joint-stock companies, as well as most of the recent crises in our sample. Differences in the extent and speed of deregulation of financial markets and banks are pointed out as a major cause of the lending boom and the associated difficulties in the Japanese asset price bubble (see, e.g., Hoshi and Kashyap, 2000; Posen, 2003). Finance became less dependent on banks due to the deregulation

Bubbles and Central Banks: Historical Perspectives 501

of bond and stock markets (e.g., the opening of foreign bond markets and less stringent collateral requirements). Remaining relatively strictly regulated, banks lost their best clients and were not able to enter into new fields of business. Therefore, they responded with a rapid expansion of lending to small firms, to foreign borrowers, and especially to the real estate sector. By 1990, real estate loans in Japan had doubled from the beginning of the 1980s.

3 Severity of Crises

All bubble episodes in our sample are characterized by strong increases in asset prices, but not all of them ended in deep depressions. In this section, we ask how the severity of crises was related to the characteristics of bubbles and their economic environments. The role of policy responses is discussed in the next section.

In our sample, no clear relationship exists between the types of bubble assets and the severity of crises. Bubbles involving real estate often lead to a severe recession. However, the same is true for many bubbles not involving real estate. For example, the bubble in grain and sugar in 1763, the Latin America Mania and the Railway Mania (both involving securities and commodities), and the French crisis of 1882 (involving securities) all had severe real consequences. This is important because it suggests that an overly narrow focus on bubbles in real estate markets – which appears to have happened following the recent crisis due to the prominence of real estate bubbles at that time – is misplaced. A prominent example of a real estate bubble not leading to a deep depression is the real estate bubble in the United States during 1920–26 (see Alston et al., 1994; White, 2009). This period saw a boom and bust in housing prices similar to that during the recent financial crisis. Nevertheless, the immediate effects on both the banking system and the real economy were rather modest.[1] An interesting question is whether this can be explained by specific policy responses, as will be discussed later.

Generally, the *financing* of asset bubbles seems to be more relevant than the *type* of bubble asset. Since real estate is typically debt-financed, such bubbles tend to be severe. But the same can be true for other asset bubbles if debt financing is pervasive. In fact, the severity of a crisis is clearly related to the presence of a lending boom. Compare, for example, the two early

---

[1] Postel-Vinay (2014) has a less benign view of real estate lending in that period. She argues that it was an important determinant of subsequent bank failures during the Great Depression, but due not to low loan quality but to its effect on banks' liquidity.

commodity bubbles in our sample, the Tulipmania and the crisis of 1763. The former was not accompanied by a lending boom given that the purchase of tulips was partly equity-financed and the extension of loans was limited to a rather small share of the population. Moreover, loans were granted directly by the sellers of the bulbs without the involvement of financial intermediaries. When the bubble collapsed, market participants experienced painful losses, but these did not spread to the rest of the economy.

The situation in 1763 was very different. Through chains of bills of exchange, credit expanded greatly, especially among financial institutions. When asset prices collapsed, highly leveraged financial institutions failed, leading to fire sales and a large-scale financial crisis with severe repercussions for the real economy (Schnabel and Shin, 2004). Another comparison can be made between the Railway Mania in England during the 1840s and the dot-com crisis. In both instances, the displacements were technological innovations – railways and the Internet, respectively. Wide parts of the population were captured by the euphoria surrounding the new technologies. But only the former crisis was accompanied by a lending boom, whereas the purchase of stocks in the dot-com crisis was, to a larger extent, financed by equity. Consequently, the Railway Mania was accompanied by a severe banking crisis followed by a serious recession, whereas the dot-com crisis ended in a rather mild recession and did not involve any major bank failure. Lending booms in the banking sector, especially when accompanied by decreasing lending standards as in Australia in 1893 or in Japan during the 1980s, are dangerous especially because they make the occurrence of banking crises more likely. And banking crises are a major determinant of the severity of a crisis. Indeed, almost all crises in our sample that were accompanied by a banking crisis led to a severe recession. In contrast, none of the crises without a banking crisis ended in a severe recession.

The mildest crises were those where the leverage of market participants was limited. One example of this phenomenon is the Chicago real estate boom of 1881–83, which was characterized by rather low leverage of market participants and did not end in a severe recession.

In several episodes, financial institutions were directly affected by the bursting bubbles because they themselves were participating in the speculation and were therefore holding the assets in question on their balance sheets. Important examples are the crisis of 1763 in Northern Europe and the Panic of 1893 in Australia. In both instances, the banking crisis was accompanied by fire sales, which accelerated the asset price decline even further. In other cases, such as the German stock price bubble of 1927, one

Bubbles and Central Banks: Historical Perspectives   503

can argue that the decline in asset prices (in this case, stocks) weakened banks' balance sheets and laid the groundwork for the ensuing deep crisis.

4 Policy Responses

The existing literature presents little empirical evidence of the role that policy can play in dealing with asset price bubbles. Our twenty-three bubble episodes offer a broad spectrum of policy responses in different phases of asset price bubble cycles. We broadly distinguish between four types of policies: cleaning up the mess, leaning interest rate policy, macroprudential measures, and central bank communication (or "talking down the market").

The category "(only) cleaning" contains those bubbles where no significant policy reaction was observed before the bubble burst. Meanwhile, a policy reaction is called "leaning" if it has the potential to dampen the bubble in the run-up phase. It is difficult to distinguish between deliberate and unintentional leaning, and we do not attempt to do so. For deriving policy implications, it is relevant whether these policy responses had an effect or not, regardless of the initial intentions. Extreme forms of leaning are policy actions resulting in the bursting of bubbles, sometimes called "pricking" in the literature. Pricking can be understood as a leaning policy that comes too late or is too strong, bursting the bubble rather than deflating it slowly.

Leaning can involve interest rate increases (called "leaning interest rate policy" in this paper) or other types of measures that would nowadays be called "macroprudential" or "quantity instruments." These include limits on the loan-to-value ratios for banks and explicit credit restrictions. Note that "leaning" is sometimes used in a narrower sense, including only interest rate changes.[2] In our analysis, macroprudential instruments are also considered leaning instruments.

Finally, central banks could also lean by "talking down" overvalued assets. Given that private agents broadly have access to the same information as central banks, it is not a priori clear whether mere statements – without any implied news about future interest rate movements or macroprudential policy responses – can in fact shift asset prices. Abreu and Brunnermeier (2003) offer one potential explanation for the suggested link between purely verbal communication and actual asset prices:

---

[2] Such a definition was, for example, used by Jean-Claude Trichet, former president of the European Central Bank, who in a June 8, 2005 speech described leaning as follows: "The leaning against the wind principle describes a tendency to cautiously raise interest rates even beyond the level necessary to maintain price stability over the short to medium term when a potentially detrimental asset price boom is identified."

Rational investors (bubble arbitrageurs) may understand that the bubble market will eventually collapse, but choose not to exit because they cannot synchronize their actions with the other arbitrageurs. A central bank declaration can coordinate the exit behavior and so lead to a quick deflation of the bubble.

Our discussion of policy responses will take place along a number of hypotheses. In all cases, it should be kept in mind that our analysis by design can only suggest the underlying trade-offs, rather than yield definitive policy recommendations for the present.

4.1 Hypothesis 1: "Pure Cleaning" Is Costly

A pure cleaning policy implies that interventions occur only when the bubble bursts by itself. This may be particularly costly because of the large adjustment needed at this point in time. One example of a cleaning policy is offered by the crisis of 1763, when no authority felt responsible for or was capable of intervening to mitigate the enormous lending boom, leading to a deep depression and the breakdown of a significant part of the financial system. Another example is the Australian crisis of 1893. Again, there was no policy intervention trying to mitigate the bubbles in mining shares and land or the accompanying lending boom. And again, the disruptions in both the financial sector and the real economy were severe.

Hence, the evidence supports the view that pure cleaning is costly. However, the evidence also shows that pure cleaning strategies are found only in relatively immature financial systems. Most advanced systems show some form of policy responses, many of which can be characterized as leaning. Even the Greenspan policy was not a pure cleaning strategy.

4.2 Hypothesis 2: Leaning Interest Rate Policy May Mitigate Crises

The most well-known example of successful leaning is the Australian real estate bubble in the early 2000s. When the Reserve Bank of Australia became more and more alarmed by rising housing prices and strong credit expansion, it first used communication to emphasize the long-term risks from these developments. Later, the Reserve Bank tightened interest rate policy in several steps beginning in mid-2000. Although these steps were officially motivated by inflationary pressures and not explicitly targeted to asset prices, their effect was a deceleration of housing price rises without any severe disruptions. The success of this leaning policy also appears intimately linked to its timing: The central bank reacted at a relatively early stage, long before the bubble could reach dangerous proportions, and so deflation of the bubble required no *substantial* rate hikes.

In other episodes, such as the Norwegian crisis of 1899, the relatively mild recession may partly be due to an early increase in interest rates mitigating the real estate bubble, although the evidence is less clear than for the Australian case. Overall, these episodes suggest that a leaning interest rate policy can in principle be effective and avoid or mitigate crises.

However, some caveats are in order. First, it is – in the case of the Australian crisis – difficult to cleanly disentangle the effect of the leaning interest rate policy from the impact of macroprudential measures, which were introduced at around the same time (as discussed later). Second, we see leaning interest rate policies in many other episodes in our sample, and most of these episodes nevertheless led to severe recessions. This suggests that the implementation of leaning policies is far from trivial. Leaning interest rate policy may become ineffective if it comes too late or is too weak and it can be harmful if it is too strong, leading to our next two hypotheses.

4.3 Hypothesis 3: Leaning Interest Rate Policy May Be Ineffective if It Is Too Weak or Comes Too Late

In many of our sample episodes, we see interest rate increases prior to the crisis, but these seem to have been too weak to curb the bubble. A telling example is the U.S. subprime bubble. The Fed raised interest rates starting as early as 2004. However, the level of interest rates was still low and housing prices continued to rise until 2006. Another example is the Gründerkrise of 1872–73, when interest rate increases were not sufficient to mitigate the boom in stocks and real estate.

In other cases, interest rates were raised at a very late stage of the crisis. For example, in the Railway Mania in England during the 1840s, the Bank of England reacted relatively late to speculation, and the bursting of the bubble led to a deep recession and one of Britain's worst banking panics. Another example is the U.S. stock price bubble in the late 1920s, when interest rates were raised after the bubble had already grown to an unsustainable level. Similarly, the increase in interest rates came very late in the Japanese crisis, and the economy entered into a long-lasting depression sometimes called the "lost decade." When interest rates were finally raised, the response was often quite harsh, leading to the bursting of the bubble, discussed next.

4.4 Hypothesis 4: Leaning Interest Rate Policy May Be Harmful if It Is Too Strong

In both of the just mentioned episodes (the United States in 1929 and Japan in 1990), the interest rate response was late but strong, contributing to the bursting of the respective bubbles ("pricking"). White (1990, p. 82) criticizes the Federal Reserve for having pushed the U.S. economy even further into recession. Similarly, the Bank of Japan was criticized for having promoted the recession by pricking the bubble (Patrick, 1998, p. 12). However, the counterfactual is unclear. It is well conceivable that a further expansion of the bubble would have led to an even more severe recession. Once asset prices have risen to unsustainable levels, all policy options can be costly.

But there are also episodes in our sample where the pricking of a bubble was not followed by a severe recession. For example, the deflation of share prices by Scottish financier John Law in the Mississippi bubble does not seem to have led to a severe disruption. Similarly, the possibly unintentional pricking of the dot-com bubble by Greenspan led to a sharp decrease in stock prices and huge losses for the holders of dot-com stocks, but the effect on the overall economy was modest and the financial system was hardly affected. Hence, it is far from clear whether "pricking" is worse than not intervening at all and letting the bubble collapse.

Overall, this substantial heterogeneity in experiences is an important reason for our wariness to derive definitive policy recommendations. Nevertheless, a policy preventing the emergence of bubbles in the first place seems preferable to a late pricking.

An alternative to interest rate instruments are macroprudential tools. Under this category, we consider all measures that attempt to reduce lending through means other than interest rates. Examples are quantity restrictions for lending or the imposition of loan-to-value ratios. In fact, such instruments were used in a number of bubble episodes, and the evidence yields some interesting insights.

4.5 Hypothesis 5: Macroprudential Instruments May Mitigate Crises

In the early crises in our sample, we do not observe the use of macroprudential instruments. However, such instruments seem to have gained importance since the beginning of the twentieth century. An early and successful use of macroprudential instruments occurred in the 1920–26 real estate bubble in the United States (see White, 2009). According to the National Banking Act of 1864, national banks outside of the central reserve

Bubbles and Central Banks: Historical Perspectives 507

cities were subject to loan-to-value restrictions of 50 percent for real estate loans with a maturity of up to five years. Moreover, total real estate lending was limited to 25 percent of a bank's capital. This may help explain why most banks survived the bursting bubble relatively well and why the stability of the entire financial system was not threatened. Another positive example is the Australian real estate bubble in the early 2000s, when the authorities imposed higher capital requirements for certain loans, such as home equity loans. In combination with leaning interest rate policy, this seems to have been quite successful in avoiding disruptions.

But macroprudential policy is subject to the same pitfalls as leaning interest rate policy. In several episodes, macroprudential policy was not able to prevent crises or may even have been counterproductive. In the stock price bubbles of 1927 in Germany and 1929 in the United States, central banks also applied macroprudential tools. Reichsbank President Schacht curbed stock market lending by threatening banks with restricted or even denial of access to rediscount facilities. Similarly, the Federal Reserve denied access to the discount window for banks granting further loans on securities. In both cases, these policies were very effective in reducing stock lending, but at the same time they induced a severe crash in stock markets, causing disruptions in the economy. Similar to other episodes discussed earlier, the measures seem to have come too late and were too strong. With respect to the German case, it has been argued that the central bank pricked a non-existent bubble. Although the ensuing recession was mild, the economy may have evolved much more favorably in the absence of pricking (Voth, 2003). Moreover, the decline in stock prices weakened banks' balance sheets. The pricking of a nonexistent bubble (through leaning interest rate policy or macroprudential tools) is certainly undesirable.

There are other examples where macroprudential measures that seem reasonable in principle were ineffective in practice. For example, the Japanese central bank introduced quantitative restrictions in 1990 to limit the growth rate of banks' real estate loans, which could not exceed the growth rate of their total loans. This measure is said to be one reason why the increase in real estate prices came to a halt (Kindleberger and Aliber, 2011, p. 285); nevertheless, the economy did not recover for a long time. In Finland, the authorities tried to limit credit expansion by allowing for raising reserve requirements up to 12 percent for banks that did not reduce their lending. It seems, however, that this measure was not strong enough to stop the credit expansion as some banks preferred to continue lending (Nyberg and Vihriälä, 1994, p. 15). In Thailand, the central bank required banks and finance companies to hold higher cash reserves for short-term deposits owned by foreigners. Again, this measure was implemented relatively late and seems to have had a minor effect on foreign borrowing.

Finally, the most well-known example of macroprudential policies is that of the Spanish authorities during the recent housing bubble. In fact, Spain was the first country to introduce countercyclical measures in the form of dynamic provisioning. Interestingly, these measures did little to limit the overall credit expansion in good times because 1) credit was substituted through other sources, and 2) the measures were simply not strong enough. In contrast, they were quite effective in mitigating the credit crunch in bad times (Jiménez et al., 2012).

Overall, the evidence suggests that macroprudential measures *can* be successful in mitigating crises. Their main advantage is that they are much more targeted than monetary policy measures because they can be applied directly to the sectors where bubbles emerge. However, just as with leaning interest rate policy, the timing and dosage of macroprudential measures are of the essence. When applied too late, they become ineffective. Moreover, a late response may force sharp actions that often have disruptive effects. The Spanish experience points to another potential shortcoming of macroprudential tools, which is just the other side of the coin of being more targeted: They may be circumvented when credit is substituted from other sources not covered by the regulation. This, in turn, is an advantage of the blunt measures, which capture all parts of the financial system.

4.6 Hypothesis 6: Central Banks Cannot Simply "Talk Down" Bubbles

During various bubble episodes in our sample, central bank communication appears to have had a clear impact on asset prices. For example, in Germany in the late 1920s, Hjalmar Schacht, then President of the Reichsbank, publically voiced his displeasure with equity price developments and urged banks to curb lending for equity purchases. Similarly, in the Australian crisis of the early 2000s, the central bank very explicitly telegraphed its policy goals. Private-sector expectations duly adjusted, and the bubble slowly deflated. However, the common theme in these and many other verbal interventions was the close link between verbal message and future *threatened* or *clearly signaled* policy interventions. Without a credible threat or promise of a later policy response, it is not clear whether the mere verbal statement would in fact have sufficed to move asset prices in the desired direction. Indeed, recent experience in the United States reinforces this skepticism. In the late 1990s, Fed Chairman Greenspan on multiple occasions warned that equity prices were excessive, credit spreads too narrow, or bank lending terms too

Bubbles and Central Banks: Historical Perspectives 509

generous. However, asset prices did not respond markedly in the intermediate run to the Chairman's comments, suggesting that investors barely update their beliefs about fair valuation after a mere verbal declaration by central bankers (Kohn and Sack, 2003). Overall, then, there is no clear empirical evidence that pure verbal communication – unaccompanied by any credible outlook for actual future policy adjustments – is in fact capable of substantially moving valuations.

5 Conclusions

Our paper has given an overview of interesting bubble episodes in the past 400 years. While being highly selective, we hope to provide some interesting lessons for today. By the very nature of our analysis, we cannot hope to derive any definitive policy recommendations and so, in particular, cannot present a simple solution that will work under all circumstances. All of the considered instruments worked well in some instances but failed in others. The particular characteristics of the bubble matter, as does the economic environment. Nevertheless, we can distill the following general lessons.

First, contrary to popular wisdom, the *financing* of bubbles is much more relevant than the *type* of bubble asset. Bubbles in stocks may be just as dangerous as bubbles in real estate if the financing runs through the financial system. The fallout from bursting bubbles appears to be most severe when the bubble is accompanied by a lending boom, high leverage and a liquidity mismatch of market players, and financial institutions participating in the buying frenzy.

Second, a policy of passively "cleaning up the mess" is likely to be expensive. The historical episodes we reviewed suggest that policy measures in many cases can indeed be effective in mitigating crises. This general thrust of the evidence notwithstanding, the complexities of a swift and precise identification of bubbles, coupled with the difficulty of gently deflating them, remain serious impediments to such proactive approaches.

Third, the timing of interventions – should they be desired – is of the essence. Late interventions can be ineffective or even harmful if they enforce sharp measures that would suddenly burst the bubble and cause severe disruptions. This emphasizes the need for a continuous macroprudential analysis that monitors important time series and tries to detect the emergence of bubbles in certain market segments at an early stage, thus allowing for an early and preventive intervention.

Fourth, no particular instrument is found to be dominant in dealing with asset price bubbles. Interest rate tools are blunt and also affect parts of the economy not showing any signs of overheating; however, they have the advantage of being less subject to circumventing behavior. To minimize the adverse effects on the rest of the economy – and, more fundamentally, to ensure that asset prices remain at all sensitive to interest rate fluctuations – early intervention is necessary, underlining yet again the need for constant monitoring. In contrast, macroprudential tools can be targeted at specific market segments or institutions, which can be useful in many circumstances. But they are always subject to regulatory arbitrage. Both instruments can be accompanied by verbal declarations, but such communication may not by itself be sufficient to appreciably change valuations.

Overall, leaning interest rate policies and macroprudential instruments appear to be complementary. Should a central bank indeed decide that an active stance against bubbles is desirable, then a combination of macroprudential tools and active interest rate policy seems preferable in many cases. As long as problems are detected in specific sectors or within particular institutions, targeted macroprudential measures are sufficient. If the bubble is more widely spread or if regulatory arbitrage is a serious threat, then a proactive interest rate policy may well be the best way to go.

So what does our paper imply for the current situation? This situation is different from most episodes in our sample in that rising asset prices coincide with overall weakness, both in the real and the financial sectors, at least in Continental Europe. In a post-bust phase there is a trade-off between preserving financial stability and getting the economy growing again. Essentially, central banks try to induce market participants to invest and take on more risk. This tends to lead to more financial risk-taking and, hence, less financial stability. In such a situation, high asset prices are driven by the central bank's cleaning strategy rather than by euphoria.

When banks are vulnerable and leverage is high in all parts of the economy, leaning interest rate policy seems to be a bad option. The Swedish example is telling in that respect: When the Swedish central bank raised interest rates in 2010 to dampen the boom in real estate prices and the overborrowing of households, inflation fell sharply and even became temporarily negative, raising the burden on debtors and plunging the economy back into recession. This example shows quite plainly that policy options are to be judged differently after a financial crisis than in boom times. If the macroeconomic environment is weak, leverage is high, and the financial system is fragile, leaning interest rate policy can be very costly. Macroprudential tools may be more appropriate in that context. The appearance of bubbles in the immediate aftermath of a financial crisis has no precedent in our sample of bubbles. Further research is desperately needed.

Event	Tulipmania	Mississippi bubble	Crisis of 1763
Time	1634–37 (crisis: Feb. 1636)	1719–20 (crisis: May 1720)	1763 (crisis: Sept. 1763)
Place **Overview**	Netherlands Tulipmania is one of the first prominent speculative bubbles in history. It refers to the extraordinary rise in prices for tulips in the Netherlands during the 17th century. The mania went along with the introduction of futures markets, where the bulbs, which were considered luxury products, were pre-sold during the year for the season from June to September. Prices rose dramatically, with nonprofessional traders buying bulbs on credit provided by the sellers. While no severe recession followed, economic activity declined after tulip prices fell.	Paris The Mississippi bubble goes back to John Law, a Scottish immigrant, who acquired the Compagnie d'Occident in August 1717 to administer trade with the colony of Louisiana and with Canada. Speculation in Compagnie stocks emerged when the Compagnie expanded its economic activity greatly: Under the new name Compagnie des Indes, it controlled trade outside Europe, acquired the right to mint coins and to collect taxes, and finally purchased most national French debt. Law aimed at reviving the economy after the bankruptcy induced by the wars of Louis XIV and at establishing an economic system where the ample supply of finance fosters economic activity. Thus, he facilitated the supply of credit by introducing	Amsterdam, Hamburg, Berlin The Seven Years' War (1756–63) was accompanied by an economic boom and a rapid growth of credit. Credit expansion was fueled by the financial innovation of the "acceptance loan," a sophisticated form of bills of exchange. Important features were the strict regulation regarding the enforceability of the loan (Wechselstrenge) as well as the joint liability of all signatories for obligations from the bill. At that time, Holland took the role as main creditor, whereas Prussia can be considered an "emerging market" economy and Hamburg was in an intermediary position. The easy availability of credit-fueled commodity speculation, especially regarding sugar and grain, precipitated a sharp increase in

(*continued*)

Event	Tulipmania	Mississippi bubble	Crisis of 1763
Time	1634–37 (crisis: Feb. 1636)	1719–20 (crisis: May 1720)	1763 (crisis: Sept. 1763)
		paper money and by founding the private Banque Générale in June 1716, which became Banque Royale, a public entity, in 1719. With the Banque Royale increasing issuance to facilitate stock sales of the Compagnie, the amount of banknotes in the market and share prices spiked. Inflation set in and, with the beginning of 1720, market expectations changed: Investors started seeking more solid investment opportunities, and confidence in the paper money eroded. The Banque Royale was taken over by the Compagnie des Indes in February 1720, which stopped backing its own share prices with banknotes. Share prices were pegged to banknotes, and direct conversion became possible. Law started deflating share prices, gradually dismantling the bubble.	asset prices. The bubble burst when commodity prices declined dramatically with the coming of peace and credit conditions tightened. Merchants suffered direct and indirect losses. Eventually, the failure of the De Neufville, a major banking house in Amsterdam, caused a panic, which rapidly spread from Amsterdam and Hamburg to Berlin.

	Tulips	Stocks of John Law's Mississippi Company	Grain, sugar
Bubble asset	Tulips	Stocks of John Law's Mississippi Company	Grain, sugar
Type of bubble asset	Commodities	Securities	Commodities
Displacement	Financial innovation (futures)	Fiat money, the "Law system"	Financial innovation (acceptance loans), war
Holder of asset	Small-town dealers, tavern keepers, horticulturalists, wealthy individuals	Wealthy people, the King as a principal shareholder, former stockholders of Banque Générale	Merchant bankers
Financier of asset	Equity and credit from sellers of the bulbs; no financial intermediaries	Financing through bills of state, Banque Générale/Banque Royale	Bills of exchange (Amsterdam investors)
Economic environment during the emergence of the bubble			
(1) Expansive monetary policy	No	**Yes:** "(. . .) the commercial scheme chosen was to print money" (Garber, 2000, p. 98)	No
(2) Lending boom	No	**Yes:** "Expansion of circulating credit was the driving force for economic expansion" (Garber, 2000, p. 107)	Yes
(3) Foreign capital inflows	No	**Yes:** Stocks of Compagnie d'Occident and Compagnie des Indes were bought by British and Dutch investors	**Yes:** Holland as a major creditor, Prussia as a debtor country
(4) General inflation	No	**Yes** "[..] the average monthly inflation rate from August 1719 through September 1720 was 4 percent, with a peak of 23 percent in January 1720" (Garber, 2000, p. 101)	**Yes:** "At the same time inflation became a widespread phenomenon in northern Europe, as many German states and other countries like Sweden financed the war by debasing their currencies" (Schnabel and Shin, 2004, p. 13)

(*continued*)

(continued)

Event	Tulipmania	Mississippi bubble	Crisis of 1763
Time	1634–37 (crisis: Feb. 1636)	1719–20 (crisis: May 1720)	1763 (crisis: Sept. 1763)
Severity of crisis			
(1) Severe recession	**No:** Negative impact on household consumption but no serious distress	**No:** No indication of a severe recession	**Yes:** Decline in industrial production and stagnation of credit; relatively quick recovery in Amsterdam and Hamburg, long-term recession in Berlin
(2) Banking crisis	No	**No:** No general banking panic, but run on Banque Royale	**Yes:** Wave of bank failures, contagion due to Wechselstrenge, fire sales; but rather a liquidity crisis than solvency crisis
(3) Spillover to other countries	No	**Yes:** Close connection to South Sea Bubble; speculation in the two crises affected Dutch and northern Italian cities as well as Hamburg	**Yes:** Repercussions on London, Scandinavia
Policy reactions			
(1) Cleaning	No	**Yes:** Issuance of a decree to liquidate the Compagnie des Indes and the Banque Royale and to readjust public debt on January 26, 1720; exchange of existing bills and stocks against new public obligations (value between 100% and 5% of original obligations, depending on the extent of speculation)	**Yes:** In Berlin, Friedrich II assisted merchants, easing the pressure on credit markets by recalling old coins and minting new ones in Amsterdam on the basis of credits from the Dutch bankers; no direct public intervention in Amsterdam and Hamburg

(2) Leaning monetary policy	No	**Yes:** Law stops supporting the Compagnie des Indes' stock price with banknotes in February 1720; peg of share prices to banknotes at 9000 livres and possibility of conversion of shares into banknotes between March 5 and May 21 (monetization of shares); decree on May 1 to deflate share prices to 5000 livres until December 1	No
(3) Pricking	No	**Yes:** After the decision of May 1, 1720 to deflate share prices to 5000 livres until December 1, those share prices dropped faster than intended: to 2000 in September and to 1000 in December 1720	No
(4) Macroprudential instruments	No	No	No
Sources	Garber (1989), Garber (2000), Kindleberger and Aliber (2011)	Conant (1915), Garber (2000), Kindleberger and Aliber (2011)	Kindleberger and Aliber (2011), Schnabel and Shin (2004)

Event	Crisis of 1772	Latin America Mania	Railway Mania
Time	1772–73 (crisis: June 1772)	1824–25 (crisis: Dec. 1825)	1840s (crises: April/Oct. 1847)
Place	England, Scotland	England (mainly London)	England
Overview	The bubble of 1772 was accompanied by the early industrial revolution, thus an increase in manufacturing, mining, and civic improvement. London speculators excessively traded stocks and futures of the East India Company, while shares of turnpikes and canals, as well as enclosures and building construction, surged. Speculation was accompanied by a lending boom. Following the restrictive policy of chartered banks in Scotland, competitors expanded credit. Ayr Bank in Scotland was founded to increase the money supply. When the bank's starting capital was exhausted, it drew a chain of bills on London. The bubble burst, when a main creditor of Ayr, the London banking house Neal, James, Fordyce and Down, closed on June 10, 1772. Ayr Bank had to	The Latin American Mania, which resulted in a panic in December 1825, refers to a stock market boom, related especially to speculation in securities of real and fictitious South American governments (e.g., Poyais) and mines. Joint stock companies as well as cotton were further objects of speculation. In the peace years after the Napoleonic Wars, expansionary monetary policy fueled a lending boom and banks tended to make riskier loans. Similar developments took place in France, where speculation also extended to buildings. When the bubble burst in London, the panic precipitated a systemic banking crisis and a severe recession. When trade slowed, distress stretched out to banks in France, Leipzig, Vienna, and Italy. Latin America	The Railway Mania refers to the speculative frenzy during the 1830s and 1840s, which was halted by several crises. Speculation in railway stocks and related assets was mainly financed by cheap credit and foreign capital. Large amounts of capital were bound in railway investments. Moreover, imports became necessary due to a bad harvest and famine, forcing the Bank of England to increase interest rates. Both aspects led to a tightening of money markets. The bubble burst in 1845, when tensions about the situation in the railway market and expectations of a bad harvest entailed declining share prices. However, the situation became tenser and escalated into two panics in 1847. While the crisis of April was precipitated by a reversal of monetary policy,

	suspend payments and the panic spread. Having widespread repercussions in England, Scotland, Amsterdam, Stockholm, St. Petersburg, and the colonies, the situation only calmed after the cooperative intervention by several central banks and rich men.	experienced its first sovereign debt crisis.	distress in October emerged when the Bank of England had difficulties due to a severe internal and external drain of reserves. In both cases, investors were no longer able to meet calls for the subscription of new shares. Britain experienced one of its worst banking panics, and the government decided to suspend the Bank Act (gold backing). When the Bank of England finally intervened, the tightening of monetary policy worsened the crisis.
Bubble asset	East India Company, turnpikes, canals, enclosures, building construction	Securities of South American governments and mines, joint stock companies, cotton	Railway related securities, corn
Type of bubble asset	Securities, real estate	Securities, commodities	Securities, commodities
Displacement	Technological innovation (industrial revolution), financial innovation (swiveling, foundation of the Ayr Bank in 1769)	Independence of former colonies, privatization of mines, lower returns on British government bonds	Technological innovation (railways)
Holder of asset	London speculators, businessmen	Widely held: "All classes of the community in England seem to have partaken" (Conant, 1915, p. 620)	Widely held: ". . . from the clerk to the capitalist the fever reigned uncontrollable and uncontrolled." (Evans, 1848, p. 2)

(*continued*)

(continued)

Event	Crisis of 1772	Latin America Mania	Railway Mania
Time	1772–73 (crisis: June 1772)	1824–25 (crisis: Dec. 1825)	1840s (crises: April/Oct. 1847)
Financier of asset	Bank credit (Ayr Bank, country banks), bills of exchange (money brokers), trade credit	Bank credit (country banks, Bank of England)	Bank credit, acceptances, foreign investments, also savings

Economic environment during the emergence of the bubble

	Crisis of 1772	Latin America Mania	Railway Mania
(1) Expansive monetary policy	**Yes:** No centralized monetary policy. Expansive policy by the Bank of England after 1763. Chartered banks in Scotland adopted restrictive policy. This encouraged competitors (e.g., British Linen Company, local and private banks) to follow an expansive policy and issue new notes	**Yes:** Liberal policy by the Bank of England "to commodate the government's fiscal demands" (Bordo, 1998, p. 79) until 1825; expansion of monetary base enabled an increasing number of country banks to freely replace coinage in the domestic circulation and issue small-denomination banknotes; also open market operations by the Treasury	**Yes:** "era of cheap money" (Ward-Perkins, 1950, p. 76), e.g, in 1842, rates of interest were reduced to 4%; market discount rates were below 2% and then below 3% in 1844
(2) Lending boom	**Yes:** "Accompanying the more tangible evidence of wealth creation was a rapid expansion of credit and banking leading to a rash of speculation and dubious financial innovation" (Sheridan, 1960, p. 171)	**Yes:** "credit was the universal currency" (Evans, 1859, p. 15)	**Yes:** Cheap credit: "From 1842 discounts had been easy and money plentiful, the funds maintained a high rate; low interest only could be obtained" (Evans, 1848, p. 2)

518

(3) Foreign capital inflows	No	**No:** Rather capital exports and outflow of gold; decrease of foreign holdings of British debt	**Yes:** Substantial amount of foreign railway investment
(4) General inflation	**No:** "... expanding output of goods kept pace with the increase in the supply of money..." (Hamilton, 1956, p. 411)	**Yes:** In 1825: "sharp increase in [...] the prices of commodities [...]. The rising prices in the latter half of the year 1825 reduced purchases" (Conant, 1915, p. 621); also compare Silberling (1924)	**Yes:** Prices increased from 1843 to early 1847
Severity of crisis			
(1) Severe recession	**Yes:** The Gentleman's Magazine stated that "no event for 50 years past has been remembered to have given so fatal a blow both to trade and public credit" (Sheridan, 1960, p. 172); credit crisis, decrease in trade, unemployment, rising average number of bankruptcies (310 in the eight years preceding the panic, 484 in 1772, and 556 in 1773)	**Yes:** Serious recession in early 1826, "massive wave of bankruptcies" (Neal, 1998, p. 65), severe unemployment, contraction of loans	**Yes:** Serious recession similar to 1825, bankruptcies throughout the U.K.
(2) Banking crisis	**Yes:** Wave of bank failures in London and Edinburgh; Ayr Bank had to suspend payments, later also failures in Amsterdam	**Yes:** "systemic stoppage of the banking system" (Neal, 1998, p. 53), widespread failures (73 out of 770 banks in England, 3 out of 36 in Scotland)	**Yes:** One of the worst British banking panics; bank runs, hoarding of money

(continued)

(continued)

Event	Crisis of 1772	Latin America Mania	Railway Mania
Time	1772–73 (crisis: June 1772)	1824–25 (crisis: Dec. 1825)	1840s (crises: April/Oct. 1847)
(3) Spillover to other countries	**Yes:** Crisis had severe effects in Amsterdam, which also spread to Hamburg, Stockholm, St. Petersburg (but without "serious disaster" in the latter three; see Clapham, 1970, Volume I, p. 248) as well as to colonies in India and America	**Yes:** As a result of declining continental sales, the crisis spread from England to Europe (especially banks in Paris, Lyon, Leipzig, and Vienna were affected) and Latin America, where it caused a sovereign debt crisis	**Yes:** Banks and brokers failed in Paris, Frankfurt, Hamburg, and Amsterdam due to declining share prices; also effects were felt in New York; impact on trade between India and Britain
Policy reactions			
(1) Cleaning	**Yes:** Bank of England discounted heavily (had to hire additional clerks), government bailout of the East India company (loan of £1.4 million and export concessions), the Bank in Stockholm supported sound banks, Empress Catherine assisted British merchants	**Yes:** First "Policy of contraction during the first days of panic caused absolute paralysis of business" (Conant, 1915, p. 621) then change in policy; critical debate as to who should act as lender of last resort; finally Bank of England granted advances on stocks and exchequer bills, also heavy discounting, aid by the Banque de France to prevent suspension of convertibility	**No:** Bank of England was criticized for not acting as a lender of last resort; suspension of the Bank Act
(2) Leaning monetary policy	**Yes:** Early in 1772, Bank of England increased the discount rate and "tried to put a brake on over-trading by a selective limitation of	**Yes:** In view of declining reserves and "Alarmed at the speculative spirit abroad, the Bank of England were the first to adopt	**Yes:** Rise in interest rates due to drain of bullion, especially after food imports since October 1845, when bubble had already burst;

	its discounts, a policy which it had often adopted before" (Clapham, 1970, Volume I, p. 245)	precautions, by contracting their circulation; and the example was followed by the country banks" (Evans, 1859, p. 15). Contractive policy by the Bank of England, mainly through divesting Exchequer bills to cut circulation beginning in March 1825, again in May and June, and from September	criticism that Bank of England reacted too late to speculation worsened the panic; increase in minimum interest rate (3% in October 1845, 3.5% in November until August 1846, 4% in January, 5% in April 1847)
(3) Pricking	No	**Possibly:** "unclear what caused the April 1825 collapse, but the Bank of England had in March sold a very large block of Exchequer bills, presumably to 'contract the circulation'" (Bordo, 1998, p. 77)	No
(4) Macroprudential instruments	No	No	No
Sources	Clapham (1970), Hamilton (1956), Hoppit (1986), Kindleberger and Aliber (2011), Sheridan (1960)	Bordo (1998), Conant (1915), Evans (1959), Kindleberger and Aliber (2011), Neal (1998), Silberling (1924)	Clapham (1970), Dornbusch and Frenkel (1984), Evans (1848), IMF (2003), Kindleberger and Aliber (2011), Ward-Perkins (1950)

Event	Panic of 1857	Gründerkrise	Chicago real estate boom
Time	1856–57 (crisis: Oct. 1857)	1872–73 (crisis: May 1873)	1881–83 (no crisis)
Place	United States	Germany, Austria	Chicago
Overview	The crisis of 1857 is considered the first worldwide crisis. Having its origins in the United States, it quickly spread to Britain, continental Europe, and the colonies. The speculative bubble preceding the turmoil emerged against the backdrop of gold discoveries, railway extension, and a global boom. Foreign investors additionally contributed to rising values of railroad securities and land in the U.S. However, increasing uncertainty about the future status of slavery (Dred Scott decision) reduced the territories' attractiveness. While conditions in the money market had already tightened several years before the crisis, interest rates in New York rose sharply from June to August of 1857. The situation escalated in September after the failure of the Ohio Life	Excessive speculative activities in stocks and real estate were one of the main underlying causes of the severe crisis at the end of the 19th century in continental Europe. Over-expansion during the so-called Gründerjahre in Germany and Austria was facilitated by an expansion of bank credit – for example, through new types of banks (e.g., Maklerbanken and Baubanken). In addition, French war reparations were used to expand the money supply. Optimistic expectations and euphoria in the context of the World Exhibition as well as reform of the stock corporation law further fueled speculation. Whereas signs of trouble had been evident before, the bubble burst in May, when the World Exhibition in Vienna opened with disappointing sales. The sharp	The Chicago real estate boom at the beginning of the 1880s was rooted in the recovery from the serious depression of 1877. Against the backdrop of improving economic conditions, Chicago, considered an important economic center, benefited from increasing wages and profits. Thus, nearly every class of society accumulated large wealth, and real estate was considered the most attractive investment. In combination with increasing immigration, this led to soaring rents, demand for housing, and growing apartment construction. In reference to the latter, this period is also known as "the flat craze." However, with the beginning of the recession of 1883, the bubble burst, albeit without severe consequences.

and Trust Company, which had been involved in fraudulent practices. Depositors hoarded their money, and deposit withdrawals peaked with a bank run in New York. Distressed sales aggravated the situation among banks and farmers. The federal government was unable to intervene effectively. A severe recession, including numerous failures and price declines, was the result. Only the joint efforts of banks finally calmed the situation.	drop in stock prices and the closure of the Vienna stock exchange ("Black Friday") were followed by a banking crisis. Despite bailouts and other emergency measures, the crisis could not be contained and it developed into a ruinous depression		
Bubble asset	Railroad stocks and bonds, land	Stocks, railroads, houses, land	New buildings, houses from foreclosure proceedings, land
Type of bubble asset	Securities, real estate	Securities, real estate	Real estate
Displacement	Gold discoveries, railway extension	End of war, World Exhibition, liberalization (banks, stock corporation law)	Innovation (apartments, skyscrapers), railroad construction, immigration
Holder of asset	Widely held	Widely held, also by banks (cf. Wirth, 1890, pp. 474 ff.)	Widely held: capitalists, businessmen, mechanics, laborers, railroad and manufacturing companies
Financier of asset	Bank credit (domestic and foreign banks), promissory notes (sellers), debt-for-equity swaps (railroad companies), foreign investments, private capitalists	Bank credit	To a large extent equity-financed

(*continued*)

(*continued*)

Event	Panic of 1857	Gründerkrise	Chicago real estate boom
Time	1856–57 (crisis: Oct. 1857)	1872–73 (crisis: May 1873)	1881–83 (no crisis)
Economic environment during the emergence of the bubble			
(1) Expansive monetary policy	**Yes:** Note issuance not centralized; New York banks could expand loans due to increase in specie	**Yes:** War reparations were used to strike new gold coins, and some federal states increased money emission rights for some banks or founded new central banks	**Yes:** Mortgage interest rates were at extremely low levels in 1877; rate of growth of U.S. money stock was extraordinarily high from 1879 to 1881: over 19% p.a. (Friedman and Schwartz, 1963, p. 91)
(2) Lending boom	**Yes:** Despite a rapid increase in the number of banks, they were not able to meet the demand for loans	**Yes:** "credit at banks was stretched to the limit" (Kindleberger and Aliber, 2011, p. 52)	**No:** Rather equity-financed; large wealth had been accumulated by 1879 among all ranks of society and was made available for investment
(3) Foreign capital inflows	**Yes:** Foreign capital from England, also Germany and France	**Yes:** French war reparations	**No**
(4) General inflation	**No:** "Prices did not advance in proportion to the increase in the volume of metallic money [...] because a large part of the new money was absorbed by the lateral expansion of commerce in quantity" (Conant, 1915, p. 637)	**Yes:** "All of this had the combined effect of raising the prices of everything, especially rents, wages and the products of industry" (McCartney, 1935, p. 79); peak in 1873 with an index of 114.3 based on prices in 1860	**Yes:** "Rising prices and profits margins speeded up production, increased employment, and furnished the funds for a brief era of speculation that culminated in 1883" (Hoyt, 1933, p. 128)

Severity of crisis			
(1) Severe recession	**Yes:** 8.6% GDP contraction in the U. S. (Bordo, 2003, p. 65), wave of company failures, decreasing prices	**Yes:** Manufacturers suffered since purchasing power was greatly reduced; "ruin of German industry seemed to be at hand" (McCartney, 1935, p. 78) numerous insolvencies in Austria	No
(2) Banking crisis	**Yes:** Wave of bank failures, hoarding of money, and deposit withdrawals, bank run in New York on October 13; suspension of convertibility throughout the country	**Yes:** Sharp decrease in profitability and credit volume; increase in insolvencies, also fire sales	No
(3) Spillover to other countries	**Yes:** First worldwide crisis; spread to continental Europe and Britain, had effects in South America, South Africa, and Far East	**Yes:** Immediate effects on Italy, Switzerland, Holland, and Belgium; in September panic reached the United States; spillover to Great Britain, France, Russia	No
Policy reactions			
(1) Cleaning	**No:** "An analysis of the crisis of 1857 suggested that the Federal government was incapable of intervening effectively and that the public, including the banks, was left without guidance to stem	**Yes:** In Austria, bailout of the Bodencredit-Anstalt by the central bank and a bank consortium; suspension of the Bank Act of 1862 to allow for central bank assistance in case of a	No

(continued)

(*continued*)

Event	Panic of 1857	Gründerkrise	Chicago real estate boom
Time	1856–57 (crisis: Oct. 1857)	1872–73 (crisis: May 1873)	1881–83 (no crisis)
	the crisis" (Kindleberger and Aliber, 2011, p. 219)	liquidity crunch; syndicate of bankers was established to make advances on sound securities; the Treasury granted loans	
(2) Leaning monetary policy	No	**Yes:** But probably too late and too little to prevent the crisis; National Bank of Austria-Hungary raised interest rates in July 1869, in 1872, and in March 1873 up to 5 % for exchange and 6% for Lombard loans	No
(3) Pricking	No	No	No
(4) Macroprudential instruments	No	No	No
Sources	Conant (1915), Calomiris and Schweikart (1991), Evans (1859), Kindleberger and Aliber (2011), Gibbons (1858), Riddiough (2012), Riddiough and Thompson (2012)	Burhop (2009), Conant (1915), McCartney (1935), Schwartz (1987), Wirth (1890)	Hoyt (1933)

Event	Crisis of 1882	Panic of 1893
Time	1881–82 (crisis: Jan. 1882)	1890–93 (crisis: Jan. 1893)
Place	France	Australia
Overview	The French stock market bubble emerged during a boom period and mainly involved the Bourses in Paris and Lyon. Due to the success of national securities, investors believed in the safety of all kinds of securities. Masses of the French population fell into euphoria. A main trigger was the financial innovation of negotiable securities and forward contracts, implying that purchasers made a down payment and borrowed the rest from an agent de change who himself borrowed in the call-money (reports) market. Besides the system of reportage, capital inflows contributed to the boom. Confronted with falling reserves, the Banque de France was forced to contract monetary policy in autumn 1881, even though it intended to avoid a sharp increase of the discount rate. Consequently, interest rates for reports increased. When the Austrian government refused to grant a concession to the Banque de Lyon, share prices fell. In January, Union Générale, which played a crucial role during the boom, failed and panic broke out. The values of all classes of securities plummeted. Investors in the forward market experienced huge losses, and the Bourse de Lyon had to close. Despite efforts by a	After the gold rushes, Australia experienced a long boom period during the 1880s, which went along with a speculative boom in real estate values and mining shares. The Australian financial system was relatively immature: No central bank existed, while little legal regulation restricted banks. Stock exchanges were only established to create a market for mining stocks, and speculation in the latter was more important than transactions in industrial shares. The speculative bubble was supported by a lending boom, while the banks themselves were heavily engaged in these markets and accumulated more and more risks. Distress manifested when British capital was withdrawn after the Baring failure. In addition, more and more depositors withdrew their money, since they expected banks would be unable to roll over debt. Eventually, panic broke out in January, when the relatively newly established Bank of Melbourne collapsed. The consequence was severe financial distress. By May, 14 commercial banks had failed, while only 12 weathered the crisis. Besides severe real effects on the Australia economy, the crisis also had an international dimension. It spread to the United States,

(continued)

(*continued*)

Event	Crisis of 1882	Panic of 1893
Time	1881–82 (crisis: Jan. 1882)	1890–93 (crisis: Jan. 1893)
	consortium of banks, as well as the Banque de France, to fight the financial crisis, their interventions could not avert a deep recession	and repercussions were felt also in Berlin, Vienna, and Italy
Bubble asset	Securities in general, stocks of new banks	Mining shares, land
Type of bubble asset	Securities	Securities, real estate
Displacement	Financial innovation (negotiable securities), payment of war reparations after the Franco-Prussian war	Gold discoveries, population growth, financial deregulation (e.g., land accepted as collateral, no limit on note issuance)
Holder of asset	Widely held: "masses of the French people" (Conant, 1915, p. 659)	Banks, foreign investors, households
Financier of asset	Bank credit (banks, caisses de reports), also equity-financed (French people)	Credit by nonbanks (pastoral companies, building societies, land mortgage companies) and banks (trading banks)
Economic environment during the emergence of the bubble		
(1) Expansive monetary policy	**Yes:** Mean discount rate of the Banque de France in 1875 was 4% compared to 2.5% in 1880; mean circulation increased between 1875 and 1880	**Yes:** No central bank, but trading banks were note-issuing banks and expanded the monetary base
(2) Lending boom	**Yes:** Expansion of credit through a system of delayed payments (reportage), existence of "many different institutional avenues for the expansion of credit" (Kindleberger and Aliber, 2011, p. 63), rapid increase in the number of trust companies, investment societies, and syndicates	**Yes:** "... nearly every little community supported branches of all the leading banks, and obtained excessive loans on property which could not be converted into quick assets" (Conant, 1915, p. 695)

(3) Foreign capital inflows	No	**Yes:** British public, investment and financial companies that invested heavily in Australian mines and speculated in Australian real estate
(4) General inflation	**No:** (Maddison, 1991)	**No:** Prices relatively stable between 1870 and 1890
Severity of crisis		
(1) Severe recession	**Yes:** "The spectacular crash of the French stock market in 1882 inaugurated a deep recession that lasted until the end of the decade" (White, 2007, p. 115)	**Yes:** "The eventual downturn in the property market led to a severe financial crisis and a depression unequalled in Australia's experience" (Bloxham et al., 2010, p. 12); 10% real output decline in 1892 (1893: -7%), large investment activity dampened for almost twenty years, deflation
(2) Banking crisis	**Yes:** After bankruptcies among many brokers and clients, banks and their caisses collapsed, runs and subsequent failures of the Banque de Lyon and Union Générale	**Yes:** Small number of banks failed in 1892, 13 of 22 note-issuing banks failed in 1893, "collapse of a significant proportion of the Australian financial system" (Kent, 2011, p.126), especially nonbank financial institutions
(3) Spillover to other countries	No	**Yes:** Shock spilled over to the United States and also affected stock markets in Berlin, Vienna, Austria-Hungary, and Italy
Policy reactions		
(1) Cleaning	**Yes:** Assistance to Union Générale as well as to brokers by a consortium of Paris banks headed by the Banque de Paris et des Pays-Bas (Parisbas) and another group headed by the Rothschild house to win some time until the end of January settlement and to work out arrangements; later Lyon brokers received 100 million francs from the Banque de France upon securities that	**Yes:** Crisis was solved without intervention by the colonial governments; Queensland government rescued National Bank; government intended to prevent liquidity crisis by passing temporary legislation making privately issued bank notes legal tender; Victoria government urged banks to give financial assistance to one another, proclaimed bank

(continued)

(*continued*)

Event	Crisis of 1882	Panic of 1893
Time	1881–82 (crisis: Jan. 1882)	1890–93 (crisis: Jan. 1893)
	would not ordinarily have been accepted; the Paris agents of exchange received 80 million francs upon the guarantee of a syndicate of bankers; Banque de France itself received aid from the Bank of England.	holiday; in the end restructuring of the Commercial Bank as well as other banks, which ended the crisis
(2) **Leaning monetary policy**	**Yes:** The Banque de France was confronted with declining reserves due to bad crops and increasing gold flows to the U.S.; Banque de France tried to avoid a sharp increase in the discount rate and therefore paid light coin and charged a premium for bullion, but had to raise interest rates by 1 percentage point on October 20, 1881	**No**
(3) **Pricking**	**No**	**No**
(4) **Macroprudential instruments**	**No**	**No**
Sources	Conant (1915), Kindleberger and Aliber (2011), Maddison (1991), White (2007)	Bloxham et al. (2010), Conant (1915), Kent (2011), Lauck (1907), McKenzie (2013), Merrett (1997)

Event	Norwegian crisis	Real estate bubble in the U.S.	German stock price bubble
Time	1895–1900 (crisis: July 1899)	1920–26 (no crisis)	1927 (crisis: May 1927)
Place **Overview**	Norway Increasing exports and economic activity in 1894 and 1895 propelled a bubble in the Norwegian real estate market. At the same time, banks could take advantage of the booming stock market to get cheap capital. While interest rates declined, reaching a low in 1895, bank lending growth accelerated. However, the gold standard put limits on the scope of Norges Bank. The Bank was forced to raise interest rates throughout 1898 as a result of declining exports. Prior to the crisis, the Bank had low reserves as a result of large credit growth. Consequently, as the Bank became prone to gold drains, uncertainty spread and liquidity conditions tightened. The crisis broke in the summer of 1899 and was triggered by the failure of	United States The U.S. housing bubble of the 1920s can partly be attributed to postwar recovery and coincides with an agricultural boom. Loose monetary policy ignited a lending boom and contributed to increasing values of residential real estate. In addition, securitized mortgages played a central role. However, mortgages were rather short-term and financial regulation prescribed a low loan-to-value ratio. Banks remained prudent lenders and were relatively well capitalized. When the bubble burst and real estate values declined, the number of foreclosures increased; however, further, if any, distress was contained regionally. Since the riskiest securitized assets were primarily in the hands of investors but not held by financial institutions, the latter	Germany The stock market crash of 1927 is sometimes referred to as the onset of Germany's Great Depression. Following the recovery of the severe post-World War I hyperinflation, the German economy experienced a boom with rising employment and exports and stable inflation. At the same time, stock prices rose, and speculative purchases financed by bank credit as well as foreign capital inflows increased. Investment was largely financed by short-term money market credit instead of capital market lending. To counter both, Reichsbank president Schacht successfully urged banks to reduce lending for speculative use in May 1927. As a consequence, the stock market fell by 11% in one day ("Black Friday 1927"). The crash reduced margin

(continued)

(*continued*)

Event	Norwegian crisis	Real estate bubble in the U.S.	German stock price bubble
Time	1895–1900 (crisis: July 1899)	1920–26 (no crisis)	1927 (crisis: May 1927)
	Chr. Christophersen, a highly leveraged nonfinancial firm. While financial distress mainly concerned banks in Oslo, several Norwegian cities were affected by a real estate crash. Due to stable international growth as well as support from the central bank, the crisis in 1899 and 1900 was moderate. Norges Bank also played a central role in restructuring and liquidating insolvent banks. Hence, the crisis of 1899, considered the first major banking crisis in Norway, was less severe than later crises. Nonetheless, the net wealth of households and firms declined due to a fall in asset prices, and credit conditions throughout the country worsened.	were less affected and no systemic banking crisis emerged. Losses for banks were modest	lending and thereby investment. Confidence eroded, stock market liquidity declined, and firm balance sheets weakened, further curtailing investment. When Germany slid into recession, the economy was in a weak position due to already deteriorated balance sheets.
Bubble asset	Land, new homes, real estate shares	Residential housing, also securitized mortgages	Stocks

Type of bubble asset	Real estate	Real estate	Securities
Displacement	Export boom, 1894 Parliament decision to expand railways	Low interest rates, postwar recovery, deregulation (legalization of private mortgage insurance)	End of hyperinflation and economic recovery
Holder of asset	Construction sector, manufacturers, brokers, stock market investors	Banks, private individuals (domestic)	Wealthy individuals, institutional investors, banks
Financier of asset	Bank credit (especially commercial banks)	Bank credit (savings and loans, mutual savings banks, commercial banks, insurance banks), informal lending (family, friends, etc.)	Stock market lending (banks, foreign investors)
Economic environment during the emergence of the bubble			
(1) Expansive monetary policy	**Yes:** The monetary base increased in the 1890s due to specie inflows from exports; Norges Bank did not sterilize the inflow; discount rate began decreasing in January 1892, reaching its low in 1895	**Yes:** Interest rate was lowered in 1925, remained at low levels in 1926	**Yes:** Discount rate was reduced in several steps (10 % on average in 1924, 9% in February 1925, and a reduction in four steps to 6% in June 1926), but Reichsbank lost power over money supply due to gold standard (free capital flows); discount rate was higher than the money market rate
(2) Lending boom	**Yes:** Acceleration of bank lending growth since the mid-1890s; "the share of overall credit outstanding granted by banks rose markedly" (Gerdrup, 2003, p. 9)	**Yes:** Especially rapid expansion of mortgage credit	**No:** Sharp increase in stock market lending during 1926 and 1927, but level was still below prewar volume

(continued)

(*continued*)

Event	Norwegian crisis	Real estate bubble in the U.S.	German stock price bubble
Time	1895–1900 (crisis: July 1899)	1920–26 (no crisis)	1927 (crisis: May 1927)
(3) Foreign capital inflows	**No:** Inflows of foreign exchange due to the repatriation of incomes from shipping services and exports, net foreign claims of private banks in 1899	**No:** USA as a major net lender	**Yes:** Inflow of long- and short-term foreign funds during 1926, but sharp decline after Reichsbank intervention at the end of the year
(4) General inflation	**No:** Price level fell in the first half of the 1890s, but a sharp increase occurred in 1898	**No:** "Great moderation of inflation after World War I" (White, 2009, p. 11)	**No:** After hyperinflation, low and stable inflation in 1925 and 1926
Severity of crisis			
(1) Severe recession	**No:** Impact on credit conditions and confidence, but only moderate effects during 1899 and 1900; more broad-based recession and deflation from 1901 to 1905 due to international recession	**No**	**No:** Mild recession (investment fell, no effect on consumer spending), which later turned into the Great Depression
(2) Banking crisis	**Yes:** But concerned mainly banks in Oslo; moderate bank runs	**No:** Decline in housing prices and increase in foreclosure rates, but only modest losses for banks; 80% of failures were in rural areas and mainly related to	**No:** But bursting bubble weakened banks' balance sheets, which may have contributed to the banking crisis of 1931

		expectations in agriculture; runs and failures of certain bank chains, but no general banking crisis: "failures did not imperil the whole of the banking system" (White, 2009, p. 46)	
(3) Spillover to other countries	**No**	**No**	**No**
Policy reactions			
(1) Cleaning	**Yes:** Norges Bank provided liquidity support and was involved in the orderly restructuring process and liquidation of insolvent banks, private liquidation of smaller commercial banks; government support to *Industribanken*; Norges Bank experienced losses in the aftermath of the crisis	**No**	**No**
(2) Leaning monetary policy	**Yes:** Restrictions due to gold standard; increase of the discount rate from 4 % to 5.5% through 1898 due to drop in exports, then a rise from 5% to 6% in February and March one year later	**No:** No change in interest rates; rather, use of macroprudential instruments	**No:** Only a few months before the crisis, beginning in October 1926; discount rate was reduced from 6 % to 5% toward the end of 1926

(continued)

(*continued*)

Event	Norwegian crisis	Real estate bubble in the U.S.	German stock price bubble
Time	1895–1900 (crisis: July 1899)	1920–26 (no crisis)	1927 (crisis: May 1927)
(3) Pricking	No	No	**Yes:** Reichsbank intervention pricked the bubble, "...crash induced by the curtailment of margin lending..." (Voth, 2003, p. 87)
(4) Macroprudential instruments	No	**Yes:** Long-standing quantitative regulations; National Banking Act of 1864: For national banks outside the central reserve cities (New York, Chicago, St. Louis) the loan-to-value ratio for real estate loans with maturity up to five years had to be less than 50%; total real estate loans were limited to 25% of bank's capital; somewhat weaker state regulation; also increase in real estate taxes	**Yes:** Reichsbank President Schacht addressed stock market lending by threatening to decrease or even deny bank access to rediscount facilities
Sources	Gerdrup (2003)	Alston et al. (1994), White (2009)	Balderston (1993), Voth (2003)

Event	U.S. stock price bubble	"Lost decade"	Scandinavian crisis: Norway
Time	1928–29 (crisis: Oct. 1929)	1985–2003 (crisis: Jan. 1990)	1984–92 (crisis: Oct. 1991)
Place	United States	Japan	Norway
Overview	The late-1920s U.S. stock price bubble culminated in one of the most shattering stock market crashes in U.S. history, the "Black Tuesday" of October 1929. Owing to the prosperity and increasing profits of the Roaring Twenties, speculation blossomed in the United States. More and more Americans invested heavily in stocks. Restrictive policy by the Federal Reserve to contain the credit boom and curb speculation was ineffective. While broker loans by banks declined, other financiers substituted for it. However, in view of an oncoming recession, expectations began to change in the summer of 1929. When the Federal Reserve Bank of New York raised interest rates in August, it pricked the bubble and precipitated the crisis. While	During the 1980s, Japan's economy was spurred by euphoria and an economic boom, liberalization, and financial innovation. When deregulation of financial markets deprived Japanese banks of large customers and increased the competitive pressure, they rapidly expanded lending, seeking new customers. These factors in combination with low interest rates led to the emergence of a massive asset price bubble in stock and property markets. Especially financial institutions, but also households, were engaged in these investments. Realizing the unsustainability of these developments, the Bank of Japan decided to increase interest rates at the end of 1989. Even when equity prices had already declined, the Bank further raised	Beginning in 1983, Norway experienced a period of accelerating growth. Widespread financial deregulation accompanied by foreign capital inflows contributed to a lending boom. In this environment, a bubble emerged in the market for real estate. Increasing competitive pressure on banks led to declining lending standards and augmented risk taking. At that time, Norges Bank pursued monetary policy to meet the government's main objective of a low, stable interest rate. Real interest rates were close to zero or even negative. However, beginning in 1986, declining oil prices, high wages, and speculative currency attacks challenged the economy. Fiscal policy was tightened and, for

(continued)

(*continued*)

Event	U.S. stock price bubble	"Lost decade"	Scandinavian crisis: Norway
Time	1928–29 (crisis: Oct. 1929)	1985–2003 (crisis: Jan. 1990)	1984–92 (crisis: Oct. 1991)
	the direct effects of the crash were first confined to the stock market due to prompt actions by the New York Fed, increasing interest rates, distressed sales, and falling industrial production soon aggravated the situation. The crash thus marked the beginning of the Great Depression, affecting all industrialized economies.	the policy rate in the summer of 1990 and held it stable for about one year. However, the sharp reversal in monetary policy pricked the bubble and precipitated a stock market crash. The persistent decline in asset prices resulted in a large proportion of nonperforming loans, causing serious difficulties for financial institutions. The bursting of the asset price bubble is therefore associated with what is referred to as Japan's "lost decade," a protracted period of economic stagnation.	Norges Bank, the defense of the fixed exchange rate regime became the priority. Consumption and investment started to decline in 1987 and the bubble deflated. The crisis began with the failure of several smaller banks in autumn of 1988. Others followed and a systemic banking crisis evolved, reaching its peak in 1991. Norges Bank delivered liquidity support on several occasions and reduced interest rates considerably. Moreover, the Norwegian government provided capital injections and banks were nationalized through the Government Bank Insurance Funds. Norway experienced a severe recession and had to de-peg its currency in 1992.
Bubble asset	Stocks (companies, utilities)	Stocks, convertible bonds, real estate	Commercial real estate, residential housing

Type of bubble asset	Securities	Securities, real estate	Real estate
Displacement	Innovation (development of an industrial securities market, productivity improvements)	Lending boom due to financial deregulation and innovation, euphoria about the "new economy"	Broad-based financial deregulation
Holder of asset	Widely held; also commercial banks (and their securities affiliates)	Widely held (especially corporations, also banks)	Firms, households
Financier of asset	Stock market credit (domestic banks, later private investors, corporations, and banks in Europe/Japan)	Bank and mortgage loans (banks, finance companies, government financial institutions)	Credit (domestic and foreign banks)
Economic environment during the emergence of the bubble			
(1) Expansive monetary policy	**Yes:** New York Fed had already decreased discount rate from 4.5 % in April to 3% in August 1924; discount rates of all Fed banks decreased from 4% to 3.5% from July to September 1927; also open market purchases	**Yes:** Interest rates were reduced from 5.5 % in 1982 to 5% in 1983, to 3.5% at the beginning of 1986, and to 2.5% one year later	**Yes:** Until the end of the 1980s, Norges Bank followed the government's goal of a low interest rate. Norges Bank had to sell foreign exchange to counter several speculative attacks on the krone, but sterilized the policy by increasing its loans to banks
(2) Lending boom	**Yes:** "This eagerness to buy stocks was then fueled by an expansion of credit in the form of brokers' loans that encouraged investors to become dangerously leveraged" (White, 1990, p. 68)	**Yes:** Deregulation of financial markets, but not banks, and financial innovations increased competitive pressure on banks and fueled an expansion of loans, also accompanied by declining lending standards ("... there is a	**Yes:** Increasing demand for credit; "real lending growth at both commercial and savings banks increased rapidly after 1982" (Gerdrup, 2003, p. 22)

(*continued*)

(*continued*)

Event	U.S. stock price bubble	"Lost decade"	Scandinavian crisis: Norway
Time	1928–29 (crisis: Oct. 1929)	1985–2003 (crisis: Jan. 1990)	1984–92 (crisis: Oct. 1991)
	but credit conditions in general were tight	consensus view among economists on how partial financial deregulation in Japan in the 1980s led to a lending boom," Posen, 2003, p. 214)	
(3) Foreign capital inflows	**Yes:** Loans from foreign banks in Europe and Japan substituted for bank loans after the intervention by the Fed	**No:** Japan as a major creditor	**Yes:** Capital inflows after relaxation of fixed exchange rate in 1984; "…this time an inflow of foreign capital supported and reinforced their high lending growth"(Gerdrup, 2003, p. 22)
(4) General inflation	**No:** In 1928 and 1929, the consumer price index declined; no significant increase in the monetary base	**No:** Inflation remained low	**Yes:** Increasing rates of inflation: 1985: 5.7 %, 1986: 7.2%, 1987: 8.7%, and 1988: 6.7% (Moe et al., 2004, p. 32)
Severity of crisis **(1) Severe recession**	**Yes:** Only moderate direct effects on wealth, but confidence and households' balance sheets were weakened; later came Great Depression with 29.7% contraction in GDP (Bordo, 2003)	**Yes:** Very protracted, credit crunch	**Yes:** Worst recession since interwar period

(2) Banking crisis	**No:** Later; at first a banking panic was prevented, owing to interventions by the New York Fed, and the direct financial effects of the crash were limited to the stock market (also included distressed sales and margin calls)	**Yes:** High volume of nonperforming loans and failures of three large banks, but no runs or losses to depositors; "many financial institutions were de-capitalized and remained in business only because of the implicit support of the government" (Kindleberger and Aliber, 2011, p. 115)	**Yes:** Systemic banking crisis, large losses for banks across all asset classes
(3) Spillover to other countries	**Yes:** No direct effects of the crash, but reduction in U.S. lending had impact on Germany, Latin America, and Australia. Later, the Great Depression affected countries worldwide	**Yes:** Impact on Hawaii, Taiwan, and South Korea (close economic relations)	**Yes:** But strictly limited to Scandinavian countries
Policy reactions **(1) Cleaning**	**No:** Restrictive policy by the Fed, a result of fears about excessive speculation, worsened the recession; however, actions by the New York Fed (despite resistance from the Board) shortly after the crash made sure that money market rates remained stable and member banks were not threatened by defaulting loans on securities	**Yes:** Reduction of the discount rate to 4 % until spring 1992 and further, but still above 3% at the end of that year and later reduced to almost zero; loan purchasing program by the government in 1993, capital injections, nationalizations, fiscal stimulus package	**Yes:** Considerable interest rate reductions in 1993; Norges Bank provided liquidity support; loans below market rates, capital injections by the government, and nationalizations through Government Bank Insurance Funds

(*continued*)

(continued)

Event	U.S. stock price bubble	"Lost decade"	Scandinavian crisis: Norway
Time	1928–29 (crisis: Oct. 1929)	1985–2003 (crisis: Jan. 1990)	1984–92 (crisis: Oct. 1991)
(2) Leaning monetary policy	**Yes:** A few months before the crash, beginning in early 1929; the New York Fed argued against selective credit control and voted in favor of interest tools, but was frequently turned down by the Board; eventually the Fed was permitted to increase the discount rate from 5 % to 6% in August 1929	**Yes:** Very late; after being held at 2.5 % until May 1989, the discount rate was increased to 4% late that year; despite equity price declines, it was increased further to 6% in 1990, remaining at that level until mid-1991	**Yes:** In order to defend the currency peg, the central bank was forced to raise the discount rate despite decelerating economic growth due to rising interest rates in Germany
(3) Pricking	**Yes:** Restrictive policy possibly contributed to the bursting of the bubble and worsened the recession; "Instead of allowing the stock market bubble to expand and burst of its own accord, the Federal Reserve's policies helped to push the economy further into a recession" (White, 1990, p. 82)	**Yes:** Leaning was probably too strong; "the Bank of Japan finally began to raise interest rates sharply in a series of steps, puncturing the bubbles, and leading to eventual economic growth slowdown, and then stagnation" (Patrick, 1998, p. 12); "the decision [..] to restrict the rate of growth of bank loans for real estate pricked the asset-price bubble" (Kindleberger and Aliber, 2011, p. 285)	**No**

542

| (4) Macroprudential instruments | **Yes:** Board applied "direct pressure"; no access to the discount window for banks granting loans on securities; also decision by Massachusetts regulators to deny a request for splitting stocks to counter speculation | **Yes:** Quantitative restrictions in 1990; central bank regulation instructing banks to restrict the growth rate of their real estate loans (must not exceed the growth rate of their total loans); increase in taxes on capital gains from investments in land | **No** |
| Sources | Friedman and Schwartz (1963), Kindleberger and Aliber (2011), White (1990) | Hoshi and Kashyap (2000, 2004), Okina and Shiratsuka (2003), Kindleberger and Aliber (2011), Patrick (1998), Posen (2003) | Gerdrup (2003), Moe et al. (2004), Vale (2004) |

Event	Scandinavian crisis: Finland	Asian crisis: Thailand	Dot-com bubble
Time	1986–92 (crisis: Sept. 1991)	1995–98 (crisis: July 1997)	1995–2001 (crisis: April 2000)
Place	Finland	Thailand	United States
Overview	A large economic boom at the end of the 1980s provided the backdrop for a real estate and stock market bubble in Finland. Overheating was also facilitated by a lending boom (especially in foreign currency) and generous tax schemes. At the same time, banks and financial markets were widely deregulated without intensifying banking supervision. The Bank of Finland recognized the adverse developments, especially the excessive expansion of credit, and decided to tighten monetary policy slightly in early 1989. In 1991, declining exports to the Soviet Union, associated with decreasing output and devaluation of the markka, and slowing domestic consumption dampened the economy. Market interest rates were rising and reduced the ability of debt	The crisis had its origins in high growth and a credit boom, spurring bubbles in the real estate sector and in the stock market. Current-account liberalization entailing capital inflows from abroad after the bursting of the bubble in Japan, as well as financial deregulation and strong tax incentives for foreign borrowing, contributed to the lending boom. While regulatory and corrective measures generally lagged behind the rapid growth of banks, some Thai banks also circumvented regulations by funding nonbank financial intermediaries. The scope of monetary policy in Thailand was limited due to the pegged exchange rate. It remained relatively loose at the beginning of the 1990s. In winter of 1996, the unregulated finance company	The dot-com bubble refers to the speculative stock market boom in the United States and other industrialized countries at the end of the 1990s related to the founding of new Internet companies, called "dot-coms." The period is associated with a considerable economic boom in the United States. After the Long Term Capital Management crisis in 1998, the Fed eased monetary policy and also provided additional liquidity toward the end of 1999. Venture capital for new firms was widely available, while American households invested heavily in new technology shares, also encouraged by the massive media response to the boom. Asset prices surged. In his famous speech in December 1996, former Fed Chairman Alan Greenspan

servicing. Eventually, the serious difficulties of Skopbank, a commercial bank acting as central bank for savings banks, triggered a systemic banking crisis. The government and the Bank of Finland had to step in to provide guarantees, take over banks, and provide monetary assistance. Yet, financial distress spilled over to the real economy. Several hundreds of firms failed and output dropped rapidly. Due to intense speculative pressure, the markka was left to float in September 1992

sector suffered the first losses, causing mistrust among foreign investors. When the Thai economy was confronted with increasing oil prices, declining exports, and a sudden reversal of capital inflows, confidence in the regional banking system collapsed. Massive speculative attacks on the Thai baht forced the government to de-peg the currency in the summer of 1997. The crisis spread to most of Southeast Asia. Thailand suffered from a credit crunch and a deep but short recession. Troubled financial institutions received official backing by the central bank. The IMF stepped in and initiated stabilization programs

warned that "irrational exuberance" might have contributed to overvalued asset prices. During the course of 1999, the Fed modestly tightened monetary policy to sterilize former operations, but also because of increasing concerns about a general bubble and inflationary pressures. The bubble collapsed during 1999 and 2001. The Nasdaq dropped 20% in April and May of 2000 and 42% from September to January. Nevertheless, real consequences were modest, while financial markets continued to function smoothly

Bubble asset	Land, residential housing, stocks	Stocks, commercial and residential real estate	New technology company stocks
Type of bubble asset	Real estate, securities	Real estate, securities	Securities
Displacement	Broad-based financial deregulation	Liberalization, capital inflows after implosion of the bubble in Japan, export boom	Technological innovation (Internet, information technologies), capital inflows after burst of Asian bubble

(*continued*)

(*continued*)

Event	Scandinavian crisis: Finland	Asian crisis: Thailand	Dot-com bubble
Time	1986–92 (crisis: Sept. 1991)	1995–98 (crisis: July 1997)	1995–2001 (crisis: April 2000)
Holder of asset	Firms, households	Professional housing developers and individuals (Renaud et al., 2001)	Households, retail investors
Financier of asset	Credit (domestic and foreign banks, finance companies)	Credit (finance and securities companies, banks)	To a large extent equity-financed
Economic environment during the emergence of the bubble			
(1) **Expansive monetary policy**	**Yes:** Constrained monetary policy due to the fixed exchange rate regime, accelerating growth of the money supply (13.5% in 1987, 23.6% one year later) as a result of increasing demand	**Yes:** Relatively loose monetary policy (reduced from 12% at the beginning of the 1990s to 9% in 1993, held until mid-1994), but no independent monetary policy due to pegged exchange rate	**Yes:** Reversal of tightening policy of 1994, further easing in 1998 due to concerns about fragile monetary arrangements after the LTCM crisis; toward the end of 1999, abundant liquidity was provided to prevent problems related to the transition to the next millenium
(2) **Lending boom**	**Yes:** "Households as well as businesses started to borrow as never before" (Nyberg and Vihriälä, 1994, p. 13); in 1988, bank lending growth peaked at 30%	**Yes:** Bank lending growth accelerated and peaked at 30.3% in 1994; lending boom in Thailand was the largest among the Asian countries	**No:** Proceeds from securities sales were used to buy more securities; "margin lending for the purchase of equities rose sharply, albeit to still low levels …" (BIS, 2000, p. 5)
(3) **Foreign capital inflows**	**Yes:** "Particularly foreign borrowing was widely used, starting in the mid-1980s, although more than	**Yes:** "Thus the expansion of the asset price bubbles in the Asian capitals followed from the	**Yes:** Capital inflows due to a change in the trade balance with Mexico in 1995 and 1996; also inflows

	half of this financing was intermediated by the banks" (Nyberg and Vihriälä, 1994, p. 7)	implosion of the asset price bubble in Tokyo and the surge in the flow of money from Japan [. . .]. The flow of money from Tokyo to Thailand and Indonesia. . . " (Kindleberger and Aliber, 2011, p. 178), intermediated by local banks	after the collapse of the bubbles in Southeast Asia, when these countries repaid their debt
(4) General inflation	No: Inflation was declining since 1984 (8.9%, 1985: 5.1%, 1986: 4.6%), but increase since 1987 (5.3%, 1988: 6.9%)	No: Moderate and stable inflation (1991: 5.70 %, 1992: 4.07%, 1993: 3.36%, 1994: 5.19%, 1995: 5.69%, 1996: 5.85%, and 1997: 5.61%; Corsetti et al., 1999, p. 323)	No: "The U.S. economy boomed in the 1990s. The inflation rate declined from above 6% at the beginning of the 1990s to less than 2% at the end of the 1990s [. . .]" (Kindleberger and Aliber, 2011, p. 181)
Severity of crisis **(1) Severe recession**	Yes: "The rapid decline in output that had begun during 1989 continued all through 1991 and 1992" (Nyberg and Vihriälä, 1994, p. 22); decline of total demand by 6.5% and unemployment rate of 11% in 1991; real GDP dropped by 3.5% in 1992; 800 business failures in October 1992 alone	Yes: Sharp recession and credit crunch, but relatively quick recovery in 1999	No: "The recession that began in the United States in 2001 was relatively mild and brief" (Kindleberger and Aliber, 2011, p. 85); especially the new technology firms were hit hard

(continued)

(continued)

Event	Scandinavian crisis: Finland	Asian crisis: Thailand	Dot-com bubble
Time	1986–92 (crisis: Sept. 1991)	1995–98 (crisis: July 1997)	1995–2001 (crisis: April 2000)
(2) Banking crisis	**Yes:** Rapid increase in nonperforming assets; bank losses soared (reaching a peak of FIM 22 billion in 1992); numerous banks came close to failure and required assistance; considerable bank losses until 1995	**Yes:** "The results were widespread corporate bankruptcies, collapse in the confidence of the regional banking system, and further declines of asset prices" (Collyns and Senhadji, 2002, p. 12); "losses were particularly heavy in the largely unregulated finance company sector" (ibid., p. 12); 56 finance companies failed	No
(3) Spillover to other countries	**Yes:** But strictly limited to Scandinavian countries	**Yes:** Regional turmoil in Southeast Asia had global spillovers; economic growth worldwide slowed	**Yes:** Nasdaq as the main anchor, thus worldwide decline of technology indexes
Policy reactions **(1) Cleaning**	**Yes:** Government declared it would secure financial stability by all means; Bank of Finland provided liquidity support; Government Guarantee Fund, creation of bad banks, reorganization of supervision	**Yes:** Bailouts and official backing for troubled financial institutions, e.g., central bank's Financial Institutions Development Fund (FIDF), IMF support	**Yes:** Sharp decrease in the federal funds rate, starting in early 2001

(2) Leaning monetary policy	**Yes:** The defense of the exchange rate peg was the main target; however, restrictive interest rate policy in late 1988 and early 1989 due to excessive credit growth and increasing inflationary pressures	**Yes:** More restrictive monetary policy since 1994, due to currency depreciation induced by loose monetary policy; more restrictive (0.5 increase to 9.5 % in September 1994 and 10.5% in March 1995), but ineffective due to capital inflows	**Yes:** But relatively late and with another focus; the dot-com bubble itself was not a concern; officially Greenspan (2002) emphasized the intention to "focus on policies to mitigate the fallout when it occurs and, hopefully, ease the transition to the next expansion"; modest increase in interest rates from mid-1999 to May 2000, by 150 basis points, in order to reverse previous rate cuts and owing to concern about general bubble in equity markets and inflationary pressures
(3) Pricing	**No**	**No**	**Yes:** "The late 1990s bubble in U.S. stock prices was pricked by the Federal Reserve in 2000 when it sought to withdraw some of the liquidity that it had provided in anticipation of the Y2K problem" (Kindleberger and Aliber, 2011, p. 102)

(*continued*)

(continued)

Event	Scandinavian crisis: Finland	Asian crisis: Thailand	Dot-com bubble
Time	1986–92 (crisis: Sept. 1991)	1995–98 (crisis: July 1997)	1995–2001 (crisis: April 2000)
(4) Macroprudential instruments	**Yes:** At the beginning only strong statements; later in February 1988, increase of special reserve requirement in accordance with the banks (cash reserve requirement could be increased up to 12 % [from 8%] in case lending was not reduced), but "some banks in the savings bank sector chose to pay the new penal rates rather than curtail their rapid credit expansion. Furthermore, as markets were now free, borrowing in foreign currencies continued to increase" (Nyberg and Vihriälä, 1994, p.15)	**Yes:** In mid-1996, the central bank obliged banks and finance companies to hold higher cash reserve requirements for short-term deposits owned by foreigners	No
Sources	Bordes et al. (1993), Nyberg and Vihriälä (1994), Vihriälä (1997)	Bank of Thailand, Collyns and Senhadji (2002), Corsetti et al. (1999), Lauridsen (1998), Renaud et al. (2001)	BIS Annual Report (2000, 2001), Greenspan (2002), Cochrane (2003), Kindleberger and Aliber (2011), Ofek and Richardson (2008)

Event	Real estate bubble in Australia	Subprime housing bubble	Spanish housing bubble
Time	2002–04 (no crisis)	2003–10 (crisis: 2007)	1997–2012 (crisis: 2007)
Place	Australia	United States	Spain
Overview	The Australian bubble at the beginning of the millennium is commonly known because of the interventions of the Reserve Bank of Australia. Thereafter, housing prices declined smoothly without severe consequences. Previously, financial market deregulation, increasing competitive pressures on banks, financial innovation in securitization, and a more favorable tax treatment for housing investors had spurred a massive increase in housing values. Banks heavily expanded credit and shifted toward household lending, but focused on high credit quality and low loan-to-value ratios. The Reserve Bank of Australia became more and more attentive to potential problems arising from these developments and first tried to openly communicate potential	The recent U.S. housing bubble is associated with the most severe financial crisis since the Great Depression. What began as distress in the U.S. subprime sector developed into a global financial crisis. In the early 2000s, financial deregulation and innovation including securitization and new financial instruments, accompanied by the rapid growth of the shadow banking sector, contributed to a credit boom in the housing sector. Soaring housing values and optimistic expectations spurred the real estate bubble. However, with the decelerating economy and rising interest rates, price increases slowed in 2005 and reversed in mid-2006. Deliquency rates increased and the values of mortgage-backed securities and other structured	The Spanish economy relied heavily on domestic demand and the real estate sector since the mid-1990s. Low interest rates in the eurozone, increasing competition among banks, population growth, foreign house purchases, and a booming construction sector further fueled the housing bubble. It burst when the U.S. subprime crisis spread to Europe. Spanish banks were hit very hard by the spillovers as they were strongly engaged in financing construction and property development activities. While the direct exposure to subprime losses was limited, changing expectations regarding the development of housing prices, as well as the credit crunch in the interbank market and the wholesale market for mortgage-financing products (on which

(*continued*)

551

(continued)

Event	Real estate bubble in Australia	Subprime housing bubble	Spanish housing bubble
Time	2002–04 (no crisis)	2003–10 (crisis: 2007)	1997–2012 (crisis: 2007)
	long-term risks. Later, it tightened monetary policy in mid-2000. However, the steps were officially motivated by inflationary pressures and not explicitly targeted to asset prices. In addition, regulators and other official bodies participated in the discussion and also took some actions. Having modest adverse effects on consumption, the deceleration of housing prices proceeded without severe disruptions	products dropped. While uncertainty spread, severe distress for financial institutions in and beyond the shadow banking sector emerged. The crisis entered a new phase when the U.S. government let the investment bank Lehman Brothers fail in September 2008. Concerns about the soundness of the financial system became paramount, severely reducing lending to the real economy and in the interbank market. The crisis spread to different markets and around the globe	Spanish institutions relied heavily), had a great impact. The crisis had dramatic effects on the real economy, leading the government to reorganize the banking sector in 2010 and to strengthen prudential regulation. Bank bailouts, decreasing tax revenues from the construction sector, the severity of the recession, and failing confidence in the eurozone caused the fiscal situation to deteriorate markedly. As a consequence, sovereign bond spreads rose and a sovereign debt crisis evolved. Spain applied for EU rescue financing under the European Financial Stability Facility (EFSF) on June 25, 2012 and left the European Stability Mechanism (ESM, the EFSF's successor institution) program after 18 months in January 2014

Bubble asset	Residential housing	Subprime mortgages, securitized assets	Residential housing
Type of bubble asset	Real estate	Real estate	Real estate
Displacement	Financial innovation (securitization), financial deregulation	Financial innovation (securitization), financial deregulation, savings glut	Spillover from the U.S.
Holder of asset	Households	Widely held	Widely held
Financier of asset	Credit (banks, mortgage originators)	Credit (banks, shadow banks), international investors (especially banks)	Credit (banks, especially cajas)
Economic environment during the emergence of the bubble			
(1) Expansive monetary policy	**Yes:** Reduction in several steps from 6.25 % in 2000 to 4.25% in 2001	**Yes:** Lax policy by the Fed; 1% key rate from mid-2003 to mid-2004, when house prices increased significantly	**Yes:** The ECB's interest rate was too low for the Spanish situation (Garcia-Herrero and de Lis, 2008); reference rate for housing loans decreased from 9.6% in 1997 to 3.3% in 2007
(2) Lending boom	**Yes:** Rapid credit growth and shift toward household lending	**Yes:** "This combination of cheap credit and low lending standards resulted in the housing frenzy that laid the foundations for the crisis" (Brunnermeier, 2009, p. 82)	**Yes:** Credit expansion; "the housing boom was reflected in a credit boom, with rates of growth that peaked above 25 % in 2006" (Garcia-Herrero and de Lis, 2008, p. 3); loans to the construction and housing sector amounted to approximately 45% of GDP in 2007

(continued)

(continued)

Event	Real estate bubble in Australia	Subprime housing bubble	Spanish housing bubble
Time	2002–04 (no crisis)	2003–10 (crisis: 2007)	1997–2012 (crisis: 2007)
(3) Foreign capital inflows	**No**	**Yes:** "U.S. economy was experiencing a low interest rate environment, both because of large capital inflows from abroad, especially from Asian countries, and because the Federal Reserve had adopted a lax interest rate policy" (Brunnermeier, 2009, p. 77)	**Yes:** "…the purchase of secondary homes by other EU countries' citizens, especially in the Mediterranean coast (net foreign investment in housing ranged between 0.5% and 1% of Spanish GDP for each year between 1999 and 2007)"(Garcia-Herrero and de Lis, 2008, p. 3)
(4) General inflation	**No:** "…low and stable inflation envirnment through the early 1990s" (Bloxham et al., 2010, p. 15); 1991–2000: 2.2%, 2001: 4.4% 2002: 3.0%, and 2003: 2.8% (BIS, 2004)	**No:** "…quiescence of underlying inflation…" (BIS, 2006, p. 60); 1991–203: 2.7%, 2004: 2.7 %, 2005: 3.4%, and 2006: 3.2 % (BIS, 2006, p. 11)	**Yes:** Higher inflation in Spain compared to eurozone: 1993–2003: 3.3%, 2004: 3.1%, 2005: 3.4 %, and 2006: 3.6% (eurozone: 1991–2003: 2.4%, 2004: 2.1%, 2005: 2.2%, and 2006: 2.1%) (ECB)
Severity of crisis **(1) Severe recession**	**No:** In 2003 "Australia continued to expand briskly" (BIS, 2004, p. 13); consumption decelerated in 2004 and 2005 but was weaker than expected; "the welcome deceleration in house prices seen so far has had benign effects relative to more disruptive potential scenarios" (BIS, 2005, p. 66)	**Yes:** Worst recession since Great Depression	**Yes:** Sharp recession; GDP fell 6.3 % in the first quarter of 2009; a short period of positive growth came in 2011; negative rates since then, as well as severe unemployment (rose from 8.3% in 2007 to 20.1% in 2010); credit crunch

(2) Banking crisis	No	Yes: Runs, liquidity hoarding, and massive failures; also fire sales and margin calls	Yes: Banks in highly precarious position: high risk concentration, refinancing problems, asset value losses amounted to 9% of GDP, failures and rescues
(3) Spillover to other countries	No	Yes: Global financial crisis	Yes: After the bubble burst, the economy went into recession; tax revenues collapsed and deficits soared; Spain entered this recession at rather low levels of government debt, but domestic banks relied heavily on finance from abroad; in what followed, Spain became a major source of spillovers to other European countries' government bond markets (cf. Claeys and Vašíček, 2012)
Policy reactions (1) Cleaning	No	Yes: Bailouts, liquidity facilities, reduction of interest rates to almost zero, recapitalization, TARP, unconventional monetary policy (e.g., quantitative easing, extension of collateral eligibility), Economic Stimulus Act	Yes: Bailouts and nationalization, fiscal consolidation, and reorganization of the banking sector: Fund for Orderly Bank Restructuring (FROB), measures to restore confidence (stress tests, transparency etc.), equity, etc.

(continued)

(*continued*)

Event	Real estate bubble in Australia	Subprime housing bubble	Spanish housing bubble
Time	2002–04 (no crisis)	2003–10 (crisis: 2007)	1997–2012 (crisis: 2007)
(2) Leaning monetary policy	**Yes:** Timely; motivated by inflationary pressures, but also by rises in house prices and household borrowing; increase in interest rates in 2002 by 0.5 basis point, in 2003: no cut rates through the year (in contrast to all other developed countries); increase of the cash rate by 0.25 in November and December to 5.25%, "close to levels seen as consistent with long-run non-inflationary sustainable growth" (BIS, 2005, p. 65) but also justified by the desire to contain the developments in the housing sector (ibid., p. 66)	**Yes:** But not intentional; according to Fed Chairman Bernanke, regulatory policy and not central bank should deal with bubble; however, the Fed raised the interest rate from 1% in June 2004 in 17 steps up to 5.25% in June 2006	**Yes:** Leaning timely enough, but a loosening of provision requirements occurred in Q1:2005: "a net modest loosening in provisioning requirements for most banks (i.e., a tightening of the provision requirements offset by a lowering of the ceiling of the dynamic provision fund)" (Jiménez et al., 2012, p. 4); magnitude of shock further curtailed effectiveness
(3) Pricking	No	**No:** After the Fed had raised interest rates, mortgage rates continued to decline one more year; however, increasing mortgage rates later induced refinancing problems for homeowners, and deliquencies increased	No

(4) Macroprudential instruments	Yes: "Open mouth policy" (Bloxham et al., 2010) to raise public awareness: clear communication, central bank was "telegraphing their intention," clarification of policy goals resulted in "verbal tightening" (forward-looking behavior of private sector due to change in expectations) (BIS, 2004, p. 75); higher capital requirements for nonstandard loans (e.g., home equity loans) and lenders' mortgage insurers after stress test; securities and competition regulators (ASIC and ACCC) reinforced investigation of illegal activities by property marketers	No: But some efforts were made to address poor underwriting standards by developing guidance for nontraditional mortgage products in cooperation with other regulators	Yes: Tightening of prudential regulation (regulatory capital and loan loss provisioning requirements for real estate exposures); dynamic provisioning introduced in third quarter of 2000, modification at the beginning of 2005; sudden lowering of the floor of the dynamic provision funds in late 2008 from 33% to 10%; countercyclical capital buffers with positive real effects
Sources	BIS Annual Report (2003, 2004, 2005, 2006), Bloxham et al. (2010), RBA Annual Report (2003)	Brunnermeier (2009), FCIC (2011), Gorton and Metrick (2012), Reinhart and Rogoff (2009), Shiller (2008)	Carballo-Cruz (2011), Claeys and Vašíček (2012), Garcia-Herrero and de Lis (2008), Jiménez et al. (2012), Müller (2011)

558   *Markus K. Brunnermeier and Isabel Schnabel*

References

Abreu, Dilip and Markus K. Brunnermeier (2003): "Bubbles and Crashes," *Econometrica*, 71(1), 173–204.

Alston, Lee J., Wayne Grove, and David C. Wheelock (1994): "Why Do Banks Fail? Evidence from the 1920s," *Explorations in Economic History*, 31(4), 409–431.

Assenmacher-Wesche, Katrin and Stefan Gerlach (2008): "Financial Structure and the Impact of Monetary Policy on Asset Prices," *Swiss National Bank Working Paper*.

Balderston, Theo (1993): "The Origins and Course of the German Economic Crisis," in *Schriften der Historischen Kommission zu Berlin, Band 2: Beiträge zu Inflation und Wiederaufbau in Deutschland und Europa 1914–1924*, Gerald D. Feldman, Carl-Ludwig Holtfrerich, Gerhard A. Ritter, and Peter-Christian Witt (eds.). Berlin: Haude and Spener.

Bank for International Settlements (2000): *70th Annual Report*. Basel.

(2001): *71st Annual Report*. Basel.

(2003): *73rd Annual Report*. Basel.

(2004): *74th Annual Report*. Basel.

(2005): *75th Annual Report*. Basel.

(2006): *76th Annual Report*. Basel.

Bank of Thailand: Interest Rates in Financial Market (1978–2004) FM_RT_001, available at www2.bot.or.th/statistics/ReportPage.aspx?reportID=222&language=eng.

Bernanke, Ben S. and Mark Gertler (1999): "Monetary Policy and Asset Price Volatility," *Economic Review*, Federal Reserve Bank of Kansas City, Fourth Quarter, 17–51.

(2001): "Should Central Banks Respond to Movements in Asset Prices?" *American Economic Review Papers and Proceedings*, 91(2), 253–257.

Blanchard, Olivier and Jordi Galí (2007): "Real Wage Rigidities and the New Keynesian Model," *Journal of Money, Credit and Banking*, 39(s1), 35–65.

Bloxham, Paul, Christopher Kent, and Michael Robson (2010): "Asset Prices, Credit Growth, Monetary and Other Policies: An Australian Case Study," *Reserve Bank of Australia Research Discussion Paper 2010–06*.

Bordes, Christian, David Currie, and Hans T. Söderström (1993): *Three Assessments of Finland's Economic Crisis and Economic Policy*. Bank of Finland.

Bordo, Michael D. (1998): "Commentary," *Federal Reserve Bank of St. Louis Review*, 80(3), 77–82.

(2003): "A Historical Perspective on Booms, Busts, and Recessions," Chapter II, *World Economic Outlook*, April, International Monetary Fund, Washington, D. C., 64–66.

Bordo, Michael D. and John Landon-Lane (2013): "Does Expansionary Monetary Policy Cause Asset Price Booms? Some Historical and Empirical Evidence," *Journal Economía Chilena (The Chilean Economy)*, Central Bank of Chile, 16(2), 4–52.

Borio, Claudio and Philip Lowe (2002): "Asset Prices, Financial and Monetary Stability: Exploring the Nexus," BIS Working Paper No. 114, Bank for International Settlements.

Brunnermeier, Markus K. (2009): "Deciphering the Liquidity and Credit Crunch 2007–2008," *Journal of Economic Perspectives*, 23(1), 77–100.

Brunnermeier, Markus K. and Martin Oehmke (2013): "Bubbles, Financial Crises and Systemic Risk," in *Handbook of the Economics of Finance*. Amsterdam: Elsevier.

Burhop, Carsten (2009): "Banken- und Finanzkrisen in Deutschland im 19. und 20. Jahrhundert," unpublished manuscript.

Calomiris, Charles W. and Larry Schweikart (1991): "The Panic of 1857: Origins, Transmission, and Containment," *The Journal of Economic History*, 51(4), 807–834.

Carballo-Cruz, Francisco (2011): "Causes and Consequences of the Spanish Economic Crisis: Why the Recovery Is Taken So Long?" *Panoeconomicus*, 58(3), 309–328.

Cecchetti, Stephen G., Hans Genberg, John Lipsky, and Sushil Wadhwani (2000): "Asset Prices and Central Bank Policy," The Geneva Report on the World Economy No. 2.

Claeys, Peter and Bořek Vašíček (2012): "Measuring Sovereign Bond Spillover in Europe and the Impact of Rating News," *Czech National Bank, Working Paper 7*.

Clapham, Sir John (1970): *The Bank of England: A History. Volumes I and II.* Cambridge University Press.

Cochrane, John H. (2003): "Stocks as Money: Convenience Yield and the Tech-Stock Bubble," in *Asset Price Bubbles: The Implications for Monetary, Regulatory and International Policies*, William C. Hunter, George G. Kaufman, and Michael Pomerleano (eds.), 175–204. MIT Press.

Collyns, Charles and Abdelhak Senhadji (2002): "Lending Booms, Real Estate Bubbles and the Asian Crisis," *IMF Working Paper WP/02/20*.

Conant, Charles A. (1915): *A History of Modern Banks of Issue*. New York: G. P. Putman's Sons.

Corsetti, Giancarlo, Paolo Pesenti, and Nouriel Roubini (1999): "What Caused the Asian Currency and Financial Crisis?," *Japan and the World Economy*, 11(3), 305–373.

Dornbusch, Rudiger and Jacob A. Frenkel (1984): "The Gold Standard and the Bank of England in the Crisis of 1847," in *A Retrospective on the Classical Gold Standard, 1821–1931*, Michael D. Bordo and Anna J. Schwartz (eds.), 233–276. Chicago University Press.

Evans, David M. (1848): *The Commercial Crisis, 1847–1848*. London: Letts, Son and Steer.
(1859): *The History of the Commercial Crisis 1857–1858 and the Stock Exchange Panic of 1859*. London: Groombridge and Sons.

Financial Crisis Inquiry Commission (FCIC, 2011): *The Financial Crisis Inquiry Report: Final Report of the National Commission on the Causes of the Financial and Economic Crisis in the United States*. U.S. Government Printing Office.

Friedman, Milton and Anna J. Schwartz (1963): *A Monetary History of the United States 1867–1960*. Princeton University Press.

Garber, Peter M. (1989): "Tulipmania," *Journal of Political Economy*, 97(3), 535–560.
(2000): *Famous First Bubbles: The Fundamentals of Early Manias*. MIT Press.

Garcia-Herrero, Alicia and Santiago Fernández de Lis (2008): "Dynamic Provisioning: Some Lessons from Existing Experiences," *ADBI Working Paper Series, No. 218*.

Gerdrup, Karsten R. (2003): "Three Episodes of Financial Fragility in Norway Since the 1890s," *BIS Working Papers No. 142*.

Gibbons, James S. (1858): *The Banks of New York, Their Dealers, the Clearing-House, and the Panic of 1857. With a Financial Chart*. New York: D. Appleton & Co.

Goodhart, Charles (2001): "What Weight Should be Given to Asset Prices in the Measurement of Inflation?," *The Economic Journal,* 111, F335–F356.

Gorton, Gary B. and Andrew Metrick (2012): "Getting Up to Speed on the Financial Crisis: A One-Weekend-Reader's Guide," *Journal of Economic Literature,* 50(1), 128–150.

Greenspan, Alan (1999): Testimony of Chairman Alan Greenspan Before the Committee on Banking and Financial Services, U.S. House of Representatives, July 22, 1999.

   (2002): "Economic Volatility," speech at a symposium sponsored by the Federal Reserve Bank of Kansas City, Jackson Hole, Wyoming, August 30, 2002.

Hamilton, Henry (1956): "The Failure of the Ayr Bank, 1772," *The Economic History Review,* 8(3), 405–417.

Hoppit, Julian (1986): "Financial Crises in Eighteenth-Century England," *The Economic History Review,* 39(1), 39–58.

Hoshi, Takeo and Anil Kashyap (2000): "The Japanese Banking Crisis: Where Did It Come From and How Will It End?" in *NBER Macroeconomics Annual 1999, Volume 14,* Ben S. Bernanke and Julio J. Rotemberg (eds.), 129–212. MIT Press.

   (2004): "Japan's Financial Crisis and Economic Stagnation," *Journal of Economic Perspectives,* 18(1), 3–26.

Hoyt, Homer (1933): *One Hundred Years of Land Values in Chicago: The Relationship of the Growth of Chicago to the Rise in Its Land Values, 1830–1933.* Chicago University Press.

International Monetary Fund (IMF, 2003): *World Economic Outlook, April 2003 – Chapter II: When Bubbles Burst.* Washington, D.C.

Jiménez, Gabriel, Steven Ongena, José-Luis Peydró, and Jesús Saurina (2012): "Macroprudential Policy, Countercyclical Bank Capital Buffers and Credit Supply: Evidence from the Spanish Dynamic Provisioning Experiments," *National Bank of Belgium Working Paper No. 231.*

Kent, Christopher J. (2011): "Two Depressions, One Banking Collapse: Lessons from Australia," *Journal of Financial Stability,* 7(3), 126–137.

Kindleberger, Charles P. and Robert Z. Aliber (2011): *Manias, Panics, and Crashes: A History of Financial Crises. Foreword by Robert M. Solow.* Sixth Edition. New York: Palgrave Macmillan.

Kohn, Donald L. and Brian P. Sack (2003): "Central Bank Talk: Does It Matter and Why?," *Board of Governors of the Federal Reserve System Working Paper No. 2003-55.*

Lauck, W. Jett (1907): *The Causes of the Panic of 1893.* Boston/New York: Houghton, Mifflin and Company.

Lauridsen, Laurids S. (1998): "The Financial Crisis in Thailand: Causes, Conduct and Consequences?," *World Development,* 26(8), 1575–1591.

Maddison, Angus (1991): *Dynamic Forces in Capitalist Development: A Long-Run Comparative View.* New York: Oxford University Press.

McCartney, E. Ray (1935): *Crisis of 1873.* Minneapolis: Burgess Publishing Company.

McKenzie, Colin (2013): "Australia's Deflation in the 1890s," *RIETI Discussion Paper Series 06-E-017.*

Merrett, David T. (1997): "Capital Markets and Capital Formation in Australia 1890–1945," *Australian Economic History Review,* 37(3), 181–201.

Moe, Thorvald G., Jon A. Solheim, and Bent Vale (2004): "The Norwegian Banking Crisis," *Norges Banks skriftserie/Occasional Papers No. 33.*

Müller, Stefanie C. (2011): "The Real Estate Bubble in Spain Has Been Pumped Up by All of Us," *AESTIMATIO, the IEB International Journal of Finance,* 2, 2–11.

Neal, Larry (1998): "The Financial Crisis of 1825 and the Restructuring of the British Financial System," *Federal Reserve Bank of St. Louis Review,* 80(3), 53–76.

Nyberg, Peter and Vesa Vihriälä (1994): "The Finnish Banking Crisis and Its Handling (An Update of Developments through 1993)," *Bank of Finland Discussion Papers 7/94.*

Ofek, Eli and Matthew Richardson (2008): "DotCom Mania: The Rise and Fall of Internet Stock Prices," *The Journal of Finance,* 58(3), 1113–1138.

Okina, Kunio and Shigenori Shiratsuka (2003): "Japan's Experience with Asset Price Bubbles: Is It a Case for Inflation Targeting?," in *Asset Price Bubbles: The Implications for Monetary, Regulatory and International Policies,* William C. Hunter, George G. Kaufman, and Michael Pomerleano (eds.), 81–99. MIT Press.

Patrick, Hugh (1998): "The Causes of Japan's Financial Crisis," *Columbia University, Center on Japanese Economy and Business Working Paper 146.*

Posen, Adam (2003): "It Takes More Than a Bubble to Become Japan," *Institute for International Economics Working Paper No. 03-9.*

Postel-Vinay, Natacha (2014): "What Caused Chicago Bank Failures in the Great Depression? A Look at the 1920s," unpublished working paper.

Reserve Bank of Australia (RBA, 2003): "Annual Report 2003," Reserve Bank of Australia, Sydney.

Reinhart, Carmen M. and Kenneth Rogoff (2009): *This Time Is Different: Eight Centuries of Financial Folly.* Princeton University Press.

Renaud, Bertrand, Ming Zhang, and Stefan Koeberle (2001): "Real Estate and the Asian Crisis: Lessons of the Thailand Experience," in *A Global Perspective on Real Estate Cycles,* Stephen J. Brown and Crocker H. Liu (eds.), 25–61. New York: Springer.

Riddiough, Timothy J. (2012): "The First Sub-prime Mortgage Crisis and Its Aftermath," *BIS Papers No. 64.*

Riddiough, Timothy J. and Howard E. Thompson (2012): "Déjà vu All Over Again: Agency, Uncertainty, Leverage and the Panic of 1857," *HKIMR Working Paper No.10/2012.*

Schnabel, Isabel and Hyun Song Shin (2004): "Liquidity and Contagion: The Crisis of 1763," *Journal of the European Economic Association,* 2(6), 929–968.

Schwartz, Anna J. (1987): "Real and Pseudo-Financial Crises," in *Money in Historical Perspective,* Anna J. Schwartz (ed.), 271–288. Chicago University Press.

Sheridan, Richard B. (1960): "The British Credit Crisis of 1772 and the American Colonies," *The Journal of Economic History,* 20(2), 161–186.

Shiller, Robert J. (2008): *The Subprime Solution: How Today's Global Financial Crisis Happened, and What to Do About It.* Princeton University Press.

Silberling, Norman J. (1924): "British Prices and Business Cycles, 1779–1850," *The Review of Economics and Statistics,* 5(2), 223–247.

Vale, Bent (2004): "Chapter 1: The Norwegian Banking Crisis" in *The Norwegian Banking Crisis,* Thorvald G. Moe, Jon A. Solheim, and Bent Vale (eds.), 1–21, Norges Banks skriftserie/Occasional Papers No. 33.

Vihriälä, Vesa (1997): "Banks and the Finnish Credit Cycle 1986–1995," *Bank of Finland Studies E:7* 1997.

Voth, Hans-Joachim (2003): "With a Bang, Not a Whimper: Pricking Germany's 'Stock Market Bubble' in 1927 and the Slide into Depression," *The Journal of Economic History*, 63(1), 65–99.

Ward-Perkins, C. N. (1950): "The Commercial Crisis of 1847," *Oxford Economic Papers*, 2(1), 75–94.

White, Eugene N. (1990): "The Stock Market Boom and Crash of 1929 Revisited," *Journal of Economic Perspectives*, 4(2), 67–83.

(2007): "The Crash of 1882 and the Bailout of the Paris Bourse," *Cliometrica*, 1(2), 115–144.

(2009): "Lessons from the Great American Real Estate Boom and Bust of the 1920s," *NBER Working Paper No. 15573*.

White, William R. (2006): "Is price stability enough?" *BIS Working Papers No. 205*, Bank for International Settlements.

Wirth, Max (1890): *Geschichte der Handelskrisen*. Frankfurt am Main: J. D. Sauerländer's Verlag.

13

Central Banks and Payment Systems

The Evolving Trade-off between Cost and Risk

Charles Kahn
University of Illinois at Urbana-Champaign

Stephen Quinn
Texas Christian University

William Roberds
Federal Reserve Bank of Atlanta

Central banks and payment systems evolved together. Many early central banks were founded as payments institutions: examples include Barcelona's 1401 *Taula di Canvi* (Usher 1934), Genoa's 1408 *Banco di San Giorgio* (Sieveking 1934a), Venice's 1587 *Banco di Rialto* (Luzzatto 1934), the Bank of Amsterdam in 1609 (Van Dillen 1934), the Bank of Hamburg in 1619 (Sieveking 1934b), and Nuremberg's 1621 *Banco Publico* (Denzel 2012). While some central banks were initially established as government fiscal agents (most famously, the Bank of England in 1694; see Clapham 1944), in most cases these institutions were soon drawn into a payments role (Roberds and Velde, 2014).

Today, payment systems continue to be a key part of central banking, and central banking remains at the center of payments. Private payment systems are important throughout Europe and North America. Innovative private systems are ubiquitous, from systems for small retail payments, such as PayPal or Square, through large-value systems like CHIPS and EURO1, and up to the international CLS system. But central bank systems – Fedwire, TARGET, CHAPS, and so on – continue to be the backbone for the rest of payments.

We thank participants in the Bank of Norway's Pre-Conference at the Graduate Institute, Geneva, April 25–26, 2013 and the discussant Ben Norman for many valuable comments and suggestions. The opinions expressed here are the authors' own and do not reflect those of the Federal Reserve Bank of Atlanta or the Federal Reserve System.

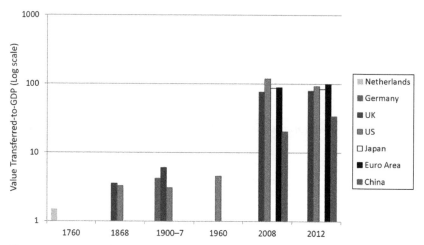

Figure 13.1. Large-value payments to GDP ratios, selected economies

Notes: Ratios represent sum of annual value transferred over all large-value systems for a given country or currency, divided by annual GDP. Sources are Cannon 1910; Carter et al. 2006; Committee on Payment and Settlement Systems 1980, 2002, 2013; Dehing 2012; De Vries and Van der Woude 1997; Hills, Thomas, and Dimsdale 2010: Matthews 1921; Riesser 1911; Ritschl and Spoerer 1997; and Stähler 1909. Figures for 2008 and 2012 include prorated shares of CLS activity. Pre-1955 values are highly approximate.

The importance of payments activity has expanded dramatically since the 1970s with the growth of financial markets, especially the growth in foreign exchange (FX) trading post–Bretton Woods. Figure 13.1 summarizes the historical evolution of "payments intensity" for selected countries, measured as annual value transferred over wholesale systems relative to nominal GDP. Payments activity at the eighteenth-century Bank of Amsterdam was already about 1.5 times contemporaneous Dutch GDP. This ratio did not change greatly over the next three centuries: by 1960 the United States was turning over 4.5 times its GDP through the Federal Reserve's wholesale system (Fedwire). Post–Bretton Woods this ratio increased rapidly in most developed countries, but by 2012 it appears to have leveled out at about 90–100 times GDP, at least for the time being.[1] Payments intensity is still increasing in other parts of the world, For example, China's ratio went from twenty times GDP in 2008 to thirty-four times GDP in 2012.

---

[1] In the U.S. case, about 60 percent of wholesale payments (by value) can be directly attributed to settlement of FX trades, since they take place over systems (CHIPS, CLS) that are specialized to this function. We suspect that FX has a similar share of large-value payments in other countries.

The dramatic expansion in payments activity has created new worries for policymakers. System-wide disasters are of course of great concern. The experience of Fedwire during the events of 9/11 has led systems to pay increased attention to backup and recovery facilities. The experience of individual payment failures in large-value systems and the potential for knock-on effects have led to large-scale reforms, culminating in movement to gross settlement (Bech and Hobijn 2007), the introduction of liquidity-saving mechanisms (i.e., queuing schemes; see Martin and McAndrews 2008), and development of CLS (Continuous Linked Settlement; see Kahn and Roberds 2001, as well as Section 4 in this chapter). And on a day-to-day basis, the overlap in services provided by private and public systems leads to a persistent question for regulatory bodies: to what degree should the private systems, that simultaneously compete with and depend on the public backbone systems, be encouraged or restricted?

In this paper, we will present a simple theoretical framework to illustrate the evolution of central bank payment systems and, importantly, their interactions with private systems. Deficiencies in a payment system create opportunities for a central bank to improve efficiency by offering a privileged form of money. Successfully introducing central bank money then causes the payment system to adjust to its new settlement anchor. Central bank money contributes to the effectiveness of the wider payment system and its characteristics depend on the structure of the central bank. Furthermore, this co-evolution of the elements of a domestic payment system is sensitive to the pressures and opportunities created by international demand for its payment services.

To demonstrate these dynamics, we consider examples of the development of payment systems before, during, and after the introduction of central banks. First, we examine the Early Modern system of bills of exchange prevalent on the European Continent. Next, we examine the Anglo-American experience with banknotes and checks. Finally, we consider modern wholesale payments arrangements for FX, which work through multiple central banks but do not have a unifying central bank.[2]

1 Analytical Framework

In order to make a transaction, a buyer and seller must establish not only the terms of the purchase – price, quantity and quality – but also the terms

---

[2] For other approaches linking the history of payment systems to the development of central banks, see Giannini 2011 and Norman et al. 2011.

of the payment: when, where, and, above all, how.[3] Nowadays, transactors have a variety of payment methods available to them: cash, checks, and various payment cards and internet arrangements. But as illustrated in the following sections, economic agents in earlier centuries often faced complex menus of payment methods as well.

Choosing among the alternative means of payment involves trade-offs. As a result, an economy uses a variety of payment methods. For example, cash has high liquidity and finality, but people resist using it because cash is expensive to acquire and protect. Credit cards, in contrast, are cheaper for consumers to use, but expensive for retailers. They are also contingent and have limited secondary market liquidity. We will call the collection of these methods at any particular time, along with their supporting infrastructures, *the payment system.*

Each method of payment has a different profile of advantages and disadvantages,[4] making it most suitable for a different segment of money demand.[5] For example, if the parties to the transaction trust each other, or if the payment is relatively small, they might prefer a technique with higher risks but lower costs. As the costs of particular payments methods change, those payments methods become larger or smaller parts of the overall system.

Conceptually, sources of payments friction can be assigned into two broad camps: *resource costs* and *risk of use.* Payment instruments that have no relative advantage in either resource cost or risk are shunned, and the monies people do use have a relative advantage in one or the other dimension. The set of payment technologies actually used thus exhibits the trade-off between cost and risk (Berger, Hancock, and Marquardt 1996).

Resource costs include costs of record keeping in accounts-based payments arrangements and cost of verification in store-of-value

---

[3] Integrating the multiple dimensions of transactions into an Arrow-Debreu context presents serious challenges. One way of solving this problem is illustrated in Geanakoplos 2009, which treats each different set of terms for a purchase (in this case the collateral requirements) as a different Arrow-Debreu commodity.

[4] A host of recent research has investigated the considerations that lead individuals to choose one means of payment over another in particular transactions. See, for example, Arango and Welte 2012; Foster, Meijer, Schuh and Zabek, 2011; Kahn and Liñares-Zegarra 2012; Klee 2008; Kosse 2012; Leinonen 2008; Schuh, and Stavins 2010.

[5] The term "money" refers to a liquid asset that serves in multiple roles, the most important of them being a means of payment. Most means of payment can be classified as monies. Usefulness as a means of payment is a primary driver of demand for money (the so-called "transactions motive"), although other considerations ("speculative" and "precautionary" motives) also influence demand for money.

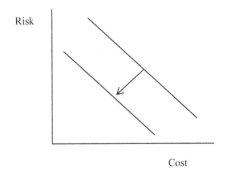

Figure 13.2. Payment system evolution
Source: Adaptation of Berger, Hancock and Marquardt 1996: 700.

arrangements (see Kahn and Roberds 2009). But the most important resource costs can often be summarized by the cost of the collateral tied up in the operation of the payment method.[6] There are several dimensions to the risks in using a payment system, but today, the most relevant are *liquidity risks*[7] and risks associated with *failure of settlement finality*. Historically the risk of loss of value, through inflation or outright default, was also an extremely important consideration when a transactor adopted a payments method. This risk is not a major concern for participants in established systems in developed countries today, but the recent experiences of hyperinflation in Zimbabwe, as well as persistent high rates of inflation in other developing economies, remind us that these concerns are ongoing in some payment systems.[8]

Evolution of the payment system occurs when a technological or institutional innovation reduces the costs or risks of using a payment method. Increased demand for the improved arrangement allows the innovators to earn profits. Figure 13.2 puts this into a schematic, where payment system evolution is that movement of a risk/cost frontier toward a zero cost, zero risk origin, rendering the old frontier feasible but inferior.

---

[6] In historical contexts the cost of the collateral backing the payment system (sometimes the cost of specie) is absolutely clear as will be seen later. In practical contexts it is also clear that the disadvantages of some modern systems stem from the amount of collateral or of central bank funds needed to run them (Martin and McAndrews 2008).

[7] Recent approaches to modeling liquidity risk include Holmström and Tirole 2011 and Brunnermeier and Pedersen 2009.

[8] And despite the remoteness of the risk, the possibility of default by large financial institutions and associated international payment disruption (so-called Herrstat Risk) was the underlying driver in the development of CLS.

568 Charles Kahn, Stephen Quinn, and William Roberds

Such evolution should not be confused with any instantaneous global jump to best practices. There are several reasons for institutions to be sluggish in reaching the technologically feasible frontier. Clearly network externalities and economies of scale are of major importance in the adoption of a particular means of payment. Thus when an incumbent is in place, entrants may not be able successfully to introduce new technologies with combinations of cost and risk that are too similar to existing systems. Instead, outsiders' innovations are more likely to arise in a different region of the efficiency frontier. Political power can also restrict the introduction of superior technologies – either through the state's use of naked power to protect its own monopoly or through influence of a powerful private system's lobbying the state. Still, over time we expect that as inferior payment instruments remain far enough behind the moving frontier, they fall into obscurity, and gradually the payment system does adjust the better to satisfy the economy's money demands.

1.1 State Money

Different types of institutions may control different parts of the payment system. At one extreme are payments arrangements run by private, for-profit corporations; at the other extreme are arrangements which are explicitly arms of the state. Most modern systems lie somewhere in between. Central banks today are state institutions, but they are typically kept insulated from control by other parts of government. Private systems are often cooperative arrangements established by otherwise competing institutions. Typically they are charged with the dual tasks of seeking profits and providing service to their members. Even state institutions can be interested in operating payment systems so as to turn a profit. Nonetheless, for this section we will simplify the discussion by considering the relation between a state sector providing an official means of payment and private entities competing with it.

Among competing payment systems, what distinguishes "state money," supplied by governments or their agents, from the rest? Relative to private suppliers, governments have potential "natural advantages." A sufficiently-stable government can, through its taxing authority and coercive powers, create a degree of credibility and coordination that other institutions cannot match (Kocherlakota 2001; Holmström and Tirole 2011, chapter 5). For example, political credibility might allow a government to develop a fiat money, avoiding expensive collateral. Or a legal tender law might widely and cheaply coordinate a benchmark for debt settlement. Or

The Evolving Trade-off between Cost and Risk 569

government might use state power to incorporate the most reliable and stable privately-provided money available into a state money. We classify state money as *successful* when transactors choose to use it.

History shows that the success of state money is not assured. A state, or the central bank acting as its agent, might lack stability or it might lack a mechanism to confer credibility onto its money, so private arrangements may dominate. One important source of failure is a conflict between the state's short-term profits (seigniorage) and its long term goals for a payment system. The history of coinage provides many examples. For millennia, states produced coins and tried to monopolize their production. Successful mints created confidence in the intrinsic content of their coins, but many regimes gained seigniorage through the debasement of their coins. Yet other coins never became established standards, so that few of them were ever produced and little seigniorage was collected by their issuers. Other illustrations are provided by the history of central banks. Successful central banks have been able to offer a payments medium with advantages over private arrangements; nonetheless there are many examples of institutions that either never gained traction as payment providers, or that collapsed following excessive monetary expansion.[9]

Even if not abusive, state monies may be displaced if they are inferior to the competition. State monies compete not only with private rivals, but with the monies of other states. Historically, the most successful mints created coins that circulated around the world. Similarly, the money of a dominant central bank could attract liquidity from abroad in excess of the nation's role in international trade. Important examples from earlier eras include the British pound (Flandreau and Jobst 2005) and the Dutch guilder (Flandreau et al. 2009; Dehing 2012).

Nowadays the U.S. dollar is the prime example of this "reserve currency" status; it remains to be seen whether the Euro, or possibly the renminbi, eventually supplants the dollar in this role. If it begins to happen, we can expect that the dollar won't give in without a fight. A state has many tools at its disposal in such a struggle. It may attempt to subvert competition by setting legal restrictions that favor its own money. Such legal tender rules

---

[9] Early (pre-Napoleonic) examples of public bank failures or collapse include Genoa in 1444 (Sieveking 1934a), Venice in 1638 (Luzatto 1934), Stockholm in 1664 (Heckscher 1934), Vienna in 1705 (Bidermann 1859), and the 1720 breakdown of John Law's System in France (Velde 2007). The Napoleonic era saw the collapse of many public banks, For example, in Amsterdam (Quinn and Roberds 2014a) and again in Vienna (Raudnitz 1917). More recent examples of hyperinflation-induced collapse are (sadly) too numerous to list here: see Siklos 1995 for a survey.

can strengthen a currency. Promoting usage reinforces network externalities: as a particular type of money becomes more popular, the marginal benefits of holding it increase. On the other hand, efforts to impose an inferior type of money can degrade an entire payment system. Here, a relevant asymmetry is that it is usually easier to impose legal restrictions on centralized systems, so legal tender will have greater effect on debt settlement (when economically centralized through clearing operations and legally centralized through contract enforcement) than on decentralized spot transactions. Otherwise put, it is easier to use illegal money in a side-alley purchase than in a clearinghouse. Nonetheless, legal restrictions, if sufficiently severe, can even push clearing arrangements into the shadows – or nowadays, out of the jurisdiction entirely and into foreign control. Access to private means of payment constrains a state's ability to impose costly public payment systems, and thus its ability to conduct restrictive monetary policies (Kahn 2013). Similarly, the state's powers in the monetary and payments arena limit the kinds of private arrangements that can develop.

1.2 Anchor

Nonetheless, the relation between the private and public spheres of payment is not simply competition between substitutes. If the public authority provides an adequate anchor, then a private system can develop from it. History provides examples of successful coins becoming payment system anchors. For a Renaissance or Early Modern city, coins (and the city's regulations regarding those coins) were the standard of finality and liquidity. Innovators responded by developing alternative payment systems that reduced costs relative to coins: mercantile credit, bills of exchange, and bank accounts. These technologies deferred the need for coin. Additional innovations avoided the use of coin through netting. Bankers learned to clear offsetting claims and merchants learned to clear offsetting bills of exchange (Velde 2009; Börner and Hatfield 2012). Eventually, multilateral netting further avoided usage of coin, so bankers centralized with clearinghouses (for their development in the United States and in the United Kingdom, see Cannon 1910 and Matthews 1921, respectively) and merchants centralized with fairs. Innovation meant that the anchor, coins, moved less and less. But each innovation depended on the stable anchor.

Like coin, successful central bank money can anchor a payment system. Unlike coin, central bank money does not contain intrinsic value – it is not itself made of gold or silver. Rather, central bank money derives value from

The Evolving Trade-off between Cost and Risk

its backing – be it precious metal, sovereign debt, or the state's full faith and credit. Compared to a system anchored by coin, a central bank can reduce or eliminate usage of coin. Displacing a commodity-money anchor, however, creates new challenges for the establishment of commitment mechanisms. Again, such efforts can fail, but when a central bank succeeds, private innovators must find their spot on the efficient frontier. Relative to successful state money, private innovators can either lower costs (at the expense of risk) or lower risk (at the expense of cost). As a consequence, a new and successful state money can set off rapid innovation – a "punctuated evolution" – as the private side of the payment system responds to the new anchor.

In fact, the private system usually directs its efforts toward cost reduction. When well deployed, the natural advantages of the public provider make it particularly challenging for private arrangements to offer a lower risk profile. This is somewhat paradoxical – after all, as we have seen, the state system has the power to renege on its promises in so many ways. But precisely because of that, a successful state system must develop strong assurance of controls on its growth – a high degree of commitment. The success of state money usually relies on credible limits on supply, and a limited supply increases the costs of this most useful resource.

As a result, confidence in an immediate means of payment has generally required assurance of some controls on its growth. But the necessary commitment makes such systems intrinsically inflexible. In the case of metals, the inflexibility was compounded by dependence on the vagaries of discovery. But more fundamentally, and particularly in fiat systems, the assurance was dependent on a belief that the rules of the game were difficult to change.

On the other hand, this inflexibility means that it is hard to improve on the backing of a stable government in periods of economic stress. The public system is likely to be most expensive but most reliable, thus serving as a refuge in times of crisis. Indeed, the contrast between the need for commitment within the central system and the need for flexibility within the economy as demand for payment grows is the tension which provides space for private systems to develop and compete. The resulting opportunity for private innovation is to offer payment services at a lower cost (but at higher risk) that many transactors find desirable. Figure 13.2 gives a schematic view of the process. To begin, a new state money moves inward the high cost, low risk end of the payment system frontier. Then innovation grows a new frontier toward lower costs/higher risks. The new private system builds on the stability of the anchor.

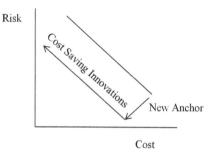

Figure 13.3. Punctuated evolution

1.3 System Risk

Participants choose the payments method that fits best with their preferences for mixing costs and risk. But the social costs of risk may be greater than the private costs. There can be externalities associated with the use of a payment system: misuse or failure of a payment system imposing costs on agents in the economy beyond the participants in the particular transaction. Systemic risk is inherent in any payment system: like national security, the very existence of a payment system enables the economy to rely on it to get things done, and therefore encourages production and investment; its disappearance damages everyone. More narrowly, the use of a payment system requires buying into its specific arrangements. There is value tied up in this, and so the destruction or degradation of the system causes losses to other participants in the system: the more widespread its use the greater these costs. The provider of a system will internalize these values in determining the right level of safety in order to maximize the value for the membership in its payments community, for example, through its specification of amounts of collateral to be posted by participants. To the extent that there are spillovers to non-participants, or to the extent that limited liability on the part of the system provider leaves him unaffected by systemic losses, the state may demand a higher level of collateral than even the system operator would prescribe.

The other half of this trade-off, the cost of the protective collateral, is also the potential source of a wedge between private and social costs. The costs of providing collateral are real enough to the participants who are required to bear them. But central banks have natural advantages in the creation of reserves which can be used as backing in payment systems. A fundamental puzzle in monetary theory is the extent to which costs of central bank reserves used as collateral are truly social costs.[10]

So far we have described a situation in which there is a strict distinction between the backbone public payment system and peripheral private systems. This is an oversimplification in several important respects. First, over time, as the peripheral systems become more central to the economy, the government will extend its rule-making powers to cover them as well. Reserves to back bank notes or deposits become not just a matter of the bank's desire to maintain its business, but also a requirement of public policy – sometimes, as pointed out by Giannini (2011), under pressure from the more reliable among the peripheral providers, in their quest for quality control. Moreover, as the peripheral systems centralize, the central authority tends to provide its capital to them as well. In part this makes perfectly good sense economically: the center is the low-cost provider of reputational capital and it values the preservation of peripheral systems, at least under some circumstances. There are two limits to this process: moral hazard and sheer size. The moral hazard dimension has long been recognized, but the size problem has become important in recent years, as in Iceland, for example, where the peripheral system became so large as to swamp even the sovereign's reputational capital. Finally of course, the decision to provide that reputational capital is only partly voluntary. ("Too big to fail" is not only a phenomenon of the current age; the Bank of Amsterdam felt compelled to lend to the Dutch East India Company despite prohibitions in its charter; see Uittenbogaard 2009). And so the need for rule making by the center is in part a defense against its inability to refuse to bail out private institutions.

1.4 The Role of Information

Information is central to the working of payment systems. As emphasized in Kahn and Roberds (2009), the success of a system requires the ability of participants to distinguish legitimate from counterfeit tokens in "store-of-value" systems and the ability to distinguish identities of counterparties in "account-based" systems. More basically, it requires the ability to distinguish one payment system from its imitators: in other words successful payment systems must be "name brands." The ability to police one's brand

---

[10] The presumed power of central authorities to provide real money balances costlessly underpins much of the debate about optimal money supplies and the Friedman rule. See Lagos and Wright 2005.

is a crucial aspect of the necessary generation of confidence in the system. Historically, sovereigns executed counterfeiters for treason, and developed techniques and institutions for preserving the value of the coin.[11]

Private arrangements band together in guild-like organizations (think of Visa and Mastercard as their modern-day equivalents), not only in order to maintain oligopoly power against rivals, but also to set standards for safety of instruments and guarantee that the public not confuse inferior versions with their own. For both of these reasons payments organizations appeal to the sovereign for protection and exclusive powers, moving down the road from purely private to quasi-public organizations.

One advantage emphasized nowadays in "store-of-value" systems is their ability to provide *anonymity*: payments may be made successfully without disclosing the identity of the payer (Kahn, McAndrews, and Roberds 2005). While this side-benefit has become of increasing interest in recent years with the ever-increasing concern with privacy, this does not seem to us to have been a primary driver in the origination of any payment system before the internet era. Aside from coin, the earliest monetary instrument that permitted privacy was the bearer note. The introduction of bearer notes by the Bank of England in 1694 allowed for anonymity of transactions, but early notes were used for large value, business-to-business payments (Clapham 1944: 22–23). Their primary benefit was to facilitate finality, by allowing an alternative to chains of debt transactions. In other words the important aspect of the trail of information in earlier payment systems is not that an individual did not leave any trail, but that no one needed to worry about following the trail others had left.

The other aspect of information crucial to running a successful payment system is knowledge of counterparty quality. Consistent with the difference in risk, private systems are often confined to smaller groups of participants than the public system. The risk associated with the private system can be reduced by carefully restricting membership to individuals deemed sufficiently reliable, or by limiting transactions to those counterparties whom one can monitor readily. Indeed demand for public systems with improved guarantees only arises when the extent of the community of transactors begins to exceed the confines of such groups.

---

[11] The most famous of these is an elaborate procedure for testing a random sample of newly minted coin for weight and fineness, known in England as the "Trial of the Pyx" (Stigler 1999). This procedure was in use as early as the thirteenth century. Virtually identical procedures were applied in other countries, see, e.g., Polak 1998 for a description of its use in the seventeenth-century, the Netherlands.

1.5 Preview

In the following sections we consider several historical examples in which a central bank or central bank innovation is introduced into an existing payment system. We examine the adjustments that occur as the rest of the payment system develops around the new anchor. We also consider the verdict on the effectiveness of the innovation, as evidenced by international participation in the system.

2 Exchange Banks[12]

The first generation of central banks in Continental Europe offered accounts rather than currency. With the exceptions of Naples and Genoa, the early public banks did not circulate monetary liabilities outside their bank. Instead, Barcelona, Venice, Amsterdam, Hamburg, and others offered only giro transfer within each bank. These early central banks were limited because their goal was to bolster bills of exchange: a private part of the payment system that moved liquidity over long distances. Exchange banks sought to replace coins as a medium of debt settlement. They did not try to displace coins from circulation as a medium of exchange. Even so, the Continental exchange banks were mostly ineffectual, or even counterproductive. An exception was in Amsterdam, where the Bank of Amsterdam did eventually innovate to create a successful anchor money for international payments.

2.1 Coins and Bills of Exchange

In the Early Modern Era, the anchor of the European payment systems was coin. Coins of the finest reputation like the Venetian ducat, the Spanish dollar, or the Dutch rixdollar circulated widely as low risk means of payment for large-value spot transactions. By "low risk" we mean that the likelihood of such coins being of a lower fineness than expected was low for international merchants and their money changers. Gandal and Sussman (1997: 444), for example, put the accuracy of touch-stone assay at around 3 percent and the accuracy of weight at ⅓ percent, so confidence in the fineness of coins was a critical competitive advantage.

Using trade coins, however, was expensive. For example, for the mid-eighteenth century, Nogues-Marco (2013: 468) calculates a 2 percent cost

---

[12] This section is based on Dehing (2012) and Quinn and Roberds (2009, 2012, 2014a, 2014b).

of acquiring and moving silver from London to Amsterdam: perhaps the shortest, safest and busiest international trade route in the world at the time. Costs include brokerage, loading, freight, and assay. Insurance adds another 1–2 percent during peace, and even more during war (Nogues-Marco 2013: 469).

To avoid such costs, merchants used bills of exchange. A bill was an "order instrument," for example an instruction by a merchant in London to a merchant in Amsterdam to pay a sum in Dutch guilders. Instead of buying and transporting coin, a merchant could spend English pounds to buy a bill drawn on Amsterdam.[13] Usually, the exchange rate within the bill delivered more Dutch guilders per English pound than could be acquired by shipping metal. The exchange rate included a charge for time, typically around ¼ percent between London and Amsterdam. Add in brokerage and postage, and total cost might reach 1 percent, or one-third the cost of shipping coin.

The trade-off, however, was risk. Foremost, the person supposed to pay the bill in Amsterdam might not pay. This was called a protest, and it left the creditor seeking compensation at law in Amsterdam or even back in London. Micro-level analysis of bill protest rates is very rare, but Santarosa (2010: 13) does find 44 percent of bills were protested in Marseille around 1780. London and Amsterdam protest rates were likely less, but we have no good estimate, and, as with other debts used as money, the likelihood of default would suddenly increase during a crisis. For our purposes, the relevant point is that compared to coins, bills of exchange were a high-risk, low-cost means of payment supplied by private parties. Government, however, did play a crucial role supporting this part of the payment system by enforcing bill contracts. And here is where the early public banks emerge.

Beyond assuring that contracts would be enforced expeditiously, local-ities sought to clarify the terms of debt settlement. Most commonly, governments would assign an ordinance value to coins denominated in the local unit of account. For example, a legal tender law might say that a particular coin is worth one guilder for settlement of debts public and private. In this way, creditors would know what coin they were due, and thus bills of exchange encouraged. Such legal restrictions could also be self-serving, for they could create demand for coins produced by local mints, and local mints paid profits from seigniorage to domestic government.

---

[13] This form of payment persists in the modern world. For example, a recent *Wall Street Journal* (McMahon 2014) describes the use of bank drafts (bills drawn on commercial banks, payable at a future date) in contemporary China.

The Evolving Trade-off between Cost and Risk 577

To gain this advantage, however, domestic coin had to deliver more unit of account per ounce of silver (or gold) than rival coins. The ratio of value per ounce of metal is called the mint equivalent. If a coin's mint equivalent was high enough, merchants would convert bullion or foreign coin into domestic coin at the local mint (Sargent and Velde 2003).

In spot transactions, merchants could circumvent this process by valuing foreign coins more than ordinances assigned the coins (Rolnick, Velde, and Weber 1996). In debt contracts, however, debtors could insist on repayment at ordinance values. In this, debtors and the local mint had a shared desire to create local coins that disadvantaged creditors. This dynamic was acute in the Early Modern Netherlands because a number of mints could produce legally-favored coins. The competition between mints damaged the reputation of coins by encouraging incremental debasement. Slightly less silver per coin meant a large mint equivalent ratio. In other words, legal restrictions often made local coins the anchor of the international payment system, but those same ordinances could promote the degradation of those same coins. The incentive came from an ability to shift the cost of coin debasement onto creditors, so an imperfect anchor undermined the private sector payment technology built on it. In effect, mints and debtors appropriated some of the cost savings created by bills of exchange.

2.2 Enter the Public Bank: The Case of Amsterdam

Around 1600, Amsterdam was becoming the commercial and financial hub of northern Europe (Gelderblom 2013). The quality of Dutch coinage, however, was suffering mild debasement, and merchants in Amsterdam thought it bad for the bill business. So, in 1609, the city created a bank, the Bank of Amsterdam, whose design was based on an earlier institution in Venice. The city required that bills of exchange settle on the bank's books rather than in coin, and it pledged that at withdrawal its bank would deliver coins of a consistently high quality. The Bank of Amsterdam would protect creditors.

To do this, the bank would suffer an asymmetry: it would accept at deposit Dutch coins with slightly less silver per coin than it would subsequently give out. To prevent arbitrage, the Bank of Amsterdam charged a 2 percent withdrawal fee plus additional fees for coins in high demand. These fees were greater than the difference between circulating coins and the coins the Bank of Amsterdam was obliged to deliver at withdrawal. The high withdrawal fee also meant that a secondary market developed. Instead

578   *Charles Kahn, Stephen Quinn, and William Roberds*

of withdrawing coin, a broker would match an existing bank customer wanting out with a prospective customer wanting in. One person would transfer money within the bank at no fee, and the other would deliver coin outside the bank at a brokerage fee less than the bank's withdrawal fee. In time, brokers became market makers ready to buy or sell at all times.

All this is an example of a new type of secondary market and private intermediary developing to lower the cost of using anchor (Bank of Amsterdam) money. Risk, of course, also went up because dealers did not assure the quality of their coinage with the same credibility as the Bank of Amsterdam. Dealers further reduced costs by offering accounts for non-bill payments outside the Bank of Amsterdam. The secondary market now swapped Bank of Amsterdam balances for private bank balances. And again, risk increased, for now customers had to worry about the private bank's liquidity in addition to the quality of coin they might eventually get at withdrawal.

The Bank of Amsterdam was itself not without risk. In concept, the Bank of Amsterdam was to be a fee-driven, full-reserves "narrow" bank. In practice, the city used its bank to lend to the city's lending bank, the Dutch East India Company, to the Province of Holland, and to important quasi-public persons such as mint masters and tax receivers. After a few decades of heavy lending, the Bank of Amsterdam learned to restrain its credit creation. This conservative position allowed the bank to survive a large run in 1672 when French troops almost overran Holland. Similarly structured public banks in other Dutch cities (Mees 1838) and Hamburg (Sieveking 1934b) did not fare nearly as well, and were forced into lengthy suspensions.

But even the Bank of Amsterdam found it difficult to flourish during the Dutch Golden Age. High withdrawal fees meant coin only infrequently left the bank, but coin deposits were even less frequent. As a result, the Bank of Amsterdam was slowly losing coin in the 1660s and 1670s. It offset the leakage with open market purchases, so the total amount of bank money remained steady. Still the demand for bank money was limited and merchants were unwilling to deposit coin at the Bank of Amsterdam for short term purposes. Coins flowed through the city of Amsterdam to the Baltic, the Mediterranean, and especially Asia, but those coins did not pass through the Bank of Amsterdam.

2.3 From Public Bank to Central Bank

In response to this stagnation, the Bank of Amsterdam made a small but important change. Starting in 1683, deposits were given account balances

The Evolving Trade-off between Cost and Risk 579

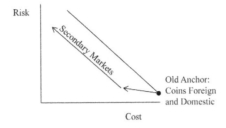

Figure 13.4. Adding the Bank of Amsterdam

and a receipt for the specific coins deposited. Receipts allowed the Bank of Amsterdam to separate the right of coin withdrawal from account balances. After creating that separation, the bank stripped the inherent right of withdrawal from accounts. By themselves, Bank of Amsterdam balances became a type of fiat money. This new system proved popular with Europe's merchants, and demand for bank money grew even among those not compelled by legal restrictions. Bank of Amsterdam money became the leading international currency of the eighteenth century, and new banking structures emerged in Amsterdam because of it.

How did the nexus of receipts and fiat money revolutionize the Bank of Amsterdam as a central bank? It lowered both costs and risk. The development of receipts made it possible to offer withdrawals at very low fees (typically ¼ percent) because customers could no longer arbitrage between types of coin. With a receipt, one got the same coins originally deposited. The bank was scrupulous in not lending these coins, and receipt commitments seem to have also deterred the city of Amsterdam from taking these coins as seigniorage. Receipts created a credible narrow bank within the larger bank, so accounts with a receipt got lower costs and less risk.

Accounts without a receipt also benefitted. Receipts were transferable, so account holders could purchase this low-cost option from other customers instead of paying the bank the higher traditional fees. As this secondary market now served the demand for coin withdrawals, traditional withdrawal fell into disuse except, potentially, during a run on the Bank of Amsterdam. Mindful of this remaining risk, the Bank of Amsterdam quietly ended the right to withdraw accounts without a receipt. Without a receipt, bank balances became a type of fiat money. Customers could transfer them within the bank but could not compel the bank to surrender assets in exchange for them. Limiting the scale of a deposit run to the amount of coin under receipt meant that the Bank of Amsterdam could not be driven

580   *Charles Kahn, Stephen Quinn, and William Roberds*

to failure. Collective action against the bank could only weaken the exchange rate; it could not force the bank to suspend payments.

The 1683 introduction of quasi-fiat money had a strong impact on the bank's payment business. Dehing (2012: 140) estimates that total "giro" turnover through the bank's accounts increased from 204 million florins in 1676 to 249 million florins in 1695. Payments through the bank increased further in the eighteenth century, reaching a peak of perhaps 400 million florins during the Seven Years' War (1756–1763).[14] As noted in the introduction, this is about 1.5 times contemporaneous Dutch GDP, a remarkable level of payments intensity for the time, comparable to that attained by the United States roughly two centuries later (Figure 13.1).

The popularity of the Bank of Amsterdam's post-1683 payment regime is also reflected in the price of bank money. Figure 13.5 gives the fee markets charged month by month from January 1700 to January 1790. During this time, except for periods of war, the price to sell bank money (relative to circulating coin) rarely climbed over 1 percent and rarely fell below zero.

This price stability, combined with Amsterdam's lack of capital controls and advanced financial markets, made Bank of Amsterdam money a successful anchor for the international payment system. Intermediaries responded by developing new types of credit systems that settled using bank money. The most important new players were merchant banks. Unlike commercial banks funded by deposits, merchant banks were funded using bills of exchange. They offered borrowers credit by accepting the bills of exchange drawn abroad (known as acceptance credit). The merchant bankers then issued new bills to fund the acceptance credit. The greatest of these firms (Hope, Pels, and Clifford) became famous in their age. These merchant banks used the Bank of Amsterdam to settle a credit network that extended to most commercial hubs in Northern Europe.

The Bank of Amsterdam's role in bank settlement also opened the opportunity to act as lender of last resort. When a major merchant bank failed in 1763, the acceptance credit market convulsed. Suddenly, banks could not sell new bills to finance bills due, so banks rushed coin to the Bank of Amsterdam to get the liquidity they needed. The Bank of Amsterdam even created a new liquidity facility that helped a couple of especially troubled banks. In all, the Bank of Amsterdam succeeded in saving

---

[14] Authors' extrapolation based on payments volume estimates given in Dehing (2012: 82).

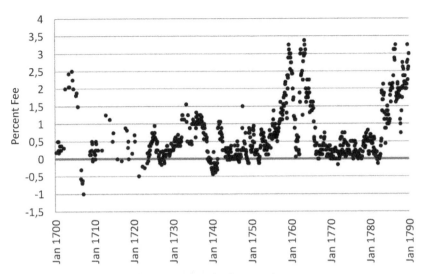

Figure 13.5. Domestic market price of Bank of Amsterdam money
Notes: Sources are McCusker; Gillard; Amsterdam Municipal Archives. Derived by subtracting the market domestic exchange rate (current guilder/bank florin) from the deposit rate of the silver rixdollar coin (1.05 current guilder/bank florin)

Amsterdam's merchant banks, but it could not assist the international customers of those banks. In other words, the financial system that settled in Amsterdam extended well beyond Holland, and this mismatch limited the Bank of Amsterdam's ability to as lender of last resort.

As successful as the Bank of Amsterdam was for most of the eighteenth century, it suffered from a brittle design. Receipts created credibility but very limited fee revenue (approximately 50 basis points per year). Supplementary bank lending to the Dutch East India Company brought extra revenue but also fractional reserve risk. The Bank of Amsterdam kept such lending modest until around 1780. Dutch shipping under the flag of neutrality during the American Revolution angered Britain to the point of declaring war in 1780. The war forced the Dutch East India Company to spend heavily to arm its ships while disrupting the return of cargo from Asia. To finance this situation, the company borrowed heavily from the Bank of Amsterdam and others, but soon the company was unable to repay. The Bank of Amsterdam became insolvent. Fearing some type of default, receipt customers removed coin. The remaining customers, lacking receipts, could not withdraw coins, so the price of bank money broke trend (see Figure 13.5). The end of the war with Britain in 1784 did not restore the Bank of Amsterdam's credibility. Bank money endured,

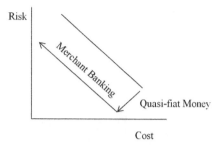

Figure 13.6. Mature Bank of Amsterdam

but it was no longer the "reserve currency" of Europe. One consequence was that merchant banks moved operations across the channel to London (Carlos and Neal 2011).

3 Anglo-American contrast

The Anglo-American evolution of central banks and payment systems took a different direction than on the Continent. Instead of municipal exchange banks, London, and then Philadelphia, focused on banks that issued currency backed by sovereign debt. Privileged note issue brought the central banks fiscal strength, yet central bank existence and independence remained a challenge to secure. And when that failed, commercial banks created quasi-central banking arrangements to support the payment system. The role of central banks in payments makes the United States a compelling contrast to England (James 2012b: 289–291). The two countries' payment system histories are similar enough that the differences outline the role of a central bank's money in the evolution of a payment system.

3.1 Central Bank Innovation: The Bank of England

Silver coins in seventeenth-century London suffered from clipping. This created uncertainty regarding their weight or additional assay costs. Some Londoners avoided coin by adopting what was called the "banking habit." In the 1650s, goldsmith-bankers began to offer checkable deposits for local payments and to arrange bills of exchange for international payments. Some banknotes were issued at this time, but these appear to have been a minor payment instrument (Quinn and Roberds 2003). Alternative payment services reduced costs relative to coin, but, of course, banks were subject to the risk of failure – despite being conservative fractional reserve operators by modern standards. For example, in 1685, loans comprised

The Evolving Trade-off between Cost and Risk 583

42 percent of the assets of Child's bank (Quinn 1994:48), and in 1702 loans were 38 percent of the assets of Hoare's bank (Temin and Voth 2013: 67).

Early bankers also created infrastructure that further reduced the cost of payments. London bankers had bilateral clearing arrangements (Quinn 1997). At least one banker kept agents in foreign ports to facilitate reliable acceptance of bills of exchange (Neal and Quinn 2001). And the largest bankers acted as both tax collectors and sovereign creditors, so taxes due the Treasury could net debt repayments due the bankers.

Exploiting scale economies, the Bank of England's incorporation scheme of 1694 built on this infrastructure. Unlike banker-led syndicates, the corporation was able to raise large amounts of outside capital because its limited-liability stock was easily transferable. And rather than deal in large amounts of coin, the Bank of England issued large amounts of currency when lending and then accepted it back for subscription payments. The business model was a successful application of network externalities: the Bank of England made large-scale issuances of currency to acquire sovereign debt that then backed the currency. As large amounts of the currency circulated in London, expectation of acceptance became routine.

While the Bank of England's money competed with that of other banks, its favored position meant lower risk. Just two years after its founding, the recoinage of England's silver coins created a liquidity crisis and a run. The Bank of England suspended payments, and it would do so again when it was unable to meet its convertibility obligations. While not explicit in law, the Treasury granted this privilege in 1696, 1797, and 1914. While infrequently resorted to, this opt-out was important. Whereas the Bank of Amsterdam could not fail because a portion of its money was always inconvertible, the Bank of England did not fail because all of its money could become temporarily inconvertible.

The Bank of England also secured the stream of seigniorage from note issue. In 1697, the Bank of England gained a monopoly on corporate banking in England and Wales, and forgery of its notes was made a capital offense analogous to counterfeiting coins. As a result, its seigniorage from currency would suffer no large-scale threat until joint-stock banking finally emerged in 1833. Even then, the new corporate banks were kept from issuing currency if they operated in London. This fiscal strength lowered the risk of Bank of England notes, for they were backed by both sovereign debt and by the discounted present-value of currency seigniorage.

The primary risk for the early Bank of England was political. The Bank of England's charter was not perpetual, and the government repeatedly negotiated extensions when the Treasury needed new funds from the Bank

584 *Charles Kahn, Stephen Quinn, and William Roberds*

of England (Broz and Grossman 2004). In effect, the state clawed back some seigniorage through new, below-market borrowing. What is remarkable, however, is how much the government did not take. The Bank of England regularly paid seigniorage profits to shareholders through dividends (Clapham 1944: 292). In contrast, the Bank of Amsterdam passed all its profits to the city, just as central banks today pay their profits to their controlling political authorities.

How the Bank of England gained secure seigniorage appears to have been something of an accident. The Bank of England's start as a corporation was a gamble at a time of intense fiscal stress on the English state. Then, the corporate form proved useful in 1697 to the state as an instrument for debt-for-equity swaps. The swaps let the Treasury convert short-term debt during a rollover crisis. Political winds, however, then blew against the Bank of England when the Tory party came to power in 1710 (Stasavage 2008: 99–129). Tory governments issued Exchequer bills that competed against banknotes, and supported the South Sea Company's gambit to displace the Bank of England in 1720 (Kleer 2012). But the collapse of the South Sea Bubble swung political support back to the Bank of England, and the mood of the era, embodied in the Bubble Act of 1720, emphasized the importance of stability (Harris 1994). The Bank of England endured as a for-profit quasi-arm of the British Treasury.

With stable political backing after 1720, Bank of England notes became the anchor of London's payment system. Again, sovereign debt and seigniorage made them low risk, but scarcity made them costly to use. Before 1760, the Bank of England focused on sovereign lending, so the supply was inelastic to aggregate demand (but elastic to war finance). Private lending was small and limited to customers who lived in London and were engaged in commerce. When the Bank of England relaxed standards enough to lend to banks (called re-discounting), the Bank of England still limited itself to buying high quality paper from the few banks that kept an account. As late as 1793, only a third of London commercial banks had balances with the Bank of England (James 2012b: 297).

3.2 Failed Attempts at Innovation: Banks of the United States

Against political opposition, Alexander Hamilton succeeded in chartering English-style central banking in the new United States in 1791. The First Bank of the United States was a nationally chartered, for-profit corporation whose primary asset was sovereign debt. Its primary liability was privileged banknotes. The U.S. bank had the only interstate charter while most state-chartered banks could not even open intra-state branches. Furthermore, the U.S. bank's notes were legal payments for all debts to the U.S. government.

Unlike in England, the First Bank of the United States did not have a war-time crisis with which to negotiate its first charter renewal. Instead, the war came a year after President Jefferson blocked renewal of the First Bank of the United States. Financing and supplying the War of 1812 over the length of the Atlantic seaboard convinced many, including military leaders, of the need for a central bank as an agent of the Treasury. In the meantime, the U.S. Treasury issued emergency notes, inflation surged, and state banks suspended specie redemption (Rockoff 2000: 654–655).

After the war and the election of a new president, the Second Bank of the United States was chartered for twenty years starting in 1817. The Second Bank was larger than its predecessor, but similar otherwise, and again political opposition was unrelenting. Andrew Jackson campaigned for President twice with the goal of ending the Second Bank, and, in 1832, he famously vetoed the re-charter authorization. The United States then entered a long period without a central bank, and, in the 1840s, the U.S. Treasury withdrew government funds from banks and the financial system altogether. This outcome is in sharp contrast to the post-1720 political equilibrium that supported the Bank of England.

3.3 Private Sector Innovation in Check Payments

In London, as a substitute for Bank of England notes, banks offered access to bank payment services on less restrictive terms. Most lending was at, or near, usury limits, so credit rationing was the binding constraint of the era (Temin and Voth 2013: 73–94). The payment instrument of choice, however, was the check. London banks with six or fewer partners could issue notes, and some did in limited amounts, but none did in any substantial quantity. Perhaps London banks lacked the credibility to directly compete with the Bank of England, perhaps the Bank of England somehow threatened issuing banks, or perhaps most wholesale customers preferred checks. In contrast, Bank of England notes did not usually circulate outside of London, and country banks (located outside of London) issued notes for regional payments. The primary country bank payment service, however, was to supply bills payable on a London correspondent bank (James 2012a).

Because London banks used checks to lower costs, the payment system developed a thick interconnectedness. Checks gain network externalities as local banks accept checks drawn on their rivals. In the process, banks gain routine obligations on each other in the form of checks due for payment. This new system made extensive use of Bank of England notes as a settlement asset. Banks were likely settling checks bilaterally in Bank of England notes even before they created the London Clearinghouse in 1776. The clearing house adopted multilateral netting in 1841, and so reduced the amount of Bank of England notes that participants needed (James 2012a: 135). In this way, Bank of England notes became the anchor of the London banking system and, in time, the center of the English banking system. Country banks and foreign banks used London correspondent banks to secure acceptance of their bills in London, to secure access to the stock and debt markets, and to secure access to the international payments market. London clearing arrangements lowered costs and centralized risk for the nation and much of the rest of the world. When corporate banks emerged in mid-nineteenth-century England, branch networks centered on London, and the system's reliance on the Bank of England continued.

In the United States, the note-check divide was over time instead of over space. Before the Civil War, state-chartered banks issued banknotes, so commerce could avoid the use of coin. While U.S. banknotes were cheaper to acquire than coin, they certainly were riskier. The era famously had such a diversity of note issuing banks that entrepreneurs published guides to help merchants judge authenticity and quality, and dealers used superior information in a manner similar to coin-based moneychangers. Still, such cost- and risk-reducing operations developed because state bank notes did circulate widely. Within a city, most notes passed at par, and railroads and telegraphs reduced the discounts of notes that traveled beyond their city of origin (Gorton 1996; Jaremski 2011). Country banks set up correspondent relationships with trade-center banks (Weber 2003). In some respects, at least, the central bank anchor was not missed in its absence: Inter-city exchange fees were less after the Second Bank of the United States than under it (Bodenhorn 1992; Knodell 2003). And, as with England, the U.S. inter-regional system of notes and bills grew increasingly centered on the metropolis. By the Civil War, New York banks were the hub of inter-regional payments (James and Weiman 2011).

The National Banking Acts of 1864 and 1865 drove state banks into checking and limited the stock of notes that national banks could issue. Check use had been growing before the civil war in local, wholesale payments (James and Weiman 2010: 238). Indeed, by 1860, the level of deposits in the United States roughly equaled the level of bank notes, and

The Evolving Trade-off between Cost and Risk 587

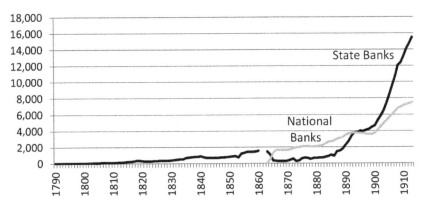

Figure 13.7. Number of U.S. Banks, 1790–1913
Sources: Wright 2001 (1790–1820), Bodenhorn 2001 (1820–1860), Grossman 2003 (1863–1913).

banks in many major cities had already created clearinghouses to settle them. After the Civil War, the volume of checks continued to grow faster than notes and surged well past notes after 1890. New York was the center of settlement as banks across the United States used correspondents in New York for inter-regional transfers, access to the markets, and for FX. Like London, the epicenter was the clearinghouse.

The lack of a central bank did not stop the growth of the American banking system, and the prevalence of unit-bank regulations caused that that growth to be in the number of banks. Figure 13.7 gives the number of state banks, and national banks after 1863. The surge in state banks after 1880 relied on the inter-regional system of check clearing.

3.4 Systemic Implications

Despite their differences, the nineteenth century British and American check payment systems appear to have supported comparable levels of payments activity. In 1868 (the first year for which data becomes available, since settlement occurs through Bank of England accounts rather than with notes), the London Bankers' Clearing House settled £3.4 billion in London-area payments through the Bank of England (Matthews 1921: appendix II), which is about 3.6 times contemporaneous GDP (see Figure 13.1). That same year, the New York Clearing House handled payments of $28.5 billion or 3.3 times GDP (Cannon 1910, 217). The British system expanded to all of England by 1907 and cleared over six times GDP, while the U.S. ratio (based on New York only) declines slightly to 3.1. However, by the early twentieth century there were over 200 regional check clearing houses operating in the United States (for which statistics are unavailable), so the aggregate ratio for the United States may be substantially higher.

Checks, bills, and their settlement infrastructure lowered costs and increased volume, but also created systemic risk. Troubles with an individual bank could spread via clearing and settlement to other banks. In this way, the supplier of money used for clearinghouse settlement gained the opportunity to act as a systemic lender of last resort. In London, this role was played by the Bank of England. In New York, the clearinghouse itself became a LOLR. And here crucial dissimilarities develop.

The Bank of England's (implicit) ability to suspend payments backstopped the system and could prevent commercial banks from suspending (James 2012b). Moreover, the Bank of England could expand lending to banks. This it did aggressively when it suited the Bank of England's operational goals, such as when convertibility was suspended (1797–1825) because of the Napoleonic Wars. Such lending, however, was limited when it went against the Bank of England's internal interests, such as during the Panic of 1825 (Neal 1998). Even when the Bank of England did clearly lend to support the system, it denied any obligation to do so (Bignon, Flandreau, and Ugolini 2012).

In New York, the clearinghouse could, and did, create emergency liquidity during crises, but the amount it could produce was limited to the collective assets of its member banks. The New York clearinghouse had no external reserves the way the Bank of England had its own holdings of gold and sovereign debt, separate from members of the London clearinghouse. As a result, when a crisis pushed the English system to its breaking point, the Bank of England could suspend convertibility into gold, so London banks did not have to suspend their convertibility into Bank of England notes. In contrast, when a crisis pushed the New York clearinghouse to suspend convertibility, it took member banks with it. "Such temporary suspensions were staple strategies of American bankers in times of crisis. . . . In London there was never a general suspension of payments during times of panic (James 2012b: 290)."

James, McAndrews, and Weiman (2013) argue that the U.S. system had grave macroeconomic consequences. With general suspensions, local means of payment suddenly came into short supply, so both payroll and debt servicing were imperiled for otherwise healthy firms. Also, interregional payments propagated the suspension to other cities, as respondent

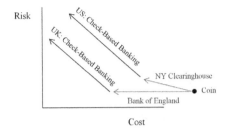

Figure 13.8. Anglo-American contrast, circa 1900

banks had to scramble for alternative sources of liquidity or default on their own payment commitments.

How serious was this difference in deep-crisis performance? The ultimate judgment seems to rest in the FX markets. The world's money favored London, and Amsterdam before it, but not New York (Flandreau et al. 2009). Indeed, one reason the New York banks campaigned for adoption of the Federal Reserve System was to improve the dollar's international attractiveness (Broz 1999). Despite similar payment systems, how the English anchor disconnected from coin (the Bank of England suspending payments) seems an important advance relative to how the United States's disconnected (general bank suspensions).

In our conceptual framework, both the United Kingdom and the United States developed anchors distinct from coin, but the British anchor was less prone to suspension, and so was the resulting payment system built upon it. As a result, Figure 13.8 shows London's check-based payment operating with less systemic risk (at any given cost profile) than New York's. As a result, the British pound became a reserve currency, and much of the world's finance occurred in London (Flandreau and Jobst 2005: 990).

When the Federal Reserve was finally created a century ago, its initial structure was designed to address both domestic and foreign payment system challenges. Foremost, the new system held reserves distinct from those of member banks. It created a system of inter-regional check clearing that helped reduce propagation of liquidity shocks (Gilbert 2000).[15] It actively promoted the international banker's acceptances (Ferderer 2003). As a result, the dollar slowly became a world reserve currency (Eichengreen and Flandreau 2012).

---

[15] Though still imperfectly, see Richardson 2007; Mitchener and Richardson 2013.

4 CLS[16]

The rise of national central banking in the nineteenth and twentieth centuries did not do away with the old problem of how to move international liquidity. Under the gold standard, in principle individuals could acquire FX by redeeming local currency for gold, and then shipping the gold abroad in order to acquire foreign currency. Few did so. Instead, bankers avoided those costs through a variety of financial instruments for interbank transfer, such as bills of exchange and banker's acceptances.

Post–Bretton Woods, people could no longer redeem gold, and interbank financial instruments became the only method available for transmission. Meanwhile, technological advances rapidly decreased the cost of interbank transfer. Indeed, the most striking empirical regularity in payments is the worldwide increase in payments intensity since 1970 (Figure 13.1). Judged by this metric, the nature of the payments business has changed more during the past forty-four years than during the preceding two centuries. The increase in payments intensity mirrors the increase in financial markets trading, particularly trading in the markets for FX. But while the volume has changed dramatically over this period, the nature of the transactions has not. FX transactions are commonly thought of as instantaneous trades of fiat money – one central bank's liabilities against another. But, at least up until 2002, they were simply faster versions of the old interbank transfer mechanisms.

Since 2002, however, central banks have increasingly detached themselves from FX trades, by delegating their settlement to a private institution, the CLS Bank. Traditionally, banks used bilateral financial instruments to bridge different units of account. Now CLS can make those connections, and its account transfers replace the instruments. By operating simultaneously in multiple currencies, CLS is able to control risks of settlement in a way that no single central bank could. CLS may be the most unusual financial institution ever established. By day, it is the largest institution on the planet. By night, it hardly exists. It handles about half of the world's FX transactions, but it is also privately owned and operates with fewer than 500 employees. It was originally designed to do one job – settle international payments – and it does it with extraordinary efficiency. Pressure from the world's central banks more-or-less forced CLS into

---

[16] The discussion of CLS here is based on Kahn and Roberds (2001). See Committee on Payment and Settlement Systems (2008) and the CLS website (www.cls-group.com) for additional information.

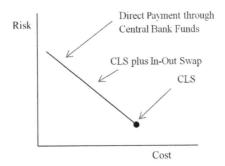

Figure 13.9. CLS spanning domestic payment systems

existence, but its position leads to extremely thorny policy questions for those same central banks.

In terms of our conceptual structure, CLS is a twist. From the point of view of a financial institution "paying" for the purchase of FX, CLS becomes the anchor technology: conducting the transaction through CLS is less risky (and slightly more expensive) than paying directly with central bank money. In order to economize on the collateral costs of conducting its business, CLS has incorporated a large number of collateral-saving devices (some of them inducing slight increases in the risk of the system). Finally banks have available to them bilateral transactions ("in-out swaps") officially outside of CLS, which can further reduce the collateral costs of using CLS, again with increases in the risk of delivery failure. Figure 13.9 illustrates this space of alternatives.

4.1 CLS, a Private Sector Innovation

CLS came into being in 2002, as a result of regulatory dissatisfaction with traditional arrangements for settling FX transactions (Committee on Payment and Settlement Systems 1996, 1998). Settling FX trades poses special challenges both because of the sheer size of the post–Bretton Woods FX markets, and because the underlying nature of FX creates risks that are resistant to traditional risk-limiting strategies such as netting and counterparty substitution. The initial impetus behind CLS was to move the payments used to settle FX trades away from traditional large-value systems (mostly run by central banks) to a specialized institution that could better handle these risks. Although in many cases there is no legal compulsion to use CLS, it has nonetheless enjoyed considerable success. The most recent statistics available on the CLS website (as of this writing, February 2014) indicate that CLS is currently settling a little over $5 trillion daily (counting transactions on both sides) or roughly 50 percent of the world's daily FX turnover (Bech and Sobrun 2013). Measured by value transferred, it is the world's largest payment system (Committee on Payment and Settlement Systems 2013, table PS3), surpassing even the largest single-currency systems.

Payments made through CLS occur as transfers on the books of a limited-purpose U.S. bank (CLS Bank) supervised by the Federal Reserve in cooperation with other central banks.[17] CLS has access to the Fed's large-value system (Fedwire) and also to large-value payment systems in all of the currencies it operates in. "Deposits" into (known as *pay-ins*) and "withdrawals" from CLS Bank (*pay-outs*) occur in central bank funds and occur immediately via the appropriate large-value, real-time gross settlement (RTGS) system.[18] Thus, CLS functions as a "daylight bank" with no deposits in its accounts overnight. Payments (account transfers) over CLS can be made by "member" commercial banks in any of its participating currencies, with about 45 percent of CLS payments occurring in U.S. dollars.

Approximately seventy-five banks are members of CLS.[19] Reflecting the immense turnover in the FX markets, daily turnover at CLS is also enormous. Following days of heavy market activity or U.S. legal holidays (when two days of settlements must be compressed into one), the value of payments made through CLS can be breathtaking–the current record daily value is $10.3 trillion on March 19, 2008, in the wake of the Bear Stearns collapse.[20]

4.2 How CLS Operates: Examples[21]

The special problems of FX settlement, the operation of CLS, and its interaction with traditional large-value payment systems can be illustrated through a series of examples.

---

[17] Actual processing of payments is carried out by a separate U.K. company (CLS Services). Both CLS Bank and CLS Services are owned by a holding company, that is in turn owned by seventy-five financial institutions worldwide (Committee on Payment and Settlement Systems 2008a).

[18] A notable exception occurs for pay-ins and pay-outs in Canadian dollars, which are sent through a net settlement system (the Large-Value Transfer System or LVTS), whose payments are guaranteed by the Bank of Canada. For purposes of the discussion here, these can be regarded as the equivalent of RTGS payments.

[19] CLS also provides indirect settlement services to over 11,000 "third parties," that is, customers of CLS member banks who must settle through a designated member.

[20] Given these magnitudes, it comes as no surprise that the CLS Bank has been designated a "systemically important financial market utility" by U.S. regulators.

[21] The examples and discussion in this section are taken from Kahn and Roberds (2001).

The Evolving Trade-off between Cost and Risk 593

Example 1. On day T, a trader for Bank A buys dollars from a trader for Bank B in return for pounds. For simplicity, say that the agreed-upon exchange rate is \$2/£, and that \$2 million is traded for £1 million. Even though this is a "spot" trade of one currency for another, like most financial market trades it is really an exchange of promises to deliver something (in A's case, dollars; in B's case, pounds) in the near future – day $T+2$ for the canonical spot FX trade.[22]

The first difficulty in settling FX trades occurs because there is limited scope (in this initial example, none) for reducing A's and B's settlement exposures through netting: B has promised to deliver something (dollar funds) which is (traditionally) only deliverable through the U.S. banking and payment systems, subject to U.S. law, while A's delivery must be routed through U.K. institutions.[23] There exists no natural choice of a "third asset" or numeraire that could serve as the basis for netting. The second difficulty is how to enforce conditionality of settlement without the use of a central counterparty – to span both sides ("legs") of an FX transaction, a traditional central counterparty would need to be able to simultaneously replace trading obligations within the constraints imposed by the national institutions of each leg of the trade. For the present time, such centralization remains an impractical option for most FX trades; see however the discussion later.

The traditional method for settling a FX trade relies on separate, unco-ordinated settlement actions by each party to the trade.[24] On day $T+2$, Bank A is obligated to send £1 million to B over the U.K. large-value system (CHAPS) and Bank B is obligated to send \$2 million to A over a dollar payment system (traditionally, CHIPS). Suppose that, due to time zone differences, the sterling transaction is executed first. In most cases, the dollar funds transfer then occurs, settling the trade. But the traditional system can lead to problems, given the finality of payments made in each

---

[22] FX trades also commonly occur as forward transactions or FX swaps (a spot combined with a forward). Issues involving settlement of these types of trades are similar to those arising from spot trades.

[23] Again there are exceptions. One is in the case of *non-deliverable forwards*, which are forward trades of a convertible currency (e.g., dollars) against another currency which may be thinly traded or not fully convertible (e.g., yuan). Non-deliverable forwards are typically settled in the convertible currency, as a cash payment in the difference in the contracted value against the spot value of the nonconvertible currency.

[24] For purposes of illustration, Example 1 assumes that each bank directly makes payments over a large-value payment system to settle the hypothetical trade. In fact, banks often effect settlement by instructing a correspondent to make such payments. Hence the traditional method is referred to as the *correspondent banking method* of settlement.

594   *Charles Kahn, Stephen Quinn, and William Roberds*

currency.[25] If, for example, Bank B is closed down before its funds are sent to Bank A, there is the risk that Bank A may lose its entire principal in the trade.[26] On the other hand, if Bank A is shut down early on date $T+2$, then in practice Bank B is also likely to suffer a loss even if the shutdown occurs before any settlement takes place, because it can be difficult for either bank to cancel its leg of transaction, should it learn of the failure of its counterparty.[27]

The key precept of CLS is to avoid the possibility of loss of principal by requiring both legs of an FX transaction to settle simultaneously, on the books of a single institution (CLS Bank). While CLS does not formally operate as a central counterparty across currencies, its ability to enforce this conditionality allows it to function in many circumstances as a "virtual central counterparty."

For purposes of illustration, assume that Banks A and B are both members of CLS, and that no other transactions take place on day T. On the morning of day $T+2$, each CLS member is required to make a payment (i.e., a *pay-in*) on its short positions. (For the moment we will assume that the payments required are equal to the full value of the trade; more complicated cases are considered later.)

Each bank begins the settlement process by making its pay-in to CLS. These payments are made through RTGS systems in central bank funds – in the example, through Fedwire for the dollar payment and through CHAPS for the sterling payment. The following table shows the holdings of each bank and CLS at that point.

Once CLS has both currencies available to it, settlement is effected through a paired set of payments on the books of CLS, as is shown in Table 13.1A and 13.1B.[28] These payments occur automatically once there are sufficient funds in each bank's account. Note that settlement is on a gross basis; each bank pays and receives the full amount of the funds due in the trade, in the form of balances on the books of the CLS Bank.

---

[25] The payments in this example occur over large-value systems where all payments are irrevocable.

[26] In the literature this risk is variously referred to as *principal risk, Herstatt risk, and (cross-country) settlement risk*.

[27] These difficulties are often attributed to the high degree of automation in settlement processes. For example, KfW Bankengruppe, a German state bank, is reported to have sent €300 million to Lehman Brothers as an automated settlement of a swap, on the same day Lehman filed for bankruptcy (Kulish, 2008).

[28] Formally, payment over CLS does not constitute legal settlement of FX trades but of "the payment instructions arising from the trades" (Committee on Payment and Settlement Systems 2008a, 24, fn 31). For our purposes, the distinction is inessential.

The Evolving Trade-off between Cost and Risk

Table 13.1A. *CLS system after full pay-in*

Bank *A*	
Assets	Liabilities
+ \$2M due from Bank *B*	+ £1M due to Bank *B*
+ £1M due from CLS Bank	
− £1M CB Funds	

Bank *B*	
Assets	Liabilities
+ £1M due from Bank *A*	+ \$2 M due to Bank *A*
+ \$2M due from CLS Bank	
− \$2M CB Funds	

CLS Bank	
Assets	Liabilities (Accounts)
+ £1M CB Funds	Currency Sub Accts.
+ \$2M CB Funds	£ \$
	Bank *A* £1M
	Bank *B* \$2M

Table 13.1B. *CLS system after settlement*

Bank *A*	
Assets	Liabilities
+ \$2M due from CLS Bank	
− £1M CB Funds	

Bank *B*	
Assets	Liabilities
+ £1M due from CLS Bank	
− \$2M CB Funds	

CLS Bank	
Assets	Liabilities (Accounts)
+ £1M CB Funds	Currency Sub Accts.
+ \$2M CB Funds	£ \$
	Bank *A* \$2M
	Bank *B* £1M

596 Charles Kahn, Stephen Quinn, and William Roberds

After that, the currencies can be sent out to the banks via the same RTGS systems that were used for the pay-ins.

Under CLS, final settlement of each side of a transaction is simultaneous and mutually conditional (in payments jargon, this feature is known as *payment versus payment* or PVP, similar to *delivery versus payment* or DVP for domestic securities transactions). As this example shows, with CLS there is never a point at which one leg is settled and the other is not settled. Under the traditional arrangement there is an instant where one bank (Bank *A* in our example) has paid out funds to its counterparty but not received funds in return. Were Bank B to fail at this moment then Bank *A*, as its creditor, would be vulnerable. By contrast, at no point in the CLS process is either bank a net creditor of the other. Under CLS, if Bank *B* fails before settlement, the transaction does not go through, and the funds paid in by Bank *A* are returned to Bank *A*. If Bank *B* fails after settlement, Bank *A* is unaffected.

Of course after settlement, Bank *A* is now a creditor of CLS until CLS sends it the payments to Bank *A*. CLS is an improvement over traditional arrangements, because CLS Bank is a better credit risk than any individual bank. In this simple example, because CLS Bank is never the creditor of any bank, it is invulnerable to failures of other banks. The finality of payments on RTGS systems is key to this arrangement. Because the CLS Bank's assets are simply "good funds," not "due froms," they won't disappear if the bank that paid them in goes bankrupt.

Example 1 is an extreme case: both sides pay in full before settlement. In practice, CLS allows members to overdraft their accounts, so that settlement may occur before all net funds have been paid in.[29] As a result, a (very modest) level of risk creeps back into the arrangement. The next example considers a case where settlement takes place after only a small initial pay-in. Table 13.2A and 13.2B illustrate the settlement process illustrates the settlement process for this example.

Example 2. As before, but suppose that initially Bank *B* pays in $200,000 or 10 percent of its due-to position in its short currency, and Bank *A* pays in a corresponding amount: £100,000. As before, settlement occurs by transferring the required balances between the sub-accounts of the two banks on the books of CLS: £1M from Bank *A*'s sterling sub-account to Bank *B*'s sterling sub-account and $2M from Bank *B*'s dollar sub-account to bank *A*'s dollar sub-account. Now, however, these transactions leave overdrafts in a sub-account for each of the banks. Once sufficient pay-ins are made, the situation is the same as in Example 1, and pay-out can proceed safely. But until pay-in is completed, the system is vulnerable to a failure by either of the banks. For example, if Bank *B* fails before completing its pay-in, CLS Bank will owe Bank *A* $1 million but will only have $100,000 in good funds.

---

[29] CLS however sets a minimum pay-in schedule for each member on a daily basis.

The Evolving Trade-off between Cost and Risk

Table 13.2A. *After initial pay-ins*

Bank A	
Assets	Liabilities
+ \$2M due from Bank B	+ £1M due to Bank B
+ £0.1M due from CLS Bank	
− £0.1M CB Funds	

Bank B	
Assets	Liabilities
+ £1M due from Bank A	+ \$2M due to Bank A
+ \$0.2M due from CLS Bank	
− \$0.2M CB Funds	

CLS Bank	
Assets	Liabilities (Accounts)
+ £0.1M CB Funds	Currency Sub Accts.
+ \$0.2 M CB Funds	£ \$
	Bank A £0.1M
	Bank B \$0.2 M

Table 13.2B. *After settlement*

Bank A	
Assets	Liabilities
+ \$2M due from CLS Bank	+ £0.9M Overdraft at CLS
− £0.1M CB Funds	

Bank B	
Assets	Liabilities
+ £1M due from CLS Bank	+ \$1.8 M Overdraft at CLS
− \$0.2M CB Funds	

CLS Bank	
Assets	Liabilities (Accounts)
+ £0.1M CB Funds	Currency Sub Accts.
+ \$0.2M CB Funds	£ \$
	Bank A −£0.9M \$2M
	Bank B £1M −\$1.8 M

598   *Charles Kahn, Stephen Quinn, and William Roberds*

Although CLS permits member banks to have overdrafts during the settlement process, the overdrafts are subject to limits. A transaction is not settled if it causes a member to exceed its position limits; instead both legs of the transaction are held in a queue until sufficient funds flow into the bank's account. The overdraft limits include limits on each sub account, as well as a separate limit on the sum of overdrafts.[30] Most importantly, a member's net position *across all currencies* is required to be positive at all times. Again, CLS Bank is never in the position of being an overall creditor to any member bank. Thus failure of Bank B does not adversely affect the value of the CLS Bank.

In order to handle the possibility of a failure by a bank with an overdraft, the CLS Bank has arranged lines of credit in each of its currencies with a set of "liquidity providers."[31] Since CLS essentially carries no credit risk, it can obtain these credit lines at extremely small costs. It is clear why the liquidity providers can trust CLS Bank; it is less clear why the CLS Bank should be satisfied with the reliability of its liquidity providers – who turn out to be owners of the CLS Bank, that is, the member banks themselves. Then might the protection offered by them be illusory? There are two counterarguments: first it is the group of liquidity providers as a whole that provides protection to the CLS bank against failure of any individual member. Second, the limits on overdrafts under CLS, while explicitly protecting existing liquidity providers, also serve to convince any potential additional liquidity providers – conceivably including, in extreme situations, central banks – of the ultimate safety of their liquidity infusions.

In the absence of exchange rate fluctuations, settlement could begin before the pay-in of any funds, without violating the principle that a bank's net position at CLS must not be negative. When exchange rates fluctuate, the "out-of-the-money party" (at least) must make some pay-in before settlement can begin.[32]

Thus far, the examples have dealt with a single payment. In fact participants in FX markets make large numbers of exchanges during

---

[30] The limit on the sum of the overdrafts is called the member's *aggregate short position limit*. It is adjusted by CLS according to factors such as capital and credit rating of the member (Committee on Payment and Settlement Systems 2008a, 79–80).

[31] CLS generally has contracts with at least three liquidity providers in each currency.

[32] Thus the net positive balance requirement plays much the same role as margin requirements under "marking-to-market" in a futures clearing arrangement. See, for example, Baer, France, and Moser, (2004), or Moser (1998).

The Evolving Trade-off between Cost and Risk   599

the day, repeatedly swapping currencies back and forth in offsetting or near-offsetting trades.

Example 3. Suppose that Bank A buys $4 million from Bank B for £2 million during the first trade of day T, and then buys £1 million from Bank B for $2 million during the second trade of the same day, with all trades at $2/ £. As before, assume that the dollar rises to £1 = $1.80 by the close of trading on day $T+1$, so that each bank's initial pay-in requirement would be the same as in example 2. That is, at the beginning of day $T+2$, Bank B is net short $2 million and long £1 million, so once again B would need to pay in $200,000.

When settlements occur depends on the size of the two banks' permitted overdrafts. For simplicity we will assume that overdrafts are sufficient to handle each trade. Nonetheless, a trade cannot settle until the pay-ins are adequate to ensure that each bank have a net positive post-trade balance. Since bank B is out of the money $400,000 on the first trade, that trade will not settle until bank B puts a further $200,000 in its account. Once it does, the first trade will settle. Although A is out of the money on the second trade, the settlement of the first trade leaves the net position of A sufficiently positive to enable the second trade to settle as well.

Although the trades are settled, the CLS Bank still lacks the funds to make a payout. These must await the pay-in of additional funds by each of the banks. As those funds appear, payouts are made on settled trades subject to two restrictions: 1) the CLS Bank can never overdraw its account with any RTGS system and 2) all settlement banks' accounts with CLS must remain net positive. Pay-ins, settlement, and pay-outs continue on an ongoing basis until all transactions have been settled and all funds paid out.[33]

4.3 Liquidity Saving and In-Out Swaps

For many of its participants a major advantage of the CLS system is the opportunity it provides to economize on the use of currency through the "liquidity recycling" arrangement described in example 3. For the purpose of settlement the CLS arrangement is *not* a netting arrangement. Each trade settles or fails separately: Given a pair of bilateral trades between two banks, it would be possible for one to settle and the other not to, due for

---

[33] The exact choice of which transactions to pay out first is made according to a proprietary algorithm. The algorithm accords preference to members and currencies with the highest balances and to currencies with the earliest large-value payment system closing times (Committee on Payment and Settlement Systems 2008a, 78).

example to a subsequent failure of a bank to make a pay-in. On the settled trade, payouts become the responsibility of CLS Bank. On the unsettled trades, each bank is returned its initial pay-ins. Nonetheless, CLS shares one important feature with traditional netting arrangements: it economizes on the use of central bank funds. In our simple example, each bank only need pay in its net position in the short currency for CLS to be able to complete the payment process. With stricter caps on overdraft positions a greater pay-in may be required, but as a bank engages in larger numbers of transactions the difference becomes small.

This "quasi-netting" property of CLS settlement generates liquidity savings that are comparable to the savings available through multilateral net settlement. According to the CLS website, quasi-netting reduces pay-in amounts to about 4 percent of the gross amounts due. But (.04) × \$5 trillion is still a lot of money, even by the rarefied standards of today's large-value payment systems. CLS's need for liquidity is exacerbated by its need for immediacy: to enable simultaneous worldwide settlement, CLS must begin processing payments very early in the American and European business days, when traditionally little liquidity is available except through central banks.[34]

CLS's liquidity demand could, in principle, be entirely met by borrowing from central banks, but CLS member banks have been reluctant to tie up their available intraday credit capacity in this fashion. Instead, as a way of reducing the liquidity costs of CLS pay-ins, they have developed a private intraday lending mechanism known as the *in-out swap*. In-out swaps are coordinated through CLS but are technically side agreements that are outside of the CLS system. An in-out swap consists of a pair of transactions that occur on the same day. In the first transaction, a CLS member exchanges, within CLS, a position in a currency in which it is long against a currency in which it is short, thereby reducing both its pay-ins and pay-outs. The second transaction happens later the same day and occurs outside CLS, and reverses the first transaction at exactly the same exchange rates. As with other intraday credit mechanisms, these intraday swaps are not priced and traded; CLS identifies potential swaps the night before and members are free to agree to exchanges "at par" or not.

---

[34] Pay-ins to CLS begin at 7 a.m. Central European Time. Settlement begins at the same time and is normally complete by 9 a.m. CET, but pay-outs (and additional pay-ins) may continue until 10 a.m. CET for Asian currencies, and noon CET for all other currencies.

The Evolving Trade-off between Cost and Risk 601

By using in-out swaps, CLS settlement members have been able to reduce the liquidity required for their pay-ins to less than 2 percent of gross amounts due (Committee on Payment and Settlement Systems 2008a), that is, less than $100 billion equivalent across all currencies on an "average" CLS day.[35] As usual there is no free lunch: since the "outside" transaction in an in-out swap is settled through the traditional "correspondent banking" method of settling FX transactions, the use of in-out swaps represents a partial retreat from the conditionality guarantee of the CLS system. Discussions of this issue usually point out that the residual amount of principal or Herstatt risk that has been reintroduced by the use of in-out swaps is small relative to the risk present before the introduction of CLS.

4.4 Policy Issues for Central Banks

The foregoing discussion shows how payments made through CLS can substitute for payments in central bank money, and provide protection against principal risk in situations where traditional forms of FX settlement could not. The design of CLS, while robust, cannot protect against all types of risks in FX trades in all situations. In particular, CLS cannot guarantee the liquidity of its participants. A CLS member might, for example, fail to pay in its obligation, in which case CLS deletes that member's trades from its system. This protects the principal of the remaining members but may subject them to liquidity pressures due to unexpected shifts in their pay-in requirements. Similarly, a failure of multiple liquidity providers in a given currency could lead to widespread stresses. Thanks to the rule that CLS is never in a negative net position, such an event would not endanger the solvency of CLS, but its ability to make pay-outs in the affected currency could be impaired. In such cases, CLS rules allow for the CLS Bank to complete pay-outs in currencies where sufficient liquidity is available. This again would preserve principal but possibly subject the remaining members to unexpected liquidity demands.

The examples presented earlier should also make clear that any CLS-induced liquidity strains would not necessarily be confined to a single currency. A failure by one member to pay in say, Euro to its CLS account, could lead to a short of liquidity and cause disruptions to large-value

---

[35] For single-currency, large-value payment systems a common ratio of net to gross payments is approximately 1 percent (Bech and Hobijn 2007), which would represent a lower limit on liquidity needed for CLS settlement. CLS does not quite attain this limit but comes close.

payment systems in other currencies. Defenders of CLS have pointed out that cross-currency linkages existed before but were only less apparent, and, because they did not control principal risk, were potentially even more disruptive. However, the ultimate allocation of residual risks, and the extent to which these are borne by central banks, is yet to be resolved.

To date, doubts about the integrity of CLS settlement have remained in the realm of the hypothetical. Notably, CLS was able to continue normal settlement processes in the wake of the market disruptions of 2007 and 2008. A watershed event was the September 2008 failure of Lehman Brothers. Lehman was a "user member" of CLS that relied on another CLS member (Citigroup) for settlement services. The decision by Citigroup to continue to settle the failed member's trades enabled CLS settlement to proceed without disruption. However, use of in-out swaps is reported to have contracted in wake of the Lehman bankruptcy, leading to some reduction in liquidity savings (Foreign Exchange Contact Group and Operations Managers Group 2009).

CLS' ability to withstand the shocks experienced during the recent crisis appears to have blunted movement toward additional centralization of FX clearing. Notably, a recent ruling by U.S. regulators (United States Treasury 2012) has granted FX markets a specific exemption from the clearing requirements of the 2010 Dodd-Frank Act. The ruling makes frequent mention of the efficacy of CLS in controlling settlement risk.

The main business of CLS is settling FX transactions, but it has branched out into other activities. In early 2008 it launched a service (in cooperation with DTCC[36]) for settling credit derivatives trades. By virtue of CLS' connections to multiple large-value payment systems, there is no technological barrier to using it to settle other types of trades as well. Another unresolved policy issue is to what extent future expansions of CLS would be consistent with its original purpose of managing risks in FX markets.

5 Conclusion

From their beginnings, central banks have had a role in payments. This role has rarely been static, however, and as central banks have innovated, these innovations have been matched, and indeed in many cases outpaced, by the private sector. The result has been a steady if not always monotone

---

[36] Depository Trust and Clearing Corporation, which owns several major U.S. financial market utilities.

The first example described the payments role of the Bank of Amsterdam, the most prominent of the Early Modern "exchange banks" – account-based public banks whose principal function was settlement of a form of private payments (bills of exchange) prevalent during that era. In 1683, the Bank of Amsterdam enacted a reform which provided its users cheap access to liquidity, and so was able to take on a dominant payments role within eighteenth-century European commerce. Ultimately the Bank failed, however, because it could not successfully reconcile its payments role with demands on it from fiscal authorities.

Our second example described the payments role of an ultimately more successful institution, the Bank of England. Like the exchange banks, the Bank of England offered accounts, but more important to its operations were the bearer notes that it issued on an unprecedented scale. Lacking the legal and financial resources to compete as note issuers, private banks responded by developing check payments into a viable alternative to notes. However, the private banks remained dependent on the Bank of England for settlement services, and especially for access to liquidity during financial crises. The nineteenth-century U.S. banking system sought to imitate the British success with checks, but a lack of a strong central bank made the highly fragmented American system susceptible to frequent crises, and therefore less attractive to international participants.

Modern RTGS systems retain aspects of both of these earlier systems, and remain the backbone of payments in most countries. Yet our third example shows how a private-sector payment system, CLS, has been able to take payments beyond the confines of any single-currency system. Through an innovative design, CLS has reduced the chances that FX market participants will suffer a loss of principal in a trade. For FX transactions, CLS is now the anchor; central banks play a vital, but secondary role in this design. But CLS has also helped to increase the interconnectedness of the world's large-value payment systems. The end result may be only to extend central banks' responsibilities for the integrity of payments.

References

Arango, C., and Welte, A. 2012. "The Bank of Canada's 2009 Methods-of-Payment Survey: Methodology and Key Results." Discussion Paper 2012–16, Bank of Canada.

Baer, H., France, V.G., and Moser, J.T., 2004. "Opportunity Cost and Prudentiality: An Analysis of Collateral Decisions in Bilateral and Multilateral Settings." *Research in Finance* 21: 201–227.

Bech, M. L., and Hobijn, B. 2007. "Technology Diffusion within Central Banking: The Case of Real-Time Gross Settlement." *International Journal of Central Banking* 3 (3): 147–181.

Bech, M., and Sobrun, J. 2013. "FX market trends before, between, and beyond Triennial Surveys." *BIS Quarterly Review* (December), 45–54.

Berger, Al., Hancock, D., and Marquardt, J. 1996. "A Framework for Analyzing Efficiency, Risks, Costs, and Innovations in the Payments System." *Journal of Money Credit and Banking* 28: 696–732.

Bidermann, H. I. 1859. *Die Wiener Stadt-Bank.* Archiv für Kunde österreichischer Geschichtsquellen, Vienna.

Bignon, V., Flandreau, M., and Ugolini, S. 2012. "Bagehot for Beginners: The Making of Lender-of-Last-Resort Operations in the Mid-Nineteenth Century." *Economic History Review* 65(2): 580–608.

Bodenhorn, H. 1992. "Capital Mobility and Financial Integration in Antebellum America." *Journal of Economic History* 52(3): 585–610.

  2001. "Antebellum Banking in the United States." *EH.Net Encyclopedia,* edited by Robert Whaples. September 5, 2001. http://eh.net/encyclopedia/article/bodenhorn.banking.antebellum.

Börner, L., and Hatfield, J. W. 2012. "The Design of Debt Clearing Markets: Clearinghouse Mechanisms in Pre-Industrial Europe."

Broz, J. L. 1999. Origins of the Federal Reserve System: International Incentives and the Domestic Free-Rider Problem." *International Organization* 53(1): 39–70.

Broz, J. L., and Grossman, R. S. 2004. "Paying for the Privilege: The Political Economy of Bank of England Charters, 1694–1844." *Explorations in Economic History* 41: 48 72.

Brunnermeier, M. K., and Pedersen, L. H. 2009. "Market Liquidity and Funding Liquidity." *Review of Financial Studies* 22(6): 2201–2238.

Cannon, J. G. 1910. *Clearing Houses.* Vol. 6 of the Report by the National Monetary Commission to the U.S. Senate, 61st Cong., 2nd sess., Doc. 491, Government Printing Office, Washington, D.C.

Carlos, A. M., and Neal, L. 2011. "Amsterdam and London as Financial Center in the Eighteenth Century." *Financial History Review* 18(1): 21–46.

Carter, S. B., Scott Sigmund Gartner, Michael R. Haines, and Alan L. Olmstead (eds). 2006. *Historical Statistics of the United States.* Cambridge University Press, Cambridge.

Cavalcanti, R. de O., and Wallace, N. 1999. "Inside and Outside Money as Alternative Media of Exchange." *Journal of Money, Credit and Banking,* 31 (3): 443–457.

Cavalcanti, R. de O., Erosa, A. and Temzelides, T. 1999. "Private Money and Reserve Management in a Random-Matching Model." *Journal of Political Economy* 107(5): 929–945.

Clapham, J. 1944. *The Bank of England, a History.* Cambridge University Press, Cambridge.

Committee on Payment and Settlement Systems. 1980. *Payment Systems in Eleven Developed Countries.* Bank for International Settlements, Basel.

  1996. *Settlement risk in foreign exchange transactions.* Bank for International Settlements, Basel.

The Evolving Trade-off between Cost and Risk 605

1998. *Reducing foreign exchange settlement risk: A progress report*. Bank for International Settlements, Basel.

2002. *Statistics on Payment and Settlement Systems in Selected Countries: Figures for 2000*. Bank for International Settlements, Basel.

2008. *Progress in Reducing Foreign Exchange Settlement Risk*. Bank for International Settlements, Basel.

2013. *Statistics on Payment, Clearing, and Settlement Systems in the CPSS Countries: Figures for 2012*. Bank for International Settlements, Basel.

Dehing, P. 2012. *Geld in Amsterdam: Wisselbank en wisselkoersen, 1650–1725*. Uitgeverij Veloren, Hilversum.

Denzel, M. A. 2012. *Der Nürnberger Banco Publico, seine Kaufleute und ihr Zahlungsverkehr*. Franz Steiner Verlag, Stuttgart.

De Vries, J., and Woude, Ad V. der. 1997. *The First Modern Economy: Success, Failure and Perseverance of the Dutch Economy, 1500–1815*. Cambridge University Press, Cambridge.

Eichengreen, B., and Flandreau, M. 2012. "The Federal Reserve, the Bank of England, and the Rise of the Dollar as an International Currency, 1914–1939." *Open Economies Review* 23(1): 57–87.

Ferderer, P. J. 2003. "Institutional Innovation and the Creation of Liquid Financial Markets: The Case of Bankers' Acceptance, 1914–1934. *Journal of Economic History* 63(3): 666–694.

Flandreau, M., and Jobst, C. 2005. "The Ties That Divide: A Network Analysis of the International Monetary System, 1890–1910." *Journal of Economic History* 65: 977–1006.

Flandreau, M., Galimard, C., Jobst, C., and Nogués-Marco, P. 2009. "Monetary Geography before the Industrial Revolution." *Cambridge Journal of Regions, Economy and Society* 2:149–171.

Foreign Exchange Contact Group and Operations Managers Group. 2009. *Report on Operational Lessons from the Demise of Lehman Brothers in Autumn 2008*. European Central Bank, Frankfurt.

Foster, K., Meijer, E., Schuh, S., and Zabek, M. A. 2011. "The 2009 Survey of Consumer Payment Choice." Public Policy Discussion Paper 11-1, Federal Reserve Bank of Boston.

Gandal, N., and Sussman, N. 1997. "Asymmetric Information and Commodity Money: Tickling the Tolerance in Medieval France." *Journal of Money, Credit, and Banking* 29(4): 440–457.

Geanakoplos, J. 2009. "The Leverage Cycle" NBER Macroeconomics Annual Vol. 24, No. 1.

Gelderblom, O. 2013. *Cities of Commerce: The Institutional Foundations of International Trade in the Low Countries, 1250–1650*. Princeton University Press.

Giannini, C. 2011. *The Age of Central Banks*. Edward Elgar, London.

Gilbert, R. A. 2000. "The Advent of the Federal Reserve and the Efficiency of the Payments System: The Collection of Checks 1915–1930." *Explorations in Economic History* 37(2): 121–148.

Gorton, G. 1996. "Reputation Formation in Early Bank Note Markets." *Journal of Political Economy* 104(2): 346–397.

Grossman, R. 2003. "US Banking History, Civil War to World War II," *EH.Net Encyclopedia*, edited by Robert Whaples. March 17, 2003. http://eh.net/encyclo pedia/article/grossman.banking.history.us.civil.war.wwii.

Harris, R. 1994. "The Bubble Act: It's Passage and Its Effects on Business Organization." *Journal of Economic History* 54: 610–627.

Heckscher, E. F. 1934. "The Bank of Sweden in Its Connection with the Bank of Amsterdam." In *History of the Principal Public Banks*, ed. J.G. van Dillen, 161–199. Martinus Nijhoff, The Hague.

Hills, S., Thomas, R., and Dimsdale, N. 2010. "The UK Recession in Context – What do Three Centuries of Data Tell Us?" *Bank of England Quarterly Bulletin* 50(4): 277–291.

Holmström, B., and Tirole, J. 2011. *Inside and Outside Liquidity*. MIT Press.

James, J. 2012a. "English Banking and Payments before 1826." *Research in Economic History* 28: 117–149.

2012b. "Panics, Payments Disruptions and the Bank of England before 1826." *Financial History Review* 19(3): 289–309.

James, J., and Weiman, D. F. 2010. "From Drafts to Checks: The Evolution of Correspondent Banking Networks and the Formation of the Modern U.S. Payments System." *Journal of Money, Credit and Banking* 42: 237–265.

2011. "The National Bank Acts and the Transformation of New York City Banking During the Civil War Era." *Journal of Economic History* 71(2): 338–362.

James, J., McAndrews, J., and Weiman, D. F. 2013. "Wall Street and Main Street: The Macroeconomic Consequences of New York Bank Suspension, 1866–1914." *Cliometrica* 7: 99–130.

Jaremski, M. 2011. "Bank-Specific Default Risk in the Pricing of Bank Note Discounts." *Journal of Economic History* 71(4): 950–975.

Kahn, C. M. 2009. "Collateral Policy in a World of Round-The-Clock Payment" working paper, University of Illinois Department of Finance University of Illinois College of Business working paper 10-0100.

2013. "Private Payment Systems, Collateral, and Interest Rates." *Annals of Finance*, 9(1): 83–114.

Kahn, C. M., and Liñares-Zegarra, J. M. 2012. "Identity Theft and Consumer Payment Choice: Does Security Really Matter?" working paper, University of Illinois, Urbana-Champaign.

Kahn, C. M., and Roberds, M. 2001. "The CLS Bank: A Solution to the Problem of International Payments Settlement?" *Carnegie-Rochester Conference Series on Public Policy*, 191–226.

2009. "Why Pay? An Introduction to Payments Economics." *Journal of Financial Intermediation* 18(1): 1–23.

Kahn, C. M., McAndrews, J., and Roberds, W. 2005. "Money Is Privacy." *International Economic Review* 46(2): 377–399.

Klee, E. 2008. "How People Pay: Evidence from Grocery Store Data," *Journal of Monetary Economics* 55(3): 526–541.

Kleer, R. 2012. "The Folly of Particulars: The Political Economy of the South Sea Bubble." *Financial History Review* 19(2): 175–197.

Knodell, J. 2003. "Duty and Profit in the Second Bank of the United States Exchange Operation." *Financial History Review* 10(1): 5–30.

Kocherlakota, N. R. 2001, "Risky Collateral and Deposit Insurance." Advances in Macroeconomics 1, art 1 1.

Kosse, A. 2012. "Do Newspaper Articles on Card Fraud Affect Debit Card Usage?" research paper, Cash and Payment Systems Division De Nederlandsche Bank, the Netherlands Version: March 2012.

Kulish, N. 2008. "Uproar over German Bank's Payout to Lehman." *New York Times*, September 18.

Lagos, R. 2006. "Inside and Outside Money," Federal Reserve Bank of Minneapolis Research Department Staff Report 374, May 2006.

Lagos, R., and Wright, R. 2005. "A Unified Framework for Monetary Theory and Policy Analysis." *Journal of Political Economy* 113: 463–484.

Leinonen, H. (ed.). 2008. *Evolving Payment Habits*, Proceedings of the Bank of Finland Payment Habits Seminar, 2008.

Luzatto, G. 1934. "Les Banques publiques de Venise (Siècles XVI–XVIII)." In *History of the Principal Public Banks*, ed. J.G. van Dillen, 39–78. Martinus Nijhoff, The Hague.

Martin, A. and McAndrews, J. "An Economic Analysis of Liquidity-Saving Mechanisms." *Federal Reserve Bank of New York Economic Policy Review*, September 2008, 25–39.

Matthews, P. W. 1921. *The Bankers' Clearing House: What It Is and What It Does*. Sir Isaac Pitman & Sons, London.

McMahon, D. 2014. "With Yuan Scarce, Firms Get Stuck with IOUs." *Wall Street Journal*, April 4.

Mees, W. C. 1838. *Proeve eener geschiedenis van het bankwezen in Nederland geduerende den tijd der Republiek*. W. Messcuert, Rotterdam.

Mitchener, K., and Richardson, G. 2013. "Shadowy Banks and Financial Contagion during the Great Depression: A Retrospective on Friedman and Schwarz." *American Economic Review* 103(3): 73–78.

Moser, J. T. 1998. "Contracting Innovations and the Evolution of Clearing and Settlement Methods at Futures Exchanges." Working paper, Federal Reserve Bank of Chicago.

Neal, L. 1998. "The Financial Crisis of 1825 and the Restructuring of the British Financial System." *Federal Reserve Bank of St. Louis Review* 80(3): 53–76.

Neal, L., and Quinn, S. 2001. "Networks of Information, Markets, and Institutions in the Rise of London as a Financial Center, 1660–1720." *Financial History Review* 8: 7–26.

Nogues-Marco, P. 2013. "Competing Bimetallic Ratios: Amsterdam, London, and Bullion Arbitrage in Mid-Eighteenth Century." *Journal of Economic History* 73 (2): 445–476.

Norman, B., Shaw, R., and Speight, G. 2011. "The History of Interbank Settlement Arrangements: Exploring Central Banks' Role in the Payment System" Working Paper No. 412, Bank of England.

Nosal, E., and Rocheteau, G. 2011. *Money, Payments, and Liquidity*. MIT Press.

Polak, M. 1998. *Historiografie en Economie van de "Muntchaos."* NEHA, Amsterdam.

Quinn, S. 1994. "Tallies or Reserves? Sir Francis Child's Balance Between Capital Reserves and Extending Credit to the Crown, 1685–1695." *Business and Economic History* 23(1): 39–51.

1997. "Goldsmith-Banking: Mutual Acceptances and Inter-Banker Clearing in Restoration London." *Explorations in Economic History* 34: 411–432.

Quinn, S., and Roberds, W. 2003. "Are On-Line Currencies Virtual Banknotes?" *Federal Reserve Bank of Atlanta Economic Review* 88: 1–15.

2009. "An Economic Explanation of the Early Bank of Amsterdam, Debasement, Bills of Exchange and the Emergence of the First Central Bank." In *The Evolution of Financial Institutions from the Seventeenth to the Twentieth-First Century* 2009, ed. Jeremy Atack and Larry Neal, 32–70. Cambridge University Press, Cambridge.

2012. "Responding to a Shadow Banking Crisis: The Lessons of 1763." Federal Reserve Bank of Atlanta Working Paper 2012-8.

2014a. "Death of a Reserve Currency." Federal Reserve Bank of Atlanta Working Paper.

2014b. "How Amsterdam got Fiat Money." *Journal of Monetary Economics* 66: 1–12.

Raudnitz, J. 1917. *Das Österreichische Staatspapiergeld und die Priviligierte National-bank: erster Theil 1762 bis 1820.* Kaiserliche und königliche Staatsdruckerei, Vienna.

Richardson, G. 2007. "The Check Is in the Mail: Correspondent Clearing and the Collapse of the Banking System, 1930 to 1933." *Journal of Economic History* 67 (3): 643–671.

Riesser, J. 1911. *The German Great Banks and their Concentration in Connection with the Economic Development of Germany.* Vol. 14 of the Report by the National Monetary Commission to the U.S. Senate, 61st Cong., 2nd sess., Doc. 593. Government Printing Office, Washington, D.C.

Ritschl, A., and Spoerer, M. 1997. "Das Bruttosozialprodukt in Deutschland nach den amtlichen Volkseinkommens- un Sozialproduktsstatistiken 1901–1995." Accessed at www.gesis.org.

Roberds, W., and Velde, F. R. 2014. "Early Public Banks." Federal Reserve Bank of Chicago Working Paper No. 2014-03.

Rockoff, H. 2000. "Banking and Finance, 1789–1914." *Cambridge Economic History of the United States* II: 643–684.

Rolnick, A. J., Velde, F. R., and Weber, W. E. 1996. "The Debasement Puzzle: An Essay on Medieval Monetary History." *Journal of Economic History* 56 (4): 789–808.

Santarosa, V. 2010. "Financing Long-Distance Trade Without Banks: The Join-Liability Rule and Bills of Exchange in 18th-Century France." Yale Working Paper

Sargent, T., and Velde, F. R. 2003. *The Big Problem of Small Change.* Princeton University Press.

Schuh, S., and Stavins, J. 2010. "Why are (Some) Consumers (Finally) Writing Fewer Checks? The Role of Payment Characteristics." *Journal of Banking & Finance* 34: 1745–1758.

Sieveking, H. 1934a. "Das Bankwesen in Genua und die Bank von San Giorgio." In *History of the Principal Public Banks*, ed. J.G. van Dillen, 15–38. Martinus Nijhoff, The Hague.

1934b. "Die Hamburger Bank." In *History of the Principal Public Banks*, ed. J.G. van Dillen, 125–160. Martinus Nijhoff, The Hague.

Siklos, P. 1995. *Great Inflations of the 20th Century*. Edward Elgar, Aldershot.

Stähler, P. 1909. *Der Giroverkehr: seine Entwicklung und international Ausgestaltung*. A. Deichert, Leipzig.

Stasavage, D. 2008. *Public Debt and the Birth of the Democratic State*. Cambridge University Press, Cambridge.

Stigler, S. M. 1999. *Statistics on the Table: The History of Statistical Concepts and Methods*. Harvard University Press, Cambridge.

Temin, P. and Voth, H-. J. 2013. *Prometheus Shackled*. Oxford University Press, New York.

Uittenbogaard, R. 2009. "Lending by the Bank of Amsterdam (1609–1802)." In *The Bank of Amsterdam*, ed. Marius van Nieuwkerk, 120–131. Sonsbeek, Amsterdam.

United States Department of the Treasury. 2012. "Determination of Foreign Exchange Swaps and Foreign Exchange Forwards Under the Commodity Exchange Act." *Federal Register* 77(224), 69694–69705.

Usher, A. P. 1934. *The Early History of Deposit Banking in Mediterranean Europe*. Harvard University Press, Cambridge.

Van Dillen, J. G. 1934. "The Bank of Amsterdam." In *History of the Principal Public Banks*, ed. J.G. van Dillen, 79–124. Martinus Nijhoff, The Hague.

Velde, F. R. 2007. "John Law's System." *American Economic Review* 97: 276–279.

2009. "The Case of the Missing Public Bank: Early Modern France." Draft presented at the XVth World Economic History Congress, Utrecht.

Wallace, N. 1983. "A Legal Restrictions Theory of the Demand for 'Money' and the Role of Monetary Policy." *Federal Reserve Bank of Minneapolis Quarterly Review Winter 19*, 7(1): 1–7.

Weber, W. 2003. "Interbank Payments Relationships in the Antebellum United States: Evidence From Pennsylvania." *Journal of Monetary Economics* 50(2): 455–474.

Wright, R. 2001. "Origins of Commercial Banking in the United States, 1781–1830." *EH.Net Encyclopedia*, edited by Robert Whaples. August 15, 2001. http://eh.net/encyclopedia/article/wright.banking.commercial.origins.

14

Central Bank Evolution

Lessons Learnt from the Sub-Prime Crisis

C.A.E. Goodhart

Financial Markets Group, London School of Economics

1 Some Background History

The global financial system that had been developing in the decades up until 1914 was shattered by the two World Wars and the inter-war crisis. The reliance on exchange controls over international capital movements by countries with weak Balance of Payments after World War II further segmented banking systems into separate national silos, especially in Europe. Thus banking in France, West Germany, Spain, etc., was then done primarily, almost solely, by respectively French, German, Spanish, etc., banks. With (almost) all banking done by their own national banks, each country could develop its own national arrangements and traditions of regulation and supervision.

In such a fragmented, nationally based context, regulation, and supervision could, and did, develop separately in each country along lines that depended on the idiosyncrasies of that country's own history, institutional developments and thinking. Thus banking supervision was done within Central Banks in some countries, but in specialised supervisory institutions in others, with a variety of links to the Central Bank. Given the restricted nature of banking, especially in those countries with direct controls on bank lending, there was little need for much direct supervision; in the United Kingdom, the Bank of England undertook limited supervision through the Discount Office, staffed by the Principal with a handful of more junior officials, and this sufficed well enough until the Fringe Bank crisis of 1973/4. There were few bank failures and no bank crises between 1945 and the 1970s.

This separate development of national banking systems in Europe led to differing approaches towards the interactions between Central Banks and their respective commercial banks in the provision of liquidity support, and thus in the definition and requirements for holdings of liquid assets. Prior to the 1970s official controls over liquid assets ratios (and cash ratios) were regarded as more important than capital ratios and requirements. But, just as with differing treatment of liquidity, Central Banks, and separate supervisory institutions, also developed separate definitions, and preferred norms, for the capital funds that they would prefer their own banks to maintain.

The country where the banks had the greatest exposure abroad was the United States. It was then, after World War II, by far the economically most powerful nation, with the largest number of multinational companies. When abroad these companies naturally looked to their own US bank(s) for help with trade finance and other forms of financial support. Having benefited economically from being the arsenal of the West in World War II (and then again with Cold War rearmament and the Korean War), the United States felt no need for exchange controls in the post-war period. So large, reputable European companies, faced with financing constraints in their own country, could borrow in dollars from US banks and swap the funds into domestic currency for use at home. Such capital inflows were generally welcomed.

The Cold War had, meanwhile, been a major factor in the genesis of the euro-dollar market. Institutions of various kinds from Communist countries which earned dollars, for example from trade, did not want to place these with US banks, particularly when sited in the United States; for fear that they might be blocked, should the Cold War flare up. So they began depositing such dollars with European banks, especially in London, and a market for such euro-dollar deposits sprang up there, encouraged by the Bank of England which was keen to see a revival of London's entrepot trade in foreign currencies. So long as sterling did not flow out, such entrepot trade was free of exchange controls.

The central role of the euro-dollar, or more generally the euro-currency, market was given a strong further impetus by the shock quadrupling of oil prices following the (fourth) Arab-Israeli war in October 1973 and the formation of OPEC. The oil producing countries received huge inflows of dollars, which initially they had no means of using domestically. So they placed these, in dollar form, primarily with the largest banks, and mostly in the euro-dollar market.

In particular, the growth of the Euromarkets, with large volumes of such deposits being channelled through the branches and subsidiaries of foreign banks in host countries (especially, but not only, in London), led directly on to the question of what were the relative responsibilities of the home,

612 C. A. E. Goodhart

and host, authorities respectively for the solvency and liquidity of such foreign banks. This question was deemed sufficiently important to engage the direct interest of politicians, in the guise of a meeting of G6 Finance Ministers, together with their Central Bank governors, in France in September 1974. The French Minister, M. Fourcade, then,

went somewhat further in his Press Conference than had been anticipated, and gave the impression that the G10 Central Bank Governors *would* be making an announcement at their subsequent Basel meeting, on the following two days, of measures to monitor and support the euro-markets. So, the Governors found themselves under intense pressure to come up with some form of words to that general effect. (See Goodhart 2011, p. 38.)

The communique that the G10 Govenors then agreed reads as follows:-

At their regular meeting in Basle on 9th September, the Central-Bank Governors from the countries of the Group of Ten and Switzerland discussed the working of the international banking system. They took stock of the existing mechanisms for supervision and regulation and noted recent improvements made in these fields in a number of major countries.

They agreed to intensify the exchange of information between central banks on the activities of banks operating in international markets and, where appropriate, to tighten further the regulations governing foreign exchange positions.

The Governors also had an exchange of views on the problem of the lender of last resort in the Euro-markets. They recognized that it would not be practical to lay down in advance detailed rules and procedures for the provision of temporary liquidity. But they were satisfied that means are available for that purpose and will be used if and when necessary. (BIS Press Communique, 10 September 1974: Also see Goodhart 2011, p. 39.)

So such national separation broke down in the early 1970s under the influence of:

    i. the growth of the euro-dollar international wholesale financial market;
    ii. the arrival in Europe, especially in London, of cross-border (primarily US) banks;
    iii. the imbalances resulting from the oil shock; and
    iv. the growing porosity of exchange control barriers.

This led to a shift of financial regulation to the newly (1975) established Basel Committee on Banking Supervision (BCBS). In some ways this title is a misnomer, since the BCBS has remained throughout the main centre for the promulgation of banking *regulation*, whereas such international *supervision* as has been done (as contrasted with national supervision) has been done heretofore by the IMF; though from 2014 onwards the ECB will also be acting as a supervisory body in the Eurozone.

There then, post 1975, followed decades of increasing financial liberalisation, especially in lending to persons, in the shape of credit and loans, mortgages offered to a wider range of potential borrowers (e.g. subprime), automobile loans, student loans, etc. As Lord Turner (2010) has noted banks were lending relatively much less to industry, where the bigger firms were now looking more to capital markets for finance, and were now intermediating primarily between borrowing and lending individuals. Meanwhile, this financial liberalisation was causing the growth rate of (bank) credit to be significantly greater than that of bank deposits (Schularick and Taylor 2009; Jorda, Schularick and Taylor 2012). In the previous century before about 1970, indeed as far back as the data enable one to go, bank credit expansion and bank deposit expansion had risen hand in hand. Over the next thirty years they diverged, with bank credit growing considerably faster than bank deposits. This was facilitated both by the process of securitisation and by increasing resort to wholesale funding, plus the associated rapid expansion in shadow banking.

Such developments were partly driven by regulatory arbitrage, and this worried the regulators. In particular, securitisation was intentionally shifting the best private sector assets out of the banks, and leaving such banks with the worst quality private sector assets. Basel I appeared to be having the effect of turning 'good' banks into 'bad' banks, and that was unacceptable. This was the background context in which work on Basel II got under way towards the end of the 1990s.

The other main feature of the time, the mid- to late 1990s, was that the analysis of risk (and of potential return), especially by commercial banks, was becoming far more quantitative, i.e. based on mathematical models, and hence supposedly more 'scientific' than before. The key innovation in the field of risk measurement was the development, by Harry Markowitz (1952), of portfolio analysis that led on to the Value at Risk (VaR) metric. So, when the officials at the BCBS turned to the assessment of Market Risk in the mid-1990s, and circulated a draft paper based on their prior system of separate risk buckets, they were told, correctly, by the banks to whom they had circulated their Working Papers that their analytical procedure was old-hat and deficient. The regulatory officials accepted this criticism, and rushed to catch up on their model-building analytical technique, setting up modelling sub-committees, etc. But the private sector could hire more, better-trained 'quants', and the regulatory community became 'cognitively captured' in the sense that it was not only prepared, but actually keen, to use techniques and methods for risk assessment developed by the industry for regulatory purposes.

This was a mistake. This is *not* because the techniques and measurements developed by the private sector were consciously biased and self-serving, but because they were developed for different purposes. The objective of the VaR metric was to tell top management how risky its own portfolio was currently. And almost all the time (risk/return) conditions are (log) normal. But financial returns exhibit fat-tails (excess kurtosis) and downwards skew. So VaR, based on an assumption of normality, is a poor measure of extreme risk. This is of less consequence to the bank manager, since in major crises the authorities will have to respond with policy measures, but the effect of such crises should, of course, be central to the concern of the relevant authorities. Historically based measures of VaR are not so subject to this critique so long as a major crisis occurred during the data period. But long periods of crisis-free outcomes, for example 1993–2007 in most of Europe, led to a diminishing appreciation of risk, and in a supposedly 'scientific' manner to boot.

This was then the context from which Basel II emerged. It sought to correct the distortions to the patterns of credit expansion that Basel I had engendered, primarily by adjusting regulatory requirements to align with the risk metrics developed in the private sector for their own (perfectly proper) purposes. While it did do some good work, e.g. in clarifying the relationship between off- and on-balance sheet requirements, it not only increased the complexity of regulation, now a rising complaint, but it also made the whole system much more procyclical and fragile in a way that was difficult, even, perhaps especially, for regulators to observe. This procyclicality was further exacerbated by the generalised adoption of mark-to-market, 'fair value', accounting procedures. While for most purposes this may well be the best possible practice, for regulatory purposes one needs, instead, to know the likely valuations in the event of stressed, panicky markets, i.e. mark-to-crisis, (Caccioli, Bouchard, and Farmer 2012).

Anyhow most banking systems seemed highly profitable and on a Basel II RWA basis well capitalised in the early summer of 2007, (including Northern Rock). Some economists, White at the BIS, Ragu Rajan, and several of us at the Financial Markets Group (2001) worried that the inherent fragility of the system was being obscured by the procyclicality of Basel II, but, given the temper of the times, nothing was, or probably could have been, done then.

2 Lessons from the Sub-Prime Crisis

The years between 1992, when the European Exchange Rate Mechanism (ERM) collapsed, and 2007 were, perhaps, the most successful economic era of all time. In the developed economies, growth was steady, inflation was held low at around the 2 percent at which most inflation targets were set, unemployment was relatively low, altogether Non-Inflationary Continuous Expansion (NICE, as Governor King christened the period). Although growth in developed economies was slower than in the decades immediately following World War II, during these years growth was much faster in the developing economies, especially in Asia, with more people taken out of poverty during these fifteen years than in any other period of history.

It is still extremely difficult to apportion the responsibility for such a good outcome between good luck and good policy, but some of this beneficial outturn will have been due to good policies, especially those arising from the generalised adoption of a combination of inflation targets and independent central banks. The central banking fraternity was at the acme of its reputation, with the central bank governor frequently being regarded as the second most important person in his/her own country. This bred a certain confidence, the unkind might even describe it as complacency, among central banks during the period.

In particular, prior to 2007/8, there were three comfortable myths, which were commonly accepted not only by central bankers, but also by markets and most commentators.

1) The first myth was that so long as central banks successfully achieved price stability, interpreted as the achievement of inflation targets, and operationally managed by varying the short-term policy interest rate to that effect, then no generalised macro-economic disturbance could, or would, arise. Of course, during these years there had been quite a number of periods of financial disturbance, coinciding with the continuation of macro-economic stability. These included:

   a) 1987: stock market crash
   b) 1991/2: Exchange Rate Mechanism (ERM) collapse
   c) 1994: US bond market panic
   d) 1997/8: Asian financial crisis
   e) 2000/1: NASDAQ Tech equity market crisis

   But all of these had been successfully weathered, in most cases and in large part by generating a sharp decline in the official interest rate after the onset of the financial disturbance. Given the difficulty of either observing, or specifically responding to, a particular asset bubble, there appeared to have been a generalised success in cleaning up any such financial disturbances, coexisting with a continuing stable macro-economic context, after the event, otherwise known as the 'Greenspan put'.

So, the general experience had been that it was both easier, better and more effective to 'clean up' after a financial disturbance arises, than to try to 'lean' into the prior asset boom through a generalised increase in interest rates, which would hit the economy more broadly, (rather than just dampening each particular asset boom).

The lesson that Minsky (1982, 1992) had described and taught, that the very success of stabilising actions would lead to a reduction in volatility and to financial intermediaries reaching for yield, for example via much enhanced leverage, was forgotten; not that Minsky ever became part of the mainstream of economic analysis. Indeed such mainstream economic analysis, in the modern guise of Dynamic Stochastic General Equilibrium (DSGE) models, continued to treat money and finance as a pure veil, with all the action occurring in the real sector of the economy. In such models, default and financial failure was simply assumed away, as were all possible shocks emanating from the financial sector, which was assumed to be perfectly behaved; an assumption which was carried through into the Efficient Markets Hypothesis.

So, the main function of central banks was to vary interest rates to offset the (real) shocks affecting the real economy. Financial stability could be left largely to look after itself.

2) Central bankers on the whole never fully bought this argument that financial stability could be largely disregarded, and left to the efficient workings of the financial system. While some, particularly in the United States, tended in this direction, most others, notably in Europe, always thought that various market inefficiencies and externalities could lead to financial instability, even when the macro economy was behaving itself. But the general view was that any resulting financial disturbances could be absorbed within the system, notably within the central, crucial, and potentially fragile banking system, by ensuring that all banks maintained sufficient *capital* to meet unexpected losses. There had been, as noted earlier, concerns that Basel I was leading to the securitisation of banks' better assets, with the worser ones left on banks' balance sheets. But it was thought

that, absent generalised macro-disturbances, the Basel II Capital Accord, which had been recently negotiated, would guarantee bank solvency. While, with the benefit of hind-sight, this appreciation now looks wildly misplaced, it must be realised that markets, and most commentators, accepted exactly this same optimistic view. Thus, CDS spreads for banks in developed economies, which measure, subject to certain qualifications, the market's view of their probability of failure, were at an all-time low in the early summer of 2007, shortly before the balloon went up.

As noted earlier, the generalised adoption of mark-to-market, 'fair value', accounting practices led to asset price increases, at least in the trading book, feeding directly into banks' accounting profits, and, to the extent retained, to their accounting capital base. But, in so far as such profits and higher capital were due to higher asset prices, they were of course subject to sharp reversal as and when the underlying asset markets reversed.

Moreover, there was little appreciation how little potentially loss-absorbing equity was actually held by banks in their Tier 1 capital base. Particularly in Europe, where there was no underlying simple leverage ratio to act as a constraint, the ratio of overall assets to equity rose in this decade to over 40 or even 50:1. It only required a significant down-turn in the valuations of a major asset class held by the banks to wipe them out. Such underlying fragility was not perceived at the time by regulators, supervisors, monetary authorities, most economic commentators, nor indeed by the bankers themselves. A discussion of why this was so will follow shortly.

3) Prior to the development of wholesale funding markets, with the euro-dollar being the first in the late 1960s, bank liquidity had mostly taken the form of asset liquidity. In particular banks in most countries, partly as a result of the aftermath of World War II, held a sizeable proportion of their assets in the form of their own government public sector treasury bills and bonds. Prior to the 1970s, the British banks held over 30 percent of their portfolio in such liquid assets. These were, of course, relatively low yielding, and, as access to the more flexible wholesale funding markets developed, banks tended to substitute their funding liquidity, i.e. the ability to borrow from such markets as and when needed, in place of asset market liquidity. In the late 1980s, the BCBS had sought to check this trend by agreeing an Accord on Liquidity to accompany the Accord on Capital. But they failed to do so for several reasons, partly that liquidity

management differed from country to country and no important central bank was keen to give up its own operational system in pursuit of a more generalised harmony. In any case it was thought that access to funding liquidity could, indeed, largely replace market liquidity, so long as the banks were perceived as safe, which it was thought that adherence to the Basel II Capital Adequacy Requirement would ensure.

So, absent any concerns about bank solvency, liquidity, it was thought, would always be available via deep, efficient wholesale markets. So, banks in most countries did, indeed, turn to wholesale markets for funding and liquidity, largely running off their liquid assets. By 2007 the main British banks held virtually zero British Government Securities. This same process allowed for a systematic shift in loan/deposit ratios, with lending, especially to the private sector, growing much faster than deposits in most economies. As Schularick and Taylor (2009) have demonstrated, the trend increase in bank loans began to diverge from, and grow faster than, the trend growth of deposits in most developed countries from 1970 onwards. Whereas loans in almost all countries over all prior documented banking history had grown at almost exactly the same rate as deposits, from 1970s onwards they grew much faster. Moreover, the wholesale market financing, whether via repos, commercial CDs, commercial paper, or whatever, was generally uninsured and came from relatively well-informed investors. While most private-sector deposit holders were either insured, uninformed, and/or generally trusting in the safety of their banks, this new trend towards a larger proportion of bank funding being done through wholesale markets left the banks very much at an elevated risk of what Gary Gorton and Metrik (2012) have described as 'the run on the repo', though this could, and should, be generalised, to a run by informed institutional investors, including the banks themselves, on any bank which was perceived as fragile.

Indeed the commercial banks themselves, who appreciated, better than the regulators, how fragile they were themselves, were amongst the first to withdraw their interbank lending to their banking counterparts. The interbank market was one of the first casualties of the Great Financial Crisis (GFC).

These various sources of financial instability were not well perceived in advance by the authorities, markets, commentators, or by the banks themselves, though financial markets, and to some extent bankers, reacted when the sub-prime crisis first hit in the summer of 2007 rather quicker than several of the regulators. In particular, there are quotes from both Bernanke and King at the time indicating that they did not believe that the initial sharp asset market downturn, focussed on the sub-prime US market, could have a generalised effect in bringing about a near-collapse of financial markets either in the United States or more widely in other developed countries. Initially, the scale of asset value declines in the sub-prime market appeared to be relatively low compared to the prior profitability and capital strength of the banking systems, with regulators partly failing to see how the latter had been blown up by fair value accounting.

As everyone knows, the trigger for the Great Financial Crisis was the bubble in the housing market, primarily in the United States, but also in some, but not all, countries in Europe, such as Spain, Ireland and the United Kingdom. Responsibility for the development and continuation of the housing bubble is widespread among the various agents of the economy. In some large part, government policies, especially in the United States, helped to stoke the rise in housing prices. In particular in the United States the government mandated Fannie Mae and Freddie Mac began to provide guarantees for lower quality mortgages, which they had not been prepared to do beforehand, in order to encourage conditions which would allow the less-advantaged in the United States to get onto the housing ladder. In most countries encouragement of wider house ownership was an objective of official policy, and was supported by a range of such policies, both fiscal and otherwise.

Although the credit rating agencies are now accused of conflicts of interest, and being too keen to curry business from the banks involved in securitisation, the actual main failing was over-reliance on formal econometric models. There were excellent monthly data on virtually all aspects of mortgage finance in the United States starting from the 1950s. By the 2000s such data provided over fifty years (600 plus observations) of all aspects of US mortgage finance. During this period, there had only been a very few months in which the value of houses, and mortgages related to them, of a regionally diversified portfolio of housing assets over the United States as a whole had faced a loss, and then only a very small one. While there had been sharp declines in housing valuations in certain specific regions, i.e. the North East in 1991/2, the oil producing states in the mid-1980s, etc., a regionally diversified portfolio virtually never showed a loss, and then only a minor one, over these fifty years. Put those data into a regression analysis, and then what you will get out at the far end is an estimate that any loss of value, in a regionally diversified portfolio of mortgages, of greater than about three or four percent, would be a two standard deviation event, in other words highly improbable. Of course, such econometric regressions are based on the implicit assumption that the future will be like the past, and a better appreciation either of US history, or of experience with housing markets outside the United States, could have led sceptics to realise that these fifty years, from which these data were taken, were unusually favourable.

Nor were most economists much better. It was argued that the remarkably low level of both nominal and real interest rates in the run-up to 2007 would be consistent with asset prices, including housing, rising relative to income. Moreover, with housing prices increasing, the value of assets held by persons was rising faster than their liabilities. Again there was a failure to appreciate that the assets were in illiquid, equity form, whereas the liabilities were in nominal, fixed interest form. So if one marked to crisis, the resulting effect on the private sector could be relatively devastating. Furthermore, it was argued that any wealth effects from the housing price increases were small, or even in some cases negative, so there was no cause to worry about rising house prices having any major effect on conditions in the real economy.

Perhaps not surprisingly, this confidence in the continuation of high, or even further rising, housing prices, fed through onto bankers as well. Lehman Brothers failed not because of proprietary gambling bets on exotic financial instruments. Indeed, their derivative book remained profitable throughout, but because their CEO, Fuld, was confident that he would make money by taking a larger and larger position on Mortgage-Backed Securities (MBS). Whereas there have been several occasions of 'rogue traders', only with AIG, which can be regarded as a failure to control concentrated lending, (a standard banking problem), and earlier with Barings, did such trading imperil the financial institution involved, (and with AIG the system as a whole). Instead, the major banking problem, both in the GFC, and with previous crises, had involved excessive credit extension based on property-related loans, either mortgages, or especially, commercial real estate. Northern Rock, HBOS, Anglo-Irish, the Cajas in Spain, and the Co-op in the United Kingdom, are all examples.

Indeed, virtually everyone was sucked into the general conventional wisdom that housing prices were almost sure to continue trending generally upwards. In this context, of course, sub-prime made perfect sense both to borrowers and lenders. With housing prices increasing, sub-prime borrowers could re-finance after a few years even more easily because their own equity in the house would have increased; they could move from one low teaser rate context to another, without ever having to reset onto the much higher rate which they would have found difficult to repay. But even in those cases when they could not repay, and the lenders had to foreclose, the lenders would not have lost money, again because the housing prices would have gone up, and they could resell at a profit. So, in 2005/6 almost everyone was happy with sub-prime, politicians, rating agencies, economists, lending banks and borrowers. Indeed, it was then frequently considered one of the best examples of great financial innovation ever discovered.

Of course, a few people did see that the market trends were likely to be unsustainable, and some made a lot of money from that perception. Michael Lewis (2011) has written about those who did foresee this in his book, *The Big Short*. What is remarkable about that book is that most of the characters who did foresee the downturn were non-sociable loners, who did not buy into the conventional wisdom.

What I find remarkable is that this narrative has been submerged by a totally different narrative, which is that bankers, almost single-handedly, brought about the collapse of the financial system by consciously taking excessive risk, especially in exotic financial instruments in their investment banking arms, in the expectation of bail-out by the taxpayers. As several articles by Stulz, (e.g. with Fahlenbrach 2009: also see Foote et al. 2012), has revealed, the real problem was that bankers did not realise that they were taking risks with their banks, nor, perhaps, until the very end, was there any expectation that they would either need to be, or would be, bailed out by the taxpayer. They thought that their positions were relatively safe. The high profits and enhanced capital generated by the application of 'fair value' accounting helped to blind both bankers and regulators to the underlying fragility of the system. The basic problem was not that the 'casino banks' were putting the 'utility banks' at risk, but that the 'utility banks' themselves were doing what they have always done, which is to get caught up in a real estate bubble, with excessive credit extension and far too much leverage.

3 Implications

Prior to 2007, there was widespread agreement that the best contribution that monetary policy could make to medium and longer term growth would be to maintain price stability. The medium and long-term Phillips curve was believed to be vertical. Once inflation diverged from a low and stable level resources would be utilised, unnecessarily, to try to offset its deleterious effects. Real growth should be enhanced by real supply-side reforms. So, there was a dichotomy, with the government responsible for growth-enhancing supply-side reforms, and monetary policy responsible for maintaining a context of (price) stability.

Since 2007, however, growth has continued to be extremely disappointing, with only a very sluggish recovery from the sharp downturn in 2008/9. Moreover, fiscal policy has been constrained by the extraordinarily high (for peacetime) levels of both deficits and debts, which has put their long-term sustainability into question. Meanwhile, supply-side reforms are politically difficult to introduce, and usually slow in effect. So, it seemed that the use of monetary policy for improving the growth rate of the economy might be increasingly necessary. These years have, in practice, been ones of generalised deflation, with continuing high unemployment. Nevertheless, even in those cases and in those countries where inflation was seen as a potential danger, there were significant calls for a temporary overshoot of inflation, beyond the target, to be entertained and allowed; indeed some influential commentators sought to bring about conditions in which central banks would commit to allowing a temporary blip of inflation in the future, in order to balance the prior deflationary pressures.

This became a contentious issue. In such conditions should central banks be prepared to put their inflation target at some risk, in order to encourage a faster recovery? Some of the best academic economists, e.g. Woodford and Svensson, advocated that central banks should do just this. On the whole, central bankers themselves were both wary and chary about the virtues of a (temporary) burst of future inflation, as a means of exiting from the present sluggish and reluctant recovery. Perhaps the most important example of the view that expansionary monetary policy should accompany other growth policies is to be found currently in Japan, where the 'three arrows' of Abenomics are being used to try to extricate Japan from two decades of stagnation.

It was always the case that inflation targeting should be applied in a 'flexible' manner, because in the shorter run there was always seen to be a trade-off between inflation and output growth; thus in short periods the Phillips curve is downwards slopping. But now, following the GFC, there are more questions about the medium-term objectives of monetary policy; in particular whether there should be some kind of 'dual mandate'. Should monetary policy aim to promote growth, even if that should put the price stability objective in the medium term at some risk? Whereas some commentators now believe that such a risk is worth taking, on the whole central bankers continue to hold to the maintenance of price stability as being their primary, main objective.

But the GFC has shown that central banks must also consider a secondary objective, in the form of the maintenance of financial stability. If there are to be two objectives, then, according to the Tinbergen principle, there should be at least two sets of instruments, if both objectives are to be hit exactly. This consideration had led to the search for another set of instruments, for the achievement of financial stability. Such instruments have been described, and characterised, as 'macro-prudential instruments'. Effectively their main function is to operate counter-cyclically against booms and busts in asset markets, in particular the property market, both in residential housing and in commercial real estate. This can either be achieved by measures to influence bank loans to such asset markets, in the form of required variations in officially set capital or liquidity ratios held against such specific lending, or in the form of more direct measures to affect such asset markets, whether by margin limitations, for example loan-to-value or loan-to-income controls, or alternatively in the form of fiscal measures, i.e. changing taxes on transactions in such markets.

There are several problems relating to the application of such controls by central banks, even for macro-prudential purposes. As already indicated, it is frequently difficult to observe when a boom is occurring. If people perceive such a boom as unsustainable, then ordinary market processes would bring it to an end. So the fact that a boom is continuing implies that many, possibly most, observers in the system do not believe that it is unsustainable. If so, it is politically difficult, and generally highly unpopular, for a central bank to step in and make housing purchases during a house price boom more expensive. In any case the distinction between a direct quantitative margin control, and a fiscal measure, is quite thin. If the authorities are to be operating directly in the housing or real estate markets more generally, it is arguable that such intervention should be done by the government, rather than by the central bank.

The central bank is on rather firmer grounds, when it intervenes to try to check, during booms, credit expansion by the banks in particular fields, or alternatively to encourage them during busts. Even then, however, the central bank, in trying to use such macro-prudential instruments, will be operating against the momentum and grain of the market. This is quite difficult to do, even during booms. Then it will be unpopular, and since the constraint will, perforce, be granular, it may be relatively easy to avoid by disintermediation either to banks abroad, to shadow banks, or even to lending for non-control purposes which then gets shunted back into the controlled sector. Given the difficulties and unpopularity of measures to try to check a credit boom, the danger is that it would be done too gently to have much effect. For example, the Spanish Dynamic Provisioning Scheme was a successfully designed counter-cyclical macro-prudential measure; and it worked! But it was not sufficiently sizeable, by itself, to prevent the Spanish banking system from running into massive difficulties during the course of the GFC. The problem will be to strengthen the backbone of central bankers in order to impose sufficiently strong macro-prudential measures during the upturn, always realising that it is impossible to foresee when a generalised good outcome is in practice an unsustainable boom.

The difficulties of applying counter-cyclical policies are, however, far greater than busts. During booms, both the micro-prudential and the macro-prudential objectives of strengthening banks go together hand in hand. During busts, however, the micro-prudential authority is even more strongly determined to try to strengthen banks' capital and liquidity ratios. By the very fact that a bust has occurred, it has been demonstrated that, before then, banks must have had insufficient capital and liquidity to survive the bust. So the immediate response is 'that must never happen again'. Capital and liquidity ratios are raised. In that context, how can it be possible to bring about some counter-cyclical macro-prudential easing?

The question of how to undertake macro-prudential counter-cyclical easing during a bust has become acute, of course, during the course of the current GFC. It is clear that banks would have done far better had they had much more loss-absorbent equity capital in the recent crisis. But, if one just asks banks to raise the equity ratio now, then the likely response will be that they will seek to do so by deleveraging, i.e. to reduce their total assets, rather than to increase the amount of equity they have on their books, because the latter would lead to considerable dilution of equity and to a lowering of the Return on Equity (RoE). A partial answer to this quandary is to introduce incentives on bankers to raise equity directly, rather than ask them to raise equity *ratios*. This latter has been done much more successfully in the United States than in Europe.

There are, perhaps, rather fewer problems in trying to adjust liquidity ratios in a counter-cyclical fashion. Liquidity and reserve ratios could be increased, fairly dramatically, during significant upturns in asset booms; and again such required ratios could be lowered, at least somewhat, in the aftermath of severe downturns. After all, in downturns, the central bank is usually striving to inject masses of liquidity; so requiring banks to hold a larger reserve of liquidity themselves at such junctures is, perhaps, less, rather than more, necessary.

Again, more thought needs to be given to separating marginal from average control mechanisms. Thus the United Kingdom's Funding for Lending Scheme (FLS) relaxes both liquidity and equity conditions on new lending, at the same time as the required ratios on existing loans is raised. Similarly, during downturns, the payment, by central banks, of a high average return on banks' deposits held with themselves helps to maintain such banks' profitability. But, if the rate of return on such *marginal* deposits, held by banks with the central bank, was lowered as far as possible, even perhaps made negative, then at the margin the banks would have an inducement to use such marginal reserves to go out and make additional loans and buy additional assets. More thought and innovation about separating the marginal from the average, or divorcing requirements on new lending from those on old lending, could help to facilitate the utilisation of successful counter-cyclical macro-prudential measures in a severe downturn. More thought needs to be given to this difficult issue.

Anyhow, central banks have now been given additional responsibilities, in the field of achieving financial stability through macro-prudential measures, as well as their price stability objective. This raises the question of whether central banks have now been given an overload, and whether this overload might even imperil their independence. Especially if macro-prudential measures should spill over from controls over banks to controls over the asset markets themselves, there will be questions whether the central banks are not infringing into areas which should be the responsibility of the government, rather than for an unelected, but independent, authority. Will the pressures and responsibility on the central bank (governor) simply become too much?

Another potential threat to central bank independence could be that the massive increase in their balance sheet, resulting from unconventional expansionary measures, such as Quantitative Easing (QE), could lead in future to very large losses, as and when interest rates return towards normal. With the central bank being part of the public sector, such losses on Central Bank holdings would actually be internalised within the public sector, with no net economic effect whatsoever. Nevertheless the political and presentational effect of such losses could be made to appear damaging to the continued independence of such central banks.

Finally, the advent of the GFC made it abundantly clear that neither central banks nor economists fully understood the working of the economic system. We, central bankers and economists, no doubt have learnt many lessons as a result of the GFC. But, do we yet really understand enough about the workings of the financial system as a whole? Probably

626   *C. A. E. Goodhart*

not! The very fact, as outlined earlier, that there are several narratives about the main causes of the GFC, indicate that there remain many uncertainties about the way our system works. We cannot be sure that we have learnt the right lessons; uncertainty remains endemic.

References

Bank for International Settlements, (1974), Press Communique, 10 September.

Caccioli, F., Bouchard, J.P., and J.D. Farmer, (2012), 'Impact-Adjusted Valuation and the Criticality of Leverage', *Risk*, 74 (7), December.

Fahlenbrach, R., and R.M. Stulz, (2009), 'Bank CEO Incentives and the Credit Crisis', NBER Working Paper 15212, National Bureau of Economic Research, July.

Financial Markets Group, (2001), 'An Academic Response to Basel II', Financial Markets Group Special Paper No. 130, May.

Foote, C.L., Gerardi, K.S., and P.S. Willen, (2012), 'Why Did So Many People Make So Many Ex Post Bad Decisions? The Causes of the Foreclosure Crisis', Public Policy Discussion Paper, No. 12-2, Federal Reserve Bank of Boston, May 2.

Goodhart, C.A.E., (2011), *The Basel Committee on Banking Supervision: A History of the Early Years, 1974–1997*, Cambridge, UK: Cambridge University Press.

Gorton, G., (2012), 'Some Reflections on the Recent Financial Crisis', National Bureau of Economic Research Working Paper No. 18397, September.

Gorton, G., and A. Metrick, (2012), 'Securitized Banking and the Run on Repo', *Journal of Financial Economics*, 104, 425–451.

Jorda, O., Schularick, M., and A.M. Taylor, (2012), 'When Credit Bites Back: Leverage, Business Cycles, and Crises', Federal Reserve Bank of San Francisco Working Paper 2011-27.

Lewis, M., (2011), *The Big Short: Inside the Doomsday Machine*, London, UK: Penguin.

Markowitz, H.M., (1952), 'Portfolio Selection', *The Journal of Finance*, 7(1), 77–91.

Minsky, H.P., (1982), *Can 'It' Happen Again? Essays on Instability and Finance*, Armonk, NY: M.E. Sharpe.

    (1992), 'The Financial Instability Hypothesis', Working Paper 74, Jerome Levy Economics Institute, Annandale on Hudson, NY.

Schularick, M., and A.M. Taylor, (2009), 'Credit Booms Gone Bust: Monetary Policy, Leverage Cycles and Financial Crises, 1870–2008', NBER Working Paper No. 15512, November.

Turner, A., (2010), 'What do Banks Do? Why Do Credit Booms and Busts Occur? What Can Public Policy Do About It?', Chapter 1 in, *The Future of Finance: The LSE Report*, by A. Turner, et al., London, UK: London School of Economics and Political Science.

15

The Evolution of Central Banks

A Practitioner's Perspective

Andrew G. Haldane
Bank of England

Jan F. Qvigstad
Norges Bank

1 The Purpose of Central Banks

History will show the twentieth century to have been an unprecedented boom period for central banking. At the start of the century, there were low single-figure numbers of central banks globally. By the end of that century, their numbers had swelled to almost 180. This boom reflected, in part, the emergence of new countries. In that sense, the emergence of new central banks was simply part and parcel of the process of state-building. But that begs the question – why have central banks been seen as such essential ingredients of state-building?

History shows that a well-functioning and stable monetary and financial system is a necessary condition for a thriving economy and rising living standards. Or, put differently, a failure to provide such conditions has tended historically to have adverse and far-reaching repercussions, social every bit as much as economic. Financial crises and hyperinflation – the extremities of financial and monetary instability – have often been the catalyst for poverty, war and revolution. They have torn the social as well as economic fabric, with scarring effects on social welfare lasting generations. Monetary and financial stability are, in that sense, public goods.

We have received useful comments from participants at the Norges Bank conference "Of the uses of central banks: Lessons from history", 5–6 June 2014, and especially the discussant of this paper, Anders Vredin. We would also like to thank our colleagues including Farooq Akram, Oliver Bush, Øyvind Eitrheim, Karsten Gerdrup, Victoria Kinahan and Emma Murphy for their comments and contributions. The views and opinions expressed in this paper are our own and must not be reported as those of the Bank of England, Norges Bank and their staff. Contact information: andy.haldane@bankofengland.co.uk; jan.qvigstad@norges-bank.no.

In principle, the public goods of monetary and financial stability could be provided by anyone. In practice, the unconstrained actions of private sector participants have shown themselves incapable of providing these public goods on a sustained and reliable basis. Private money and unregulated banking, despite having their supporters through the ages, have not historically been a recipe for sustained monetary and financial stability. As with the provision of all public goods, left to itself the market has historically tended to under-provide monetary and financial stability.

It does not take an economic theorist to explain why. At root, both fiat money and commercial bank finance are underpinned by trust – and often by little more than trust. Paper money is underpinned by promises, not gold, diamonds or shale gas. So too are bank deposits. Leaving the manufacture of trust or promises to something as amorphous and myopic as the market was unlikely to sustain a steady and reliable supply. And so, historically, it has proved. The world has had banking panics and hyperinflation – catastrophic losses of trust in finance and money – for as long as it has had a recognisable monetary and financial system.

In principle, government or the state could provide trust in money and credit. And for lengthy periods in history, right up until the dawn of the twentieth century, the state was indeed the de facto guarantor of monetary and financial stability in a great many countries. As Giannini (2011) notes: "The evolution of monetary institutions appears to be above all the fruit of a continuous dialogue between economic and political spheres, with each taking turns to create monetary innovation, to menace the stable value of money, and to safeguard the common interest against abuse stemming from partisan interests".

But the twentieth century marked something of a structural break from the past. Central banks, rather than governments, began to play a progressively more pivotal role in safeguarding the stability of money and finance. For some central banks, this role began with the central bank being granted monopoly powers over the issuance of legal tender. More recently, it has taken the form of operational independence over the setting of monetary policy or the regulation and oversight of the financial system.

The reasons for this shift were largely steeped in experience. This had shown governments could act in ways which undermined financial and monetary stability. Sometimes this revealed itself as pressures to print money, or coerce banks, to finance wars; at others, as incentives to over-stimulate monetary policy, or over-relax regulation, for electoral purposes. In either respect, a government shoring up its finances or popularity risked undermining longer-term stability in money and finance. In the language of economic theory, putting power over money and finance in the hands of an elected

The Evolution of Central Banks: A Practitioner's Perspective   629

government sowed the seeds of a time-consistency problem – promising to be chaste, just not yet (Kydland and Prescott, 1977).

Through the twentieth century, central banks have progressively come to be seen as an institutional safeguard against this time-consistency problem.[1] They enabled operational, day-to-day decisions over the stability of money and finance to be delegated to an institution with greater immunity from short-term electoral pressures. Because central banks combined long memories of the past – financial crises, hyperinflation and all – and longevity for the future – an ability to look beyond today's wars or elections – they fitted the institutional bill.[2] What followed was a twentieth century boom in central banks' stock of responsibilities.

As these responsibilities have grown, so too have the demands placed on central banks by governments and wider society. There has been an understandable democratic demand for greater accountability and transparency. In response, frameworks for monetary and financial stability have evolved which place constraints on central banks' actions. These include government-set success targets – for example, for inflation or financial stability – and requirements to explain and account for decisions – for example, through published minutes, reports and parliamentary appearances.

The result has been the creation of monetary and financial policy regimes of what is often described as "constrained discretion" (Bernanke, 2003; Bernanke and Mishkin, 1997). Discretion is delegated to central banks, but is bounded. Inflation-targeting has over the past twenty-five years become the dominant regime for the execution of monetary policy globally. It is one example of a constrained discretionary regime. Although more embryonic, so too are the macro- and micro-prudential policy frameworks which are being built among a number of central banks in the light of the global financial crisis.

Although the language of constrained discretion may be new, the principle itself is not. The essence of central banking through the ages has been exercising discretion within constraints, to learn by doing, to observe and then adapt.[3] This bounded flexibility has been essential for

---

[1] King (2004) argued, given that we live in an uncertain world, it is unlikely that we would want to embed any policy rule deeply into our decision making structure such as giving it the force of law or making it part of a constitution.

[2] Milton Friedman, despite being a strong proponent of rule-based monetary policy, saw a necessary role for the central bank within the monetary system to maintain the sanctity of contract and ensure its effective working (Friedman, 1962).

[3] Eitrheim and Øksendal (2014) study how the division of responsibility between the government and Norges Bank (= "the monetary authorities") has changed over two hundred years, including during crisis management.

preserving trust, both in monetary and financial stability and in the central bank institutions charged with securing them. The actions taken by central banks over the past few years, many new and innovative, provide no better example of this flexibility.

This essay discusses the evolution of central banks as public policy institutions. Given the authors' respective positions, we do so with particular reference to the Bank of England and Norges Bank. This has the advantage not just of familiarity, but also a relatively rich history with together over 522 years of institutional (if not personal) experience. We begin by outlining briefly the institutional history of the two institutions – the past. We then discuss some of the key institutional pillars of the two central banks as they currently operate – the present. Finally, we discuss some of the open issues which are likely to be important to their evolution – the future.

2 Central Banking in the Past

2.1 The Old Lady of Threadneedle Street

The Bank of England was born in 1694. Back then, it had none of the core purposes it has today – namely, maintaining monetary and financial stability. Back in the last years of the seventeenth century, its primary role was to serve as banker to the monarchs of the day, William III and Mary II, along with government. It acted as a financial arm of the monarch and state. Specifically, during its early years, the Bank of England's primary focus was on meeting a seemingly insatiable demand for financing wars.

To set up the institution, monarchs and other private subscribers deposited money balances with the Bank, which were then lent to the government of the day. As a reward, the Bank was allowed to be the sole "limited liability" bank in the United Kingdom. Every other bank in the United Kingdom could at that time have no more than six partners. Because at this stage the Bank was actively competing with commercial competitors for business, this made for an acrimonious relationship between the Bank and the banks (Haldane, 2013).

As the Bank grew larger and more powerful, other banks and important merchants also began to deposit their money with it. With a surplus of funds, the Bank lent out these deposits to other banks, typically by the practice of 'discounting' bills of exchange. The Bank became banker to the banks. The Bank was also allowed to issue its own notes. Indeed, within London it held a monopoly on note issue. Due to the implicit backing of the government, these notes were trusted and circulated freely

The Evolution of Central Banks: A Practitioner's Perspective   631

as currency with the public – the Bank became a banker to the public as well as the banks.

This role, as banker to the banks and the public, was the precursor to the Bank being given a specific remit, underpinned by statute, for putting money on a sound footing. In 1844 the Bank Charter Act was passed, extending the London monopoly on note issuance across the whole of England and Wales, together with a requirement that Scottish banks back their issuance of bank notes with Bank of England notes. At that point, the Bank became the sole issuer of legal tender – public money – in the United Kingdom and has remained so ever since.

Yet, even then, this power was conferred within a well-defined constraint – the Bank could only issue new notes if they were tied to gold reserves. This, together with a fixed price for gold, laid the foundations for the gold standard. In effect, the 1844 Act placed well-defined limits on the Bank's ability to develop its own commercial business interests. In so doing, it moved the Bank decisively towards being a quasi-public institution.

2.2 A New Bank for a New Norway

The Bank of England, together with the Swedish *Riksbank* (established in 1668), are examples of early central banks that initially fulfilled only limited functions. Norges Bank (established in 1816) belongs to another generation, born in the decade after the end of the Napoleonic wars.[4] Despite their individual circumstances differing, these institutions were rooted in the same basic desire – to put the currency on a secure footing after the economic and political havoc of the war years.

An additional factor in the origins of Norges Bank was the restoration of Norway as a nation state as part of the peace dividend in 1814. Having joined forces with the French emperor in 1807, Denmark had ceded Norway to Sweden. But before Sweden could take possession of her prize, the Norwegian national assembly passed a liberal constitution and declared independence. Following a short war, Sweden accepted the new constitution giving Norway sovereignty in all domestic issues, including currency, but under the conditions of a common King and foreign policy.

Establishing a currency was a key challenge for the new state. The monetary system was in chaos as the need to fund the war had led the

---

[4] The Danish (1818), Dutch (1814) and Austrian (1816) central banks were among those belonging to this group.

previous Danish king to use his printing press freely. Rampant inflation followed: from 1807 to 1817 prices increased more than fifty-fold and the currency was eventually devalued by 98 percent. This experience taught Norway's founding fathers some valuable lessons: giving day-to-day responsibility for the currency to the King entailed dangerous temptations; and in order to fulfil the requirements of well-functioning money, currencies had to be stable.

The first lesson generated an institutional response: the chartering of Norges Bank by the Storting (Norwegian parliament) in 1816 as a private joint stock bank with what became a de facto note-issuing monopoly. Although the state was the major shareholder, control of the Bank rested with the Storting, not the King and his government. Moreover, it was agreed in principle that the Bank could not lend to the government or the King.

Symbolising the distance between the Bank and the state, the headquarters of the Bank was situated in a city 500 kilometres (and a mountain range) away from the seat of central government and even further from Stockholm where the King resided.[5] When chartered, Norges Bank was the first bank in the country. Even after the establishment of savings banks in 1822 and commercial banks in 1848, Norges Bank continued to lend directly to the public in competition with other financial intermediaries, in much the same way as had the Bank of England in its early life. Only in the last few years before the First World War did rediscounting for private banks become a main part of Norges Bank's activities.

A new unit of account was defined as a given weight of silver. In theory, any note-holder should have been able to redeem her notes in silver at par. In reality, this was not attained until 1842. That establishing currency convertibility should take some twenty-five years not only reflected the strained economy of the 1820s, but also more fundamental questions of credibility and trust.

Norges Bank had the means to back the note issue – a forced contribution levied on wealth had assembled a considerable silver fund.[6] But to prevent the risk of a run depleting the silver reserves, a strategy fittingly described as *the long promise* was pursued – a strategy aimed at gradually

---

[5] Christiania is current day's Oslo. When the headquarters was finally moved to Christiania in 1897, central bank independence was so ingrained in the prevailing thinking that the distance from the central government no longer was an issue.

[6] The contributors quite unwillingly thereby found themselves as shareholders in Norges Bank.

The Evolution of Central Banks: A Practitioner's Perspective 633

achieving silver convertibility. From 1823 to 1842, the premium commanded by silver over notes was only progressively lowered by the monetary authorities. Eventually, delivering on the long promise became the starting point for a period of monetary stability associated with the silver and later gold standard that lasted until the start of the First World War.[7]

2.3 Banker to the Banks

Banking crises have historically been pivotal in reshaping central bank practices. During the early centuries of its life, the Bank of England's financial stability role was, to say the least, not well articulated. For the whole of the eighteenth century, and a good chunk of the nineteenth century, the Bank was a powerful, direct competitor to other banks. As the ultimate provider of sterling, and the bankers' bank, the Bank was at the fulcrum of the financial system. This allowed commercial banks to piggyback on some of its trust and credibility when their own was at a low ebb. But the Bank's quasi-commercial incentives meant liquidity support to other banks in the system could never be 100 percent assured – a periodic source of friction among commercial banks.

The succession of banking crises over the course of nineteenth century saw the Bank playing an increasingly influential role as liquidity provider of last resort. This meant mobilising its own resources – and those of the City – if a single bank's demise threatened to spill over into the financial system. This was true, in particular, of the banking panics of 1857 and 1866. In this way, the Bank slowly adopted the 'responsibility doctrine' proposed by Walter Bagehot in *Lombard Street*, subsuming its private interest to the public interest (Bagehot, 1873; Roberts, 1994, p. 158). The Barings crisis of 1890 is typically held to be a pivotal event in defining the Bank's role as last resort lender, a role that has continued to the present day.

The story was not dissimilar in Norway. A series of financial crises over the same period led to Norges Bank's gradually establishing its last-resort lending function. In the nineteenth century, three crises stand as milestones. In response to the international crises of 1847–1848, the commitment of Norges Bank to maintain de jure convertibility and protect her silver reserves meant it came close to stopping lending altogether.

---

[7] Norway followed the general European move towards the gold standard in the 1870. Gold replaced silver as the external anchor effectively from 1 January 1874. However, from the perspective of Norwegian monetary stability this was a non-event.

634 *Andrew G. Haldane and Jan F. Qvigstad*

Norges Bank, in her eagerness to stand by her legal commitments, ended up undermining de facto convertibility by restricting specie payments.[8]

Ten years later, the response to the international crisis of 1857 in the wake of the Crimean war was quite different. Norges Bank maintained de facto convertibility, including by sending a steamer to Hamburg loaded with silver to support her own international drafts when the bankers there failed to honour them and by increasing its domestic lending to the public to maintain a well-functioning payment system. In 1899, at around the same time the Barings crisis was hardwiring the Bank of England's liquidity-provision role, Norges Bank for the first time acted as lender of last resort to banks in response to a severe crisis in Christiania (now Oslo) caused by the bursting of a property price bubble – in the words of the then Governor Karl Gether Bomhoff, "to avert or at least limit economic disaster" (Norges Bank, 1899, p. 6). The bank of issue had become a central bank.[9]

Slowly, then, during the course of the nineteenth century central banks transitioned from being competitors *within* the financial system to being guardians *of* that system. This was, in many respects, a natural evolutionary step from central banks having been granted monopoly powers over money issue. Central banks' list of core responsibilities had doubled, from safeguarding the value of the currency to ensuring the smooth functioning of the financial system.

2.4 Central Banks and the Payment System

Banking and payment systems, in one form or another, predate central banks by a millennium or more. Tenth-century Arabic sources point to well-developed banking activities within Muslim territories with cheques being inherited from the Byzantines. In most of Western Europe, coinage was popular and moneychangers expanded their specialist role of valuing coins to offer payment and other banking services based on the deposits held with them (Kohn, 1999; Mueller, 1997).

---

[8] To readers unfamiliar with the particulars of Norwegian geography, this is like telling a Christiania trader: "Yes, of course we will give you silver for your notes. You just have to travel 500 kilometres by horse to pick it up."

[9] A monetary policy reform was enacted in 1892, giving the central bank more flexibility and room to act as lender of last resort. The new act was a product of a long process of discussion and it resembled the British system at the time. First of all, it introduced a more flexible framework for convertibility, but it also allowed temporary breaches during crises, making lender of last resort operations permissible also de jure.

The origins of banking in London can be found among the goldsmiths who developed a banking business based on their specialist service of providing safekeeping facilities. By the 1660s, London goldsmiths were carrying out a banking business by issuing notes against deposits and creating money by issuing further notes to borrowers. The claims that banks accepted on each other were then redeemed on a bilateral basis every few days with the difference settled in coins – in other words, an interbank clearing mechanism saw the light of day.

As economic activity grew, ever more payments needed to be made over greater distances and so volumes and values of interbank obligations increased. To avoid having directly to exchange precious metals or currency in settlement of their obligations, banks sought arrangements by which they could instruct their banks to settle claims on their behalf, either by transferring deposits across their own books or by transferring deposits via interbank arrangements. In that way, claims arose between banks that somehow needed to be settled.

To effect this clearing, the banks had to select a settlement asset that was acceptable to all and establish a set of rules by which such settlements could take place. In short, they needed a payment system. In response, banks' clearing and settlement arrangements became more formalised as a set of rules or conventions. For much of the eighteenth and nineteenth centuries, private clearing houses often played the role of settlement agent for interbank transactions. And often, but not always, these clearing houses provided the settlement asset.

But once central banks were given monopoly powers over legal tender, and stood ready and willing to extend emergency liquidity, central bank money emerged naturally as the asset best able to perform the role of settlement medium. Clearing of interbank payments came increasingly to occur across the books of central banks, typically at end of the business day. That role has largely continued to the present day, though usually with settlement occurring more frequently than daily, often in close to real time.

At least for large-scale interbank payment systems, settlement is usually discharged in central bank liabilities, gross and in real time. In many countries, central banks also have a role in setting or overseeing the rules and obligations which underpin these large-value systems to ensure their robustness (Bank for International Settlements, 2012). In a number of countries, including the United Kingdom and Norway, central banks have gone one step further in providing the infrastructure which enables the operational functioning of the wholesale payment system.

Central banks' role in other pieces of market infrastructure has evolved more slowly and indirectly. For example, central bank involvement in retail or small-value payment systems shows a mixed picture across countries – some providing the settlement asset and overseeing system rules, others not. The same is true of other market infrastructures, from securities settlement systems to central counterparties.

2.5 The Growth of Financial System Oversight

By the early part of the twentieth century, the core tools of central banks' financial stability trade were in place – last resort lending and the provision of a settlement asset to lubricate payment systems. With liquidity provision to the banking system now occurring daily and in scale, this strengthened the case for central banks improving their understanding of the financial strength of the banking counterparties to whom they were now running large credit exposures.

At times of crisis, last resort lending against collateral came with considerable credit risk because of the difficulty of identifying liquidity and solvency risks. Even day-to-day money market operations entailed a degree of counterparty risk. Managing those risks called for an understanding of the balance sheet strength of counterparty banks. Out of this balance sheet concern grew an informal and unofficial form of banking supervision by central banks. This had no statutory backing, relying instead on informal credit risk checks and the occasional raised eyebrow by the Governor of the day.

In the period immediately after the Second World War, regulatory constraints and restrictions on banks tightened. So too did exchange controls to support the Bretton Woods system of fixed-but-adjustable exchange rates. These constraints suppressed bank balance sheet growth and dampened risk-taking. The world experienced an extended period of financial repression. In this environment, informal oversight of banks was more than adequate for keeping the financial system in check. The incidence of banking failures was low and there were no notable systemic financial crises.

Moving into the 1970s, that position began to change. The breakdown of Bretton Woods heralded a slow but progressive dismantling of exchange restrictions internationally. Regulatory constraints on banks were also progressively relaxed. The incidence of bank failure began to rise. In the United Kingdom, the crisis among some small "secondary" banks in the early 1970s brought this home to the Bank of England. In response, the Bank began to formalise its supervisory approach and augment its oversight resources, though the approach remained non-statutory.

The Evolution of Central Banks: A Practitioner's Perspective   637

That changed in 1979 with the first Banking Act granting the Bank of England statutory powers of supervision over deposit-taking institutions. This framework was augmented in 1987 following the failure of Johnson Matthey Bank. Further updates to the statutory framework came with the Financial Services and Markets Act in 1998 and the Financial Services Act in 2012. As with earlier statutory acts, these came as a direct response to crisis – BCCI's failure in 1991, Barings' failure of 1995 and the global financial crisis of 2008.

The course of supervisory history has not run smoothly for central banks. In 1998, the Bank of England was stripped of its banking supervisory responsibilities which were delegated to an arms-length supervisory agency, the Financial Services Authority (FSA). A number of other countries subsequently followed suit.

In Norway, Norges Bank has never had responsibility for the supervision of individual financial institutions. Nonetheless, most central banks have through their history maintained active oversight of the financial system as a whole – so-called macro-prudential oversight. This has been true of both the Bank of England and Norges Bank for most of the recent past. Prior to the crisis, a number of central banks began publishing financial stability reports, giving their assessment of risks to the financial system as a whole. The Bank of England was the first central bank to do so in 1996. Norges Bank began producing internal reports on financial stability in 1995 and has been publishing them since 1997, first in its Economic Bulletins and since 2000 as a separate *Financial Stability Report*. At last count, eighty-six countries are now producing such reports.

Since the global financial crisis, these macro-prudential frameworks, like the micro-prudential frameworks of the past, have been formalised, strengthened and given statutory force in a number of countries. For example, the Financial Services Act (2012) in the United Kingdom not only returned micro-prudential supervision to the Bank of England, but also created a formal structure for macro-prudential regulation with a Financial Policy Committee (FPC) charged with the task. A number of other countries are following suit, though not always with the central bank at the helm.

2.6 The Emergence of Modern Monetary Policy

Through its financial system oversight role, the central bank has an incentive to safeguard the stability of private sector money creation. With its liabilities as the ultimate settlement asset, a central bank also has an incentive to maintain their value by varying the terms – or interest rates – on which they are made available to the banking system. This is the essence, and origin, of monetary policy.

The course of monetary policy, as that of financial stability, has not always run smoothly. Prior to the twentieth century, monetary arrangements generally took the form of commodity standards, generally linking the currency to gold. With periodic interruptions, these arrangements generally lasted through until the start of the First World War. In the main, they were seen as relatively successful in providing a nominal anchor for prices, in particular during the "classic" gold standard era in the latter part of the nineteenth century and early part of the twentieth during which period the price level was fairly stable.

Relative to earlier centuries, the twentieth century was one of considerable flux for monetary policy arrangements. Attempts to repeg to gold after the First World War were disastrous both in the United Kingdom and Norway. After the Second World War, responsibility for monetary policy management in the United Kingdom and Norway lay in the hands of government. A range of instruments were brought to bear, in addition to short-term interest rates, to regulate the supply of liquidity and credit in the economy. This included liquidity and credit restrictions. During the 1950s and 1960s, no real distinction was made between what would today be called monetary and macro-prudential policy tools. The role of central banks was largely to act as operational agent, rather than decision-making principal, over these tools.

Financial liberalisation from the early 1970s onwards heralded a re-orientation in monetary policy frameworks. The rise of Monetarism led to progressively greater focus being placed on the setting of monetary supply targets as the centrepiece of monetary policy arrangements. In the United Kingdom, these were introduced progressively through the 1970s. But the setting of these targets, and the monetary instruments to hit them, remained in the hands of government.

During the 1980s, monetary policy frameworks became more discretionary in many countries, relative to earlier eras of fixed exchange rates and money supply targets. A broader range of intermediate indicators was used to gauge the monetary stance. After a brief period when sterling was part of the European Exchange Rate Mechanism (ERM), the United Kingdom adopted inflation-targeting in 1992. This was a far clearer regime than its predecessors, with a singular, well-defined objective and a singular, well-defined instrument. Although still a discretionary regime, harder constraints were placed on this discretion.

The Evolution of Central Banks: A Practitioner's Perspective 639

At the same time, the Bank of England began publishing a quarterly *Inflation Report*, setting out its view on the inflation outlook to underpin its advice to government on the appropriate setting of short-term interest rates. Minutes of the monthly deliberations of the Governor and Chancellor were published soon after. For the first time in its history, the Bank's advice to government on the monetary policy stance was open to public scrutiny. This increased the Bank's indirect influence over monetary policy decisions.

In 1997, the Bank was granted operational independence for the setting of monetary policy to hit the inflation target, with the setting up of a Monetary Policy Committee (MPC) to make those decisions. The regime was still one of constrained discretion, but with discretion now exercised by the MPC. With relatively few modifications, this flexible inflation-targeting regime has remained in place since. It has proven to be the most durable of all the post-war monetary policy arrangements in the United Kingdom – and arguably the most durable in the Bank's 320-year history.

In Norway, monetarism played far less of a role in the evolution of its monetary policy framework. Fixed, or quasi-fixed, exchange rate regimes characterised much of the post-war period. During 1978–1986 a fixed exchange rate regime prevailed, but with frequent devaluations, some disguised as technical adjustments in the currency basket against which the krone was fixed. An important change came in May 1986, with the exchange rate peg becoming notably more fixed and with policy set to maintain the same inflation rate as the countries against which the currency was fixed.

This strict fixed exchange rate regime broke down in December 1992 and was followed by a "managed float". Norway informally adopted an inflation targeting regime in 1999, and formally did so in March 2001. Monetary policy decisions are taken by the Bank's Executive Board, which includes a majority of government-appointed external members. The deliberations of the Executive Board on monetary policy are summarised in Norges Bank's quarterly *Monetary Policy Report*, which also includes an assessment of financial stability issues.

3. Central Banks at Present : What Makes a 'Good' Central Bank?

If history shows us why we need central banks, can it also illustrate what makes a successful one? In his Adam Smith Lecture in 2006, former Bank of England Governor Mervyn King laid out some criteria for a good institution (King, 2006):

1. clear objectives
2. tools and competence to meet these objectives
3. accountability
4. designed to reflect history and experience

These are timeless characteristics. Using them, it is possible to evaluate the role and responsibilities of central banks today, including in the light of the crisis as these responsibilities have expanded.

3.1 Clear Objectives

Over the course of the past century or so, central banks have been delegated the task of maintaining a well-functioning and stable monetary and financial system. In fact, these objectives can be found in the original mandates of many central banks, albeit often using less precise language. For example, among the objectives of the Bank of England in its 1694 charter was: "to promote the public Good and Benefit of our People". The same could be said of Norges Bank's original charter of 1816. Although not stated explicitly, the objectives could be easily derived from the charter's paragraphs on the Bank's silver fund, note coverage and an explicit horizon to resume note convertibility at par.

The objectives of maintaining a well-functioning and stable monetary and financial system are, by themselves, rather imprecise. In a world of delegated responsibility – the central bank world of the past few decades – they need to be made operational and, ideally, measurable. This is desirable to help reinforce external understanding of the policy framework and policy actions and to ensure a degree of consistency in these actions. It is also important if central banks are to be held to account for the objectives, as delegated agents.

Through history, targets for monetary stability have evolved considerably. In earlier centuries, they often took a clear and unambiguous form – for example, a direct link to the price of a precious metal, as under the gold standard. From the First World War through to the late twentieth century, targets often became somewhat more indirect and at one remove from the ultimate target. This included the use of exchange rates as targets under the post-war Bretton Woods system of fixed-but-adjustable exchange rates. It was also true of the ensuing period of monetary targeting from the early 1970s onwards. Monetary policy targets were "intermediate".

The breakdown of these intermediate targets in turn gave birth to direct targets, in particular quantitative targets for inflation. From their introduction in the late 1990s, inflation targeting frameworks have proved to be fairly robust to various shocks, real, nominal and financial, at least compared with their historical predecessors. As a result, they have attracted a growing swell of central bank followers, within both advanced and emerging economies. In a number of countries, the inflation target is augmented with a growth or employment target to give a dual mandate, as in the United States.

In the light of the crisis, there has been some questioning of whether inflation targeting has been too narrowly cast – for example, because the framework may have paid insufficient attention to financial sector factors (Borio, 2014b). This debate continues today, even among those who recognise that macro-prudential actions can help shoulder some of the policy burden when financial imbalances emerge. For example, Stein (2014) sets out the conditions under which such a "leaning against the wind" approach to monetary policy might be optimal in the face of financial sector vulnerabilities. This is likely to remain a live policy issue for some years to come.

Operational targets for the stability of the financial system have been less easy to specify, at least in clear, quantitative terms. It is clear in intuitive terms what financial *in*stability looks like, i.e. systemic financial crises with large costs for the wider economy. It is more difficult to define precisely financial stability success. Is crisis avoidance enough? Or should central banks define a more ambitious set of objectives, such as the avoidance of booms and busts in credit or the avoidance of distortionary asset price bubbles? This, too, has been the subject of an active recent debate (Borio, 2014a; Galati and Moessner, 2013).

Perhaps for these reasons, central banks have for many years shied away from publishing a clear framework to underpin their financial stability objectives. For example, when last resort lending formed the fulcrum of central banks' financial stability mandate, there was a reluctance to provide a clear description of its framework, in part to avoid the risk of moral hazard (Goodhart, 1999). But that has changed materially over the past decade or so, and in particular since the crisis, as central banks have published frameworks, often suitably flexed or augmented, for the provision of liquidity insurance to the banking system.

This evolution towards clearer frameworks can also be seen on the regulatory front. Informal methods of regulation, with rather imprecise objectives, have given way to formal statutory approaches with clear and often measurable policy objectives. For example, the Financial Services Act (2012) in the United Kingdom gives the Bank of England a very clear set of statutory objectives for the supervision of financial firms and the financial sector as a whole, with distinct objectives for the micro-prudential and macro-prudential arms of policy.

There is a clear link between these frameworks and the operational issue of whether policy should be pursued by following a policy rule or by exercising discretion. Rules require greater clarity about objectives and greater discipline about their implementation, whereas discretion may be more appropriate to a world of multiple and diffuse objectives. There is a large body of literature suggesting that when the objectives are price stability and economic growth, policy can be enhanced by central banks responding to deviations of these variables from their target paths. Proponents argue that such rules not only reduce policy mistakes, but also improve the transparency of policy while limiting political influence on the central bank (Cox, 1990; Hetzel, 1997; Goodfriend, 1997; Cukierman, 1992).

These are among the reasons why monetary policy exhibited rule-like behaviour through much of its history. These regimes made sense in a world of still-fledgling, and potentially unstable, democracies in a great many countries. They were a robust defence against short-term political interference. The establishment of Norges Bank and the silver standard in 1816 marked a monetary policy watershed in Norway, signalling the end of the inflationary policies of the Napoleonic war. In much the same way, the United Kingdom's inflationary experience of wars throughout the eighteenth and into the nineteenth centuries led to a desire to restore the currency to a sound footing through the Bank Charter Act of 1844 and the introduction of the gold standard.[10]

Yet at the same time there are theoretical arguments, as well as ample historical experience, suggesting that strict rules-based policy can be a mixed blessing. Proponents of discretion reject rules because they reduce, perhaps eliminate, the role of judgement in policy making. King (2004) outlines how this is needed to allow policymakers to learn from experience and to adapt to a changing economic environment (Lear, 2000). And historical experience suggests that a failure to adapt monetary policy to a changing world can have dire policy consequences.

---

[10] But even under the classical gold standard, there was some room for discretion, which was used especially during crises, see for example Øksendal (2012).

In Norway, Governor Nicolai Rygg's rigid pursuit of parity policy – reestablishment of purchasing power parity under the gold standard system prior to 1914 – was highly controversial. It was believed to be instrumental in the deflationary and recessionary forces of the 1920s and 1930s. The same is generally held to be true of sterling's return to the gold standard in 1925, its adherence to strict monetary targets in the early 1980s, and its period in the European Exchange Rate Mechanism in the early 1990s. The lack of flexibility of these arrangements in the face of changed circumstances made for recession or depression.

In the light of this experience, a large number of central banks have adopted regimes based on "constrained discretion" (Bernanke, 2003; Bernanke and Mishkin, 1997). These tend to specify some clear, sometimes quantitative, over-arching objectives, but then give central banks discretion to execute policy to meet these objectives. This discretion is typically subject to the usual accountability safeguards. The framework is intended to strike a balance between the benefits of rules (in creating clarity and time-consistency) and discretion (in allowing flexibility and adaptation). Indeed, increasingly this constrained discretionary framework has been used in financial stability and regulatory settings, as well as monetary policy ones.

None of this is to say that the framework-setting process for central banks today is somehow completely solved. The financial crisis has brought with it a demand to look at broader sets of objectives or has reinforced existing ones – from financial stability to banking competition to high employment. It has also spawned new responsibilities and new committees. While these new objectives, responsibilities and committees operate broadly speaking in a framework of constrained discretion, they have added to the challenge of central bank policy-setting. For example, more active choices then need to be made about how different objectives are weighed and, on occasion, traded off – for example, inflation versus employment or systemic risk versus competition. This places even greater demands on co-ordination across the different arms of central bank policy and on transparency about what each arm is seeking to achieve.

Today, central banks are still in the early stages of re-crafting their communication and co-ordination strategies in the face of this brave new world. The challenge is partly analytical, as the existing academic literature gives surprisingly few clues on issues such as how monetary and macro-prudential policies should best be coordinated (Antipa and Matheron, 2014), or the trade-off between stability and competition in finance (Allen and Gale, 2004). But it is also partly a communication challenge in explaining these policies to the wider world at a time when the frameworks themselves are still taking shape.

3.2 Tools and Competence

Being able to meet assigned and clear objectives relies on having an appropriate set of policy tools. These tools need to be effective in their impact on the final objective. But, as importantly, the central bank needs to be competent in its control of these instruments. There are many factors that bear on the effectiveness of tools and the competence of central banks. Here we focus on three: the structure of the financial system; the staffing model of central banks; and the process of decision-making.

Stable money and credit relies on a strong and stable financial sector. Financial instability weakens the strength and stability of the monetary and financial transmission mechanism. A broken financial system risks rendering impotent standard monetary and financial policy transmission mechanisms, as the crisis illustrated only too clearly. That is one reason why central banks' pursuit of financial stability is intimately linked to their pursuit of price stability.

The monetary and financial policy transmission mechanism is also shaped importantly by structural and technological changes. The evolution of the choice of monetary and regulatory policy tools can be seen as a reflection of those changes. For much of the nineteenth and some of the twentieth centuries, only a small share of firms and households had access to financial capital and bank loans. With credit and financial markets under-developed, interest rates and bank regulatory policies would have had limited effect on demand and inflation. In these circumstances, direct control of the money supply – for example, through metallic currency standards or exchange rate arrangements – was a more effective means of affecting monetary and credit control.

As banks grew in scale during the twentieth century, and financial markets were progressively liberalised, other means of monetary and credit control became more effective. This included direct, quantitative restrictions on banks' balance sheets and credit provision. These tools formed the bedrock of monetary and regulatory policies from the Second World War up until the 1970s. Indeed, during this period, monetary and regulatory policies were largely indistinguishable. Both operated in a way which effectively used credit rationing to hold in check the economy and the financial sector.

Entering the 1970s, that situation began to change once more. Successive waves of financial and capital account liberalisation rendered direct controls over banks' balance sheets much less effective. For example, these controls could then be obviated by banks' borrowing from overseas. In response, central banks were drawn increasingly to price-based controls over money and credit – short-term interest rates – to maintain price stability. At the same time, international regulatory rules, such as the Basel capital adequacy rules, were being drawn up in an attempt to level the regulatory playing field and thereby reduce the scope for financial instabilities to spread cross-border. These monetary policy and regulatory tools remained the mainstay of central bank policy right up until the financial crisis.

Since then, the number of central bank tools has grown, perhaps as never before. New tools have been deployed and some old tools rediscovered. Faced with a severe liquidity crisis, central banks' liquidity provision policies have been flexed and adapted to crisis circumstance – for example, by lending against wider collateral, at longer tenors and to a wider set of institutions. With conventional monetary transmission mechanisms damaged, and with monetary policy at the effective zero lower bound, a number of central banks resorted to policies of "quantitative easing" – direct purchases of assets, public or private. A larger-still number of central banks have begun to use regulatory tools to help meet macro-economic ends – so-called macro-prudential policy. These have been significant evolutionary responses in central banks' toolkit in the face of a changed financial environment over the past few years.

None of these tools is likely to be effective unless central banks have the competence and experience necessary to adjust them appropriately. While the academic literature has paid considerable attention to the role of central bank governors' preferences in effective policy-making, the availability and importance of a competent staff has largely been taken for granted. This view stands at odds with the views of central bank practitioners, including ourselves (Bernanke, 2014; Oritani, 2011). The latter study looked at the internal organisation of a central bank, highlighting the need for highly qualified staff. A staff possessing knowledge of recent advances and mastering state-of-the art techniques appears to be crucial for formulating well-founded policy options (see Apel et al, 2013).

Yet, historically, this was not always the case. Central banks evolved from being staffed like large manufacturing firms at the start of the twentieth century to looking like quasi-academic departments by its end. In the middle of the nineteenth century, Bagehot criticised the Bank of England's senior management on the grounds that the primary consideration in determining who was Governor was age – the oldest and most senior Director who had not been in office almost inevitably became Deputy Governor and then immediately Governor. Bagehot proposed a reform that there should be a permanent Deputy Governor in order to provide continuity.

From the turn of the century, there appears to have been an increasing emphasis on experience and capability within central banks. Relatively few Directors before Montagu Norman's time had a university education. But Norman had 'always been convinced of the desirability of full-time professionals on the Court' and when he became Governor the whole composition began to change. There was a gradual swing from traditional City figures to industrialists. In line with Bagehot's suggestion, he introduced a full time Deputy Governor from 1929.

Despite the remark from a Governor in the 1950s that the "Bank of England is a bank, not a study group", over the past fifty years or so we have seen a steady move towards greater professionalisation in central banking (Capie, 2012, p. 54). Most central banks these days, including the Bank of England and Norges Bank, have moved towards a staffing model heavily reliant on highly educated research staff, many with higher degrees in economics and finance. At the same time, there has been a steady reduction in the numbers of staff carrying out some traditional central bank tasks such as note printing. In some cases, these tasks have been outsourced. For example, at Norges Bank the number of central banking staff has been reduced from about 1200 to 300 over the past fifteen years, with the Bank no longer printing notes or minting coins, nor compiling and publishing financial statistics.

A final aspect in the effective deployment of central bank policy tools is the process of decision-making. For most of central bank history, the choice of decision-maker was not of especially great importance since central banks had relatively few decisions to make. When those decisions did have to be made, they fell naturally to the Governor of the day – for example, at times of last resort lending.

Over the past few decades, as decision-making responsibilities have increased, so too has the formality of the decision-making process within central banks. In particular, a number of central banks have moved towards a model of committee-based decision-making for their highest level decisions. A wide-ranging survey undertaken by Fry et al. (2000) found that seventy-nine central banks out of a sample of eighty-eight use some form of committee structure when setting monetary policy. Even for

The Evolution of Central Banks: A Practitioner's Perspective   647

those countries with a long track record of committee-based decision-making – the US Federal Open Market Committee has been in existence since 1935 when the Federal Reserve Act was revised – we have seen a shift towards a more democratic and collegiate monetary policy decision-making process over time.

The rationale for such a shift is also now better understood. Studies suggest committees tend on average to make better decisions than individuals (Blinder and Morgan, 2005; Lombardelli et al, 2005). The latter study suggests that committees perform significantly better than all but their best member. Given the difficulty of detecting ex-ante who that might be, on balance this points clearly to making decisions by committee. This research also showed that committees do more than just eliminate the poor decisions of a minority of members. They also allow members to learn by observing the behaviour of others.

3.3 Accountability

Richard Ely (1885) said good central bankers should "acknowledge our ignorance, and if we claim superiority to others it is largely on the very humble ground that we know better what we do not know". Central bank accountability is a necessary condition for sustaining its operational independence. Independence without accountability is likely to be interpreted as a dilution of democracy. And a central bank which hands the levers of power to a single individual, rather than a more diverse set of committee members, might be particularly susceptible to a democratic deficit. It was not ever thus. In the 1930s, the Bank of England Deputy Governor of the day told the Macmillan Enquiry that "it is a dangerous thing to start to give reasons".

Since then, economic theory has begun to identify the channels through which transparency and accountability might improve the performance both of central banks and the wider economy. Transparency can help agents solve the signal extraction problem of whether it is incompetence or under-handedness that is driving policy decisions (Briault, Haldane and King, 1996). King (2004) outlines the need to build credibility by 'doing it' and so resisting the temptation to deviate from time-consistent policy.[11] This is perhaps especially important at the outset of a new regime or when the inherited stock of policy credibility is low (Garfinkel and Oh, 1995; Stein, 1989).

---

[11] We refer to Barro and Gordon (1983) and Jansson and Vredin (2004) for a discussion of "time-consistent policy" in theory and practice.

There has been a radical transformation of both the Bank of England's and Norges Bank's approach to external transparency over the past twenty years or so. The degree of transparency of Norges Bank's interest rate decisions has increased gradually since inflation targeting was formally introduced in 2001. Since 2005, Norges Bank has published three-year-ahead key policy rate forecasts, indicating the interest rate path that it believes provides an appropriate balance between different monetary policy considerations. This is intended to enhance the predictability of interest rate policy. Norges Bank is also open about the basis for its monetary policy decisions, with the quarterly *Monetary Policy Report* providing forecasts for key macroeconomic variables for the next three years, together with a press conference led by the Governor.

The Bank of England has produced a quarterly *Inflation Report* since 1993 and a biannual *Financial Stability Report* since 1996. Press conferences now accompany both, followed by scheduled appearances before Parliamentary Committees. The Bank of England's *Inflation Report* now presents forecasts for a wide range of macroeconomic variables, the set of key assumptions and judgments underlying these forecasts and alternative scenarios. In 2013 the Bank has issued forward guidance on the conditions that are likely to determine the future path of short-term interest rates in the United Kingdom.

Whether central banks publish voting records and the minutes of their deliberations depends on the character of the committees. At the Bank of England, each MPC member is individually responsible for their vote under statute, with the decision made by majority voting. In line with this, the Bank of England publishes the minutes of the MPC's deliberations and its voting pattern, though individual members remain anonymous.

In Norway, the Executive Board is a "collegial committee" where members seek consensus in their decision. This means that the committee takes decisions by consensus and that members collectively stand behind the final decision. Norges Bank does not publish the minutes of the Executive Board's deliberations. Instead the Board's assessment and discussion is published without naming individual members. A detailed account explaining the background to the interest rate decision is published to enhance accountability and transparency.[12]

---

[12] The interest rate decision is based on a strategy that is described in the *Monetary Policy Report*. The *Report* also presents the analyses underlying the strategy. The basis for interest rate decisions is thus available to the general public, see Qvigstad (2013).

The Evolution of Central Banks: A Practitioner's Perspective 649

The Bank of England's Financial Policy Committee (FPC) is, in some respects, a middle ground between these two models. The preferred basis for decision-making is by consensus. The aim here is to reduce any uncertainty that might result from differences of view across the FPC. There is no vote unless a consensus cannot be reached, in which case votes are cast and the result and the balance of arguments set out in a published quarterly Record. This procedure aims to strike a balance between the needs of the financial system – a clear policy signal – and the need to maintain high levels of external accountability for decisions.

3.4 Central Banks Reflect History and Experience

Most central banks have a long history, encompassing past episodes of monetary and financial instability. This gives them two institutional attributes crucial for effective public policy: memory and patience. Institutional memory is important for guarding against the sins of the past, be it high and variable inflation or financial crises. Understanding and avoiding both is made easier with a deep appreciation of past events and, indeed, past errors. For example, institutional memory of Germany's hyperinflationary past has been maintained by the Bundesbank in the post-war period. And institutional, or at least historical, memory of the Great Depression helped in convincing central banks of the need for extraordinary monetary accommodation to help cushion the effects of the recent global financial crisis (Bernanke, 2013).

Patience – a willingness to take action today for the good of tomorrow – is also crucial in delivering price and financial stability. Central banks, as institutions with long time horizons, are likely to be better placed to make choices that deliver those public goods. For example, inflationary episodes of the past were often rooted in a desire to trade off output today for inflation tomorrow. And past crisis episodes were often rooted in a desire to trade off a credit or asset price boom today for a bust tomorrow. Both such tendencies can be neutralised by delegating policy to a patient institution with a low discount rate (Haldane, 2013).

Both of these institutional features – memory and patience – are likely to result in a degree of caution in central bank decision-making. This needs to be balanced against the need for adaptability in response to changed circumstances. Central banks' historical record on this front is somewhat mixed. In adhering strictly to its legal mandate, Norges Bank was slow to supply liquidity in the crisis of 1848. The same accusation was frequently levelled at the Bank of England in the second half of the nineteenth century. Both central banks had to learn "through experience of several financial crises how to respond when a sudden demand for liquidity arose" (Capie, 2012, p. 585).

By 1857, Norges Bank was providing liquidity to Norwegian banks where needed, even though its legal mandate was the same as in 1848. And by the end of the nineteenth century, the Bank of England was going above and beyond its formal remit when it constructed a financial 'lifeboat' to stop the solvent but illiquid Barings bank from failing in 1890. In 1914, at the outbreak of the First World War, the Bank faced perhaps the largest liquidity crisis in its history. It responded with an imaginative liquidity provision scheme – the 'cold storage scheme' – which averted disaster (Roberts, 2013).

Almost a century later, many central banks have once more had to act imaginatively to avert a systemic liquidity crisis. This has involved the use of schemes and facilities that make liquidity available on a historically unprecedented scale; for historically unprecedented tenors; against historically unusual sets of collateral; and to a historically unprecedentedly wide set of institutions. Adaptation, at speed and in scale, has been the order of the day.

4 Central Bank Issues for the Future

A key lesson of the global financial crisis is that no central bank can afford to rest on its laurels or become complacent about the stability of the monetary and financial system. The period of the Great Moderation may have dulled the risk senses of central banks and market participants to instabilities in the financial sector. Too great a focus on price stability may have contributed to that lack of peripheral vision.

The crisis has tended to endow central banks with greater sets of responsibility and greater numbers of instruments. As a corollary, it has also exposed central banks to greater criticism and placed increasing demands on their transparency and accountability practices. In the light of the crisis, it is interesting to consider the issues that might shape the future evolution of central banks. We discuss six.

4.1 Central Bank Independence

The concept (and reality) of independence for central banks has gone from a 'relative rarity to the norm' for monetary policy regimes over the

The Evolution of Central Banks: A Practitioner's Perspective   651

past twenty years.[13] This case has been well-built analytically and is now widely accepted operationally. But until the financial crisis, the analytical case for central bank independence on financial stability issues had by no means been articulated as clearly. Yet the arguments for central bank independence are every bit as strong, if not stronger, for financial policy as monetary policy (Haldane, 2013).

First, independence of central banks is important in helping to reduce the moral hazard otherwise associated with financial sector support during a crisis. The credibility of regulatory action, including lender of last support to banks, can undermine incentives if the central bank is not perceived to be independent. Expectations of liquidity support to effectively insolvent banks, or expectations of systematic regulatory forbearance, may encourage excessive risk taking, thereby laying the ground for future financial crises. Central bank independence may also be important in the efficient management and resolution of crises.

Second, institutional memory is particularly important when dealing with financial cycles. These cycles are longer than typical business cycles, increasing the chances of policymakers falling prey to myopia. A "This Time is Different" mentality has presaged most systemic financial crises. Central banks unencumbered by the electoral cycle and with embedded institutional memory are less prone to this mentality.

Third, financial cycles also tend to exhibit wider fluctuations, thereby imposing potentially larger costs, than the typical business cycle. Deeper financial integration has probably added to those costs, by increasing the size and incidence of tail risk in the financial system. These larger costs increase the incentives to act time inconsistently with financial stability policy – for example, by forbearing on failing banks or bailing out insolvent institutions.

Fourth, the distribution of these costs is likely to be uneven, with stronger cohorts of 'winners and losers' than the business cycle. For example, asset owners benefit from asset price booms, borrowers benefit from credit booms – and banks benefit from both. These powerful vested interests can harness strong lobbying power, increasing the need for an independent institution to lean against financial cycles through tough regulatory actions (Olson, 1971).

---

[13] See, for example Cukierman (2008), Berger et al, (2001) Kuttner and Posen (2013) and Haldane (2013).

Encouragingly, in at least some countries there is evidence of these lessons being heeded, with prudential responsibilities being handed to operationally independent central banks. For example, in the United Kingdom responsibilities for both micro-prudential regulation (through the Prudential Regulation Authority or PRA) and macro-prudential regulation (through the Financial Policy Committee or FPC) returned to the Bank of England in 2012.

But this is by no means agreed best-practice internationally for regulatory regimes. For example, of the large number of new macro-prudential frameworks put in place internationally since the crisis, only around half have had central banks in the driving seat (Lim et al., 2013). As with monetary policy independence, the case for independence of financial stability policy is likely to be built gradually in the light of experience, perhaps over decades.

Even when central banks are granted operational independence for monetary and financial stability, the specification of statutory objectives can be crucial for averting time-consistency problems. For example, the Bank of England's FPC has two objectives – guarding against the build-up of systemic risk to enhance financial stability and, *subject to that*, supporting the Government's objectives for growth and employment. This lexicographic ordering means the Committee is tasked with avoiding pressures to go for growth today if it is at the expense of instability tomorrow. The FPC can help provide the long-sightedness required for future financial stability.

Yet independence is not absolute. Central banks are part of the executive branch of government. They are also rightly subject to strict transparency and accountability requirements. As some central banks have taken on broader sets of responsibility – in particular prudential policy – questions have been raised about whether this reduces their degree of de facto independence (IMF, 2013). For example, some macro-prudential instruments, such as the setting of Loan-to-Value (LTV) limits on mortgages, can have overt distributional consequences. So too can unconventional monetary policy measures. This places additional demands on central banks when accounting for their actions.

Facing those additional constraints, safeguarding independence will in future require central banks to be clearer than ever in explaining their decisions publicly and their importance for fulfilling their statutory functions of monetary and financial stability. It also increases the importance of central bank constituency-building for these objectives.

4.2 Building a Constituency for Central Bank Objectives

Delegating responsibility for monetary policy, and in some cases financial stability, to a central bank has become an accepted policy-making model over the past couple of decades. But delegated responsibility, if it is to be durable, relies on sustaining support within wider society. It relies on building public understanding of central bank actions and trust in them. This, in turn, depends on credible accountability mechanisms vis-a-vis the general public.

What counts as a credible accountability framework will depend, among other things, on the statutory framework within which a central bank operates. For example, in the United Kingdom policy-making officials are called to regular parliamentary hearings where they explain their actions and account for their performance in meeting statutory objectives. Press conferences accompany the publication of the quarterly *Inflation Report* and bi-annual *Financial Stability Report*. In Norway, a press conference is held after each monetary policy meeting and the Governor appears before the Storting (Norwegian parliament annually). These arrangements, often formalised in statute, ensure that there are mechanisms in place for unelected technocrats to be held accountable to the electorate, as represented by national parliaments.

For central banks to be trusted institutions, these statutory accountability arrangements, while necessary, are unlikely to be sufficient. To be effective over the longer-term, a central bank needs to build a wider and broader constituency of support. In particular, as the ultimate stakeholders affected directly by central bank policy actions, the general public need to be part of this broader constituency.

During the late 1990s and into the early twenty-first century, this has been recognised by a widening array of central banks, including the Bank of England and Norges Bank. For example, the Bank of England embarked on a campaign to build a 'constituency for low inflation' in the United Kingdom from the early 1990s onwards. This meant spending time and resources on ensuring that the wider public knew that the Bank had a target for inflation and why this was in the long-term interests of the public. As an example of an attempt to widen this understanding, the Bank set up a schools competition involving students simulating setting monetary policy to hit an inflation target.

Transparency initiatives aim to help anchor inflation expectations by influencing wage and price-setting behaviour, thereby making hitting the inflation target somewhat easier. The benefits of this anchoring of expectations have been well-illustrated by events over recent years. In the aftermath of the financial crisis, measured inflation was consistently, and sometimes materially, above the Bank of England's inflation target. Yet throughout this period the general public's longer-term inflation expectations remained closely anchored to the 2 percent target. Constituency-building over an extended period helped buttress the credibility of the regime.

Firmly anchored expectations are no less important, and could even be more so, when it comes to financial stability. Trust in commercial bank money and credit is, in some respects, even more difficult to sustain than trust in central bank money. That is why bank runs and credit crunches – in effect, losses of trust in money and credit – have littered financial history. An ever-more interconnected financial network heightens the difficulty of sustaining trust, as it increases the potential for local runs and panics to contagiously spread into systemic ones (Haldane and May, 2011).

Two areas of policy where expectations are crucial are deposit insurance and macro-prudential policy. Public knowledge of the protection provided by deposit insurance schemes was shown during the crisis to be very low. Pre-crisis, many countries offered 100 percent deposit insurance, but only up to a specified limit. Neither aspect was, in the event, well-understood by the general public. That is why, when facing liquidity pressures during the crisis, a number of countries made public declarations that deposit insurance was effectively unlimited in an attempt to stem depositor panic.

But unlimited insurance, ex post, is a sure-fire recipe for ex-ante moral hazard and excessive risk-taking. It is much better to have the general public understand the scope and limits of deposit insurance up front and plan their finances accordingly. This would reduce the chances of a panic-induced portfolio shift when shocks strike. In the light of crisis experience, the UK authorities launched a campaign to increase awareness of the deposit insurance scheme among the general public to assist their understanding of their degree of protection.

Expectations are also likely to be crucial for the efficacy of macro-prudential policy. Credit booms are built on hubris or over-optimistic expectations about the future. Credit busts are, conversely, built on over-pessimistic expectations about the future. One of the roles of macro-prudential policy is to curb those booms and busts in credit provision. Given their origins, macro-prudential actions are most likely to be effective when they act directly on expectations. If macro-prudential actions are anticipated, they may reshape risk-taking activities and nip incipient risk

The Evolution of Central Banks: A Practitioner's Perspective   655

problems in the bud. This might include curtailing lending decisions by banks in an incipient boom. Equally important, it may also affect the borrowing behaviour of consumers and firms. In effect, this is the expectations channel of macro-prudential policy (Aikman et al, 2014).

For this signalling channel to be effective, macro-prudential policy signals need to be clear and systematic. Policy statements, regular publications, stress tests and speeches can all help in conditioning policy expectations, as can a systematic approach. For example, the Bank of Korea has pursued a systematic approach to moderating house price fluctuations using macro-prudential tools (Columba et al., 2011). This appears to have had considerable success, in part due to the potency of the expectations channel. More recently, the Bank of England's FPC has applied the tools at its disposal to counteract the adverse effects of a housing market boom (FPC, 2014).

At present, with macro-prudential frameworks still fledgling, relatively few countries are operating a macro-prudential regime that is sufficiently systematic and predictable to be well-understood by financial market participants, much less the general public. That underscores the importance of efforts by central banks (every bit as great as those that accompanied the early years of inflation-targeting) to garner and sustain a constituency for financial stability. This is no easy task. It may call for central banks using imaginative new ways of conveying their messages to the wider public, including greater use of conventional and social media. One or two central banks have already begun to take steps in this direction.

4.3 Interventions in Financial Markets and Institutions

Traditionally, the focus of central bank interventions in financial markets has been relatively narrow and targeted, in two senses. First, these interventions have tended to centre on short-term money markets, consistent with controlling short-term money market interest rates (for monetary stability reasons) and providing central bank liquidity to markets or institutions (for financial stability reasons). Second, these interventions have tended to centre on commercial banks, rather than a wider class of financial institutions. At least until the crisis, these targeted interventions were felt to be necessary and sufficient to achieve central bank objectives.

Over the course of the recent financial crisis, this orthodoxy has been forced by events to adapt. This is in part a reflection of changes in the underlying structure and topology of the financial system. External finance to non-financial corporations is increasingly being provided from non-bank, capital market sources, including commercial paper, corporate bonds and securitisations. And providers and holders of these instruments extend beyond commercial banks to investment banks, mutual and other funds and institutional investors, including insurance companies and pension funds. Central counterparties have also become increasingly important as risk repositories as more financial transactions are centrally cleared. This set of institutions is sometimes collectively referred to as "shadow banks" (Pozsar et al., 2013).

As the crisis vividly illustrated, disturbances in a broader (than short-term money market) set of financial markets, and among a broader (than commercial banks) set of financial institutions, are more important today than perhaps ever previously. In response, central banks in a number of countries expanded their conventional operations to support a wider set of institutions and markets during the crisis. This included interventions in asset markets such as commercial paper, corporate bonds and securitisations and in sectors such as money market mutual funds, trust companies and parts of the corporate sector.[14] In crisis, some central banks moved from lenders of last resort to de facto market makers of last resort (MMLR).

This is a significant shift and raises a host of important analytical and operational questions. Among these is whether it is possible, or desirable, to avoid such crisis-induced interventions in future. This is a re-run, in some respects, of the lender of last resort debate from the mid-nineteenth century. At that time, the Bank of England and Norges Bank were resistant to any ex-ante lender of last resort commitment. Yet experience in the latter half of the century, with repeated interventions, undermined the credibility of the threat not to intervene next time. Having played the role of MMLR once, there is a question about the credibility of a "never again" statement by central banks today.

If a no-intervention policy lacks time-consistency, there is then a potential benefit from being somewhat clearer about the criteria and modalities for such intervention. This reduces uncertainty on the part of market participants about the central bank's crisis reaction function. It also increases the chances of the central bank adhering to this reaction function in a time-consistent fashion and in a way which is operationally effective. For example, these interventions often place heavy informational demands on central banks. This includes information on the prudent price of assets

---

[14] See for example Adrian, Kimbrough and Marchioni (2011) and Panetta et al., (2009).

The Evolution of Central Banks: A Practitioner's Perspective   657

used as collateral at times when observable market prices may not be reliable.[15] It may require on-going operational relationships with a wide set of firms and in a wide range of financial markets, together with standardised information collection.

During the course of the crisis, a number of central banks have moved closer towards this type of framework, by making more systematic and expansive their liquidity insurance facilities on a permanent basis. This has often included expanding the range of assets which central banks have been willing to accept as collateral; extending the term over which liquidity is provided; and expanding the range of counterparties with which the central bank deals. For example, the Bank of England announced an extension along all three lines in 2009 and again in 2013. In 2014, it announced the extension of liquidity insurance facilities to broker-dealers and central counterparties.[16]

As the structure of the financial system continues to evolve, not least in the light of the regulatory reform agenda, it seems likely that central bank operations in financial markets will need to remain under constant review in the period ahead. It took 150 years for central banks to go from lender to effective market maker of last resort. Given the dynamism in financial markets, the next evolutionary step may not take that long.

4.4 Policy Decision-Making under Uncertainty

The dominant paradigm for studying decision-making in economics and finance is based on rational agents who operate with known, calculable risks. Many of these frameworks are descendants of the Arrow-Debreu general equilibrium framework with a fully-defined, and fully priced, set of state-contingent risk factors (Arrow, 1964; Debreu 1959). Some key policy design principles flow from this framework, which have often found their way into central bank policy practice. For example, in this Arrow-Debreu set up more information is always better than less and decisions should optimally weight all relevant factors. Policymakers act as mean-variance optimisers, focusing policy on keeping the central paths for the economy and financial system broadly in line with their targets.

---

[15] Of course, acting as LOLR also entails heavy informational requirements although such information or data may be more readily available from the institutions themselves.

[16] Further details on these changes are available in the Bank of England's 'Red Book' available here: www.bankofengland.co.uk/publications/Pages/news/2014/144.aspx.

This intellectual framework underpins the monetary policy and regulatory policy frameworks operated by most central banks. Monetary policy under flexible inflation-targeting is underpinned by central projections for inflation and output and is based on a large, complex set of informational and model inputs. And regulatory frameworks are underpinned by central estimates of risk factors, based on a large, complex set of informational and model inputs. To these are then added policymaker discretion or judgment – hence "constrained discretion".

In practice, of course, policy decisions are typically made in an environment of acute uncertainty, as well as risk, in the sense of Knight (1921). The sources of these uncertainties are many and various, including data uncertainties, uncertainties about the functioning of the economy or financial system and uncertainties about the impact of policies on this system. There is ample evidence of all three of these uncertainties over the past few years. They are especially acute during crisis when the data are changing fast, the economy or financial system is in transition and the time for decision-making is short.[17]

There is no perfect safeguard against, or antidote to, these uncertainties. But in situations where policy is navigating through thick (data, behavioural and policy) fog, decision-making can often benefit from some simple guard-rails or principles. One such principle is simplicity: the more complex and uncertain the environment, the greater the robustness of relatively simple rules of the road is likely to be (Gigerenzer, 2014). Although on the face of it counter-intuitive, the rationale is straightforward enough. In an uncertain environment, there is a premium on the avoidance of big errors. Simple rules are an effective way of doing so. They also help prevent policy making a bad situation worse.

To some extent this principle already plays some role in the monetary and regulatory policy process. For example, it is the rationale for making reference to simple rules, such as a Taylor rule, when setting monetary policy (Taylor, 1993), alongside more complex policy formulations. Counter-factual simulation studies have consistently shown that this rule performs fairly well in avoiding serious policy errors, such as the inflationary episodes of the 1970s.

Another simple cross check is to observe if the inflation gap and output gap have opposite signs, which is a characteristic of optimal monetary

---

[17] See for example Poloz (2014) for a discussion on how central banking is evolving in light of recent experience, with particular emphasis on the incorporation of uncertainty into policy decision-making.

The Evolution of Central Banks: A Practitioner's Perspective   659

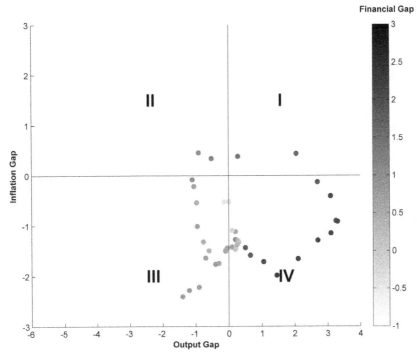

Figure 15.1: A Qvigstad plot for Norway
Source: Norges Bank calculations. Notes: The chart plots the Norwegian output gap (Norges Bank estimates) and inflation relative to target (2.5 percent) together with a heat map based on a financial instability indicator. This indicator is calculated as the first principal component of four financial stability indicators used by Norges Bank (credit to GDP gap, house price to income gap, real commercial property price gap, wholesale funding gap), where the gaps and principal component are calculated recursively. The sample period is 2004Q1–2013Q4.

policy under discretion with flexible inflation targeting. This idea was developed by one of the authors of the present paper in Qvigstad (2006). In a recent paper, Carl Walsh referred to this as the "Qvigstad rule" and illustrated the rule with a cross-plot of the inflation gap against the output gap for the United States (Walsh, 2014).

Figure 15.1 shows a similar Qvigstad plot for Norway over the past ten years, but with a twist. It has been extended along a third dimension, with a measure of financial stability shown as a colour plot using different shades of grey. The rationale is that the recent financial crisis has demonstrated that low and stable inflation is not by itself sufficient and that it is also necessary to safeguard financial stability. So even if monetary policy is "appropriate" – with dots in quadrants II and IV – this may still sometimes

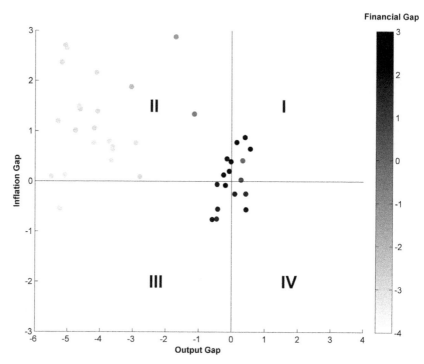

Figure 15.2: A Qvigstad plot for the United Kingdom
Source: Bank of England calculations; Office for National Statistics; British Bankers' Association; Nationwide and Halifax house price indices; Investment Property Databank. Notes: The chart plots the UK output gap (Bank of England estimates) and inflation relative to target (2 percent) together with a heat map based on a financial instability indicator. This indicator is calculated as the first principal component of four financial stability indicators (credit to GDP gap, house price to income gap, real commercial property price gap, wholesale funding gap), where the gaps and principal components are calculated recursively. The sample period is 2004Q1–2013Q4.

be inconsistent with financial stability. Indeed, Figure 15.1 suggests that this has been the case in Norway in the past, with darker grey dots occurring in quadrant IV where the output gap is positive and the inflation gap is negative, indicating the building of financial imbalances. This is, in effect, a simple cross-check on whether the policy mix (both monetary and financial stability) is an appropriate one.

Figure 15.2 shows the same plot for the United Kingdom over the same period, 2004Q1–2013Q4. The majority of dots fall in quadrants II and IV, suggesting that monetary policy has been "appropriate" over that period on the simple Qvigstad criterion. But although the output gap and deviations of inflation remained relatively stable around the origin before

The Evolution of Central Banks: A Practitioner's Perspective   661

the crisis, these dots were developing a darker shade of grey, suggesting that financial imbalances were building. While the monetary policy seas appeared calm, the same was not true of financial stability where a storm was brewing.

Clearly, there could have been worse outcomes for both countries – for example, if we had seen darker grey dots scattered in the corners of quadrants I and III. But these charts highlight the importance these days of considering the multi-dimensional nature of central bank policy. The plot also provides a rough-and-ready cross-check on whether these multiple policy dimensions are being appropriately weighed in the setting of monetary and financial stability policy.

On the regulatory front, the simplicity principle is one rationale for using a simple leverage ratio, alongside more complex regulatory rule formulations, in countering crises. Counter-factual simulation studies have shown this performs well in detecting past crises relative to more complex alternatives (Haldane and Madorous, 2012). There is probably further to go in enshrining the simplicity principle in central bank decision-making. Existing central bank policy frameworks may have over-weighted complexity, perhaps as a result of having under-emphasised uncertainty.

A second policy principle, given uncertainty, is pluralism. Model or epistemological uncertainty can to some extent be neutralised by using a diverse set of models or approaches. It can help avoid the large policy errors that might result from choosing a single model or approach and it proving wrong. The workhorse macro-economic model, without banks and with little role for risk and asset prices, was unable to account for macro-economic events during the crisis, perhaps unsurprisingly. Using a suite of models, with some emphasising banks, asset prices and risk transmission channels, is likely to have given a better picture of macro-economic trends through the crisis (Taylor, 2013).

As important as model diversity is diversity of thought. This calls for having staff and decision-makers who are drawn from a heterogeneous set of disciplines and backgrounds. This is one of the strongest rationales for committee-based decision-making, in particular with a mix of internal and external representation. While some progress has been made towards increasing the diversity of skills and experience within central banks, there is a case for greater investment in understanding the models and approaches used in other disciplines, both in the natural and social sciences. For example, in the light of the crisis some progress has been made towards modelling the financial system as a complex adaptive web using techniques from evolutionary biology (Haldane and May, 2011). There is also a case for greater use of inductive methods, alongside more traditional deductive methods, for understanding the changing dynamics of as complex and adaptive a system as the economy.

A third principle, given uncertainty, is robustness. In a world of uncertainty, the best-response strategy can often be to avoid the worst possible outcome (Hansen and Sargent, 2007). That same principle ought to apply to central bank policy too. There are some indications of this beginning to be the case. For example, regulatory policy is increasingly being drawn towards the use of stress tests to evaluate the resilience of the financial sector to extreme shocks. These are, in effect, a form of "minimax" methodology, predicated if not on a worst-case scenario than one which is in the far right-hand tail of the distribution. They are a means of evaluating how much insurance the financial system might need to buffer against an extreme-tail loss.

There is also greater, and increasing, use of scenario analysis in the monetary policy setting process. For example, the Bank of England has published alternative scenario forecasts in its *Inflation Reports* since 2013 to assess the impact of more fundamental changes in the functioning of the economy. This mirrors the sorts of scenario-based analysis common in some commercial companies. Nonetheless, there is certainly further for central banks to go in better capturing the impact of uncertainty in their quantitative evaluation of risks and in their policy decision-making.

4.5 Future of Money and Banking

At root, money and credit are about trust. Stable money and credit means sustaining that trust in the face of competing incentives - to inflate, to risk-take, to counterfeit. At different stages in financial history, technology has dictated different solutions to this trust problem for money and credit. The earliest, and most obvious, solution to this problem was to give money itself some real value – for example, by having it made from, or backed by, a valued commodity. It was for this reason that commodity monies dominated for many centuries in various civilisations, often using precious metals such as gold and silver. As well as having intrinsic value, such commodity monies were relatively divisible, portable and verifiable.

Towards the latter part of the second millennium, commodity monies gave way to commodity standards – that is, paper obligations backed by a commitment to redeem into a commodity. These aimed to preserve trust in money by preserving the link to a real commodity, while saving on the transaction costs of using that commodity day to day (as a result of

The Evolution of Central Banks: A Practitioner's Perspective

theft, handling and transportation costs). Private goldsmiths began the practice of issuing notes backed by gold in their vaults. But once they had given themselves monopoly rights over paper money, governments and central banks followed hard on their heels. The gold standard was the best known, and most durable, of these commodity money standards.

When the gold standard was abandoned in phases through the first half of the twentieth century, its replacement was a fiat money standard. The transaction cost efficiencies of paper money were preserved, but the provision of trust in money shifted from a centralised commodity (such as gold) to a centralised institution (the central bank and its ultimate guarantor, the state). Through the passage of time, the foundation of people's trust moved from a tangible physical material to an intangible human institution.

Until recently, this fiat money standard had remained largely unchanged and unchallenged. Private monies have, over the centuries, come and subsequently gone. What ultimately caused their obsolescence was that they could not provide a secure, centralised, trustworthy means of discharging obligations. Or at least not as secure, centralised and trustworthy a mechanism as the state backed by future generations of tax-payers.

Recently, digital currencies such as Bitcoin have arrived on the scene. These are digital means of discharging obligations, created and sustained using state-of-the-art cryptographic techniques (Ali et al., 2014a). A great many monetary economists, and some policymakers, have dismissed Bitcoin as but the latest in a long line of private monies, doomed to failure due to their lack of a trustworthy means of verification. The wild fluctuations in Bitcoin's value have tended to reinforce this perception.

Yet Bitcoin has generated a different response from technologists and some policymakers who see Bitcoin as a potentially important technological breakthrough. Underpinning Bitcoin is a cryptographic technology which allows trust to be created and sustained in a *distributed*, rather than centralised, way – a "distributed ledger" (Ali et al., 2014b). In effect, Bitcoin uses the information embedded in its payments network to be self-policing. Discharging obligations can be achieved without the need for verification and guarantees from a central third party, whether a commodity or the state.

If this technology proves to be robust, it would be an important step forward in thinking about how trust in money is created and sustained and hence the future of money and payments. For a variety of reasons, it seems unlikely that Bitcoin itself will change the landscape for money and payments. But the technology underlying Bitcoin perhaps could. In some respects, IT companies have already over the course of the past few years been changing fundamentally the nature of global payment systems through vehicles such as PayPal and Google Money.

Some have predicted the end of central banks if a next-generation of Bitcoin were to sweep in. That is overly pessimistic. History suggests it is also unlikely. As with the goldsmiths back in the seventeenth century, there is no reason why, even if a new technology took hold, central banks could not follow suit. For example, there is no reason in principle why central banks could not themselves issue a digital currency as a next evolutionary step in money issuance. Central banks have rarely been technological first movers. But the games of money and credit are repeated ones. And in repeated games it is usually the last mover that matters most.

4.6 Optimal Degrees of Central Bank Transparency

The openness and transparency of central bank operations has undergone a complete transformation over the course of the past century. A century ago, the prevailing ethos was well-summarised by the Bank of England Governor of the day, Montagu Norman: "never apologise, never explain". This was not just about an aversion to external scrutiny and criticism. Central bank mystique was felt to be a key weapon in the central bank armoury – for example, in surprising the market with monetary policy or when guarding against moral hazard in lender-of-last-resort operations. For reasons good and bad, mystique was guarded preciously.

The period since has seen successive waves of greater transparency. Many of these were accompanied by changes in central bank responsibilities, in particular the delegation of greater monetary and financial stability powers and responsibilities to central banks. That generated an understandable desire for greater external scrutiny and, ultimately, accountability. A generation ago, central bank publications were scarce, press conferences scarcer still, media appearances few and far between. Central banks were rarely seen and infrequently heard. They were back page news most of the time.

A generation on the situation could not be more different. Publications from central banks are now regular and frequent. Forecasts, projections and stress tests of the future path of the economy and financial system are commonplace. Press conferences are now a staple, not a luxury, of central bank communications. Minutes of policy meetings have become common currency. Media appearances come thick and fast, as do appearances

The Evolution of Central Banks: A Practitioner's Perspective 665

before parliamentary committees. Rarely are central banks far from the front pages of newspapers.

This remarkable shift does not only reflect the increased accountability demands placed on central banks given their new responsibilities. It also reflects an intellectual or philosophical shift as some of the broader benefits of transparency have been recognised. Prominent among these is the benefit of acting systematically and time-consistently. Doing so is made easier with greater ex-ante transparency about actions and intentions. This is, in turn, then reflected in better anchored expectations of inflation and systemic risk.

In an important sense, central bank transparency is a one-way street: there is no going back. The interesting question for the future is then whether central banks should, or will be required, to go further still down this transparency path. There is already some pressure to do so. For example, a number of central banks have moved to a monetary regime of "forward guidance" over the past few years, in which more of their future monetary policy hand is revealed, including Norges Bank and the Bank of England. The ECB has begun publishing minutes of the meetings of its monetary policy Governing Council. And the Bank of England is to publish with a lag transcripts of MPC meetings, following the practice of the US Federal Reserve.

Yet at the same time there are some important debates to be had about the potential limits, or disadvantages, of greater transparency. Is it possible to have too much of a good thing? If central banks become the focus of excessive attention, that itself may be problematic. Financial market prices may become excessively sensitive to public signals and insensitive to private ones (Morris and Shin, 2002). This can be problematic if public signals are noisy and destabilising and if private information is invested in insufficiently by market participants.

In a similar vein, transcripts of monetary policy meetings ought in principle to increase transparency about central bank reaction functions. But the act of publishing may itself alter the nature of the monetary policy decision-making process in ways which may make this information less useful in the first place. For example, studies of the US FOMC meetings, before and after the decision to publish transcripts, indicate a significant shift in behaviour by participants, with interventions becoming longer and more formulaic (Meade and Stasavage, 2008). It is unclear whether this shift towards greater transparency has materially improved the quality of FOMC debates and decisions. This was an important factor weighing in the Bank of England's announcement in December 2014 about how and when it would publish transcripts of MPC meetings (Warsh, 2014). More generally, it will be important to assess critically the pros and cons of further great leaps forward in central bank transparency in the period ahead.

5 Concluding Remarks

This chapter forms part of a book to celebrate the bicentenary of Norges Bank. This book is inspired by a work published in 1994 to celebrate the tercentenary of the Bank of England (Capie et al., 1995). Around that time, much of the academic and policy-making focus was on issues around central bank independence in the setting of monetary policy. Back then, this was not a widely accepted feature of monetary policy globally, though it was becoming more so. Today it is. Societal thinking has evolved and with it central bank practice. That has very much been the pattern of central bank evolution, with a near-continuous process of experimentation, adaptation and trial and error.

Between the period of the Bank of England's tercentenary and Norges Bank's bicentenary, the world has experienced a jarring and scarring financial crisis. This period has, once again, been defined by central bank experimentation, adaptation and trial and error. Today, the focus of academic and policy-making debate is on issues around central bank independence in respect of financial stability policy. As in 1994, this is not a widely-accepted feature of financial stability policy globally, though it is becoming more so. In thirty years' time, when the Banco de Portugal celebrates its bicentenary, will financial stability policy independence be as firmly established as monetary policy independence is today? It remains to be seen.

Back in 1994, Charles Goodhart wrote:

The lasting qualities – the philosophy if you will – that seem to me the hallmark of central banking are a triumvirate:

- Continuity and all that implies for experience and nurturing a long view;
- Competence and all that implies for a high degree of professionalism and careful deliberation and communication; and
- Integrity and all that implies for accountability and simple honesty.

We think that captures perfectly the essence of this paper and the evolution of central banking, past, present and future. Provided central banks continue to adhere to these qualities, there is no reason twenty-first century central banking cannot repeat the evolutionary successes of the twentieth.

References

Adrian, T., Kimbrough, K. and Marchioni, D. 2011. "The Federal Reserve's commercial funding facility", *Economic Policy Review* 17: 25–39

Aikman, D., Galesic, M., Gigerenzer, G., Kapadia, S., Katsikopoulos, K., Kothiyal, A, Murphy, E. and Neumann, T. 2014. 'Taking uncertainty seriously: simplicity versus complexity in financial regulation', *Bank of England Financial Stability Papers* 28

Ali, R., Barrdear, J., Clews, R. and Southgate, J. 2014a. "Innovations in payment technologies and the emergence of digital currencies", *Bank of England Quarterly Bulletin* 54: 262–275

2014b. "The economics of digital currencies", *Bank of England Quarterly Bulletin* 54: 276–286

Allen, F. and Gale, D. 2004. "Competition and financial stability", *Journal of Money, Credit and Banking* 36: 453–480

Antipa, P. and Matheron, J. 2014. "Interactions between monetary and macroprudential policies", *Banque de France Financial Stability Review* 18: 225–239

Apel, M., Claussen, C. A., Gerlach-Kristen, P., Lennartsdotter, P. and Røisland, Ø. 2013. "Monetary policy committees – comparing theory and 'inside' information from MPC members", *Norges Bank Working Papers* 2013/03. Available at: www.norgesbank.no/pages/92821/Norges_Bank_Working_Paper_2013_03.pdf

Arrow, K. J. 1964. "The role of securities in the optimal allocation of risk-bearing", *Review of Economics and Statistics* 31: 91–96

Bagehot, W. 1873. *Lombard Street: A description of the money market.* New York, New York: Scribner, Armstrong & Co.

Bank for International Settlements 2012. *Payment, clearing and settlement systems in the CPSS countries volume 1 and 2.* Basel: Bank for International Settlements

Barro, R. and Gordon, D. B. 1983. "A positive theory of monetary policy in a natural rate model", *Journal of Political Economy* 91: 589–610

Berger, H., De Haan, J. and Eijffinger, S. C. 2001. "Central bank independence: An update of theory and evidence", *Journal of Economic Surveys* 15: 3–40

Bernanke, B. S. 2003. "Constrained discretion' and monetary policy", remarks before the money marketeers of New York University. New York, New York, 3 February 2003. Available at: www.federalreserve.gov/boarddocs/Speeches/2003/20030203/default.htm

2013. "Monetary policy and the global economy", speech at the Department of Economics and STICERD (Suntory and Toyota International Centres for Economics and Related Disciplines) Public Discussion in Association with the Bank of England. London, United Kingdom, 25 March 2013. Available at: www.federalreserve.gov/newsevents/speech/bernanke20130325a.pdf

2014. "The Federal Reserve: Looking back, looking forward", speech at the Annual Meeting of the American Economic Association. Philadelphia, Pennsylvania, 3 January 2014. Available at: www.federalreserve.gov/newsevents/speech/bernanke20140103a.htm

Bernanke, B. S. and Mishkin, F. S. 1997. "Inflation targeting: A new framework for monetary policy?", *Journal of Economic Perspectives* 11: 97–116

Borio, C. 2014a. "(Too) great expectations for macro-prudential?", *Central Banking* 25: 79–85

2014b. "Monetary policy and financial stability – what role in prevention and recovery?", *BIS Working Papers* 440. Available at: www.bis.org/publ/work440.pdf

Briault, C., Haldane, A. G. and King, M. 1996. "Independence and accountability", *Bank of England Working Papers* 49. Available at: www.bankofengland.co.uk/archive/Documents/historicpubs/workingpapers/1996/wp49.pdf

Blinder, A. S. and Morgan, J. 2005. "Are two heads better than one? Monetary policy by committee", *Journal of Money, Credit and Banking* 37: 789–811

Capie, F. 2012. *The Bank of England: 1950s to 1979*. New York: Cambridge University Press

Capie, F., Fisher, S., Goodhart, C. and Schnadt, N. 1995. *The future of central banking*. Cambridge: Cambridge University Press

Columba, F., Costa, A., Kongsamut, P., Lim, C., Otani, A., Saiyid, M., Wezel, T. and Wu, X. 2011. "Macroprudential policy: What instruments and how to use them? Lessons from country experiences", *IMF Working Papers* 11/238. Available at: www.imf.org/external/pubs/ft/wp/2011/wp11238.pdf

Cox, W. M. 1990. "Two types of paper: The case for Federal Reserve independence", *FRB Dallas Annual Report*: 6–17

Cukierman, A. 1992. *Central bank strategy, credibility and independence: Theory and evidence*. Cambridge, Massachusetts: MIT Press

2008. "Central bank independence and monetary policymaking in institutions – past, present and future", *European Journal of Political Economy* 24: 722–736

Debreu, G. 1959. *Theory of value – an axiomatic analysis of economic equilibrium*. New Haven, Connecticut: Yale University Press

Eitrheim, Ø. and Øksendal, L. F. 2014. "1899 and the Christiania crash revisited: Crisis management and the interplay between monetary authorities in Norway over two centuries", unpublished paper prepared for the Arne Ryde Symposium: Macro policy in crisis, University of Lund

Ely, R. T. 1885. *Recent American socialism*. Baltimore, Maryland: Johns Hopkins University

FPC 2014. Financial Policy Committee statement on housing market powers of Direction from its policy meeting, 26 September 2014. Available at: www.bankofengland.co.uk/financialstability/Documents/fpc/statement021014.pdf

Friedman, M. 1962. "Should there be an independent monetary authority?", in Yeager (ed.), *In search of a monetary constitution*, pp. 219–243. Cambridge, Massachusetts: Harvard University Press

Fry, M., Julius, D., Mahadeva, L., Roger, S. and Sterne, G. 2000. "Key issues in the choice of monetary policy framework", in Mahadeva and Sterne (eds.) *Monetary frameworks in a global context*, pp. 1–216. London: Routledge

Galati, G. and Moessner, R. 2013. "Macroprudential policy – a literature review", *Journal of Economic Surveys* 27: 846–878

Garfinkel, M. R. and Oh, S. 1995. "When and how much to talk credibility and flexibility in monetary policy with private information", *Journal of Monetary Economics* 35: 341–357

Giannini, C. 2011. *The age of central banks*. Cheltenham: Edward Elgar

Gigerenzer, G. 2014. *Risk Savvy: How to make good decisions*. London: Penguin

Goodfriend, M. 1997. "Monetary policy comes of age: A 20th century odyssey", *FRB Richmond Economic Quarterly* 83: 1–22

The Evolution of Central Banks: A Practitioner's Perspective 669

Goodhart, C. A. E. 1999. "Myths about the lender of last resort", *International Finance* 2: 339–360

Haldane, A. G. 2013. "Why institutions matter (more than ever)", speech given at the Centre for Research on Socio-Cultural Change (CRESC) Annual Conference, School of Oriental and African Studies, London, 4 September 2013. Available at: www.bankofengland.co.uk/publications/Pages/news/2013/102.aspx

Haldane, A. G. and Madouros, V. 2012. "The dog and the Frisbee", speech given at the Federal Reserve Bank of Kansas City's 36th economic policy symposium, "The Changing Policy Landscape", Jackson Hole, Wyoming, 31 August 2012. Available at: www.bankofengland.co.uk/publications/documents/speeches/2012/speech596.pdf

Haldane, A. G. and May, R. M. 2011. "Systemic risks in banking ecosystems", *Nature* 469: 351–355

Hansen, L. P. and Sargent, T. 2007. *Robustness.* Princeton, New Jersey: Princeton University Press

Hetzel, R. L. 1997. "The case for a monetary rule in a constitutional Democracy", *FRB Richmond Economic Quarterly* 83: 45–66

IMF 2013. "The interaction of monetary and macroprudential policies", *International Monetary Fund Policy Papers*

Jansson, P. and Vredin, A. 2004. "Preparing the monetary policy decision in an inflation-targeting central bank: The case of Sveriges Riksbank", in the conference volume Practical Experience with Inflation Targeting, hosted by the Czech National Bank

King, M. 2004. "The institutions of monetary policy", *American Economic Review* 94(2): 1–13

2006. "Trusting in money: From Kirkcaldy to the MPC", The Adam Smith Lecture, Bank of England. Available at: www.bankofengland.co.uk/archive/Documents/historicpubs/speeches/2006/speech288.pdf

Kohn, M. 1999. "Bills of exchange and the money market to 1600", *Dartmouth College, Department of Economics Working Papers* 99/04. Available at: www.dartmouth.edu/~mkohn/Papers/99-04.pdf

Knight, F. H. 1921. *Risk, uncertainty and profit.* Boston, Massachusetts: Houghton Mifflin Company

Kuttner, K. N. and Posen, A. S. 2013. "Goal dependence for central banks: Is the malign view correct?", paper presented at the 14th Jacques Polak Annual Research Conference hosted by the International Monetary Fund Washington, District of Columbia. Available at: www.imf.org/external/np/res/seminars/2013/arc/pdf/posen.pdf

Kydland, F. E. and Prescott, E. C. 1977. "Rules rather than discretion: The inconsistency of optimal plans", *Journal of Political Economy* 83: 473–492

Lear, W. V. 2000. "A review of the rules versus discretion debate in monetary policy", *Eastern Economic Journal* 26: 29–39

Lim, C. H., Krznar, I., Lipinsky, F., Otani, A. and Wu, X. 2013. "The macroprudential framework: Policy responsiveness and institutional arrangements", *IMF working papers* 13/166. Available at: www.imf.org/external/pubs/ft/wp/2013/wp13166.pdf

Lombardelli, C., Proudman, J. and Talbot, J. 2005. "Committees versus individuals: An experimental analysis of monetary policy decision making", *International Journal of Central Banking* 1: 181–206

670   *Andrew G. Haldane and Jan F. Qvigstad*

Meade, E. E. and Stasavage, D. 2008. "Publicity of debate and the incentive to dissent; evidence from the US Federal Reserve", *The Economic Journal* 118: 695–717

Morris, S. and Shin, H. S. 2002. "Social welfare and public information", *American Economic Review* 92: 1521–1534

Mueller, R. C. 1997. *The Venetian money market: Banks, panics, and the public debt 1200–1500*. Baltimore and London: John Hopkins University Press

Norges Bank 1899. *Annual report.* Oslo: Norges Bank, Norway
     2013. "Criteria for an appropriate countercyclical capital buffer", *Norges Bank Memo* 1/2013
     2014. "Monetary policy report with financial stability assessment 1/14". Oslo, Norway

Øksendal, L. F. 2012. "Freedom of manoeuvre: the Norwegian gold standard experience, 1874 -1914", in Ögren and Øksendal (eds.), *The gold standard periphery: Monetary policy, adjustment and flexibility in a global setting*, pp. 37–57. London: Palgrave MacMillan

Olson, M. 1971. *The logic of collective action: Public goods and the theory of groups.* Cambridge, Massachusetts: Harvard University Press.

Oritani, Y. 2011. "Public governance of central banks: an approach from new institutional economics", working Paper, *BIS Working Papers* 299. Available at: www.bis.org/publ/work299.pdf

Panetta, F., Faeh, T., Grande, G., Ho, C., King, M., Levy, A., Signoretti, F. M., Taboga, M. and Zaghini, A. 2009. "An assessment of financial sector rescue programmes", *BIS Papers* 48

Poloz, S. S. 2014. "Integrating uncertainty and monetary policy-making: A practitioner's perspective", *Bank of Canada Discussion Papers*

Pozsar, Z., Adrian, T., Ashcraft, A. B. and Boesky, H. 2013. "Shadow banking", *FRB New York Economic Policy Review* 19(2): 1–16

Qvigstad, J. F. 2006. "When does an interest rate path 'look good'? Criteria for an appropriate future interest rate path", *Norges Bank Working Papers* 2006/5. Available at: www.norges-bank.no/Upload/import/publikasjoner/arbeidsnotater/pdf/arb-2006-05.pdf
     2013. "Monetary policy committees and communications", *Norges Bank Staff Memo* 6/2005

Roberts, R. 1994. "The bank and the city", in Roberts and Kynaston (eds.) *The Bank of England: Money, power, and influence, 1694–1994*, pp. 152–184. Oxford: Clarendon Press
     2013. *Saving the city: The great financial crisis of 1914.* Oxford: Oxford University Press

Stein, J. C. 1989. "Cheap talk and the Fed: A theory of imprecise policy statements", *American Economic Review* 79: 32–42
     2014. "Incorporating financial policy considerations into a monetary policy framework", speech at the International Research Forum on Monetary Policy, Washington D.C. Board of Governors of the Federal Reserve System, Washington, District Of Columbia, 13 April 2014. Available at: www.federalreserve.gov/newsevents/speech/stein20140321a.pdf

Taylor, J. B. 1993. "Discretion versus rules in practice", *Carnegie Rochester Conference Series on Public Policy* 39: 195–214

2013. "Simple rules for financial stability", keynote address at the Financial Markets Conference "Maintaining Financial Stability: Holding a Tiger by the Tail" hosted by FRB Atlanta, Stone Mountain, Georgia, 9 April 2013. Available at: www.frbatlanta.org/-/media/Documents/news/conferences/2013/fmc/13fmctaylorpres.pdf

Walsh, C. E. 2014. "Multiple objectives and central bank trade-offs under flexible inflation targeting", *CESifo Working Papers* 5097. Available at: http://people.ucsc.edu/~walshc/MyPapers/cesifo1_wp5097.pdf

Warsh, K. 2014. "Transparency and the Bank of England's Monetary Policy Committee", Review conducted for the Bank of England. Available at: www.bankofengland.co.uk/publications/Documents/news/2014/warsh.pdf

Index

Abreu, Dilip, 503–504
ACAM. *See* Mutual Insurance Supervisory Authority
acceptance credit, 580
acceptance market, 151–152
Accominotti, Olivier, 366–367
accountability, 63–64, 647–649, 652–653, 665
ACP. *See* Autorité de Contrôle Prudentiel
Act for Competition and Credit Control (CCC), 456–457
active reserve, 12, 282–283
agio, 23, 26–27, 29–30
Aguiar, Mark, 408
Aizenman, Joshua, 391–392, 397–398, 401, 403–404
Aldrich-Vreeland Act, 243, 451
Alesina, Alberto, 198–199
Aliber, Robert Z., 231, 233–234, 496–497
American Account economies, 307–308
American National Monetary Commission, 441–442
Amsterdamsche Wisselbank. See Bank of Amsterdam
Anand, Rahul, 407
The Anguish of Central Banking (Burns), 100–104
Annual Report on Exchange Arrangements and Exchange Restrictions (AREAER), 421–422
annuities, 20–22, 24–25
Ansaldo, 450
anti-Semitism, 266
Arab-Israeli War, 611–612
AREAER. See Annual Report on Exchange Arrangements and Exchange Restrictions

Argentina, 237–238, 330, 344–345, 401, 403
The Art of Central Banking (Hawtrey), 255–256
Ashton, T. S., 234–235
Asian financial crisis (1997–1998), 294, 344–345, 400–401, 411, 413–414, 500–501
  emerging market economies and, 394–398
  RBNZ and, 139
asset liquidity, 617–618
asset price bubbles, 14, 261, 406–407
  conclusions to, 509–510
  introduction to, 493–496
  overview of episodes, 496–501
  policy responses and, 503–509
  severity of crises, 501–503
Association of Limited Liability Companies, 450
Australia, 196, 212–213, 222–223, 263, 312–313, 332–333, 338–339, 508
  Bretton Woods and, 126–127
  CBA, 125–127, 216–217
  as high trust society, 217
  New Zealand and, 136–137
  RBA, 125–127, 216–217, 504–505
  real estate bubble of, 496–497, 504–507
Austria, 167–168, 177–178, 240, 254, 256, 282, 295–296, 298–300
  active exchange rate policy in, 158
  classical gold standard and, 324–326
  government debt in, 40
  market interest rates in, 172–173
  second-generation public banks in, 40
  War of Austrian Succession, 26–27
Austro-Prussian War, 330

673

674 *Index*

autonomy, 63–64, 70–71
  monetary, 398–402
  monetary nonautonomy, 398–399
Autorité de Contrôle Prudentiel (ACP), 470
Autorité des Marchés Financiers, 470
Ayr Bank, 244

Bade, R., 198–199
Bagehot, Walter, 11, 235, 262, 291, 425,
  427–428, 645–646. *See also Lombard
  Street: A Description of the Money
  Market*
  Bernanke and, 246
  inherent fragility and, 264
  Liberal Party and, 292–293
  LOLR and, 233–234
  Responsibility Doctrine and, 3, 115, 633
Bagehot's rule, 246–247, 257–259
Bai-Perron test, 83–84
balance of payments, 196, 343, 356–357, 363,
  378–379, 610
balance sheets, 45–46, 280–282, 368–369,
  377–378, 636–637
  consolidated, 12–13
  expansion of, 5, 14–15
  of Federal Reserve, 128–131
  money demand and, 20
  money markets and, 153–162
Balkan War, 330
Ball, L., 63–64, 77–78
Banca di Genova, 152–153
Banca d'Italia, 67, 240–241, 434–435, 442–443
  inflation and, 123–124
  World War I and, 123, 449–451
Banca Nazionale del Lavoro, 460
Banca Nazionale nel Regno d'Italia, 152–153,
  433, 442
Banco de España, 217–219
Banco de la República, 453–455, 465–467,
  474–475
Banco de Portugal, 296, 666
Banco del Giro, 27–28, 40, 44, 48–50
Banco di Rialto, 27–29, 44, 52–53
Bank Act (1833), 326–327
Bank Act (1844), 3, 326–327, 439–440
Bank Act (1891), 437–438
Bank Act (1900), 437–438
Bank Act (1926), 450–451
Bank Act (1936), 460–461, 470
Bank Act (1941), 469–470
Bank Act (1946), 470–471

Bank Act (1947), 470–471
Bank Act (1967), 464–465
Bank Act (1993), 471–472
Bank Act Amendment (1924), 453
Bank Charter Act (1833), 430–431
Bank Charter Act (1844), 236–237, 430–431,
  630–631, 642
Bank Circulation Redemption Fund, 437–438
Bank deutscher Länder, 152–153
Bank for International Settlements (BIS), 256,
  280, 333, 339, 347, 476–477
  asset price bubbles and, 494
  banking statistics and, 363–364
  bilateral cooperation and, 347–348
bank holidays, 252–253, 461–462
Bank Law (1926), 450–451
Bank of America, 233–234
Bank of Amsterdam (*Amsterdamsche
  Wisselbank*), 32, 46–47, 51–53, 580,
  602–603
  founding of, 29
  as LOLR, 580–581
  receipts and, 578–580
Bank of Canada (BoC), 64, 67, 70–71, 131–136,
  464–465
Bank of Canada Act, 133–134
Bank of Credit and Commerce International
  (BCCI), 477–478
Bank of England, 18–19, 35–36, 46–47,
  114–117, 151–152, 175–176, 327–328,
  610–611, 629–630
  banknotes and, 2, 32–33
  Baring Crisis and, 262–265
  bearer notes and, 574
  check payments and, 585–586
  credibility and, 104–105
  deposit banking and, 439–441
  discount rates and, 172–173
  foreign assets and, 158
  forward guidance and, 4–5
  FSM and, 430–431
  gold and, 247
  gold standard and, 107–108
  good collateral and, 3
  government debt and, 35–36
  Group Arrangement and, 340–341
  as LOLR, 234–239, 633
  open market operations and, 177–178
  origins of, 67
  in past, 630–631
  payment systems and, 582–585

Index

675

Prudential Regulation Authority and, 468
Smith on, 244
structure of, 51–52
suspension of convertibility and, 55–56
World War I and, 446–447
World War II and, 116, 455–456
Bank of France. *See* Banque de France
Bank of Hamburg, 30–31, 46–47, 51–53
Bank of Japan, 67, 288–289, 320–321, 324, 328–329, 506
credibility and, 96
as LOLR, 239
Bank of Spain, 24–25, 284, 296
Bank of the Parliament (*Riksens Ständers Bank*), 34–35
Bank of United States, 257, 264–267
Bankers Industrial Development Corporation (BIDC), 447
Bankers Trust Company, 371–372
Banking Act (1874), 434
Banking Act (1921), 218–219
Banking Act (1933), 462
Banking Act (1935), 462
Banking Act (1941), 458–459
Banking Act (1946), 218–219
Banking Act (1962), 219
Banking Act (1979), 457, 636–637
banking crisis (1930s), 177–178
Banking in the early stages of industrialization: a study in comparative economic history (Cameron), 1
Banking Law (1865), 438–439
Banking School, 285–286, 304
banknotes, 14, 154, 430, 443
Bank of England and, 2, 32–33
convertibility of, 446–447
protection of, 430–439
in Sweden, 34
Banque de France, 38–39, 117–119, 301–302, 324, 326–328, 431–433
deposit banking and, 441–442
domestic lending and, 165–167
gold exchange standard and, 300–301
as LOLR, 239–240
World War I and, 448–449
Banque générale (Banque Royale), 36–38, 56
Banque Nationale de Crédit (BNC), 457–458
Banque Royale (Banque générale), 36–38, 56
Barcelona, Spain, 23–25, 44–46, 49–51
Baring, Francis, 235, 244–245, 255–256

Baring Brothers and Company, 237–238, 262–263, 330, 440
Baring Crisis, 238, 262–265, 442–443, 633
Barro, Robert, 198, 220–221
Basel Committee on Bank Supervision (BCBS), 476–477, 479–480, 612–614, 617–618
Basel I agreement, 477–479, 613, 616–617
Basel II agreement, 477, 479–480, 614, 616–618
Basel soft laws, 471–472
BCCI. *See* Bank of Credit and Commerce International
BCSC. *See* Basel Committee on Bank Supervision
Bear Stearns, 270–271, 592
Beckhart, B. H., 437–438, 441–442
Beenstock, Michael, 205–206
Belgium, 152–153, 158, 167–168, 207–210, 282, 295, 298–299, 304–306
collateralized lending and, 169–170
credit controls and, 178
National Bank of Belgium, 287–288
Berg, Carl, 413–414
Berman, U. Michael, 409–410
Bernanke, Ben, 11, 73–74, 104, 107–108, 255, 267–268, 273, 618–619
asset price bubbles and, 493–494
Bagehot and, 246
cost of financial intermediation and, 261–262
FSM and, 424
global financial crisis and, 68, 346–347
Beyer, A., 78–106
Bhundia, Ashok J., 398, 401
BIDC. *See* Bankers Industrial Development Corporation
Big Bang (1986), 467–468
The Big Short (Lewis), 621
Bignon, Vincent, 231, 248–249, 431
bills of exchange, 23–24, 29, 37–38, 164, 168–169, 570, 602–603, 630–631
Early Modern system and, 14
exchange banks and, 575–577
foreign, 41–44
Bimetallic system, 117, 218–219
BIS. *See* Bank for International Settlements
Bitcoin, 57, 663–664
Black Monday, 250–251
Black Tuesday, 250–251
Blessing, Karl, 70–71
Blinder, Alan, 62, 428
BNC. *See* Banque Nationale de Crédit

676 *Index*

BoC. *See* Bank of Canada
Bolshevik Revolution, 297, 329–330
Bomhoff, Karl Gether, 633–634
Bonaparte, Napoleon, 28, 39
bons de la Defense Nationale, 448–449
boom-bust economic cycle, 268–269, 359, 388–389, 408–409
Bordo, Michael D., 79, 131–132, 231, 499–500
Borio, Claudio, 75, 280–282, 362
Bouey, Gerald, 134
Braude, Jacob, 198–226
Brazil, 324–326, 347, 401, 403, 412–413
Bretton Woods, 196–197, 215, 254–255, 298–299, 335–336, 345–346, 471–472, 636–637
   Australia and, 126–127
   Canada and, 71, 132–134
   central bank reserves and, 304–312
   collapse of, 106, 309–310
   DBB and, 122
   emerging economies and, 389–390
   Federal Reserve and, 129–130
   France and, 118–119
   gold-exchange standard and, 304–306
   international monetary regime and, 336–342
   interwar gold standard and, 322–323
   Italy and, 123–124
   Norway and, 120
   Sweden and, 113–114
   Switzerland and, 124–125
   UK and, 116
Britain, 152–153, 165–167, 174–175, 246. *See also* Bank of England
   classical gold standard and, 324
   credibility and, 69
   credit controls and, 178
   Exchange Equalization Accounts in, 302
   Financial Revolution of, 1–16
   Glorious Revolution of, 1–16
   gold standard and, 201, 319–320, 367
   as high trust society, 216–217
   LOLR in, 3
   monetary policy debates in, 285–286
   Napoleonic Wars and, 35–36, 246–247
   standing facilities in, 174–175
British Government Securities, 618
Brown, William Arthur, 446–447
Brunner, Karl, 62, 198–226
Brunnermeier, Markus K., 495–496, 503–504
Bubble Act (1720), 583–584
bullion, 2, 54, 158, 281–287

Bundesbank (DBB), 71–85, 95–96, 113–114, 338–339, 346–347
Bureau of Economic Analysis, 375–376
Bureau of Internal Revenue, 200
Burgess, W. Randolph, 452
Burns, Arthur, 71, 100–104, 129–130, 341
Bussière, Matthieu, 413–415

Cagan, Philip, 198–199
Caisse de Dépôts de Consignations, 459
Caisse des Comptes Courants, 39, 46–47
Caisse d'Escompte, 36, 38–39, 55
Caisse Nationale de Crédit Agricole, 459
Caja de Crédito Agrario, 465–466
Caldwell and Company, 251–252
Calomiris, C. W., 263–264, 330
Cameron, Rondo, 1
Canada, 13, 71–72, 81–82, 197, 304, 312–313, 337–338, 483. *See also* Bank of Canada
   Bretton Woods and, 71, 132–134
   Coyne Affair in, 125–127, 134–135
   deposit banking in, 445
   deregulation in, 473–474
   FSM and, 437–438
   global financial crisis and, 134–135
   globalization in, 473–474
   Great Depression and, 464–465
   IT and, 72
   World War I and, 452–453
   World War II and, 132
Canada Deposit Insurance Corporation (CDIC), 464–465
Canadian Bankers Association, 437–438, 445, 452–453, 464–465
Capie, Forrest, 198–202, 206–207, 215–216, 231, 249–250, 456–457
capital, 443
   closed markets, 390
   foreign, 303–304, 500
      inflows, 497–498
   free movements, 328–329
   mobility of, 413–414
   openness of, 396–397
   social, 247
   Tier 1 capital base, 616–617
capital accounts, 12–13, 357–358
   IMFS and, 356–357
   liberalization of, 311–312
   shocks, 412–413
Capital Assistance Program, 269

Index

677

capital controls, 125, 321–322, 343, 345, 415, 479
  elimination of, 469
  in Germany, 333–335
  index, 392
capital exports, 293
capital flight, 370–371
capital flows, 196–197, 328, 366–367, 373–378, 412–413
  cross-border, 391–392
  external, 222–223
  gross, 361–362, 375–376
  international, 370
  measuring, 361–364
  net, 357–358, 361–363, 376–377
  private, 396–397
  reversals of, 387
  round-trip, 375–376
  short-term, 158–160
  World War II and, 282–283
capital inflows, 14, 408–409
  foreign, 497–498
capital markets
  closed, 390
  malfunctioning of, 222
  short-term, 293–294
Capital Purchase Program, 269
capital ratios, 623–624
capital requirements, 21, 472–473
Carney, Mark J., 64
Carr, Jack, 453
carry trades, 296–297
Carter, Jimmy, 130
Casa di San Giorgio, 25–27, 37–38, 51–52
cash, 566
casino banks, 621
Cassa Depositi e Prestiti, 460
Catalonia, Spain, 23–25, 48–50
Catao, Luis, 413–414
Catholic banks, 450–451
Cavour (Prime Minister), 433–434, 439
CBA. *See* Commonwealth Bank of Australia
CCC. *See* Act for Competition and Credit Control
CDIC. *See* Canada Deposit Insurance Corporation
CECEI. *See* Credit Institutions and Investment Firms Committee
Central America, 323–324
central bank communication, 139, 508–509
central bank cooperation, 336–342

central bank independence, 2, 10, 12, 82–83, 93–94, 650–653
  contracts, examples of, 215–220
  conventions and, 198–200
  free banking in high trust societies, 221–222
  GDP and, 223–224
  high trust societies and, 204
  instructions and, 201–204
  introduction to, 195–197
  openness, degree of, 221–227
  role of law and, 198–200
  small open economies and, 204–205, 211–212
  trust and, 198–200
Central Bank Money, 122–123
central bank reserves
  Bretton Woods and, 304–312
  conclusion to, 312–313
  early history of, 283–288
  Europe and, 288–293
  foreign exchange reserves, 293–297
  Genoa and, 297–304
central banking operations, 5
central banks. *See also specific topics*
  conclusion to, 666–668
  future issues, 650–666
    constituency-building, 653–655
    decision-making under uncertainty, 657–662
    independence, 650–653
    interventions in financial markets and institutions, 655–657
    money and banking, 662–664
    transparency, 664–666
  in past, 630–639
    Bank of England, 630–631
    financial system oversight, 636–637
    modern monetary policy, 637–639
    Norges Bank, 631–638
    payment system and, 634–636
  at present, 639–650
    accountability, 647–649
    clear objectives, 640–644
    history and experience, 649–650
    tools and competence, 644–647
  purpose of, 627–630
Chamon, Marco, 402
CHAPS, 563–564, 593–594
chartered banks, 464–465
cheap money, 132–133
check payments, 585–587

678 *Index*

Checkland, S. G., 244
Chen, Qianying, 413–414
Chicago flat craze, 498–499
Chicago real estate boom (1881–1883),
    496–497, 502–503
Chile, 332–333, 403
China, 294, 342–343, 347, 361–362, 375–376,
    388, 403
  bank drafts in, 576
  renminbi and, 311–313, 343
  reserve accumulation and, 411–413
  silver standard and, 323–327
Chinn, Menzie, 392, 397–398, 412–414,
    422–423
CHIPS, 593–594
Chrysler, 268–269
Chung, H., 75–76
Churchill, Winston, 332
CIA Factbook, 421–422
Citigroup, 602
City of Glasgow Bank, 237–238
Civil Code, 433–434
Civil War
  of Colombia, 438–439
  of Spain, 218–219
  of U.S., 324–326, 330–332, 436–437,
    586–587
classical gold standard, 322–331, 361, 637–638
  in Austria, 324–326
  Britain and, 324
  Napoleonic Wars and, 323–324
  World War I and, 69, 323–324
clear objectives, 640–644
Clearing House Association, 265–266
clearinghouse loan certificates, 241–243
clearinghouses, 240–243, 570, 585–586, 635
closed capital markets, 390
closed economies, 205
CLS. *See* Continuous Linked Settlement
Coase, Ronald, 201–202
Code of Liberalization, OECD, 310–311
coevolution
  of monetary policy, 147–151
  of money markets, 11, 147–151
Coinage Act (1792), 435
coins and coinage, 23–24, 27, 569–570
  debasement of, 30–32
  exchange banks and, 575–577
  gold, 25–26, 39
  multiple-coin commodity money system, 49
  recoinage, 35

silver, 39, 54, 582–583
  transactions, 20–21
  virtual, 54
Cold War, 610–612
collateral, 572–573, 636, 656–657
  good, 3, 249–250
  trust and, 262
collateralized lending, 162–170, 262
collateralized loan markets, 180
collateral-saving devices, 590–591
collegial committee, 648–649
Colombia, 13, 332–333, 401, 403
  deposit banking in, 445–446
  deregulation in, 474–475
  FSM and, 438–439
  globalization in, 474–475
  gold standard and, 465
  Great Depression and, 465–467
  World War I and, 453–455
Comité de Réglementation Bancaire et
    Financière, 470
commercial bank finance, 1–16
commercial bills, 163–164
Commercial Code, 431–434
commercial corporations, 41
Commercial Revolution, 286
Commission Bancaire, 458–459, 469–470
Commission de Contrôle des Banques,
    458–459
committee-based decision-making, 646–649,
    661
commodity bubbles, 502
commodity exporters, 402
commodity money system, 20–21,
    662–663
  multiple-coin, 49
commodity prices, 284–285
commodity standards, 319–320, 662–663
Common Law, 199, 202
common shocks, 221–222
Commonwealth Bank of Australia (CBA),
    125–127, 216–217
Commonwealth Trust Company, 473–474
communication
  of central banks, 139, 508–509
  with public, 70–71
Community Development Capital Initiative,
    269
Companies Act, 430–431
comparative analysis, 146–147
comprehensive net worth, 20

Index

679

Comptoir d'Escompte, 239–240, 441–442, 457–458
Concordat, 477–479
Connally, John, 320, 341
Conseil d'Etat, 432
Consortium for Industrial Finance, 450
constituency-building, 653–655
constrained discretion, 629, 642–643, 657–658
contagion of fear, 232
Contamin, 295–296
continuity bias, 7
Continuous Linked Settlement (CLS), 565, 590–603
  in-out swaps and, 599–601
  liquidity saving and, 599–601
  operation of, 592–599
  policy issues and, 601–602
  as private sector innovation, 591–592
conventions, 198–200
convergence periods, 11
convertibility, 298–299, 328
  of banknotes, 446–447
  of bullion, 283–285
  current account, 337–339
  of gold, 113
  of silver, 632–633
  specie, 117
  suspension of, 55–56, 434
Core Principles for Effective Banking Supervision (BCBS), 479–480
correspondent banking method, 593, 600–601
Coulibaly, Brahima, 410–411
countercyclicality, 410–411, 415–416, 623–625
counter-factual simulation, 658, 661
counterparties, 180, 574
Coyne, James, 70–71, 133–134
Coyne Affair, 125–127, 134–135
CPI inflation, 96–98
crawling peg regime, 137–138
credibility, 10
  Bank of England and, 104–105
  Bank of Japan and, 96
  Britain and, 69
  conclusions to, 107–108
  data, 81–83
  empirical evidence for, 83–107
  Federal Reserve and, 100–104
  gold standard and, 10, 68–69, 93–94
  history of, 68–74
  introduction to, 62–68
  Japan and, 71–72, 96

  measuring over long time span, 80–81
  methodological considerations for, 81–83
  oil price shock and, 78–106
  quantifying, 74–81
  shocks, 10, 68
  in UK, 104–105
  in U.S., 96–104
credit booms, 360, 368–369, 373–374, 654–655
credit cards, 566
credit controls, 178, 180–181, 456–457
credit expansion, 357–359
Credit Institutions and Investment Firms Committee (CECEI), 470
Crédit Lyonnais, 469–470
Crédit Mobilier, 239
Crédit National, 448–449
credit rationing, 459–460, 585, 644–645
credit risk, 148–149, 162–163, 636–637
Creditanstalt crisis, 121
Crimean War, 330, 633–634
Crispi (Prime Minister), 442
cross-border borrowing, 409
cross-border capital flows, 391–392
cross-border cooperation, 56–57
cross-country settlement risk, 594
Cukierman, Alex, 63–64, 82–83, 206–207
culture of stability, 73–74
Cunliffe report, 115–116
currency crisis (1984), 137–138
currency internationalization, 311–312
currency jurisdiction, 364
Currency Reform (1923), 121
Currency Reform (1948), 122
currency repos, 301–302
Currency School, 285–286
currency wars (1930s), 8, 337
current accounts, 361–362, 366–367, 379–381
  balances, 396–397
  convertibility, 337–339
  IMFS and, 356
  surpluses, 356–357
current money, 23, 30–32
cyclical factors, 154–158

Danat. *See* Darmstädter- und Nationalbank
Dannhauser, Jamie, 204–205
Darmstädter- und Nationalbank (Danat), 372–373
Darwinian model, 10, 18–19, 51–52
Dawes Plan, 303–304
DBB. *See* Bundesbank

680   *Index*

de Cecco, Marcello, 293–294
debt-to-equity conversion, 37–38
decision-making, 646–649, 657–662
  internal, 280
  units, 12–13, 358, 363–364
deflation, 79, 86, 106, 131–132, 621–622
  global, 297
  in Japan, 86–90
  periods of, 67–68
DeGaulle, Charles, 118–119
Dehing, Pit, 32, 579–580
delivery versus payment (DVP), 596
demand deposits, 244–245
demand management, 407–408
demand notes, 244–245
demandable deposits, 44, 48
denier resort, 244–245
Denmark, 119–120, 631
Denmarks Nationalbank, 240
Denzel, Markus A., 47, 53–54
Department of Insurance, 474
dependency, 213
deposit banking, 439–446
  in Canada, 445
  in Colombia, 445–446
  in France, 441–442
  in Italy, 442–443
  in UK, 439–441
  in U.S., 443–445
deposit certificates (*fede di credito*), 26–27, 34
deposit insurance, 263–264, 444–445, 653–655
deposit-currency ratio, 256–259, 265–266
Depository Trust and Clearing Corporation
  (DTCC), 602
deposit-reserve ratio, 257–259, 265–266
deregulation, 426, 467–475, 497–498, 500–501
  in Canada, 473–474
  in Colombia, 474–475
  in France, 468–470
  in Italy, 470–472
  in UK, 467–468
  in U.S., 472–473
Deutsche Bank, 371–373
Deutschemark, 122
Deutsches Lander Bank, 122
Devaluation of 1967, 116
Diamond, D. W., 232, 263–264
Dickens, Charles, 4
Diefenbaker, John, 133–134
digital currency, 663
diplomatic alliances, 290–291
Disconto Gesellschaft, 372–373
discount market, 162, 175–176, 180

discount rates, 170–173, 177–178
discount window, 177–178, 180
discretion-based supervision, 452, 483–484
displacement, 360, 367–368, 498–499
Disyatat, Piti, 362
divergence periods, 11
diversity of thought, 661
Dodd–Frank Wall Street Reform and
  Consumer Protection Act, 271–272,
  428, 602
dollar, 12, 113–114, 282, 342–343, 377–378,
  569–570
  global liquidity and, 308–309
  IMFS and, 358
  liquidity of, 281
  phases of, 343–344
  rivals to, 312–313
  shortage of, 376–377
  swap lines, 347–348
  in UK, 309
domestic assets, 182
domestic bonds, 367–368
domestic economy, 7–8
domestic lending, 165–168
domestic liabilities, 368–369
domestic liquidity, 158–160
domestic markets, 162
domestic monetary operations, 158–160
Dominion Act, 437
Dominion notes, 437, 452–453
dot.com crashes, 425, 498–499, 502, 506
double liability, 272–273
Douglas, Roger, 138–139
Dow Jones Industrial Average, 250–251
Draghi, Mario, 289–290
Drexel Burnham Lambert, 266–267
DSGE. *See* Dynamic Stochastic General
  Equilibrium
DTCC. *See* Depository Trust and Clearing
  Corporation
Dunbar, Charles F., 439
Dutch East India Company (VOC), 30, 573,
  578, 580–581
Dutch Republic, 29–30
DVP. *See* delivery versus payment
Dybvig, Philip H., 232, 263–264
Dynamic Stochastic General Equilibrium
  (DSGE), 616

Early Modern system, 14, 565
East India Company, 160–161
EBU. *See* European Banking Union
ECB. *See* European Central Bank

Index

Eccles, Marriner S., 320
economic contractions, 232–233
economic freedom, 206–207, 213, 215
economic growth performance, 66–67
Economic Journal, 295–296
economic objectives, 62–63
economic shocks, 62–63
economic territory, 362–364, 379–380
economies of scale, 567–568
The Economist, 476–477
EEC. *See* European Economic Community
Efficient Market Hypothesis, 616
Eggertsson, G., 64–65
Eichengreen, Barry, 6–7, 251, 319,
    366–367
Einzig, Paul, 300–301
Eitrheim, Øyvind, 629
Ely, Richard, 647
Emergency Banking Act (1933), 461–462
emergency loans, 248
emerging economies
    future conjectures, 415–416
    international trilemma and, 389–398
    introduction to, 387–389
    monetary policy, describing, 398–411
    reserve accumulation and, 411–415
    self-insurance and, 411–415
Emmanuel, Rahm, 267–268
EMS. *See* European Monetary System
EMU. *See* European Monetary Union
encadrement du crédit, 459–460, 468–469
engineering sectors, 450
enhanced shareholder liability, 272–273
Ennis, Huberto M., 263–264
Equity Funding Corporation of America,
    266–267
equity ratios, 624–625
ERM. *See* Exchange Rate Mechanism
ERS. *See* exchange rate stability
Esdaile, Grenfell, Thomas & Co., 238
Esdaile, James, 238
Estey Commission, 473–474
Estonia, 298, 403
EU. *See* European Union
euro, 105–106, 122–123, 311–313, 342–343,
    569–570
euro crisis (2010), 343
Eurodollar market, 467, 476
Euromarkets, 611–612
Europe. *See also specific countries*
    central bank reserves and, 288–293
European Banking Union (EBU),
    480–482

European Central Bank (ECB), 65–66,
    73–85, 146, 179–180, 342–343, 426,
    469–470
European Economic Community (EEC), 137,
    344–345
European Monetary System (EMS), 118–119,
    123–124, 323, 469
European Monetary Union (EMU),
    480–481
European National Banks of Issue, 124
European Payments Union, 337–338
European Stability Mechanism, 294, 343
European System of Central Banks, 219
European Union (EU), 344–345, 471–472,
    480–482
Eurosystem, 165, 343, 469–470
Eurozone, 311, 376–377, 388–417, 612–613
evolutionary process of public banks, 44–56
    conclusion to, 56–57
    evolution and, 50–56
        external evolution, 52–53
        fiat money, 53–54
        general features, 50–51
        internal evolution, 52–53
        state and bank, 55
        stumbles and adaptations, 55–56
        three eras, 51–52
    origins of, 47–50
        private failings, 48–49
        public failings, 49–50
    quantitative overview of, 45–47
ex ante liquidity, 148–149, 163–165
excess financial elasticity, 12–13, 357–361,
    379–380
excess saving, 357–358
exchange banks, 575–582, 602–603
    Amsterdam and, 577–578
    bills of exchange and, 575–577
    coins and, 575–577
    public banks to central banks, 578–582
exchange controls, 132, 302, 610
Exchange Equalization Accounts, 302
Exchange Fund Account, 132
Exchange Rate Mechanism (ERM), 114, 615,
    638, 642–643
exchange rate pass through, 406–407
exchange rate peg, 398–399
exchange rate stability (ERS), 7–8, 328–329,
    391–396, 422
exchange rates. *See also* fixed exchange rates;
    floating exchange rates
    active policy, in Austria, 158
    fluctuations in, 20–21, 49, 598

682   *Index*

exchange rates (cont.)
  managed, 319–320, 347
  nominal, 363
  non-market, 53–54
  pegged, 107–108, 122, 132–133, 196–197
  real exchange rate depreciation, 210–211
  regimes, 319–322
    fixed, 322
  as shock absorbers, 394–396
  system, 12
  uncertainty, 303
  volatility, 301, 392
Exchequer bills, 235, 244–245, 583–584
Executive Board, 648–649
exogenous factors, 11, 180–181
exogenous shocks, 182, 329–330, 498–499
expansive monetary policy, 497–498
external capital flows, 222–223
external credit, 360
external drain, 248–249
external evolution, 52–53
external imbalances, 396–397
external shocks, 391, 471–472
external stability, 319–321, 324–326, 349
extraordinary times, 7–8

fair value, 614, 616–617, 621
Fannie Mae (Federal National Mortgage
    Association), 269–270, 619–620
FCI. *See* Financial Corporation for Industry
FDIC. *See* Federal Deposit Insurance
    Corporation
fear of floating, 344–345
fede di credito (deposit certificates), 26–27, 34
Federal Business Development Bank, 464–465
Federal Deposit Insurance Corporation
    (FDIC), 462–463
Federal Deposit Insurance Corporation
    Improvement Act, 472–473
Federal Home Loan Mortgage Corporation
    (Freddie Mac), 269–270, 619–620
Federal National Mortgage Association (Fannie
    Mae), 269–270, 619–620
Federal Reserve, 146, 151, 177–180, 249,
    254–255, 280–281
  balance sheet of, 128–131
  Board of Governors, 253
  Bretton Woods and, 129–130
  comprehensive net worth of, 20
  credibility and, 100–104
  dollar liquidity and, 281

  forward guidance and, 4–5
  gold reserve of, 260–261
  gold standard and, 71, 128
  inflation and, 96–98
  Meltzer on, 260
  profits of, 18
  World War I and, 128
  World War II and, 65–66, 129–130
Federal Reserve Act, 303–304, 444–445,
    451–452
Federal Reserve's Open Market Committee
    (FOMC), 63–64, 129–130, 665–666
Fed-Treasury Accord, 71
Fedwire, 563–565, 591–592, 594
Feldstein, Martin, 428
Ferguson, T., 69, 372–373
fiat money, 1–16, 246–247, 568–569, 578–579,
    590, 628, 662–663
  invention of, 53–54
  quasi-fiat money, 579–580
FIMBRA. *See* Financial Intermediaries,
    Managers and Brokers Regulatory
    Association
Finance Act (1914), 452–453
Financial Commission, 297–298
Financial Corporation for Industry (FCI), 455
financial crisis (1763), 502
financial crisis (1793), 244–245
financial crisis (1797), 235, 244–245
financial crisis (1825), 235
financial crisis (1847), 174–175, 237
financial crisis (1857), 174–175, 239–240
financial crisis (1866), 2–7, 174–175
financial crisis (1870), 174–175
financial crisis (1873), 113, 174–175
financial crisis (1907), 8, 113
financial crisis (1931), 256
financial globalization, 415
Financial Institutions and Deposit Insurance
    Amendment Act, 473–474
Financial Intermediaries, Managers and
    Brokers Regulatory Association
    (FIMBRA), 467–468
financial liberalization, 180–181, 391–392, 638
Financial Markets Group, 614
financial openness, 391–394, 396–397
financial openness/integration (KAOPEN),
    422–423
Financial Policy Committee (FPC), 637,
    648–649, 651–652
Financial Revolution, 1–16

Index

Financial Services Act, 426, 637, 641–642
Financial Services and Markets Act, 467–468, 637
Financial Services Authority (FSA), 467–468, 637
financial stability mandate (FSM), 13
  conclusion to, 482–485
  deposit banking and, 439–446
  deregulation and globalization of banking and, 467–475
  Great Depression and, 455–467
  internationalization of bank regulation, 475–482
  introduction to, 424–427
  in ordinary and exceptional times, 427–430
  origins of, 430–439
  protection of banknotes and, 430–439
  World War I and, 446–455
Financial Stability Report, 637
financial type influence, 198–199
Finland, 206, 240–241
First Bank of the United States, 435–436, 584–585
First Consul of the Republic, 39
First National Bank, 265–266
First National Loan, 449–450
First World War. *See* World War I
first-generation public banks, 22–32
  in Barcelona, 23–25
  in Catalonia, 23–25
  characteristics of, 42–43
  common themes of, 32
  in Dutch Republic, 29–30
  early German municipal banks, 28–29
  in Genoa, 25–27
  in Hamburg, 30–31
  in Nuremberg, 31–32
  in Venice, 27–28
fiscal agents, 41–44
fiscal debt, 336
fiscal deficits, 409–410
fiscal policy, 399
Fischer, Stanley, 222
Fisher, Irving, 329–330, 333–335
fixed exchange rates, 196–197, 337, 349–350, 389–390
  regimes, 322
  systems, 12, 196–197
fixed-but-adjustable rates, 196–197
fixed-income securities, 312–313
fixed-price offering, 37–38

Flandreau, Marc, 231, 248–249, 431
Flannery, Mark J., 272–273
flexible inflation target, 223
floating exchange rates, 195–196, 306–307, 319–320, 337–338, 342–350
  Greenback paper money, 128
  regimes, 322
  Riksbank and, 114
  unsustainability of, 12
Flood, Robert P., 413–414
florin, 28–29, 295–296, 301
FLS. *See* Funding for Lending Scheme
FOMC. *See* Federal Reserve's Open Market Committee
Fondo de Garantías de Instituciones Financieras, 474–475
forbearance, 484–485
foreign assets, 154–158
foreign bills of exchange, 41–44
foreign capital, 303–304, 500
  inflows, 497–498
foreign exchange (FX), 182, 288–289, 590–592
  clearing, 41–44
  inflows, 175, 178
  management, 12
  markets, 162, 180–181, 281–282
    interventions, 301–302
  reserves, 282, 286, 293–297, 396–397
  trades, 593–594
Foreign Exchange Control Board, 132
foreign liabilities, 368–369
foreign reserve management, 280–281
foreign-currency-denominated claims, 286–287
formal constraints, 168–169
Forssbæck, Jens, 147
forward guidance, 4–5, 665
Fourcade, M., 612
FPC. *See* Financial Policy Committee
France, 13, 36, 51–52, 81–82, 152–153, 158–160, 165–167, 174–175, 177–178, 282. *See also* Banque de France
  Bretton Woods and, 118–119
  bullion controversy in, 2
  collateralized lending and, 169–170
  credibility and, 69
  credit controls and, 178
  deposit banking in, 441–442
  deregulation in, 468–470
  geopolitical influence of, 283
  Germany and, 326–327

684 *Index*

France (cont.)
globalization in, 468–470
gold standard in, 117–118, 367
Great Depression in, 118, 457–460
IMFS and, 365–366
inflation in, 69–70
interest-rate smoothing and, 295–296
market interest rates in, 172–173
Netherlands and, 30–31
second-generation public banks in, 36–39
Venice and, 28
Wales and, 244–245
World War I and, 117–118, 448–449
Franco-German War, 117–118
Franco-Prussian War, 120–121, 291, 319–320, 326–327, 329–330
francs, 118–119, 287–289, 291, 299, 333
French securities, 299–300
stabilization of, 302
Frankel, Jeffrey, 407, 409–410
Franklin, Benjamin, 62–63
Franklin National Bank, 266–267
Fratzscher, Marcel, 412–413
Freddie Mac (Federal Home Loan Mortgage Corporation), 269–270, 619–620
Frederick the Great, 32, 39
free banking, 221–222, 247
free capital movements, 8, 328–329
Free Silver threat, 128
"Free to Choose" (TV series), 265–266
Fregert, K., 113–114
French bank (1716–1720), 19
French Indies Company, 37–38
French Revolution, 38, 244
French Wars, 284–285
Friedman, Milton, 6, 11, 77–78, 256–261, 264–266, 629. *See also specific works*
central bank independence and, 199–200
Federal Reserve and, 249, 251
free banking and, 221
pegged rates and, 196–197
rescue operations and, 266–267
Fringe Bank crisis, 610–611
fringe banking sector, 457
Fry, M., 646–647
FSA. *See* Financial Services Authority
FSM. *See* financial stability mandate
Fullarton, John, 236–237
Funding for Lending Scheme (FLS), 624–625
FX. *See* foreign exchange

Gaitskell, Hugh, 455–456
Galati, Gabriele, 280

Gallatin, Albert, 241–242
Gandal, Neil, 575–576
GDP. *See* gross domestic product
Geanakoplos, John, 300–301
Geithner, Timothy, 270–271
General Motors, 268–269
genetic drift, 52–53
Genoa, Italy, 25–27, 46–47, 49–52, 54, 297–304
Genoa Conference, 297–298
Genoa International Economic Conference, 332
Genoa Order, 297–299
Germany, 158–160, 167–169, 175–176, 310–311, 335, 343–346. *See also* Bank of Hamburg; Bundesbank
capital controls in, 333–335
capital flight in, 370–371
classical gold standard and, 324–326
credibility in, 105–107
culture of stability in, 73–74
early municipal banks in, 28–29
France and, 326–327
Franco-German War, 117–118
gold standard and, 319–320
Gründerkrise and, 499–501, 505
Hamburg, 30–31, 239–240
hyperinflation in, 69–70, 87, 120–121
IMFS and, 364–366, 370–373
macroprudential policy in, 506–507
Nuremberg, 31–32
positive inflation shocks in, 95–96
short-term debt of, 369
stock price bubble in, 502–503
Gertler, Mark, 493–494
Ghosh, Atish R., 397–398, 402, 411–412
ghost money, 20–21, 49
Giannini, Curzio, 439–440, 573, 628
Glass, Carter, 462
Glass-Steagall Act, 462
global deflation, 297
global financial crisis (2007–2009), 81, 84, 146, 348–349, 424
Bernanke and, 68, 346–347
Canada and, 134–135
Great Moderation and, 4, 130–131
IT after, 403–406
Global Financial Data, 82
Global Financial Stability Report, IMF, 374–375
globalization, 426, 467–475, 484–485
in Canada, 473–474
in Colombia, 474–475

Index

financial, 415
in France, 468–470
in Italy, 470–472
in UK, 467–468
in U.S., 472–473
Glorious Revolution, 1–16
gold coin, 25–26, 39
gold convertibility, 113
gold exchange standard, 69, 367
gold inflows, 128–129
gold specie standard, 356
gold standard, 115, 158–160, 201, 212–213, 215, 219–220, 367, 391, 642–643. *See also* classical gold standard
 Bagehot's rule and, 246–247
 Bank of England and, 107–108
 BoC and, 131–132
 breakdown of, 115–116
 Britain and, 201, 319–320, 367
 CBA and, 125–126
 Colombia and, 465
 credibility and, 10, 68–69, 93–94
 Federal Reserve and, 71, 128
 France and, 117–118, 367
 Germany and, 319–320
 interest rates and, 295
 interwar, 322–323, 331–336
 Italy and, 123
 in Japan, 324
 LOLR and, 233–235
 mobility of financial capital, 356–357
 monetary policy and, 389
 in Norway, 632–633
 pre-war, 297–298
 Switzerland and, 124–125
gold-exchange standard, 297–301, 304–306
Goldstein, Morris, 401
good collateral, 3, 249–250
Goodfriend, Marvin, 84, 272, 427–428
Goodhart, Charles, 75, 231, 248–249, 428, 476–477, 493–494, 666
Google Books, 255–256
Google Money, 663–664
Google Trends, 267
Gopinath, Gita, 408
Gordon, David, 198, 220–221
Gorton, Gary, 263–264, 272, 618
Goschen, George, 440
Gourinchas, Pierre-Olivier, 413–414
government debt, 38, 44, 50–51, 161, 169–170, 180–181
 annuities and, 22
 in Austria, 40

Bank of England and, 35–36
 long-term, 161–162
 market, 151–152
gradualism, 127, 134
Gramm-Leach Bliley Act, 472–473
Grassman, S., 205–206
Grassman Adjustment, 206
Great Canadian Slump, 73–85
Great Contraction, 128–129, 249, 265–266
Great Depression, 69–70, 330, 335–336, 348–349, 366–367, 379, 426, 483–484
 Bank of United States and, 264–266
 BoC and, 131–132
 in Canada, 464–465
 CBA and, 125–126
 in Colombia, 465–467
 Federal Reserve and, 100–104
 in France, 118, 457–460
 FSM and, 455–467
 Germany and, 121
 intercept break of, 84
 in Italy, 450–460
 LOLR and, 250–262
 progressive narrative of, 6
 RBNZ and, 136–137
 Switzerland and, 124–125
 in U.S., 461–463
Great Financial Crisis, 13, 356–358, 373–381
Great Inflation, 73–75, 98–100, 116, 122–123, 129–130
 credibility and, 71
 Germany and, 73–85
 Switzerland and, 125
Great Moderation, 66–67, 98–100, 116–117, 130, 323, 343–344, 424–425
 credibility and, 71–72, 104
 global financial crisis and, 4, 130–131
Great Nordic War, 34–35
Great Recession, 4, 6
Greenback paper money floating exchange rate, 128
Greenspan, Alan, 73–74, 104, 130, 346–347, 494–496, 506, 508–509
Greenspan put, 494–495, 615–616
Greuter, Eduard, 370–371
gross capital flows, 361–362, 375–376
gross domestic product (GDP), 207, 223–224, 238, 256–257
Grossman, Richard S., 272–273
Group Arrangements, 309, 340–341
Group de Contact, 476–477

686   *Index*

Gründerkrise, 499–501, 505
Grupo Colombia, 474–475

Haldane, A. G., 5
"Halfway Down" (Milne), 5
Hamburg, Germany, 30–31, 239–240
Hamilton, Alexander, 584–585
Hannah, Leslie, 447
hard pegs, 400–401
Hausgenossenschaften, 28
Hausmann, Ricardo, 415–416
Havenstein (president), 120–121
Hawtrey, R. G., 11, 231, 255–256
Heath, Alexandra, 280
Herstatt Risk, 567, 594, 600–601
Hibberts, Fuhr, & Purrier, 238
high inflation, 198–199
high trust societies, 11, 202–204, 213
   Australia as, 217
   Britain as, 216–217
   free banking in, 221–222
   New Zealand as, 215–216
high-powered money, 148–149, 396–397
Hirschman-Herfindahl indices, 304
History of Financial Crises under the
   National Banking System (Sprague),
   251–252
Hitler, Adolf, 121
Hodrick-Prescott filter, 74–75
Home Bank, 452–453
Hope, Pels, and Clifford, 580
Hori, Akinari, 309–310
Horne, Robert, 297
Huang, Haizhou, 264
Hume, David, 356
Humphrey, Thomas, 231–233
Hungary, 282, 295–296, 298, 401, 403
Hutchison, Michael, 401, 403–405, 409–410
hyperinflation, 69–70, 87, 120–121, 566–567

IDB. *See* Industrial Development Bank
IG Chemie (Internationale Gesellschaft für
   Chemische Unternehmungen AG),
   370–371
IG Consortium, 370–371
IG Farben, 370–371
Imai, Masami, 272–273
IMF. *See* International Monetary Fund
IMFS. *See* international monetary and financial
   system
implementation frameworks, 146

implicit price stability anchor, 398–399
"In Search of a Monetary Constitution,"
   199–200
independence. *See also* central bank
   independence
   MI, 391–394, 397–398, 421–422
   operational, 115, 628–629
   statutory, 214
India, 172–173, 293–294, 323–327, 403,
   412–413
Industrial Development Bank (IDB), 132,
   464–465
Industrial Revolution, 1–16, 446–447
inflation, 67–68, 79–80, 225–226, 323,
   343–346, 615. *See also* credibility;
   deflation; Great Inflation; low inflation
   breaks in, 106
   CPI, 96–98
   credit rationing and, 459–460
   drifting of, 74–75
   expectations, 64–65, 71–72, 78, 222–223
   expected value and, 66–67
   in France, 69–70
   high, 198–199
   hyperinflation, 69–70, 87, 120–121, 566–567
   mean rates, 86
   median rates, 86
   near-term control, 360
   negative rates, 86–87
   New Deal and, 472
   in Norway, 631–632
   objectives, 62–63, 74–76, 84
   paper-money, 33, 36
   performance, 10, 62–63, 70–71
   target, 77–78
      achievement, 65
      implied, 77–78
   time-varying objectives, 90–91
   transparency and, 653–654
inflation gap, 74
Inflation Report, 639, 647–648
inflation shocks, 79–80, 91–93, 95–96
inflation targeting (IT), 80, 107–108, 120,
   196–197, 401–402, 415–416, 641
   in Canada, 72
   flexible, 223
   after global financial crisis, 403–406
   macro factors not addressed by, 406–408
   macroprudential issues and, 408–409
   in New Zealand, 134–135, 400–401
   output growth gap and, 401–402

Index

prerequisites and, 409–411
RBA and, 127
Switzerland and, 125
inflation targeting lite, 398–399, 401
inherent credit risk, 148–149
inherent fragility, 264
in-out swaps, 590–591, 599–601
Inspectorate for the Safeguarding of Savings
and for Credit Activity, 460–461
institutional memory, 649, 651
intercept break, 84
interest rates, 248–249, 260, 287, 308–309,
637–638
differentials, 289
in emerging economies, 387–388
leaning policy, 503–506, 510
market vs. bank, 170–180
official, 170–172, 174–175, 178
real, 346–347
short-term, 178–179, 397–398, 644–645
smoothing of, 75, 77, 295–296, 406
internal decision-making, 280
internal drain, 248
internal evolution, 52–53
international bimetallism, 322–326
international capital flows, 370
*International Convergence of Capital
Measurement and Capital Standards.
A Revised Framework*, 479–480
international currencies, 289–290, 319–321,
324–326, 349, 364
international monetary and financial system
(IMFS)
analytical reference points and, 358–364
conclusion to, 379–381
Great Financial Crisis and, 373–379
interwar experience of, 364–373
introduction to, 356–358
International Monetary Fund (IMF), 337–339,
341–342, 345, 374–375, 421–422
international monetary regime, 12
Bretton Woods and, 336–342
central bank cooperation and, 336–342
classical gold standard and, 323–331
comparison of, 322
conclusion to, 349–350
floating exchange rates and, 342–349
interwar gold standard and, 331–336
introduction to, 319–323
rise of central banks and, 342–349
international trilemma, 389–398

choices and, 390–392
emerging economies standing apart,
392–398
historical context of, 389–390
Internationale Gesellschaft für Chemische
Unternehmungen AG (IG Chemie),
370–371
interregional payments, 588–589
interwar gold standard, 322–323, 331–336
Iraq, 268–269, 338–339
Ireland, 222–223, 618–619
IRI. *See* Istituto per la Ricostruzione Industriale
Israel, 222–223, 401
Istituto per la Ricostruzione Industriale (IRI),
460
IT. *See* inflation targeting
Italy, 13, 81–82, 123–124, 152–153. *See also*
Banca d'Italia
deposit banking in, 442–443
deregulation in, 470–472
FSM and, 433–435
Genoa, 25–27, 46–47, 49–52, 54,
297–304
globalization in, 470–472
gold standard and, 123
in Great Depression, 450–460
Naples, 33–34, 44, 51
Venice, 21, 27–28, 44, 46–49
World War I and, 449–451
World War II and, 123
Ito, Hiro, 392, 397–398, 422–423

Jackson, Andrew, 584–585
James, John, 588–589
Japan, 70, 311, 324–326, 343–346, 361,
411–412, 500–501, 622–623. *See also*
Bank of Japan
credibility and, 71–72, 96
deflation in, 86–90
gold standard in, 324
macroprudential measures in, 507–508
yen internationalization and, 310–311
Jefferson, Thomas, 241–242, 584–585
Jewish immigrants, 266
Jobst, Clement, 295–296
Johnson, Lyndon B., 129–130
Johnson Matthey Bank, 457, 637
Joint Stock Banking Companies Act, 431
Jonung, Lars, 113–114
JP Morgan Chase, 233–234, 269–270, 286–287,
303–304, 367–368

688 *Index*

Kahn, Charles M., 77, 573–574
Kaminsky, Graciela L., 400–401, 413–414
Kansallis-Osake-Pankki, 240–241
KAOPEN. *See* financial openness/integration
Kapstein, Ethan B., 476–477
Keating, Paul, 126–127
Keister, Todd, 263–264
Kemmerer, Edwin, 332–333, 453–454, 465–466
key currencies, 289–293, 298–300, 304–306
Keynes, John Maynard, 253, 295–296, 333–335
Keynesian doctrine, 129–130, 232–233
Kindleberger, Charles P., 231–234, 261, 360, 367–368. *See also specific works*
King, Mervyn, 197, 618–619, 639–640, 642, 647
King, Robert, 84, 427–428
Kipper- und Wipperzeit, 30–32
Klein, Michael W., 415
Knickerbocker Trust, 251–252, 266–267
Knight, F. H., 657–658
Knights Templar, 21
Königliche Hauptbank (Royal Main Bank), 39, 39–40, 53–54, 152–153, 167–168, 172–173
Königliche Seehandlung (Maritime Enterprise), 39–40
Korean War, 132–133, 610–611
Kostdevisen, 301–302
Kozicki, S., 76–78
Kreditanstalt, 254, 256
krona, 113–114
Kryzanowski, Lawrence, 453, 464

Lafitte, Jacques, 239
Lancashire Cotton Corporation, 447
Landon-Lane, John, 499–500
Large Scale Asset Purchase programs (LSAP), 161–162
Latin America, 237–238, 356–357, 360, 387–388, 413–414. *See also specific countries*
Latin America Mania, 499–501
Latin Monetary Standard, 123
Latin Monetary Union, 124, 218–219, 291
Law, John, 36–38, 51–53, 55, 506
League of Nations, 254, 297–300, 332–333
leaning interest rate policy, 503–506, 510
Lehman Brothers, 267–272, 376–377, 602, 620
lender of last resort (LOLR), 64–66, 368–369, 425, 427–428, 444
    Bank of Amsterdam as, 580–581
    Bank of England as, 234–239, 633

in Britain, 3
conclusions to, 273
controversies of, 232–234
definitions of, 232–234
development of theory, 243–250
in early twentieth century, 239–243
evolution of, 11
Great Depression and, 250–262
introduction to, 231
in nineteenth century, 239–243
Norges Bank as, 633–634
re-emergence of, 81
rescue operations and, 262–267
subprime crisis and, 267–273
three pillars of, 2–3
in U.S., 240–243, 250–255
lending booms, 14, 497–500
Lescure, Michel, 448–449
leverage, 18–19
Lewis, Michael, 620–621
Ley 45 (1923), 453–454
Ley 45 (1990), 474–475
Liberal Party, 292–293
LIBOR. *See* London Interbank Offered Rate
Lidderdale, William, 238
limited liability corporation, 432
Lindert, Peter, 288–289
liquid assets, 617–618
liquidity, 153–154, 160–161, 175, 636
    asset, 617–618
    creation powers, 50
    discount rates and, 172–173
    of dollar, 281
    domestic, 158–160
    ex ante, 148–149, 163–165
    funding, 162–163
    global, 308–309
    liability-side, 162–163
    market, 162–163, 286, 301–302
    providers of, 598
    structural, 175–176
    structural demand, 161–162
liquidity insurance, 641–642
liquidity ratios, 623–625
liquidity recycling, 599–600
liquidity risks, 566–567
liquidity saving, 599–601
liquidity shocks, 443–444, 589
liquidity-saving mechanisms, 565
lira, 123, 333, 339–340
Lisack, Noëmie, 413–414

Index

689

Lithuania, 403
Lo Duca, Marco, 412–413
loan/deposit ratios, 618
loan-to-value (LTV), 652
LOLR. *See* lender of last resort
Lombard facility, 25–26
Lombard Street: A Description of the Money Market (Bagehot), 2–3, 231, 246–250, 255, 265–266, 273, 292, 326
London Clearinghouse, 585–588
London Interbank Offered Rate (LIBOR), 171–172
London Stock Exchange, 467–468
long promise, 632–633
lost decade, 505
Louvre Accord, 348–349
Lovell, Michael C., 234–235
low inflation, 79, 87–90, 98–100, 195–196, 202–203, 220–221
    Maastricht criteria, 114
    threshold for, 79
low trust societies, 215–216
LSAP. *See* Large Scale Asset Purchase programs
LTV. *See* loan-to-value
Luther, Hans, 333–335
Luzzatti, Luigi, 8
Lyon Bourse, 441

Maastricht criteria, of low inflation, 114
Maastricht Treaty, 118–119
MacMillan Commission, 131–132
macroeconomic shocks, 67–68
macroeconomic stabilization, 388–389
macroprudential instruments and measures, 503, 505–508, 510, 622–623, 625, 645–646
macroprudential issues, 408–409, 506
macroprudential policy, 653–655
macroprudential regulation, 4–5, 14–15
macro-systemic shocks, 427, 485
Madison, James, 241–242
Malaysia, 338–339, 401, 403
managed exchange rates, 319–320, 347
managed float, 639
managed floating plus, 401
Manias, Panics, and Crashes (Kindleberger), 232, 260–261
margin control, 623
margin trading, 164
marginal borrowing facility, 178–179

marginal deposits, 625
Marion, Nancy P., 413–414
Maritime Enterprise (*Königliche Seehandlung*), 39–40
mark banco, 30–31
market discipline, 479–480
market functioning, 152
market infrastructure, 635–636
market interest rates, 170–180
market liquidity, 162–163, 286, 301–302
market makers of last resort (MMLR), 656–657
market mechanisms, 182
market prices, 149–150
Markowitz, Harry, 613
marks, 289, 292–293
Marshall Aid, 339
Marshall Plan, 120
Martin, William McChesney, 71
Martín-Aceña, P., 284
Martínez-Ruiz, Elena, 284, 296
Mary II (queen), 630
Masaaki Shirakawa, 2–3
Masciandaro, D., 198–199
Masson, Paul R., 409–410
Mathewson, Frank, 453
Matsukata (Count), 288
maturity, 153–154, 168
MBS. *See* mortgage-backed securities
McAndrews, James, 588–589
McCauley, R., 377–378
McDonald, Ramsay, 201
McGuire, P., 377–378
MCI. *See* monetary conditions index
McKenna, Reginald, 370
McKenna rule, 446–447
mean inflation rates, 86
Mecenseffý, Emil, 164
median inflation rates, 86
medieval banks, 48
medieval money, 20–22
Melitz, Jacques, 459, 469
Meltzer, Allan H., 128–129, 251, 260, 272
memory, 9, 649–651
mercantile credit, 570
Metallgesellschaft, 371
Metallwerte, 371
Mexico, 324–327, 344–345, 401, 403, 474, 478–480
Meyer, Eugene, 320–321
MI. *See* monetary independence
Middle Ages, 52

690 *Index*

Midland bank, 370
Milesi-Ferretti, Gian-Maria, 413–414
Milne, A. A., 5
minimax methodology, 661–662
minimum capital requirements, 479–480
*Minimum standards for the supervision of
 international banking groups and their
 cross-border establishments* (BSBC),
 477–478
Ministro de la Hacienda y Crédito Público,
 466–467
Ministry of Agriculture, Industry and
 Commerce, 434
Minsky, Hy, 615–616
Mishkin, Frederic S., 64
Mitchell, B. R., 263–264
Mlynarski, Feliks, 298–300, 306–307
MMLR. *See* market makers of last resort
modern monetary policy, 637–639
Modigliani-Miller benchmark, 22–23
Mody, Ashok, 388–417
monarchies, 55
moneta in obligatione (money owed), 21–22
moneta in solutione (money repaid), 21–22
Monetarism, 638
monetary autonomy, 398–402
monetary conditions index (MCI), 139
A Monetary History of the United States
 (Friedman and Schwartz), 6, 255,
 255–261, 265–266
monetary independence (MI), 391–394,
 397–398, 421–422
monetary intervention, 152
monetary nonautonomy, 398–399
monetary operations, domestic, 158–160
monetary policy, 4–5, 10, 54, 100–104,
 146–147
 coevolution of, 147–151
  central banks to money markets, 149–150
  conceptual issues, 150–151
  money markets to central banks, 148–149
 debates of, 285–286
 describing, 398–411
  IT and, 403–406
  macro factors and, 406–408
  macroprudential issues and, 408–409
  monetary autonomy and, 398–402
  prerequisites and, 409–411
 design of, 11
 evolution of, 13, 388–389
 expansive, 497–498

gold standard and, 389
microeconomic aspects of, 146–147
modern, 637–639
performance, 66–67
strategy, 63–64
in U.S., 303
Monetary Policy Committee (MPC), 639
Monetary Policy Report, 647–648
monetary power, division of, 9
monetary reform, 128
monetary regimes, 360–361
monetary stability, 15, 66, 81–82, 627–628, 640
monetary statistics, 258
monetary targeting strategy, 125, 134, 217
monetary theory, 572–573
money anchor, 398–399
money demand, 20
money growth instrument, 78–106
money market funds, 289
money markets
 coevolution of, 11, 147–151
 composition of assets, 155–166
 conclusions to, 181–182
 domestic lending, share of advances in, 166
 motivation and, 145–147
 quantitative evidence and, 151–181
 short-term, 655–656
 structure of, 11
money owed (*moneta in obligatione*), 21–22
money repaid (*moneta in solutione*), 21–22
money supply target, 93–94
money with a zero maturity (MZM), 271–272
Monnet, Eric, 118
Montiel, Peter J., 398–399
moral hazard, 473, 573, 641–642, 651
moral suasion, 132
Moreau, Emile, 69–70, 121, 301–302
mortgage-backed securities (MBS), 620
MPC. *See* Monetary Policy Committee
Mueller, R. C., 21
multilateral net settlement, 600
multilateral netting mechanisms, 48–49, 570
multiple-coin commodity money system, 49
Mundell, Robert, 222–223
Mussolini, Benito, 123, 450
Mutual Insurance Supervisory Authority
 (ACAM), 470
MZM. *See* money with a zero maturity

Naples, Italy, 33–34, 44, 51
Napoleon Bonaparte, 28, 39

Index

Napoleonic era, 10, 18–19, 33, 39–40, 57
Napoleonic Wars, 51–52, 115, 320–321,
 331–332, 588, 631
 Austria and, 40
 Britain and, 35–36, 246–247
 classical gold standard and, 323–324
 government debt and, 161
 Norway and, 119–120
National Bank Act, 436–437
National Bank Holiday, 252–253
National Bank of Belgium, 287–288
National Banking Act (1864), 506–507,
 586–587
National Banking Act (1865), 586–587
National Banking System, 443–444
National Credit Council, 458–459
National Development Plan, 474
National Monetary Commission, 365–366
National Shipbuilders Security Ltd, 447
National Socialism, 121
nationality, 363–364
near-term inflation control, 360
Nederlandsche Bank, 175, 240
net capital flows, 357–358, 361–363, 376–377
Netherlands, 152–153, 165–167, 175, 177–178,
 207–210, 576–577. *See also* Bank of
 Amsterdam
 classical gold standard and, 324–326
 credit controls and, 178
 Dutch Republic, 29–30
 France and, 30–31
 IMFS and, 364–366, 370–372
 market interest rates in, 172–173
netting, 48–49, 593
Neue Zürcher Zeitung, 371
New Deal, 462, 472
New Keynesian models, 494
New York Clearing House, 587–588
New York Stock Exchange, 451–452
New Zealand, 116–117, 136–139, 196–197,
 338–339
 as high trust society, 215–216
 inflation in, 195
 IT in, 134–135, 400–401
NICE. *See* Non-Inflationary Continuous
 Expansion
Niebuhr, M., 164
Niemeyer, Otto, 242, 332–333
Nixon, Richard, 320, 341
Nogues-Marco, Pilar, 284, 296, 575–576
non-deliverable forwards, 593

Non-Inflationary Continuous Expansion
 (NICE), 615
non-key currencies, 300
"Nonmonetary effects of the financial crisis in
 the propagation of the great
 depression" (Bernanke), 255
Norges Bank, 15, 119–120, 240–241, 426, 629,
 642, 649–650
 as LOLR, 633–634
 in past, 631–638
Norges Bank Act (1816), 219–220
Norman, Montagu, 69–70, 121, 282–283, 332,
 646, 664–665
Norway, 152–153, 196, 198–226, 240. *See also*
 Norges Bank
 Bretton Woods and, 120
 classical gold standard in, 361
 gold standard in, 632–633
 inflation in, 631–632
 Monetarism in, 639
 Napoleonic Wars and, 119–120
 positive inflation shocks in, 95–96
 Qvigstad rule and, 659–660
Norwegian crisis (1899), 496–497, 505
Noy, Ilan, 401, 403–405
Nuremberg, Germany, 31–32
Nurkse, Ragnar, 297
Nürnberger Banco Publico, 31–32

Obama, Barack, 267–268
Obstfeld, Maurice, 409, 413–414
OC. *See* optimal control
OCC. *See* Office of the Comptroller of the
 Currency
OECD, 310–311, 343–344
Oehmke, Martin, 495–496
Oesterreichische Nationalbank, 167–168
Office of the Comptroller of the Currency
 (OCC), 436–437, 444, 461–462
Office of the Inspector General of Banks, 474
Office of the Superintendent of Financial
 Institutions (OSFI), 474
Office of the Superintendent of Financial
 Institutions Act, 473–474
official interest rates, 170–172, 174–175, 178
oil price shock (1970s), 84, 113–114, 122–123,
 130, 134, 468–469, 611–612
 credibility and, 78–106
 in New Zealand, 137–138
 slope breaks and, 84
 UK and, 104–105

692   *Index*

oil price shock (1970s) (cont.)
  Volcker disinflation policy and, 96–98
Okun's Law, 77–78
open market
  operations, 54, 145–146, 160–161, 172–173,
    177–180, 260
  rates, 171–172
Open Market Committee, 251
openness
  degree of, 221–227
  financial, 391–394, 396–397
  measuring, 205–206
operational independence, 115, 628–629
operational targets, 641
optimal control (OC), 78
original sin, 388–389, 409, 415–416
Orphanides, A., 76–78
OSFI. *See* Office of the Superintendent of
  Financial Institutions
Ostry, Jonathan, 222–223, 397–398, 402,
  411–412
output gap, 75–78, 404–405
  positive, 84
  real GDP and, 74
output growth gap, 401–402
Overend Gurney, 3, 6–7, 115, 237–238,
  289–292
Oxelheim, Lars, 147

panel estimates, 83–96
Panic of 1819, 496–497
Panic of 1825, 248–249
Panic of 1857, 500
Panic of 1893, 500
Panic of 1907, 128, 444–445, 496–497
Panic of 2008, 11
panics, 232–234, 263–264
*Panics, Manias, and Crashes: A History of
  Financial Crises* (Kindleberger and
  Aliber), 496
Panizza, Ugo, 415–416
paper-money inflations, 33, 36
Paris Bourse, 239, 441
Paris Siege, 291
Parkin, M., 198–199
path dependence, 56
patience, 9, 649–650
Pattillo, Catherine, 413–414
Paulson, Henry, 270–271
pay-ins, 591–592, 594–595, 598–599

payment systems, 48–51, 148, 426–427,
  563–565, 634–636
  analytical framework for, 565–575
    anchor and, 570–571
    information and, 573–574
    preview and, 575
    state money and, 568–570
    system risk and, 572–573
  Anglo-American contrast, 582–589
    Bank of England and, 582–585
    First and Second Banks of America and,
      584–585
    private sector innovation in check
      payments, 585–587
    systemic implications and, 587–589
  CLS and, 590–602
  conclusion to, 602–603
  exchange banks and, 575–582
  large-value, 56–57
payment versus payment (PVP), 596
payments
  balance of payments, 196, 343, 356–357, 363,
    378–379, 610
  check, 585–587
  DVP, 596
  interregional payments, 588–589
  means of, 429–430, 433–434, 463
payments friction, 566
payments intensity, 563–564, 590
pay-outs, 591–592
PayPal, 563–564, 663–664
Peel, Robert, 236–237
Peel's Act, 236–237, 285–286
peer pressure, 7
pegged exchange rates, 107–108, 122, 132–133,
  196–197
penalty rate, 248–249
Penn Central Railroad, 266–267
Penn Square Bank, 267
People's Bank of China, 343
peripheral countries, 388–417
peripheral currencies, 301
peripheral systems, 573
permanent shocks, 206
Perron, P., 81
Persian Gulf States, 338–339
Peru, 332–333, 401, 403
Peseta, 218–219
peso, 301
pessimism, 232–233

Index

Philippines, 401, 403
Phillips curve, 120, 129–130
Pill, Huw, 222
Pitt, William, 235
Plaza Agreement, 348–349
Plessis, Alain, 239–240
pluralism, 661
Poincare, Raymond, 117–118
Poland, 401, 403
policy rate changes, 74–75
policy regimes, 68–69, 82
Policy Targets Agreement (PTA), 138–139
policy type influence, 198–199
political conditionality, 294
political supervision, 302
politics
  factors of, 290–291
  influence of, 12, 198–199, 282–283
  of key currencies, 289–293
Polyphonwerke, 371
Popular Front, 457–458
portfolio management, 12, 282–283
Portugal, 282, 296, 324–326
Posen, Adam, 195–196
positive feedback loops, 408–409
positive supply-side developments, 360
Postel-Vinay, Natacha, 501
pound sterling, 136–137, 295–296
PRA. *See* Prudential Regulation Authority
Prados, Leandro, 213
Prasad, Eswar S., 391–392, 407
precautionary motives, 566
press conferences, 653
Preußische Bank, 152–153, 167–168, 174–175
pre-war gold standard, 297–298
price behavior, 149–150
price controls, 132, 137–138
price formation, 152
price instability, 336, 400–401
price level targeting, 329–330
price of risk, 359
price variable, 152–153
price volatility, 150
pricking, 503, 506–508
primary credit facility, 178–179
principal reserve assets, 282
principal risk, 594, 600–602
private banking, 21, 49–50
private bills, 171–172
private capital flows, 396–397
private currency, 243
private debts, 21–22, 44
private failings, 48–49

private ownership, 41–44
private sector, 49–50, 154–158
  CLS as innovation of, 591–592
  innovation in check payments, 585–587
procyclicality, 400–401, 409–411, 415, 614
profit sharing arrangements, 161
profitability, 286–287
profit-making, 41–44
"A Program for Monetary Stability"
  (Friedman), 221
proportional systems, 284
protocentral banks, 18–19
Prudential Regulation Authority (PRA), 468,
  651–652
Prudential Supervisory Authority, 470
Prussia, 39–40, 55, 167–168
  Austro-Prussian War, 330
  classical gold standard and, 324–326
  Franco-Prussian War, 120–121, 291,
    319–320, 326–327, 329–330
  market interest rates in, 172–173
Prussian Bank, 324
PTA. *See* Policy Targets Agreement
public banks, 10, 18–19
  Amsterdam and, 577–578
  conclusion to, 56–57
  evolutionary process of, 44–56
  first-generation, 22–32, 42–43
  money demand and, 20
  second-generation, 32–40, 51
pure cleaning policy, 504
Putnam, Robert, 476–477
PVP. *See* payment versus payment

quantitative easing (QE), 4–5, 130–131,
  412–413, 625, 645–646
quantity theory, 77–78, 256–257
quasi-fiat money, 579–580
quasi-netting, 600
Quigley, Neil, 453
Qvigstad rule, 659–661

Radcliffe Committee, 116, 456–457
Railway Mania, 500–502, 505
Rajan, Raghuram, 387, 614
Rasminsky, Louis, 133–134
Rasminsky directive, 134
RBA. *See* Reserve Bank of Australia
RBNZ. *See* Reserve Bank of New Zealand
RBNZ Act, 138–139
Reagan, Ronald, 130, 478–479
"Real and pseudo-financial crises" (Schwartz),
  261

694   *Index*

real GDP, 74, 84
real shocks, 206
real-time gross settlement (RTGS), 591–592, 594, 603
receipts, 578–580
recession within the depression (1937–1938), 254
recoinage, 35
Reconstruction Finance Corporation, 461–462
Redemption Fund, 452–453
re-discounting, 584
Redish, Angela, 131–132
Regulation Q, 462
regulatory arbitrage, 150, 443–444, 473, 481, 510, 613
Reichsbank, 67, 69–72, 106, 120–123, 152–153, 167–168, 372–373
Reinhart, Carmen M., 65–66, 76, 263–264, 330–331, 400–401, 413–414
Reis, Ricardo, 296, 426
renminbi, 311–313, 343
reputation, 63–64, 68–74
rescue operations, 231, 243, 249–250, 262–267
reserve accumulation, 411–415
Reserve Advisory Management Program, 312
Reserve Bank of Australia (RBA), 125–127, 216–217, 504–505
Reserve Bank of New Zealand (RBNZ), 136–139
Responsibility Doctrine, 3, 115, 633
return on equity (RoE), 624–625
Revolutionary Wars, 35–36, 39
Rey, Helene, 360–361, 415
Reynolds, Jackson, 265–266
Riefler-Burgess doctrine, 251
Riksbank, 65, 113–114, 324
Riksens Ständers Bank (Bank of the Parliament), 34–35
risk management, 479
risk of use, 566
Roberds, William, 573–574
Roberts, Gordon S., 453, 464
robustness, 84, 661–662
RoE. *See* return on equity
Rogoff, Kenneth S., 65–66, 76, 263–264, 330–331
Roman law, 22, 199
Romer, Christina, 63–64, 210–211, 213, 220–221, 267–268
Roosevelt, Franklin D., 128–129, 252–253, 320, 335–336
Rose, Andrew, 406, 415–416
Rothschild, 262–263, 286–287

Rouble crisis (1999), 344–345
round-trip capital flows, 375–376
Royal Commission (1933), 464
Royal Main Bank (*Königliche Hauptbank*), 39, 39–40, 53–54, 152–153, 167–168, 172–173
RTGS. *See* real-time gross settlement
Rudebusch, G., 75
Rueff, Jacques, 118–119
Russia, 294, 301, 330, 347, 403, 411–413
Rygg, Nicolai, 119–120, 642–643

SA. *See* société anonyme
sacrifice ratio, 71–72
Safety-Funds System, 436
Salandra (Prime Minister), 449–450
Santarosa, Veronica, 576
Sargent, T. J., 48–49
Saskatoon Monetary manifesto, 134
Sayers, Richard S., 242, 447, 455–456
SBI. *See* Società Bancaria Italiana
Scandinavian Currency Union, 219–220
scenario analysis, 661–662
Schacht, Hjalmar, 69–70, 121, 506–508
Schenk, C. R., 309
Schularick, M., 69, 263–264, 366–367, 618
Schwartz, Anna, 231, 249–251, 264–265, 273, 427–428. *See also specific works*
rescue operations and, 267
Second Bank of the United States, 128, 152–153, 286, 435, 584–587
Second World War. *See* World War II
second-generation public banks, 32–40, 51
in Austria, 40
common themes of, 32–33
in England, 35–36
in France, 36–39
in Naples, 33–34
in Prussia, 39–40
in Sweden, 34–35
Securities and Exchange Commission, 252–253
Securities and Investments Board, 467–468
Security Trust Company, 473–474
self-insurance, 294, 411–415
Seven Years War, 38, 50, 579–580
shadow banking systems, 6–7, 289–290, 374–376, 655–656
Shambaugh, Jay, 415, 421–422
Sheridan, Richard B., 63–64
Sherman Silver Purchase Act, 233–234
Shin, H. S., 375–376
shocks. *See also* oil price shock
capital accounts, 412–413

Index

common, 221–222
credibility, 10, 68
economic, 62–63
exogenous, 182, 329–330, 498–499
external, 391, 471–472
inflation, 79–80, 91–93, 95–96
liquidity, 443–444, 589
macroeconomic, 67–68
macro-systemic, 427, 485
permanent, 206
real, 206
trade, 195–196, 406–408
short-term money markets, 655–656
Sieveking, H., 30–31
SIFI. *See* systemically important financial
  institution
Siklos, Pierre, 79, 82–83
Silber, W. L., 461–462
silver, 632–633, 642
  coin, 39, 54, 582–583
Single Deposit Guarantee Scheme, 480–481
Single Resolution Mechanism, 482
Single Supervisory Mechanism, 480–481
small open economies, 197, 204–205, 211–212
  changes in statutory independence, 214
  data and methods, 206–207
  figures for, 207–215
  measuring openness and, 205–206
  studies of, 222–223
Smets, Frank, 222
Smith, Adam, 202, 244–246, 273
Smithsonian Agreement, 341–342
Snake in the Tunnel, 118–119, 123–124
SNB. *See* Swiss National Bank
social capital, 247
Società Bancaria Italiana (SBI), 442–443
société anonyme (SA), 432
Société de Dépôts et Comptes Courants,
  441–442
Société Générale, 152–153, 448
soft law, 477–478, 484–485
Sorkin, Andrew Ross, 269–270
South Sea Company, 35–38
sovereign debt, 388–389, 480–481
Spain, 196, 217–219, 282, 296–297, 618–619
  Bank of Spain, 24–25, 284, 296
  Barcelona, 23–25, 44–46, 49–51
  Catalonia, 23–25, 48–50
  civil war of, 218–219
  credit booms in, 373–374
  macroprudential measures in, 507–508
Spanish Dynamic Provisioning Scheme,
  623–624

Spanish-American War, 330
Special Drawing Rights, 309–310
speculative motives, 566
Sprague, O. M. W., 251–252, 264–265
Spufford, P., 47
Stabilization Bills, 104
Stabilization Fund, 466–467
State Bank of the Russian Empire, 324
state money, 568–571
Statement on the Conduct of Monetary Policy,
  127
statutory independence, 214
Steagall, Henry, 462
Stein, Jeremy, 495–496, 641
sterling, 12, 116, 282, 292–293, 306–307, 333,
  339–340
  decline of, 309
  float of, 341–342
  pound, 136–137, 295–296
Sterling Agreements, 340–341
Sterling Area, 303–304, 307–309
sterling crisis (1931), 303–304
Stock, J. H., 83–84
Stock Banking Act, 430–431
stock exchange crisis (1882), 175
stock market crash (1928), 250–251
stock price bubble (1920s), 505
Stockholms Banco, 34, 44, 52–53
Stone, Mark R., 398, 401
Storting, 631–632, 653
Straub, Roland, 412–413
Stringher, Bonaldo, 449–450
Strong, Benjamin, 69–70, 121, 251, 282–283,
  320–321, 332
Stulz, R. M., 621
subprime crisis, 267–273, 497–498, 500–501
  background history and, 610–614
  implications of, 621–626
  lessons from, 615–621
Substitution Accounts, 309–310
Superintendencia Bancaria, 453–455, 465–466,
  474–475
supranational currency, 56–57
Sushko, V., 377–378
Sussman, Nathan, 575–576
Svensson, Lars, 65, 621–622
Sweden, 51, 55, 81–82, 86–87, 113–114, 240,
  631. *See also* Riksbank
  banknotes in, 34
  Bretton Woods and, 113–114
  real estate in, 510
  second-generation banks in,
  34–35

Index

Swiss National Bank (SNB), 67, 71, 73–85, 124–125, 346–347, 426
Switzerland, 71–74, 81–82, 86–87, 122–123, 152–153, 291, 411–412
  Bretton Woods and, 124–125
  Exchange Equalization Accounts in, 302
  Great Inflation and, 125
  IMFS and, 364–366, 370–372
  positive inflation shocks in, 95–96
swiveling, 500
systemically important financial institution (SIFI), 440–442, 483

Tabellini, G., 198–199
Tale of Two Cities (Dickens), 4
TARP. *See* Troubled Asset Relief Program
Taula de Canvi, 23–25, 44–46, 49–50
Taylor, J. B., 74, 76, 263–264, 366–367, 618
Taylor rule, 74–77, 130–131, 401, 403–404, 658
  regressions, 404–405, 407
Temin, Peter, 251, 372–373
Term-Asset Backed Loan Facility, 262
Thatcher, Margaret, 104–105, 116–117
"Theory of Moral Sentiments" (Smith), 202
Thiessen, Gordon, 134–135
Thirty Years War, 206
Thornton, Henry, 11, 244–246, 273, 427–428
Tier 1 capital base, 616–617
time series, 81–82
time-consistency problem, 628–629
time-varying inflation objectives, 62–63, 90–91
Tinbergen principal, 622–623
Tinsley, P. A., 76–78
Toniolo, Gianni, 341
Tooke, Thomas, 236–237
toxic assets, 268–270
trade shocks, 195–196, 406–408
Trading with the Enemy Act, 451–452
transferable bearer liabilities, 52
transparency, 63–64, 70–71, 200, 642, 647, 652–654, 664–666
Treasury bills, 115–116, 154, 168–169, 235
Treasury-Fed Accord, 463
Trial of the Pyx, 574
Trichet, Jean-Claude, 503
Triffin dilemma, 298–300, 306–307
Tripartite agreement, 118
triple liability, 272–273
Troubled Asset Relief Program (TARP), 268–269
trust, 1–4, 198–200, 262, 628, 653–654, 662–663. *See also* high trust societies
Tsangarides, C., 397–398, 411–412

Tulipmania, 497–498, 502
Turgot, Anne Robert Jacques, 38
Turkey, 197, 324–326, 403

Ugolini, Stefano, 231, 248–249, 287, 431
UK. *See* United Kingdom
uncollateralized lending, 162–170
Union Générale, 239, 441
United Kingdom (UK), 71–72, 81–82, 114–117, 207–210, 338–339, 618–619. *See also* Bank of England
  Bretton Woods and, 116
  credibility in, 104–105
  credit booms in, 373–374
  deposit banking in, 439–441
  deregulation in, 467–468
  dollar in, 309
  European Economic Community and, 137
  globalization in, 467–468
  in Great Depression, 455–457
  IMFS and, 365–366
  oil price shock and, 104–105
  Qvigstad rule and, 660–661
  World War I and, 446–447
United States (U.S.), 8, 13, 66–67, 81–82, 128–131, 320, 375–376, 610–611. *See also* Bank of United States; First Bank of the United States; Second Bank of the United States
  Civil War of, 324–326, 330–332, 436–437, 586–587
  clearinghouses in, 240–243
  credibility in, 96–104
  deposit banking in, 443–445
  deregulation in, 472–473
  Exchange Equalization Accounts in, 302
  FSM and, 435–437
  globalization in, 472–473
  gold standard in, 324
  in Great Depression, 461–463
  IMFS and, 365–368
  LOLR in, 240–243, 250–255
  monetary policy in, 303
  payments systems and, 582–589
  primary credit facility in, 178–179
  as protectionist, 207–210
  in World War I, 451–452
United States Postal Savings System, 257
universal banking, 472–473
U.S. *See* United States
usury, 174–175, 180
utility banks, 621

Index

697

value at risk (VaR), 613–614
Végh, Carlos A., 400–401, 409–410
Velde, François R., 48–49
Venice, Italy, 21, 27–28, 44, 46–49
Verdier, Léon, 301–302
Vereinigte Glanzstof-Fabriken AG, 371
Vichy regime, 457–459
Victory bonds, 132–134
Viennese Municipal Bank (*Wiener Stadtbank*),
    40, 46–47, 55
Vietnam War, 129–130, 342
VIX index, 360–361
VOC. *See* Dutch East India Company
Volcker, Paul, 63–64, 71, 96–98, 104, 130,
    346–347, 478–479
Vuletin, Guillermo, 409–410

W. & J. Brown & Co., 238
wage controls, 132, 137–138
Wagner, Adolph, 164
Walsh, Carl, 659–660
Walters, Alan, 116–117
War of 1812, 584–585
War of a Thousand Days, 438–439
War of Austrian Succession, 26–27
War of Spanish Succession, 24–25, 37
war plans, 11
Warburg Plan, 128
Warburton, Peter, 205–206
wartime controls, 217
Watson, M. W., 83–84
weak anchor, 398–399
Wealth of Nations (Smith), 244
Weiman, David F., 588–589
Wheelock, David C., 251
White, Harry Dexter, 320
White, Thomas, 464
Wicksell, Knut, 329–330
Wiener Stadtbank (Viennese Municipal Bank),
    40, 46–47, 55
Wiggin-Layton committee, 369, 371–372
William III (king), 630
Williams, J., 78
Willis, H. P., 437–438, 441–442
Witte, Sergei, 294
Wood, Elmer, 198–202, 206–207, 215–216, 231
Woodford, M., 64–65, 74–75, 621–622
Working Papers, 613–614
World Economic Outlook forecast, 414
World War I, 160–161, 180–181, 216–217, 254,
    292–293, 329–330, 336, 483–484,
    637–638
    active reserve and, 282

Banca d'Italia and, 123, 449–451
bond financing and, 367
Canada and, 452–453
classical gold standard and, 69, 323–324
collateralized lending and, 169–170
Colombia and, 453–455
Federal Reserve and, 128
France and, 117–118, 448–449
FSM and, 446–455
gold standard and, 115–116
government debt and, 161
in Italy, 449–451
liquidity and, 164–165
Norges Bank and, 632–633
Norway and, 119–120
official reserves before, 288–289
open market rates and, 171–172
Reichsbank and, 120–121
state-building and, 332
Sweden and, 113
Treasury bills and, 168
U.S. and, 451–452
World War II, 98–100, 160–161,
    168–169, 178, 254, 298–299,
    483–484, 615
asset liquidity and, 617–618
Bank of England and, 116, 455–456
Bank of Japan and, 96
Canada and, 132
capital flows and, 282–283
discount rates and, 170
Federal Reserve and, 65–66, 129–130
France and, 118
government debt and, 161
inflation and, 87–90, 122
Italy and, 123
Norway and, 119–120
RBNZ and, 137
regulatory constraints and, 636–637
Sweden and, 113
Switzerland and, 124–125
UK and, 104–105

yen, 310–311, 341–342
Yokohama Specie Bank, 324

zero lower bound (ZLB), 75–76, 135–136
Ziegler, Dieter, 167–168
Zingales, Luigi, 428–429
ZLB. *See* zero lower bound

Øksendal, Lars F., 629
Österreichische Nationalbank, 40

Other books in the series (continued from page iv)

Aurel Schubert, *The Credit-Anstalt Crisis of 1931*, 1992

Trevor J. O. Dick and John E. Floyd, *Canada and the Gold Standard*, 1992

Kenneth Mouré, *Managing the Franc Poincaré*, 1991

David C. Wheelock, *The Strategy and Consistency of Federal Reserve Monetary Policy, 1924–1933*, 1991

CPSIA information can be obtained
at www.ICGtesting.com
Printed in the USA
LVHW111730150120
643605LV00005BA/536